CHICAGO

PHILADELPHIA

NORTH
EAST
NEW
YORK
LAKES

WASHINGTON D.C.

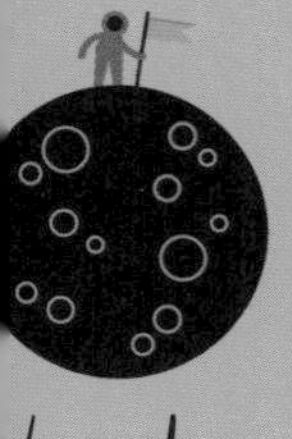

NEW
Orleans

ATLANTA
SOUTH
EAST

MIAMI

The New York Times

36 HOURS

EDITED BY BARBARA IRELAND

The New York Times

HOURS
USA & CANADA

TASCHEN

Contents

NORTHEAST

SOUTHEAST

MIDWEST & GREAT LAKES

SOUTHWEST & ROCKY MOUNTAINS

WEST COAST

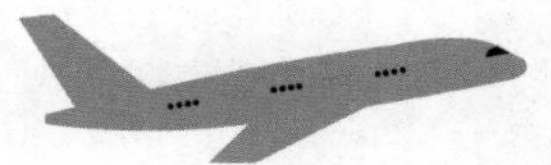

Foreword

The 36 Hours *column made its first appearance on the pages of* The New York Times *in 2002, became an immediate hit with readers, and has been inspiring trips, wish lists, and clip-and-saves ever since. Created as a guide to that staple of crammed 21st-century schedules, the weekend getaway, it takes readers each week on a carefully researched, uniquely designed two-night excursion to an embraceable place. With a well-plotted itinerary, it offers up an experience that both identifies the high points of the destination and teases out its particular character.*

This second edition of The New York Times 36 Hours: 150 Weekends in the USA and Canada *includes 29 new* 36 Hours *columns, based in destinations not covered in the first edition, and 121 revised and updated versions on cities that were featured before. No matter what the choices, amid all the richness of the vast territory of the United States and Canada, from glittering cities and eccentric small towns to heart-stopping mountains and seacoasts, even 150 places is not very many. The task of selection, difficult the first time around, was even harder with new work from the* Times *Travel section to choose from for this new edition.*

Some destinations, of course, remain obvious musts: the marquee metropolises like New York, Montreal, and Los Angeles; the world-famous natural wonders at Niagara Falls and the Grand Canyon; the national icons of Washington, D.C., and Quebec City. But the process of choosing among rest brings home how much more there is to find and see over a territory stretching from Juneau to Miami and Quebec to Kauai. There are discoveries to be made: the Connecticut coast, with its tidal marshes and old Yankee towns; the Laurel Highlands of Pennsylvania, where Frank Lloyd Wright's masterpiece, Fallingwater, is hidden away in the woods. So-called "secondary" Rust Belt cities like Duluth and Detroit turn out to be rich repositories of spirit and culture. And the work of some of the best and most renowned Times *staff writers was ready to be plucked for the book, too —David Carr on his former home city of Minneapolis, William Grimes on Manhattan and Sam Sifton on Brooklyn, Bill Pennington on ski towns in both East and West.*

As one of the dozens of editors who have worked on 36 Hours *over the years—along with hundreds of writers, photographers, graphic artists, and designers—I've come to feel that the column's popularity is based on its special feeling of accessibility. The framework is the weekend. The audience is broad—with a little adapting, these itineraries are meant to work for both the backpacker and the jet-setter. And the destination might be anyplace where there is fun to be had and a quirk or two to discover.*

This book is not a conventional guidebook, and 36 Hours *was never intended to replicate the guidebook formula. It was meant from the beginning to give a well-informed inside view of each place it covers, a selective summary that lets the traveler get to the heart of things in minimal time. Travelers who have more days to spend may want to use a* 36 Hours *as a kind of nugget, supplementing it with the more comprehensive information available on bookstore shelves or on the locally sponsored Internet sites where towns and regions offer exhaustive lists of their attractions. Or, since the book is organized regionally, two or three of these itineraries could easily be strung together to make up a longer trip. (I did this myself in Kentucky and eastern Tennessee, using the* 36 Hours *for Louisville, Lexington, and Knoxville.)*

Whatever the journey or the wanderer's choice, the star of the book is still North America itself, shining out page after page in all of its amazing variety, energy, and grandeur. — BARBARA IRELAND, EDITOR

PAGE 2 The Statue of Liberty, icon and inspiration since 1886, lifts her famous torch in New York Harbor.

OPPOSITE Delicate Arch at sunset in Arches National Park outside Moab, Utah.

ISLAND
hollywood
George Wallace
BALLYS
planet hollywood
ph
MIRACLE MILE SHOPS
Monte
NEW YORK
NEW YORK
ROK
ZUMANITY
CIRQUE DU SOLEIL
SPORTS

Tips for Using This Book

Plotting the Course: Travelers don't make their way through a continent alphabetically, and this book doesn't, either. Each of its sections is based on a region — Northeast, Southeast, Midwest & Great Lakes, Southwest & Rocky Mountains, and West Coast — and introduced with a regional map. Each begins in a prominent city and winds from place to place the way a touring adventurer on a car trip might. An alphabetical index appears at the end of the book.

On the Ground: Every *36 Hours* follows a workable numbered itinerary, which is both outlined in the text and shown with corresponding numbers on a detailed destination map. The itinerary is practical: it really is possible to get from one place to the next easily and in the allotted time, although of course many travelers will prefer to take things at their own pace and perhaps take some of their own detours. Astute readers will notice that the "36" in *36 Hours* is elastic, and the traveler's agenda probably will be, too.

The Not So Obvious: The itineraries do not all follow the same pattern. A Saturday breakfast choice may or may not be recommended; after-dinner night life may or may not be included. The destination dictates, and so, to some extent, does the personality of the author who researched and wrote the article. In large cities, where it is impossible to see everything in a weekend, the emphasis is on the less expected discovery over the big, highly promoted attraction that is already well known. In New York, for example, the Metropolitan Museum of Art is left for art lovers to find on their own.

Travel Documents: The United States and Canada are friendly neighbors, but they are still separate countries. A passport is required for travel between them; and where a visa is required, travelers should be prepared to show that, as well, at the international border. Goods and luggage may be inspected by customs agents.

Seasons: The time of year to visit is left up to the traveler, but in general, the big cities are good anytime; the smaller northern towns are usually best visited in warm months, unless they are ski destinations; and the Deep South and Southwest may be unpleasantly hot in July and August. The most tourist-oriented towns are often seasonal — some of the sites featured in Provincetown or Bar Harbor, for example, may be closed from November to April.

Updates: While all the stories in this volume were updated and fact-checked for publication in 2014, it is inevitable that some of the featured businesses and destinations will change in time. If you spot any errors in your travels, please feel free to send corrections or updates via email to 36hours@taschen.com. Please include "36 Hours Correction" and the page number in the subject line of your email to assure that it gets to the right person for future updates.

OPPOSITE The fantasyland skyline of Las Vegas, the uniquely American oasis of hope, abandon, and glittering commercialism in the Western desert.

THE BASICS

A brief informational box for the destination, called "The Basics," appears with each *36 Hours* article in this book. The box provides some orientation on transportation for that location; for instance, whether a traveler arriving by plane should rent a car to follow the itinerary. "The Basics" also recommends two or three reliable hotels.

PRICES

Since hotel and restaurant prices change quickly, this book uses a system of symbols, based on 2014 United States dollars.

Hotel room, standard double:
Budget, under $125 per night: $
Moderate, $126 to $250: $$
Expensive, $251 to $375: $$$
Luxury, $376 and above: $$$$

Restaurants, dinner entree:
Budget, under $15: $
Moderate, $16 to $29: $$
Expensive, $30 to $44: $$$
Very Expensive, $45 and up: $$$$

Restaurants, full breakfast, or lunch entree:
Budget, under $10: $
Moderate, $10 to $20: $$
Expensive, $21 to $29: $$$
Very Expensive, $30 and up: $$$$

NORTH EAST

160 Mont TREMBLANT

166 Quebec City

154

Montreal

150 Ottawa

52 Lake Placid

146 Burlington

46 the Hudson Valley

New Haven 84

NEW YORK CITY 12

38 Queens

58 Princeton

32

GETTYSBURG 80

70

PHILADELPHIA

Brooklyn

the Brandywine Valley 76

CAPE MAY 64

172
Charlevoix

Prince
Edward
Island
176

Bar
Harbor
140

Midcoast
Maine 134

Bretton Woods
124

182
the Bay
of fundy

Halifax
186

130
PORTLAND

BOSTON
114

120
Cambridge

PROVINCETOWN
108

PROVIDENCE
92

the
Connecticut
Coast
88

Newport
96

MARTHA'S
100 VINEYARD

26
Harlem
APOLLO

22 Broadway

Lower
Manhattan
18

42 East
Hampton

NANTUCKET
104

NOW
RENTING

New York City

The English writer Michael Pye came up with a clever title for his book on New York: Maximum City. *That says it all in two words. The place is just too much. It's an all-out assault on the five senses, exhilarating but unnerving, that even hardy New Yorkers struggle to contain. Visitors, all too often, are simply crushed, but there are ways around the problem. The most effective is to divide and conquer. When it's split up into bits and pieces, neighborhood by neighborhood, or even block by block, the city shows a more human scale and a softer side. Quirks come to the surface, odd corners reveal themselves, and unexpected pleasures turn up, not all of them wallet-draining experiences. New York can be tamed.* — BY WILLIAM GRIMES

FRIDAY

1 *Art Crawl* 3 p.m.

For gallery hopping, Chelsea is the place, with hundreds of art galleries clustered in the far west of streets numbered in the teens and 20s. While high rents have driven smaller operators to the Lower East Side and the East Village, big names like Gagosian, Pace, and David Zwirner have expanded, creating megagalleries that can accommodate huge installation shows. The smaller fry still carry on at buildings like 547 West 27th Street, a warren of small exhibition spaces like the artist-run **Painting Center** (212-343-1060; thepaintingcenter.org). For guidance, pick up a free *Gallery Guide*; it's found at most galleries.

2 *Rail and River* 5:30 p.m.

Stroll the hugely popular **High Line** (thehighline.org), an abandoned elevated rail line transformed into a garden walkway, and enjoy the view. While you're up there, look west toward the Hudson River and behold your next destination, **Chelsea Waterside Park** (hudsonriverpark.org), another emerald in a necklace of riverside parks. This one begins at 23rd Street, near the Chelsea Piers, and combines play areas, curving walks, artfully landscaped beds, and grassy areas ideal for plopping down, watching the boats sail past, and resting tired feet.

3 *Sole on Ice* 7 p.m.

The **Ace Hotel** (20 West 29th Street, at Broadway) is one of the landmarks in a district of hip hotels and spiffy restaurants that has grown up north of Madison Square and has acquired, inevitably, a nickname: NoMad. The **John Dory Oyster Bar** (1196 Broadway; 212-792-9000; thejohndory.com; $$$), in the hotel, is a tiled, clamorous seafood brasserie with oysters on the half shell, multilevel seafood plateaus served with the restaurant's Parker House rolls, and small plates like chorizo-stuffed squid with smoked tomato. This is your chance to try whelks on toast.

SATURDAY

4 *Lone Star Eats* 9:30 a.m.

The neighborhood around the **Flatiron Building** (23rd Street, Broadway, and Fifth Avenue), on Madison Square, enjoyed its heyday in the late 19th and early 20th centuries, when the square was ringed with fashionable restaurants, theaters, and, of course, the grand entertainment venue named after it: Madison Square Garden (now in a newer incarnation

OPPOSITE Manhattan at dusk.

RIGHT Madison Square Park, a welcoming green space with changing displays of public art, attracts lawn loungers, strolling art lovers, and canine athletes.

on 34th Street). Today, the square and its splendidly renovated park anchor a neighborhood known for unusual specialty shops and terrific restaurants at all price points. To kick off the day, it is hard to beat breakfast at **Hill Country Chicken** (1123 Broadway, at 25th Street; 212-257-6446; hillcountrychicken.com; $). The décor is 1940s diner, the menu robust: egg and cheese or chicken biscuits with sausage or bacon, breakfast tacos, and flaky two-cherry turnovers made on site.

5 *Pop Quiz* 10:30 a.m.

The **National Museum of Mathematics** (11 East 26th Street; 212-542-0566; momath.org) offers a change of pace from the Museum of Sex a few blocks north. Pull the oversize "pi" door handles, and a hands-on wonderland awaits, a mathematical fun house that lets children and their parents explore Platonic solids, fractals, and other heroes of the mathematical universe. Visitors can ride tricycles with square wheels around a series of arcs radiating from the center of a circular track. The ride is smooth because the length of each side of the square is equal to the length of the arc in each bump. Those who struggled with high school geometry, and you know who you are, can amuse themselves at the miniature roller coaster, arranging dips and climbs to achieve maximum speed for the little car that runs along its rails.

6 *Asia on a Plate* Noon

It's a short walk to **Num Pang** (1129 Broadway; 212-647-8889; numpangnyc.com), an Asian sandwich shop just a few doors north of Hill Country Chicken. The specialties include a five-spice-glazed pork belly sandwich, a Khmer sausage sandwich with Asian slaw, and a grilled ear of corn swabbed with chili mayonnaise and coconut flakes.

7 *Dogging It in the Park* 12:30 p.m.

Walk off lunch in **Madison Square Park**, whose expansive lawns, sinuous paths, and comfortable benches make it one of the city's most welcoming green spaces. The dog run is a treat, with top-quality canine athletes eager to show off their skills. On the lawn, an ever-changing program of public art catches the eye. In one commissioned work, *Ideas of Stone*, the Italian artist Giuseppe Penone balanced large boulders in three bronze trees.

8 *Blood, Sweat, and Sweets* 1:30 p.m.

The shopping is eclectic in these parts. Well-known chains line Fifth Avenue, but interesting holdouts still populate the side streets. The **New York Cake and Baking Distributor** (56 West 22nd Street; 212-675-2253; nycake.com) contains thousands of baking pans, cookie cutters, and decorative doodads in every conceivable shape and size. That includes margarita-shaped birthday candles, with

little lime slices, and sheet molds that turn out insect-shaped cookies. **Bxl Zoute** (50 West 22nd Street; 646-692-9282; bxlrestaurants.com) is good for a break, with a stellar lineup of Belgian beers on tap as well as a house specialty, Cuvee Bxl, an amber beer brewed with orange peel, curacao, coriander, and grains of paradise. **Abracadabra** (19 West 21st Street; 212-627-5194; abracadabrasuperstore.com) is your headquarters for zombie blood and vampire teeth. There's a magic department, a deli counter with body parts and brains, and a nice selection of classic gag items like joy buzzers and red-hot chewing gum. Dressed dummies, available for rental, lurk in every corner. Step up to the wretch bent over a drum of toxic waste near the front door and press the button. You'll get a big surprise.

9 *Destination Italy* 7 p.m.

Eataly (200 Fifth Avenue, near 24th Street; 212-229-2560; eataly.com), a mammoth Italian food market, has a life of its own from its opening at 10 a.m., when a human tide rolls in, drawn by the superabundance of cheeses, salumi, pastas, vegetables, breads — anything and everything Italian and food-related. At dinner time, choose from its seven restaurants. Only Manza, linked to the meat counter, takes reservations. At La Piazza, an enoteca with standing marble tables, the accent is on cheeses, salumi, and Italian wines by the glass. You can also order inventively garnished slices of raw fish in olive oil from the crudo bar, Eataly's answer to Japanese sashimi. On the way out, pick up a take-home gift from the fresh-pasta department. Say, pumpkin-filled ravioli or spaghetti alla chitara.

OPPOSITE ABOVE The High Line rises above Chelsea along a former elevated train track.

ABOVE At Columbus Circle, the Museum of Arts and Design stands out in silvery tones below the skyscrapers.

SUNDAY

10 *East Riv Vu* 10 a.m.

Uptown, across from East End Avenue, a street so discreet that most city residents have never heard of it, **Carl Schurz Park** (carlschurzparknyc.org) overlooks the East River from 84th Street to 90th Street. It has two priceless features. The first is a raised riverside esplanade that offers views of Ward's Island and the once-dangerous tidal strait known as Hell Gate. The second is Gracie Mansion, the stately official residence of New York City's mayor.

11 *Art With Umlauts* 11:30 a.m.

A ride on the 86th Street bus, crossing that more famous green space, Central Park, leads directly to

the **Neue Galerie** (1048 Fifth Avenue, at 86th Street; 212-994-9493; neuegalerie.org), a small museum created by the philanthropist Ronald S. Lauder to honor the dealer Serge Sabarsky and to showcase both men's collections of German and Austrian modernist art. The museum specializes in small-scale, focused exhibitions of artists like Ernst Ludwig Kirchner and Wassily Kandinsky, or movements like the Blaue Reiter. The sweet conclusion awaiting every visitor is **Café Sabarsky** (212-288-0665; kg-ny.com) on the ground floor, which replicates a traditional Viennese cafe right down to the Meinl coffee. The menu includes wursts, sandwiches, and salads, but these are mere distractions from the stunning parade of Viennese and Hungarian pastries.

ABOVE A view of New York Harbor.

OPPOSITE New York's iconic Flatiron Building, at the confluence of Fifth Avenue and Broadway.

THE BASICS

Fly into Kennedy, LaGuardia, or Newark Liberty. Take a taxi to Midtown or connect to a commuter railroad via the AirTrain from J.F.K. or Newark. Taxis are plentiful. The subway is convenient and safe.

Ace Hotel
20 West 29th Street
212-679-2222
acehotel.com/newyork
$$-$$$$
Haute-hipster.

NoMad Hotel
1170 Broadway
212-796-1500
thenomadhotel.com
$$$
Luxurious but understated.

Eventi Hotel
851 Avenue of the Americas
212-564-4567
eventihotel.com
$$$
New-wave boutique hotel.

Lower Manhattan

One World Trade Center, the new tallest building in New York, has risen where the Twin Towers once dominated, at the tip of Manhattan Island. The 9/11 Memorial is there, too, drawing hushed and respectful visitors from around the world. No one will ever forget the terrorist attacks, but the neighborhoods nearby long ago recovered from both the physical devastation and the economic jolt several years later. The financial district is bustling, Chinatown is as quirky and enticing as ever, and TriBeCa is bursting with new restaurants, bars, and hotels. With the exception of those seeking a night of relentless club-hopping, travelers hardly need venture north of Canal Street for a complete New York weekend. — BY SETH KUGEL

FRIDAY

1 *Cruising the Harbor* 2 p.m.

Been there (the Statue of Liberty) and done that (taken the free Staten Island Ferry)? There are other options for harbor cruises, and what better way to get an overview of Lower Manhattan? One possibility is a 90-minute sail on the *Clipper City* tall ship, a replica of a 19th-century lumber-hauling schooner (Manhattan by Sail; 212-619-0907; manhattanbysail.com), which departs from the South Street Seaport. Another is a one-hour harbor cruise with **Statue Cruises** (201-604-2800; statuecruises.com). The company has even launched a Hornblower Hybrid, which relies on several power sources, including hydrogen fuel cells, solar panels, and wind turbines.

2 *Sugar and Shopping* 4 p.m.

Venture to TriBeCa for a lemon tart or a "magic cupcake" at **Duane Park Patisserie** (179 Duane Street; 212-274-8447; duaneparkpatisserie.com) on the shaded pocket park it is named after. Then wander into the nearby shops, which range from the cute to the serious, sometimes in the same store. **Torly Kid** (51 Hudson Street; 212-406-7440; torlykid.com) has funky, functional clothes for babies to tweens. **Patron of the New** (151 Franklin Street; 212-966-7144; patronofthenew.com) sells aggressively fashion-forward clothes and shoes. Pay tribute to the craftsmanship of Detroit at **Shinola** (177 Franklin Street; 917-728-3000; shinola.com), which specializes in bicycles, watches, and leather goods, many of which are made in Detroit or at least assembled there.

OPPOSITE One World Trade Center, America's tallest building, overlooks the site once occupied by the Twin Towers.

3 *Bankers' Happy Hour* 6:30 p.m.

If you resent investment bankers' salaries and bonuses, then here's something else to be envious of: the cobblestone stretch of Stone Street. What might be New York's greatest outdoor drinking spot happens to be right next to Goldman Sachs's former headquarters. When it's warm, this quaint block, lined with 19th-century Greek Revival buildings, is practically blocked by tables occupied by financial types, a few sundry locals, and knowledgeable tourists. Choose a table outside **Adrienne's Pizzabar** (212-248-3838; 54 Stone Street; adriennespizzabar.com; $$) and order a bottle of wine and a meatball and broccoli rabe pizza, enough for three people.

4 *Latin Rhythms* 10 p.m.

New York has plenty of flashy nightclubs, but for throwback grit, try the Friday night party at **2020** (20 Warren Street; 212-962-9759; 2020latinclub.com), where Latinos working in every kind of downtown job come to dance to the D.J.-supplied rhythms of the Spanish-speaking Caribbean.

SATURDAY

5 *In Memoriam* 9 a.m.

Buy your passes online in advance to avoid long lines at the **National September 11 Memorial** (911memorial.org), with its pair of one-acre reflecting pools in the footprints of the fallen towers, names of victims inscribed in bronze panels, and rustling swamp white oak trees overhead. The on-site museum that has taken shape is designed to be deliberately labyrinthine, meant to jar those who view its exhibitions on the original World Trade Center and the attacks. No pass is needed to visit the nearby **St. Paul's Chapel** (209 Broadway; trinitywallstreet.org), which became a refuge for rescue workers in the days after the attacks.

6 *Manahatta* Noon

Most people don't put the Smithsonian on their New York must-do list. But the **National Museum of the American Indian** (1 Bowling Green; 212-514-3700; nmai.si.edu), in the Beaux Arts splendor of the old Customs House near Battery Park, is a reminder that Manhattan and the rest of the Western Hemisphere has a long and vibrant cultural history. The Infinity of Nations exhibition has everything from a macaw and heron feather headdress from Brazil to a hunting hat with ivory carvings from the Arctic. To get an up-close view of a wampum belt and corn pounder used by the Lenape Indians, who called the island Manahatta, head to the museum's resource center and ask. The museum is free—not far from the price for which the Lenapes famously sold Manhattan to the Dutch.

7 *Doctoral Downtown* 2 p.m.

Continue your historical education with a **Big Onion tour**. Downtown is a complicated place, with layers upon layers of history: Dutch, African-American, Revolutionary, and financial, among others. It takes a doctoral candidate to decode it, and that is who will probably lead you on a two-hour tour that might include "Historic TriBeCa," "Revolutionary New York," or "The Financial District." Times vary; see bigonion.com.

8 *Wine by the T-Shirt* 7 p.m.

At the wine bar **Terroir Tribeca** (24 Harrison Street; 212-625-9463; wineisterroir.com), the young servers dressed in wine-themed T-shirts don't look as though they could know what they are talking about, but don't get them started. (Actually, do get them started.) A glass of wine can be had at many prices, and the menu is full of nonstandard temptations to go with it: fried balls of risotto, wine, and oxtail, for example, are a perfect way to spend your allotment of deep-fried calories.

9 *Salvage and Bruschetta* 9 p.m.

Who knows how many diners have walked out of Robert DeNiro and company's Locanda Verde, the big northern Italian spot, and wondered what was going on in the tiny, bustling restaurant across the street? Decked out with salvaged materials that evoke an old factory or warehouse, **Smith and Mills** (71 North Moore Street; 212-226-2515; smithandmills.com; $$) seats 22 at tables shoehorned between the standing, drinking crowds. The menu includes items like tomato bruschetta, oysters with horseradish, burgers, and brioche bread pudding. One must-see: a restroom in a turn-of-the-century iron elevator.

10 *Drinks on Doyers* 11 p.m.

Head east to Chinatown, where **Apotheke** (9 Doyers Street; 212-406-0400; apothekenyc.com)

is a non-Chinese intruder sitting on the elbow of L-shaped Doyers Street, the spot known as the Bloody Angle for the gang-related killings there in the early 20th century. Here you'll find one of the city's top cocktail bars, with old-time décor and dim lighting. Try a drink like the Deal Closer, made with cucumber, vodka, mint, lime, vanilla, and "Chinatown aphrodisiacs."

SUNDAY

11 *Brooklyn Bridge Crossing* 9 a.m.

With the arrival of the dog days, you have to get up pretty early to walk across the **Brooklyn Bridge** in comfort. As romantic as ever, a walk along the elevated pedestrian walkway provides a photo opportunity a minute. On your way back, stop by **City Hall Park**, and then head west across Chambers Street to pick up bagels and smoked salmon from **Zucker's** (146 Chambers Street; 212-608-5844; zuckersbagels.com).

OPPOSITE The view of Lower Manhattan from across the East River, at Brooklyn Bridge Park in Dumbo.

ABOVE A sightseeing cruise heads up the East River between Manhattan and Brooklyn.

THE BASICS

Getting around is easy on foot and by subway, but the street layout here, well south of the city's famous regular street grid, can be confusing. You'll need a good map or a practical app.

Greenwich Hotel
377 Greenwich Street
212-941-8900
thegreenwichhotel.com
$$$$
In the heart of TriBeCa.

Gild Hall
15 Gold Street
212-232-7700
thompsonhotels.com
$$
Well-appointed boutique hotel.

Blue Moon Hotel
100 Orchard Street
212-533-9080
bluemoon-nyc.com
$$$$
Converted tenement is a reminder of the immigrant past.

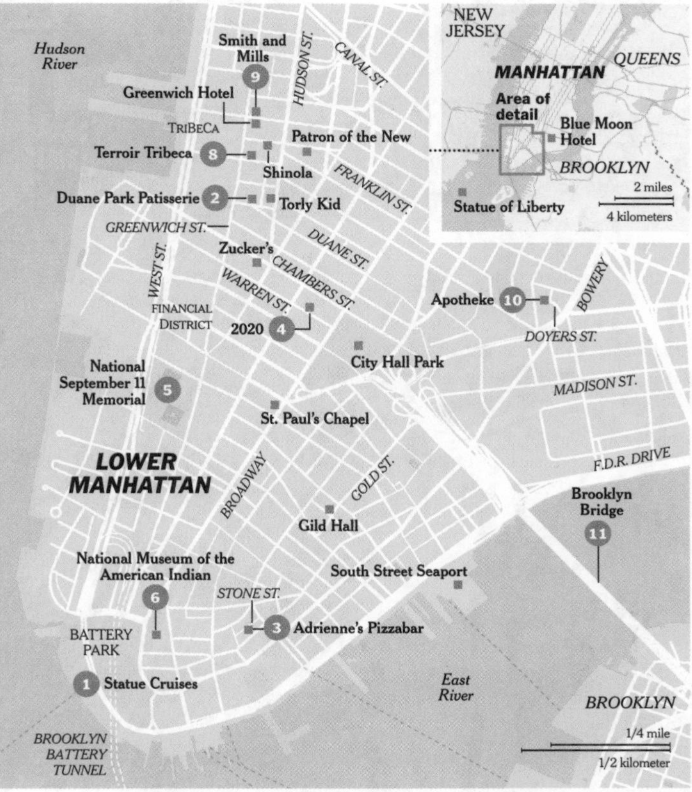

Hudson River
Smith and Mills 9
Greenwich Hotel
TRIBECA
HUDSON ST.
CANAL ST.
Terroir Tribeca 8
Shinola
Patron of the New
FRANKLIN ST.
Duane Park Patisserie 2
Torly Kid
GREENWICH ST.
DUANE ST.
Zucker's
CHAMBERS ST.
WEST ST.
WARREN ST.
FINANCIAL DISTRICT
2020 4
Apotheke 10
BOWERY
DOYERS ST.
City Hall Park
National September 11 Memorial 5
MADISON ST.
St. Paul's Chapel
LOWER MANHATTAN
BROADWAY
GOLD ST.
F.D.R. DRIVE
Brooklyn Bridge 11
Gild Hall
National Museum of the American Indian 6
South Street Seaport
STONE ST.
BATTERY PARK
3 Adrienne's Pizzabar
1 Statue Cruises
East River
BROOKLYN
BROOKLYN BATTERY TUNNEL
1/4 mile
1/2 kilometer
NEW JERSEY
MANHATTAN
QUEENS
Area of detail
Blue Moon Hotel
BROOKLYN
Statue of Liberty
2 miles
4 kilometers

MARY POPPINS
ON BROADWAY
Prudential
HSBC
100% Colombian Coffee
Juan Valdez
The Addams Family
ROBERT DOWNEY JR.
ZACH GALIFIANAKIS
DUE DATE
NOVEMBER 5
ankook
riving emotion
INGLOT
give it back
maxell
INVENTIVE
Kodak
ONLY
ONLY
ONLY

Broadway

Four plays in one weekend? Why not? On Broadway, the best of American theatrical talent comes together in 40 theaters within a tight cluster of walkable New York City blocks. The schedules are right, the marquees are bright, and the variety of the productions gives you plenty to choose from. Between shows, follow celebrity footsteps into some hangouts of the theater people and learn some Broadway history. This district has been home of the best (and worst) of what the New York stage has to offer for more than a century.
— BY MERVYN ROTHSTEIN

FRIDAY

1 *Ticket Strategy* 2 p.m.

Lengthy treatises have been written about how to get Broadway tickets. One option is to join the line at the discount **TKTS** booth at the north end of Times Square (tdf.org/tkts), sponsored by the nonprofit Theater Development Fund. The latest hits aren't likely to show up here, but good productions well into their runs may be available, and savings can be 25 percent to 50 percent. Lines form well before the booth opens at 3 p.m. Whether you buy at TKTS, pay full price at a theater box office, or book weeks ahead through **Telecharge** (telecharge.com) or **Ticketmaster** (ticketmaster.com), study the reviews and listings first. To span the Broadway experience, plan to see a mix of shows — light and serious, traditional and daring.

2 *Evening Joe* 6:15 p.m.

Join pre-theater crowds at **Joe Allen's** (326 West 46th Street; 212-581-6464; joeallenrestaurant.com; $$). It's a very busy, very New York place. While you're eating your meatloaf or pan-roasted Atlantic cod, check out the wall displays of posters for the biggest flops in Broadway history. You no doubt know the book, and the movie, of *Breakfast at Tiffany's*. But did you know there was also a 1966 musical version? It starred Mary Tyler Moore and Richard Chamberlain. The world may have forgotten, but the stars no doubt haven't.

3 *Song and Dance* 7:45 p.m.

Get your theater weekend off to a high-energy start with a musical. Broadway is most famous for its musicals, and the top 14 longest-running shows in Broadway history (No. 1 is *The Phantom of the Opera*) are creatures of song and dance. A tip: musicals that have been playing for years can sometimes be tired, with sets shopworn and stars long gone. Choose one that's still fresh, and arrive early. Latecomers are despised almost as much as people who forget to turn off their cellphones.

4 *Fisticuffs Optional* 10:30 p.m.

Head off for a drink at **Angus McIndoe** (258 West 44th Street; 212-221-9222; angusmcindoe.com), where producers, critics, stagehands, directors, and sometimes even actors show up to discuss what's playing, what's in rehearsal, and what's in trouble. A notorious incident here: the director David Leveaux, angry with Michael Riedel of *The New York Post* for making snide comments about his show at the time, a 2004 revival of *Fiddler on the Roof*, pushed, or maybe it was punched, Riedel. It's unlikely there will be another boxing match, but you never know.

SATURDAY

5 *45 Seconds Away* Noon

The legendary **Cafe Edison** (Hotel Edison, 228 West 47th Street; 212-840-5000; edisonhotelnyc.com; $)

OPPOSITE Times Square is at the heart of Broadway and home to the TKTS booth for discounted theater tickets.

RIGHT A production of *The Book of Mormon*, one of Broadway's success stories, at the Eugene O'Neill Theater.

looks like a plain deli, but to Broadway it is something like what the Polo Lounge is to Hollywood. Producers, writers, even old-time comedians have been known to hang out here — yes, that could have been Jackie Mason you saw here once, telling a bad joke. Neil Simon wrote a play called *45 Seconds From Broadway* about the Cafe Edison, but the restaurant is better than the play. August Wilson used to sit for hours over coffee working on his dramas. And another kind of star — Joe DiMaggio — lived at the Edison when he was hitting the kind of home runs that aren't just a metaphor for success. The cafe is also known as the Polish Tea Room, but you can order much more than tea — from bagels and lox to potato pancakes and applesauce to pastrami on rye.

6 *Get Serious* 1:45 p.m.

You want to see at least one meaty serious play, the kind with a chance of showing up someday on college reading lists. Schedule it for today's matinee, and you'll leave yourself time afterward to think about what you've seen and maybe even discuss it over dinner. While you're waiting for the show to begin, check out the "At This Theater" feature in your *Playbill* to see what giants of yesteryear appeared on the stage you'll be viewing. Humphrey Bogart became a star at the Broadhurst in 1935 in *The Petrified Forest.* Marlon Brando made his Broadway debut in 1944 in *I Remember Mama* at the Music Box (which was built by Irving Berlin) and astonished audiences as Stanley Kowalski in *A Streetcar Named Desire* in 1947 at the Ethel Barrymore.

7 *Dinner Break* 6:15 p.m.

Rebuild your strength with a French-inspired dinner at **Chez Josephine** (414 West 42nd Street; 212-594-1925; chezjosephine.com; $$$). It's run by Jean-Claude Baker, the adopted son of the chanteuse Josephine Baker. There's a pianist accompanying the meal — and whoever's playing that evening counts among his predecessors Harry Connick Jr. If you'd rather go Japanese, try **Kodama Sushi** (301 West 45th Street; 212-582-8065; kodamasushi.com; $$), a home away from home for chorus lines, supporting casts, stage managers, and other theatrical types. Stephen Sondheim and William Finn have been spotted at the sushi bar, and the autographed posters on the wall from recent hits (and misses) add to the ambience. It's a neighborhood place, but the neighborhood is Broadway.

8 *Seeing Stars* 7:45 p.m.

For the biggest night of the week, find a show with top-tier leads. Then file in with the rest of what's likely to be a full audience, and share the night with the other star watchers. Seeking autographs? Head for the stage door right after the curtain drops, and don't be dismayed if you're part of a crowd. Celebrity actors are usually willing to pause before entering their limos and sign all of the *Playbill* copies thrust at them. Before the show, check out the theater itself: many Broadway houses are stars in their own right. Notice the ornate decoration, and remember the history. **The Lyceum** on West 45th Street, for example, dates to 1903 and was put up by a producer named David Frohman. The story has it that he

ABOVE A cluster of theater marquees along West 45th Street between Eighth Avenue and Broadway.

BELOW Breakfast at Cafe Edison on West 47th Street, a regular gathering spot for Broadway royalty.

OPPOSITE Queuing for theater tickets at the TKTS booth in Times Square.

built an apartment high up inside with a small door for observing the stage — and that he would wave a white handkerchief to warn his actress wife, Margaret Illington, that she was overacting.

9 *And More Stars* 11 p.m.

The post-performance star gazing is usually good at **Bar Centrale** (324 West 46th Street; 212-581-3130; barcentralenyc.com), where actors often retire for a cocktail after two or three hours of performing. It's run by Joe Allen, above his eponymous restaurant. Don't seek autographs here, though — the performers expect post-play privacy.

SUNDAY

10 *Brunch, Anyone?* 12:30 p.m.

If the weather's good, the idyllic garden of **Barbetta** (321 West 46th Street; 212-246-9171; barbettarestaurant.com; $$$) is an enchanting space for a light pasta and a lighter wine, giving you a feel of northern Italy.

11 *Grand Finale* 2:45 p.m.

Make your last play memorable. Broadway and its audiences have fallen under the spell of Hollywood-style special effects, and if you want something splashy, you can probably find it. In theater, you're seeing the pyrotechnics live (despite all the publicity, accidents are rare), and producers can't rely as much on computer-generated sleight of hand. Sit back and enjoy the spectacle.

THE BASICS

Taxis, trains, buses, and subways all converge on Times Square. Everyplace in the theater district is walkable from anyplace else in the theater district.

Marriott Marquis
1535 Broadway
212-398-1900
marriott.com
$$$-$$$$
In the heart of Broadway, with a theater inside.

W Times Square
1567 Broadway
212-930-7400
starwoodhotels.com/nyc-hotels
$$$-$$$$
Stylish and luxurious.

Hilton Times Square
234 West 42nd Street
212-840-8222
hilton.com
$$$-$$$$
Spacious rooms, many amenities.

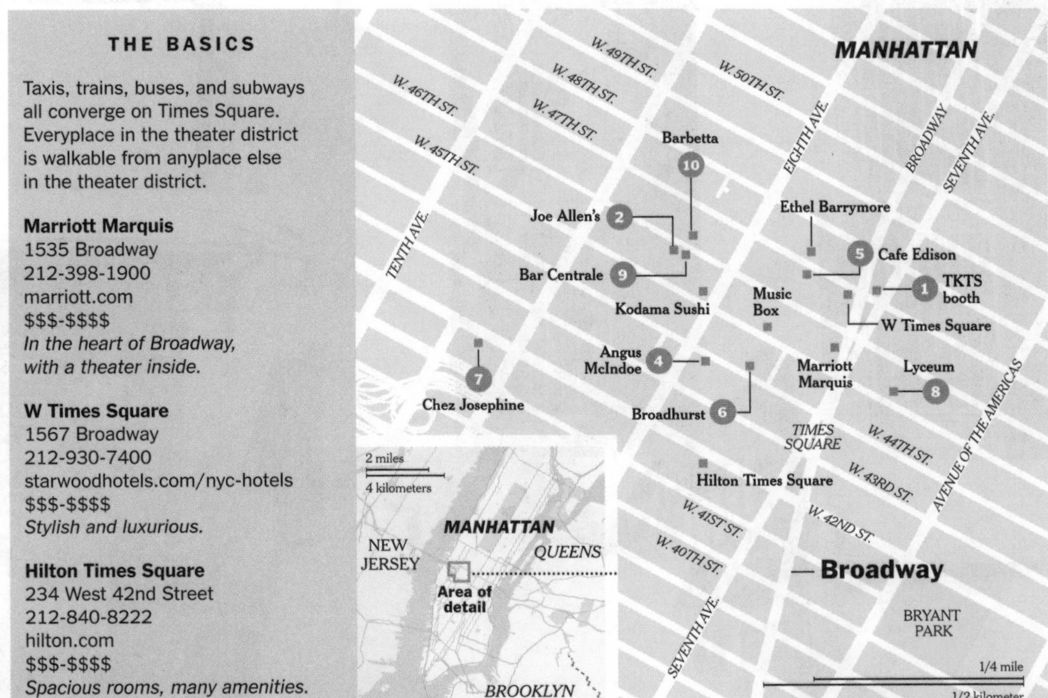

2370

Harlem

In Harlem, the first years of the 21st century may best be remembered for a seismic demographic shift: an influx of whites and a drop in the black population that put it below 50 percent for the first time in decades. This shifting landscape has brought with it a new cultural scene with a distinct cosmopolitan vibe. But even with the arrival of new doorman buildings, luxurious brownstone renovations, and chichi boutiques and restaurants, this swath of Upper Manhattan still brims with the cultural landmarks that made it the capital of black America.

— BY JOHN ELIGON

FRIDAY

1 *The Collector* 4 p.m.

Stop in at the **Schomburg Center for Research in Black Culture** (515 Malcolm X Boulevard; 212-491-2200; nypl.org/locations/schomburg), a trove of manuscripts, rare books, photos, videos, and recordings. Its exhibitions have included photos of early-20th-century Harlem life, private papers of Maya Angelou, and an exploration of the influence of jazz on the visual arts. It is named for Arturo A. Schomburg, a visionary Puerto Rican-born black private collector who amassed a significant portion of this material before his death in 1938. Check the schedule for films, lectures, discussions, and musical performances.

2 *Strivers' Row* 6 p.m.

The timing may not have been great when a group of elegant townhouses went up in Central Harlem in the late 19th century — it was shortly before an economic panic. But the development, on 138th and 139th Streets between Adam Clayton Powell Jr. and Frederick Douglass Boulevards, survived. Today it is one of New York's most graceful and integrated examples of period architecture. Stroll past Italian-palazzo and neo-Georgian former homes of the high achievers like Scott Joplin and Bill Robinson (Bojangles) who gave this section its nickname, **Strivers' Row**. Don't miss a nod to the past, painted on some of the entrances to the rear courtyard: "Private Road; Walk Your Horses."

3 *Culinary Eclectic* 8 p.m.

Marcus Samuelsson, true to his heritage as Ethiopian born and Swedish raised, has done with his restaurant, **Red Rooster Harlem** (310 Lenox Avenue; 212-792-9001; redroosterharlem.com; $$), what few can: attracted a clientele diverse in both color and age. The menu pulls from all cultural corners (blackened catfish, lemon chicken with couscous, steak frites with truffle Béarnaise). Stick around after dinner for a drink at the horseshoe-shaped bar or in the basement lounge.

4 *Old-World Charm* 11 p.m.

After eating at Red Rooster, head downstairs to Samuelsson's other creation, **Ginny's Supper Club**. Although both are housed in the same building, Ginny's has its own unique speakeasy vibe and a different menu of creative small plates and cocktails. With a D.J. spinning tunes, you can dance off your dinner.

SATURDAY

5 *The Main Drag* 10 a.m.

The 125th Street corridor stands at the convergence of old and new. On the sidewalks, vendors sell fragrant oils and bootleg DVDs. Indoors, you can find shops like **Atmos** (203 West 125th Street;

OPPOSITE Italianate and neo-Georgian townhouses line Harlem's Strivers' Row, once home of Scott Joplin.

RIGHT Named for one of New York's first black-owned bars, 67 Orange Street is on Frederick Douglass Boulevard.

212-666-2242; atmosnyc.blogspot.com), with cool sneakers and street wear, and **Carol's Daughter** (24 West 125th Street; 212-828-6757; carolsdaughter.com), the flagship store of a successful local maker of cosmetics and lotions. In the midst of it all is the **Apollo Theater** (253 West 125th Street; 212-531-5300; apollotheater.org), where black entertainers have gotten their start for generations. Group tours are available by appointment; if you're not traveling with a pack, you may be able to tag along with one. (Call to check availability.) To catch the famed Amateur Night, return on a Wednesday.

6 *El Barrio* Noon

Harlem's east side is El Barrio, a repository for Spanish culture. Have an authentic Puerto Rican meal at **La Fonda Boricua** (1702 Lexington Avenue; 212-410-7292; fondaboricua.com; $$), which started as a lunch counter and expanded with a simple dining room. There is no printed menu, but you can't go wrong with the pernil (roast pork). Walk off lunch with a tour of the murals on nearby buildings. A mosaic at 106th Street and Lexington Avenue honors Julia de Burgos, a 20th-century poet. The four-story-tall *Spirit of East Harlem*, on Lexington at 104th Street, includes men playing dominoes, a woman holding a baby, and the Puerto Rican flag. Stop at **Justo Botanica** (134 East 104th Street; 212-534-9140), a musty store founded in 1930 that offers spiritual readings and sells African and Native American carvings as well as prayer cards, candles, and beads. For a history of Spanish Harlem, visit **El Museo del Barrio** (1230 Fifth Avenue; 212-831-7272; elmuseo.org).

7 *The New Renaissance* 3 p.m.

The true Harlem Renaissance was centered on art, and now new galleries and art spaces are popping up again. **Casa Frela Gallery** (47 West 119th Street; 212-722-8577; casafrela.com), in a Stanford White brownstone, exhibits small collections and screens films. The **Renaissance Fine Art Gallery** (2075 Adam Clayton Powell Jr. Boulevard; 212-866-1660; therfagallery.com) and the **Dwyer Cultural Center** (258 St. Nicholas Avenue; 212-222-3060; dwyercc.org) celebrate black culture through art. **The Studio Museum** (144 West 125th Street; 212-864-4500; studiomuseum.org) shows fine art, photography, and film.

8 *The Scene* 6 p.m.

Hard to believe, but the stretch of Frederick Douglass Boulevard where the 1970s drug lord Frank Lucas boasted he made $1 million a day selling heroin is now Harlem's Restaurant Row, a stretch of inviting restaurants and lounges. If the weather's nice, enjoy a drink in the neighborhood's best outdoor space at **Harlem Tavern** (No. 2135;

212-866-4500; harlemtavern.com). Find an ode to multiculturalism at **bier international** (No. 2099; 212-280-0944; bierinternational.com), a twist on the German beer garden. Check out **Moca Restaurant & Lounge** (No. 2210; 212-665-8081; mocalounge.com) for the latest in hip-hop tracks. At No. 2082 and named for the address of one of New York's first black-owned bars, **67 Orange Street** offers exotic cocktails and a speakeasy vibe.

9 *Soul Food* 8 p.m.

Those who know soul food know that it is best prepared at home. So it should come as no surprise that good soul food restaurants are difficult to find even in Harlem. **Sylvia's** (328 Lenox Avenue; 212-996-2669; sylviassoulfood.com) gets the most buzz, but it's more about the restaurant's history than the food. Better options are **Amy Ruth's** (113 West 116th Street; 212-280-8779; amyruthsharlem.com; $), where dishes are named for famous African-Americans, or **Miss Mamie's Spoonbread Too** (366 West 110th Street; 212-865-6744; spoonbreadinc.com; $-$$) and its sister restaurant **Miss Maude's** (547 Lenox Avenue; 212-690-3100).

10 *A World of Music* 11 p.m.

For a great combination of live music and dance space, take a seat at **Shrine** (2271 Adam Clayton Powell Jr. Boulevard; 212-690-7807; shrinenyc.com), a no-frills restaurant and bar where everyone feels like a local. This is a true melting pot of music. Jazz, reggae, hip-hop, pop, and more might be played by the live bands on a single night. And with lots of floor space to maneuver in, you'll be dancing until your feet are sore.

OPPOSITE Manuel Vega's mosaic tribute to the poet Julia de Burgos at East 106th Street and Lexington Avenue.

ABOVE The Abyssinian Baptist Church, where the Sunday-morning service is as theatrical as a Broadway production.

LEFT Dr. Harold Cromer puts on a tap dance show at the Dwyer Cultural Center.

SUNDAY

11 *Gospel and Brunch* 11 a.m.

Gospel churches are a staple of Harlem visits. A tourist favorite is **Abyssinian Baptist Church** (132 Odell Clark Place; 212-862-7474; abyssinian.org), a megachurch with a Broadway-like music production. For something more serene, yet still inspiring, attend a service at **Mount Olivet Baptist Church** (201 Lenox Avenue; 212-864-1155; mountolivetbaptistchurch.org). Afterward, have your Sunday brunch at **Kitchenette Uptown** (1272 Amsterdam Avenue; 212-531-7600; kitchenetterestaurant.com; $$). The restaurant is designed like a rural porch, providing a home-style feel with hearty dishes to match. Try the baked crème brulee French toast, turkey sausage, or one of the thick omelets.

ABOVE A Rafael Ferrer exhibit at El Museo del Barrio in Spanish Harlem. The museum tells the neighborhood's story with a focus on its artistic landscape.

OPPOSITE The interior of Mount Olivet Baptist Church on Lenox Avenue, one of the Harlem churches that welcome Sunday morning visitors.

THE BASICS

Harlem spans a section of northern Manhattan roughly from 110th Street to 155th Street.

Get around on the subway, or hail taxicabs.

Aloft Harlem
2296 Frederick Douglass Boulevard
212-749-4000
alofthotels.com/harlem
$$
A bona fide luxury hotel to represent Harlem's changing face. High design in contemporary style.

The Harlem Flophouse
242 West 123rd Street
347-632-1960
harlemflophouse.com
$$
Charming four-room bed and breakfast in an 1890s brownstone.

Mount Morris House
12 Mount Morris Park West
917-478-6214
mountmorrishouse.com
$$$
Four-room B&B in a restored mansion with elegantly carved woodwork.

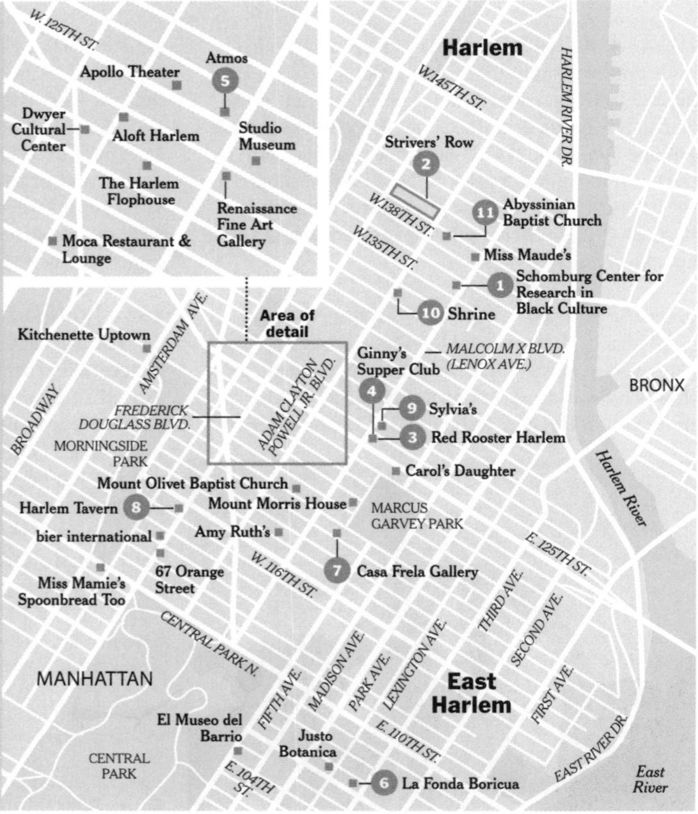

Brooklyn

The Brooklyn Cruise Terminal on the Buttermilk Channel has picturesque views even when the Queen Mary 2, *which docks there regularly, is at sea. There is verdant Governor's Island across the water and, behind it, the heaving, jagged rise of Manhattan. To the north are the great bridges of the East River. To the west, the Statue of Liberty. And to the east, beyond chain link and forbidding streets, there is Brooklyn itself, New York City's most populous borough, a destination in its own right.* — BY SAM SIFTON

FRIDAY

1 *Waterfront Stroll* 4 p.m.

The cobblestone streets under the Manhattan Bridge are home to small shops and shiny new condominium buildings, and to **Saint Ann's Warehouse** (29 Jay Street, at Dock Street; 718-254-8779; stannswarehouse.org), a theater that has been a mainstay of the Brooklyn arts scene for more than three decades. Across from Fulton Ferry State Park, it is an excellent destination after a walk along the **Promenade** in Brooklyn Heights (parallel to Columbia Heights, a grand old street of towering brownstones, running from Remsen to Orange Streets). Check ahead to see what's playing and then wander down to the box office to pick up your tickets.

2 *Walk in the Park* 5 p.m.

Alternatively, head inland, toward the leafy precincts of Fort Greene, for a show at the **Brooklyn Academy of Music** (bam.org) or the **Mark Morris Dance Group** (markmorrisdancegroup.org). Atlantic Avenue, which runs deep into the borough, will lead you most of the way, through a stretch of antiques shops and restaurants.

3 *Pre-theater Dinner* 6:30 p.m.

Once you get strolling, it is difficult not to drift into other pretty residential neighborhoods: Cobble Hill and Carroll Gardens nearby and, slightly farther afield, Park Slope and Prospect Heights. There is excellent eating along the way. At the bottom of Court Street in Carroll Gardens: **Prime Meats** (465 Court Street at Luquer Street; 718-254-0327; frankspm.com), a chic Germanish steak and salad restaurant. A block or so farther south, on the corner of Huntington Street: **Buttermilk Channel** (524 Court Street; 718-852-8490; buttermilkchannelnyc.com), where you can get local cheeses and pastas and a superlative duck meatloaf. Ten minutes before the end of your meal, have the host call for a car, and go to the performance you've chosen.

4 *Drink After the Curtain* 10 p.m.

Fort Greene abounds in bars suitable for a late-evening drink. A cocktail at the minimalist and homey **No. 7** is no-risk (7 Greene Avenue at Fulton Street; 718-522-6370; no7restaurant.com). Those seeking rougher charms can venture to the **Alibi** (242 DeKalb Avenue between Clermont Avenue and Vanderbilt Avenue), where there are cheap drinks, a pool table, and a crowd that runs equal parts artist and laborer.

SATURDAY

5 *Breakfast Paradise* 9 a.m.

Tom's Restaurant in Prospect Heights (782 Washington Avenue at Sterling Place; 718-636-9738) has been a crowded, friendly mainstay of this neighborhood for decades, and is a winning place to begin a day in Kings County (that's Brooklyn, to you outsiders; each of New York City's five boroughs

OPPOSITE Brownstone-lined streets invite long strolls in Park Slope and Prospect Heights.

RIGHT Boutiques like the Brook Farm general store flourish in Brooklyn's Williamsburg and Greenpoint neighborhoods.

is a separate county). Eat pancakes and waffles in a room filled with tchotchkes and good cheer, and watch the marvelous parade.

6 *Parks and Arts* 10 a.m.

A Tom's breakfast provides a strong foundation for a visit to the exhibitions of the nearby **Brooklyn Museum** (200 Eastern Parkway at Washington Avenue; 718-638-5000; brooklynmuseum.org). It is also useful in advance of a walk through the **Brooklyn Botanic Garden** (900 Washington Avenue; 718-623-7200; bbg.org), a 19th-century ash dump that is now home to some of the best horticultural displays in the world. And of course there is **Prospect Park** (prospectpark.org), Frederick Law Olmsted and Calvert Vaux's triumphant 1867 follow-up to Central Park in Manhattan. Those with children may wish to visit the zoo (450 Flatbush Avenue near Empire Boulevard; 718-399-7339; prospectparkzoo.com), where the daily feedings of the sea lions are a popular attraction.

7 *A Visit to Hipchester* 2 p.m.

Boutiques, coffee bars, and restaurants continue to flourish in Williamsburg and Greenpoint, north Brooklyn's youth-culture Marrakesh. Amid these, **Brook Farm**, a general store in south Williamsburg, offers an aesthetic of farmhouse cosmopolitanism (75 South Sixth Street, between Berry Street and Wythe Avenue; 718-388-8642; brookfarmgeneralstore.com). **Artists and Fleas** is a weekend market where artists, designers, collectors, and craftspeople show their work (70 North Seventh Street between Wythe

ABOVE A storefront on Eighth Avenue in Brooklyn's Chinatown, in Sunset Park.

LEFT The much loved and well used Prospect Park, designed by Frederick Law Olmsted and Calvert Vaux after they completed Central Park in Manhattan.

OPPOSITE Diners in the back room of Williamsburg's Fatty 'Cue, the Southeast Asian-inspired barbecue restaurant.

Avenue and Kent Avenue; 917-488-4203; artistsandfleas.com). And **Spoonbill and Sugartown, Booksellers** offers an eclectic mix of art and design books and academic tracts (218 Bedford Avenue at North Fifth Street; 718-387-7322; spoonbillbooks.com). For a pick-me-up or a new coffee machine for home, try **Blue Bottle Coffee** (160 Berry Street between North Fourth and North Fifth Streets; 718-387-4160; bluebottlecoffee.net), an impossibly nerdy outpost of the original Oakland coffee bar. Siphon? French press? Cold drip? All available, along with all the crazy coffee talk you like. Get your geek on.

8 *Dinner for Kings* 7:30 p.m.

Those enamored of the Williamsburg scene may stay in the neighborhood for a smoky dinner at **Fatty 'Cue**, Zak Pelaccio's antic and awesome Southeast Asian barbecue joint (91 South Sixth Street between Berry Street and Bedford Avenue; 718-599-3090; fattycue.com/home). In Greenpoint, there is the excellent and slightly more adult-themed **Anella**, where the chef works marvels with vegetables and duck (222 Franklin Street at Green Street; 718-389-8100; anellabrooklyn.com). Parents with children might try the pizzas at **Motorino** (739 Broadway; 718-599-8899; motorinopizza.com) or scoot back to Park Slope, where the brothers Bromberg offer a welcoming family atmosphere with food to match at their **Blue Ribbon Brooklyn** (280 Fifth Avenue, between First Street and Garfield Street; 718-840-0404; blueribbonrestaurants.com).

9 *Pazz and Jop* 10 p.m.

Brooklyn's music scene continues to expand. Three places to hear bands are **Union Pool** in Williamsburg (484 Union Avenue at Meeker Avenue; 718-609-0484; union-pool.com); **Brooklyn Bowl**, also there (61 Wythe Avenue between North 11th and North 12th Streets; 718-963-3369; brooklynbowl.com); and **Southpaw**, in Park Slope (125 Fifth Avenue, between Sterling Place and St. Johns Place; 718-230-0236; spsounds.com). Jazz heads should make their way to **Barbès** in Park Slope (376 Ninth Street at Sixth Avenue; 347-422-0248; barbesbrooklyn.com), where a rich calendar of readings and concerts can take a visitor from early Saturday evening well into Sunday morning.

SUNDAY

10 *Dim Sum à Go-Go* 10 a.m.

Brooklyn's Chinatown, along Eighth Avenue in the Sunset Park neighborhood, is not as large as Manhattan's but it offers great pleasures. Arrive early for a dim sum meal at **Pacificana** (813 55th Street at Eighth Avenue; 718-871-2880), and watch as the dining room fills into an approximation of a rush-hour subway car. Then stop in at **Ba Xuyen** (4222 Eighth

Avenue, between 42nd and 43rd Streets) for a banh mi brunch sandwich and a Vietnamese coffee, or at **Yun Nan Flavour Snack** (5121 Eighth Avenue; 718 633-3090) for a fiery sweet and sour soup with dumplings.

11 *History in the Ground* 1 p.m.

Walk off all the food with a tour of **Green-Wood Cemetery** (500 25th Street at Fifth Avenue; 718-768-7300; green-wood.com), the hilly and beautiful parkland where generations of New Yorkers have moved after death. Admission is free, as are the maps available at the entrance. Look for Boss Tweed, for Jean-Michel Basquiat, for Leonard Bernstein, and for other once-boldfaced names, as parrots (really!) fly about and the wind ruffles the trees and that view of Manhattan opens up in the distance once more. It appears smaller from this vantage, as if placed in perspective.

ABOVE The view of Manhattan from the Battle Hill Monument at Green-Wood Cemetery, which was a popular tourist attraction in the 19th century.

OPPOSITE The pedestrian path on the Brooklyn Bridge.

THE BASICS

Take a taxi from LaGuardia or Kennedy Airport. From Kennedy, the AirTrain to Jamaica Station is also an option. From Manhattan, take the subway. Use the subway, buses, and car services, which are easier to find than yellow cabs.

Marriott at the Brooklyn Bridge
333 Adams Street
718-246-7000
marriott.com
$$$
Comfortable rooms and easy access to bus and subway.

Hotel Le Jolie
235 Meeker Avenue
718-625-2100
hotellejolie.com
$$
Boutique hotel in Williamsburg, near shops and restaurants.

Hotel LeBleu
370 Fourth Avenue
718-625-1500
hotellebleu.com
$$$
Sublime views of the harbor and near two subway stations.

Hudson River
MANHATTAN
East River
Anella
GREENPOINT
MANHATTAN BRIDGE
FULTON FERRY STATE PARK
BROOKLYN BRIDGE
Area of detail
WILLIAMSBURG
Saint Ann's Warehouse 1
Promenade
BROOKLYN HEIGHTS
New York Marriott at the Brooklyn Bridge
GOVERNOR'S ISLAND
Motorino
Buttermilk Channel
COBBLE HILL
CARROLL GARDENS
FORT GREENE
Area of detail
PROSPECT HEIGHTS
PARK SLOPE
Brooklyn Cruise Terminal
3
Prime Meats
Buttermilk Channel
Barbès
PROSPECT PARK
Zoo
Brooklyn Botanic Garden
FLATBUSH AVE.
GOWANUS EXPWY.
11 Green-Wood Cemetery
Ba Xuyen
SUNSET PARK
Yun Nan Flavour Snack
MCDONALD AVE.
10 Pacificana
278
BROOKLYN
1 mile
2 kilometers

Spoonbill and Sugartown, Booksellers
KENT AVE.
Brooklyn Bowl
Artists and Fleas
Blue Bottle Coffee
Hotel Le Jolie
WILLIAMSBURG BRIDGE
BERRY ST.
BEDFORD AVE.
BROOKLYN-QUEENS EXPWY.
9 Union Pool
Brook Farm 7
8 Fatty 'Cue
BROADWAY
WYTHE AVE.

FORT GREENE PARK
DEKALB AVE.
Mark Morris Dance Group
Alibi
LAFAYETTE AVE.
4 No. 7
Brooklyn Academy of Music 2
FULTON ST.
ATLANTIC AVE.
FLATBUSH AVE.
Tom's Restaurant 5
Southpaw
Blue Ribbon Brooklyn
Hotel Le Bleu
Brooklyn Museum 6

NEW JERSEY
QUEENS
Statue of Liberty
Area of detail
STATEN ISLAND
BROOKLYN

佳美旅遊
美盛
入籍中心
移民留學
TOP ONE
MEDICAL BILLING
安捷醫務
帳管公司
718-886-8180
135-27 三樓
미용
135-31 40 RD.
CHINA
星島日報
和平統一促進會
NEW YORK ASSOCIATION FOR
PEACEFUL UNIFICATION OF CHINA
紅蘋果
駕駛學校
型屋
SALON
咖喱葉
新温州
718 886-7768
脚底按摩
1小时$28元
免费肩膀按摩
拔罐 $20元
刮痧 $20元
卓悦 二樓
美容
LIQUORS
亞美國際旅遊
718-358-6413
Shining Salon
靚點 髮型屋
名媛美容
미용 SKIN CARE
718-961-4888
135-31 40RD 3A
CURRY LEAVES RESTAURANT INC.
咖喱葉
馬來風味
TEL:718-762-9313
135-31
臺北
酷狗
髮型設計
消費者保險
CONSUMERS INSURANCE

Queens

Remember old New York, where immigrants strived, cultures collided, grit outshone glamour, and ethnic restaurants were filled with ethnic crowds rather than Instagramming foodies? That city lives on in Queens, where the forces of gentrification have barely nipped at the edges. Queens is the city's most expansive borough, home to 2.2 million people from (it seems) 2.2 million backgrounds. It is full of sights and sounds unlike anything you'll find a short subway ride away, and across the East River, in Manhattan.

— BY SETH KUGEL

FRIDAY

1 *Tinseltown, Astoria* 5 p.m.

Hollywood gets all the publicity, but Astoria, one of Queens's most energetic neighborhoods, is home to Kaufman Astoria Studios, where the Marx Brothers shot *Animal Crackers* in 1930 and where Big Bird still resides. One building is now the **Museum of the Moving Image** (36-01 35th Avenue; 718-777-6888; movingimage.us), which is free on Fridays from 4 to 8 p.m. The displays cover not just television (Dr. Heathcliff Huxtable's sweater and Mork from Ork's spacesuit) and film (telegrams sent by Orson Welles, Winona Ryder's prosthetic legs from *Black Swan*), but also digital entertainment, including functioning Donkey Kong, Space Invaders, and Ms. Pac-Man machines, as well as special exhibitions.

2 *Little Egypt* 8 p.m.

Long known as a Greek neighborhood, Astoria is now wildly diverse, with Colombians, Brazilians, and Slavs, and, at the end of Steinway Street, a big Middle Eastern commercial district known as Little Egypt. You are unlikely to find better, more simply prepared fish than at **Sabry's Seafood** (24-25 Steinway Street; 718-721-9010; $$), an informal, popular spot where whole snapper, bronzini, and tilapia are grilled, fried, or barbecued Egypt style. Start with the grilled calamari, and try an Egyptian lemonade. (No alcohol is served.)

OPPOSITE An agglomeration of street signs proclaim the vibrancy of the Chinatown in Flushing, Queens.

3 *Hookahs and Tea* 10 p.m.

Little Egypt is filled with the informal hookah lounges called shisha bars. For a lavish version, head up the stairs from Sabry's to **Layali Dubai** (24-17 Steinway Street; 718-728-1492; layalidubainy.com). The dress code for the mostly Muslim crowd is shocking in its range, from conservative to the near scandalous. Groups of men and women (often separated) sip mint tea and fruit juice, smoke hookahs, and take in live music and belly-dancing until late.

4 *Choose Your Party* Midnight

Drink like a hipster at **Dutch Kills** (27-24 Jackson Avenue; 718-383-2724; dutchkillsbar.com), a fashionable cocktail hideaway in the Queens neighborhood of Long Island City, for a Rum Buck, Bloody Knuckle, or—why not?—a Manhattan. (The specialty drinks are likely to be several dollars cheaper than those you'd find at similar Manhattan joints.)

SATURDAY

5 *Eat, Drink, Shop* 10:30 a.m.

Walk out of the subway at the Roosevelt Avenue-Jackson Heights stop, and you have entered a land of diversity you previously assumed was metaphorical. How else to explain Jackson Heights, a place where a pharmacy sign reads "Bangladesh Farmacia" (to

RIGHT A belly dancer at Layali Dubai, a night spot that draws a mostly Muslim crowd.

appeal to both South Asian and South American constituencies) and where a Guatemalan shop closes and is fast replaced by a Russian deli? Head north up 74th Street, stopping in **Patel Brothers** supermarket (No. 37-27; 718-898-3445) to ogle exotic produce, **India Sari Palace** (No. 3707; 718-426-2700) to shop for saris, and **Al Naimat** (No. 3703; 718-476-1100) to buy South Asian sweets. Take a right on 37th Avenue, Jackson Heights's main thoroughfare. Pick up a Colombian salpicón, halfway between fruit salad and juice, at **La Paisa Bakery** (37-03 82nd Street; 718-779-2784) to tide you over until you reach **La Gran Uruguaya** (85-06 37th Avenue; 718-505-0404) for coffee and buttery soft Uruguayan-Colombian pastries.

6 *Chez Satchmo* 1 p.m.

At the **Louis Armstrong House Museum** (34-56 107th Street; 718-478-8297; satchmo.net), the décor was more or less frozen in time when Armstrong, the jazz giant, died in his sleep (in the bed you'll see) in 1971. His wife, Lucille, lived on in the house until 1982 but left most things untouched, down to the reel-to-reel tape recorders in Satchmo's office-studio, a bottle of his cologne, and the gilded bathroom fixtures. Why did a celebrity like Armstrong choose to live the last three decades of his life in a modest house in the working-class Corona neighborhood of Queens? That question is explored on the guided tour.

7 *Panoramic View* 3 p.m.

Take the No. 7 train two stops down from the Armstrong house to **Flushing Meadows-Corona Park**. The borough's biggest park, it hosts sporting events ranging from the annual United States Open tennis championships to hardscrabble immigrant cricket games. Walk toward the 12-story-high Unisphere sculpture, built for the 1964 World's Fair, and seek out the etched granite work nearby in which the artist Matt Mullican recounts the history of the park. Then head into the **Queens Museum of Art** (718-592-9700; queensmuseum.org), home to the Panorama of the City of New York, an astonishing scale model of the five boroughs with 895,000 houses and buildings. (There are even planes taking off from La Guardia Airport.)

8 *Eat Uzbek* 8 p.m.

Of course Queens has a restaurant specializing in Bukharan Jewish cuisine from Uzbekistan—need you even ask? **Cheburechnaya** (92-09 63rd Drive; 718-897-9080; $) is a dinerlike restaurant in the Rego Park neighborhood with food not like that of any diner you've ever seen. This area's so-called "Russian" Jewish community is largely from Central Asia, and foods from that region are the specialties here. The namesake chebureki may look like the stuffed fried pockets of countless other cultures, but the Central Asian spice blend makes it clear these are no empanadas. Even better are the samcy—flaky savory pastries filled with pumpkin or ribs.

9 *Taste of Home* 10 p.m.

Despite its international flair, Queens is situated (did you forget?) in the United States. Two subway stops farther down Queens Boulevard is **Forest Hills**, a suburban-feeling neighborhood where a buzzing

ABOVE Reel-to-reel tape recorders at the Louis Armstrong House Museum, where many things remain as they were when Armstrong died in 1971.

BELOW Well stocked with memorabilia, the Museum of the Moving Image is a must-see for television and movie fans, especially if they have long memories.

night-life spot is, surprisingly, an American bakery that gets as packed on late evenings as it does for weekend brunch. **Martha's Country Bakery** (70-30 Austin Street; 718-544-0088; marthascountrybakery.com) serves cappuccino and tantalizing desserts like red velvet cheesecake and absurdly scrumptious sour cream apple pie.

SUNDAY

10 *Chinese Massage* 10 a.m.

New York's most vibrant Chinatown — in Flushing, Queens — is packed with massage parlors. Some are fronts for more risqué businesses, but not so the very legit **Winnie Foot & Spa** (135-05 40th Road, 2nd floor; 718-961-3599). The reflexology practitioners here know their way around the human paw; just don't expect much conversation during your 30-minute foot massage unless you're fluent in Mandarin. Instead, listen to soothing music and relax in an old-fashioned recliner as if you were the fictional Queens resident Archie Bunker (though he might have scoffed at the Hello Kitty pillows).

11 *Upstairs, Downstairs* 11:30 a.m.

It's difficult to spot a non-Asian customer in **Grand Restaurant** (136-20 Roosevelt Avenue; 718-321-8258; $$), a mind-bogglingly huge dim sum palace on the third floor of the New World Mall. Choose from delicate shrimp dumplings, sticky rice with chicken wrapped in lotus leaves, and tofu rolls stuffed with pork and mushroom. For more variety and even lower prices, visit the food court downstairs and choose from a continent's worth of noodles, soups, and dumplings — from mainland China, Hong Kong, Taiwan, Korea, and beyond.

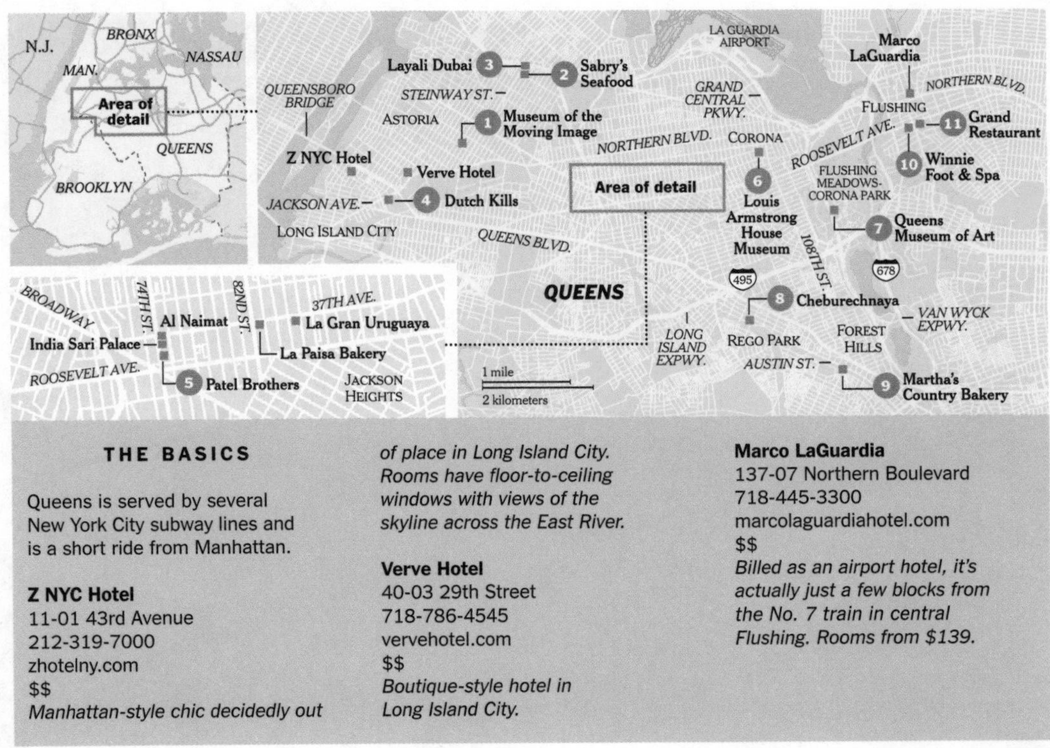

THE BASICS

Queens is served by several New York City subway lines and is a short ride from Manhattan.

Z NYC Hotel
11-01 43rd Avenue
212-319-7000
zhotelny.com
$$
Manhattan-style chic decidedly out of place in Long Island City. Rooms have floor-to-ceiling windows with views of the skyline across the East River.

Verve Hotel
40-03 29th Street
718-786-4545
vervehotel.com
$$
Boutique-style hotel in Long Island City.

Marco LaGuardia
137-07 Northern Boulevard
718-445-3300
marcolaguardiahotel.com
$$
Billed as an airport hotel, it's actually just a few blocks from the No. 7 train in central Flushing. Rooms from $139.

East Hampton

On the east end of Long Island, New York, the Atlantic Ocean crashes onto the shores of the lavish string of villages known as the Hamptons. When New York City's movers and shakers migrate here in the summer for sunning, surfing, fishing, and flirting, the center of the social swirl is historic East Hampton. Lately a raft of luxurious boutiques and restaurants have opened in town. Beloved old hotels and barrooms have been renovated. And celebrities — including Madonna — keep snapping up property in the area.
— BY STEPHANIE ROSENBLOOM

FRIDAY

1 *Social Calendar* 4 p.m.

Want to plunge into the Hamptons social scene? Then your first order of business is to grab the free newspapers and glossy magazines — *Social Life, Hampton Life, Hamptons, Hampton Sheet, Dan's Papers, The East Hampton Star* — and scan them for the weekend's fete, charity event, or oceanfront screening of *Jaws*. You'll find them near the door of many boutiques in East Hampton, but perhaps the most indulgent place to get them is **Scoop du Jour** (35 Newtown Lane; 631-329-4883), the ice cream parlor where waffle cones are stacked with cavity-friendly flavors like cake batter and cotton candy. This is also where you can buy Dreesen's doughnuts, a Hamptons staple since the 1950s. Need a gift for a party host (or yourself)? Shops have sprouted along Main Street, including **Hugo Boss** (No. 46) and **Roberta Freymann** (No. 21).

2 *Pizza Patio* 7 p.m.

It's not just socialites who flee New York for the Hamptons in summer. Manhattan restaurateurs migrate here, too. One establishment is the Italian standby **Serafina** (104 North Main Street; 631-267-3500; serafinarestaurant.com; $$$). Yellow umbrellas poke up like daffodils from its sidewalk patio and vine-covered pergola. Fresh pastas and seafood are on the menu, though the brick oven pizzas — in more than two dozen varieties, including pesto — are among the most popular picks. On a typical night, couples canoodle at the bar while well-manicured families stream into the dining room. If your taste leans toward fried seafood, homemade chowder, and frosty drinks, however, head to **Bostwick's Chowder House** (277 Pantigo Road; 631-324-1111; bostwickschowderhouse.com; $$), which has new indoor-outdoor digs.

3 *Water Music* 9 p.m.

Watching boats glide along the horizon is perhaps the simplest and most peaceful of Hamptons pleasures. Happily, a favorite haunt, the **Andrra Restaurant & Lounge** (39 Gann Road; 631-329-3663; andrra.com), occupies a secluded spot overlooking Three Mile Harbor, where Bostwick's was previously located. The open-air decks of this gleaming restaurant are an idyllic perch from which to watch boats dock. But on weekends, as the night progresses, Andrra morphs into an indoor-outdoor lounge where the lithe and tanned sip and sway to beats from a D.J.

SATURDAY

4 *Farm Fresh* 10 a.m.

Before men in golf shirts roamed the Hamptons, it was the purview of farmers. Thankfully, there are still some left. Pick up fresh eggs, local produce, and

OPPOSITE At the Pollock-Krasner House and Study Center visitors don slippers to walk on the paint-splattered floor of Jackson Pollock's studio.

RIGHT A converted storage barn, which Jackson Pollock and Lee Krasner used as their studio, is open to tours at the Pollock-Krasner House and Study Center.

home-baked muffins and scones for breakfast at **Round Swamp Farm** (184 Three Mile Harbor Road; 631-324-4438; roundswampfarm.com). Be sure to buy enough for lunch so you can skip the interminable snack bar line at the beach.

5 *Where to Tan* 11 a.m.

Choosing a favorite Hamptons beach is not unlike choosing a favorite child. Still, there are distinctions. In 2013, Stephen P. Leatherman, director of the Laboratory for Coastal Research at Florida International University, named **Main Beach** (in East Hampton) as America's best beach, beating out beaches in Hawaii and Florida, by ranking it No. 1 in his annual Top 10 Beaches rankings (drbeach.org). In 2010, **Coopers Beach** (in Southampton) captured the No. 1 spot. Both are wide and clean and—very important—sell food. Many beaches require seasonal parking permits, though visitors can park at Coopers Beach for $40 a day. Parking at Main Beach is $20 a day, but weekdays only; on weekends visitors must walk or ride bikes. (For details, go to the Long Island Convention & Visitors Bureau's Web site, discoverlongisland.com.)

6 *East End Expressionism* 3:30 p.m.

The wetlands and dunes that draw pleasure-seekers today also inspired some of the greatest abstract and landscape artists of our time. Go see why at **LongHouse Reserve** (133 Hands Creek Road; 631-329-3568; longhouse.org), a sprawling but less-visited garden and sculpture park with works by Buckminster Fuller, Dale Chihuly, Willem de Kooning, and Yoko Ono. Founded by the textile designer Jack Lenor Larsen, the 16-acre reserve is open to the public Wednesdays through Saturdays during the summer. Nearby is the **Pollock-Krasner House and Study Center** (830 Springs-Fireplace Road; 631-324-4929; pkhouse.org), which Jackson Pollock and Lee Krasner bought for $5,000 in 1946 and turned into their home and studio. Visitors must don booties to enter the barn because the floor is splattered with paint that Pollock dripped and flung for his masterpieces. In fact, some of his paint cans are still there.

7 *Clams and Cocktails* 8 p.m.

Norman Jaffe, the American architect, designed the once popular (and now defunct) restaurant known as Laundry. The space now has life as **Race Lane** (31 Race Lane; 631-324-5022; racelanerestaurant.com; $$$)—a sleek yet cozy spot with a tree-shaded patio seemingly engineered for tête-à-têtes over breezy cocktails and clams from the raw bar. Inside, well-heeled couples dine at tables or on couches in the spare, airy space. You'll find beef in many forms and seafood dishes like scallops with parsnip purée, chanterelle mushroom, hearts of palm, and tomato.

8 *No Velvet Rope* 10 p.m.

The Hamptons nightclub scene has quieted in recent years as action shifts to the tip of Long Island at Montauk, where shabby motels and quaint restaurants are being remade into boho-chic establishments. But there are still plenty of pleasures to be had in East Hampton after sunset. The music continues to thump at clubs like **Lily Pond** and **South Pointe**. For a chiller affair, head to **c/o The Maidstone** (207 Main Street; 631-324-5006; themaidstone.com). The hotel's Living Room restaurant and lounge lure a lively, attractive crowd.

SUNDAY

9 *Morning Runway* 11:30 a.m.

Catch a tennis match or baseball game on flat screens while enjoying panini or frittatas at **CittaNuova** (29 Newtown Lane; 631-324-6300; cittanuova.com; $$$), a Milan-inspired cafe with a facade that peels back to provide indoor-outdoor seating along the village's prime shopping strip. A backyard patio has more tables. The pretty space can be jammed during events like the World Cup. Should there be no games to hold your attention, people-watching (O.K., fashion-policing) from the outdoor tables will.

10 *Artful Afternoon* 1 p.m.

Many of the artists who settled in the Hamptons exhibited at **Guild Hall** (158 Main Street; 631-324-0806;

guildhall.org), the region's celebrated arts center, and current artists still do. Performances are held all summer long.

11 *Behind the Hedges* 2:30 p.m.

Real estate is a blood sport here. And one of the most coveted addresses is Lily Pond Lane. Take a leisurely drive along the wide road where beyond the hedges you can glimpse houses that belong to the likes of Martha Stewart. Grey Gardens, once the decayed home of Edith Ewing Bouvier Beale and her daughter, can be found where Lily Pond meets West End Road. Along the way you're likely to spot many material girls, but if you are desperately seeking the original, head over to Bridgehampton, where Madonna owns a horse farm on Mitchell Lane.

OPPOSITE Tanning at Main Beach, one of the East Hampton beaches frequently rated among the best places in the United States to sun and swim.

ABOVE The Roberta Freymann store on Main Street.

THE BASICS

The hundred-mile drive from Manhattan can be frustrating in summer traffic. Alternatives are the Long Island Railroad and buses run by Hampton Jitney (hamptonjitney.com) and Hampton Luxury Liner (hamptonluxuryliner.com). In town, ride a bike.

c/o The Maidstone
207 Main Street
631-324-5006
themaidstone.com
$$$$
19 modish rooms, vintage Scandinavian bicycles, beach parking permits, and yoga classes.

The 1770 House Restaurant & Inn
143 Main Street
631-324-1770
1770house.com
$$$$
Feels like the home it once was.

The Huntting Inn
94 Main Street
631-324-0410
thepalm.com/Huntting-Inn
$$$-$$$$
A pretty inn that is also home to the popular Palm restaurant.

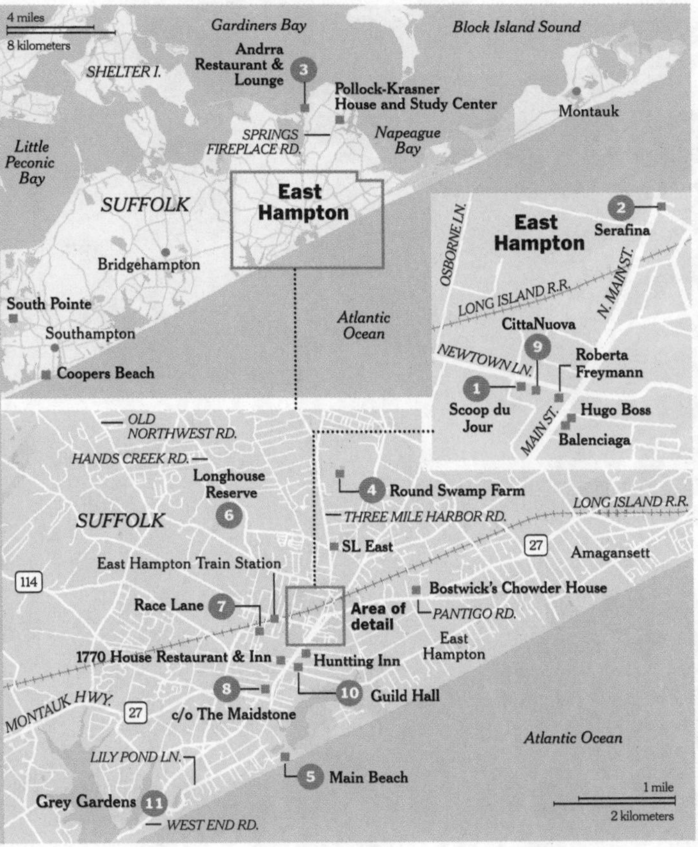

The Hudson Valley

The Hudson Valley is miles of sandstone and granite cliffs, cattail-lined riverbanks, former factory towns, orchards, farmland, and forests. The constant is the wide and beautiful Hudson River, pushing south toward its mouth at New York City. It's a one-hour train trip from Manhattan to Peekskill, at the doorstep of the mid-Hudson Valley, but the region can be fully explored only on a road trip—skirting one side of the river and winding down the other; hopscotching between historic estates, reawakened old villages, and sizable arts institutions; and detouring for farm stands, roadside diners, and seductive swimming holes.

— BY FREDA MOON

FRIDAY

1 *Peek Into Peekskill* 4 p.m.

Escape the city early and arrive in Peekskill in time for "hoppy hour" at **Peekskill Brewery** (47-53 South Water Street; 914-734-2337; peekskillbrewery.com), a 7,000-square-foot space. Or you might choose the **Birdsall House** (970 Main Street; 914-930-1880; birdsallhouse.net), where there's an antique cash register, live music on weekends, and a good craft beer list. While you're in town, drop into **Bruised Apple Books and Music** (923 Central Avenue; 914-734-7000; bruisedapplebooks.com), which has a section devoted to the Hudson Valley's past and present, a pulp-mystery reading room, and a vinyl-record listening station.

2 *Merci Beaucoup* 7:30 p.m.

Drive north to Hyde Park for dinner at the **Bocuse Restaurant** (Hyde Park; 845-471-6608; ciarestaurants.com; $$) of the Culinary Institute of America, the prestigious cooking school housed in a former seminary. The restaurant's name is a homage to the Lyonnaise chef Paul Bocuse, and the French-inspired menu includes Bocuse's black truffle soup with a puff pastry lid among the appetizers. Entrees like roasted meats and seared fish arrive with pleasing accompaniments.

OPPOSITE Olana, the painter Frederic Church's home high above the river in Hudson, New York.

RIGHT Paddling in the Hudson near Cold Spring.

3 *Folkies and Newbies* 10 p.m.

Backtrack south to Beacon to stretch out the evening at **Dogwood** (47 East Main Street, Beacon; 845-202-7500; dogwoodbar.com), a combination cocktail bar, restaurant, and music venue, or the vintage pub **Max's on Main** (246 Main Street; 845-838-6297; maxsonmain.com). On some Saturdays, there's another option: though the Band's former drummer, Levon Helm, has died, the **Midnight Rambles** (levonhelm.com) at his Woodstock studio endure as once- or twice-monthly hootenannies.

SATURDAY

4 *Active Outdoors* 9 a.m.

Dip south to Cold Spring for biscuits with sausage gravy or raspberry cornmeal pancakes at **Hudson Hil's Cafe & Market** (129-131 Main Street; 845-265-9471; hudsonhils.com; $$) and then walk to **Hudson River Expeditions** (14 Market Street; 845-809-5935; hudsonriverexpeditions.com) for advice on local hikes, like the not-for-novices Breakneck Ridge Trail (nynjtc.org/hike/breakneck-ridge-trail), or kayak rentals. Take your pick for an active morning. Afterward, you'll be ready to tackle the Texas-style dry-rubbed, hickory-smoked barbecued brisket, sausage, or ribs at **Roundup Texas Barbeque** (2741 Route 9; 845-809-5557; rounduptxbbq.com; $$). It is

housed in a trailer parked alongside a former gas station, and also serves Lone Star beer and classic sides like Frito pie and jalapeño mac 'n' cheese.

5 *Tasting Trails* 2 p.m.

In 2007, the **Tuthilltown Distillery** (14 Grist Mill Lane, Gardiner; 845-255-1527; tuthilltown.com) became New York State's first post-Prohibition whiskey distillery, operating in an old grist mill and selling its four-grain bourbon, Manhattan rye, and single-malt whiskey under the Hudson Whiskey label. Tours include a tasting. If wine's your thing, the Shawangunk Wine Trail (shawangunkwinetrail.com) winds to 14 wineries, including **Benmarl Winery** (56 Highland Avenue, Marlboro; 845-236-4265; benmarl.com), which claims to be the oldest vineyard in the country. And the Web site of the **Hudson Valley Cider Alliance** (cideralliance.com) offers yet another beverage-themed option, directing you to apple cider makers.

6 *Walking on Water* 4 p.m.

Cross the Hudson on foot on the **Walkway Over the Hudson** (walkway.org), a 1.28-mile former railroad bridge transformed into a park. Then take a drive through New Paltz and out on Mountain Rest Road, past the 144-year-old Mohonk Mountain House lake resort, to the Mohonk Preserve (mohonkpreserve.org). Continue through the hamlets of High Falls and Stone Ridge, and over the Ashokan Reservoir, one of New York City's pristine water sources. Along the way, stop in at the **Last Bite** (103 Main Street, High Falls; 845-687-7779) for a cup of Catskill Mountain Coffee or at the kitschy, 1970s-era **Egg's Nest Saloon** (Main Street, High Falls; 845-687-7255; theeggsnest.com) for a Sicilian egg cream.

7 *Old World Redux* 6 p.m.

Take two-lane back roads to **Gunk Haus Restaurant** (387 South Street, Highland; 845-883-0866; gunkhaus.com; $$). Sit on the biergarten deck and look out over apple orchards and "the Gunks"—the Shawangunk Mountains, one of the country's best-known rock-climbing ridges. The menu lives up to the Teutonic promise of the name with dishes like pork loin jäger schnitzel served with wild mushroom ragout and spaetzle, and the addictive obatzda, a Bavarian cheese dip that's a potent mix of cheeses, beer, and spices and is served with a chewy house-made pretzel.

8 *The Kingston Trio* 10 p.m.

Relax with drinks and music in Kingston, a small city that served as the capital of New York State in the 18th century. **Stockade Tavern** (313 Fair Street; 845-514-2649; stockadetavern.com) sells sophisticated cocktails in a one-time Singer sewing machine factory in the 17th-century Stockade

District. **BSP Lounge** (323 Wall Street; 845-481-5158; bsplounge.com) hosts local and touring bands in a former vaudeville theater. Near the waterfront, the casual **Rondout Music Lounge** (21 Broadway; 845-481-8250; rondoutmusiclounge.com) has a maritime aesthetic that evokes the shipyard-and-seafaring ambience of the nearby **Hudson River Maritime Museum** (hrmm.org).

SUNDAY

9 *Hike in the Hills* 9 a.m.

Drive into the hills beyond Woodstock to the 900-acre **Overlook Wild Forest** (www.dec.ny.gov/lands/73982.html). Look for the parking lot of the Overlook Mountain Fire Tower trail across Meads Mountain Road from the Tibetan Buddhist monastery strung with prayer flags. The hike follows a wooded former carriage road to the eerie ruins of a 19th-century Catskills resort and onto the 60-foot fire tower; climb the steel structure for views that extend from the Berkshires to the Catskills.

10 *Hudson on the Hudson* 11 a.m.

With its dozens of showrooms selling midcentury furniture with five-figure price tags, the old river port city of Hudson feels incongruously cosmopolitan. For brunch, sit in the backyard patio at **Cafe Le Perche** (230 Warren Street, Hudson; 518-822-1850; cafeleperche.com; $$) and choose from dishes like spiced brioche French toast with poached pear or a roasted four-mushroom tartine with melted Brie, baguette, micro greens, and truffle oil. Then

OPPOSITE A rocky shore at Cold Spring, with a view of the hilltops across the Hudson River.

BELOW Inside Olana, the Persian-inspired home overlooking the Hudson River that Frederic Church designed for himself and his family.

spend some time coveting antiques on Warren Street. The Hudson Antiques Dealers Association (hudsonantiques.net) has a guide to the 40-plus artfully curated shops.

11 *Far From the Old School* 2 p.m.

Drive out of town to the **Olana State Historic Site** (5720 Route 9G, Hudson; 518-828-0135; olana.org), the 250-acre estate of the 19th-century painter Frederic Edwin Church. Crisscrossed with trails and planted with Church's "designed landscape," the property is crowned by the painter's elaborate Persian-style home that now holds a collection of works by Hudson River School painters. If you have time to see more on your way back to the big city, stop in Beacon at the sprawling contemporary museum **DIA Beacon** (3 Beekman Street, Beacon; 845-440-0100; diaart.org) for art that's equal parts intriguing, bewildering, and bizarre.

ABOVE A meal of rainbow trout at the Gunk Haus.

OPPOSITE A perfect Hudson Valley weekend mixes indulgences like shopping and upscale dining with hiking and outdoor sports. This trailhead is near Cold Spring.

THE BASICS

Drive north from New York City on the expressways, and then exit for village main streets and country roads.

Buttermilk Falls Inn + Spa
220 North Road, Milton
845-795-1310
buttermilkfallsinn.com
$$$
On 75 acres along the river, with 17 rooms and suites, a farm-to-table restaurant, and a spa with an indoor pool.

Roundhouse at Beacon Falls
2 East Main Street, Beacon
845-765-8369
roundhousebeacon.com
$$$$
In an old mill in Beacon; rooms overlook a waterfall.

The Rhinecliff
4 Grinnell Street, Rhinecliff
845-876-0590
www.therhinecliff.com
$$$
Queen Anne-style inn built in the 1850s and revived in the 21st century as a riverside hotel.

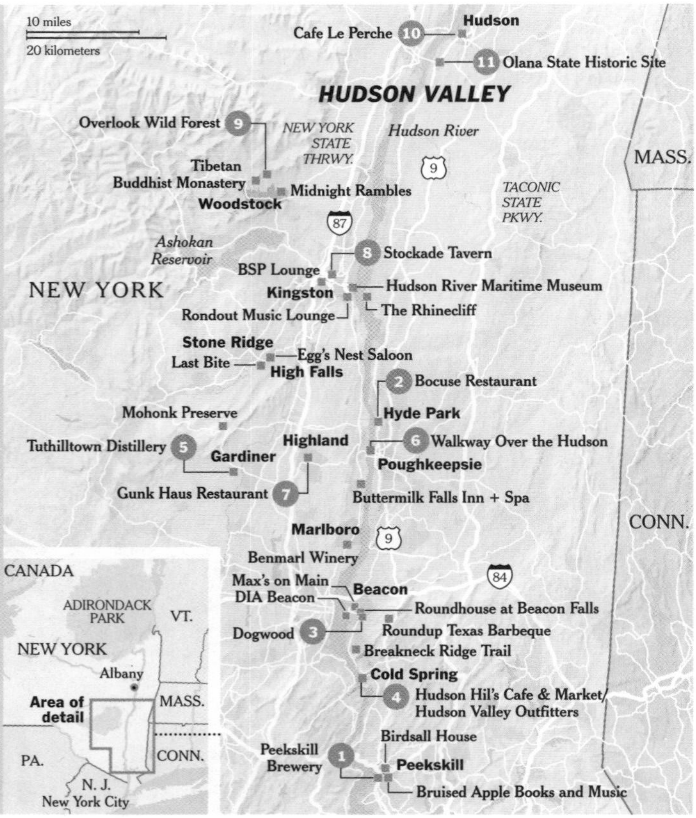

STATE OF NEW YORK
TRAIL
MARKER
TACONIC
REGION
PARKS, RECREATION & HISTORIC PRESERVATION
TRAIL
MAPS

Lake Placid

In any trip to Lake Placid, there will be a moment when you catch yourself thinking: Do you believe this little place was the host of two Olympic Games? Not because something so symbolic and global does not fit in a tiny upstate New York village of 3,000, but, more striking, because it will dawn on you that it is the perfect place. While the Olympics have become outsized, intimate Lake Placid retains ties to simpler times, whether 1932, when the Winter Games first came to visit, or 1980, a time remembered fondly by Americans for the Miracle-on-Ice United States hockey team. Still, a visit is less about the Olympics as they were than about life as it was. Lake Placid has the rhythm of a small town, albeit one with the sophistication to have played host to the world, and its pace is spiked by active people who embrace the mountain and lake setting that has attracted visitors for centuries. In the end, at least occasionally, you have to buy into the Olympic motto — Swifter, Higher, Stronger — and just go with it. Oh, and hold on for dear life. — BY BILL PENNINGTON AND LIONEL BEEHNER

FRIDAY

1 *Reason to Scream* 7 p.m.

Park your car in the center of the village, get out, and follow the screaming. It will lead you to a metal and wood three-story ramp next to Mirror Lake. Buy a ticket to rent a four-person toboggan. (Don't look up.) Climb to the top of this converted ski jump and place your toboggan on the solid-ice runway. (Don't look down.) Someone will push you down the steep chute, and after a few harrowing seconds at 40 miles an hour, you will be flung out across the frozen lake. (Don't get out.) The toboggan often does 360-degree turns before it stops. Then get up and do it again. (Don't forget to scream this time.) You have just experienced the **Lake Placid Toboggan Chute** (Parkside Drive; 518-523-2591; northelba.org/government/park-district/toboggan-chute.html).

OPPOSITE Olympic trails and rinks, Adirondack views, and some of the best skiing in the East keep the winter weekenders coming to Lake Placid.

RIGHT Snow-season downtime in one of the cozy common rooms at the Mirror Lake Inn.

2 *Toast Your Triumph* 8 p.m.

Now that you have been baptized in the ways of the Olympic village, your bravery will be rewarded at the **Lake Placid Pub and Brewery** (813 Mirror Lake Drive; 518-523-3813; ubuale.com), a few steps from the toboggan chute. Its signature Ubu Ale, a dark, smooth brew, will quickly calm your nerves.

3 *Window or Hearth?* 9 p.m.

A short trip up the hill overlooking the village of Lake Placid, on Olympic Drive, is a wonderful way to get the lay of the land, even at night. That frozen patch where your toboggan flew, Mirror Lake, is the dominant feature of the village. (Lake Placid itself is to the north.) This view of the village is best from **Veranda** (101 Olympic Drive; 518-523-3339; lakeplacid.com/dining; $$$), where you can warm up at a table by the fire or look out from a table with lake and mountain views. This is the Adirondacks, so order the duck.

SATURDAY

4 *Sourdough Breakfast* 8 a.m.

At **Saranac Sourdough** (2126 Saranac Avenue; 518-523-4897; lakeplacidmenus.com; $), Eileen and John Black have been serving up yeasty sourdough breads and tangy sourdough pancakes since 1998. The building is a converted log cabin, and the dining room is encased in swirling twigs and Impressionist paintings of the Adirondacks. Try the Mountain Man, a formidable stack of pancakes, eggs, meats, and sourdough toast.

5 *Into Thin Air* 9 a.m.

Although *Ski Magazine* has periodically called **Whiteface Mountain** (518-946-2223; whiteface.com), about seven miles from Lake Placid, the best ski area in the Eastern United States, somehow the place remains perhaps the most underrated snow sports destination in North America. People used to say it was too hard and too cold. It is true Whiteface's black diamond runs include the steep trails used for the 1980 Olympic races, but the mountain has expanded its terrain to soften the harsh edges. There is something good for everyone now at Whiteface, most of all, a speedy — and warm — gondola.

6 *Wine, Cheese, Venison* Noon

The **J. Lohr Vineyards and Wines Café** ($$), at the Whiteface base lodge, serves up tasty platters of French cheeses as well as chef's salads, panini, and Cajun-seared salmon on ciabatta rolls. They all go well with a Belgian hot chocolate or hot mulled wine.

7 *Hockey and More* 2 p.m.

Smack in the middle of town is Lake Placid's main attraction: the **Olympic Center** (2634 Main Street; 518-523-1655; lakeplacid.com). It is a draw for not just hockey dads but also winter sports buffs. The museum displays an impressive collection of miscellany, like coach Herb Brooks's natty suit (or at least the one worn by Kurt Russell, who played him in *Miracle on Ice*), monogrammed ice skates, and Olympic torches that look like medieval weapons. A motion theater simulates the feeling of soaring off a

ABOVE The Olympic speed skating oval, where Eric Heiden won five gold medals in the 1980 Winter Games, is open to the public for skating.

LEFT Whiteface Mountain, where Olympic skiers raced.

ski jump or barreling down a bobsled run. The main attraction remains the hockey rink—a smallish arena whose rafters are festooned with American flags.

8 *Tasty Inventions* 7 p.m.

Don't be fooled by the dive-bar facade and no-frills interior of **Liquids and Solids** (6115 Sentinel Road; 518-837-5012; liquidsandsolids.com; $$). It's a gastro-pub with an inventive, frequently changing menu of dishes like rabbit crepinette and beef heart ragout. This place also has the tastiest burger around, smothered in aioli on a focaccia roll and served with sides like maple baked beans.

9 *Consider the Atmosphere* 9 p.m.

Lake Placid's Main Street retains its party atmosphere all winter, luring tourists and townies alike to commingle over pints of local lager. **Zigzags** (134 Mirror Lake Drive; 518-523-8221), named for the deadliest pair of turns on the old bobsled course, is a lively bar that doubles as a shrine to bobsled paraphernalia, yellowed world maps, and vintage signs. By 10 p.m., the place fills up with rugged-looking locals in floppy dog-eared hats and flannel shirts, as a live band belts out oldies. For something less crowded, you could head to the **Cottage** (77 Mirror Lake Drive; 518-523-2544; mirrorlakeinn.com), a rustic spot that offers a late-night happy hour.

SUNDAY

10 *Mush Much?* 10 a.m.

Greet the morning with the sounds of eight Alaskan huskies barking and pulling a sled across

ABOVE Dogsledding on frozen Mirror Lake.

RIGHT The view from the top of the Lake Placid bobsled run, which was used in the 1932 and 1980 Olympics.

a glistening Mirror Lake. Just off Main Street, **Thunder Mountain Dog Sled Tours** (across from the High Peaks Resort; 518-891-6239) provides the sled, the dogs, and the musher. Watch out for flying toboggans.

11 *Devil's Highway* Noon

Take the bobsled ride at the **Olympic Sports Complex**, if you dare (220 Bobsled Run Lane; 518-523-4436; whiteface.com/activities/bob.php). As you speed down the track, a squiggly chute of steel, concrete, and ice, you'll share the sled with a pair of pros who look like members of the Navy Seals. To go it alone, choose the skeleton, a face-first solo thrill ride aboard what feels like a cafeteria tray affixed to steel runners. If you'd prefer something tamer (and cheaper), go instead to the **Olympic Jumping Complex** (52 Ski Jump Lane; 518-523-2202) and take the glass-enclosed elevator up 120 meters to the top for spectacular sunset views of the Adirondacks' majestic peaks.

ABOVE Professional sledders swoosh paying thrill-seekers down the Olympic bobsled run.

OPPOSITE Mirror Lake in Lake Placid on a fall day, before the Adirondack snowfalls and the winter rush.

2 miles
4 kilometers
Whiteface Mountain 5
NEW YORK
Lake Placid
6 J. Lohr Vineyards and Wines Café
Lake Placid Lodge
ADIRONDACK PARK
Saranac Sourdough 4
Area of detail
CANADA
L. Champlain
NEW YORK
Lake Placid
ADIRONDACK PARK
VT.
11 Olympic Jumping Complex
1 Olympic Sports Complex

Lake Placid
Interlaken Inn
Mirror Lake Inn
Cottage
MIRROR LAKE DR.
High Peaks Resort
10 Thunder Mountain Dog Sled Tour
NORTHWOOD RD.
Zigzags 9
Mirror Lake
Veranda 3
OLYMPIC DR.
1 Lake Placid Toboggan Chute
PARKSIDE DR.
Olympic Center 7
MAIN ST.
2 Lake Placid Pub and Brewery
Lake Placid
86
Liquids and Solids 8
SENTINEL RD.
1/4 mile
1/2 kilometer

THE BASICS

Drive five hours from New York City or fly into Albany, New York; Burlington, Vermont; or Montreal, each two and a half hours away.

Mirror Lake Inn
5 Mirror Lake Drive
518-523-2544
mirrorlakeinn.com
$$$$
Resort overlooking Mirror Lake.

Lake Placid Lodge
144 Lodge Way
518-523-2700
lakeplacidlodge.com
$$$$
Woodsy Adirondack elegance.

The Interlaken Inn
39 Interlaken Avenue
518-523-3180
theinterlakeninn.com
$$-$$$
Small inn close to downtown.

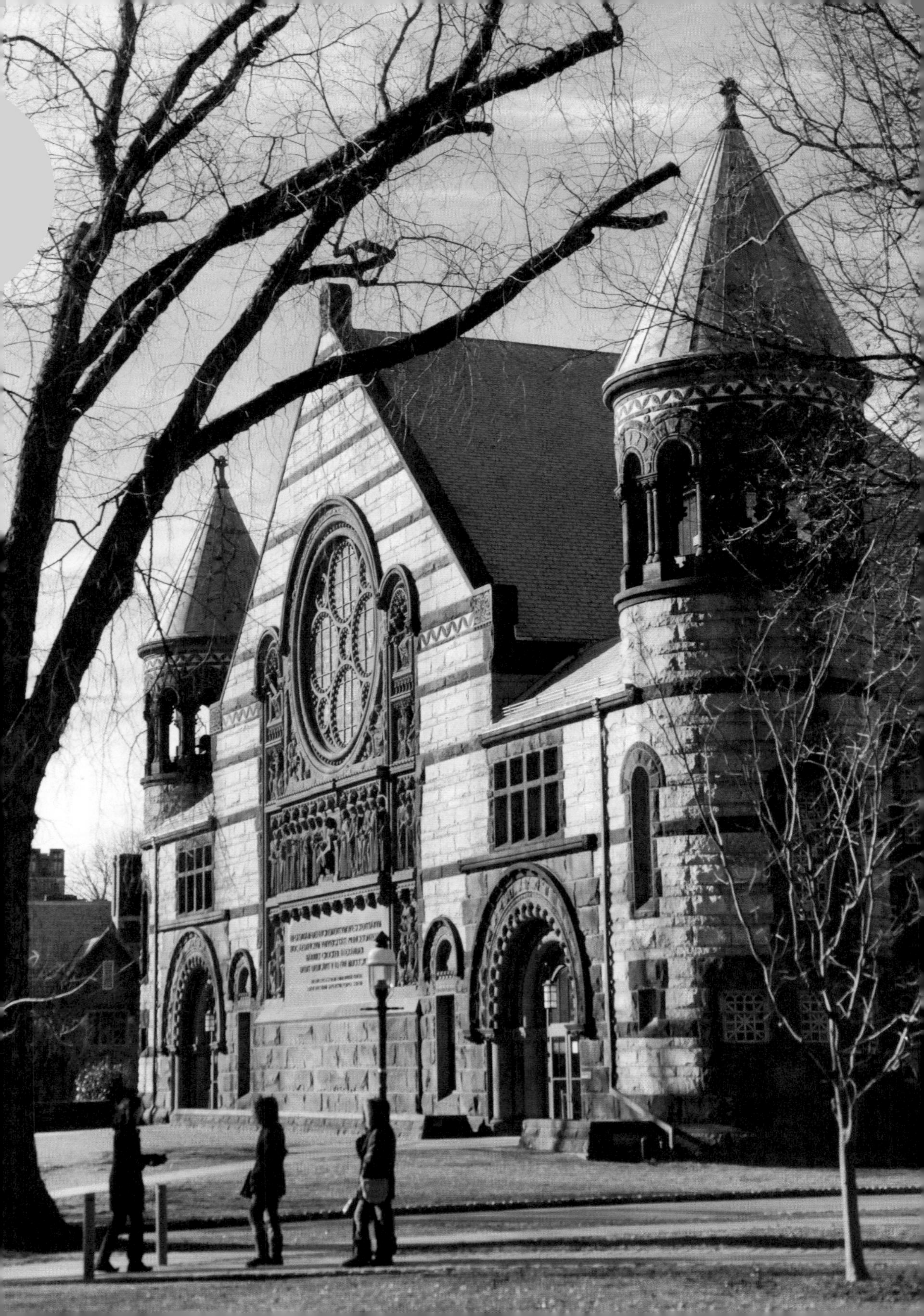

Princeton

"I think of Princeton as being lazy and good-looking and aristocratic—you know, like a spring day," F. Scott Fitzgerald wrote in This Side of Paradise. *Ninety years later, the appraisal still fits. From the century-old wrought-iron FitzRandolph Gate of Princeton University to the sleek rowing shells on sparkling Lake Carnegie, this small New Jersey town retains an air of easygoing noblesse. It is studded with landmarks, from a Revolutionary War battlefield to Albert Einstein's workplace, but nevertheless lives firmly in the present—traditional but not stuffy, charming but not quaint. In the tree-shaded downtown, Colonial-era buildings and high-end spots coexist with jeans-and-corduroy vegetarian hangouts and ice cream shops. And the campus is its own luxurious green city, in the words of Raymond Rhinehart, author of a guide to campus architecture, "a marketplace of ideas, set in a garden."* — BY LOUISE TUTELIAN

FRIDAY

1 *Catch of the Day* 6 p.m.

There's great fishing at the **Blue Point Grill** (258 Nassau Street; 609-921-1211; bluepointgrill.com; $$-$$$). The menu typically lists 20 fish specials, from Barnegat bluefish to a whole Greek bronzini. It's B.Y.O., but not to worry: **Nassau Liquors Grape & Grain** (264 Nassau Street; 609-924-0031) is a handy half-block away.

2 *The Flavor of the Place* 8 p.m.

Get out onto Nassau Street, Princeton's main street, to window-shop the bookstores and boutiques, check out vintage buildings, and peek down side streets at beautifully kept Victorian houses. The red-brick **Bainbridge House** (158 Nassau Street), dating to 1766, houses the **Historical Society of Princeton**. The Tudor Revival building at 92 Nassau Street, built in 1896, was once a Princeton dormitory.

SATURDAY

3 *Stack 'em Up* 8 a.m.

Get up and go early to **PJ's Pancake House** (154 Nassau Street; 609-924-1353; pancakes.com; $$), Princeton's breakfast nook since 1962, with the initial-carved wooden tables to prove it. Students, young families, and gray-haired couples rub elbows while plunging their forks into the tender pancakes—buttermilk, blueberry, buckwheat, and more—served with eggs and bacon. After breakfast, stroll down to the **Princeton University Store** (114 Nassau Street; 609-921-8500; pustore.com) and pick up a map of the university campus. (Online maps are at princeton.edu.)

4 *Take a Tiger by the Tail* 9 a.m.

The bronze tigers flanking the entrance to Nassau Hall are a fitting invitation to the architecturally rich Princeton University campus, though their dignity is compromised by the generations of children who have clambered over them. Built in 1756, Nassau Hall survived bombardment in the Revolution and now holds the office of the university president. Alexander Hall has echoed with the words of speakers from William Jennings Bryan to Art Buchwald; Prospect House, deeper into the campus, was Woodrow Wilson's home when he was president of the university. Don't be surprised if a wedding is under way at University Chapel, a Gothic-style landmark. The Frank Gehry-designed Peter B. Lewis math and science library, opened in 2008, adds swooping stainless steel curves to Princeton. The 87,000-square-foot building includes a second-floor "tree house" with 34-foot-high ceilings and clerestory windows framing the trees outside. All over campus, look for unusual spires and

OPPOSITE Alexander Hall has echoed with the words of speakers from William Jennings Bryan to Art Buchwald.

BELOW The 18th-century Nassau Inn.

whimsical gargoyles of cackling monkeys, dinosaurs, and dragons.

5 *Art in the Heart of Campus* 10:30 a.m.

Besides giving Princeton one of the richest endowments of any university in the world, wealthy benefactors have provided it with a wealth of outstanding art from many eras at the **Princeton University Art Museum** (609-258-3788; artmuseum.princeton.edu). Don't rush it—there are more than 60,000 works, and the galleries are spacious, peaceful, blessedly uncrowded—and free. The pre-Columbian and Asian collections are notable, but you can also see Monet's *Water Lilies and Japanese Bridge* and Warhol's *Blue Marilyn.* If you remember reading the 2004 best-selling novel *The Rule of Four*, set on the Princeton campus, picture the student heroes sneaking around these premises in the dark.

6 *Follow the Icons* 12:30 p.m.

Pick up a sandwich on excellent fresh bread at the **Terra Momo Bread Company** (74 Witherspoon Street; 609-688-0188; terramomo.com; $) and set out to trace the footsteps of giants. "It's a fine fox hunt, boys!" George Washington is said to have cried to his troops as the British fled from them on Jan. 3, 1777, at **Princeton Battlefield** (500 Mercer Road in neighboring Princetown Township; 609-921-0074; state.nj.us/dep/parksandforests/parks/princeton.html). The victory helped restore faith in the American cause at a critical time in the war. Check out the small museum and picture the troops clashing where students now sunbathe. Back toward town on Mercer Road, turn right onto Olden Lane to reach the **Institute for Advanced Study** (Einstein Drive; 609-734-8000; ias.edu). Einstein used to walk to work there from his house at 112 Mercer Street—sometimes, legend has it, after forgetting to put on his socks. The buildings, still a rarefied haven for distinguished scholars, are closed to the public, but the 500-acre Institute Woods, where violets bloom along the banks of the Stony Brook, is open to the public year-round.

7 *Relativity and Retail* 3 p.m.

Only in Princeton will you find a store that combines an Einstein mini-museum with great deals on woolens. Walk directly to the rear of **Landau of Princeton** (102 Nassau Street; 609-924-3494; landauprinceton.com) to see the Einstein photos, letters, and sketches. Then check out the pop-top mittens made of Alpaca yarn, perfect for texting. Steps away in Palmer Square, dozens of shops sell

ABOVE Lewis Library, designed by Frank Gehry.

OPPOSITE ABOVE The tap room at the Nassau Inn.

OPPOSITE BELOW Bronze tigers guard Nassau Hall.

well-designed and indulgent goods from eye kohls to stemware and sandals. Revive at the **Bent Spoon** ice cream shop (35 Palmer Square West; 609-924-2368; thebentspoon.net), whose owners pledge to use local, organic, and hormone-free ingredients whenever possible in the treats they make fresh every day. Who knew nectarine sorbet could taste so good?

8 *For the Record* 5 p.m.

Since 1980, the **Princeton Record Exchange** (20 South Tulane Street; 609-921-0881; prex.com) has been dispensing used vinyl, CDs, and DVDs at irresistible prices (from $2 for some LPs to under $12 for used DVDs.) The store, which is open to 9 p.m., crams 150,000 items onto its floor at any one time.

9 *Sustainable Dining* 8 p.m.

One relaxing choice for dinner is **Mediterra** (29 Hulfish Street; 609-252-9680; terramomo.com; $$$), where wines from 10 countries line the walls; look for paella or locally raised chicken. Locally sourced and sustainable food is the focus at **elements** (163 Bayard Lane; 609-924-0078; elementsprinceton.com; $$$). Golden tilefish, black bass, and monkfish are all from area waters.

10 *Brews and Blues* 10 p.m.

You may hear anything from pop to blues to classic rock 'n' roll for a modest cover at **Triumph Brewing Company** (138 Nassau Street; 609-924-7855; triumphbrewing.com), where the crowd is student-heavy but not raucous. A busy bar dispenses handcrafted beers, and physics graduate students rub elbows with 40-somethings escaping their teenage children.

SUNDAY

11 *The Tow Path* 11 a.m.

Rent a mountain bike at **Jay's Cycles** (249 Nassau Street; 609-924-7233; jayscycles.com) and cruise southeast on Alexander Street for about a mile and a half until you see Turning Basin Park on the right. You'll be next to the Delaware-Raritan Canal tow path, a level dirt trail that is a delightful place to walk, bike, or jog. If you'd rather be on the water, you can stow the bike at **Princeton Canoe & Kayak Rental** (483 Alexander Street; 609-452-2403; canoenj.com) and rent a watercraft. Make your way a half-mile up to the Washington Road Bridge and look for impossibly fit young Princetonians sculling under a bright blue spring sky on Lake Carnegie.

ABOVE Regulars can browse the 150,000 or so titles at the Princeton Record Exchange, open since 1980. The store is known for its selection of vinyl.

OPPOSITE Students walk the Princeton University campus, which in the words of Raymond Rhinehart is "a marketplace of ideas, set in a garden."

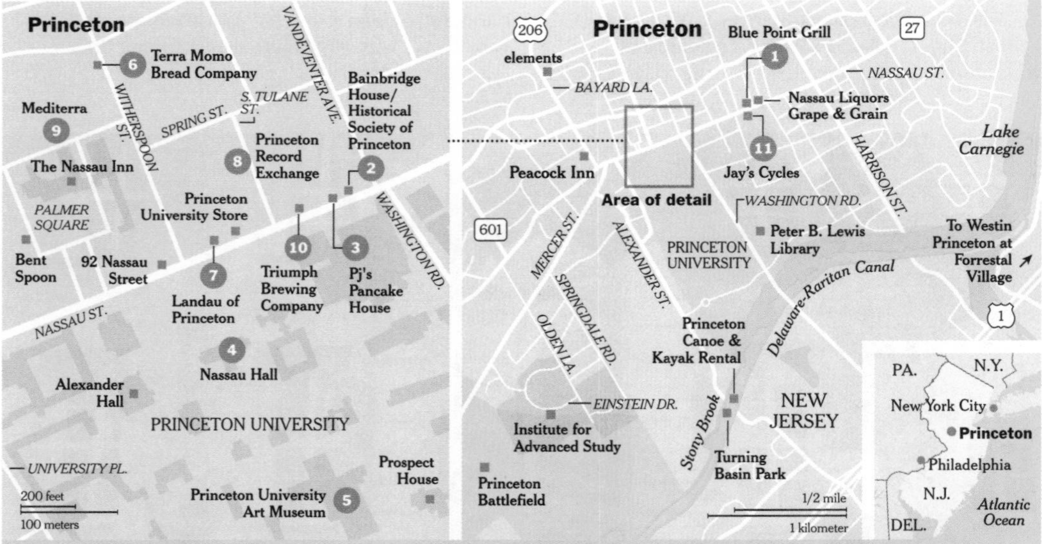

Princeton
6 Terra Momo Bread Company
9 Mediterra
The Nassau Inn
8 Princeton Record Exchange
2 Bainbridge House/ Historical Society of Princeton
Princeton University Store
10 Triumph Brewing Company
3 Pj's Pancake House
7 Landau of Princeton
Bent Spoon
92 Nassau Street
4 Nassau Hall
Alexander Hall
PRINCETON UNIVERSITY
5 Princeton University Art Museum
Prospect House
200 feet
100 meters

Princeton
elements
Blue Point Grill 1
Nassau Liquors Grape & Grain
11 Jay's Cycles
Peacock Inn
Area of detail
Peter B. Lewis Library
PRINCETON UNIVERSITY
Lake Carnegie
To Westin Princeton at Forrestal Village
Delaware-Raritan Canal
Princeton Canoe & Kayak Rental
Institute for Advanced Study
Turning Basin Park
Princeton Battlefield
NEW JERSEY
1/2 mile
1 kilometer
PA. N.Y. New York City Princeton Philadelphia N.J. DEL. Atlantic Ocean

THE BASICS

Princeton is about an hour from New York City by car or New Jersey Transit rail.

The Peacock Inn
20 Bayard Lane
609-924-1707
peacockinn.com
$$-$$$
Boutique hotel in a building dating to 1775. Multimillion-dollar renovation in 2010.

The Nassau Inn
10 Palmer Square East
609-921-7500
nassauinn.com
$$$
In the heart of town, with 18th-century-style furnishings.

Westin Princeton at Forrestal Village
201 Village Boulevard
609-452-7900
westinprinceton.com
$$-$$$
Just outside town.

Cape May

The images of the Jersey Shore conjured up by reality television bear little resemblance to Cape May, the southernmost town on the New Jersey coast. One of the oldest seaside resorts in the nation, this 3.5-square-mile island has welcomed vacationers for more than 200 years. The entire city is a National Historic Landmark, with hundreds of sturdily built Victorian houses; but Cape May knows how to embrace a more modern persona as well. Several of its once-faded grande dame hotels and low-slung motels have been updated and transformed into chic escapes for stylish beachgoers. Located on the Atlantic Flyway, Cape May is also an internationally renowned birding hot spot, especially busy with the bird-watching crowd during the avian migration seasons in spring and fall.

— BY MICHELLE HIGGINS AND LOUISE TUTELIAN

FRIDAY

1 *Catch of the Day* 4:30 p.m.

Crowds gather early at **The Lobster House** on Fisherman's Wharf (906 Schellengers Landing Road; 609-884-8296; thelobsterhouse.com; $$), which serves up traditional surf 'n' turf dishes, with the catch often hauled in by its own fleet of commercial fishing boats. Because the restaurant doesn't take reservations, securing a spot in one of its traditional dining rooms often involves a wait of at least an hour. To avoid the bedlam, head to the dockside Raw Bar and order a lobster platter and a beer. Then stake out a shaded table alongside the ships in Cape May Harbor. Another option: hop aboard the *Schooner American*, a 130-foot-long sailing vessel turned cocktail lounge that's moored alongside the restaurant, for appetizers. Have kids? Call in your order to the Lobster House's Take-Out shop (609-884-3064), which offers a kids' menu online, so it's ready when you arrive.

2 *Shop and Stroll* 7 p.m.

Burn off your meal with a stroll along the **Washington Street Mall** (washingtonstreetmall.com), a three-block pedestrian concourse between Perry and Ocean Streets that is lined with clothing boutiques, kitschy souvenir shops, toy stores, and candy and ice-cream shops. Many stores stay open until 9 p.m. or later on Fridays and Saturdays in summer. Then make your way to Cape May's so-called boardwalk, a paved promenade just a few blocks away that runs parallel to the beach for nearly two miles. Stop in at the **Family Fun Arcade** (732 Beach Drive; 609-884-7020) for Skee-Ball, photo booth shots, and other games.

3 *Bar Below* 9 p.m.

Duck into the cavelike Boiler Room, in the basement of the **Congress Hall hotel** (Beach Avenue and Congress Street, with an entrance on Perry; 609-884-8421; caperesorts.com/hotels/capemay/congresshall/) for drinks, dancing, and live music. Exposed brick walls, low red lighting, and fixtures from days when this really was a boiler room all lend the bar a cool industrial feel.

SATURDAY

4 *On the Wing* 7:30 a.m.

Cape May is on the Atlantic Flyway, one of the planet's busiest bird migratory corridors, navigated

OPPOSITE The Cape May Lighthouse, a favorite symbol of this traditional summer beach town. The entire city is a National Historic Landmark.

RIGHT It's 199 steps to the top (and 199 back down), but the panoramic view of New Jersey and Delaware from the top of the lighthouse is worth the climb.

by hundreds of species in spring and fall. Because of its location amid barrier islands and wetlands, fresh water and ocean, birds come to rest, eat, and nest. Things are calmer in summer, but there are still plenty of birds to be seen, especially with the help of a good guide. **The Cape May Bird Observatory** (701 East Lake Drive, Cape May Point; 609-884-2736; birdcapemay.org) sponsors naturalist-led walks early on many Saturdays and also offers free maps for self-guided walks. Not a birder? Start your day with a flowing yoga class offered on either the beach or the expansive lawn in front of the **Congress Hall hotel** (251 Beach Avenue; 609-884-8421; caperesorts.com/hotels/capemay/congresshall/), depending on the heat. Sign up and grab a mat at the check-in desk in the hotel lobby. Afterward, load up on carbs with a pancake platter at **Uncle Bill's Pancake House** (261 Beach Avenue; 609-884-7199; unclebillspancakehouse.com).

ABOVE Quiet, smoothly paved streets and a bicycle-friendly attitude make cycling one of the best ways to get around in Cape May. Rentals are easy to find, and some inns provide bikes for their guests.

OPPOSITE ABOVE Hundreds of substantial and well preserved Victorian houses and inns give Cape May its distinctive architectural look. Many have multi-level porches facing the water and cooled by the ocean breeze.

5 *Hit the Beach* 11 a.m.

You can pick up your beach tags (required on summer days) at any beach entrance. Need chairs? **Steger Beach Service** (609-884-3058; stegerbeachservice.com), which rents umbrellas, chairs, and other beach gear from 12 locations along Cape May's wide stretch of beach, will stake out your spot in the sand.

6 *Family Affair* 2 p.m.

Beachgoers line up for American fare with a Greek twist and a seat at one of the cozy booths at **George's Place** (301 Beach Avenue; 609-884-6088; $$), originally opened by George Tsiartsionis, the father-in-law of the current owner, John Karapanagiotis, in 1968. Family portraits line the walls. The Lemon Chicken Greek salad is a good bet after the beach, but if you need a reminder that you are close to Philadelphia, order the substantial cheese steak. Another option: just down the block, the **Y.B.** (314 Beach Avenue; 609-898-2009), run by George's brother, Peter, who has cooked under the chef Georges Perrier at Le Bec-Fin in Philadelphia, offers a range of salads and sandwiches in a small but inviting space decorated in black and white. Both restaurants are cash-only.

7 *Just a Summer Cottage* 3:30 p.m.

Now that you've crisscrossed the streets amid Cape May's majestic Victorian houses, satisfy your

curiosity about what lies behind the gingerbread with a tour of the **Emlen Physick Estate** (1048 Washington Street; 609-884-5404; capemaymac.org), a mansion constructed for a Philadelphia physician in the Stick style of the late 1800s. Fifteen of the rooms have been restored with historical accuracy, and the lavish interiors shed some light on how the privileged social leaders of Cape May's affluent summer colony vacationed in their 19th-century heyday.

8 *Beach Shack Update* 6:30 p.m.

Order a beer and a bucket of peel-and-eat shrimp at the bustling **Rusty Nail** (205 Beach Avenue; 609-884-0017; beachshack.com/rusty-nail.php; $), an updated twist on a surfer bar that occupied the same spot in the '70s. It's equal parts hip, family-friendly, and laid-back, depending on the spot you snag. Families congregate around the fire pit and picnic tables, a young crowd lines the bar inside, and heavily tanned locals gather around the outdoor tap, singing to the Grateful Dead and Melissa Etheridge covered by local musicians.

RIGHT When the summer crowd has departed, the birders take over, drawn in spring and fall by migrators stopping off on their seasonal journeys. Cape May is well known as a prime spot for seeing birds in variety and abundance.

SUNDAY

9 *The Pig Is Blue* 8:30 a.m.

Fuel up for a morning bike ride at **Congress Hall's Blue Pig Tavern** (251 Beach Avenue; 609-884-8422; caperesorts.com/restaurants/capemay/bluepigtavern; $$), which serves fresh and simple American fare and offers crayons for the kids. Ask for a seat in the outdoor courtyard next to the trickling fountain and order a side of turkey sausage for sustenance.

10 *On Two Wheels* 9 a.m.

Rent some wheels at nearby **Shields Bike Rental** (11 Gurney Street; 609-898-1818;

shieldsbikerental.com). Flat roads, wide shoulders, and slow-moving traffic make Cape May perfect for the casual bike rider. If you want to make the beachfront promenade part of your ride, do so before 10 a.m.; later than that, bikes are not allowed.

11 *One Last Look* 11 a.m.

If you have the energy to keep pedaling, take Broadway to Sunset Boulevard to visit the **Cape May Lighthouse** (609-884-5404; capemaymac.org), built in 1859. It's in Cape May Point State Park. Climb the spiraling 199-step staircase, and at the top, you'll be rewarded with a panoramic view of the Cape May Peninsula, with views of the coast from Wildwood to the north to — on a clear day — Cape Henlopen, Delaware, to the west.

ABOVE The wildlife refuge at Cape May Point is a rest stop on the migratory path along the Atlantic Seaboard for millions of birds. This guest is a cedar waxwing.

OPPOSITE Elaborate gingerbread exteriors, a hallmark of lavishly decorated Victorian houses, survive in style in Cape May. This building is the Virginia Hotel.

THE BASICS

Drive 160 miles from New York City or 95 miles from Philadelphia. A bicycle is handy to use around town.

Virginia Hotel
25 Jackson Street
609-884-5700
virginiahotel.com
$$-$$$$
Boutique hotel that looks the part, with sophisticated design and plush amenities, half a block from the beach.

Congress Hall
251 Beach Avenue
609-884-8421
congresshall.com
$$-$$$$
Steps from the beach in the center of town, with pool and spa.

Queen Victoria Bed & Breakfast
102 Ocean Street
609-884-8702
queenvictoria.com
$$$-$$$$
Choose from among 32 rooms and suites in four luxuriously renovated Victorian buildings.

1/2 mile
1 kilometer
NEW JERSEY
GARDEN STATE PKWY.
SEASHORE RD.
OCEAN DR.
109
CAPE MAY PENINSULA
Cape May Bird Observatory
4
1 Lobster House
BROADWAY
LAFAYETTE ST.
WASHINGTON ST.
606
7 Emlen Physick Estate
SUNSET BLVD.
633
Cape May Point
CAPE MAY POINT STATE PARK
Cape May
11
Cape May Lighthouse
Area of detail
Philadelphia PA.
GARDEN STATE PKWY.
N.J. TPKE.
NEW JERSEY
Atlantic City
Atlantic Ocean
Delaware Bay
DEL.
Cape May
Cape May
LAFAYETTE ST.
Steger Beach Service 5
PAGE ST.
FRANKLIN ST.
Washington Street Mall
2
HUGHES ST.
COLUMBIA AVE.
OCEAN ST.
Blue Pig Tavern
9
CARPENTER LN.
STOCKTON PL.
Virginia Hotel
GURNEY ST.
WINDSOR AVE.
CONGRESS ST.
Congress Hall
PERRY ST.
JACKSON ST.
Queen Victoria Bed & Breakfast
Shields Bike Rentals
10
GRANT ST.
Rusty Nail
8
Boiler Room 3
Y.B.
BEACH AVE.
Family Fun Arcade
Promenade
Uncle Bill's Pancake House
6
George's Place
500 feet
1/4 kilometer
Atlantic Ocean

25 Jackson

FedEx

Philadelphia

The 18th-century city tucked inside Philadelphia, where the United States was born at Independence Hall, swarms all year with curious tourists, history buffs, and children on school trips. Sprawling out from it is the other Philadelphia, firmly rooted in the 21st century and bustling with the activity of a rapidly evolving destination city. Adventurous restaurants reinforce the city's growing culinary reputation, though an obligatory cheese steak still hits the spot. Neighborhoods in transition provide hot spots for shopping and night life, while other areas keep dishing out some old-school Philly "attytood." And traditional leisure-time stops like the Schuylkill riverbanks and the venerable Franklin Institute keep right on drawing them in. — BY JEFF SCHLEGEL AND FREDA MOON

FRIDAY

1 *Another Go-to Building* 2 p.m.

Independence Hall belongs to the ages; **City Hall** (Broad and Market Streets; 215-686-2840; visitphilly.com/history/philadelphia/city-hall) belongs to Philadelphia. This 548-foot-tall 19th-century building is more than just a big hunk of granite interrupting traffic in the heart of the city—it is topped by a 27-ton bronze statue of William Penn, one of 250 statues by Alexander Milne Calder ornamenting the building inside and out. Take the elevator to the top for 35-mile views from the observation deck. For another kind of overview, take in the displays at the **Philadelphia History Museum** (15 South Seventh Street; 215-685-4830; philadelphiahistory.org), which spans 330 years of local history with objects including a belt given to William Penn by the Lenape people, Schmidt's beer cans, and a collection dedicated to the African-American experience.

2 *Sichuan Style* 5 p.m.

Across the Schuylkill River, the University City location of the locally beloved **Han Dynasty** (3711 Market Street; 215-222-3711; handynasty.net; $$) has a wide-open dining room with modern lines, rough-hewn wood, and a kitschy cocktail list including bucket-size drinks like the Scorpion Bowl and Singapore Sling. But the food is the real attraction. Plates come one after the other in family-style portions—dan dan noodles, double-cooked fish, and spicy, crispy cucumbers, each rated 1 to 10 on Han's hot-or-not index.

3 *Museum on the Move* 8 p.m.

For most of its 90-year history, the **Barnes Foundation Museum** (2025 Benjamin Franklin Parkway; 215-278-7000; barnesfoundation.org) was seven miles away in suburban Merion. But after years of controversy and construction, it relocated in the city, bringing one of the world's great collections of works by Picasso, Matisse, and Modigliani (and many others) to Museum Row. On Friday nights, the museum stays open until 10 p.m. and enlivens its atmosphere with music and wine. Day or night, reserve museum tickets well in advance.

SATURDAY

4 *Slice of Local Color* 10 a.m.

Enticing aromas of homemade sausages, cheeses, and pastries infuse the air along the **Ninth Street**

OPPOSITE AND RIGHT Philadelphia's massive City Hall is topped by a bronze statue of William Penn weighing 27 tons. Artist Alexander Milne Calder was responsible for the structure's 250-plus statues, including this likeness of Benjamin Franklin (right).

Italian Market (Ninth Street, between Wharton and Fitzwater Streets; phillyitalianmarket.com). Produce vendors ply their wares under green-and-red awnings in front of shops selling Italian specialties and assorted merchandise at this century-old South Philadelphia outdoor market. Hungry? **Lorenzo's Pizza** (Ninth and Christian Streets; 215-922-2540; lorenzospizza.net; $) is an unpretentious corner shop serving one of the city's best pizza slices. The secret: no skimping on spices.

5 *Ben's Place* 1 p.m.

Noted for its giant two-story model of a human heart and interactive displays that make it seem more like a theme park than a science museum, the **Franklin Institute** (222 North 20th Street; 215-448-1200; fi.edu) is aptly named for Benjamin Franklin, the city's favorite polymath. Flight simulators, giant locomotives parked indoors, a virtual trip to astronaut world—it's tough to know where to look. The place to start, though, may be on the Web, where you can buy tickets in advance and skip the long lines waiting at the door.

6 *Shop Your Way* 2 p.m.

Shop your way along 13th Street, visiting interesting shops like **Verde** (108 South 13th Street; 215-546-8700; verdephiladelphia.com), which sells an eclectic mix of charm bracelets, women's clothing by international designers, patent leather bags, and handcrafted Marcie Blaine chocolates. For a midafternoon sugar fix, try a scoop of Thai coconut, pistachio, or decadent dark chocolate at **Capogiro Gelato Artisans** (119 South 13th Street; 215-351-0900; capogirogelato.com).

7 *Books in the Square* 5 p.m.

Built during the booming 1850s, the **Rittenhouse Square** neighborhood was home to the city's Victorian aristocracy. The park has a reflecting pool; diagonal walkways crisscrossing beneath oak, maple, and locust trees; and bronze sculptures, like the 1832 allegory of the French Revolution, *Lion Crushing a Serpent*, by Antoine-Louis Barye. Stop in at **Joseph Fox Bookshop** (1724 Sansom Street; 215-563-4184; foxbookshop.com), a Philadelphia institution since 1951. Its crowded shelves are stocked with everything from art and architecture to fiction and poetry, and its events bring in big-name writers like David Sedaris.

ABOVE A jogger strikes a *Rocky*-esque pose atop the stairs of the Philadelphia Museum of Art.

OPPOSITE ABOVE The Philadelphia skyline

OPPOSITE Rowers make their way down the placid Schuylkill River.

8 *Farm to Philly* 8 p.m.

The Farm and Fisherman (1120 Pine Street; 267-687-1555; thefarmandfisherman.com;$$$), tucked away on a narrow side street of unassuming brick facades, is a neighborhood B.Y.O.B. with a sophisticated farm-to-table menu that changes daily. One menu featured a delicate Kona Kampachi (jack, with quince, turnip, apple, and tapioca) and squab with Seckel pear, rosemary, kabocha squash, and chestnuts.

9 *Israeli and More* 10:30 p.m.

For live music and locally brewed beer, go to **Johnny Brenda's** (1201 North Frankford Avenue; 215-739-9684; johnnybrendas.com), where the small stage attracts some surprisingly big indie music acts, like Grizzly Bear and Vampire Weekend. Across the street, **Frankford Hall** (1210 Frankford Avenue; 215-634-3338; frankfordhall.com) is less aggressively stylish and more family friendly, with Ping-Pong and picnic tables, an affinity for wood block games, and an excellent beer list. Next door, an outpost of the Brooklyn smoked meat and American whiskey joint **Fette Sau** (1208 Frankford Avenue; 215-391-4888; fettesauphilly.com) serves dry-rubbed barbecue until midnight.

SUNDAY

10 *Morning Constitutional* 8:30 a.m.

The best time to hit **Independence National Historical Park** (nps.gov/inde) is first thing in the morning, ahead of the crowds. Pick up your free tickets (the Visitor Center at 6th and Market Streets opens early) and start with the main attraction,

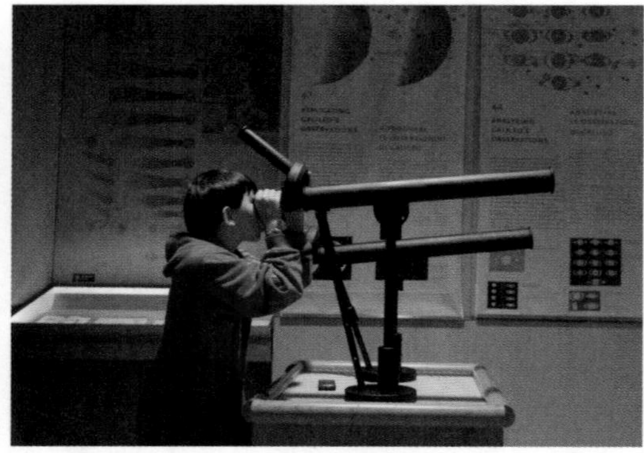

Independence Hall, where lines will soon be longest. Take a quick look at the Liberty Bell through the glass at its dedicated building, and then poke around the restored buildings and inviting lawns.

11 *Riverside* 11 a.m.

Head over to the **Philadelphia Museum of Art** (26th Street and Benjamin Franklin Parkway; 215-763-8100; philamuseum.org), take your picture with the Rocky statue out front, and then walk in to enjoy the collection. From there, walk behind the museum to the **Breakaway Bikes** shed (215-568-6002; breakawaybikes.com) to rent a bike and ride along the path paralleling the Schuylkill River in Fairmount Park. Look for elegant Victorian-era boathouses built in the heyday of the city's rowing clubs. One of the city's Olympic-level rowers was Grace Kelly's father. Watch today's rowers in their shells as they glide along the river.

ABOVE Trying out a model telescope in a Galileo exhibition at the Franklin Institute.

OPPOSITE A view from the City Hall observation deck of the grand Benjamin Franklin Parkway.

THE BASICS

Fly, drive, or take a train on Amtrak's busy Northeast Corridor. Philadelphia is a good walking city, but a car is handy to have.

The Independent
1234 Locust Street
215-772-1440
theindependenthotel.com
$$
Boutique hotel in a restored building. Some of the 24 rooms have fireplaces.

The Alexander Inn
301 South 12th Street
215-923-3535
alexanderinn.com
$$
Art Deco-inspired touches in 48 designer rooms.

Hotel Palomar
117 South 17th Street
215-563-5006
hotelpalomar-philadelphia.com
$$
Stylish new hotel near City Hall, with 230 rooms.

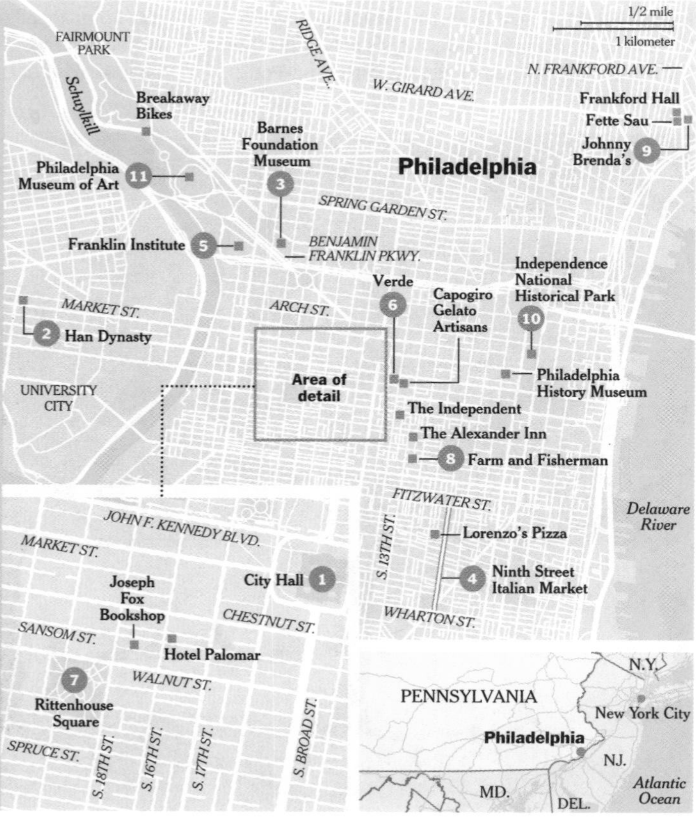

1/2 mile
1 kilometer
FAIRMOUNT PARK
Schuylkill
RIDGE AVE.
W. GIRARD AVE.
N. FRANKFORD AVE.
Frankford Hall
Fette Sau
Johnny Brenda's 9
Breakaway Bikes
Barnes Foundation Museum 3
Philadelphia
Philadelphia Museum of Art 11
SPRING GARDEN ST.
Franklin Institute 5
BENJAMIN FRANKLIN PKWY.
Independence National Historical Park 10
Verde 6
Capogiro Gelato Artisans
MARKET ST.
ARCH ST.
2 Han Dynasty
Area of detail
Philadelphia History Museum
UNIVERSITY CITY
The Independent
The Alexander Inn
8 Farm and Fisherman
FITZWATER ST.
Delaware River
JOHN F. KENNEDY BLVD.
MARKET ST.
Lorenzo's Pizza
S. 13TH ST.
City Hall 1
4 Ninth Street Italian Market
Joseph Fox Bookshop
CHESTNUT ST.
WHARTON ST.
SANSOM ST.
Hotel Palomar
7
WALNUT ST.
Rittenhouse Square
S. BROAD ST.
SPRUCE ST.
S. 18TH ST.
S. 16TH ST.
S. 17TH ST.
PENNSYLVANIA
N.Y.
New York City
Philadelphia
N.J.
MD.
DEL.
Atlantic Ocean

The Brandywine Valley

In the Brandywine Valley, spanning Pennsylvania and Delaware, one can canoe past riverbanks where George Washington placed his troops and visit the house in which he prepared for battle. Minutes away, perfectly maintained, are estates and gardens of the kind that became symbols of young America's rise to global power, all of them connected with the du Pont family of industrialists. The Wyeth clan of artists, too, left its mark, living and painting here. Preservationists have assured that there are still untrammeled vistas in the valley today, giving it the allure of landscapes that have been spared suburban sprawl. — BY GERALDINE FABRIKANT

FRIDAY

1 *A Watershed Battle* 2 p.m.

As he prepared to stop General William Howe and his British troops at Chadds Ford, George Washington took over the simple two-story stone house of Benjamin Ring, a local farmer and mill owner who was the town's most prominent businessman. Now it is part of the 52-acre **Brandywine Battlefield Park** (1491 Baltimore Pike, Chadds Ford; 610-459-3342; brandywinebattlefield.org). You can stand in the room where Washington strategized, and the park also has a 20-minute movie about the battle as well as cannons, guns, and maps. The battle, on Sept. 11, 1777, was a stinging defeat for the Americans.

2 *On the Brandywine* 3 p.m.

Whether you choose a canoe, kayak, or tube, don't miss a trip down the Brandywine from the **Northbrook Canoe Co.** (1810 Beagle Road, West Chester; 610-793-2279; northbrookcanoe.com) or **Wilderness Canoe Trips** (2111 Concord Pike/Route 202, Wilmington; 302-654-2227; wildernesscanoetrips.com). You may pass the site of Trimble's Ford, where British and Hessian forces crossed the Brandywine to flank Washington. You are also likely to see turtles, birds, and deer as you glide by walnut, oak, and sycamore trees.

3 *Jaguar on Your Plate* 7:30 p.m.

The menu is imaginative, and so is the décor, at **Krazy Kat's** (528 Montchanin Road, Montchanin; 302-888-4200; krazykatsrestaurant.com; $$$), with its washed peach walls, tapestry-upholstered side chairs, colorful dinner plates with jaguars racing across them, and portraits of cats and dogs in military uniform. Choose from dishes like corn duck with sourdough spaetzle or swordfish with fennel.

SATURDAY

4 *Breakfast With Hank* 8 a.m.

No restaurant in town is probably busier for an early breakfast than **Hank's Place** (1625 Creek Road, Chadds Ford; 610-388-7061; hanks-place.net; $) in Chadds Ford. This lively diner, with its baskets of petunias and impatiens hanging along the outdoor terrace, was a favorite of Andrew Wyeth's. Lines can be long, but the reward is corned beef hash and eggs or Italian-style scrambled eggs with mild Italian sausage.

5 *Wyeth Country* 9:30 a.m.

The Brandywine area has been home to three generations of Wyeths, and about 40 years ago the Brandywine Conservancy bought a grist mill that was set to be demolished. It created the **Brandywine River Museum** (1 Hoffman's Mill Road, Chadds Ford; 610-388-2700; brandywinemuseum.org) at a location

OPPOSITE A Gilbert Stuart portrait of George Washington decorates the dining room of Winterthur, Henry Francis du Pont's country estate.

BELOW The Benjamin Ring House, George Washington's headquarters, at the Brandywine Battlefield State Park.

along the meandering river where the views are as enchanting as the works by the three Wyeths—N.C., Andrew, and Jamie—that you will find inside.

6 *Bring On the Books* 11 a.m.

Kennett Square may be small, but it is big on books. **Thomas Macaluso Used and Rare Books** (130 South Union Street, Kennett Square; 610-444-1063) is a labyrinth of a store where readers can find historical maps and books, like a first edition of *Official Letters to the American Congress by His Excellency George Washington Commander-in-Chief of the Continental Forces*, published in 1795. Or drive out from Kennett Square along open country roads to **Baldwin's Book Barn** (865 Lenape Road, West Chester; 610-696-0816; bookbarn.com), a five-story extravaganza of a bookstore in a converted dairy farm. "We have 300,000 books on all subjects," said the owner, Tom Baldwin. "Our specialties are rare books and books on the local history."

7 *A Place of Her Own* 1 p.m.

"You might like the garden, but it is a bit overgrown," said Susan Teiser as she welcomed a guest to her casual **Centreville Café** (5800 Kennett Pike, Centreville; 302-425-5808; centrevillecafe.com; $$), a few miles over the Pennsylvania border in Delaware. She makes just about everything on the premises; two good choices were tomato soup and a hearts of palm salad with a mix of pecans, cheese, and apples.

8 *How Henry Kept Busy* 2 p.m.

Henry Francis du Pont's wife, Ruth, called it "Henry's Hobby," and the estate he named **Winterthur** (5105 Kennett Pike, Winterthur; 302-888-4600; winterthur.org) was certainly an expensive du Pont indulgence. While visiting Electra Havemeyer Webb's Vermont home in 1923, Henry du Pont experienced a coup de foudre for American furniture and decorative arts, and he soon began a shopping spree that resulted in a house filled with American antiques. Among the discoveries in Winterthur's 175 rooms are 69 of the 302 pieces of a dinner service that belonged to George and Martha Washington. The nearly 1,000-acre property includes 60 acres of gardens that are as naturalistic as the nearby Longwood Gardens, created by Henry's cousin Pierre S. du Pont, are manicured. So enamored of his trees was this du Pont that he instructed his staff that in case of a fire, they were to save the trees before the house. Along with an azalea woods, there is a charming children's garden complete with a tulip tree house and a fairy cottage.

9 *Great Style, Great Food* 7 p.m.

Don't let the mall location fool you. **Sovana Bistro** (696 Unionville Road, Kennett Square; 610-444-5600; sovanabistro.com; $$$) in Kennett Square, with its high ceilings and elaborate wood chandeliers that give off a warm glow, is one of the trendiest restaurants in the area. Mushrooms, the pride of this area, appear in dishes like grilled mushroom tart and pan-roasted

ABOVE Andrew Wyeth's studio at the Brandywine River Museum. The Brandywine area has been home to three generations of painters from the Wyeth family.

BELOW The conservatory at Longwood Gardens, one of the du Pont family estates in the area that are open to the public for tours.

chicken with mushrooms and wilted spinach (but not in the liquid-center butterscotch cake).

10 *Where the Locals Loll* 9 p.m.

Have an evening drink at the **Gables at Chadds Ford** (423 Baltimore Pike, Chadds Ford; 610-388-7700; thegablesatchaddsford.com), a converted dairy barn with red-leather-upholstered metal stools and high-backed banquettes lining the walls. A piano player entertains on weekends.

SUNDAY

11 *Pierre the Gardener* 10 a.m.

Gardens were the passion of Pierre S. du Pont, who purchased the original 202 acres of what is now **Longwood Gardens** (1001 Longwood Road, Kennett Square; 610-388-1000; longwoodgardens.org), then known as Peirce's Park, in 1906 to preserve its wealth of trees. His obsession went beyond flowers and plants to fruits and vegetables, and there is still a small house there where he grew bananas and plantains for employees and friends. As you explore the 1,077 acres, which include an outdoor topiary garden and a silver garden of succulents and cactuses in the conservatory, be sure to check out the water lily pond in a courtyard outside the hothouses. Some lily pads grow as wide as eight feet.

ABOVE Sampling the merchandise at Baldwin Books.

THE BASICS

Wilmington and Philadelphia are the gateways. Hop from town to town by car.

Inn at Montchanin Village
528 Montchanin Road, Wilmington
302-888-2133
montchanin.com
$$
Tastefully decorated cottages, a spa, and Krazy Kat's restaurant. Owned by members of the du Pont clan.

Fairville Inn
506 Kennett Pike, Chadds Ford
610-388-5900
fairvilleinn.com
$$
On the edge of both Winterthur and some lovely hiking trails.

Hotel du Pont
11th and Market Streets, Wilmington
302-594-3100
hoteldupont.com
$$$$
Venerable and luxurious.

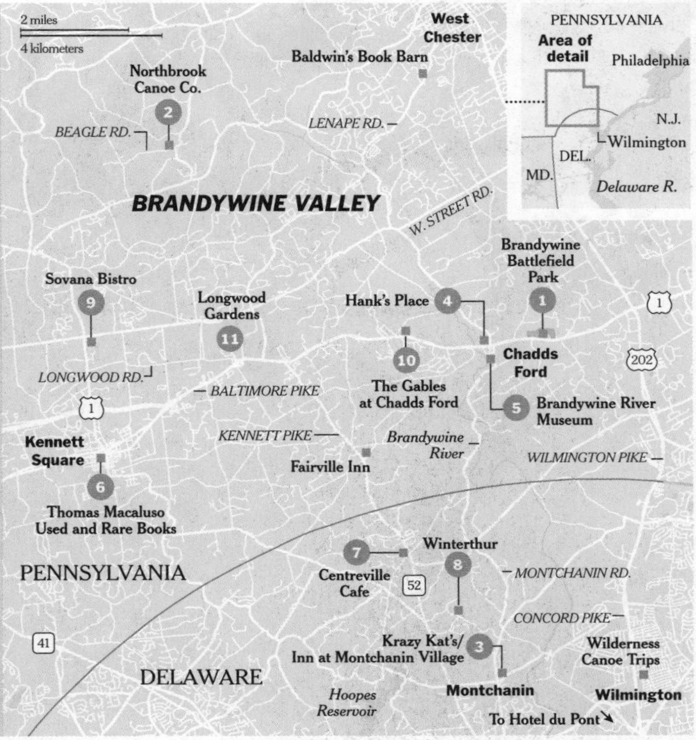

2 miles
4 kilometers
BRANDYWINE VALLEY
West Chester
Baldwin's Book Barn
Northbrook Canoe Co. 2
BEAGLE RD.
LENAPE RD.
W. STREET RD.
PENNSYLVANIA
Area of detail
Philadelphia
N.J.
Wilmington
DEL.
MD.
Delaware R.
Brandywine Battlefield Park 1
Sovana Bistro 9
Longwood Gardens 11
Hank's Place 4
Chadds Ford
The Gables at Chadds Ford 10
Brandywine River Museum 5
LONGWOOD RD.
BALTIMORE PIKE
1
202
KENNETT PIKE
Brandywine River
WILMINGTON PIKE
Kennett Square
Fairville Inn
Thomas Macaluso Used and Rare Books 6
PENNSYLVANIA
Centreville Cafe 7
Winterthur 8
52
MONTCHANIN RD.
CONCORD PIKE
41
Krazy Kat's/ Inn at Montchanin Village 3
Wilderness Canoe Trips
DELAWARE
Hoopes Reservoir
Montchanin
Wilmington
To Hotel du Pont

Gettysburg

On July 1, 1863, Confederate and Union troops descended on the grassy hills of Gettysburg, thrusting the sleepy town of 2,400 into the Civil War. The three-day Battle of Gettysburg ended the Confederate invasion of the North and resulted in staggering losses for both sides—an estimated 51,000 casualties in all for the campaign. Each year, about 1.2 million visitors journey to the Gettysburg National Military Park to see the battlefield and imagine the struggle unfolding in this peaceful setting. Gettysburg itself—still a small town, with a population of only 7,645—has a lot to offer beyond its compelling history. The town's compact but lively center, lined with Federal-style buildings, is filled with mom-and-pop shops and restaurants, and serves as a great base for exploring the region's vineyards and winding country roads. — BY EMILY BRENNAN

FRIDAY

1 *Students' Union* 3 p.m.

Founded in 1832, **Gettysburg College** (300 North Washington Street; gettysburg.edu) sits on 200 bucolic acres north of the town's center. Walk among the mostly brick Georgian and Victorian buildings and stop at the stately white Pennsylvania Hall, an administrative building that was a signal corps station and field hospital for Union and Confederate troops during the battle. Sit in the Adirondack chairs on its expansive lawn, and then step into the Musselman Library to see if there's an exhibition on view.

2 *Homegrown and Homemade* 5 p.m.

Walk down North Washington Street to **Johnny Como's Cupcakes and Coffee** (62 Chambersburg Street; 717-339-0339; johnnycomos.com), which, with its recreated pink 1950s kitchen and Betty Boop posters, is like a step back in time. Order a maple bacon or peanut butter madness cupcake. There are more cupcakes across the street at the **Wells Family Baking Company** (100 Chambersburg Street; 717-337-2900), which is also a good place for coffee and biscotti (try the lemon anise or cranberry pecan). For nearby shopping, stop in at **A & A Village Treasures** (53 Chambersburg Street; 717-398-2555; aavillagetreasures.com) for jewelry, scarves, and goat-milk soaps or at **Gallery 30** (26 York Street; 717-334-0335; gallery30.com), which sells pottery and hand-painted gourds by local artisans, as well as blankets, pillows, and tablecloths woven in Pennsylvania.

3 *Meal with a View* 8 p.m.

You used to have to drive about 30 minutes to the chef Neil Annis's restaurant Sidney in East Berlin, Pa., for his locally sourced, seasonal American menu. Now you'll find an outpost, **Sidney Willoughby Run** (730 Chambersburg Road; 717-334-3774; restaurantsidney.com/willoughby-run; $$$$), overlooking the battlefield. Menus vary; one included fall-off-your-fork-tender braised beef short ribs and a salsify purée so creamy it was like a sauce to the broccoli rabe and wild mushrooms.

SATURDAY

4 *Cup of Joe with Abe* 8:30 a.m.

Grab a quick breakfast of coffee, Amish baked goods, and fresh berries at the **Gettysburg Farmers' Market** (717-334-8151; gettysburgfarmmarket.com) in Lincoln Square, which is marked by a bronze life-size sculpture (by J. Seward Johnson Jr.) of Abraham Lincoln greeting a modern man with a wave of his stovepipe hat. For a souvenir, pick up a bottle from Torchbearer Sauces; its recipes include Pennsylvania-grown peppers, and the sauces come in tongue-in-cheek flavors like Zombie Apocalypse (ghost and habanero peppers) or Oh My Garlic.

5 *Origin Story* 9 a.m.

Arrive at the **Gettysburg National Park Service Museum and Visitor Center** (1195 Baltimore Pike; nps.gov/gett) before the crowds descend at midmorning. The most popular way to navigate the park's 26 miles of roads is by car. CDs of self-guided tours are sold in the bookstore. For a tour with a licensed battlefield guide, reserve a two-hour bus tour or take a two-hour private tour with a guide in your own car. Reservations can also be made online at

OPPOSITE The battlefield, still a focus of reverence and curiosity a century and a half after the Civil War.

tickets.gettysburgfoundation.org up to three days in advance or by phone at 877-874-2478 within three days of your visit. The museum offers a primer on the Civil War through short videos, photographs, and artifacts like Robert E. Lee's battlefield cot and desk. The short film *A New Birth of Freedom* covers the origins of the war; the debate over slavery's expansion to new territories; and the battle's legacy, immortalized by Lincoln's Gettysburg Address, as a defense of democratic ideals. The *Gettysburg Cyclorama*, a monumental 1884 painting by the French artist Paul Philippoteaux that depicts Pickett's Charge, is worth a look.

6 *Battle and Burial* 10 a.m.

Gettysburg National Military Park spans 5,989 acres of woodlands, farmlands, craggy ridges, and sloping valleys, with more than 1,300 monuments erected by the battle's veterans and state governments. Start at McPherson Ridge, where, early in the morning of July 1, 1863, fighting broke out between Union cavalry and Confederate infantry. Then drive south to Little Round Top, the craggy hill that Union soldiers, in a downhill bayonet charge, defended against Confederate troops. At the High Water Mark, look out on the open field that some 12,000 Confederate infantrymen crossed in a mile-long front known as Pickett's Charge. After their decisive defeat, Confederate troops retreated to Virginia, ending Lee's campaign into Pennsylvania. Cross the road to Soldiers' National Cemetery, where about 3,500 Union soldiers lie buried. When the cemetery was dedicated on Nov. 19, 1863, Lincoln took two minutes to deliver "a few appropriate remarks" —his Gettysburg Address.

ABOVE The Cyclorama, a wraparound depiction of the great battle at Gettysburg.

OPPOSITE The national cemetery dedicated by Abraham Lincoln in his Gettysburg Address.

7 *Sweet Break* 1:30 p.m.

For lunch at **Café Saint-Amand** (48 Baltimore Street; 717-334-2700; cafesaintamand.com: $$), a French-style bistro, try one of the savory crepes, like the Swiss cheese and caramelized onions, and then one of the sweet, like the glazed apple with ginger crumbs and candied walnuts. Or get your dessert fix nearby at **Mr. G's Ice Cream** (404 Baltimore Street; 717-334-7600).

8 *Civilian Side* 3 p.m.

A number of historic houses and foundations line Gettysburg's streets. Skip most of them and go to the **Shriver House** (309 Baltimore Street; 717-337-2800; shriverhouse.org), which gives a glimpse of the battle's effect on civilians. A guide in 19th-century costume takes you through the meticulously refurbished home of the Shrivers, a family who, having fled the battle, returned to find their house repurposed to treat wounded soldiers. At Lincoln Square, drop into the **David Wills House** (8 Lincoln Square; 717-334-2436; davidwillshouse.org), a lawyer's Federal brick home where President Lincoln stayed the night before he delivered the Gettysburg Address. A bedroom, with its original mahogany Rococo bed, is said to be where Lincoln added finishing touches to his speech.

9 *Stout Spot* 8 p.m.

You could go to the darkly lighted, laid-back **Garryowen Irish Pub** (126 Chambersburg Street;

717-337-2719; garryowenirishpub.net; $$) just for a pint of stout, but it would be a shame to miss out on its rib-sticking Irish food, like shepherd's pie or an Irish onion soup made with Guinness instead of wine. Live music ranges from Irish to alt-country.

SUNDAY

10 *Wine Way* Noon

Apple orchards and farms still blanket Adams County, and some have reinvented themselves as vineyards. Take Lincoln Highway to the **Adams County Winery** (251 Peach Tree Road, Orrtanna; 717-334-4631; adamscountywinery.com), an 1860s red barn in Orrtanna where you can taste up to six wines for free. **The Historic Round Barn and Farm Market** (298 Cashtown Road, Biglerville; 717-334-1984; roundbarngettysburg.com), in a 1914 white barn in Biglerville, sells fresh produce and its own pickled vegetables and jams. Pick up some cheeses and snacks for a picnic across the road at the **Hauser Estate Winery** (410 Cashtown Road, Biglerville; 717-334-4888; hauserestate.com). After sampling some wines here, order a glass of your favorite and set up your picnic on the patio overlooking the valley.

THE BASICS

Gettysburg's sites are spread out, so plan to make your way around by car.

Gettysburg Hotel
1 Lincoln Square
717-337-2000
hotelgettysburg.com
$$
Built in 1797.

James Gettys Hotel
27 Chambersburg Street
717-337-1334
jamesgettyshotel.com
$$
Suites in a hotel dating back to 1804; part of the building served as a hospital after the battle.

Gettystown Inn Bed & Breakfast
89 Steinwehr Avenue
717-334-2100
dobbinhouse.com
$$
Overlooks the spot where Lincoln gave his Gettysburg Address.

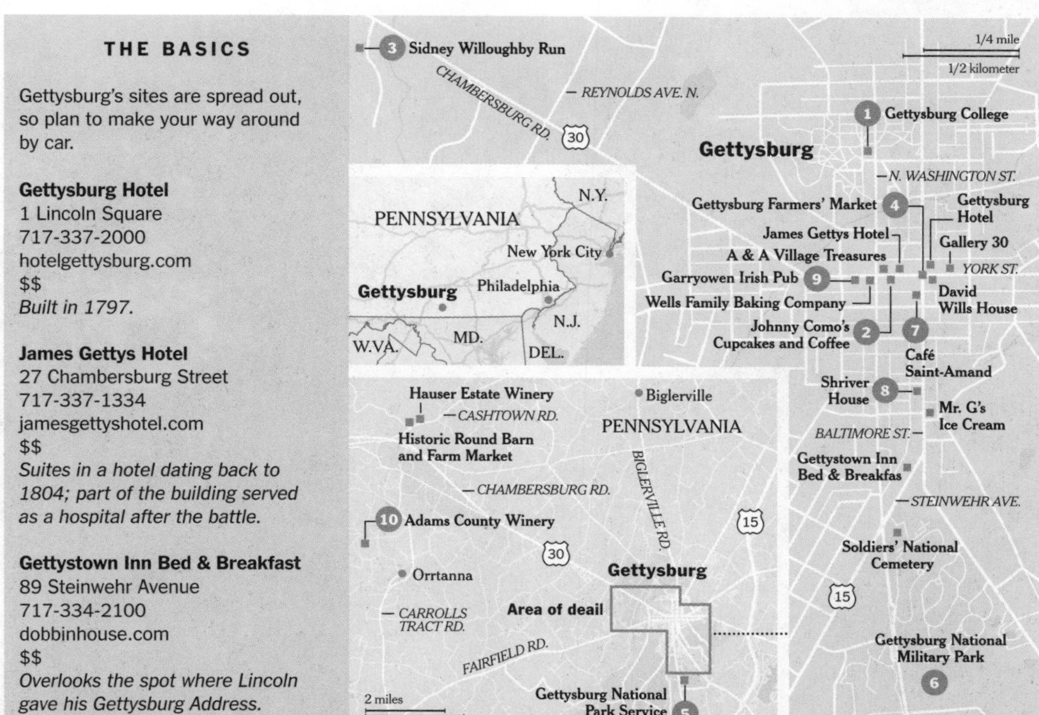

New Haven

It wasn't long ago that New Haven was a poster child for the troubled college town, a place where the graduates of prep schools rubbed shoulders with victims of the mid-'80s and early-'90s crack epidemic. While New Haven's hard-luck reputation lingers, it is no longer fully deserved. The city's historic center, which fans out around twin lawns planted with towering elms, maintains an older New England character, with neo-Gothic towers and working-class neighborhoods of faded but elegant Victorian houses. While town and gown have worked to attract brand-name businesses to downtown (among them an Apple Store and a Shake Shack), New Haven remains complex and layered—a city of taco trucks and barbecue shacks as well as high-end clothiers and stylish cocktail lounges. — BY FREDA MOON

FRIDAY

1 *Get Coastal* 5 p.m.

Take a walk along Long Island Sound, from **Sandy Point Bird Sanctuary** (Beach Street, West Haven; 203-937-3712), where birders glimpse red-billed oystercatchers and green-winged monk parakeets, to **Bradley Point Beach** (Captain Thomas Boulevard, West Haven), near the site of the British invasion of July 5, 1779. Between the two, a paved 1.7-mile promenade keeps the sand from your toes. At sunset, stop into the scuba-themed **Dive Bar & Restaurant** (24 Ocean Avenue, West Haven; 203-933-3483; divebarandrestaurant.com) for a cocktail—a margarita, Key lime martini, or spicy mojito—or a flight of five pours from the rotating tap of 10 craft beers.

2 *Apizza Aplenty* 7 p.m.

In the perennial debate over which local joint serves the superior New Haven-style pie, **Zuppardi's Apizza** (179 Union Avenue, West Haven; 203-934-1949; zuppardisapizza.com; $$), which has been around since 1934, is too often overlooked. On an otherwise residential street, behind a red, green, and white awning, Zuppardi's serves Napolitano "apizza" (pronounced "ah-BEETZ") to families crowded into orange vinyl booths. Order the fresh clam, a thin, bubbling, slightly blackened crust brushed with olive oil, garlic, and parsley and loaded with just-shucked littleneck clams.

3 *Way Off Broadway* 8:30 p.m.

New Haven is a theater town, with three well-respected playhouses, each with its own creative niche. Check schedules and find a play that interests you. Near the industrial waterfront at the foot of the city's food terminal is **Long Wharf Theatre** (222 Sargent Drive; 203-787-4282; longwharf.org), founded in 1965, where performers have included Hollywood powerhouses like Al Pacino and Kevin Spacey as well as up-and-coming Broadway talent. The **Yale Repertory Theatre** (1120 Chapel Street; 203-432-1234; yalerep.org) produces new plays and bold interpretations of classics on three stages. Lighter fare, like musicals and comedy, often predominates at the **Shubert Theater** (247 College Street; 203-562-5666; shubert.com), which has been in operation since 1914.

4 *Porter and Punk* 11 p.m.

On a two-block stretch best known for thumping multistory clubs, the **Cask Republic** (179 Crown Street; 475-238-8335; thecaskrepublic.com) is a comparably more studious place devoted to the less-than-quiet contemplation of fine ales, lagers, stouts, and porters—some 60 or so on draft alone, including rare and cask-conditioned beers. For live jazz or punk rock, Scottish folk or Texas blues, settle in at the **Cafe Nine** (250 State Street; 203-789-8281; cafenine.com), beloved by locals and dubbed the "musician's living room" for its intimate scale. Along Crown Street,

OPPOSITE Harkness Tower, a symbol of Yale.

BELOW Retro cool at the Anchor Restaurant.

notice the Walk of Fame-style stars embedded in the sidewalk, the work of the artist Sheila Levrant de Bretteville, designed to celebrate the grocers, cigar makers, and ship captains of New Haven's past.

SATURDAY

5 *Olmsted on the River* 9 a.m.

In the quiet Westville neighborhood, **Bella's Café** (896 Whalley Avenue; 203-387-7107; bellascafect.com; $$) invites brunch crowds with a menu that includes selections like crab and shrimp omelet or grilled peach shortcake. Eat your fill and then take a walk along the banks of the West River in the 120-acre **Edgewood Park** (Edgewood Avenue; cityofnewhaven.com/Parks), which was designed by Frederick Law Olmsted Jr.

6 *Art for Free* Noon

The **Yale University Art Gallery** (1111 Chapel Street; 203-432-0600; artgallery.yale.edu), which underwent a 14-year renovation that was completed in late 2012, offers expanded (and free) access to its 200,000-piece collection. Across the street, the equally impressive (also free) **Yale Center for British Art** (1080 Chapel Street; 203-432-2800; britishart.yale.edu) holds the largest collection of British art outside Britain, including dramatic George Stubbs lion-and-horse oil paintings, Surrealist triptychs by Francis Bacon, and Pop Art from the 1960s.

7 *Say Cheese* 1 p.m.

Its crowded shelves of imported artisanal pasta and olive oils are reason enough to make the trek to **Liuzzi Cheese** (322 State Street, North Haven; 203-248-4356; liuzzicheese.com), a gourmet market. But the shop also sells sandwiches made with cured meats, like Parma prosciutto and sopressata, and house-made cheeses, like ricotta salata and burrata. There's more informal fare at **Caseus Fromagerie Bistro** (93 Whitney Avenue; 203-624-3373; caseusnewhaven.com; $$), where patio tables, warmed in cold weather by heat lamps, are perfect for savoring comfort food like poutine (pommes frites, cheese curds, velouté) or a sandwich of prosciutto, fig jam, and Taleggio cheese. Next door, **Fashionista Vintage & Variety** (93 Whitney Avenue; 203-777-4434; fashionista-vintage-variety.com) sells hand-selected costumes (harem outfits, animal heads); men's clothing; and vintage wear for women, including dresses that Betty Draper would covet.

8 *The Outlook's Fine* 5 p.m.

Time your visit to the season for a drive to the top of the 426-acre **East Rock Park** (cityofnewhaven.com/Parks), where a 350-foot basalt cliff offers a magnificent vantage for catching the sunset over Elm City and Long Island Sound. The park closes at dusk.

9 *Old-World New England* 8 p.m.

A French restaurant in the high Yankee style, **Union League Cafe** (1032 Chapel Street; 203-562-4299; unionleaguecafe.com; $$$) has an inscription above the fireplace marking a 1789 visit by George Washington. This mix of history and Beaux-Arts grandeur is one reason for visiting; the other reasons are service that's formal without being finicky and food that tastes decadent—foie gras, caviar, and truffles—without being overly rich.

10 *Retro Bar Crawl* 10 p.m.

If only for the atmosphere, stop by the **Owl Shop** (268 College Street; 203-624-3250; owlshopcigars.com), a vintage cigar lounge, draped in leather and wood, where bourbon flows and tobacco is blended. Next door, **Anchor Restaurant** (272 College Street; 203-865-1512) has lighthouse-shaped lamps, blue vinyl booths, and a neon-lit Rock-Ola jukebox. **Rudy's** (1227 Chapel Street; 203-865-1242; rudysnewhaven.com) is no longer the charmingly grimy dive bar it was in a former location, but the back room still pays homage to Yale football, and the frites are still hand-cut, twice-cooked, and Samurai sauce-ready.

SUNDAY

11 *Coffee on the Lawn* 9 a.m.

In the shadow of the Corinthian portico and steeple of St. Michael's Catholic Church, designed in 1855 and among Connecticut's first Italian-American churches, **Wooster Square** is awash in church bells and bordered by cherry trees. Stop at **Lucibello's Italian Pastry Shop** (935 Grand Avenue; 203-562-4083; lucibellospastry.com) for marzipan-flavored, pine nut-topped pignoli, clam-shaped sfogliatelle, and crispy cannolis; then pick up an espresso to go at the friendly coffee shop **Fuel** (516 Chapel Street). Pass the rest of the morning wandering the Yale campus. On a peaceful Sunday, the architecture (yale.edu/architectureofyale), from the 1752 Connecticut Hall to the turtle-shaped shell of the 1958 Eero Saarinen ice skating rink, takes center stage.

OPPOSITE New Haven from East Rock Park.

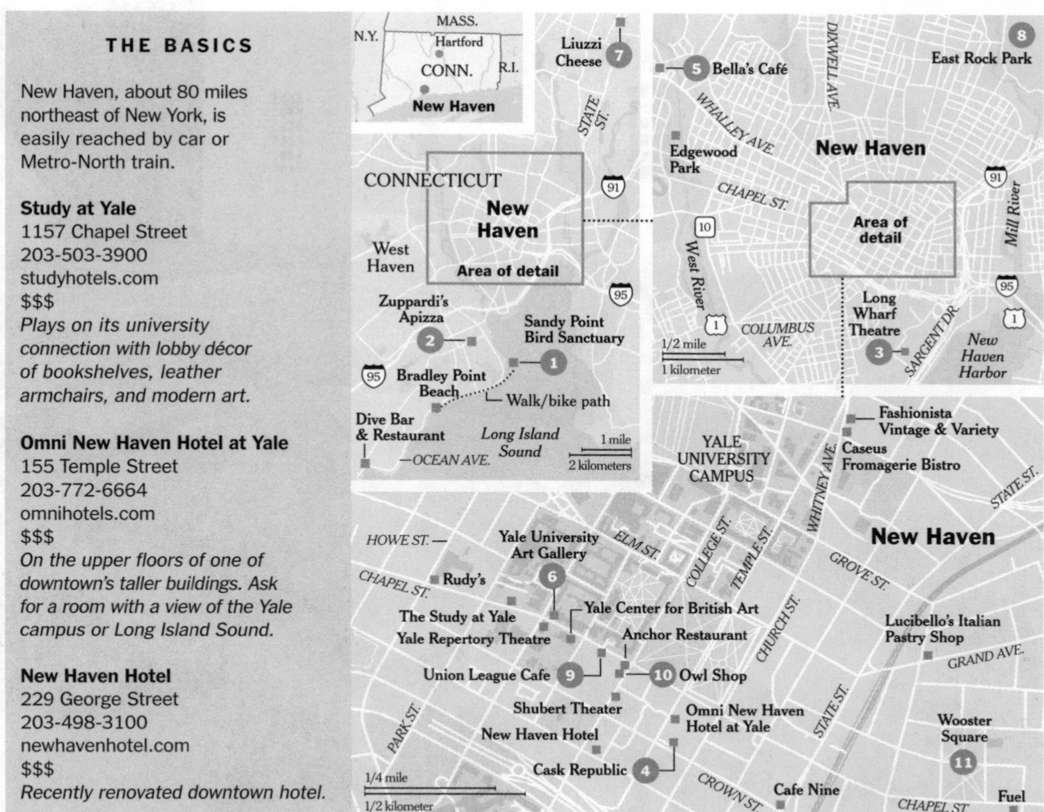

THE BASICS

New Haven, about 80 miles northeast of New York, is easily reached by car or Metro-North train.

Study at Yale
1157 Chapel Street
203-503-3900
studyhotels.com
$$$
Plays on its university connection with lobby décor of bookshelves, leather armchairs, and modern art.

Omni New Haven Hotel at Yale
155 Temple Street
203-772-6664
omnihotels.com
$$$
On the upper floors of one of downtown's taller buildings. Ask for a room with a view of the Yale campus or Long Island Sound.

New Haven Hotel
229 George Street
203-498-3100
newhavenhotel.com
$$$
Recently renovated downtown hotel.

The Connecticut Coast

A summertime drive up Connecticut's coast on Long Island Sound, from the New York City suburbs at its western end to the quiet old town of Stonington about 150 miles to the east, passes bustling marinas, peaceful green fields, and tidal marshes with nesting osprey. It's no secret that this shore is pretty. With a tutored eye and a carefully planned route of discovery, it can be enchanting. The magic is in the sights, smells, and tastes waiting for the traveler. Keep a leisurely pace and stop to spend time with the 21st-century Connecticut Yankees and the ocean waves.

— BY AMY M. THOMAS

FRIDAY

1 *The Gold Route* 1 p.m.

The initial impression of Connecticut can be deceiving. In Greenwich, just over the state line from New York, four-figure baby strollers, six-figure cars, and seven-figure yachts parade along the waterfront. The Gold Coast ambience stretches east to Fairfield, through towns like Westport, where Tiffany sells its gems not far from restaurants by Mario Batali and Danny Meyer. See a different kind of display at the **Bruce Museum of Arts and Sciences** (1 Museum Drive, Greenwich; 203-869-0376; brucemuseum.org), where natural science exhibits draw from the local sea and shore while rotating shows have featured the work of artists from Rembrandt to Chuck Close.

2 *Marsh and Sea* 3 p.m.

Soon the formality fades. The moneyed enclaves turn into relaxed seaside towns. Mansions give way to clam shacks. See open shoreline, barrier beach, and a remnant of the natural coastal marsh at the **Connecticut Audubon Society Coastal Center at Milford Point** (1 Milford Point Road; 203-878-7440; ctaudubon.org/coastal-center-at-milford-point), at the mouth of the Housatonic River. Or just head eastward to pay homage to Yale University and New Haven's justly famed pizza. Frank Pepe started it all in 1925, when he fired up his coal oven and started making tomato pies with a thin crust. **Pepe's** (157 Wooster Street, New Haven; 203-865-5762; pepespizzeria.com; $$) is now legendary, drawing everyone from the food critic Alan Richman to Bill Clinton.

3 *Roadside Cookout* 7 p.m.

Two towns over, in Guilford, is another restaurant with a cult following. **The Place** (901 Boston Post Road, Guilford; 203-453-9276; theplaceguilford.com; $-$$) occupies a roadside expanse that is partly covered by a tattered red-and-white striped tarp. Come in warm weather for classic cookout fare in a casual outdoor setting. (If you want alcohol, bring your own.) The restaurant was founded in 1971 by Gary and Vaughn Knowles, brothers looking to supplement their teachers' salaries. Today, it is a raucous backyard party, with disco and doo-wop, and tree stumps for seats. Everything from catfish to chicken to corn on the cob is cooked on the 24-foot grill, and on any summer night, you will see Yale students, families, and tourists feasting on the clams roasted in butter and cocktail sauce.

SATURDAY

4 *Book Center* 9 a.m.

Have a gouda omelet or some buttermilk pancakes at the **Wharf** restaurant in the seafront **Madison Beach Hotel** (94 West Wharf Road, Madison; 203-350-0014; madisonbeachhotel.com/the-wharf-restaurant.htm; $$), and then explore **Madison**'s town center. The don't-miss shop here is the beloved and capacious independent bookstore

OPPOSITE Stonington's First Congregational Church.

BELOW The A.C. Petersen Drive-In in Old Lyme.

R. J. Julia (768 Boston Post Road; 203-245-3959; rjjulia.com), which stocks thousands of carefully chosen books and regularly brings in well-known authors for readings and events.

5 *Salt in the Air* 11 a.m.

All along the stretch of Route 1 from Guilford to Old Saybrook, you can roll down the car window for a whiff of salty air and feel your tires rippling over steel drawbridges that cross inlets and marshlands. Canoes flit along tributaries, and cruisers and sailboats decorate the Sound. The roadside scenery is a mix of antique and bric-a-brac stores, 17th-century homes and cemeteries, bait-and-tackle shops, and farm stands selling strawberries and squash. To soak up some sun and dip a toe in the Sound, hit the state's largest public beach at **Hammonasset State Park** (1288 Boston Post Road, Madison; 203-245-2785). Then push on a few more miles to Old Lyme for a break at **A.C. Petersen Drive-In** (113 Shore Road, Old Lyme; 860-434-1998), formerly the Hallmark Drive-In, which carries on a long tradition of serving homemade ice cream.

6 *Favorable Impressions* 1 p.m.

A century ago, **Old Lyme**, with its reedy riverbanks, tidal estuaries, and bohemian air, was known as an inspiring setting for painters. The **Florence Griswold Museum** (96 Lyme Street, Old Lyme; 860-434-5542; flogris.org), set on a sloping lawn overlooking the Lieutenant River, shows the work of American Impressionists who were part of the Old Lyme art colony of that era, including Henry Ward Ranger, William Chadwick, and Childe Hassam.

7 *Among the Reeds* 3 p.m.

For a close encounter with the water, rent a kayak from **Black Hall Outfitters** (132 Shore Road; 860-434-9680; blackhalloutfitters.com), which is on the Connecticut River Estuary Canoe and Kayak Trail. In the quiet inlets, you'll paddle past regal herons and fishermen looking to land striped bass. When you're ready to get back on the road, stay close to the shore on Route 156, and then head north and pick up Route 1 again in New London.

8 *Succulent and Sculptured* 6 p.m.

Find your way to the sleepy town of Noank and join the parade of cars flocking to **Abbott's Lobster in the Rough** (117 Pearl Street, Noank; 860-536-7719; abbotts-lobster.com; $$). A Connecticut classic, it's a seasonal restaurant with picnic tables perched overlooking the water. You can't go to Connecticut and not have a lobster roll, and as all the tourists documenting their meals with digital cameras attest, the quarter-pound of succulent, buttered lobster meat at Abbott's, sculptured into a perfect round puck and served on a seeded hamburger roll, fits the bill.

9 *A Drink With the Captain* 8 p.m.

You'll be rolling into **Mystic** with just enough time left in the evening for a look at the compact downtown, with its cluster of little clothing and knickknack shops, galleries, and restaurants. Drop in for a drink at the **Captain Daniel Packer Inne** (32 Water Street; 860-536-3555; danielpacker.com), which was built in 1756 as an inn for Daniel Packer, a former square-rigger skipper who operated a rope ferry across the Mystic River. Its impressive stone foundation gives way to a cozy dark wood downstairs bar; a restaurant is upstairs.

SUNDAY

10 *Mystic Morning* 10 a.m.

Mystic Seaport (75 Greenmanville Avenue; 860-572-0711; mysticseaport.org), a 17-acre complex

on the banks of the Mystic River, simulates a 19th-century New England coastal village. Some of the buildings are authentic and have been moved to the seaport; others are reproductions of buildings that were once there or in other coastal towns. Stroll around to see maritime life recreated in buildings like the Mallory sail loft, constructed in the early 19th century and named for Charles Mallory, who made ships' sails. Museum workers use the loft to maintain sails used by the exhibition vessels that are at docks alongside the village.

11 *Last Port of Call* 1 p.m.

Stonington, the last town before Rhode Island, lives up to its name with old stone walls (built by sheep farmers a couple of centuries ago) lacing its green fields. The small borough, or village, at the waterfront is a former whaling port with plain fishermen's cottages wedged next to each other and pillared homes facing Fishers Island Sound. Out on a peninsula, a lonely stone lighthouse, which dates to 1840 and has survived Category 3 hurricanes, stands across from a wee public beach. Here, as you feel the sun, solitude, and sea air and see water in every direction, you'll know you have seen the authentic Connecticut coast.

OPPOSITE ABOVE The Seashore at Hammonasset State Park.

OPPOSITE BELOW A lobster roll at Abbott's in the Rough.

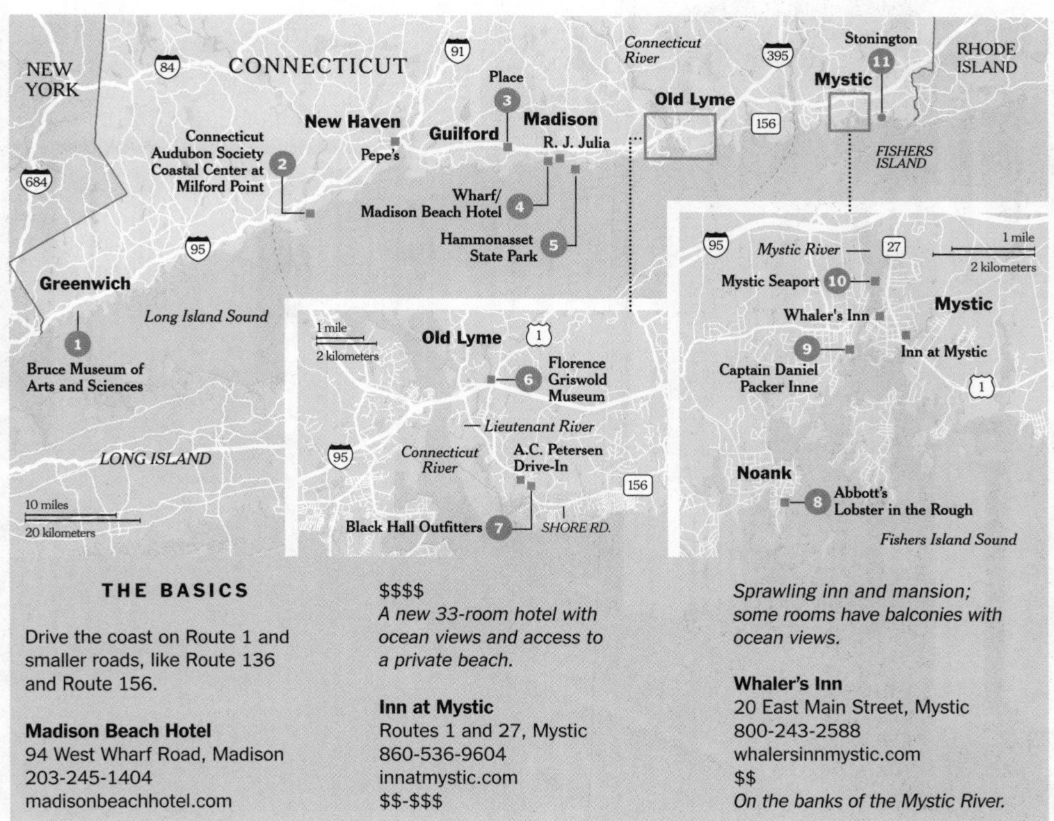

THE BASICS

Drive the coast on Route 1 and smaller roads, like Route 136 and Route 156.

Madison Beach Hotel
94 West Wharf Road, Madison
203-245-1404
madisonbeachhotel.com
$$$$
A new 33-room hotel with ocean views and access to a private beach.

Inn at Mystic
Routes 1 and 27, Mystic
860-536-9604
innatmystic.com
$$-$$$
Sprawling inn and mansion; some rooms have balconies with ocean views.

Whaler's Inn
20 East Main Street, Mystic
800-243-2588
whalersinnmystic.com
$$
On the banks of the Mystic River.

Providence

Overshadowed by Boston 50 miles up the East Coast and the mammoth New York City megalopolis a couple of hours' drive in the other direction, Providence, the smallish capital of the country's smallest state, is easy to underestimate. But spend a weekend there, and you'll discover a town many times more creative and cosmopolitan than its relative obscurity and modest population of 180,000 might suggest. Home to an Ivy League college, one of the best design schools in the United States, and a major culinary institute, Providence has exceptional food, compelling art and architecture, a thriving gay scene, and an inordinate number of very smart people. Yet it remains unpretentious and affordable.
— BY FREDA MOON AND KAREN DEUTSCH

FRIDAY

1 *Art Through the Ages* 3 p.m.

With 84,000 objects housed in its six stories, the Rhode Island School of Design's **RISD Museum** (224 Benefit Street; 401-454-6500; risdmuseum.org) could easily consume an entire day. The collection ranges from ancient Roman, Egyptian, and Greek artifacts to midcentury modern Eames furniture and Frank Lloyd Wright stained-glass windows.

2 *Hidden Beauty* 5 p.m.

Cross into downtown via one of the elegant bridges over the Woonasquatucket and Moshassuck Rivers. Both rivers were covered by concrete and rail lines until the mid-1990s, when a considerable effort was undertaken to unearth the city's waterways. Knock on the door at **Big Nazo Lab** (60 Eddy Street; 401-831-9652; bignazo.com), where gleeful monsters and alien creatures — colorful wearable sculptures made of latex — peer from storefronts. Founded by Erminio Pinque, an instructor at Rhode Island School of Design, the studio has a gracious open-door policy: "Visitors of all shapes and sizes are welcome," Pinque said.

OPPOSITE A street in the College Hill neighborhood, home to Brown University and the Rhode Island School of Design. College Hill recalls the city's colonial past.

RIGHT Gondola tours are a good fit in a city with three rivers and its own Little Italy.

3 *Bank on It* 8 p.m.

In a lesser food town, the **Dorrance** (60 Dorrance Street; 401-521-6000; thedorrance.com; $$) could rest on the laurels of its architectural splendor — stained-glass windows; gilded candelabra; and elaborate, cake-frosting molding. But it wouldn't have to. Dorrance serves food as ornate as its surroundings, the opulent lobby of the former Union Trust building. Diners at one visit had mild Peruvian ceviche with tomatillo, fried sweet potato chips, and herbs, and Rhode Island black fish crusted in quinoa, with quahogs, asparagus, and sunchokes, drowned in grass-green ramp dashi.

4 *Dim the Lights* 10 p.m.

Two of Providence's most enticing bars are hidden on a residential Federal Hill side street. Signless and easy to miss, the **Avery** (18 Luongo Memorial Square; 401-286-0237; averyprovidence.com) has dim lights, woodcuts of Art Nouveau vixens, and the varnished woodwork of a luxury yacht. Just down the block, **E&O Tap** (289 Knight Street; 401-454-4827; eandotap.com) is a raucous dive bar with a changing list of tap beers and a kitschy black velvet painting of Elvis.

SATURDAY

5 *Paisano!* 9 a.m.

Like many of the country's aging Little Italys, **Federal Hill** can feel more like a theme park attraction than an authentic neighborhood. The chef Cindy Salvato's three-hour culinary tour, **Savoring Rhode Island** (401-934-2149; savoringrhodeisland.com),

steps past the faux-Italian facades and into the back rooms of historic neighborhood businesses. Among them, a shop that's been slaughtering quail, rabbit, and geese for the city's immigrant communities since 1853; the diminutive kitchen where Venda Ravioli produces vast quantities of broccoli rabe, truffle, and lobster ravioli by hand each day; and the family-run Scialo Brothers Bakery, in business since 1916.

6 *Going Downtown* 1 p.m.

On Saturdays, there's traditional Irish music on fiddles and flutes, guitars and concertinas at **AS220 FOO(d)** (115 Empire Street; 401-831-3663), a restaurant run by the nonprofit AS220 (as220.org), which has transformed the Downcity neighborhood with its music, gallery, and art studios. Have a sandwich for lunch (maybe the Tomato Braised Lamb with tzatziki sauce, feta, greens, and onions). After lunch, check out the shops of Westminster Street, including the nautically themed men's store **Wharf** (212 Westminster Street; 401-272-1231; shopwharf.com), the women's boutique **Queen of Hearts** (222 Westminster Street; 401-421-1471; queenofheartsri.com), and **Craftland** (235 Westminster Street; 401-272-4285; craftlandshop.com), an emporium devoted to locally made ceramics, art prints, soaps, T-shirts, and more.

7 *Walk Back in Time* 4 p.m.

Take a long look at some of the architecture that gives Providence its powerful sense of place. On Benefit Street, a quaint strip that sits on College Hill, find the **Old State House** (150 Benefit Street; 401-222-3103) where, in 1776, Rhode Islanders declared independence two months before the rest of the American colonies. Nearby are the **Providence Athenaeum** (251 Benefit Street; 401-421-6970; providenceathenaeum.org) and the **John Brown House** (52 Power Street; 401-273-7507), completed in 1788 and home to one of the founders of Brown University. Turn in at the picturesque Brown campus (brown.edu), which looks just the way a venerable Ivy League university should.

ABOVE *WaterFire*, a river installation by the sculptor Barnaby Evans that comes to shimmering life downtown on some Saturday nights from May to November.

8 *A French Accent* 7 p.m.

Chez Pascal (960 Hope Street; 401-421-4422; chez-pascal.com; $$$) is a French restaurant with white tablecloths, leopard print furniture, and the open arms of a neighborhood brasserie. The menu emphasizes Rhode Island ingredients, but the food is traditional and exquisite: a selection of house-made pâtés and charcuterie, escargots à la Bourguignon, and slow-roasted duck with a seared root vegetable cake and golden raisin and red wine sauce. Across the street is the much-hyped **Cook & Brown Public House** (959 Hope Street; 401-273-7275; cookandbrown.com), one of several options for excellent craft cocktails in this cocktail-happy city.

9 *Watermark* 9 p.m.

In 1994, a Brown alumnus and artist named Barnaby Evans created a sculpture of 100 mini-bonfires that marked the convergence of the Providence, Moshassuck, and Woonasquatucket Rivers in the heart of downtown. The work, ***WaterFire*** (waterfire.org), has a mesmerizing quality and continues today, drawing crowds on about a dozen Saturday evenings between May and November. If you're not here when *WaterFire* is lighted, catch a show at **Cable Car Cinema**

and Cafe (204 South Main Street; 401-272-3970; cablecarcinema.com), where you can sip a glass of wine while watching a little-known feature film straight from the festival circuit.

SUNDAY

10 *Hair of the Dog* 8:55 a.m.

Get to **Julians** (318 Broadway; 401-861-1770; juliansprovidence.com; $$) before it opens, or plan on waiting. The brunch includes a selection of vegan dishes, like the Def Scram tofu scramble (rainbow carrots, jalapeños, pea tendrils, and sesame rice crisps), alongside carnivore-pleasing masterpieces like the Funky Boss braised short rib eggs Benedict with caramelized onion, pickled cabbage, jalapeño grits, and smoked paprika hollandaise. This is a popular hangover spot; diners can be seen gripping a tall, spicy bloody mary in one hand, a coffee cup in the other.

11 *Ethiopian Picnic* 11 a.m.

Take a lazy stroll along the **Blackstone Boulevard Walking Path** (blackstoneparksconservancy.org), which begins at Blackstone Park at Angell Street and River Road and cuts through one of Providence's most beautiful and historic neighborhoods. Then head down to Fox Point and pick up an unusual picnic: Ethiopian takeout at **Abyssinia** (333 Wickenden Street; 401-454-1412; abyssinia-restaurant.com) and sit by the water in **India Point Park** (friendsofindiapointpark.org).

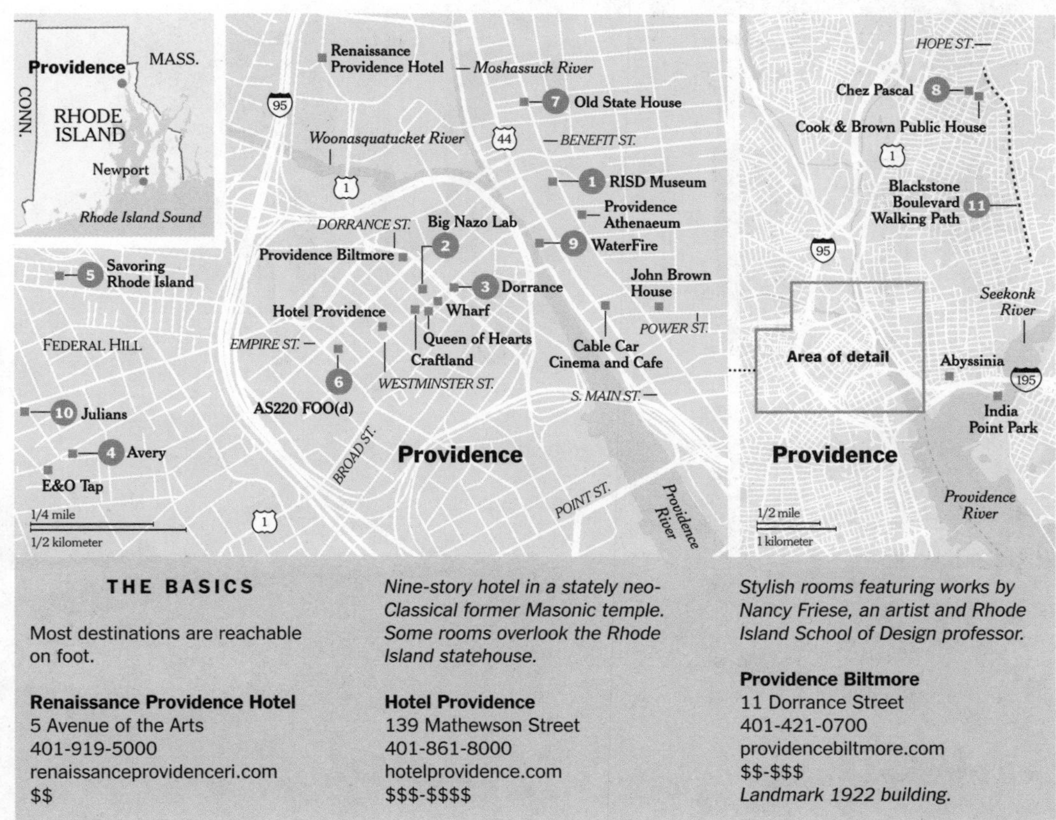

THE BASICS

Most destinations are reachable on foot.

Renaissance Providence Hotel
5 Avenue of the Arts
401-919-5000
renaissanceprovidenceri.com
$$
Nine-story hotel in a stately neo-Classical former Masonic temple. Some rooms overlook the Rhode Island statehouse.

Hotel Providence
139 Mathewson Street
401-861-8000
hotelprovidence.com
$$$-$$$$
Stylish rooms featuring works by Nancy Friese, an artist and Rhode Island School of Design professor.

Providence Biltmore
11 Dorrance Street
401-421-0700
providencebiltmore.com
$$-$$$
Landmark 1922 building.

Newport

Each summer, two million tourists head to Narragansett Bay to shuffle their way through the Gilded Age trophy homes of Newport, Rhode Island — the lumbering white elephants (or are they overdressed maiden aunts?) perched hip to hip on the city's glittering rocky coastline. You too can explore America's insatiable appetite for... darn nearly everything here, and ponder the freakishness of the wealthy. Glut your senses by driving down Newport's main drag, otherwise known as Bellevue Avenue, a weird bazaar of architectural expression that includes more Versailles references than is probably healthy. If you continue along Ocean Drive, you will note attempts by contemporary architects to be this century's Stanford White (and that is not necessarily a good thing). But keep your eyes on the rugged coast, green parks, and yacht-filled harbor, all cooled on hot summer days by the ocean breeze, and you will remember how all of this got here.
— BY PENELOPE GREEN

FRIDAY

1 *The Cliff Walk* 3 p.m.

Get a jump on the weekend crowd with a Friday afternoon trip to the Fifth Avenue of nature walks. Newport's famous **Cliff Walk** (cliffwalk.com) runs for three and a half miles along shoreline that makes everyone love an ocean view. It can be jam-packed on the weekends with tourists ogling the backyards of the Bellevue Avenue estates, many of which it slices into. Here is a strategy: Park at Easton's Beach on Memorial Boulevard, just below the Chanler at Cliff Walk hotel. You will find the path entrance right there. Follow the path to the end at Ledge Road (only if you are strong; this will take more than an hour) or to the stone staircase called the 40 Steps (about 20 minutes). Walk up Ledge Road to Bellevue Avenue, make a left, and you will see a bus stop for Newport's trolleys (if you make it only to the 40 Steps, there is a stop at Narragansett and Ochre Point). Take a trolley back into town, get off at the Newport Casino, and walk down Memorial Boulevard to your car.

2 *Find Salvation* 7 p.m.

Have drinks and dinner at the **Salvation Restaurant and Bar** (140 Broadway; 401-847-2620; salvationcafe.com; $$), the way the locals do. The tattooed waiters and vaguely Asian-hippie menu remind you that Newport is only 40 miles from the Rhode Island School of Design. Dinner can jump from a Hoisin Sticky Ribs appetizer to an entree of vegan risotto. Stick around for dessert.

SATURDAY

3 *Eggs at the Dock* 9 a.m.

Take an outdoor table for breakfast at **Belle's Cafe**, at the Newport Shipyard (1 Washington Street; 401-846-6000; newportshipyard.com; $$). The eggy burritos are good, and the yacht-people watching is, too.

4 *A Heart-Shaped World* 10 a.m.

One of Stanford White's prettiest and silliest houses is **Rosecliff** (548 Bellevue Avenue), built for the heiress Tessie Oelrichs in 1902. You can read all about it in *The Architect of Desire*, a hypnotic family memoir about the tragic and emotional legacy of the Gilded Age's favorite architect, written by his great-granddaughter, Suzannah Lessard. (Tessie died alone at Rosecliff in 1926, Lessard wrote, talking to

OPPOSITE The Breakers, one of the trophy mansions that typified Newport's golden age. Several of the most lavish and eye-popping are now open for tour.

RIGHT The 3.5-mile Cliff Walk, where the public now enjoys the same ocean views that were treasured by the mansion builders of the Gilded Age.

imaginary guests.) With its heart-shaped double staircase and baby-blue trompe-l'oeil ballroom ceiling, Rosecliff is sweeter and lighter than many of Newport's lavish hulks from the same period. Allow an hour for a tour of the house and a little more time to wander Rosecliff's green lawns, which swoop down to the cliffs. The house is one of 11 properties and landscapes owned by the Preservation Society of Newport County, which runs this and other mansion tours (401-847-1000; newportmansions.org).

5 *Rare Books* Noon

If the crowds haven't gotten to you yet, they soon will. Find an oasis at the **Redwood Library & Athenaeum** (50 Bellevue Avenue; 401-847-0292; redwoodlibrary.org), the oldest lending library in the United States. There's a collection of furniture, sculpture, and paintings, including six portraits signed by Gilbert Stuart. But even more charming is the Original Collection of 750 titles, purchased from England in 1748 by a group of Newport citizens. You may not always be able to just drop in to read them, but a look at the titles is an interesting window on the wide interests of the library's founders—from theology to bloodletting techniques to how to build a privy.

6 *Make Mine Gothic* 1 p.m.

Bannister's and Bowen's wharves, smack in the middle of Newport Harbor, make up ground zero for Newport's seafaring past. They are very scenic and wharfy. But you knew that. What you might not know is that many of the exteriors in a marvelous camp classic, the gothic soap opera *Dark Shadows*, were shot in Newport. Have a salad at the **Black Pearl** (Bannister's Wharf; 401-846-5264; blackpearlnewport.com, $$), which was known as the Blue Whale in *Dark Shadows*.

7 *Teak and Brass* 2 p.m.

Walk down to the **International Yacht Restoration School** (449 Thames Street; 401-848-5777; iyrs.org) and its affiliated **Museum of Yachting** (moy.org). The school is both a center for restoring classic yachts and a school for history-minded craftsmen learning how to be restorers. There are heartbreakingly beautiful boats everywhere, in all stages of restoration. Make sure you wander through the turn-of-the-century factory building and out to the water, where you will find the school's most ambitious project, a 133-foot schooner, built in 1885, called *Coronet*. To see more, take a water taxi (newportharborshuttle.com) to the affiliated **Museum of Yachting** (moy.org), out on a bay island at Fort Adams State Park. Its exhibitions dovetail with the restoration work, explaining and expanding on what visitors see at the school.

8 *Back to the Wharf* 7 p.m.

Have dinner (make a reservation) at **Tallulah on Thames** (464 Thames Street; 401-849-2433; tallulahonthames.com; $$$$), a small, sophisticated dining spot. It's on Thames Street, which is also the home of predictable tourist shops and restaurants, but a world apart. For a splurge, order the three-course prix-fixe menu; its creative dishes have included appetizers of corn veloute and duck confit; entrees of artfully presented seafood; and desserts like panna cotta and lemon cheesecake with rhubarb.

SUNDAY

9 *Around the Dunes* 9 a.m.

You will need a salty wind to ruffle your hair today, something brisk and fresh to blow away all that dust and glitter. Head a few miles north out of town to the **Sachuest Wildlife Refuge** (769 Sachuest Point Road, Middletown; 401-847-5511; www.fws.gov/refuge/sachuest_point/). Two-hundred-and-forty-two acres of salt and freshwater marshes, sea

ABOVE Fog over the Newport-Pell Bridge. Originally a seafaring settlement, Newport is still a boatman's town, especially if that boat is a yacht.

OPPOSITE ABOVE Harborside dining at Bannister's Wharf in the old Narragansett Bay port area.

grass, bayberry, and bittersweet and a rocky coastline are host to all manner of wildlife, including seals, nesting terns, and harlequin ducks. Take the three-mile perimeter trail so you can be constantly on the water.

10 *In the Bay* 11 a.m.

For another perspective on Narragansett Bay, drive out onto the two-mile-long Claiborne Pell Bridge, which soars some 215 feet above the bay, and take the first exit, at Jamestown. This much smaller town is overshadowed by Newport, but its waterfront is worth a visit, with its own galleries, restaurants, and shops. Pick up some provisions, find the dock for the **Jamestown-Newport Ferry** (Conanicut Marina, One East Ferry Wharf; jamestownnewportferry.com), and park your car. Then ride the ferry to its first stop, Rose Island, and eat your lunch at the **Rose Island Lighthouse** (401-847-4242; roseisland.org), which is owned and maintained by a nonprofit group and has an associated museum and wildlife refuge. You'll find yourself in the middle of the bay, with gorgeous views of boats, harbors, and the sparkling water in every direction.

THE BASICS

By car, Newport is three to four hours from New York and an hour from the airport in Providence, Rhode Island. In town, drive your car and use the RIPTA public bus system (ripta.com).

Forty 1° North
351 Thames Street
401-846-8018
41north.com
$$$$
New hotel on the water, with stylish, modern touches.

The Chanler at Cliff Walk
117 Memorial Boulevard
401-847-1300
thechanler.com
$$$$
Luxury, stunning views, and ornately decorated rooms.

Admiral Fitzroy Inn
398 Thames Street
866-848-8780
admiralfitzroy.com
$$$
Bed-and-breakfast in a former convent.

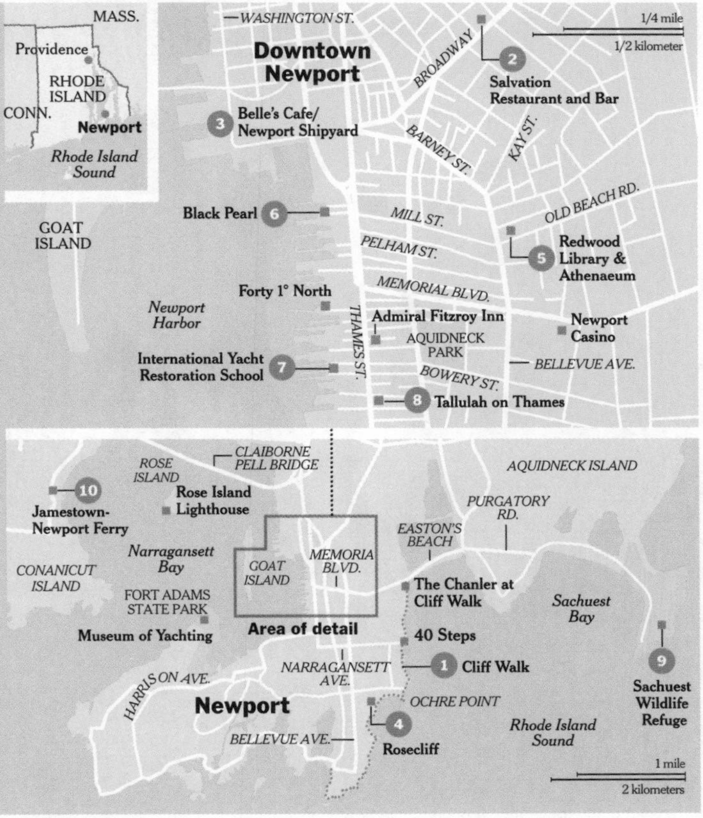

MASS.
Providence
RHODE ISLAND
CONN.
Newport
Rhode Island Sound
WASHINGTON ST.
Downtown Newport
BROADWAY
1/4 mile
1/2 kilometer
2 Salvation Restaurant and Bar
3 Belle's Cafe/ Newport Shipyard
BARNEY ST.
KAY ST.
Black Pearl 6
MILL ST.
OLD BEACH RD.
GOAT ISLAND
PELHAM ST.
5 Redwood Library & Athenaeum
MEMORIAL BLVD.
Forty 1° North
Newport Harbor
THAMES ST.
Admiral Fitzroy Inn
AQUIDNECK PARK
Newport Casino
International Yacht Restoration School 7
BOWERY ST.
BELLEVUE AVE.
8 Tallulah on Thames
ROSE ISLAND
CLAIBORNE PELL BRIDGE
AQUIDNECK ISLAND
10 Jamestown-Newport Ferry
Rose Island Lighthouse
PURGATORY RD.
EASTON'S BEACH
Narragansett Bay
CONANICUT ISLAND
GOAT ISLAND
MEMORIAL BLVD.
The Chanler at Cliff Walk
Sachuest Bay
FORT ADAMS STATE PARK
Area of detail
Museum of Yachting
40 Steps
HARRISON AVE.
NARRAGANSETT AVE.
1 Cliff Walk
9 Sachuest Wildlife Refuge
Newport
OCHRE POINT
4 Rosecliff
BELLEVUE AVE.
Rhode Island Sound
1 mile
2 kilometers

Martha's Vineyard

What is it about presidents (at least Democratic ones) and Martha's Vineyard? The Kennedys have been coming since there were actual vineyards. The Clintons turned up nearly every summer of their White House years, and the Obamas followed. Wealthy A-listers usually hover nearby, hoping for invitations to the same parties where the First Families show up. But part of the Vineyard's appeal is its easy way of shrugging off snobbery. Despite its popularity among the presidential set, this island, off Cape Cod in Massachusetts, is still a laid-back place with a lot of mopeds, fish shacks, and nice beaches. Folks here will tell you that the Vineyard is really just an old fishing community—that is, if you don't get stuck behind a motorcade. — DANIELLE PERGAMENT AND MARY SUH

FRIDAY

1 *Lobster Worship* 5 p.m.

Lobsters are practically a religion on the island, so it's fitting that some of the freshest are served in a church. On summer Fridays from 4:30 to 7:30 p.m., **Grace Church** in the tree-lined town of Vineyard Haven (Woodlawn Avenue and William Street; 508-693-0332; gracechurchmv.com) sets up picnic tables and sells lobster rolls—fresh, meaty cuts tossed lightly with mayonnaise and served on soft hot dog buns. Judging by the long lines, the church-supper prices (under $20 for lobster roll, chips, and a drink) might be the best deal in town. Sit with fellow worshipers, or take your meal down by the docks for a view of the harbor.

2 *Your Inner Oak Bluffs* 6:30 p.m.

The Vineyard is an island of small towns, and Oak Bluffs is the slightly disheveled member of the family, the one that has a hard time getting dressed for dinner. So, it's a fun place to just stroll. Start by heading for the famed **Trinity Park Tabernacle** (508-693-0525) and its campgrounds. Once a retreat for Methodists, who pitched tents there, the area has an open-air auditorium and frequent concerts. Surrounding the park are Lilliputian gingerbread cottages, many dating from the mid-1800s. Once you've seen them, it's not hard to understand why their architectural style is called Carpenter Gothic. Continue your stroll past the marina to the **Flying Horses Carousel** (508-693-9481) on Oak Bluffs Avenue, the country's oldest operating platform merry-go-round, dating to 1876. Yes, it even has brass rings. Grab one and get a free ride. Then head toward **Ocean Park**, which is ringed by beautiful old houses, many now bed-and-breakfasts. Watch people fly kites, ride bikes, and just hang out.

3 *Secret Sweets* 9 p.m.

On summer nights, in a dark parking lot in Oak Bluffs, a small crowd lines up at the screen door of the **Martha's Vineyard Gourmet Cafe and Bakery** (5 Post Office Square; 508-693-3688; mvbakery.com), waiting for warm doughnuts right out of the oven. This open secret is known as Back Door Donuts. The doughnuts are soft, sticky, and delicious, though some veterans will tell you the apple fritters are superior.

SATURDAY

4 *Egg Rolls and Wool* 9 a.m.

Get to the **West Tisbury Farmers' Market** (1067 State Road; 508-693-9561; westtisburyfarmersmarket.com) when it opens at 9 so you can watch the stalls being set up—and shop before the best produce is picked over. Take your camera along on this

OPPOSITE The Allen Sheep Farm & Wool Company, where even the livestock has an ocean view.

RIGHT By the sea in Oak Bluffs, a town of beaches, boats, and Victorian gingerbread houses.

expedition: you'll find a colorful scene of wildflowers, organic fruits and vegetables, alpaca-yarn clothing, homemade jams, and, somewhat curiously, a stall selling egg rolls.

5 *Say Baaah* 10:30 a.m.

Martha's Vineyard is like a miniature Ireland —roads wind among bright green pastures where sheep, horses, and cattle graze. Many of the farms welcome visitors. The **Allen Farm Sheep & Wool Company** in the bucolic town of Chilmark (421 South Road; 508-645-9064; allenfarm.com) has been run by the same family since 1762. Take in the views of rolling fields. Buy lamb chops or try on a handmade wool sweater in the gift shop. Those things grazing out front? They're lambs, and they're very friendly.

6 *Fried Goodness* 1 p.m.

It's a picture-perfect beach shack — without the beach. Housed in a tiny, weathered shingle house on a small side street in the old fishing port of Menemsha, the **Bite** (29 Basin Road; 508-645-9239; $$) has been serving what many regard as the island's best fried clams, oysters, squid, shrimp, and scallops since 1988. There are only two picnic tables, so bring a couple of icy beers, get a small order of clams, and take the paper bag of crispy deliciousness to the dock and watch the fishermen.

7 *Time in the Sand* 2 p.m.

The nicest beaches on Martha's Vineyard are private; you need a key to get in. But one that's open to the public is **Menemsha Beach**, a lovely stretch of sand just outside of town (ask for directions at the Bite; you're close). It is popular with families, and in the evening, it's a favorite place to watch the sunset. Swim a little, walk a little, or just hang out.

8 *Take a Hike* 4 p.m.

Yes, the Vineyard looks great from the water. But for a less-photographed view of the island's natural beauty, drive inland to **Waskosim's Rock Reservation** (mvlandbank.com), a nature reserve with 185 acres of open fields, wooded trails, and marshes. A modest, mile-long hike takes you to Waskosim's Rock, the boulder that divided the island between the English and the native Wampanoag people 350 years ago. Tempting though it may be, resist climbing the rock — Vineyarders want to make sure it's around for another 350.

9 *State Dinner* 8 p.m.

They may not be as famous as the vegetable garden on Pennsylvania Avenue, but the herb and vegetable patches that supply the **State Road** restaurant (688 State Road; 508-693-8582; stateroadmv.com; $$) have their admirers. State Road features American cuisine using local ingredients: lobster, fresh fish, locally raised chicken and lamb, and a bounty of produce from farms on the Vineyard and nearby. The dining room is simple and sleek, with hardwood floors, high ceilings, and Edison bulb chandeliers.

10 *Night at the Ritz* 11 p.m.

The Vineyard isn't known for night life, but your best bet for a nightcap is in the handful of lively bars along Circuit Avenue in Oak Bluffs. Stop by the **Ritz Café** (4 Circuit Avenue; 508-693-9851), which attracts

locals and has live music. Don't be fooled by the name; this is more of a draft beer than an appletini kind of joint.

SUNDAY

11 *Stores by the Seashore* 10 a.m.

There's a lot of good shopping between all those seagull paintings and dancing-lobster napkins. In Vineyard Haven, drop by Carly Simon's **Midnight Farm** (44 Main Street; 508-693-1997; midnightfarm.net) for its eclectic mix of gauzy sundresses, home furnishings, and, at times, signed copies of Simon's CDs. Up the street is **Nochi** (29 Main Street; 508-693-9074; nochimv.com), which sells robes, blankets, and all things cozy. And down the street is **LeRoux at Home** (62 Main Street; 508-693-0030; lerouxkitchen.com), a housewares store with a great selection of kitchen supplies, linens, cookbooks, and tableware.

OPPOSITE ABOVE The Menemsha Inn.

OPPOSITE BELOW The Bite, a clam shack in Menemsha.

ABOVE The twice-a-week West Tisbury Farmers' Market attracts farmers and shoppers from all over the island.

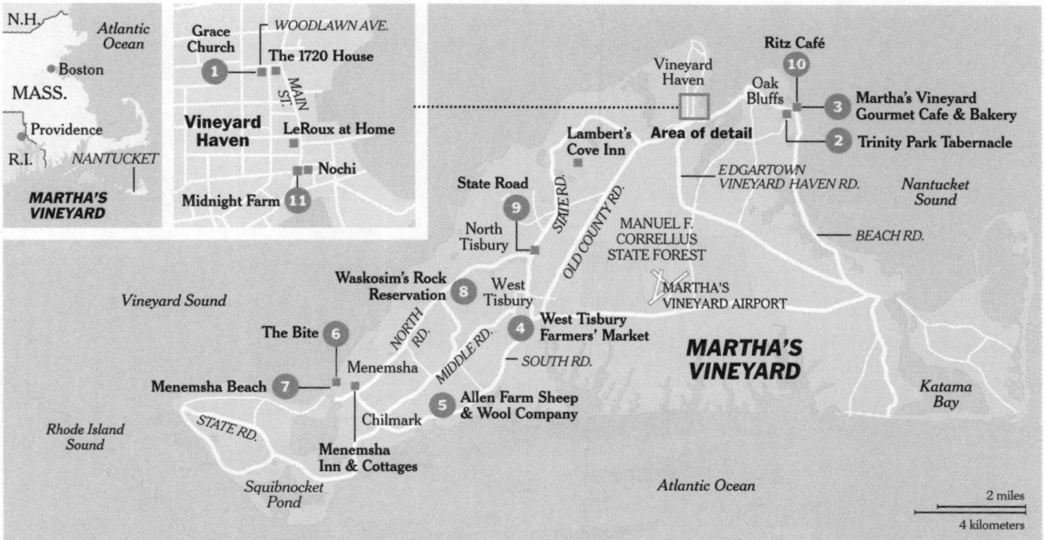

N.H.
Atlantic Ocean
Boston
MASS.
Providence
R.I.
NANTUCKET
MARTHA'S VINEYARD
Grace Church
WOODLAWN AVE.
1 The 1720 House
MAIN ST.
Vineyard Haven
LeRoux at Home
Nochi
Midnight Farm 11
Vineyard Haven
Area of detail
Ritz Café 10
Oak Bluffs
3 Martha's Vineyard Gourmet Cafe & Bakery
2 Trinity Park Tabernacle
Lambert's Cove Inn
State Road 9
North Tisbury
STATE RD.
OLD COUNTY RD.
EDGARTOWN VINEYARD HAVEN RD.
Nantucket Sound
MANUEL F. CORRELLUS STATE FOREST
BEACH RD.
Waskosim's Rock Reservation 8
West Tisbury
MARTHA'S VINEYARD AIRPORT
Vineyard Sound
NORTH RD.
4 West Tisbury Farmers' Market
The Bite 6
MIDDLE RD.
SOUTH RD.
MARTHA'S VINEYARD
Menemsha
Menemsha Beach 7
5 Allen Farm Sheep & Wool Company
Katama Bay
Chilmark
Rhode Island Sound
STATE RD.
Menemsha Inn & Cottages
Squibnocket Pond
Atlantic Ocean
2 miles
4 kilometers

THE BASICS

Fly in or arrive by ferry. Rent a car on the island.

Lambert's Cove Inn
90 Manaquayak Road
West Tisbury
508-693-2298
lambertscoveinn.com
$$$
Pool, tennis court, and beach.

The 1720 House
152 Main Street, Vineyard Haven
508-693-6407
1720house.com
$$
Cute and well located.

Menemsha Inn and Cottages
12 Menemsha Inn Road
Menemsha
508-645-2521
menemshainn.com
$$$$
A guesthouse and cottages.

Nantucket

Near the beginning of Moby-Dick, *Ishmael explains why he decided to set sail from Nantucket: "There was a fine, boisterous something about everything connected with that famous old island." Today, more than a century and a half after it was written, that characterization still rings true. Though its downtown cobblestone streets and windswept fringes are now filled with expensive restaurants and elegant cocktail bars, the island still has a swagger. To see it in full swing, linger over pints at one of the many harborside pubs, especially at sundown when sailors and fishing boats return to port.* — BY SARAH GOLD

FRIDAY

1 *Historic Bearings* 3 p.m.

Main Street is lined with 19th-century storefronts and buckled brick sidewalks that seem to require deck shoes. To bone up on island history, visit **Mitchell's Book Corner** (54 Main Street; 508-228-1080; mitchellsbookcorner.com), a bookstore that first opened in 1968. The beloved Nantucket Room holds hundreds of titles about island lore. The store also hosts weekly readings by such local authors as Elin Hilderbrand and the National Book Award winner Nathaniel Philbrick. A few blocks away, a sister store, **Nantucket Bookworks** (25 Broad Street; 508-228-4000; nantucketbookpartners.com), offers readers more shelves to browse.

2 *Preppy It Up* 5 p.m.

You can still find a bona fide pair of the pinkish chinos called Nantucket Reds at **Murray's Toggery Shop** (62 Main Street; 508-228-0437; nantucketreds.com), and buy sunscreen or fancy bath products at **Nantucket Pharmacy** (45 Main Street; 508-228-0180; nantucketrx.com), another classic of Nantucket shopping. But there are plenty of much newer boutiques to explore. **Jack Wills** (11 South Water Street; 508-332-1601; jackwills.com), the first stateside outpost of the British university outfitter, carries jaunty polos, cable-knit sweaters, and canvas totes in signal-flag colors. **Milly & Grace** (2 Washington Street; 508-901-5051; millyandgrace.com) sells youthful summer dresses and tops, jewelry, and home accessories.

3 *Fish of the Moment* 8 p.m.

Dune (20 Broad Street; 508-228-5550; dunenantucket.com; $$$) serves local seafood and produce in an intimate, warmly illuminated space. There are three dining rooms as well as a patio, but you'll need to book ahead. Changing menus have included dishes like sauteed local cod with Parmesan broth, wax beans, tomatoes, pea greens, and dill spaetzle. Stop by the petite quartzite bar on your way out.

4 *Beach Martinis* 10 p.m.

A young, tanned crowd fills the back room of **Galley Beach** (54 Jefferson Avenue; 508-228-9641; galleybeach.net; $$$). A cherished beachside restaurant, it has also become a late-night gathering spot, serving wines by the glass and drinks like pear sage martinis. The party also spills outside, where sofas and candlelit tables line the sand.

SATURDAY

5 *Island Market* 10 a.m.

The **Nantucket Farmers & Artisans Market** (Cambridge and North Union Streets;508-228-3399;

OPPOSITE Yachts rule in Nantucket Harbor, once the refuge of whaling ships.

RIGHT Brant Point Lighthouse in the harbor.

sustainablenantucket.org) offers the wares of dozens of island farmers and artisans throughout the season and hosts workshops to encourage other would-be island growers and craftsmen. Keep an eye out for handmade quilts, freshly picked blueberries and raspberries, and fresh baked goods.

6 *Surf and Seals* Noon

If you're looking for a day of sand and saltwater and don't mind company, decamp to one of the favorite public swimming beaches, like Cisco Beach in the island's southwest, where strong waves draw surfers. But to see a wilder and more natural Nantucket, drive out to the far west end, where the island tapers to the twin forks of **Eel Point** and **Smith's Point**. You'll need to rent a four-by-four — make sure it has a beach-driving permit; if not, you'll have to buy one for $150 at the Nantucket Police Station. You'll also need to reduce the tire pressure to maximize traction and minimize environmental damage. But after bumping along hillocky dune trails, you'll enter onto wide-open, mostly empty shores. There are no amenities to speak of, so bring all the supplies you'll need, including food and water. Oh, and a camera. You might spot gray seals.

7 *Brew with a View* 5 p.m.

An afternoon of salty, sandy fun can leave you pretty thirsty. So it's convenient that you're close to **Millie's** (326 Madaket Road; 508-228-8435; milliesnantucket.com), a fabled west-end watering hole. Millie's takes full advantage of the sunset location. A glassed-in second-floor bar lets you drink in panoramic vistas along with your Grey Lady or Whale's Tale Pale Ale, both from the Cisco Brewery a few miles down the road.

8 *Baja Style* 8 p.m.

Corazón del Mar (21 South Water Street; 508-228-0815; corazonnantucket.com; $$) has attracted a slavish following. This cozy, tiny papaya-orange den turns out south-of-the-border-inspired dishes like Peruvian chicken wings or soft, Baja-style tacos filled with beer-battered fish, cabbage slaw, chipotle mayo, and avocado. After dinner, take a stroll along Straight Wharf to **Nantucket Ice Cream** (44 Straight Wharf; 508-332-4949) for a cone or the seasonal specialty (one summer standout was a sandwich of lemon sugar cookies and blueberry ice cream).

SUNDAY

9 *Sea Saviors* 10 a.m.

More than 700 shipwrecks litter the treacherous shoals and surrounding waters around Nantucket. For a fascinating glimpse into the island's underwater heritage, visit the **Nantucket Shipwreck & Lifesaving Museum** (158 Polpis Road; 508-228-1885; nantucketshipwreck.org), which has vintage surfboats once used to save wreck survivors, child-friendly exhibits on Coast Guard sea dogs, and — most chillingly — grainy black-and-white 1956 film footage of one of the most infamous wrecks, the Italian ship *Andrea Doria*, shown slowly listing into the sea after its collision with a Swedish ocean liner.

ABOVE Sunbathing in the Nantucket summer.

BELOW Traditional weathered wooden shingles are everywhere, even on this luxury hotel, The White Elephant.

10 *Beachside Brunch* Noon

The **Summer House Restaurant** in Siasconset village (17 Ocean Avenue; 508-257-9976; thesummerhouse.com; $$$$) is the island's most civilized spot for lunch, especially at its umbrella-shaded Beachside Bistro. Look for jazzed-up summertime classics like crab cake with corn salsa and tarragon aioli or a warm poached lobster salad with green beans and beurre blanc.

11 *Not Quite Open House* 1 p.m.

The **Bluff Walk** in Siasconset village was once the south shore's most fiercely guarded secret. But though you will probably share the unmarked path with other visitors these days, a stroll here is still breathtaking. Pick up the trail in the village center (take a right and then a quick left at the end of Front Street) and walk along the high, Atlantic-skirting bluffs, past the backyards of some of the island's stateliest gray-shingled mansions. Erosion has left its mark (the last third of a mile, which used to extend all the way to Sankaty Head lighthouse, is now closed). But just stay on the path, keep your voice down, and wear long pants — some residents, whether intentionally or not, let their sections become overgrown.

ABOVE Surfers young and old, beginning and experienced, find waves to fit their skills at Nantucket's beaches.

THE BASICS

Fly into the Nantucket airport or take a ferry from Hyannis, Massachusetts, on Cape Cod. Buses of the Nantucket Regional Transit Authority (nrtawave.com) run all over the island.

The Cottages & Lofts at the Boat Basin
24 Old South Wharf
866-838-9253
thecottagesnantucket.com
$$$$
Shipshape cottages at the Harbor.

The White Elephant
50 Easton Street
508-228-2500
whiteelephanthotel.com
$$$$
Harborside patio, spa, and 64 rooms, suites, and cottages.

The Union Street Inn
7 Union Street
508-228-9222
unioninn.com
$$$
In a 1770 house.

Nantucket
Nantucket Bookworks
Dune 3
8 Corazón del Mar
Jack Wills
5 Nantucket Farmers & Artisans Market
Nantucket Pharmacy
Milly & Grace
1 Mitchell's Book Corner
Murray's Toggery Shop 2
Union Street Inn
Nantucket Ice Cream
Cottages & Lofts at the Boat Basin
STEAMBOAT WHARF
STRAIGHT WHARF
OLD SOUTH WHARF
COMMERCIAL WHARF
Nantucket Harbor
BROAD ST.
CHESTNUT ST.
S. WATER ST.
FEDERAL ST.
CENTER ST.
INDIA ST.
CAMBRIDGE ST.
OLD NORTH WHARF
MAIN ST.
LIBERTY ST.
FAIR ST.
ORANGE ST.
UNION ST.
WASHINGTON ST.
CANDLE ST.
SALEM ST.
NEW WHALE ST.
COMMERCIAL ST.
200 feet
100 meters
Boston
Atlantic Ocean
MASS.
R.I.
CAPE COD
MARTHA'S VINEYARD
NANTUCKET
Nantucket Sound
NANTUCKET ISLAND
COATUE-COSKATA WILDLIFE REFUGE
Head of the Harbor
Wauwinet
WAUWINET RD.
Galley Beach 4
White Elephant
Nantucket Harbor
9 Nantucket Shipwreck & Lifesavimg Museum
6 Eel Point
Area of detail
POLPIS RD.
MIDDLE MOORS
Bluff Walk 11
Smith's Point
7 Millie's
HUMMOCK POND RD.
NANTUCKET STATE FOREST
MILESTONE RD.
Siasconset
Cisco Beach
Cisco Brewery
NANTUCKET MEMORIAL AIRPORT
NANTUCKET CONSERVATION FOUNDATION
10
Summer House Restaurant
2 miles
4 kilometers

MODA FINA
birdie
good scents
for
the body

Provincetown

Park yourself anywhere on Commercial Street, the bustling main artery of Provincetown, and you will see celebrities, some real (John Waters, Paula Poundstone), some fake (that wasn't Cher). But mostly you will see ordinary people—lesbian, gay, bisexual, transgendered, and none of the above. Of the first 100 obvious couples to walk past Wired Puppy, a coffee-and-WiFi joint, one typical summer night, 28 were female-female, 31 male-male, and 41 male-female. Four hundred years after the Pilgrims arrived here on the Mayflower, *water is still Provincetown's raison d'être; it provides the gorgeous scenery and the cod, sole, haddock, clams, lobsters, and oysters that make this a food lover's paradise. The trick, as in any resort town, is to eat at odd hours, which makes it possible to avoid crowds even on weekends. And then exercise. With great places to walk, bike, and swim, Provincetown makes burning calories as much fun as consuming them.* — BY FRED A. BERNSTEIN

FRIDAY

1 *On Two Wheels* 4 p.m.

Try to arrive in Provincetown by plane or boat. A car is useless in Provincetown, and besides, you can't really appreciate the place unless you see it as the Pilgrims saw it—on the ground, with the ocean out the front door and a vast bay out the back. Have the taxi driver take you straight to **Ptown Bikes** (42 Bradford Street; 508-487-8735; ptownbikes.com) for a reasonably priced bicycle rental. Then beat the evening crowd with an early trip to **Fanizzi's by the Sea** (539 Commercial Street; 508-487-1964; fanizzisrestaurant.com; $$), where you can find cold beer and the classic fish and chips, lightly battered fried clams, or a local fishermen's platter.

2 *Dune Buggin'* 5:30 p.m.

Time to burn off some of what you just ate. Ride your bike southwest to the end of Commercial Street, turn right at the traffic circle, and pedal till you see the Herring Cove Beach parking lot. At the end of the lot, a small opening in the fence leads to the bike trail into the **Province Lands** (nps.gov/caco). It's a five-foot-wide strip of asphalt that swoops up and down the dunes like a glorious doodle. It's about four miles to **Race Point Beach**—perhaps the town's most breathtaking stretch of sand. Fill up at the water fountain and return to town in time for sunset.

3 *Night Galleries* 7:30 p.m.

Park your bike at the **Provincetown Art Association and Museum** (460 Commercial Street; 508-487-1750; paam.org). The town's premier art space, it grew with a smart addition by Machado and Silvetti (the architects of the Getty Villa restoration in Los Angeles). It's open till 10 p.m. (and free) on Friday nights. There are dozens of other galleries in Provincetown, and they, too, are open late on Fridays. Walk through the commercial district and drop in on a few.

4 *Love the Nightlife* 10 p.m.

The **Crown & Anchor** (247 Commercial Street; 508-487-1430; onlyatthecrown.com) offers one-stop shopping for gay entertainment. Arrayed around its courtyard are a disco with laser lights and throbbing speakers, a leather bar with hirsute habitués, a piano

OPPOSITE Leave the car at home. Provincetown's main drag, Commercial Street, is best navigated on foot or by bicycle.

BELOW A trail ride down the Beech Forest Trail in the Province Lands area.

bar where everyone knows the lyrics, and more. When the bars close at 1 a.m., follow the crowd to **Spiritus Pizza** (190 Commercial Street; 508-487-2808; spirituspizza.com; $). Some call it the "sidewalk sale"—the last chance for a hookup—but really it's a giant block party. The pizza, with thin crust and more marinara than cheese, is super.

SATURDAY

5 *Window Seat* 10 a.m.

If your hotel doesn't have breakfast, head to **Cafe Heaven** (199 Commercial Street; 508-487-9639; $$) for delicious omelets, house-made granola, and banana pancakes. From behind its big windows, you can peruse the local papers for concert and theater listings.

6 *Stairway After Heaven* 11:30 a.m.

You loved those pancakes. Now work them off at the **Pilgrim Monument**, a gray stone crenellated tower that has looked out over the town and out to sea since 1910 (pilgrim-monument.org). Buy a bottle of water from the machine outside and then start climbing; a mix of stairs and ramps will take you to the top of the 252-foot tower. On a clear day, you can see the tops of Boston's tallest buildings.

7 *The End of Cape Cod* 1 p.m.

Stop at **Angel Foods** in the East End (467 Commercial Street; 508-487-6666; angelfoods.com) for takeout—ask for the delicious lobster cakes and a savory curry chicken salad. With lunch in your back-pack, ride to the traffic circle at the end of Commercial Street and lock your bike to the split-rail fence. Walk out onto the breakwater, a 1.2-mile-long line of rocks the size of automobiles. After a spectacular 25-minute trek, you'll find yourself on a deserted beach.

ABOVE The West End, at Provincetown Harbor.

LEFT Provincetown is on the East Coast, but its location at the end of curving Cape Cod makes it a good place for watching sunsets, like this one at Herring Cove Beach.

8 *Retail Corridor* 4 p.m.

Time for some shopping. **Wa** (220 Commercial Street; 508-487-6355; waharmony.com) is a shop that looks more like a perfectly curated museum of Asian art and furniture. **Forbidden Fruit** (173 Commercial Street; 508-487-9800; eatmyapple.com) sells unusual home décor items that run from funky to bizarre, including shiny masks with a slightly carnal tone. At **Alice Brock Studio** (69 Commercial Street; 508-487-2127; alicebrock.com), you may meet the proprietor, who sells her artwork here. It's not her first commercial venture—she is the Alice immortalized by Arlo Guthrie in the song *Alice's Restaurant.*

9 *Inn Fare* 8:30 p.m.

You've planned ahead and made a reservation (the restaurant recommends doing so six weeks in advance), so now claim your spot at **The Red Inn** (15 Commercial Street; 508-487-7334; theredinn.com; $$-$$$), a 200-plus-year-old house that has been beautifully maintained and updated. The food is not adventurous (pan-roasted cod, Long Island duck, lamb chops with a Dijon crust), but it is well prepared, and the place is gorgeous, with tongue-and-groove paneling over a bay window in the beautiful back room, fireplaces, a great barroom, and a deck right on the water.

ABOVE AND BELOW Walkers on the breakwater and the view inland from Cape Cod Bay

SUNDAY

10 *Portuguese Breakfast* 10 a.m.

This time, breakfast at **Chach** (73 Shank Painter Road; 508-487-1530; $$), an update on the diner theme with a retro checkered floor and vinyl booths. There are plenty of typical breakfast choices, and this is a

good place for Portuguese sweet bread, a nod to the Portuguese fishermen who once dominated this town. The abundant cod that sustained them are largely fished out, but some of their descendants remain, and Provincetown celebrates their traditions with its Portuguese Festival every summer.

11 *The Windblown Shore* 1 p.m.

Take a guided trip by S.U.V. through the **Cape Cod National Seashore** with **Art's Dune Tours** (4 Standish Street; 508-487-1950; artsdunetours.com). The tour ventures out into the sand dunes on protected lands at the tip of Cape Cod, and will take you past dune shacks where such writers and artists as Eugene O'Neill, Jack Kerouac, Tennessee Williams, and Jackson Pollock once spent summers working in near total isolation. The dunes are a magical experience, and the guides are happy to share their knowledge about the people who once lived here and the hardy plants and wildlife that find sustenance in this remote and windy spot.

ABOVE Wa, an Asian-themed shop on Commercial Street.

OPPOSITE Although Provincetown today is anything but austere, the Pilgrim Monument celebrates its Puritan roots.

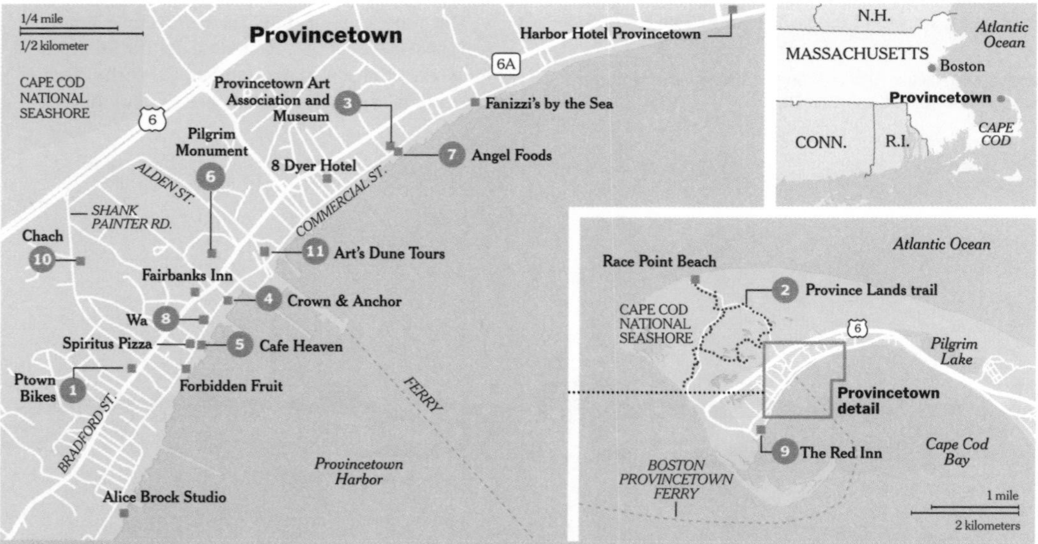

1/4 mile
1/2 kilometer
Provincetown
Harbor Hotel Provincetown
6A
CAPE COD NATIONAL SEASHORE
6
Provincetown Art Association and Museum 3
Fanizzi's by the Sea
Pilgrim Monument 6
8 Dyer Hotel
7 Angel Foods
ALDEN ST.
COMMERCIAL ST.
SHANK PAINTER RD.
Chach 10
11 Art's Dune Tours
Fairbanks Inn
4 Crown & Anchor
Wa 8
Spiritus Pizza
5 Cafe Heaven
Ptown Bikes 1
Forbidden Fruit
FERRY
BRADFORD ST.
Provincetown Harbor
Alice Brock Studio
N.H.
Atlantic Ocean
MASSACHUSETTS
Boston
Provincetown
CONN.
R.I.
CAPE COD
Atlantic Ocean
Race Point Beach
2 Province Lands trail
CAPE COD NATIONAL SEASHORE
6
Pilgrim Lake
Provincetown detail
9 The Red Inn
Cape Cod Bay
BOSTON PROVINCETOWN FERRY
1 mile
2 kilometers

THE BASICS

Flights and ferries arrive in Provincetown from Boston. The trip by car takes two and a half hours from Boston and at least five from New York.

Harbor Hotel Provincetown
698 Commercial Street
508-487-1711
harborhotelptown.com
$$
Stylishly renovated; spectacular views of Cape Cod Bay.

8 Dyer Hotel
8 Dyer Street
508-487-0880
8Dyer.com
$$-$$$$
Bright and nicely decorated.

Fairbanks Inn
90 Bradford Street
508-487-0386
fairbanksinn.com
$$
Centrally located, with rooms overlooking a courtyard.

COMMONWEALTH
ShopUsLast.Com
Exit 45 • Rte. 495 • Lawrence

Boston

Boston is known for its bricks and brownstones, but with downtown stretching unimpeded to the waterfront after the $15 billion Big Dig, these days it feels like a whole new city. High-tech exuberance, modern parks, and a reclaimed harbor add to the sheen of newness, complementing the youthful energy of the large student population. There's no danger that the city will forget its pivotal role in American history. The Freedom Trail is still there for the walking, and stately colonial houses still invite a stroll in Beacon Hill. But Boston offers some new paths to travel, too. — BY KATIE ZEZIMA

FRIDAY

1 *Everything Old Is New* 4:30 p.m.

In a city this historic, it's not every day that a new neighborhood is built from scratch. But that is essentially the story with Fan Pier, a former area of industrial blight on the South Boston waterfront being slowly transformed into a hub of fashion, art, and dining. Anchored by the **Institute of Contemporary Art** (100 Northern Avenue; 617-478-3100; icaboston.org), a glass-and-steel museum that seems to hover over the harbor, it is a go-to place for the cool crowd. Shopping's a draw, too: **LouisBoston** (60 Northern Avenue; 617-262-6100; louisboston.com), the high-end store, has a 20,000-square-foot flagship, with a restaurant, next to the museum.

2 *Taste of Dakar* 8 p.m.

There's more on Boston dinner plates than baked beans. As the city becomes more diversified, so do its culinary offerings. Case in point: **Teranga** (1746 Washington Street; 617-266-0003; terangaboston.com; $), a Senegalese restaurant that opened in May 2009 on a busy South End street, far from the well-dressed masses. An elegant space with exposed brick walls and a long banquette, it serves spicy, fragrant dishes like nems, spring rolls stuffed with vermicelli, and thiébou djeun, a popular West African dish with kingfish, jasmine rice, tomato sauce, carrots, and cabbage.

3 *Hear the Buzz* 10 p.m.

There are plenty of places to catch a show but not so many to hear live music with no cover. The **Beehive** (541 Tremont Street; 617-423-0069; beehiveboston.com), a restaurant where the lights are low and bands are chill, fills the void. Descend the staircase to be closer to the band, or stick to the quieter bar upstairs. Either way, don't leave without catching the intricate, hand-painted bathroom walls.

SATURDAY

4 *Easy as Green* 11 a.m.

Downtown was once defined by an elevated steel highway. Then by the Big Dig, the seemingly never-ending project to sink the roadway underground. After billions of dollars and untold numbers of delays, it is finally home to the **Rose Kennedy Greenway** (rosekennedygreenway.org), a mile-long ribbon of lawns, public art, and much-needed playgrounds snaking along Atlantic Avenue. To explore this emerald oasis, start at South Station and meander toward the North End, stopping to frolic in the fountains or take a spin on the carousel. At **Christopher Columbus Park**, find a spot under a wisteria-covered trellis and watch as boats bob in the harbor and planes take off from Logan Airport. It was worth the wait.

5 *Lobster Bar* 1 p.m.

It's a cliché for a reason: you can't visit Boston, smell a salt breeze, and not want to eat seafood.

OPPOSITE The landmark Custom House Tower, now a Marriott hotel, overlooking the Rose Kennedy Greenway in Boston.

BELOW Wharf District Park, one of the interconnected public spaces along the Rose Kennedy Greenway.

Steer clear of the waterfront traps and head to **Neptune Oyster** (63 Salem Street; 617-742-3474; neptuneoyster.com; $$$), a tiny spot where Sam Adams-swilling frat boys rub shoulders with fabulous Champagne sippers at the marble bar. The attraction? Why, the lobster roll, a mountain of warm, butter-slicked lobster piled into a soft brioche bun, with a side of crispy skin-on fries.

6 *Couture and Cannolis* 3 p.m.

The North End, Boston's Italian neighborhood, is now as much Milan as manicotti, with boutiques popping up between restaurants and pastry shops. **Acquire** (61 Salem Street; 857-362-7380; acquireboutique.com) melds vintage and modern housewares. The ladies win at **In.jean.ius** (441 Hanover Street; 617-523-5326; injeanius.com), where the friendly staff stops at nothing to turn up that perfect pair. This is also the neighborhood of **Old North Church** (193 Salem Street; 617-523-6676; oldnorth.com), where two lanterns in the steeple served as a signal to Paul Revere in 1775.

7 *Personalized Libations* 6 p.m.

Tired of forking over $15 for a cocktail that doesn't quite speak to your individual tastes? Then pull up to **Drink** (348 Congress Street; 617-695-1806; drinkfortpoint.com), where mixology becomes personal. Instead of providing menus, bartenders ask patrons about their tastes and liquors of choice, and try to concoct the perfect tincture. The bar is reminiscent of a booze-drenched chemistry lab, and any experiments that don't turn out right can be sent back. You can't go wrong with the Maximilian Affair, a smoky combination of mezcal, St. Germain, Punt e Mes, and lemon juice.

8 *Provence on the Charles* 8 p.m.

Boston raised its culinary game with **Bistro du Midi** (272 Boylston Street; 617-426-7878; bistrodumidi.com; $$$), run by Robert Sisca, formerly

ABOVE AND LEFT The 1909 main building and the Foster + Partners-designed American wing, opened a century later, of the venerable Museum of Fine Arts Boston.

the executive sous chef at the renowned New York restaurant Le Bernardin. Here Sisca has created a Provençal menu with a focus on local fish. Ask to be seated upstairs, where businessmen and dolled-up couples sit in buttery yellow leather chairs and gaze at unbeatable views of the Public Garden outside.

9 *Local Tallboys* 10:30 p.m.

Tourists flock to the "*Cheers* bar" at 84 Beacon Street, made famous by the television series. But there's an antidote around the corner at **75 Chestnut** (75 Chestnut Street; 617-227-2175; 75chestnut.com). Tucked on a romantic side street, this dimly lighted restaurant feels like a modern take on an old brownstone, with tin ceilings and mahogany pillars. For a younger and cooler scene, check out the **Delux Café** (100 Chandler Street; 617-338-5258), a reigning temple of kitsch with walls decorated with records, comic books, and a bust of Elvis. To get some New England hipster cred, order a tallboy Narragansett Beer, the region's answer to Pabst Blue Ribbon.

SUNDAY

10 *Art and Architects* 10 a.m.

Boston has had a first-rate art collection, spread over its well-known museums, for as long as anyone can remember. In recent years, renowned architects have arrived in town to design some of the display space. To see art and modern architecture blended at the venerable **Museum of Fine Arts** (465 Huntington Avenue; 617-267-9300; mfa.org), head to its Art of the Americas wing by Foster + Partners, which opened in 2010. The I.M. Pei-designed galleries added in the 1980s are still worth a look, too. Renzo Piano designed new breathing space for the quirky **Isabella Stewart Gardner Museum** (280 The Fenway;

TOP The Institute of Contemporary Art in Fan Pier, a new go-to neighborhood in South Boston. The museum's glass-and-steel cantilever hovers over the harbor.

ABOVE Custom mixologists at Drink, a South Boston bar.

617-566-1401; gardnermuseum.org), although its masterpieces must remain in the Venetian-style palazzo where Ms. Gardner installed them. Prefer a ballgame to a museum trip? If it's baseball season and the Red Sox are in town, get tickets for a game this afternoon at **Fenway Park** (4 Yawkey Way; redsox.com), the beloved ballpark that remains right where it was when it opened in 1912.

ABOVE Fenway Park, home of the Boston Red Sox.

OPPOSITE The North End and the Old North Church.

11 *Oysters at Brunch* 1 p.m.

Henrietta's Table (Charles Hotel, One Bennett Street, Cambridge; 617-661-5005; henriettastable.com; $$$) is known for having the richest brunch in town. The rustic, easygoing vibes belie the upscale prices. Getting your money's worth requires strategy and discipline. Bypass the breads and muffins for the raw oysters; innumerable types of smoked fish, pâtés, and cheeses; and perfectly cooked steaks, fish, and pork. Oh, yes, and the dessert table: don't miss this rare opportunity to spread crème brûlée on a Belgian waffle.

THE BASICS

Fly to Logan Airport or take a high-speed Amtrak train from New York. In the city, public transportation is plentiful (mbta.com).

The W Boston
100 Stuart Street
617-261-8700
whotels.com/boston
$$$-$$$$
Opened in 2009, with 235 sleek rooms overlooking the Theater District.

The Ames Hotel
1 Court Street
617-979-8100
ameshotel.com
$$$
Also new in 2009. Minimalist rooms and trendy décor.

Newbury Guest House
261 Newbury Street
617-437-7666
newburyguesthouse.com
$$
A brownstone with quaint touches and 32 rooms.

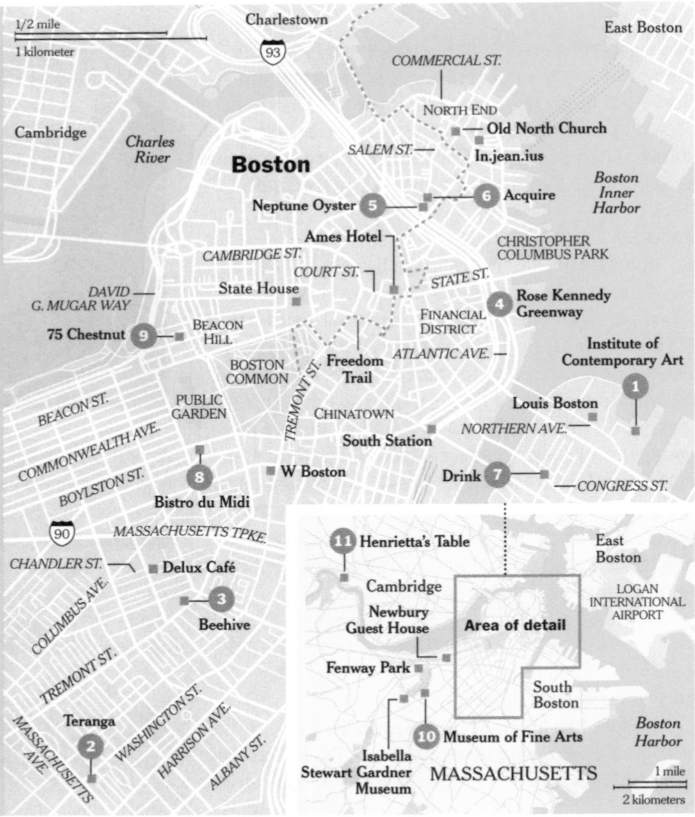

OHN W. WEEKS BRIDGE

Cambridge

Home of Harvard and the Massachusetts Institute of Technology, with a good portion of its 100,000-plus residents enrolled at one or the other, Cambridge, Massachusetts, has a well-deserved reputation as the country's academic epicenter. The life of the mind comes with plenty of perks: a collection of arty cinemas, a thriving music scene, scads of independent bookshops, and a smorgasbord of international restaurants. Though Harvard Square is the tourist center, other neighborhoods offer visitors respites from both its escalating gentrification and its Ivy League self-regard. The gritty Central Square is home to great clubs and cheap, sophisticated ethnic restaurants, and Inman Square is young and adventurous. — BY POOJA BHATIA

FRIDAY

1 *Pizza cum Laude* 7 p.m.

Locals usually delight in dissing all things Yale, but for some reason they defer to New Haven when it comes to pizza. There's really no need. The patrons lining up for seats at **Emma's** (40 Hampshire Street; 617-864-8534; emmaspizza.com; $) say it slings the best pies in the Northeast, with crackling, wafer-thin crusts; about 30 interesting but not-too-outré toppings; and the ideal crust-sauce-cheese ratio. Design your own pie; one winning combination is goat cheese, basil, thyme-roasted mushrooms, and roasted tomatoes. For some heat, try rosemary sauce, hot cherry peppers, and Italian sweet sausage. Don't overdo it. Your next stop is dessert.

2 *Creativity on Ice* 9 p.m.

Cantabrigians take their ice cream seriously. Many profess loyalty to the molto-rich versions at **Toscanini's** (899 Main Street; 617-491-5877; tosci.com), including salted saffron or double chocolate stout. Others flock to **Christina's** (1255 Cambridge Street; 617-492-7021; christinasicecream.com), where adzuki bean and ginger molasses are among the dozens of flavors and a scoop of khulfi accurately translates the cardamom-rich Indian treat. Purists, be content: both places still have good old vanilla, chocolate, and strawberry, too.

3 *Time to Improvise* 10 p.m.

Catch the second set at the dark, intimate **Regattabar** at the Charles Hotel (1 Bennett Street; 617-661-5000; regattabarjazz.com), which has long been the leading jazz spot in town—and some who have said that weren't talking only about Cambridge, but about Boston as well. Fans of jazz, blues, soul, R&B, and world music also venture across the Charles River to Allston to catch their favorites at **Scullers Jazz Club** (400 Soldiers Road; 617-562-4111; scullersjazz.com) in the Doubletree Hotel. Both spots book nationally known musicians.

SATURDAY

4 *Breakfast From the East* 8:30 a.m.

The atmosphere is eastern Mediterranean all day at **Sofra Bakery and Cafe** (1 Belmont Street; 617-661-3161; sofrabakery.com; $). At lunchtime, that means a mezze bar and shawarmas. For breakfast, it might mean haloumi cheese with your bacon and eggs. Anytime, this is a great place for Turkish coffee and something sweet, like a sesame caramel sticky bun or a pumpkin turnover. Sofra is tiny, so arrive early to get a table.

5 *Getting Beyond Euclid* 10 a.m.

At M.I.T., Cambridge's "other" university, numbers are king. They denote classes ("I've got 6012" means you're headed to microelectronic devices

OPPOSITE An autumn regatta on the Charles River.

RIGHT A view of the Frank Gehry-designed Stata Center.

and circuits) and even majors (8, for instance, is physics), and most buildings on the largely undistinguished campus are known by them. But some recent additions have not only names but also architectural verve. The undergrads living in **Simmons Hall** (229-243 Vassar Street), designed by Steven Holl, say it reminds them of a waffle or sponge, thanks to the 5,500 cut-out windows that give it a porous look. Just down the road is Frank Gehry's fanciful **Stata Center** (32 Vassar Street). Orange brick portions pay humorous homage to M.I.T.'s boxy engineering labs, but they're cut up by aluminum waves, lacking right angles, that resemble the pleats of a skirt or a chef's toque.

6 *Food for Curiosity* Noon

You're at M.I.T., so don't miss the **MIT Museum** (265 Massachusetts Avenue; 617-253-5927; web.mit.edu/museum), where inviting ongoing and rotating exhibits will absorb anyone who likes to ask "Why?" or "How does it work?" Visit with a sociable robot; step into the nucleus of a cell to watch DNA do its job; and tilt your head to see the shimmering changeability of some of the museum's hundreds of holograms. The history of invention gets its due, as well; Polaroid cameras are on view, and one exhibit showed the importance of the slide rule in the development of the modern world.

7 *The World in a Square* 3 p.m.

Give Harvard equal time with a walk in Harvard Yard, and then turn your attention to Harvard Square. Chain restaurants call it home these days, but so do quirky street performers, plotting chess masters, texting teenagers, and independent bookstores. Book lovers should plan to spend some serious time at the **Harvard Book Store** (1256 Massachusetts Avenue; 617-661-1515; harvard.com), which has been around since 1912 and has an outstanding selection of books to suit every interest, as well as a solid used-book section. Even older is the **Harvard Coop**, pronounced like the coop in "chicken coop" (1400 Massachusetts Avenue; 617-499-2000; thecoop.com), a cooperative bookstore founded in 1882. The **Grolier Poetry Book Shop** (6 Plympton Street; 617-547-4648; grolierpoetrybookshop.org) is a destination for poets and scholars from around the world. If you're looking for Camus or Cervantes in the original language, head to **Schoenhof's Foreign Books** (76A Mount Auburn Street; 617-547-8855; schoenhofs.com).

8 *The View at Dinner* 8 p.m.

The décor alone is reason enough to visit the **Soiree Room** at **UpStairs on the Square** (91 Winthrop Street; 617-864-1933; upstairsonthesquare.com; $$$). Begin your gawking at the leopard-print carpet and work your way up along the walls, painted à la Klimt, to the gilded mirror ceiling. Somehow it all adds up to whimsical charm. The food, such as cumin-crusted lamb or scallop risotto, can be as luxe as the furnishings, but even the humblest dishes are well tended.

9 *Drama and Then Some* 9:30 p.m.

Part playhouse, part nightclub, **Oberon** (2 Arrow Street; 617-496-8004; cluboberon.com) is the wilder, crazier affiliate of A.R.T., the **American Repertory Theater** at Harvard. The show is likely to be daring and dazzling, like the audience-pleasing *The Donkey Show*, an interactive disco version of *A Midsummer Night's*

ABOVE Harvard Square, Cambridge's historic center.

OPPOSITE *The Donkey Show* at the A.R.T. theater.

Dream. On the other hand, you could make an earlier evening of it and see a play at A.R.T. itself (64 Brattle Street; 617-547-8300; americanrepertorytheater.org).

SUNDAY

10 *Riverside* 11 a.m.

Six days a week, cars choke Memorial Drive on the banks of the Charles River. On Sundays from the end of April to mid-November the road closes to cars and fills up with runners, walkers, in-line skaters, and cyclists, all eager to burn off weekend excesses. The route, punctuated by boathouses, parks, and geese, is lovely in any season, especially when the sun shines and the river sparkles under an azure sky. To get out on the river, rent a kayak at **Charles River Canoe & Kayak** (500 Broad Canal Way, Kendall Square; 617-965-5110; paddleboston.com). Paddle out for some of the best views to be had of both Cambridge and Boston.

THE BASICS

Cambridge is a 15-minute cab ride from Logan International Airport in Boston. Parking is a nightmare. Plan on plenty of walking.

Hotel Veritas
1 Remington Street
617-520-5000
thehotelveritas.com
$$$
New but intentionally old-looking 31-room hotel just east of Harvard Square. Free passes to a nearby gym.

Charles Hotel
One Bennett Street
617-864-1200
charleshotel.com
$$$
Close to Harvard's quads and the Kennedy School of Government.

Hotel Marlowe
25 Edwin H. Land Boulevard
617-868-8000
hotelmarlowe.com
$$-$$$$
A Kimpton boutique hotel in East Cambridge.

Harvard Square
American Repertory Theater
BRATTLE ST.
Harvard Coop
HARVARD YARD
CAMBRIDGE ST.
BROADWAY
Regattabar/ Charles Hotel
3
MASSACHUSETTS AVE.
BENNETT ST.
Schoenhof's Foreign Books
7 Harvard Book Store
Charles River
MEMORIAL DR.
8
WINTHROP ST.
Grolier Poetry Book Shop
HARVARD ST.
Soiree Room/ UpStairs on the Square
MOUNT AUBURN ST.
Hotel Veritas
1/8 mile
1/4 kilometer
9
Oberon
Somerville
MASSACHUSETTS
Cambridge
Fresh Pond
Cambridge
BEACON ST.
LOGAN INT'L AIRPORT
2 mile
4 kilometers
Boston
Boston Harbor
BELMONT ST.
4
Sofra Bakery and Cafe
Christina's
CAMBRIDGE ST.
Area of detail
MIT Museum
6
Hotel Marlowe
1 Emma's
Toscanini's 2
Scullers Jazz Club
SOLDIERS RD.
VASSAR ST.
Stata Center
Simmons Hall 5
10
Charles River Canoe & Kayak
Boston
1/2 mile
1 kilometer

Bretton Woods

On winter weekends, the roofs of cars arriving at the Omni Mount Washington Hotel, the grand Edwardian inn in Bretton Woods, New Hampshire, are piled high with downhill and Nordic skis, snowshoes, ice skates, swimming pool flotation devices, and even rock-climbing gear. Bretton Woods is a year-round resort, and it holds global fame as the site of the 1944 conference that set the course of the postwar global economy. It is best known now for its skiing, although its variety of experiences makes it a winter weekend spot even for non-skiers. Ideally positioned at the foot of Mount Washington, the highest mountain in the northeastern United States, shielded from wind and blessed with sun and snow, it has impeccable grooming, good snow, and just lots and lots of comfortable cruising trails. In recent years, it has added new downhill terrain, new trails in a Nordic ski area that was already expansive, and new extras like zip lines, a night club, and a capacious spa.

— BY BILL PENNINGTON

FRIDAY

1 *Check-In Grandeur* Noon

The **Mount Washington Hotel** (Route 302; 603-278-1000; mountwashingtonresort.com) was, and may still be, the largest wooden structure in New England, a palace built for the rich of New York, Boston, and Philadelphia. Constructed on 10,000 acres by the New York rail and coal magnate Joseph Stickney and opened in 1902, the hotel has a Spanish Renaissance Revival exterior and French Renaissance-style interior that were created by 250 Italian craftsmen lured from Boston. A wraparound veranda extends for a quarter of a mile. Check in early if possible and assess your surroundings. The Great Hall, which includes the lobby, has 23-foot ceilings, Tiffany stained glass, and an oversize fieldstone hearth. Visit the concierge desk to plan your weekend from the hotel's long list of winter activities.

2 *Wintry Zip* 1 p.m.

Get your overview of the resort's acreage from the treetops in a **canopy tour** (603-278-4947; brettonwoods.com/activities/canopy_tour) that includes a series of zip lines and platforms high in the hemlocks. Your guide will point out the wildlife below you. More than you were bargaining for? Instead, orient yourself to the snow with a few fast slides down the resort's tubing hill.

3 *The Keynesian Past* 3 p.m.

If you don't ski and yet have heard of Bretton Woods, you probably stayed alert in high school history class or pay attention now to economic debates. In the summer of 1944, with the Allies winning World War II, about 1,000 delegates from 44 nations convened here to lay plans for reviving a wrecked global economy. Big as the hotel is, it was so crowded that some guests had to sleep in closets. The star of the conference was John Maynard Keynes — the most renowned economist of the 20th century and Britain's chief representative. (He stayed in Room 129 with his wife, Lydia Lopokova, a former Russian ballerina.) The Bretton Woods agreement, signed at a rock maple table that is still in the Gold Room, established the World Bank and the International Monetary Fund and made the American dollar the world's predominant currency. The system endured until the 1970s, when President Richard M. Nixon took the dollar off the gold standard and floating exchange rates soon prevailed. By that time, the world's other economies had had time to recover and grow. Now daily **hotel history tours** at 10 a.m. and 3 p.m. (603-278-3305; brettonwoods.com/activities/event/detail/123) explain this pivotal event.

OPPOSITE AND BELOW Two sides of Bretton Woods. Now visitors come for snow sports. In 1944, world leaders arrived to shape the post-World War II global economy. A plaque marks the room where the final articles were signed.

4 *Take the Tunnel* 7 p.m.

When Omni Resorts took over Bretton Woods in 2009, it took on a multimillion-dollar project to both restore and modernize the hotel. Among the results, along with tougher ski runs in addition to the tried-and-true, is farm-to-table dining at **Stickney's** (800-258-0330; $$$), a pub-style steakhouse with a great view of Mount Washington by day and fireside dining at night. Across from the restaurant, in the same part of the hotel, the **Cave**, a 21st-century version of an underground Prohibition-era speakeasy, maintains its hideaway ambience with a narrow, tunnel-like entranceway and a dark, distressed wood interior. It also has late-night entertainment.

ABOVE The grand Omni Mount Washington Hotel.

BELOW The hotel spa, one of many creature comforts.

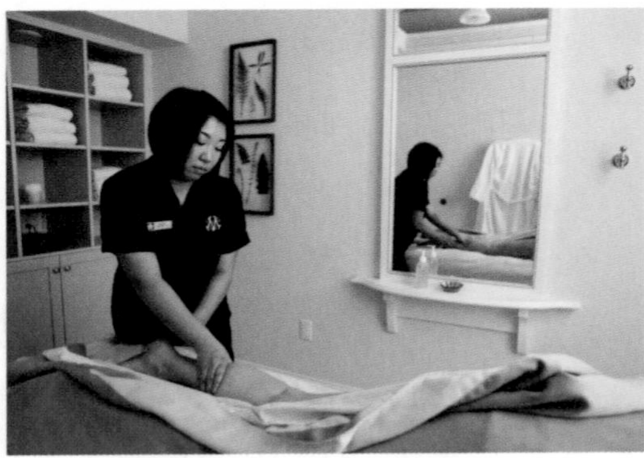

SATURDAY

5 *Glides and Glades* 9 a.m.

The **Bretton Woods ski area** (brettonwoods.com) has 464 acres of downhill ski terrain: 62 trails, 35 glades, and three terrain parks. Arrive at the base, and within minutes, thanks to high-speed lifts, you'll be flying down the renowned Bretton Woods groomers. They're not death-defying runs, but they have an old New England feel, with dips and hollows that induce an entertaining rhythm of linked turns. This is family-friendly skiing, and the trail system makes sure there are beginner routes from every lift and that every trail filters to the same base lodge so that families can congregate in the same place. Venture over to the West Mountain trails, opened in the late 1990s, to the long Starr King trail, which has several good drops and pitches that demand attention. Small detours next to Starr King cut through the woods. On the east end of the area, at Rosebrook Canyon Glades, enjoy a Bretton Woods tradition—weaving through stands of birch and pine trees. Glades on Mount Stickney, a rounded hilltop, have a slightly remote, isolated ambience and offer unparalleled views of the white hotel, with its bright red roof, on the valley floor.

6 *Steamy Interlude* 4 p.m.

Back at the hotel, a heated walkway leads to the heated outdoor pool, where you can alternate dipping into the warm water and out into the steam rising over the pool in the chilly air. Come inside to the 25,000-square-foot spa, which has treatment rooms with views of the mountains, as well as a lengthy menu of massages, facials, and grooming services.

7 *Dinner at the Arms* 7 p.m.

A short walk from the main hotel, there's fine dining at the **Bretton Arms Dining Room** (173 Mount Washington Road, Omni Bretton Arms Inn; 603-278-0330; $$$) in the Bretton Arms Inn, a smaller hotel that was once used as lodging for the hotel staff but is now an alternative to the grand hotel. The food is traditional but carefully prepared, and there's a wine bar for some extra down time.

ABOVE Live music at the Mount Washington Hotel.

BELOW The resort's pools include this one indoors and another that offers warm swimming in the open air.

SUNDAY

8 *Dogs Don't Go Straight* 10 a.m.

Both sleighing and dog sled tours are available at Bretton Woods, but of the two, being led through a winter landscape by a team of dogs is far more engaging, more like a sport. Though seated and comfortable, you watch how the lead dogs set not only the pace but also the chosen path, which is far from straight. The dogs get distracted by the things they see — deer, birds, was that a moose? — and

the sled veers hither and thither. It's part of the adventure. The solidarity, the cold, and the mission at hand—go somewhere but get back to where you started, too—delivers its own sense of purpose. And heading back to the hotel, with the dogs in an easy canter, yields its own kind of restful calm.

9 *Skim the Woods* 11 a.m.

With nearly 70 miles of trails threading through the snowy stillness of the White Mountain National Forest, Bretton Woods has one of the largest cross-country trail systems in the East, often the scene of competitions. Take advantage of it with a few hours of Nordic skiing (maps, skis, and passes at the Nordic ski center, 603-278-3322; brettonwoods.com). You can glide along easy trails like Perimeter, a flat pathlike trail that encircles a golf course. Or you can find challenges like the moderately difficult Bridle Path, which heads deep into a forest and follows the Ammonossuc River to a cascade called Middle Falls.

ABOVE AND OPPOSITE Families tackle the Bretton Woods slopes. Although most activities are at the Omni resort, skiers can also stay elsewhere and use day passes.

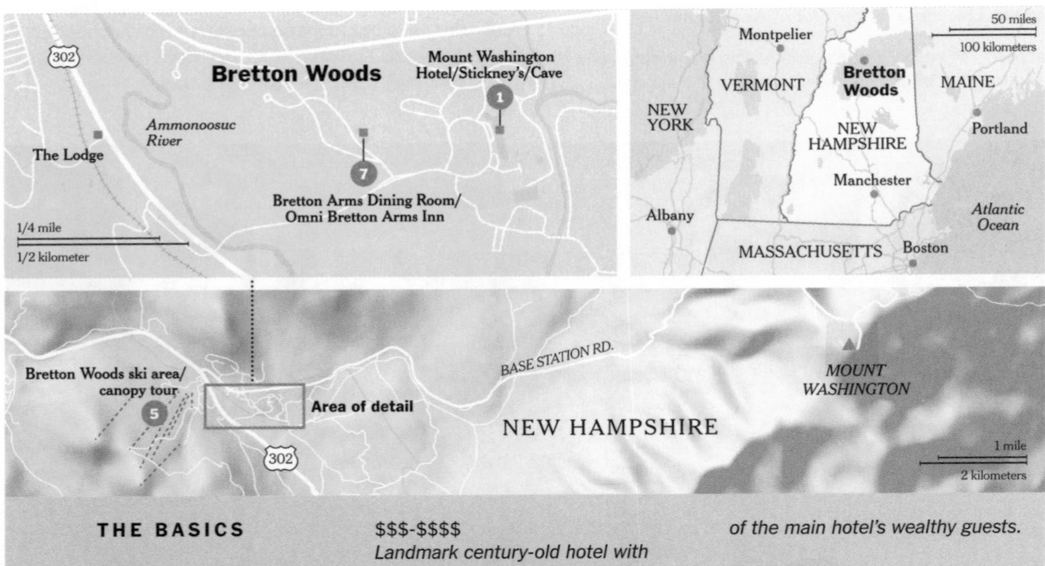

THE BASICS

Bretton Woods is on Route 302, about 160 miles from Boston. The nearest major airport is 100 miles away in Manchester, New Hampshire.

Omni Mount Washington Hotel
310 Mount Washington Hotel Road
603-278-1000
mountwashingtonresort.com
$$$-$$$$
Landmark century-old hotel with 200 rooms and suites; the center of everything at Bretton Woods.

Bretton Arms Inn
173 Mount Washington Road
603-278-3000
mountwashingtonresort.com
$$$$
Small, 34-room inn that once provided lodging for servants of the main hotel's wealthy guests.

The Lodge
2653 Route 302 East
603-278-4000
brettonwoods.com/lodging/the_lodge/overview
$$
Motel with balconies overlooking the mountains and the main hotel.

Portland

Portland is known for three L's: lobster, lighthouses, and L.L. Bean (O.K., make that four L's). Here's another: local. In recent years, this city on the coast of Maine has welcomed a wave of locavore restaurants, urban farms, and galleries that feature local artists. Abandoned brick warehouses are being repurposed as eco-friendly boutiques. In the main square, a 19th-century building has been refashioned into a farmers' market. And everywhere you look, this once-sleepy industrial town is showing signs of rejuvenation —usually by keeping things local. —BY LIONEL BEEHNER

FRIDAY

1 *West Side Story* 2 p.m.

To see bohemian Portland, stroll down Congress Street, where at least a dozen galleries, studios, and cafes have opened in recent years. David Marshall, a beret-wearing painter who moonlights as a city councilman, is among the artists who exhibit at **Constellation Gallery** (511 Congress Street; 207-409-6617; constellationart.com). An artsy crowd can be found at **Local Sprouts** (649 Congress Street; 207-899-3529; localsproutscooperative.com), an earthy, community-supported cafe as crunchy as it sounds. Nearby is the **Portland Museum of Art** (7 Congress Street; 207-775-6148; portlandmuseum.org), which has a celebrated collection including many works by Winslow Homer.

2 *Made in Maine* 7 p.m.

Portland's locavore scene has blossomed in recent years, as evidenced by attention to it on the Food Network. Among the most talked about restaurants is **Farmer's Table** (205 Commercial Street; 207-347-7479; farmerstablemaine.com; $$), which offers nice terrace views of the harbor. The owner and chef, Jeff Landry, gets his vegetables from area gardens and serves dishes like beef short ribs from grass-fed cows reared on a nearby farm. Or try **Caiola's** (58 Pine Street; 207-772-1110; caiolas.com; $$), a locals' favorite serving Mediterranean fare.

3 *Indie Playground* 9 p.m.

Live music anchors Portland's night life. The **State Theatre** (609 Congress Street; 207-956-6000; statetheatreportland.com), a Depression-era movie house with a Moorish-style interior, closed in 2006 and reopened as a concert hall in 2010, drawing touring bands. Music buffs also make their way to the **Port City Music Hall** (504 Congress Street; 207-899-4990; portcitymusichall.com), a glitzy club by Portland standards that even lifts a velvet rope for its V.I.P.'s. A younger, more relaxed crowd flocks to **Space Gallery** (538 Congress Street; 207-828-5600; space538.org), a scruffy art space by day that has films and performances at night.

SATURDAY

4 *Suburban Bagels* 8:30 a.m.

Across a drawbridge lies South Portland, a city of bungalows with a quiet beach. But the sweetest reason to visit is the **Scratch Baking Co.** (416 Preble Street, South Portland; 207-799-0668; scratchbakingco.com; $), a bakery on Willard Square that sells oven-fresh muffins, scones, and sourdough bagels. Get there before 9 a.m., as the bagels run out fast. Then snag a spot on Willard Beach, a patch of rocky sand with views of the coast.

5 *Free Island* 10 a.m.

The free spirit of **Peaks Island**, part of the archipelago that surrounds Portland, is evident the

OPPOSITE The Munjoy Hill neighborhood as seen from the ferry ride to Peaks Island.

BELOW Scratch Baking Co. in South Portland sells oven-fresh breads, muffins, and pizzas.

moment you step off the ferry. If no one is manning **Brad and Wyatt's** (115 Island Avenue; 207-766-5631), a bike rental place housed in a dusty shack, drop some money into the honor-system box. Then cruise the rocky coastline for the stuff of Maine legend: gorgeous lighthouses, osprey swooping off the surf. The island is pleasantly free of McMansions and private beaches. No wonder the natives tried (unsuccessfully) to secede from Portland a few years back.

6 *Mini-Mart* Noon

A collective moan could be heard when the Public Market, a hangar-size hall run by Maine farmers and fishermen, shuttered in 2006. Luckily, some of the vendors who had thrived there pooled their resources and opened a scaled-back version on Monument Square. Occupying a building from the mid-1800s, the **Public Market House** (28 Monument Square; 207-228-2056; publicmarkethouse.com) is stocked with bread, cheeses, local produce, and microbrewery beer. Tables sell only Maine products, and shops include specialty food purveyors like **Kamasouptra** (207-415-6692; kamasouptra.com), which makes hearty soups like grilled cheese and tomato.

7 *Vintage Maine* 2 p.m.

Search out the most adventurous shops in the maze of stores lining the Old Port, the historic warehouse district. **Madhouse Studio** (569 Congress Street; 207-518-9228; madgirlcustom.com) is a quirky spot where Meredith Alex recycles skateboards and Barbie dolls into jewelry and funky, eco-friendly dresses; the restroom doubles as a space for monthly art installations. **Ferdinand** (243 Congress Street; 207-761-2151) carries handmade goods, vintage fashions, novelty cards, and jewelry.When the Old Port palls, drive to Munjoy Hill, a traditional working-class Irish district that now looks more like Notting Hill, with a grassy promenade that overlooks the water. Among its sophisticated establishments are **Rosemont Market & Bakery** (88 Congress Street; 207-773-7888; rosemontmarket.com), which sells fresh breads and sandwiches, and **Angela Adams** (273 Congress Street; 207-774-3523; angelaadams.com), a design store that sells perky home furnishings.

8 *Divine Diving* 8 p.m.

Anchovy truffle butter? The foodie scene is old news here. A later development in Portland's dining scene is reclaimed architecture. A rundown gas station was converted into **El Rayo Taqueria** (101 York Street; 207-780-8226; elrayotaqueria.com), a Mexican cafe with yellow picnic tables. And the old Portland Savings Bank became **Sonny's** (83 Exchange Street; 207-772-7774; sonnysportland.com; $$), a Latin-themed restaurant. A fine example of this culinary invasion is **Grace** (15 Chestnut Street; 207-828-4422; restaurantgrace.com), a New American restaurant in an 1850s Gothic Revival-style church. There is something divine about drinking next to the nave, or gorging on goat cheese gnocchi surrounded by stained-glass windows.

9 *Bowl for Kicks* 10 p.m.

The bars along Wharf Street can get pretty fratty. For a more memorable evening, roll across town to **Bayside Bowl** (58 Alder Street; 207-791-2695; baysidebowl.com), a 12-lane bowling alley. Even if bowling isn't your thing, you can knock back a few pints of Shipyard ale at the sleek bar, which draws a mostly young crowd with tattoos and tie-dyed shirts. Or skip the bowling entirely and go to **Novare Res** (4 Canal Plaza; 207-761-2437; novareresbiercafe.com), a festive beer garden with long beechwood tables and more than 300 beers that feels more Munich than Maine.

SUNDAY

10 *The Mail Run* 10 a.m.

Schooner tours and lobster boat rides can be touristy, not to mention pricey. A better way to cruise around scenic Casco Bay is the mail ferry—a courier fleet that hops around five of the islands. The ferry is run by **Casco Bay Lines** (56 Commercial Street; 207-774-7871; cascobaylines.com) and departs twice a

day, seven days a week, from the main ferry terminal. The loop, which costs less than $20, takes three hours, so pack a lunch.

11 *Fermented Fun* 2 p.m.

Mead, or fermented honey, may have gone out of fashion in, oh, the 16th century, but the **Maine Mead Works** (51 Washington Avenue; 207-773-6323; mainemeadworks.com) is bringing it back. This honey winery in a gritty warehouse on the edge of town resembles a mad chemist's garage with tanks and tubes everywhere. A few blocks away but in a similar spirit is the **Urban Farm Fermentory** (200 Anderson Street; 207-653-7406; urbanfarmfermentory.com), a producer of hard cider, kombucha, mead, and other fermented comestibles that offers seminars on topics like pickling and eco-friendly mulching. It's another example of how Portland can't seem to get enough of recycling.

OPPOSITE The Portland Head Lighthouse, south of the city in Cape Elizabeth, is postcard Maine.

ABOVE A fishing boat in the Portland harbor. Maine seafood and local produce appear on city restaurant menus.

THE BASICS

Portland is two hours by car from Boston or five from New York. If you're not driving your own car, fly in and rent one at the airport.

Portland Harbor Hotel
468 Fore Street
207-775-9090
portlandharborhotel.com
$$
Recently renovated; 101 rooms include some with fireplaces.

The Danforth
163 Danforth Street
207-879-8755
danforthmaine.com
$$$
Nine-room inn dating back to the early 1800s.

Portland Regency Hotel and Spa
20 Milk Street
207-774-4200
theregency.com
$$
In the Old Port; built as an armory in 1895.

Midcoast Maine

Wedged between the indie urbanity of Portland and the great outdoors of Acadia National Park, Maine's midcoast region has long enthralled summertime travelers with its quaint towns and pastoral, pine-lined roads. The tranquil harbors and craggy beaches along U.S. Route 1 offer settings as quintessentially Maine as can be. (Lobster roll with a lighthouse view, anyone?) But lately, as Portland's arty influence creeps northward, the midcoast is flush with chic new inns; art galleries; and a modern, hyper-local food scene. For visitors, that means the best of both Maines: a cool, innovative spirit that lures city dwellers from Portland and beyond, blended with the laid-back Down East spirit that has long been a point of local pride.

— BY BRENDAN SPIEGEL

FRIDAY

1 *Modern-Day Mills* 3 p.m.

Brunswick, a former mill town that serves as the gateway to the midcoast, these days produces less lumber and textiles than artwork and craft beer. The old Fort Andross Mill, a large brick structure where textiles were once produced, is now occupied by art studios; a branch of the New York City and Portland contemporary gallery **Coleman Burke** (14 Maine Street, Brunswick; 207-725-3761; colemanburke.com); and **Frontier Café + Cinema + Gallery** (14 Maine Street, Brunswick; 207-725-5222; explorefrontier.com). Stop at Frontier's bar for a cappuccino made with organic wood-roasted beans from Matt's Coffee or a Farmhouse Pale Ale from Oxbow Brewing—both producers are local—and head into the small theater for a documentary screening or a set from a local songwriter. Then walk across the truss bridge to **Sea Dog Brewing Company** (1 Bowdoin Mill Island, Topsham; 207-725-0162; seadogbrewing.com), a former pulp mill where wheat ales accented by blueberries and apricots pair nicely with a view over the Androscoggin River.

2 *Scenic Detours* 5 p.m.

As Route 1 winds eastward, the region's major towns lie close together, but opportunities for rewarding detours are endless. Just beyond Brunswick, the area commonly called **Harpswell Peninsula**, made up of an oblong peninsula, islands, and connecting bridges, provides plenty of options for waterfront wandering. Farther east is **Reid State Park** (375 Seguinland Road, Georgetown; 207-371-2303), a pine-filled preserve with a picnic area that has views of a rocky shore and one of the area's few stretches of sand beach. Towering green pines overlook a sea of swimmers and sunset surfers.

3 *Backyard-to-Table* 7 p.m.

A good spot for farm-to-table food dining on the midcoast is **Primo** (2 South Main Street, Rockland; 207-596-0770; primorestaurant.com; $$$$), set in a century-old house on a hill just south of downtown Rockland. Walk around the restaurant's backyard organic gardens, greenhouses, chicken coops, and pig pens; then taste the fruits of all that husbandry in dishes like honey wine-braised moulard duck over roasted beets, farro, baby leeks, hazelnut, and rhubarb chutney. Choose the formal setting downstairs or head upstairs for a more modern, barnyard-chic ambience. Or pull up to the bar for house-made wild boar salami and chickpea-fried fiddleheads.

4 *Produce at the Pub* 9:30 p.m.

Just north of Rockland in the tiny harbor community of Rockport, a wood-walled former general

OPPOSITE A walk on the breakwater in Rockland, one of the harbor towns that make this section of coast a stretch of quintessential Maine.

BELOW Rockland's revitalized downtown. Galleries among the shops show and sell the work of Maine artists.

store has been remade into an artisanal pub called **Shepherd's Pie** (18 Central Street, Rockport; 207-236-8500; shepherdspierockport.com). Try one of its fruit cocktails infused with herbs and a small plate or two, perhaps fried clam tacos and pickled baby carrots.

SATURDAY

5 *Walk on Water* 10 a.m.

There is no shortage of ways to get out on the water around here, but one of the most spectacular is the 4,346-foot walk along the breakwater jutting into **Rockland Harbor** (end of Samoset Road, Rockland; rocklandharborlights.org). The narrow granite structure took 18 years to build in the late 19th century, and it stretches nearly a mile out into the harbor. In morning light the red brick lighthouse and accompanying wood-frame keeper's house set at the breakwater's end form a dramatic sight as they seem to float in the middle of the harbor.

6 *Art Crawl* 11 a.m.

The hub of the midcoast's lively art scene is Rockland's revitalized Main Street. The **Farnsworth Art Museum** (16 Museum Street, Rockland; 207-596-6457 ext. 130; farnsworthmuseum.org) is home to one of the nation's largest collections of works by Andrew, Jamie, and N.C. Wyeth. **Asymmetrick Arts** (405 Main Street, Rockland; 207-594-2020; asymmetrickarts.com) and **Carver**

ABOVE The Sea Dog Brewing Company in Topsham.

BELOW The blue sweep of Camden Harbor.

Hill Gallery (338 Main Street, Rockland; 207-594-7745; carverhillgallery.com) focus on emerging Maine artists. In Rockport, a former horse stable contains the **Center for Maine Contemporary Art** (162 Russell Avenue, Rockport; 207-236-2875; cmcanow.org).

7 *Boat Town* 1 p.m.

Camden Harbor is one of Maine's pre-eminent sailing spots. Visitors can explore it from the deck of a windjammer fishing yacht like the old schooner ***Surprise*** (Public Landing, Camden; 207-236-4687; camdenmainesailing.com). Or get even closer with a sea kayak tour from **Maine Sport Outfitters** (24 Main Street, Camden; 207-230-1284; mainesport.com). Guides teach kayaking basics before taking paddlers across the harbor and circling tree-lined Curtis Island. Kayakers may spot harbor seals and porpoises; and if they dare, they can pop in for a dip in the sub-60-degree water.

8 *Camden Thai* 7 p.m.

Camden, which looks like quintessential Maine, is not the first place you might expect to find superior Thai cuisine. Yet here it is, at **Long Grain** (31 Elm Street, Camden; 207-236-9001; $$), a 30-seat restaurant with simple décor and food made with ingredients sourced from the Maine coast but reflecting flavors of Bangkok. Try the chewy, slightly charred broad noodles, pad kee mao, which are made in-house, or the Thai beef salad. The place is justly popular; don't try coming without a reservation.

9 *Bonfire Bocce* 10 p.m.

At the working wharf a few miles north in Belfast, you'll find **Three Tides** (40 Marshall Wharf, Belfast; 207-338-1707; 3tides.com), perhaps the

ABOVE The Atlantic Climbing School shepherds rock climbers in Camden Hills State Park. The reward at the top of the cliffs is wide-angle views of Penobscot Bay, Megunticook Lake, and the forested hills.

BELOW An upstairs room at Primo, one of the best local restaurants for farm-to-table dining.

closest thing midcoast Maine has to a hipster bar scene. The nautical-themed bar (a pile of shucked oyster shells serves as décor) includes a bocce court and a bay-view bonfire pit, and the drinks include two dozen house-brewed beers.

SUNDAY

10 *Mountain Bound* 8 a.m.

Camden may be known for sailing, but for landlubber adventure-seekers it's also fast emerging as a rock climbing destination. With fewer people on the rocks than up north in Acadia, it's an excellent place to learn the basics. **Atlantic Climbing School** (207-288-2521; acadiaclimbing.com) runs half-day courses for beginners in **Camden Hills State Park,** where the climb is rewarded with views of Penobscot Bay and Megunticook Lake. The school serves experienced climbers, too.

11 *Greens to Go* 12:30 p.m.

The vegetarian restaurant **Chase's Daily** (96 Main Street, Belfast; 207-338-0555; $$) not only sources most of the menu from a family farm in Freedom, 20 miles inland, but also devotes space to an art gallery and a farmers' market. Order a pizza baked in a bread oven and topped with four local cheeses and fresh marjoram, and then grab some beet greens or Maine products like Swan's raw, unfiltered wildflower honey to take home.

OPPOSITE The old schooner *Surprise*, a windjammer fishing yacht, sails out of Camden Harbor.

THE BASICS

Drive up U.S. 1, and be ready to make frequent stops.

Camden Harbour Inn
83 Bayview Street, Camden
207-236-4200
camdenharbourinn.com
$$
A design-conscious boutique hotel in a formerly dilapidated Victorian building dating to 1874. Sweeping bay views.

Belfast Bay Inn
72 Main Street, Belfast
207-338-5600
belfastbayinn.com
$$
In two Main Street row houses, with an airy garden courtyard.

Hawthorn Inn
9 High Street, Camden
207-236-8842
camdenhawthorn.com
$$
Ten rooms, including suites with garden views.

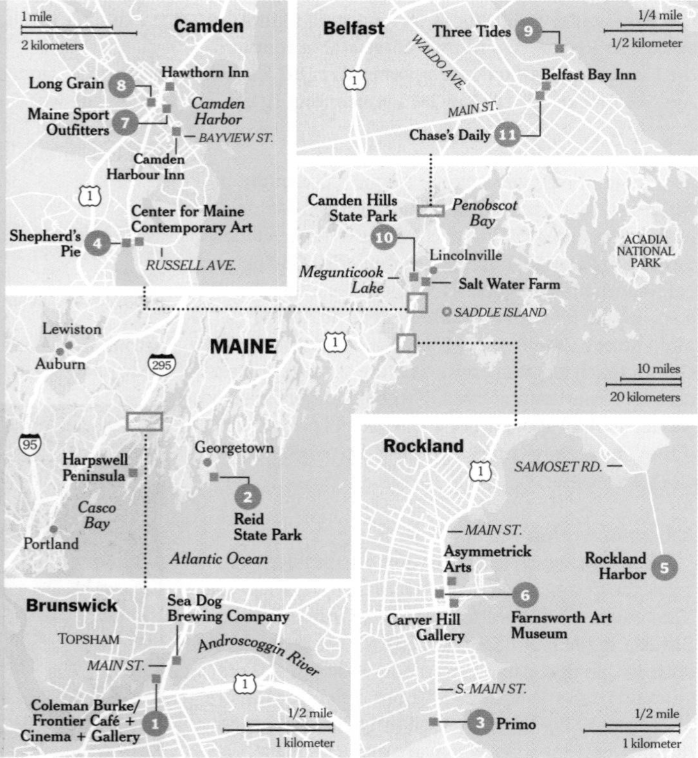

SURPRISE

BLACK DOG
SHOP
MARGARET TODD
BOAT TICKETS
Jack's Jewelry
Featuring
Tourmaline
PATRICK'S
MEET ME
SINCE 1974
COOL STUFF

Bar Harbor

There are summer resorts that get busier and more chic over the years. And then there are the ones, like Bar Harbor, Maine, that feel deliciously frozen in time. Bar Harbor is the largest town on Mount Desert Island, and nearby Acadia National Park encompasses some 50 square miles. The rest of Mount Desert belongs to residents and a tony array of summer tenants: Brooke Astor summered here, as did myriad Rockefellers; and once upon a time, the town of Northeast Harbor had so many well-to-do Philadelphia families that it was dubbed "Philadelphia on the rocks." They all came lured by the striking setting of mountains, woodlands, lakes, and ocean waves crashing against granite cliffs. Then and now, Mount Desert has served as a glorious nature camp for biking, hiking, and boating. At day's end, a visitor can cozy up with a blueberry beer and lobster. Evening strollers can watch sailboats drop anchor and the mist slip down over the hundreds of islands that dot the water. —BY GERALDINE FABRIKANT

FRIDAY

1 *Toast the Sunset* 6 p.m.

Take the two-hour cruise on the ***Margaret Todd***, a four-masted windjammer that sails through Frenchman Bay and the Porcupine Islands (207-288-4585; downeastwindjammer.com). You'll pass Ironbound Island, still owned by descendants of the painter Dwight Blaney, who with his contemporary John Singer Sargent and others painted the remarkable vistas of the bay and Acadia. A guitarist may serenade you, but if you want to toast the sunset, bring your own wine.

2 *Seafood Extravaganza* 8:30 p.m.

It may be called the **Reading Room** (7 Newport Drive; 207-288-3351; barharborinn.com/dining.html; $$), but dining in a rotunda that overlooks the harbor feels more like eating on a ship than in a library. On weekends, a pianist usually plays old favorites. Lobster lovers can opt for the lobster pie, but the broiled Maine haddock with butter crumb crust is also a treat. For a more exotic setting, dine at the red-walled **Havana** (318 Main Street; 207-288-2822; havanamaine.com; $$), which was the Obamas' choice when they visited one year. The paella with lobster, mussels, clams, and chorizo is worth the stop.

3 *Blueberry Beer* 10 p.m.

Hang with the locals at **Geddy's** (19 Main Street; 207-288-5077; geddys.com), a fun, funky pub filled with old photographs and local signage. Blueberries thrive in the local terrain, and aficionados can try the Sea Dog blueberry draft beer or a blueberry margarita.

SATURDAY

4 *Book Lover's Breakfast* 8:30 a.m.

By 8 o'clock the line is already forming at the cheerful **Cafe This Way** (14 ½ Mount Desert Street; 207-288-4483; cafethisway.com; $) on a tiny back street off the town square. Inside, tables sit near bookshelves filled with classics and poetry. Mainers don't stint on breakfast, nor should you; fill up on French toast with real maple syrup or a McThisWay

OPPOSITE Main Street in Bar Harbor, a resort town on Mount Desert Island with a history as a summer place dating back to the 19th century.

BELOW The four-masted windjammer *Margaret Todd* at rest in Bar Harbor's morning fog.

sandwich of fried eggs, tomatoes, Cheddar cheese, and bacon. Those who want some oomph can try a mimosa or a bloody mary.

5 *Bike Acadia* 10 a.m.

There are numerous entrances to Acadia National Park (207-288-3338; nps.gov/acad). Take a drive around the 27-mile Park Loop Road and head to the top of **Cadillac Mountain**, the highest point on the Eastern Seaboard. It was named after the French explorer who called himself Sieur de la Mothe Cadillac. He went on to help found Detroit, where the car was named after him. You cannot rent bikes or canoes within the park, but in Bar Harbor, **Acadia Bike** (48 Cottage Street; 207-288-9605; acadiabike.com) fills the need. If you are not inclined to bike the steep 2.5 miles into the park, pack your bike on the free Island Explorer Shuttle (207-667-5796; exploreacadia.com; daily service from 9:15 a.m. at the Village Green to the Eagle Lake Carriage Road entrance). In the park, 45 miles of biking paths wind through forests, along beaver dams, and around lakes. Take a map — even the road signs can get tricky.

6 *Popovers in the Park* 1 p.m.

Lunch at the **Jordan Pond House** (207-276-3316; thejordanpondhouse.com; $$) shouldn't be missed, and it comes with views across the park's Jordan Pond to the Bubble Mountains. Popovers as rounded as the mountaintops are a specialty and come with everything from lobster salad to vegetable quiche. If you have brought your kayak or canoe, you can use it on the pond.

7 *Maine Merchandise* 4 p.m.

Back in town, do some Maine-appropriate shopping. **Window Panes** (166 Main Street; 207-288-9550; windowpanesmdi.com) carries gifts

LEFT During a two-hour sailing cruise on Frenchman Bay off Bar Harbor, passengers take part in hoisting the sails onboard the *Margaret Todd*.

including coasters made from local granite. **Cool as a Moose** (118 Main Street; 207-288-3904; coolasamoose.com) is a place to grab a sweatshirt for a chilly night. You can immerse yourself in Maine lore at **Sherman's Book and Stationery Store** (56 Main Street; 207-288-3161; shermans.com), where you might want to pick up a copy of *Time and Tide in Acadia* by Christopher Camuto or *The Maine Wild Blueberry Cookbook*. For the Lilly Pulitzer look of hot pink, orange, and blue tops or straw hats and summer bags, check the racks at the **Romantic Room** (130 Main Street, Northeast Harbor; 207-276-4005; theromanticroom.com).

8 *It's All About Lobster* 7 p.m.

Any stay in Maine is partly about lobster. Nowhere is that fact driven home more bluntly than at **Thurston's** (Steamboat Wharf Road, Bernard; 207-244-7600; thurstonslobster.com; $$), in a half-plastic, half-canvas tent overlooking a working harbor and surrounded by stacks of lobster pots. You choose your live lobster, they cook it, and you pick it up on a plastic tray. The result: high turnover and surprisingly low prices. For variety try the lobster stew. If you prefer a cottage setting, try **Abel's Lobster Pound** (13 Abels Lane off Route 198, south of Junction 233; 207-276-5827; $$$), a lively family-owned restaurant set in a spruce grove on a fjord. Eat at picnic tables illuminated by tiki torches and overlooking the yacht basin, or indoors in the knotty pine dining room.

OPPOSITE ABOVE The rocky coast that defines the rugged beauty of Acadia National Park. Offshore, lobstermen haul a catch into their boat.

ABOVE The Reading Room, a dining rotunda with a sea view at the Bar Harbor Inn, and the yellow umbrellas of the outdoor tables on a terrace just below.

SUNDAY

9 *Garden Spots* 9:30 a.m.

At the **Asticou Azalea Garden** (Peabody Drive and Sound Drive; 207-276-3727; gardenpreserve.org; free), pines, hemlocks, Korean firs, Japanese maples, azaleas, and blueberries are set around a pond. The garden's hybrid of styles includes a small Japanese karesansui garden composed of Maine granite island stones in a sea of raked white sands; lanterns and stepping-stones add to the Japanese look. Nearby, on Peabody Drive, is the **Thuya Garden** (207-276-5130; gardenpreserve.org; free), named after the house built by the landscape architect Henry Curtis, who summered there. The lodge is now a horticultural library, and the setting features a broad array of trees and shrubs and an English-style garden with everything from wood lilies to Beverly Sills irises.

One can drive or climb to the garden; but the climb, which affords broad views of Northeast Harbor, is well worth the effort.

10 *Truly Local* 11 a.m.

Take the mail boat to **Little Cranberry Island** from Northeast Harbor, and you may find yourself helping locals unload their groceries on the dock (207-244-3575; cranberryisles.com/ferries.html). Stop at the free **Islesford Historical Museum**, with its collection of ship models, tools, and dolls (207-244-9224; acadianationalpark.com/bar_harbor_maine_attractions), and then have brunch or a drink at the **Islesford Dock Restaurant** (Marina, Islesford; 207-244-7494; islesforddock.com). The harbor setting and views capture the Maine atmosphere, and the place has been mentioned in Martha Stewart's blog (she is a Seal Harbor summer resident). Try the Maine lobster fritter and grits.

ABOVE Sunrise viewing at the top of Cadillac Mountain in Acadia National Park.

OPPOSITE Cycling up Cadillac Mountain. Rent a bicycle in Bar Harbor and take a free shuttle into the park.

THE BASICS

Drive to Bar Harbor on Routes 1A and 3 from Bangor, which is on Interstate 95 and has an airport.

Asticou Inn
15 Peabody Drive
207-276-3344
asticou.com
$$$
Overlooks the water in Northeast Harbor and has the feel of a roomy old Maine home, but one with a tennis court and heated swimming pool.

The Inns at Ullikana
16 The Field
207-288-9552
ullikana.com
$$
Cheerful B&B near the water, with each room decorated in a panoply of colors and fabrics.

Bar Harbor Inn
1 Newport Drive
207-288-3351
barharborinn.com
$$$-$$$$
Stay in the main building for the grand-old-hotel experience.

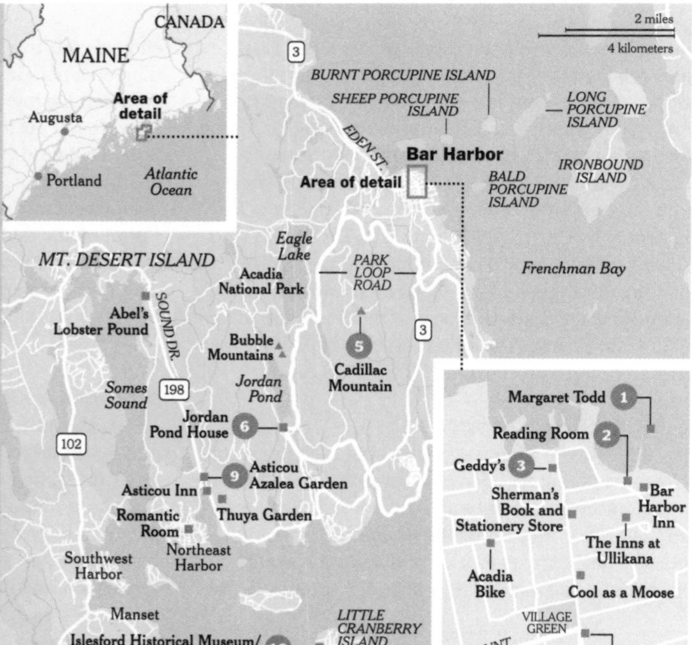

Burlington

It is no surprise that Burlington, Vermont, a city whose best known exports include the jam band Phish and Ben & Jerry's ice cream, has a hip, socially conscious vibe. But in counterpoint to its worldliness —antiglobalization rallies and fair-trade products abound—Burlington turns a discerning eye to the local. The Lake Champlain shoreline has undergone a renaissance, with gleaming hotels, bike and sailboat rental shops, and parks with sweeping views of the Adirondack Mountains. In the city's restaurants, local means locavore—urbane menus filled with heirloom tomatoes and grass-fed beef from (where else?) Vermont. And you're practically required to wash it all down with a local microbrew.

— BY KATIE ZEZIMA

FRIDAY

1 *Stroll, Shop, Snack* 4:30 p.m.

With its lively mix of students, activists, artists, families, and professors (the University of Vermont is based here), Burlington offers some interesting people-watching. Take in the sights at the **Church Street Marketplace** (2 Church Street; churchstmarketplace.com), a wide, four-block concourse that is the city's social center and home to more than 100 shops and restaurants. The pace is slow, leisurely, and crowded, so be sure to leave plenty of time to explore. Pop into **Sweet Lady Jane** (40 Church Street; 802-862-5051; sweetladyjane.biz) for funky women's clothes and accessories; **Frog Hollow** (85 Church Street; 802-863-6458; froghollow.org) to check out treasures created by Vermont artists; and **Lake Champlain Chocolates** (65 Church Street; 802-862-5185; lakechamplainchocolates.com), where a hot chocolate doubles as a meal and you'll be hard put to eat just one truffle.

2 *Chic Tables* 7:30 p.m.

Long known as a town for gravy fries, pizza, and other collegiate staples, Burlington has seen a flurry of upscale restaurants opening in recent years. **L'Amante** (126 College Street; 802-863-5200; lamante.com; $$$) helped lead the charge. If one were to take Tuscany and add a splash of Vermont, the result would be this hearty yet crunchy menu. Starters might include squash blossom fritters, and main dishes include items like grilled Vermont quail. It's sleek and low-lit, yet somehow informal, despite an expensive wine list that leans heavily on Italian reds.

3 *Music and Maple Syrup* 10 p.m.

If there are three things that Burlington does well, they are live music, beer, and coffee. **Radio Bean** (8 North Winooski Avenue; 802-660-9346; radiobean.com), a coffee bar with exposed brick walls covered in local artworks, has all three. It's like hearing a band at a friend's party, if your friend lives in a ridiculously cool loft. Scan the drinks menu for original concoctions like a "shake" of stout, espresso, and maple syrup. Check the Web site to see what bands are playing.

SATURDAY

4 *View from a Bicycle* 9 a.m.

Playing outside, whether on ski slopes, hiking trails, or lakes, is a way of life in Burlington, so it's no surprise that biking is a popular way to get around. Rent a bike at one of the many local shops like **North Star Sports** (100 Main Street; 802-863-3832; northstarsportsvt.com), for about $20 an hour or $30 a day. For those who want to see the city, marked

OPPOSITE Sunset kayaking in Burlington Harbor on Lake Champlain. The city has reclaimed its once-dingy waterfront for recreation and outdoor sports.

BELOW The Frog Hollow Gift Shop, an arts center and gallery of Vermont-made arts and crafts.

bike lanes make it look easy, but steep hills will have your quads thinking otherwise. Head out along Lake Champlain, however, and the terrain is mostly flat, joining to some 1,100 miles of trails crisscrossing through New York and Canada. Maps are available at champlainbikeways.org.

5 *Weightless Suds* 1 p.m.

Chances are **American Flatbread** (115 St. Paul Street; 802-861-2999; americanflatbread.com; $) will be packed when you get there with a crowd that ranges from kids to beer geeks. But don't panic; just order one of the Zero Gravity house beers—this place specializes in Belgian styles. The crispy flatbreads, baked in a wood-fired hearth, are essentially thin-crust pizzas topped with things like kalamata olives, sweet red peppers, goat cheese, rosemary, and red onions.

6 *Wrecks and Monsters* 3 p.m.

Lake Champlain isn't just what makes Burlington so picturesque. It's also a huge ecosystem that is the home of one of the world's oldest coral reefs (now fossilized) and hundreds of species of fish and plants. The **ECHO Lake Aquarium and Science Center** (at the Leahy Center for Lake Champlain, 1 College Street; 802-864-1848; echovermont.org) explores the scientific, ecological, and cultural and historical importance of the lake with hands-on exhibitions, including the remnants of an old shipwreck and an installation that gives visitors new respect for frogs. The center even explores Lake Champlain's biggest mystery: Is Champ a mythical lake monster or real? Try to spot him from the second-floor deck.

7 *No Page Unturned* 5 p.m.

Reading and recycling are cultivated arts in Burlington, and no place combines both better than the **Crow Bookshop** (14 Church Street; 802-862-0848; crowbooks.com). Stroll on the creaky wooden floor and browse a trove of used and rare books as well as publisher's overstocks, ranging from gardening guides to gently used copies of Shakespeare. Let the children explore their part of the store while you hang out on one of the couches and thumb through a stranger's old textbook.

8 *Paris in Vermont* 8 p.m.

In a city where style is inspired more by Birkenstocks than Birkin bags, **Leunig's Bistro** (115 Church Street; 802-863-3759; leunigsbistro.com; $$) offers a welcome dash of French flair. With its cherub lamps, cozy booths, and alfresco dining, it remains a social center. Go for a traditional beef Bourguignon or look for something with a local touch, perhaps maple-and-cardamom-marinated pork loin.

9 *On the Town* 10:30 p.m.

Follow the thumping bass to **Red Square** (136 Church Street; 802-859-8909; redsquarevt.com), a friendly nightclub that draws club kids and music lovers. If the weather is warm, you might find a band playing on the outdoor patio. Indoors, Red Square hosts both bands and D.J.'s who spin hip-hop, rock, and reggae for college students in halter tops and T-shirts. For something on the mellower side, head to **Nectar's** (188 Main Street; 802-658-4771; liveatnectars.com), the club where Phish got its start.

SUNDAY

10 *Green Eggs or Tofu* 11 a.m.

Prefer tofu in your breakfast scramble? Try the **Magnolia Bistro** (1 Lawson Lane; 802-846-7446; magnoliabistro.com; $), where eggs are always

interchangeable for tofu and homemade granola is on the menu. For meat eaters, there are choices like a meat lover's omelet with maple sausage, bacon, and Cheddar, as well as sandwich selections like open-face steak and barbecued pork. Magnolia also claims to be one of Burlington's most environmentally friendly restaurants, which means it must be really, really green. Indeed, everything is recycled, and it's certified by the Green Restaurant Association.

11 *Could This Be Stonehenge?* 1 p.m.

Not sure of the time? Find out at the **Burlington Earth Clock**, a 43-foot-wide sundial at Oakledge Park and Beach (end of Flynn Street) made of slabs of granite from local quarries. Stand in the middle and look toward the mountains; the stones in front of you represent where the sun sets during equinoxes and solstices. On the other end of the park is a studio apartment-size treehouse reachable even for kids in wheelchairs. It's an inclusive childhood fantasy come true.

OPPOSITE ABOVE On the popular Burlington Bike Path.

OPPOSITE BELOW The Earth Clock, a 43-foot sundial, shares Oakledge Park with a beach and recreation spaces.

ABOVE Church Street Marketplace, the place for shopping, people watching, and decadent hot chocolate.

THE BASICS

Burlington is a short flight or a pretty six-hour drive on Route 7 from New York City. In town, walk and bike.

Willard Street Inn
349 South Willard Street
802-651-8710
willardstreetinn.com
$$$
Antique-filled 12-room inn in a Queen Anne-style mansion close to the University of Vermont.

Courtyard by Marriott Burlington Harbor
25 Cherry Street
802-864-4700
marriott.com/hotels/travel/btvdt-courtyard-burlington-harbor/
$$
Faces Lake Champlain; easy access to Church Street Marketplace.

Hotel Vermont
41 Cherry Street
802-651-0080
hotelvt.com
$$$
New and sophisticated.

500 feet
1/4 kilometer
Burlington
BATTERY PARK
MONROE ST.
N. WINOOSKI AVE.
3 Radio Bean
PARK ST.
LAKE ST.
Church Street Marketplace 1
PEARL ST.
7 Crow Bookshop
Hotel Vermont
CHERRY ST.
Sweet Lady Jane
S. UNION ST.
Courtyard by Marriott Burlington Harbor
Lake Champlain Chocolates
BANK ST.
Frog Hollow
ECHO Lake Aquarium and Science Center
L'Amante 2
8 Leunig's Bistro
6
COLLEGE ST.
Magnolia Bistro 10
CITY HALL PARK
9 Red Square
Nectar's
North Star Sports 4
MAIN ST.
5
American Flatbread Burlington Hearth
KING ST.
BATTERY ST.
ST. PAUL ST.
MAPLE ST.
PINE ST.
Lake Champlain
11
Burlington Earth Clock
To Willard Street Inn
CANADA
Lake Champlain
Burlington
VERMONT
N.Y.
N.H.
MASS.

Ottawa

Ottawa has always had image problems. Back in 1857, when it beat out its rivals Toronto and Montreal in a bid to become Canada's national capital, the Governor General bemoaned Parliament's move to what seemed a frontier outpost on the Ottawa River as an "exile to wilderness." Since then, it has often been written off as a staid hub of government. But beneath Ottawa's buttoned-up, civil-servant demeanor lies a vibrant community, with enough green space, trails, and water within city limits to satisfy the most hyperactive of travelers. —BY KATIE ARNOLD

FRIDAY

1 *Pay Homage to the Hill* 3 p.m.

With a metropolitan-area population of about 1.2 million, Ottawa is smaller than many national capitals, but it holds the machinery of government, the requisite share of pomp and circumstance, and more than 125 embassies. You're too late today for the British-style changing of the guard on **Parliament Hill** (Wellington Street; 613-239-5000; parl.gc.ca), but there's time to get inside the stolid granite buildings with their formal neo-Gothic turrets. Just steps from downtown, across an unfenced emerald lawn, the nexus of Canada's government is thrillingly accessible. Join a free guided tour of the House of Commons chambers. Or skip the formalities and take the elevator up to the 300-foot-high **Peace Tower** for a bird's-eye panorama of downtown, the river, and Quebec's rolling Gatineau Hills.

2 *Museum Stroll* 4 p.m.

From the Peace Tower, it's an easy walk through **Major's Hill Park**, a grassy headland with unobstructed views of Parliament Hill, to the footpath across Alexandra Bridge. Beneath you is the imposing Ottawa River, once frequented by fur traders and loggers, and at this spot the border between two huge provinces, Ontario and Quebec. Just across the river in Gatineau, Quebec, the **First Peoples Hall of the Canadian Museum of History** (100 Laurier Street; 819-776-7000; civilization.ca) collects relics from Canada's 53 cultural groups, some dating as far back as 20,000 years.

3 *Breaking for Mussels* 6 p.m.

Come quitting time, government workers and others in the know descend on **Métropolitain Brasserie** (700 Sussex Drive; 613-562-1160; metropolitainbrasserie.com), with its ruby-leather banquettes, hammered zinc bar, and très Paris vibe. During Hill Hour (weeknights from 4 till 7), it dishes up plates of steaming Prince Edward Island mussels, fresh Malpeque oysters, and jumbo shrimp from Ottawa's largest bar cru.

4 *Fare of the Country* 8 p.m.

Just a block east of Sussex, **ByWard Market** is a bustling, three-by-five-block warren of hip boutiques, wine bars, and restaurants — an unexpected microplex of cool in the middle of the city. For food from one of the city's highly regarded kitchens, dine at **Restaurant 18** (18 York Street; 613-244-1188; restaurant18.com; $$$-$$$$). The cuisine is French; the décor is sophisticated. Expect fresh produce, interesting flavors, and sturdy main dishes like Quebec wild boar or Nova Scotia swordfish.

SATURDAY

5 *Run the Canal* 9 a.m.

The fastest way to wake up in Ottawa is with a sprint along the city's beloved **Rideau Canal**, part of a 125-mile-long waterway that links the Ottawa

OPPOSITE The Rideau Canal, a playground year-round.

RIGHT Berries in season at the ByWard Market.

River to Lake Ontario. It first opened in 1832 and is a Unesco World Heritage Site. Start at the hydraulic locks below Sussex Street, and head south along the paved jogging/biking/inline-skating paths. Picture the scene in winter, when the canal turns into a perfect linear rink, with skaters (including commuters headed to work) and ice sleighs crowding the glassy-smooth surface. The city's Winterlude festival, which draws hundreds of thousands of people annually, grew up around the canal. After your run, have breakfast at the sunny and simple **French Baker** (119 Murray Street; 613-789-7941; bennysbistro.ca), home to the flakiest croissants in town.

6 *Paddle the River* 11 a.m.

Switch waterways and modes of travel. Rent a flat-water kayak or canoe from **Trailhead Paddle Shack** (1960 Scott Street; 613-725-5259; ottawapaddleshack.ca) and put in at sandy **Westboro Beach** on the Ottawa River. On all but the windiest of days the flat-water basin makes for a fine two-hour tour. Just downstream, where the river funnels into the Champlain Rapids, whitewater kayakers surf "the Wall," a Class III standing wave off Bates Island.

7 *Time Out for Tea* 2 p.m.

Traditional afternoon tea is serious business at **Zoe's** ($$$) in the **Fairmont Château Laurier** (1 Rideau Street; 613-241-1414; fairmont.com/laurier-ottawa), a grand railway hotel choicely located between Parliament and the Rideau Canal, but the experience is anything but stuffy. Come as you are, and when the tea wagon rolls around, sniff from several loose-leaf black teas. Your choice is brewed in a pot at your table and served with a meal's worth of tidbits like Nova Scotia lox and tiny bagels, Canadian white Cheddar, and just-baked scones with Devonshire cream. The formality is simply meant to help you relax and savor the afternoon. It works.

ABOVE Taking in the scenery at Gatineau Park.

RIGHT Native art in the First Peoples Hall at the Canadian Museum of History.

8 *Back to ByWard* 4 p.m.

ByWard Market by day is an amateur shopper's dream: just enough unexpected finds to keep you scouting and not too many to overwhelm the brain or the bank account. Old Ottawa stalwarts like **LaPointe Fish** (46 ByWard Market Street; 613-789-6221; lapointefish.ca), which has been in operation since 1867, mingle with stylish home and apparel shops. **Zone** (471 Sussex Drive; 613-562-2755; zonemaison.com) is a glittery housewares emporium filled with mod, affordable treasures. A few doors down, **Trustfund** (493 Sussex Drive; 613-562-0999; trustfundboutique.com) collects an eclectic mix of clothes and accessories for men and women. Whether or not you need a sugar fix, stop at **BeaverTails** (69 George Street; 613-241-1230; beavertailsinc.com), a ByWard Market tourist landmark. The tiny kiosk on the corner of George and Williams Streets fries up XL whole-wheat pastries in the shape of a beaver's tail (squint and you'll see), dusted with cinnamon, sugar, and a spritz of lemon.

9 *Sing Along at the Laff* 5:30 p.m.

If you can't get a table inside the mobbed **Château Lafayette**, a.k.a. the Laff (42 York Street;

613-241-4747; thelaff.ca), park yourself on the sidewalk in front of this pleasingly seedy tavern to hear Lucky Ron (Ron Burke) belt out his own twangy brand of 1950s country music. An Ottawa favorite, he's had this Saturday afternoon gig since 1999. For better or worse, the audience sometimes joins in.

10 *Get Fresh* 8:30 p.m.

The scene is more serene at **John Taylor at Domus Café** (87 Murray Street; 613-241-6007; domuscafe.ca; $$$), a high-ceilinged, green-powered oasis where the chef and owner, John Taylor, has been offering virtuous "regional seasonal" cuisine since 1997—back when "eating locally" meant hitting the hamburger joint around the corner. Most of the menu is sourced from farmers in the Ottawa-Gatineau region. Save room for the crème brulée or a tart.

SUNDAY

11 *Gatineau Park* 10 a.m.

Across the river in Quebec, **Gatineau Park** (819-827-2020; ncc-ccn.gc.ca/places-to-visit/gatineau-park) shelters 140 square miles of wooded backcountry. The park's western boundary, the Eardley Escarpment, marks the edge of the Canadian Shield, a slab of granite bedrock that sprawls northward to the Arctic. Hike the three-mile Skyline trail, and then stop by **Café Soupe-Herbe** (168 Chemin, Old Chelsea, Quebec; 819-827-7687; soupherbe.com) for brunch on the terrace.

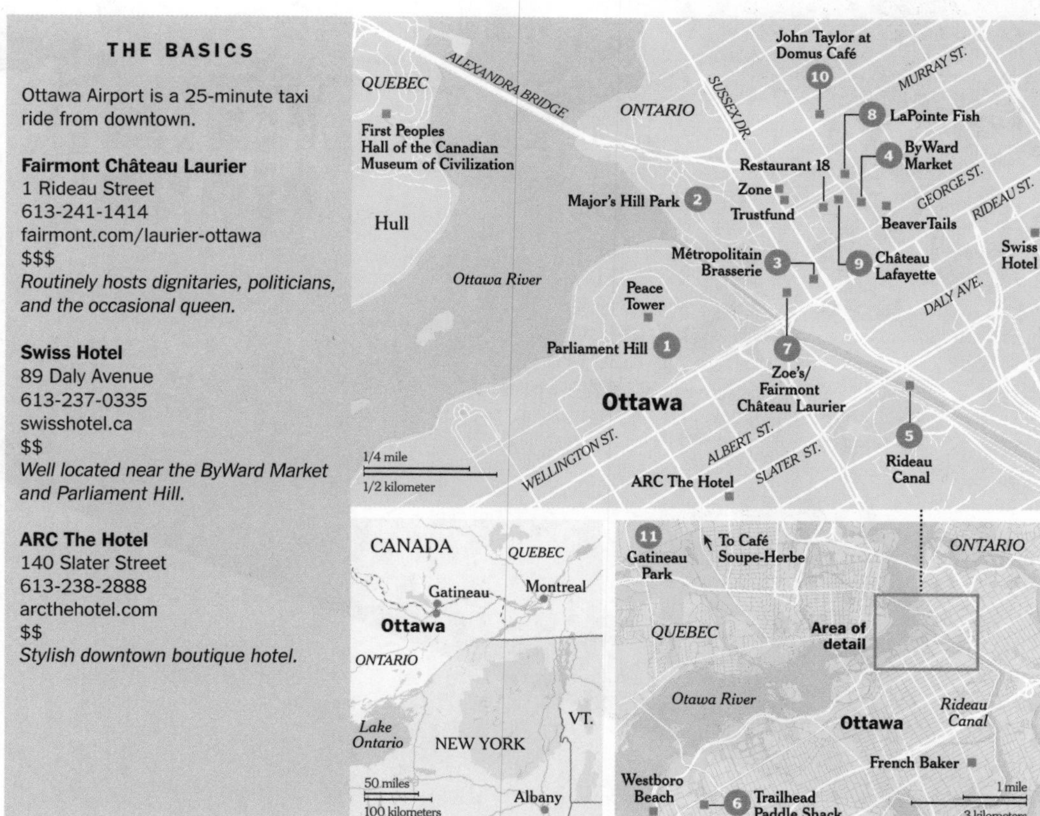

THE BASICS

Ottawa Airport is a 25-minute taxi ride from downtown.

Fairmont Château Laurier
1 Rideau Street
613-241-1414
fairmont.com/laurier-ottawa
$$$
Routinely hosts dignitaries, politicians, and the occasional queen.

Swiss Hotel
89 Daly Avenue
613-237-0335
swisshotel.ca
$$
Well located near the ByWard Market and Parliament Hill.

ARC The Hotel
140 Slater Street
613-238-2888
arcthehotel.com
$$
Stylish downtown boutique hotel.

Montreal

French or English? One of the beautiful things about Montreal is that you never know in what language you will be greeted. Which brings up a second thing: Maybe it's the good food, the open skies, or the free-spirited students who call this city their campus, but the folks of Montreal are friendly. Ask someone for directions in the Métro, part of the vast Underground City that stays toasty during the winter, and you may end up making drinks plans later. That's not a bad thing, bien sûr. With the city's music-charged night life, slaughterhouse-chic restaurants, and postindustrial revival, it helps to have a guide.
— BY DENNY LEE

FRIDAY

1 *Get Wheels* 3 p.m.

For bicycle touring, Montreal delivers, with 310-plus miles of bike lanes that crisscross the city, about half of which are physically separated from cars. The public Bixi bike program that gained considerable fanfare after opening in 2009 stalled after it ran into financial trouble, but it's easy to rent a bicycle. Get yours at **Montreal on Wheels** (27, rue de la Commune Est; 514-866-0633; caroulemontreal.com), where you can also pick up a map and get advice on routes.

2 *Downtown Roll* 3:30 p.m.

To see why Montreal was designated a Unesco City of Design, point your handlebars toward the Lachine Canal, a former industrial waterfront that has been transformed into a lush green belt. The path is dotted with architectural gems like **Habitat 67** (2600, avenue Pierre-Dupuy; habitat67.com), a Brutalist-style experiment in modular housing designed by Moshe Safdie in the heady late-'60s era of Expo 67, one of the last great world's fairs. Or pedal along Boulevard de Maisonneuve, which cuts through downtown Montreal, where a 2.1-mile path is named after the late Claire Morissette, a cycling activist.

3 *Québécois Plates* 8 p.m.

Normand Laprise, who pioneered the use of fresh Québécois ingredients at the pricey Toqué!, often praised by critics as the city's best restaurant, opened a midpriced sister restaurant, **Brasserie t!** (1425, rue Jeanne Mance; 514-282-0808; brasserie-t.com; $$$). Situated at the foot of the Contemporary Art Museum, the brasserie looks like a sleek cargo container. Inside, a contemporary French menu showcases unfussy dishes like grilled flank steak and cod brandade.

4 *Musical Mile* 10 p.m.

It's impossible to talk about the Mile End district without name-dropping bands like Arcade Fire and the gritty stages that gave them their start. The beloved Green Room closed because of a fire, but upstart bands are still jamming at **Divan Orange** (4234, boulevard St.-Laurent; 514-840-9090; divanorange.org). An alternative, with a bigger stage and sound, is **Il Motore** (179, rue Jean-Talon Ouest; 514-274-7676; ilmotore.ca).

SATURDAY

5 *Like the Marais* 10 a.m.

For shopping and a selection of cafes, head to Old Montreal, where historic cobblestones and high foot traffic ensure the survival of indie boutiques.

OPPOSITE The Biosphere, designed by Buckminster Fuller, lives on as a Montreal landmark. It was built for the 1967 world's fair called Expo 67.

BELOW The shopping is good in Old Montreal, where busy tourist traffic on the historic cobblestones provides a healthy environment for indie boutiques.

For homegrown designers like Arielle de Pinto and international fashion brands like Acne, squeeze inside **Reborn** (231, rue St.-Paul Ouest, Suite 100; 514-499-8549; reborn.ws), a small shop with a sharp eye. Down the block is **À Table Tout le Monde** (361, rue St.-Paul Ouest; 514-750-0311; atabletoutlemonde.com), an elegant store that carries exquisitely crafted ceramics and housewares. And while you're exploring the historic district, drop into **DHC Art** (451, rue St.-Jean; 514-849-3742; dhc-art.org), one of the city's leading contemporary art galleries.

ABOVE From the Lachine Canal bicycle path, cyclists can get a glimpse of this experiment in modular housing, Moshe Safdie's Habitat 67.

BELOW A charcuterie spread paired with a glass of red wine at Brasserie T!, where the sleek, ultra-modern architecture compliments contemporary French fare.

6 *City of Design* 2 p.m.

Trendy design shops are a retail staple in Montreal, but if you like your modern design on a larger scale, the **Musée des Beaux-Arts de Montreal** (1379-80, rue Sherbrooke Ouest; 514-285-2000; mmfa.qc.ca) has a strong collection, along with Old Masters and contemporary Canadian artists. And the **Canadian Centre for Architecture** (1920, rue Baile; 514-939-7026; cca.qc.ca) holds regular exhibitions on architecture and urbanism in a striking 19th-century mansion with a modern stone addition.

7 *French Bites* 8 p.m.

A neighborhood wine bar that happens to serve terrific food is one of those pleasures that make Paris, well, Paris. That's the vibe at **Buvette Chez Simone** (4869, avenue du Parc; 514-750-6577; buvettechezsimone.com; $$$), a bar in Mile End with sly design touches. The comfy brasserie menu features dishes like a roast chicken served on a carving board with roasted potatoes. If you're hankering for more inventive fare, bike over to **Pullman** (3424, avenue du Parc; 514-288-7779; pullman-mtl.com;

$$$), a high-end tapas bar that serves clever plates like venison tartare, foie gras cookies, and olives with candied lemon. The crowd at both restaurants skews young, fashionable, and chatty.

8 *Electronic Artists* 10 p.m.

In another sign of Euro-flair, techno music is huge in Montreal. And one of the coolest parties is thrown by **Neon** (iloveneon.ca), a digital music collective that has showcased a who's who of electronic artists like Glass Candy and Hudson Mohawke. Many events take place at **Le Belmont sur le Boulevard** (4483, boulevard St.-Laurent; 514-845-8443; lebelmont.com), an intimate gay-friendly club that has a pool table up front and a pulsing sound system in the rear. For a more analog vibe, head to **Velvet Speakeasy** (426, rue St.-Gabriel; velvetspeakeasy.ca), a posh club in the Old Port district.

ABOVE On the dance floor at the Velvet Speakeasy, one of a variety of music and dance clubs that make up Montreal's active night life scene.

BELOW The path along the Lachine Canal is part of a 310-mile system of bicycle routes and lanes that make Montreal an exceptionally bicycle-friendly city.

SUNDAY

9 *Eggs to Go* 9:30 a.m.

For a delightful morning meal served in an old town house with communal tables, have brunch at **Le Cartet** (106, rue McGill; 514-871-8887; lecartet.com;

$$). Part cafe, part grocery store, Le Cartet draws young families and professionals with hearty platters of eggs that come with figs, cheese, and salad greens. On your way out, feel free to stock up on crusty baguettes, French mustards, and picnic cheeses.

10 *Smooth Water, Wild Water* 11 a.m.
Join the city at play back at the **Lachine Canal**, nine miles of smooth water originally built as a bypass around the Lachine Rapids, which roil and churn in the St. Lawrence River right inside the city. Now the canal is filled in summer with sailboats, canoes, and other small craft. Secure a kayak or pedal boat from **H20 Adventures** (514-842-1306; h2oadventures.ca) or one of the other boat rental businesses along the canal, and join in. Or skip the tame canal and go jet-boating through the rapids themselves with **Les Descentes sur le St.-Laurent** (514-767-2230; raftingmontreal.com).

11 *Dancing Man* 2 p.m.
If it's sunny, join Montreal's barefoot and pierced crowd at **Piknic Électronik** (piknicelectronik.com), an outdoor rave held on Île Ste.-Hélène during the summer. At Jean-Drapeau Park, follow the slithering beats to *The Man*, a giant sculpture, created by Alexander Calder for the 1967 Expo, which hovers over the dance floor. The leafy island has other architectural ruins from the Expo. Between beats, stroll over to the **Montreal Biosphere** (biosphere.ec.gc.ca), the iconic geodesic dome that still evokes a utopian vision of technology.

OPPOSITE À Table Tout le Monde in Old Montreal.

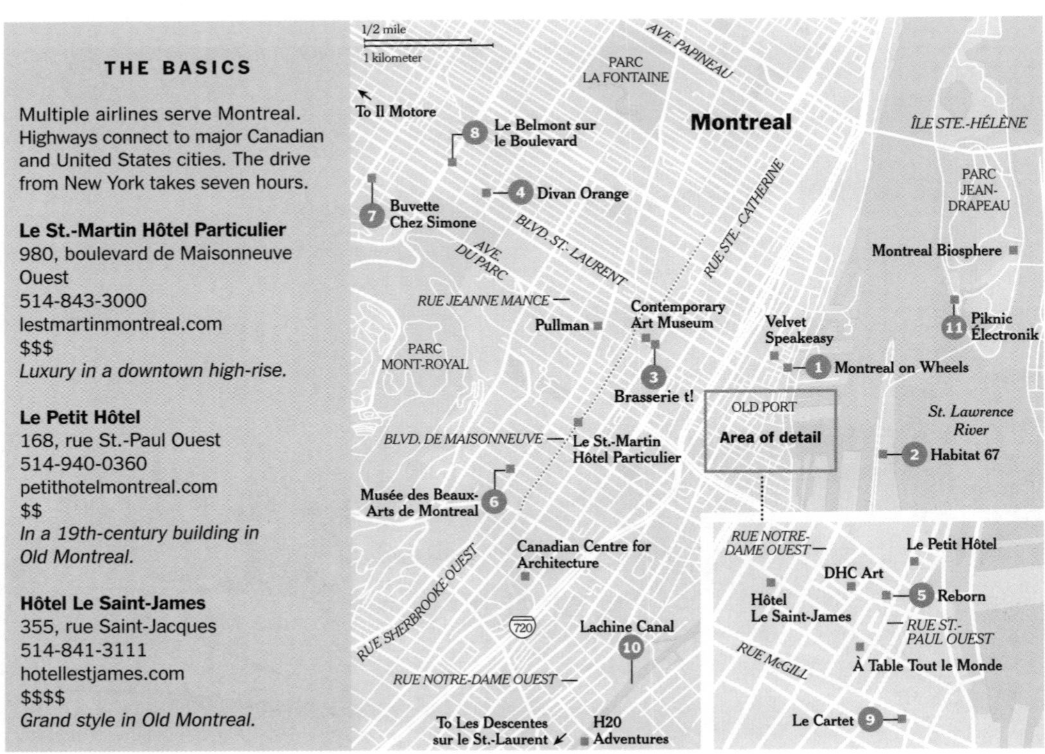

THE BASICS

Multiple airlines serve Montreal. Highways connect to major Canadian and United States cities. The drive from New York takes seven hours.

Le St.-Martin Hôtel Particulier
980, boulevard de Maisonneuve Ouest
514-843-3000
lestmartinmontreal.com
$$$
Luxury in a downtown high-rise.

Le Petit Hôtel
168, rue St.-Paul Ouest
514-940-0360
petithotelmontreal.com
$$
In a 19th-century building in Old Montreal.

Hôtel Le Saint-James
355, rue Saint-Jacques
514-841-3111
hotellestjames.com
$$$$
Grand style in Old Montreal.

TOUCHEZ AUX
TOUCH THE

TREMBLANT

Mont Tremblant

One of the oldest ski resorts in North America, with miles of runs in the evergreen-topped Laurentian Mountains, Mont Tremblant, Quebec, seems to have it all. Combining the Canadian charm of a rustic logging town with the Old World flavor of the French Alps, Tremblant is consistently ranked by Ski Magazine *readers as the East's No. 1 resort. Hotels, condos, and bed-and-breakfasts accommodate thousands of skiers, and there are enough restaurants, shops, pools, and spas to keep everyone busy after a day on the slopes. Mont Tremblant is a year-round resort, with golf courses, a casino, and a national park, but it is in winter, when 150 inches of snow keep the ski trails slippery and the rooftops white, that it really comes into its own.* — BY LIONEL BEEHNER

FRIDAY

1 *Sleigh Bells Ring* 4 p.m.

For an action-packed lay of the land, hop on a sleigh ride with the resort's **Activity Center** (Place St. Bernard; 819-681-4848; tremblantactivities.com), which offers hourlong rides for 35 Canadian dollars (despite fluctuating currency rates, the prices usually aren't too different in U.S. dollars). Two beefy Percheron horses — steam wafting from their bodies — pull a rickety yet comfortable sleigh through Quebec's boreal forest, while the tour guide animatedly regales passengers with stories about the "trembling" mountain and may even sing some Québécois folk songs. The trip is like an Alpine safari; the trail is teeming with wildlife, like white-tail deer and red foxes. Bundle up — the mercury often dips below zero. Blankets are provided, and halfway through the ride everyone gulps down some hot cocoa.

2 *Alternative Shopping* 5 p.m.

Skip the resort's pricey boutiques and head to historic St.-Jovite — a village now rechristened Centre-Ville Mont-Tremblant — a 10-minute drive from the mountain. Explore the shops on Rue de St.-Jovite. **Boutique Manège** (No. 830; 819-425-8952; boutiquemanege.com) sells cute — even sometimes hip — children's clothes; several other stores cater to the fashionable adult. For handmade golf shoes and high-end ladies' footwear, drop by **Nycole St.-Louis Collections** (No. 822; 819-425-3583; nycolestlouis.com). Folk arts and country antiques are the specialty at **Le Coq Rouge** (No. 821; 819-425-3205; coqrouge.com).

OPPOSITE The base village at Mont Tremblant, widely considered to be the No. 1 ski resort in eastern North America.

3 *Poutine Time* 7 p.m.

Foodies will appreciate the Quebec-style fusion cooking at **sEb** (444 Rue St.-Georges; 819-429-6991; resto-seb.com; $$$). A high-end restaurant with a laid-back vibe, it gives comfort food a modern twist. Traditional dishes like rabbit stew or bison strip loin steak are jazzed up with local foie gras or the hefty regional favorite known as poutine, cheese curd with fries and gravy. Sébastien Houle, the young proprietor, cut his culinary teeth as a chef on the yacht of Paul Allen, a cofounder of Microsoft.

4 *Canadian Bandstand* 9 p.m.

Find Tremblant's young partyers at **P'tit Caribou** (125 Chemin de Kandahar; 819-681-4500; ptitcaribou.com), a dive bar in the base village with beer-soaked wooden floors and bar-top dancers.

RIGHT The shops of St.-Jovite, now called Centre-Ville Mont-Tremblant, are a 10-minute drive from the mountain.

D.J.'s, popcorn, and low prices keep things lively, and if the exuberance appears particularly youthful, recall that the legal drinking age in Quebec is 18.

SATURDAY

5 *French Breakfast* 7:30 a.m.

Kick off your day with something sweet. **Crêperie Catherine** (113 Chemin de Kandahar; 819-681-4888; creperiecatherine.ca; $$), carved out of a former chalet, is famous among local skiers for its old-fashioned crepes, and the hundreds of chef-themed dolls, teapots, cookie jars, and other tchotchkes that line its walls. Order the house specialty—a crepe with hot and velvety sucre à la crème. Arrive early. Seats here are in demand.

6 *Go North, Young Skier* 8:30 a.m.

Tremblant (819-681-2000; tremblant.ca) is a mountain folded in four parts, with a south, north, and soleil (sunny) side and a segment called the Edge. Start the morning on the north side, when there is usually more sun and less wind. Long cruisers like Beauchemin let you find your balance before conquering the fast bumps on Saute-Moutons. After lunch, follow the sun over to the south side. Nansen offers marvelous views largely untainted by

condos, while speed demons should hit the steeps of Kandahar. To ski off-piste, take the Telecabine Express gondola to the top and ski down to the Edge lift, or trek over to the soleil side. Of Tremblant's 94 trails, 15 are glades. If the conditions get icy — this is the East, after all — drop by the cozy Grand Manitou summit restaurant. Or just high-tail it back to your condo's hot tub.

7 *Aprés-Ski Restorative* 3:30 p.m.

Replenish your energy after a long day of skiing with a nutrition-conscious snack from **Fluide Juice Bar** (1000 Chemin Kandahar; 819-681-4681). Try a smoothie, organic fresh-squeezed vegetable or fruit juice, or vegan snacks. Your body will thank you.

8 *Nordic Thaw* 5 p.m.

Landed a few face plants? Pamper those sore muscles at **Le Scandinave** (4280 Montée Ryan; 819-425-5524; scandinave.com), a Nordic-themed spa in a barnlike fortress on the outskirts of town. The spa's rustic-chic motif and thermal waterfalls will lull bathers into a state of relaxation. Warm up in a Finnish sauna or Norwegian steam bath before taking a cold plunge in the Diable River out back. Sadly, the 17,000-square-foot spa doesn't offer maple syrup scrubs like some of its competitors. But a Swedish massage will rejuvenate even the sorest of muscles. Take it from two of the owners, who are retired NHL hockey players.

9 *Slopeside Fondue* 7:30 p.m.

"Have you tried the fondue at La Savoie?" You'll hear that question a lot in Mont Tremblant. In the middle of the base village, **La Savoie** (115 Chemin de Kandahar; 819-681-4573; restaurantlasavoie.com; $$$) has a homey décor befitting a chateau in the Savoy region in the French Alps. The same goes for the fondue. Tabletop pierrades and raclettes let patrons cook their own shrimp, chicken, fish, or filet mignon in communal fashion, before dunking the morsels into melted cheeses, red wine, or garlic sauces. Chances are you won't have room for the chocolate fondue.

10 *Hockey-Free Zone* 9:30 p.m.

Most bars in town, it seems, are just repositories of wall-mounted moose heads and bad cover bands. A welcome exception is **La Diable** (117 Chemin de

OPPOSITE ABOVE AND BELOW Pampering is available indoors and out at Le Scandinave, a Nordic-themed spa. Warm up in a hot bath before plunging into the icy Diable River, or stick to the massages and thermal waterfalls inside.

ABOVE Mont Tremblant National Park, vast and just outside town, is laced with waterways and comes alive in summer with canoeing, hiking, and fishing.

Kandahar; 819-681-4546; microladiable.com), a low-key microbrasserie that serves up an eclectic array of devil-themed brews like the Extreme Onction—a Belgian Trappist-style ale with 8.5 percent alcohol. La Diable might also be the only mountainside bar without hockey playing on the flat screen.

SUNDAY

11 *Call of the Wild* 8:15 a.m.

Ever wanted to commandeer a caravan of canines through the Canadian wilderness? Pay a visit to **Nordic Adventure Dog Sledding** (Place St. Bernard; 819-681-4848; tremblantactivities.com). After a 40-minute bus ride, you arrive at what looks like the setting of a Jack London novel—a secluded camp in the woods surrounded by nothing but Siberian huskies. Above the din of barking dogs, the gregarious guide explains how to steer and how to stop and go ("Hop-hop!" or "Mush!"). Eight harness-linked dogs sprint at breakneck speed. The two-hour ride (about 150 Canadian dollars) winds its way through some challenging terrain, interrupted only by a cabin break for hot chocolate and a prep course in fire-starting.

ABOVE AND OPPOSITE Skiing is the preferred way to play outside, but there are others. One option is dogsledding in Mont Tremblant's reliable fresh snow, with you in the driver's seat. Count on the guide to teach you when to say "Mush!"

THE BASICS

Fly direct to Mont Tremblant from several U.S. and Canadian cities. Most hotels offer airport shuttles, but a rental car is desirable.

Hôtel Quintessence
3004 Chemin de la Chapelle
819-425-3400
hotelquintessence.com
$$$$
Elegance in 30 suites overlooking Tremblant Lake.

Château Beauvallon
6385 Montée Ryan
819-618-6611
chateaubeauvallon.com
$$$
Suites with kitchens, gas fireplaces, and private balconies.

The Crystal Inn
100 Chemin Joseph Thibault
819-681-7775
crystal-inn.com
$$
Colorful, cozy bed-and-breakfast outfitted with crazy murals and a small spa.

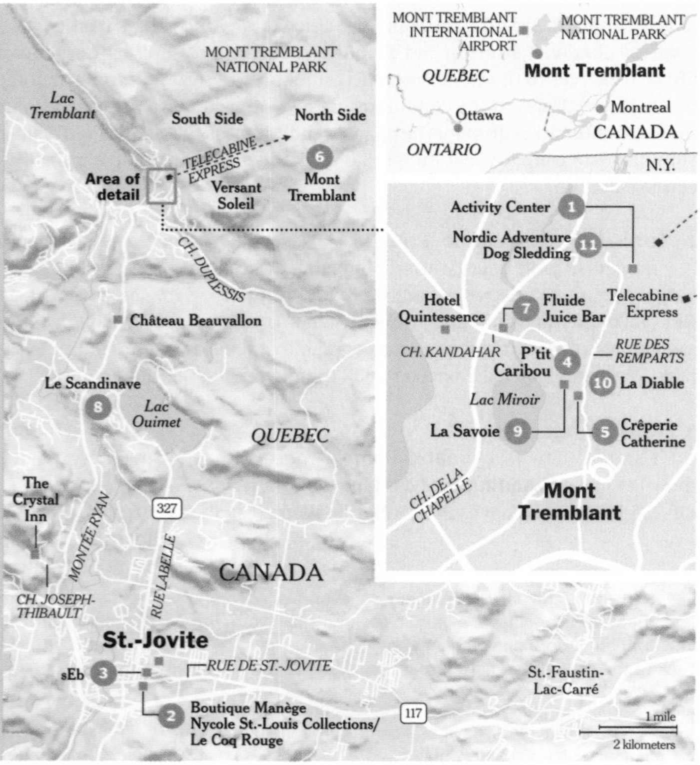

Quebec City

Quebec can give provincialism a good name. Orphaned by mother France, dominated by Britain (after what Québécois still call the Conquest) and then for years by majority-Anglophone Canada, the people of Quebec have followed Voltaire's advice to tend to their own garden. This is especially true of Quebec City, the provincial capital. Proudly dated, lovingly maintained, Quebec City has charm to spare, particularly within the city walls of the Old Town and in the Lower Town tucked between those walls and the St. Lawrence River. The city's French heart is always on its sleeve, and a stroll over the cobblestones leads to patisseries, sidewalk cafes, and a profusion of art galleries. Yet a vast wilderness is the next stop due north, putting game on restaurant menus and a kind of backwoods vigor in the city's spirit. To a Yankee it all seems European. But there is no place like this in Europe; there is nothing else like it in North America, either. And that's reason enough to celebrate. — BY SCOTT L. MALCOMSON

FRIDAY

1 *Champagne and Cigars* 5 p.m.

It's too late in the day to head out for kayaking on the St. Lawrence River, so go instead to the first-floor **St. Laurent Bar & Lounge** at the **Fairmont Le Château Frontenac** (1, rue des Carrières; 418-692-3861; fairmont.com/frontenac) for Champagne. You're atop the city's cliffs, and this semicircular room has wonderful views of the St. Lawrence. A drink in the château, as it is called (it's that enormous castle-like building, built as a grand hotel for the Canadian Pacific Railway) is always pricey, but luxury can be like that. Even the bar food is classy, running to snacks like assiette of smoked fish. This huge grand hotel is a spectacle itself, dominating the city skyline and rich in history (Franklin Roosevelt and Winston Churchill met here on one memorable occasion during World War II). Take this opportunity to explore the opulent lobby and find the cliffside boardwalk called the **Dufferin Terrace**.

2 *Lower Town Update* 8 p.m.

Fast-forward a few decades by finding your way down to St. Roch in the Lower Town, hard up against the cliff. Once a grim commercial district, it is now a hotspot of high-tech businesses, artists' studios, galleries, shops, and cafes. One of the pioneering restaurants in the transformation was the sleek **Versa** (432, rue du Parvis; 418-523-9995; versarestaurant.com; $$$), which touts its mojitos and boasts that it is the city's only oyster bar. The menu mixes bistro food and more formal entrees like duck breast dumplings or free-range chicken with roasted octopus.

3 *Dancing Feet* 10 p.m.

For a taste of St. Roch night life, drop in at **Le Boudoir** (441, rue de l'Église; 418-524-2777; boudoirlounge.com), a bar packed with young professionals. D.J.'s keep things hopping on the weekends, and the sound system boasts 60 speakers. There's a different scene on the Grande Allée, where a stretch of nightclubs including **Maurice** (575, Grande-Allée Est; 418-647-2000; mauricenightclub.com) draws a glamorous clientele.

SATURDAY

4 *On the Plains* 10 a.m.

Take a jog or a leisurely walk on the **Plains of Abraham**, an extensive, undulating rectangle on the heights above the St. Lawrence just west of the Frontenac. This is where, in 1759, British invaders led by James Wolfe defeated Louis-Joseph de Montcalm in the battle that set in motion the decline of French

OPPOSITE The guards at Quebec's Citadel may look English, but their regiment's official language is French.

BELOW For tourists, walking is the way to get around.

power in North America. Today it is a playground, an urban park (ccbn-nbc.gc.ca) where children race around the open spaces, actors stroll by in 18th-century garb, and Paul McCartney gave a free concert in 2008 to mark Quebec City's 400th birthday. For a concrete example of Quebec's mixed historical legacy, stop off at the **Citadel** (1, Côte de la Citadelle; 418-694-2815; lacitadelle.qc.ca), where an officially French-speaking regiment performs an English-style changing of the guard, complete with black bearskin hats, every summer morning at 10.

5 *Provincial Special* 2 p.m.

At least once this weekend you have to eat poutine, the concoction of French fries, cheese curd, and gravy that is close to the French Canadian soul,

if not particularly friendly to its heart. Find it at **Buffet de l'Antiquaire** (95, rue St.-Paul; 418-692-2661; $), a Lower Town institution with sidewalk tables in summer. It is a very good, very local diner that serves all kinds of Canadian comfort food and is always worth a visit at breakfast, too.

6 *That Perfect Find* 3 p.m.

Walk out into the **rue St.-Paul**, a street lined with easygoing antiques shops and art galleries, to poke through Victoriana, country furniture, Art Deco relics, and assorted gewgaws. If you still can't find the right present to take home, take the first left up into the Old Town and head for **Artisans du Bas-Canada** (30, côte de la Fabrique; 418-692-2109; artisanscanada.com), which has jewelry made from Canadian diamonds and amber as well as an abundance of Québécois tchotchkes.

7 *Take to the Ramparts* 6 p.m.

Stroll along the ramparts of the Old Town for a stirring view of the St. Lawrence. Quebec City was strategic because of its commanding position on the

ABOVE The Lower Town along the St. Lawrence River.

LEFT J.A. Moisan, a gourmet grocery store.

OPPOSITE The Château Frontenac is now a Fairmont Hotel.

river just at the point where it begins to widen and expand into the Gulf of St. Lawrence on its way to the Atlantic. Then proceed downhill for a drink at the friendly and cozy **Belley Tavern** (249, rue St.-Paul; 418-692-1694). Or try **Môss Bistro** (255, rue St.-Paul; 418-692-0233), a "bistro belge" that has a wide selection of Belgian beers, including several on tap, and many ways of preparing mussels.

8 *Haute Cuisine* 8 p.m.

Most Québécois speak English, but French, even bad French, goes over well. So use yours to ask for directions to the luxury hotel called **Auberge Saint-Antoine** (8, rue St.-Antoine). Its restaurant, **Panache** (418-692-2211; saint-antoine.com/en/dining; $$$$), is a point of reference for Quebec City's haute cuisine. Start off with Champagne cocktails, then on to an amuse-bouche and the tasting menu, which moves at a leisurely pace from an appetizer, perhaps foie gras, through seafood and meats that often include venison or other Canadian game, and finally to dessert, all with suitable wines. It is easy to drag this out—in a space that is like a rustic loft with upholstered chairs—for three hours or more. After dinner, make your way through the narrow streets to admire the restored buildings of the Place-Royal at your leisure.

9 *Québécois Cabaret* 11 p.m.

For a late night out that will connect you to the local artistic crowd, go to **Le Cercle** (228, rue St.-Joseph Est; 418-948-8648; le-cercle.ca), a sleek industrial-modern space that offers live indie, rock, dance, and folk music, as well as films, comedy shows, theater, art, and video. It's also a wine bar with a 2,000-bottle cellar and a kitchen that turns out morsels for wee-hours snacking.

SUNDAY

10 *Riverside* 11 a.m.

You've gazed at the St. Lawrence from the heights; now it's time to get close. Join the locals catching the breeze on the **Promenade Samuel de Champlain**, a riverfront strip park that opened in 2008, in time for the city's 400th anniversary celebration. The 1.5-mile-long promenade, on land between the boulevard Champlain and the river — for many years a degraded industrial area — was such a hit that the city soon set to work extending it to a length that will eventually reach for six more miles.

11 *One Last Chance* Noon

If you're still in the market for something to take home, check out **J. A. Moisan** (699, rue Saint-Jean; 418-522-0685; jamoisan.com), which claims to be the oldest gourmet grocery store in North America. Should the cheeses, chocolates, pasta, and other fare fail to charm, you'll find a selection of other high-end shops on rue Saint-Jean.

ABOVE AND OPPOSITE Quebec City's Old Town caters to tourists with shopping, restaurants and bars, and its well preserved native charm.

THE BASICS

On the Old Town's narrow streets, plan to walk. To go from Lower to Upper Town, take the funicular or the Breakneck Staircase.

Fairmont Le Château Frontenac
1, rue des Carrières
418-692-3861
fairmont.com/frontenac
$$$
A classic grand hotel with 618 rooms and river views. Quebec's gold standard.

Auberge Saint-Antoine
8, rue St.-Antoine
418-692-2211
saint-antoine.com
$$
Built around a cannon fortification; displays artifacts like coins and cannonballs.

Hotel Le Germain Dominion
126, rue Saint-Pierre
418-692-2224
germaindominion.com
$$
An airy and modern break from fleurs-de-lis and polished wood.

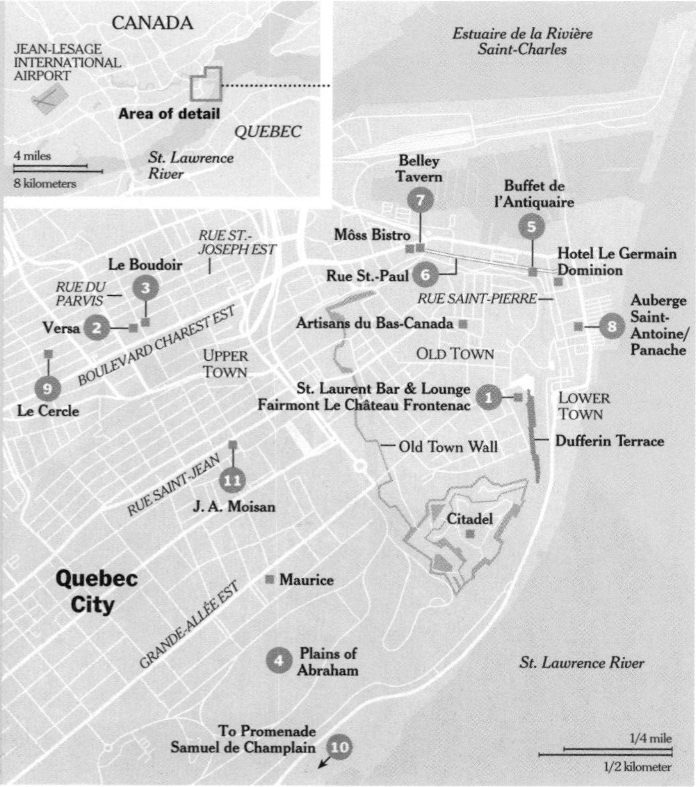

Charlevoix

The narrow, snaking roads of the Charlevoix region climb and descend past the muscular and majestic Laurentian Mountains on one side and the grand, slate-blue St. Lawrence River on the other. In between, lush, rolling valley floors are studded with saltbox and barn-style houses painted blue and gray and yellow, with neat white trim. Streams coming down from the mountains to meet the river rush through gorges and over cascades. Some 350 million years ago, a huge meteorite collided with this part of what is now eastern Canada and created the roughly 2,300 square miles of hilly terrain on which Charlevoix's 30,000 residents now live. The crater, filled and drained by various glaciers over the centuries, also developed what the locals call yellow soil, which is especially supportive of agriculture; hence Charlevoix's considerable reputation as a producer of quality vegetables and fruits, breads and beer, veal, foie gras, and cheese.
— BY JIM ATKINSON

FRIDAY

1 *The Widening River* 1 p.m.

Arrive in La Malbaie, the best town to use as your weekend focal point, in time for lunch at **Café Chez-Nous** (1075, rue Richelieu, La Malbaie; 418-665-3080; cafecheznous.com; $$), where the menu includes soups, salads, omelets, and veal skewers. You'll be coming in from the southwest, traveling downriver from Quebec City on Routes 138 and 362 along the north shore of the St. Lawrence. The river is already vast here — crossed by boats, not bridges — as it begins the great widening that transforms it eventually into the Gulf of St. Lawrence. Don't expect to rush through the next couple of days. Once here, every destination seems to be 20 or 30 miles away on winding two-lane roads often clogged with farm equipment. But that's to the traveler's advantage. Despite a long history as a summer retreat, Charlevoix still feels untrammeled and untrampled.

2 *A Walk in Town* 2 p.m.

The dominant presence in La Malbaie is a clifftop Fairmont hotel that looks like a medieval fortress and makes an excellent landmark. Walk away from it, heading north, down Richelieu Street for a look at the town's century-old houses and a few art galleries and shops. At the end of Richelieu Street, turn right on Comporte Street for a stroll on the riverfront walkway. Check out the pier, and find the **Musée de Charlevoix** (10, chemin du Havre; 418-665-4411; museedecharlevoix.qc.ca), a modern building with displays on the area's geology, history, and maritime heritage.

3 *Fortress With Spa* 5 p.m.

Spend the evening hours at the **Fairmont Le Manoir Richelieu** (181, rue Richelieu; 866-540-4464; fairmont.com/richelieu). You'll have no trouble entertaining yourself. In addition to its 400 luxury rooms, the hotel has a huge spa, a golf course, walking trails, three restaurants, a lobby bar, and a busy casino. As early as the 18th century, Scottish noblemen vacationed in this region, which was named for the Rev. François Xavier Charlevoix, a Jesuit explorer who was French Canada's first historian. By the early 20th century, La Malbaie had become a well-kept vacationing secret of the American upper crust, including a soon-to-be-president, William Howard Taft, who once commented that breathing Charlevoix air was like "drinking Champagne without the hangover." The original Manoir Richelieu

OPPOSITE Canoeing in the shadow of the mountains at Parc National des Hautes-Gorges-de-la-Riviére-Malbaie.

BELOW The Fairmont Le Manoir Richelieu, a testament to the Charlevoix region's long history as a getaway.

was built in 1899, burned in a fire, and was replaced by the present building in 1928. The region remained largely a playground for the rich until 1988, when Unesco designated it a protected biosphere reserve and eco-tourists began to show up.

SATURDAY

4 *Start with Cheese* 9 a.m.

Roam the so-called Flavour Trail (tourisme-charlevoix.com/en/circuits/flavor-trail), which links dozens of food producers spread over the pastoral valleys and meadows of Charlevoix farm country. Stop at will—especially in blueberry season in August, when you may see the berries offered in many spots along the road—and eat as you go. One interesting place right at the start is a modest shop called **Fromagerie St.-Fidèle** in La Malbaie (2815 Boulevard Malcolm Fraser; 418-434-2220; fromageriestfidele.net). The basic Cheddar here has a bright, cheerful taste, and the other samplings won't disappoint. A dozen or so patrons seem to be in line at all times.

5 *Next, Foie Gras* 10 a.m.

Proceed to the tiny town of St.-Urbain for **La Ferme Basque de Charlevoix** (813, rue St.-Èduoard; 418-639-2246; lafermebasque.ca), where foie gras and various pâtés are made according to Basque technique and tradition. Its duck liver pâté may be the earthiest you have ever tasted.

6 *Chocolate Finale* 11 a.m.

Find a change of pace at **Chocolaterie Cynthia** (66-3, rue Saint-Jean-Baptiste, Baie-St.-Paul; 418-240-2304; chocolateriecynthia.com), where, behind a modest storefront, you can feast on hot chocolate, blueberries, and chocolate in various combinations, and homemade ice cream dipped in 72 percent pure chocolate.

7 *Hike to the Heights* 1 p.m.

Do some serious hiking at one of the nearby national parks. **Parc National des Grands-Jardins** (sepaq.com/pq/grj), close to St.-Urbain and accessible from Route 381, is known for carpets of lichen on its rocky expanses and for fishing. More spectactacular is **Parc national des Haute-Gorges-de-la-Rivière-Malbaie** (High Gorges of the Malbaie River; 418-890-6527; sepaq.com/pq/hgo), about an hour's drive from La Malbaie and accessible from Route 138 via the village of Saint-Aimé-des-Lacs. Even in a short visit, you can experience this shiny, pristine place, with the clear Malbaie River meandering through deep, green gorges and thickly forested glens, all to the music of shifting, whistling winds and chirping birds. Walks are of varying lengths and degrees of difficulty, and a shuttle stops at trailheads. (Get directions from your hotel, and be sure the park is open; Haute-Gorges was closed for remedial work in 2014.)

8 *Fare to Remember* 8 p.m.

For a tour-de-force meal, make a reservation at **La Pinsonnière** (124, rue St.-Raphaël, La Malbaie; 418-665-4431; lapinsonniere.com; $$$$), the dining room of a luxury boutique hotel about 10 minutes from the center of La Malbaie in an area called Cap-à-l'Aigle. The French fare is expensive, but worth

ABOVE A riverboat cruise on the Malbaie River in Parc National des Hautes-Gorges-de-la-Riviére-Malbaie.

RIGHT Charlevoix's narrow, snaking roads climb and descend in rolling countryside between the Laurentian Mountains and the St. Lawrence River.

every penny. The three-course menu one evening included a salad of asparagus and pecorino cheese soaked in a homemade vinaigrette, with precisely calibrated tart and salty flavors, and a lamb tasting consisting of a medallion, a chop, and a shank, all rich and perfectly turned.

SUNDAY

9 *Whale Guarantee* 8 a.m.

Get up early to make the hour-and-a-half drive north along the St. Lawrence to Baie-Ste.-Catherine. There, a 10-minute ferry across the Saguenay River at its confluence with the St. Lawrence will take you to the tiny burg of **Tadoussac** and the small Zodiac boats of **Croisières AML** (866-856-6668; croisieresaml.com). Seven species of whales regularly plumb the depths, fed by saltwater, of the unusually deep Laurentian Channel (600 to 1,800 feet), which runs here from the gulf into the river. When one whale-watching tour captain promised "many whales," he was not exaggerating. The boat was suddenly surrounded by dozens of minke and fin whales — some 20 feet long — and populous harems of frolicking sea lions. The captain edged so close that the spray from the whales' blowholes tickled the passengers' faces.

ABOVE The shop at La Ferme Basque de Charlevoix, a duck and foie gras producer in St.-Urbain, is a stop on the Charlevoix Flavour Trail.

THE BASICS

The Charlevoix region is centered about 90 miles northeast of Quebec City.

La Pinsonnière
124, rue St.-Raphaël, La Malbaie
418-665-4431
lapinsonniere.com
$$$$
Boutique hotel overlooking the St. Lawrence.

Fairmont La Manoir Richelieu
181, rue Richelieu, La Malbaie
418-665-3703
fairmont.com/richelieu-charlevoix
$$$
Sprawling grand old resort hotel with beautiful views of the St. Lawrence River.

Auberge des Falaises
250 Chemin des Falaises, La Malbaie
418-665-3731
aubergedesfalaises.com
$$$
On a hillside above the river, with a pool and a tiny spa.

159230

Prince Edward Island

Prince Edward Island, Canada's smallest province, is a puffy green comforter of an island embroidered with flowers and farms and ribboned with empty roads, some of them still red clay. Nestled just above Nova Scotia in the Gulf of St. Lawrence, it is blessed with river flows and sandbars that warm its waters to 70 degrees and higher in July, a quirk of geography that makes its beaches more swimmable than most of New England's. For shellfish, this is paradise. Lobsters love it here, at least until they take a wrong turn on the ocean floor and end up in one of the countless traps you see at the ends of piers, by the sides of the roads, even on stoops. Clams and scallops flourish as well. But the biggest stars are the oysters, which go by designations or labels like Malpeque, Raspberry Point, and Colville Bay. A P.E.I. mussel is a brand with real clout in the world of gourmet cooks and restaurateurs.

— BY FRANK BRUNI AND JAMES LEDBETTER

FRIDAY

1 *Pick a Route* 1 p.m.

The eight-mile-long **Confederation Bridge**, the island's first link to the mainland, was not completed until 1997, and there are still only about 140,000 residents here, scattered over a clump of land 140 miles long. The quiet roads invite a drive. (Pick up maps at the tourist information center at the bridge, or find routes at tourismpei.com/pei-scenic-heritage-roads.) On the northern shore, just an hour's drive from the capital, Charlottetown, you stare out at what looks like infinity from a series of low-lying, red-soil cliffs with a peculiar, desolate beauty. Elsewhere there are dune-skirted beaches or forests of evergreens sloping to the water's edge.

2 *Follow the Piper* 3:30 p.m.

If you arrive before 3:30 p.m. in Summerside, west of Charlottetown, you can catch a summer mini-concert at a standout island academic institution, the **College of Piping and Celtic Performing Arts** (619 Water Street East, Summerside; 902-436-5377 or 877-Bag-PIPE; collegeofpiping.com). Affiliated with the College of Piping in Glasgow, Scotland, the school turns out specialists in Highland bagpiping, drumming, and step dancing, all much loved arts on this island. (As you watch this performance-in-plaid, you'll have no trouble guessing the ancestry of many Prince Edward Islanders.)

3 *Harbor Shopping* 5 p.m.

Stroll around **Old Charlottetown**, near the harbor. On Queen Street, exquisitely quaint shops inhabit many of the classic Victorian brick buildings. **Northern Watters Knitwear**, around a corner at 150 Richmond Street (902-566-5850; nwknitwear.com) makes and sells knitted clothing of fine British wool; this is the place to order a bespoke cardigan or a classic fisherman's sweater. **Moonsnail Soapworks** (85 Water Street; 902-771-7627; moonsnailsoapworks.com) has fine homemade soaps, some of which contain a bit of the famous red island clay. **Peakes Quay** (discovercharlottetown.com/en/see-do) is the place for waterfront restaurants and bars (some of which have live Celtic music into the evening), boat tours, and shops including the self-explanatory **Flip Flop Shop** (902-628-3526) and **Cow's** (Great George Street; 902-566-4886), a popular ice cream chain headquartered on the island.

4 *At the Source* 8 p.m.

Local seafood is a specialty at the **Claddagh Oyster House** (131 Sydney Street, Charlottetown;

OPPOSITE "Bucolic" is still the right word for Prince Edward Island, even though its beaches, warm ocean waters, and seafood bring savvy summer tourists.

BELOW Red-soil cliffs give the island's coastline a singular desolate beauty.

902-892-9661; claddaghoysterhouse.com; $$-$$$). Try the Oysters Rockefeller, with oysters from Malpeque Bay, or an Irish-inspired dish (this place and many others celebrate the Irish side of the island's heritage), like the prawns and scallops bathed in a mix of ingredients including Irish Mist.

SATURDAY

5 *Walking With the Foxes* 8 a.m.

Take a morning walk among the splendid, well-preserved dunes of **Prince Edward Island National Park** (902-672-6350; pc.gc.ca/eng/pn-np/pe/pei-ipe/visit.aspx), a half-hour drive from Charlottetown on the northern coast. Watch for the signature blue heron, and try not to trip over the stealthy red foxes that will dart across your path. To test the island's reputation for warm water, wade in at **Brackley Beach**.

6 *Lake View by the Sea* Noon

Without leaving the park, have a leisurely lunch at **Dalvay by the Sea** (902-672-2048; dalvaybythesea.com; $$), a gorgeous, stately Victorian house built in 1896 as the summer home of Alexander McDonald, a former president of Standard Oil of Kentucky, and now a resort hotel. You can sit outdoors on oversize wooden chairs overlooking one of the island's few freshwater lakes—don't worry about false advertising; the sea is close by, too. One lunch possibility is the restaurant's refined take on chowder, with scallops, haddock, lobster, and shrimp floating in a creamy broth.

BELOW Hauling in some of P.E.I.'s renowned oysters from Colville Bay.

OPPOSITE ABOVE A red fox at the national park.

OPPOSITE BELOW Countryside reminiscent of *Anne of Green Gables*, the classic children's book set on P.E.I.

7 *You Must Meet Anne* 2 p.m.

Prince Edward Island's reigning celebrity is fictional. She's Anne of Green Gables, the heroine of a series of children's books by Lucy Maud Montgomery, who made her home and set her stories here. Anne is to Prince Edward Island what Francis is to Assisi, or maybe what Mickey is to Orlando. Actually, she's a deeply revered, exhaustively merchandised combination of both. Souvenir shops hawk Anne bric-a-brac. An island theatrical production based on Anne's life story lays claim to being the longest-running musical in Canada. And a specially designated **Green Gables House** (Route 6, Cavendish; 902-963-7874; gov.pe.ca/greengables) is the island's most heavily promoted tourist destination, beloved in particular by travelers from Japan. Japanese couples have civil wedding ceremonies there, and Japanese girls have been known to show up with their hair dyed red and in pigtails, just like Anne's.

8 *Eat Your Lobster* 8 p.m.

Seafood is practically a religion on Prince Edward Island, and because the supply is fresh and essentially uniform, you can choose a restaurant by its view. **Lobster on the Wharf** (2 Prince Street, Charlottetown; 902-894-9311; lobsteronthewharf.com; $$) offers open-air tables facing the cozy harbor. The fish and chips are good, but it's hard to beat the specialty of the house.

SUNDAY

9 *Links and Bikes* 9 a.m.

A surprisingly high proportion of Prince Edward Island is taken up by golf courses, thanks to arable

soil and relatively flat topography. For a genuine challenge, try the **Links at Crowbush Cove** (Route 350, Lakeside; 800-377-8337;peisfinestgolf.com), widely considered one of the best courses in North America. The oceanside fairways make a breathtaking setting, but the winds off the Gulf of St. Lawrence have been known to add strokes on many of the holes. Not a golfer? Rent a bike and ride as much as you can of the **Confederation Trail** (tourismpei.com/pei-confederation-trail), which follows old railroad lines and will take you past enough rolling fields (most grow potatoes), hardwood forests, rivers, and charming villages to let you feel you've really gotten to know this island.

ABOVE Farms remain, but vacation homes with sea views are increasingly a part of the landscape.

OPPOSITE The dining room at the Johnson Shore Inn on the northern coast.

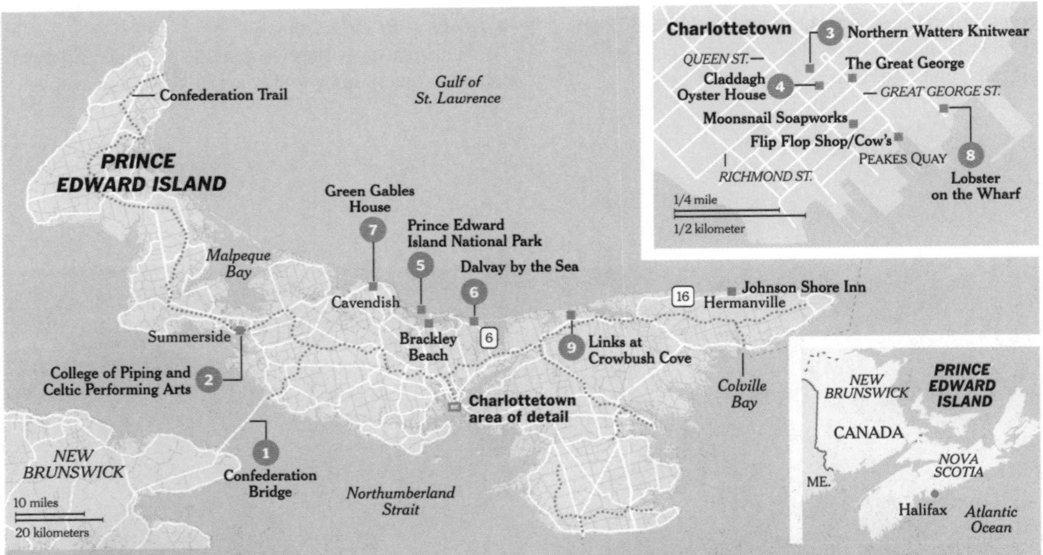

Confederation Trail
Gulf of St. Lawrence
PRINCE EDWARD ISLAND
Green Gables House 7
Prince Edward Island National Park 5
Dalvay by the Sea 6
Malpeque Bay
Cavendish
Summerside
Brackley Beach
6
Links at Crowbush Cove 9
16
Johnson Shore Inn
Hermanville
College of Piping and Celtic Performing Arts 2
Colville Bay
Charlottetown area of detail
1 Confederation Bridge
NEW BRUNSWICK
Northumberland Strait
10 miles
20 kilometers

Charlottetown
3 Northern Watters Knitwear
QUEEN ST.
The Great George
Claddagh Oyster House 4
GREAT GEORGE ST.
Moonsnail Soapworks
Flip Flop Shop/Cow's
PEAKES QUAY
RICHMOND ST.
8 Lobster on the Wharf
1/4 mile
1/2 kilometer

NEW BRUNSWICK
PRINCE EDWARD ISLAND
CANADA
NOVA SCOTIA
ME.
Halifax
Atlantic Ocean

THE BASICS

Fly in and rent a car, or drive across the Confederation Bridge from New Brunswick.

Dalvay by the Sea
Route 6, 16 Cottage Crescent
902-672-2048
dalvaybythesea.com
$$$
A 19th-century tycoon's lakefront mansion.

The Great George
58 Great George Street
Charlottetown
902-892-0606
thegreatgeorge.com
$$-$$$
Located in 17 small buildings in the city's quaint historic district.

Johnson Shore Inn
9984 Route 16, Hermanville
902-687-1340
johnsonshoreinn.com
$$
B&B on a spectacular perch atop red-soil cliffs.

The Bay of Fundy

At Fundy National Park in New Brunswick, the salty ocean air is laced with the scent of pine. The park's smooth lakes and quiet forests would be enough alone to make it one of Canada's favorites. But the real wonder here is a strange natural phenomenon: the sweeping tides of the Bay of Fundy. Residents around the bay say its tides are the highest in the world, and only a bay in far northern Quebec challenges the claim; the Canadian government diplomatically calls it a tie. Highest or not, the Fundy tides are extreme and dramatic, rising at their largest surge by 33 feet and leaving, when they recede, vast tidal flats ready for exploring. Tourists who drive north through New Brunswick on their way to Fundy will be struck by the forests stretching to the horizon and by the comfortable mix of French and English influences that has cashiers and waitresses calling out "Hello bonjour!"

— BY KAREN HOUPPERT

FRIDAY

1 *Park Central* 3 p.m.

The main attraction is **Fundy National Park** (506-887-6000; pc.gc.ca/eng/pn-np/nb/fundy/index.aspx), which covers about 50,000 acres and is laced with trails and sprinkled with campsites that make it a paradise for backpackers. Away from the hub of activity around the park headquarters (and not counting the surprising presence of a nine-hole golf course), there are few tourist services. Get your bearings at the **Visitor Reception Centre**, close to the southeastern park entrance near the gateway town of Alma. Pick up maps, find out about the interpretive programs for the weekend, and most important, check the tide tables.

2 *Fundy Fare* 6 p.m.

Drive into Alma for dinner (there's no dining in the park itself). You'll find lobster with a view at the **Tides Restaurant**, located in the **Parkland Village Inn** (8601 Main Street, Alma; 506-887-2313; parklandvillageinn.com; $$), where the dining room overlooks the bay. The choices run to the traditional and hearty, including steaks and various kinds of Atlantic seafood, good for packing it in at the start of an active weekend. Tables at the Tides can fill up fast, so take care to reserve in advance.

OPPOSITE AND RIGHT Fundy National Park's 68 miles of well-tended trails wind into forests and meadows, past waterfalls and beaver dams. Although spectacular tides, rising 33 feet, are the area's major attraction, the park is also prized for its inland natural beauty.

3 *Brushwork* 7 p.m.

Fundy's vast, muddy stretches of beach make for poor swimming, even at high tide. The water remains shallow for a quarter mile out to sea. The park does its best to compensate, offering visitors a swim in its heated salt-water pool overlooking the bay. But if the Bay of Fundy is not great for swimming, it is a sensuous delight. As evening approaches, stroll along the coastal paths to take it in. At dusk, as the fog rolls in, the hills and cliffs beyond the shore shimmer with the deep green of thousands of pines. The silky-smooth red clay of the tidal flat provides a rich saturation of complementary color. It's like stepping into a Van Gogh.

SATURDAY

4 *Sticky Fingers* 9 a.m.

You could go for the fresh home-baked bread or doughnuts, or come back at lunch for sandwiches and chili, but the star of the show at **Kelly's Bake Shop**

(8587 Main Street, Alma; 506-887-2460) is the sticky bun. Locally renowned and alluring for tourists, the buns keep customers lined up at Kelly's, which sells as many as 3,000 of them on a busy day. They're sweet, flavorful, and enormous. Don't expect to eat more than one.

5 *Reset the Clock* 9:30 a.m.

Venture to one of Alma's two small general stores to pick up provisions for later. Then consult your new clock, the lunar version that announces itself in the Fundy tides. It's important to be at the beach when the mud flats are exposed — that's the experience that draws people here. So plan your day accordingly — not by the numbers on your watch or cellphone, but by the water's flow.

6 *Out to Sea* Low Tide

At low tide the vast intertidal zone is otherworldly: endless red muddy flats, shallow pools, and sporadic, massive barnacle-covered boulders that appear to have been randomly dropped into the muddy flatness from an alien spaceship. Beachcombers can walk along the exposed ocean floor, hunting for shells and bits of sea-smoothed glass, for more than half a mile before they reach the water's edge. The impulse to scoop up the clay underfoot and squeeze it through your fingers is hard to suppress. While grown-up travelers seem to enjoy the delightful respite the wet clay of the bare ocean floor provides to tired feet after a hard day of hiking, kids have been known to do full body rolls in the squishy muck. The spot where you're standing will probably be under water again before long, but there's no need to fear. The tide's return is gradual, progressive, and orderly — very Canadian — and nicely nudges you back shoreward with small, gentle, very cold waves.

7 *Into the Woods* High Tide

When the water claims the beach, go hiking. The park's 68 miles of well-tended trails wind deep into forests and flower-strewn meadows, past waterfalls and beaver dams, and even to a covered bridge. By the standards of many busier parks, it is blissfully quiet. Even in August, the prime season, it is possible for hikers to trek the 2.8-mile **Mathews Head** trail along the park's rocky southern shore and not pass a single person. The path offers teasing ocean views from atop red-clay cliffs that drop to the sea. Amid the solitude is a silence so pervasive that even children grow pensive at the wonder of these headlands, which feel like the end of the earth.

8 *Shell and Claw* 7 p.m.

Do as the locals do and find a table at the **Harbour View Market & Restaurant** (8598 Main Street, Alma; 506-887-2450; $). You can get your daily ration of shellfish — in the seafood chowder or a lobster roll — and perhaps pick up some local gossip at the same time.

9 *Nature Theater* 8 p.m.

Don't look for rangers at Fundy National Park — here they are interpreters. The staff is serious about the job of making Fundy accessible, and in summer there is a program almost every night at the **Outdoor Theatre**. You may learn about the wildlife, from moose and bears to flying squirrels. You may hear about the rivers that wash kayakers upstream when the tide comes in, the whales and migratory

birds that thrive offshore, or the area's history—this is Acadia, where French and English cultures clashed and mingled. Expect a multimedia experience, with video, music, comedy, or even drama.

SUNDAY

10 *Water Power* 10 a.m.

For an appropriate last stop, drive about 25 miles north of Alma to Hopewell Cape, where the bay shore is littered with eroded sea stacks known as the **Flowerpot Rocks**. See them from a clifftop trail, and if it's low tide inspect them close up, at the **Hopewell Rocks Ocean Tidal Exploration Site** (Highway 114; 877-734-3429; thehopewellrocks.ca). Resembling pillars or top-heavy mushrooms, some with trees growing on their tops, the rocks are part of a rugged shoreline of caves, tunnels, and misshapen crags, all of it a testament to the relentless force of the water constantly tugged back and forth against the shore by the Fundy tides.

OPPOSITE ABOVE The world's highest tides (officially tied with those in a more remote Quebec bay) flow out to leave vast flats for exploring.

OPPOSITE BELOW Matthews Head, a high rocky headland on the Fundy coast.

ABOVE A sunrise over Owl's Head, seen from Alma Beach in Fundy National Park.

THE BASICS

Fundy National Park is a drive of three hours from the Maine-New Brunswick border and an hour and a half from the airport in Moncton, New Brunswick.

Fundy Highlands Motel and Chalets
8714 Route 114
506-887-2930
fundyhighlandchalets.com
$$
Motel rooms and colorful cabins within Fundy National Park.

Falcon Ridge Inn
24 Falcon Ridge Drive, Alma
506-887-1110
falconridgeinn.nb.ca
$$
B&B with bay views.

Cliffside Suites and Cottage
22 Bayview Drive, Alma
506-887-1022
cliffsidesuites.com
$$
Minutes from the park.

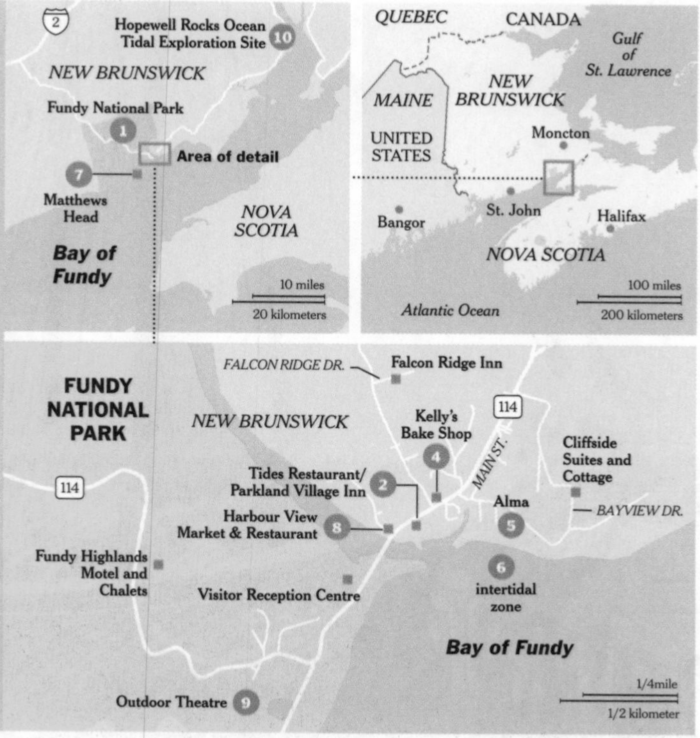

2
Hopewell Rocks Ocean Tidal Exploration Site 10
NEW BRUNSWICK
Fundy National Park 1
Area of detail
7 Matthews Head
NOVA SCOTIA
Bay of Fundy
10 miles
20 kilometers

QUEBEC
CANADA
Gulf of St. Lawrence
NEW BRUNSWICK
MAINE
UNITED STATES
Moncton
Bangor
St. John
Halifax
NOVA SCOTIA
Atlantic Ocean
100 miles
200 kilometers

FUNDY NATIONAL PARK
NEW BRUNSWICK
FALCON RIDGE DR.
Falcon Ridge Inn
114
Kelly's Bake Shop 4
MAIN ST.
Cliffside Suites and Cottage
Tides Restaurant/ Parkland Village Inn 2
Alma 5
BAYVIEW DR.
Harbour View Market & Restaurant 8
Fundy Highlands Motel and Chalets
Visitor Reception Centre
6 intertidal zone
Bay of Fundy
Outdoor Theatre 9
1/4mile
1/2 kilometer

Halifax

Halifax, Nova Scotia, is a harbor city steeped in maritime history. Founded in 1749 as a British naval and military base, it served originally as a strategic counter to French bases elsewhere in Atlantic Canada, and many years later as an assembly point for shipping convoys during World Wars I and II. Today, Halifax is better known for its lobster, which you can fill up on from morning (lobster eggs Benedict anyone?) till night while still having enough cash left for a sail around the harbor on a tall ship. A vibrant student population—the city has six universities—gives Halifax a youthful, bohemian feel, too. As a result, it's often compared to that other hilly town on the ocean, San Francisco, but you'll find that Halifax's blend of fair-trade coffee bars, wharfside lobster shacks, and public gardens has a character all its own. —BY TATIANA BONCOMPAGNI

FRIDAY

1 *A Pint and a Pirate Joke* 5 p.m.

Start the weekend right at the **Alexander Keith's Nova Scotia Brewery** (1496 Lower Water Street; 902-455-1474; keiths.ca). Take the 55-minute tour led by local actors in 19th-century garb, and you'll get not only a primer on the history of Halifax's oldest working brewery—it dates back to the 1820s—but a pint of its finest as well. Find a comfy bench in the brewery's Stag's Head Tavern, where barkeepers have been known to regale the crowd with old pirate jokes and barmaids have burst into song.

2 *Bard of Nova Scotia* 7 p.m.

Shakespeare is so much better in the grass, methinks. Grab a blanket and some cushions and head to **Point Pleasant Park** (Queen Victoria leased it to Halifax around the mid-19th century for one shilling a year, which the city still pays), where the **Shakespeare by the Sea Theater Society** (902-422-0295; shakespearebythesea.ca) stages the Bard's plays. The park overlooks the entrance to Halifax Harbor, so enjoy the sublime views, then arrive for the performance 10 minutes before show time and stake your claim in the grass. A donation is encouraged.

3 *Dinner at the Shoe Shop* 10 p.m.

For a late meal, a sophisticated spot is the **Economy Shoe Shop** (1663 Argyle Street; 902-423-8845; bigmikebass.site90.com/economyshoeshop/; $-$$), a cafe and bar that takes its name from a salvaged neon sign hanging from the side of its building. Honor Haligonian tradition by ordering seafood chowder.

SATURDAY

4 *Breakfast on the Commons* 9 a.m.

In the 18th century, town authorities set aside more than 200 acres for community cattle grazing and military use. The part that remains, called the Commons, is a municipal complex of sports fields and playgrounds—a great place for a morning jog. And for those who would rather stroll a bit and then slip into the day more gently, there's brunch nearby at the **Coastal** (2731 Robie Street; 902-405-4022; thecoastal.ca; $$), where just reading the menu can keep you entertained. Selections include Breakfast of Champignons (eggs with asparagus, mushrooms, tapenade, and other fixings); Frooty Looops (a bagel with berries, yogurt, and almond hemp seed granola); and the Elvis (a waffle sandwich with peanut butter, bananas, and bacon).

5 *Antiquing on Agricola* 10:30 a.m.

If you're in the market for well-priced antiques or reproductions, make sure you hit Agricola Street,

OPPOSITE The *Bluenose II*, a replica of the schooner on the back of the Canadian dime, docked on the waterfront.

RIGHT Firing the noon-day gun at Halifax Citadel.

where a handful of the city's best dealers have set up shop. At **McLellan Antiques & Restoration** (2738 Agricola Street; 902-455-4545; mclellanantiques.com), you'll find furniture including bureaus and cupboards, early pine pieces, and 1920s mahogany. **Finer Things Antiques** (2797 Agricola Street; 902-456-1412; finerthingsantiques.com) is the place to go for nautical antiques like old ship's wheels and compasses. For more eclectic shopping (and to pick up a snack for an on-the-go lunch), hike down to the harbor to the **Halifax Seaport Farmers' Market** (1209 Marginal Road; 902-429-6256; halifaxfarmersmarket.com), established in 1750 and now operating in a 56,000-square-foot market hall that opened in 2010.

6 *Sail On* 1 p.m.

You haven't really seen Halifax until you take a tour around its harbor — considered the second-largest natural harbor anywhere, after Sydney's — in one of the tall ships that dock along the wharf. Sail aboard the ***Silva*** (877-429-9463; tallshipsilva.com) or the ***Mar II*** (902-420-1015; mtcw.ca), and dress warmly; it can get cold on deck. You may also have another option: the ***Bluenose II*** (1675 Lower Water Street, 902-634-1963; halifaxkiosk.com/Bluenose-II.php), which sometimes sails here. It's a replica of the schooner that is engraved on the Canadian dime, an honor it earned by collecting racing trophies in the 1920s and '30s. Its home port is Lunenburg, about 60 miles away, but it travels the New England and Maritime provinces coasts.

7 *Remembrance* 4 p.m.

Halifax's role as a busy port city, sometimes complicated by the North Atlantic's infamous fog, has cursed it with a legacy of shipwrecks and catastrophe. The **Maritime Museum of the Atlantic** (1675 Lower Water Street; 902-424-7490; museum.gov.ns.ca/mma) has moving displays of artifacts from voyages gone wrong. One commemorates the disaster most horrific for Halifax. It happened in 1917, when a French ship loaded with explosives collided in the harbor with a Belgian relief ship, resulting in a blast that killed nearly 2,000 people, injured thousands more, and obliterated the north end of the city. The museum also displays an incredibly well-preserved deck chair from the *Titanic*, which sank off the Grand Banks (the famous fishing grounds northeast of here) in 1912. Of the 328 bodies recovered from the *Titanic*, 150 are buried in Halifax.

8 *Menu Study* 8 p.m.

Make your way to the neighborhood of Dalhousie University's downtown Sexton campus for dinner at **Chives Canadian Bistro** (1537 Barrington Street; 902-420-9626; chives.ca/about; $$$). Its imaginative dishes are made with local and seasonal ingredients,

ABOVE The view down to the harbor from Citadel Hill.

so selections change. Scan the menu for entrees like Lamb Mykonos or caramelized sea scallops with pork belly, spinach-and-ricotta ravioli, and mustard crème fraîche.

SUNDAY

9 *The Citadel* 11 a.m.

The best views in the city can be had from the **Halifax Citadel** (5425 Sackville Street; 902-426-5080; pc.gc.ca/lhn-nhs/ns/halifax/index.aspx), a star-shaped fort built on its highest hill. The British built four forts atop the summit, the last of which was completed in 1856, when the United States posed the greatest threat to the harbor and city. Be sure to get there in time for the "noon-day gun" firing of the cannon. Afterward watch pipers and drummers perform in the enormous gravel courtyard.

ABOVE Homage to the original brewmaster at Alexander Keith's Nova Scotia Brewery.

10 *Last Call for Lobster* 1 p.m.

It wouldn't be right to leave without a taste of sweet Nova Scotia lobster. Snag an umbrella-shaded outdoor table at **Salty's** (1869 Upper Water Street; 902-423-6818; saltys.ca; $$-$$$). Go for a steamed one-and-a-half-pounder and a side of hot sweet-potato fries, and you won't be hungry on the plane going home.

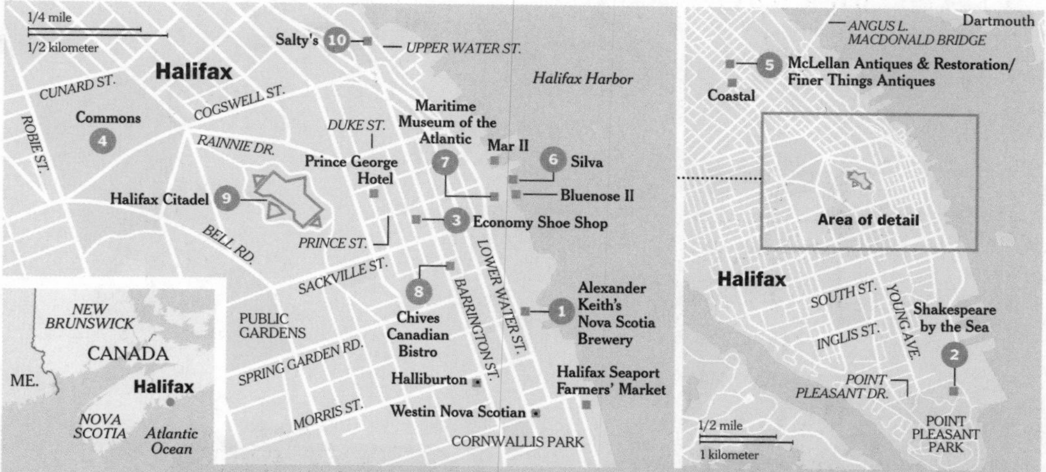

1/4 mile
1/2 kilometer
Halifax
Salty's 10
UPPER WATER ST.
Halifax Harbor
CUNARD ST.
COGSWELL ST.
ROBIE ST.
Commons 4
RAINNIE DR.
DUKE ST.
Maritime Museum of the Atlantic
Mar II
6 Silva
Prince George Hotel
7
Bluenose II
Halifax Citadel 9
3 Economy Shoe Shop
BELL RD.
PRINCE ST.
LOWER WATER ST.
SACKVILLE ST.
8
BARRINGTON ST.
Alexander Keith's Nova Scotia Brewery 1
NEW BRUNSWICK
CANADA
ME.
Halifax
NOVA SCOTIA
Atlantic Ocean
PUBLIC GARDENS
Chives Canadian Bistro
SPRING GARDEN RD.
Halliburton
Halifax Seaport Farmers' Market
MORRIS ST.
Westin Nova Scotian
CORNWALLIS PARK
ANGUS L. MACDONALD BRIDGE
Dartmouth
5 McLellan Antiques & Restoration/ Finer Things Antiques
Coastal
Area of detail
Halifax
SOUTH ST.
YOUNG AVE.
INGLIS ST.
Shakespeare by the Sea 2
POINT PLEASANT DR.
POINT PLEASANT PARK
1/2 mile
1 kilometer

THE BASICS

Fly into Halifax International Airport. Cabs and walking will work, but a car offers more options.

Westin Nova Scotian
1181 Hollis Street
902-421-1000
thewestinnovascotian.com
$$-$$$
Historic hotel, once the site of an official dinner held by Princess Diana.

The Halliburton
5184 Morris Street
902-420-0658
www.thehalliburton.com
$$
A boutique hotel in the heart of the city.

Prince George Hotel
1725 Market Street
902-425-1986
princegeorgehotel.com
$$$
Well-appointed downtown hotel.

Louisville 288

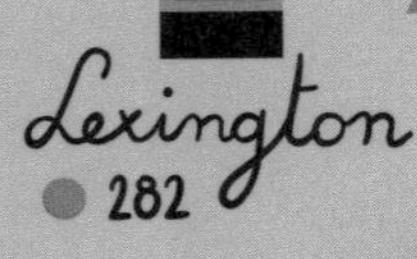

Lexington 282

NASHVILLE 292

KNOXVILLE 276

ASHEVILL 272

298 MEMPHIS

26

306 Birmingham

JACKSON 302

310 Montgomery

314

NEW Orleans

SOUTHEAST

harlottesville
208

192
WASHINGTON D.C.

BALTIMORE
198
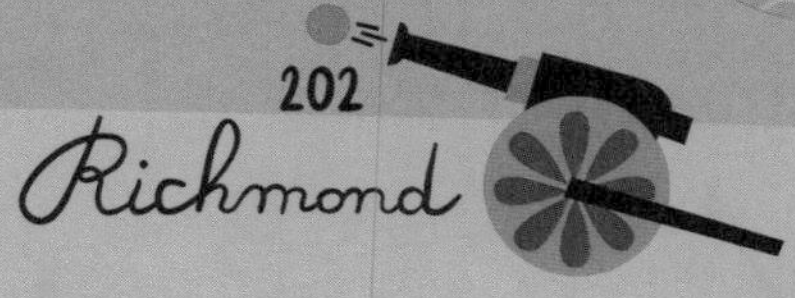
202
Richmond
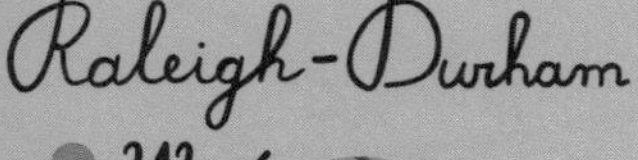
Raleigh-Durham
212

LANTA

charleston
216

SAVANNAH 220

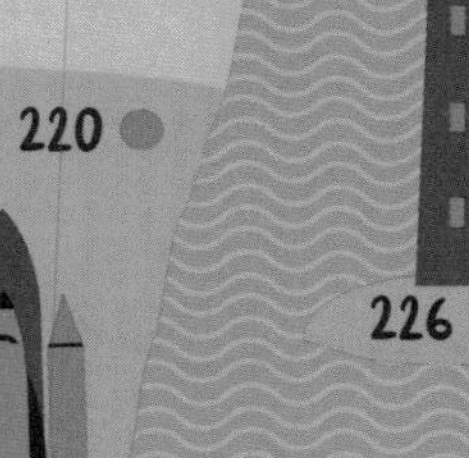

St. Simons
Island
226

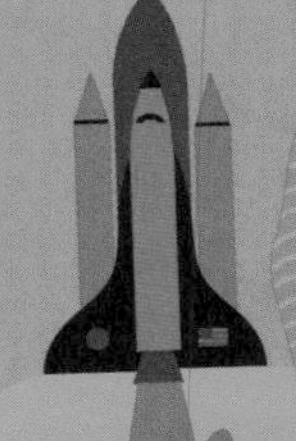

CAPE
Canaveral
236
ORLANDO
230

Sarasota
262

244
Fort
Lauderdale
South
Beach
248

Palm Beach 240
MIAMI

258
KEY WEST

254
the Everglades

Washington D.C.

The familiar monuments, symbols, and sites of Washington are American icons no visitor should miss. But there are times on a Washington weekend when it's best to leave the imperial city and spend some time with the people who live here full time. They're not all politicians, but a Washingtonian without some political connection can be hard to find. So stay alert. Someone may be trading insider gossip at the next restaurant table. — BY HELENE COOPER

FRIDAY

1 *House Party* 6 p.m.

Hobnob with the Beltway crowd at **Eighteenth Street Lounge** (1212 18th Street NW; 202-466-3922; eighteenthstreetlounge.com). Enter through the door next to the Mattress Discounters—there's no sign outside—take the stairs, and voila! A multilevel row house, with room after room of velvet couches and fireplaces, awaits you. There's a back deck for spring and summer after-work cocktails, and the crowd is a mix of political activists and Middle Eastern and European World Bank types.

2 *Eat like Oprah* 8 p.m.

Take a taxi to **Capitol Hill**, to **Art and Soul Restaurant** in the Liaison Hotel (415 New Jersey Avenue NW; 202-393-7777; artandsouldc.com; $$$). Oprah Winfrey's former chef, Art Smith, owns this restaurant, and it does a big business in D.C. parties. Yes, you've already had a cocktail, but you're not driving, so be sure to try the margarita at the bar before sitting down to eat. The menu will remind you that Washington is a Southern city. Sprinkled among the more usual listings, like seared ahi tuna and arugula salad, you'll see preparations like "country fried" and "red-eye" and foods like ribs, okra, watermelon pickles, and collard greens. Not to mention fried green tomatoes.

3 *Freedom Walk* 10 p.m.

With luck, no one in your party wore the five-inch Prada heels tonight, because you're about to walk off that pork chop as you head down the National Mall. Your destination is the **Lincoln Memorial** (nps.gov/linc), with ole Abe backlit at night. Washington's monument row is always best viewed at night, when the tourists are gone and the romantics are strolling arm in arm. The Lincoln Memorial, long the first destination for African-American visitors to Washington, has often been an emotionally charged spot: think of Marian Anderson's concert in 1939, Martin Luther King's "I Have a Dream" speech, and Election Night 2008, when Illinois learned it was sending another of its sons to Washington. In quieter times it is almost a retreat, as residents and visitors alike come to read the inscription "With malice toward none, with charity for all" and to ponder America the Beautiful.

SATURDAY

4 *Morning Sit-in* 9 a.m.

Breakfast at **Florida Avenue Grill** (1100 Florida Avenue NW; 202-265-1586; floridaavenuegrill.com; $), a soul food institution, is a dip into the past, evoking the feel of lunch counter sit-ins and the civil rights movement. The place has been serving greasy and delicious Southern cooking since 1944. Buttery grits,

OPPOSITE Inside the Capitol Hill Visitor Center, where guests can see the Capitol Dome peering through a large glass ceiling.

BELOW The Lincoln Memorial at night.

Virginia ham, biscuits and gravy, even scrapple — all surrounded by photos of past Washington bigwigs as various as Ron Brown, the former commerce secretary, and Strom Thurmond, the former South Carolina senator.

5 *1600 Pennsylvania* 10 a.m.

We know. It's the ultimate in touristy. But come on, it's the **White House** (1600 Pennsylvania Avenue; 202-456-7041; whitehouse.gov). To schedule a public tour, first you'll need to find nine friends to come with you. Then call your Congressional representative to schedule. (Foreign nationals must try months in advance to schedule tours through the United States embassies in their home countries.) These self-guided tours — which are allotted on a first-come-first-served basis about one month before the requested date — allow you to explore the public rooms and the gardens. You will get to see the East Room, the Diplomatic Reception Room, and the dining room where they have those swanky state dinners.

6 *Hello, Betsy* Noon

No, not that Betsy... there are no star-spangled banners at **Betsy Fisher** (1224 Connecticut Avenue NW; 202-785-1975; betsyfisher.com). This stylish and

ABOVE Ben's Chili Bowl on U Street Northwest, popular by day and an institution late at night.

BELOW The chorus at St. Augustine Roman Catholic Church at 15th and V Streets Northwest, one of the oldest black Catholic churches in the country.

OPPOSITE A view of the Capitol from down the Mall.

funky boutique is port of call for those well-dressed deputies in the White House. The owner, Betsy Fisher Albaugh, always has cocktails and wine on hand to occupy the men who invariably are dragged into the store.

7 *Go Represent* 2 p.m.

It took six years to complete, but the **U.S. Capitol Visitor Center** (Capitol Hill, at the east end of the Mall; 202-225-6827; visitthecapitol.gov) finally opened at the end of 2007. The subterranean center is meant to relieve the bottleneck that used to serve as the entryway for visitors to the Capitol. It does that and more, although some critics say it assumes a life of its own that is too separate from the Capitol itself. See for yourself—you can book a tour via the Web site, or just show up and wander around. The center has a rotating display of historic documents that can range from a ceremonial copy of the 13th Amendment, abolishing slavery, to the speech President George W. Bush delivered to Congress after the Sept. 11 attacks.

8 *Political Dish* 7 p.m.

O.K., enough with the federal touring, it's time to hang out with the real Washingtonians. Head to the always hopping **U Street Corridor**, and plop yourself on a stool at **Local 16** (1602 U Street NW; 202-265-2828; localsixteen.com). There are multiple lounges and, best of all, a roof deck where you can see the city lights while you sip your pre-dinner watermelon martini. Have dinner a few blocks away at **Cork Wine Bar** (1720 14th Street NW; 202-265-2675; corkdc.com; $$), which might have the best fries in town. The menu includes both small and big bites, from marinated olives and cheeses to duck confit and sautéed kale. And for goodness' sake, don't forget those fries! They are tossed with garlic, lemon, and parsley. In fact, order two helpings.

9 *Smoke-filled Room* 10:30 p.m.

Puff away the rest of your evening at **Chi-Cha** (1624 U Street NW; 202-234-8400; latinconcepts.com/chicha.php), a hookah lounge where you can smoke honey tobacco out of a water pipe and sip late-night cocktails. The eclectic crowd dances to rumba and slow salsa into the wee hours, and there's always a diplomat in a corner couch doing something inappropriate—avert your eyes, enjoy your hookah, and sway to the beat. You could be in Beirut. O.K., let's try that one again. You could be in Marrakesh. Well, maybe Marrakesh with Brazilian music. If you want to keep the night going, stop by **Ben's Chili Bowl** (1213 U Street NW; 202-667-0909; benschilibowl.com), a Washington institution so established that even then-French President Nicolas Sarkozy has stopped by for the Chili Half-Smoke hot dogs. He went at noon, but Ben's is busiest in the wee hours.

SUNDAY

10 *River Idyll* 8 a.m.

Washington is known for beautiful mornings along the Potomac River, especially on the water. **Thompson Boat Center** (2900 Virginia Avenue NW; 202-333-9543; thompsonboatcenter.com), just where Georgetown meets Rock Creek Parkway, offers canoe rentals. Paddle up the river, and you might catch a senator (or a Saudi prince) having coffee on the patio of a stately home.

11 *Lift Your Voice* 12:30 p.m.

St. Augustine Roman Catholic Church (1419 V Street NW; 202-265-1470; saintaugustine-dc.org), which calls itself "the Mother Church of Black Catholics in the United States" is one of the oldest black Catholic churches in the country. The 12:30 Sunday Mass combines traditional black spirituals with gospel music.

ABOVE Outside a fence and looking in at the White House, which is off-limits to walk-ins. Tours are allowed, but they must be requested — preferably well in advance — through a member of Congress or a foreign embassy.

OPPOSITE The Capitol as seen through a window at the Library of Congress.

THE BASICS

Washington's two airports are well served by an array of airlines. The subway, usually called the Metro, has many convenient stops.

Hotel Monaco
700 F Street NW
202-628-7177
monaco-dc.com
$$$-$$$$
A Kimpton hotel in the Penn Quarter neighborhood across from the National Portrait Gallery and near the International Spy Museum.

Hotel Palomar
2121 P Street NW
202-448-1800
hotelpalomar-dc.com
$$$-$$$$
Another Kimpton boutique hotel, in the heart of Dupont Circle.

Hotel Tabard Inn
1739 N Street NW
202-785-1277
tabardinn.com
$$
A budget alternative filled with charm. Some rooms share baths.

PAY
HERE
50%
Green Power
Cafe Hon
HON
Burger
Night
1/2 Price
Cafe Hon

Baltimore

"You can look far and wide, but you'll never discover a stranger city with such extreme style," John Waters once noted about his hometown. Maybe that's why Baltimore's trumpeted glass-and-steel Inner Harbor development, with its chain restaurants, neon-loud amusements, and brand-name shopping, feels so counterintuitive as a symbol for the city. But walk in any direction, and the city's charm reasserts itself. Indeed, Baltimore's best draws tend to be left-of-center: offbeat theater, grandly decrepit neighborhoods on the cusp of gentrification, a world-class museum devoted to outsider art, and a dive-bar culture that must be one of the nation's finest. —BY CHARLY WILDER

FRIDAY

1 *Divine Inspiration* 3 p.m.

There may be no better introduction to Baltimore than the extraordinary **American Visionary Art Museum** (800 Key Highway; 410-244-1900; avam.org), or AVAM, which is devoted to the work of self-taught and outsider artists. AVAM's collection ranges in scale and tenor from a 10-foot mirror-plated sculpture of the drag icon Divine to *Recovery*, a moving self-portrait of an anonymous British mental patient that was carved from an apple tree trunk before he committed suicide in his 30s.

2 *Crab Happy* 7 p.m.

Call it the great democratizer: it's hard to find a Baltimorean who doesn't enjoy wielding the mallet. **L.P. Steamers** (1100 East Fort Avenue; 410-576-9294; lpsteamers.com; $$) is a purist's crab house. Its waiters dump buckets of fresh-caught Old Bay-coated steamed crab onto brown paper for diners to whack, smash, pry, shuck, and suck out the tender white meat. For two people, a dozen mediums, and a pitcher of Baltimore's signature swill, National Bohemian a.k.a. Natty Boh, should do the trick. Snag a table on the restaurant's upper deck and watch the sun set over one of Baltimore's best views.

OPPOSITE "The Avenue" in Hampden, whose pink flamingoes, beehived ladies, and classic cars were made famous through the films of John Waters.

RIGHT The Inner Harbor, where recreation reigns.

3 *Arts and Drafts* 10 p.m.

Several arts districts have popped up in Baltimore in the past decade. The most successful has been **Station North** (www.stationnorth.org), the downtown area inhabited by artists, actors, and students (and dropouts) from the nearby Maryland Institute College of Art and University of Baltimore. You can see an art show, hear local sounds, or catch a screening at the **Metro Gallery** (1700 North Charles Street; 410-244-0899; themetrogallery.net) or the **Windup Space** (12 West North Avenue; 410-244-8855; thewindupspace.com). Yet when it comes to night life, what Baltimore does best is the dive bar. There may be none better than **Club Charles** (1724 North Charles Street; clubcharles.us; 410-727-8815), a grimy, kitschy little joint with a masterful jukebox and regulars like the electro-pop ringleader Dan Deacon.

SATURDAY

4 *Greasy Spoon* 9 a.m.

Grab breakfast at **Pete's Grille** (3130 Greenmount Avenue; 410-467-7698; $), a grits-and-grease diner in a rundown neighborhood dotted with liquor stores, Chinese takeout joints, and the occasional boarded-up row house. At the counter, cops, dockworkers, students, and professionals sidle up, while career waitresses trade barbs with regulars (the Olympian Michael Phelps sometimes among them) and sling plates of fried eggs, home fries, and blueberry pancakes touted as the best in town.

5 *Beside the Point* 11 a.m.

The more artistically minded can walk breakfast off with a trip to **Normals** (425 East 31st Street; 410-243-6888; normals.com), a trove of used records and books. From there, head to **Fell's Point**, a historic waterfront neighborhood that has transformed over the years from salty fisherman's quarter to touristy night-life district. Skip the collegey bar scene along cobblestoned Thames Street, and appreciate the area's daytime incarnation as an emerging hub for boutique shopping. Shops include the midscale designer clothing store **Babe** (1716 Aliceanna Street; 410-244-5114; babeaboutique.com); **Poppy and Stella** (728 South Broadway; 410-522-1970; poppyandstella.com), a girlie emporium of accessories and shoes; and **Katwalk Boutique** (1709 Aliceanna Street; 410-669-0600), a cultish clothing boutique.

6 *Patrician Beans* 1 p.m.

Board the free shuttle bus that began service in 2010 under the jocular title Charm City Circulator and get off in Mount Vernon, an area filled with leafy blocks of 19th-century row houses. Stroll around the original Washington Monument, completed in 1829 when the neighborhood was home to the city's most fashionable families. The Mount Vernon Place Conservancy (mvpconservancy.org) oversees the monument and organizes free concerts, screenings, and other events in the square. For a snack, stop at locavore hangout **Milk & Honey Market** (816 Cathedral Street; 410-685-6455; milkandhoneybaltimore.com; $), an organic cafe, deli, and food shop.

7 *Art Hopping* 3 p.m.

Go west to see works by some of Baltimore's best emerging art-makers. A 117-acre swath of downtown's west side is a state-designated arts district. The gallery **sophiajacob** (510 West Franklin Street; sophiajacob.com) has been host to works by the Baltimore artists Christopher LaVoie and Zach Storm and the curatorial project Szechuan Best, which transformed the white-walled gallery into the office of a travel agency catering to vampires. The **Bromo Seltzer Arts Tower** (21 South Eutaw Street; 443-874-3596; bromoseltzertower.com), the tallest building in the city when it went up in 1911, has been converted to artist studios that open to the public one Saturday a month, usually the first. Call ahead and pay a visit to **Nudashank** (405 West Franklin Street; 443-415-2139; nudashank.com), an independent artist-run space that provides not only a platform but also a home to many of the city's creative vanguard.

8 *Exotic Meats* 6 p.m.

The northwest neighborhood of **Hampden**, traditionally working-class, is now shared by its original demographic and a younger, arty set that began to settle here in the '90s Hampden's quirky boutique-lined main drag, a part of 36th Street called "The Avenue," is packed with galleries and shops selling vintage clothing, books, and eccentric home décor. This is also where you'll see 20-somethings in jeans and T-shirts sharing cigarettes with "Hons," the brassy women with 10-ton beehive hairdos and cat's-eye glasses who are now deified as Hampden's central characters. (They're celebrated every June in Baltimore's "Honfest.") More recently, there's been a restaurant boom on West 36th Street. **Corner BYOB** (850 West 36th Street; 443-869-5075; cornerbyob.com; $$), a bistro under the stewardship of the eccentric Belgian-born chef Bernard Dehaene, offers a changing menu featuring refined European peasant food — coq au riesling and Ghent-style waterzooi — and dabbles in exotic beasts like kangaroo.

9 *Stage Women* 8 p.m.

Catch a show at the **Strand Theater** (1823 North Charles Street; 443-874-4917; strand-theater.org), a 55-seat space in the Station North district that is a platform for female directors, writers, performers, and designers. The Strand made headlines when Rain Pryor, daughter of the comedian Richard Pryor, became its artistic director.

SUNDAY

10 *Comfort Brunch* 11 a.m.

Yet another neighborhood to undergo renewal is **Hamilton**, a northeastern area with bakeries, coffee shops, and restaurants opening along once-depressed Harford Road. Slide into a repurposed pew at retro-rustic **Clementine** (5402 Harford Road; 410-444-1497; bmoreclementine.com; $$) for chipped beef with biscuits or an "Elvis Special," waffle with pecans, bacon, banana, and Nutella whipped cream. Nearby, one of the owners has opened a deli and corner store with farm-to-table leanings, the **Green Onion Market** (5500 Harford Road; 410-444-1718; greenonionmarket.blogspot.com).

OPPOSITE ABOVE A Dalton Ghetti pencil-tip sculpture at the American Visionary Art Museum.

OPPOSITE BELOW Night life at the Windup Space, which hosts screenings and art shows as well as music and dancing.

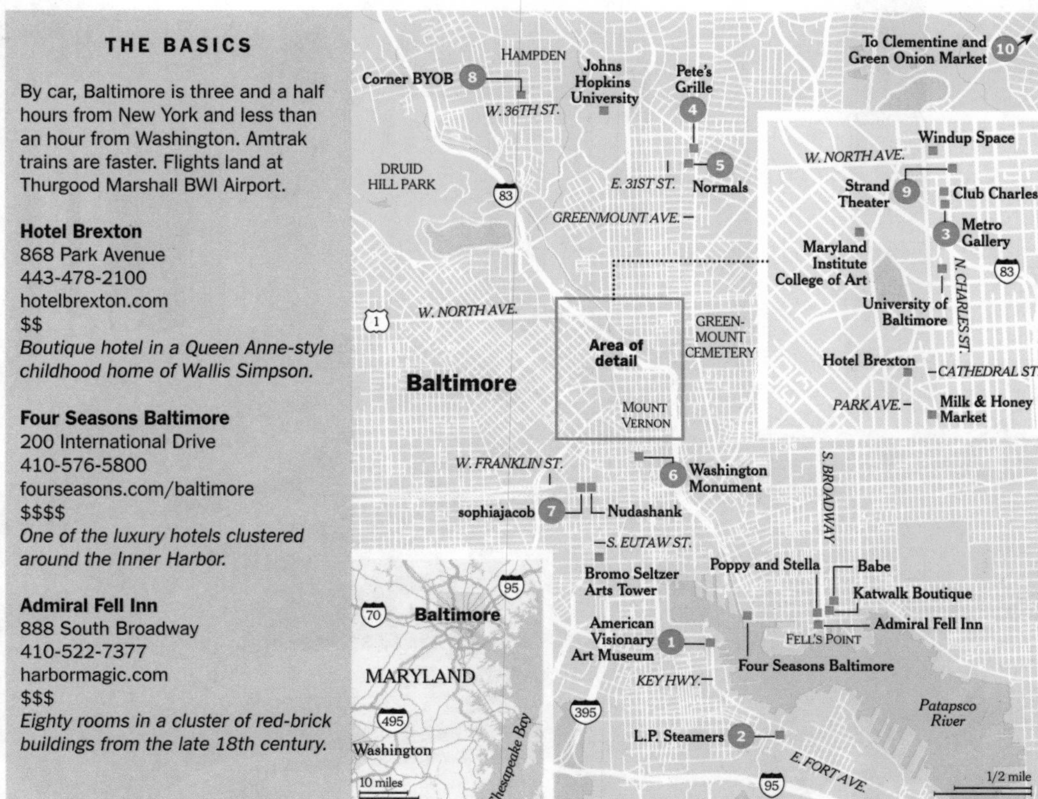

THE BASICS

By car, Baltimore is three and a half hours from New York and less than an hour from Washington. Amtrak trains are faster. Flights land at Thurgood Marshall BWI Airport.

Hotel Brexton
868 Park Avenue
443-478-2100
hotelbrexton.com
$$
Boutique hotel in a Queen Anne-style childhood home of Wallis Simpson.

Four Seasons Baltimore
200 International Drive
410-576-5800
fourseasons.com/baltimore
$$$$
One of the luxury hotels clustered around the Inner Harbor.

Admiral Fell Inn
888 South Broadway
410-522-7377
harbormagic.com
$$$
Eighty rooms in a cluster of red-brick buildings from the late 18th century.

Richmond

As the heart of the old Confederacy, Richmond, Virginia, will always have a claim as the capital of the South, a place to find Southern tradition and a center of Civil War history. But for decades in the late 20th century, it watched with envy as cities like Atlanta and Charlotte leaped ahead economically and culturally. Now Richmond is surging back to life in the present. A building boom in the last few years has seen century-old tobacco warehouses transformed into lofts and art studios. Chefs are setting up kitchens in formerly gritty neighborhoods. And the city's once buttoned-up downtown has life after dusk, thanks to new bars and a performing arts complex, Richmond CenterStage. Without forfeiting all of its Old South personality, Richmond now is a player in the New South, too.

— BY JUSTIN BERGMAN AND LINDSAY MORAN

FRIDAY

1 *Tea and Wisteria* 2:30 p.m.

For a sense of what makes Richmond Richmond, take a drive in the Fan District, so named because its wisteria- and tree-lined streets spread out like a fan. Park the car and walk along Monument Avenue, one of the loveliest places anywhere for an urban stroll. The monuments are statues — of Robert E. Lee, Stonewall Jackson, J.E.B. Stuart, and Jefferson Davis — sharing space somewhat incongruously with a more recent favorite son, Arthur Ashe Jr., the tennis champion. The stately houses are Queen Anne, Victorian, Tudor, Colonial, Italianate, Greek Revival. To complete the genteel experience, take afternoon tea, with scones and finger sandwiches, in the **Jefferson Hotel** (101 West Franklin Street; 804-788-8000; jeffersonhotel.com), whose grand style dates back to 1895.

2 *Fast Forward* 5 p.m.

Jump into the 21st century in Carytown, where shoppers and people watchers make their way to a half-mile stretch of boutiques, vintage clothing stores, and cafes. This colorful strip is Richmond at its most eclectic, mixing floppy-haired musicians, gay hipsters with pierced eyebrows, and suburban mothers pushing strollers. Check out local T-shirt designs at the **Need Supply Company** (3100 West Cary Street; 804-355-5880; needsupply.com). Examine the retro ball gowns, tiaras, and cigarette cases at **Bygones** (2916 West Cary Street; 804-353-1919; bygonesvintage.com). Or seek Japanese anime, underground graphic novels, and comics at **Chop Suey Books** (2913 West Cary Street; 804-422-8066; chopsueybooks.com).

3 *Fed in Virginia* 6:30 p.m.

The Grace Street corridor, a long moribund area near the Capitol, has come back to life with new stores and restaurants in old, ironwork-decorated storefronts. Stop in at **Pasture** (416 East Grace Street; 804-780-0416; pasturerva.com; $$) for cocktails flavored with house-made jams and smoked ginger syrup. **Rappahannock Restaurant** (320 East Grace Street; 804-545-0565; rroysters.com/restaurants.htm; $$$) specializes in Chesapeake Bay oysters and has a raw bar and entrees like bacon-fat-poached Virginia scallops.

4 *Stage Two* 8 p.m.

A major element in the Grace Street revival is **CenterStage**, a performing-arts complex centered in an old Loew's movie palace, the Carpenter Theatre (600 East Grace Street; 804-592-3400; richmondcenterstage.com), that has been restored to its former grandeur. Check the schedule; you may

OPPOSITE The Fan District, a bastion of old Richmond.

BELOW Belle Isle, now an island park accessible by footbridge from the bank of the James River, was used as a prison camp during the Civil War.

find the Virginia Opera, the Richmond Symphony, or other local or traveling performances.

SATURDAY

5 *Three-Sided War* 10 a.m.

A few diehards still call the Civil War the War of Northern Aggression, but the **American Civil War Center at Historic Tredegar** (500 Tredegar Street; 804-780-1865; tredegar.org) takes a less pro-Southern approach. With interactive displays, it tells the story of the war from three perspectives: those of the Union, the Confederacy, and the slaves. The museum building itself is a giant relic, the old 1861 Tredegar Gun Foundry, a major munitions factory during the war. At the adjacent **Richmond National Battlefield Park** (470 Tredegar Street; nps.gov/rich), recorded voices read written wartime accounts by local witnesses. Garland H. White, a former slave, tells of entering defeated Richmond as a Union soldier and being reunited with his mother, "an aged woman," from whom he had been sold as a small boy.

ABOVE The American Civil War Center, which tells the story of the war from the three different perspectives of the Union, the South, and the slave population, is in the old Tredegar Gun Foundry.

6 *Battle of the Lunch* Noon

There's a new war being waged at the **Black Sheep** (901 West Marshall Street; 804-648-1300; theblacksheeprva.com; $$), a cozy restaurant with barn-wood wainscoting and church pews for benches. Brave eaters attack two-foot-long subs named after Civil War-era ships in what the menu calls the "War of Northern Ingestion." Served on French baguettes,

the CSS Virginia is topped with fried chicken livers, shredded cabbage, and apples, while the USS Brooklyn has jerk barbecued chicken and banana ketchup. A warning: each behemoth can feed at least two.

7 *Into the Trees* 2 p.m.

Need an adrenaline boost? How about maneuvering through the trees like Tarzan? Across the James River in the Stratford Hills section, instructors at **Riverside Outfitters** (6836 Old Westham Road; 804-560-0068; riversideoutfitters.net) lead expeditions that include zip lines and harnessed walks along limbs 40 feet above the ground. Expect to pay at least $150 for two hours. If you prefer lower altitudes — and prices — stay on the Capitol side of the river and find **Belle Isle** (jamesriverpark.org), an island accessible by footbridge from Tredegar Street. It's crisscrossed with trails and offers views of Richmond's natural urban rapids, where you are likely to see intrepid kayakers. Used as a prison camp in the Civil War, the island once held 8,000 captured Union soldiers.

8 *Haute Home Cookin'* 7 p.m.

The industrial-chic bistro **LuLu's** (21 North 17th Street; 804-343-9771; lulusrichmond.com; $$) provides comfort food done right to the polo-shirt-wearing young professionals who have moved into the historic neighborhood of Shockoe Bottom, occupying lofts in renovated tobacco warehouses. Scan the LuLu's menu for easygoing dishes like chicken and dumplings or a pork chop with grilled macaroni and cheese.

9 *Uptown Music* 9 p.m.

You can stay in Shockoe Bottom for drinks and dancing as its nightclubs begin to fill up. But for a quieter evening, head uptown to the **Camel** (1621 West Broad Street; 804-353-4901; thecamel.org), a venue to catch up-and-coming Southern rock and bluegrass bands, acoustic singer-songwriters, and jazz and funk musicians.

SUNDAY

10 *Make Mine Biodynamic* 10 a.m.

Find a breakfast with good-health credentials at the **Urban Farmhouse Market & Cafe** (1217 East Cary Street; 804-325-3988; theurbanfarmhouse.net; $), a small, attractive place in a 19th-century building near the Capitol. Urban Farmhouse assures its customers that the coffee is fresh-roasted (try yours

ABOVE AND OPPOSITE BELOW Jefferson Davis, gesturing grandly, and General J.E.B. Stuart, astride a cavalry horse, are among the sculpted Southern heroes on Monument Avenue. In the late 20th century this Confederate crowd was joined by a bronze of the tennis star Arthur Ashe.

with organic almond milk), the eggs are free-range, and the bacon is pasture-raised with no hormones or antibiotics. You may find a local musician playing acoustic guitar. Ask about the biodynamic wines.

11 *Art Factory* Noon

Once an industrial wasteland, the Manchester neighborhood has emerged as an arts district with loft apartments. The anchor is the former MeadWestvaco packaging plant, now a huge art complex with 75 studios and three galleries. Stroll through the mazelike **Art Works** (320 Hull Street; 804-291-1400; artworksrichmond.com), where artists sell their creations, many for under $200. Then, since you're in the neighorhood, head to **Legend Brewery** (321 West Seventh Street; 804-232-3446; legendbrewing.com; $), for a snack and a local microbrew.

ABOVE Saleswomen turn models at Bygones, a retro-inspired store. It's in Carytown, a strip of shops and cafes frequented by an eclectic crowd.

OPPOSITE Sipping in style at afternoon tea in the elegantly appointed Jefferson Hotel.

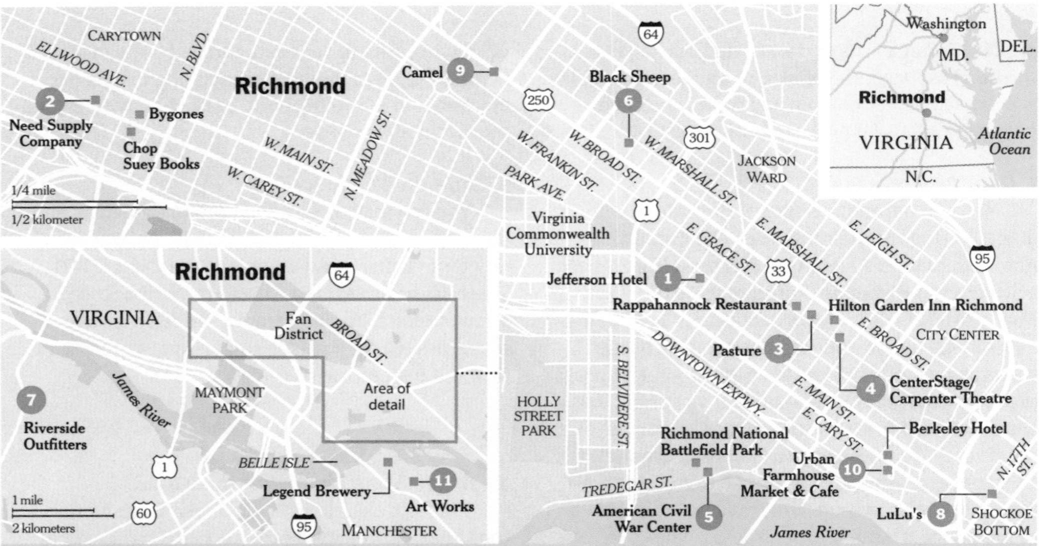

THE BASICS

Fly into the Richmond airport or drive south from Washington for two hours (much longer at rush hour). A car is the best option for getting around town.

The Jefferson Hotel
101 West Franklin Street
804-649-4750
jeffersonhotel.com
$$$
Definition of luxury since 1895.

The Berkeley Hotel
1200 East Cary Street
804-780-1300
berkeleyhotel.com
$$
Stylish comfort downtown near the river.

Hilton Garden Inn Richmond
501 East Broad Street
804-344-4300
hiltongardeninn.hilton.com
$$
Chain hotel in a renovated downtown department store.

25

Charlottesville

As far as Charlottesville is concerned, Thomas Jefferson might still be living on the hill at Monticello. There and at the University of Virginia, which he founded in 1819, he is referred to as "Mr. Jefferson" with a familiarity that suggests he might stroll past, horticulture manual in hand, at any moment. To this day an inordinate number of houses and buildings in the area resemble the back of a nickel. But Jefferson was always at the cutting edge, and the traveler today can share in some of that spirit, too, thanks to the energy emanating from the university he left behind. The active music scene has produced megastars like the Dave Matthews Band and helped to launch the modern roots-rock wave. Local chefs marry grits and fried chicken with international influences. Prize-winning vineyards checker the foothills, a development that Jefferson would have appreciated. He succeeded at nearly everything, but he couldn't coax a decent wine out of Virginia's soil.

— BY JENNIFER TUNG AND JOSHUA KURLANTZICK

FRIDAY

1 *Al Fresco Downtown* 5 p.m.

Walk through the oak-lined downtown mall, where students talk philosophy over coffee and locals gravitate for drinks. You will pass rows of restored brick buildings, street entertainers like mimes and violinists, a central plaza for public art, and al fresco cafes. Stop in just off the main mall at **Feast** (416 West Main Street, Suite H; 434-244-7800; feastvirginia.com), an artisanal cheese shop, charcuterie, and gourmet market that feels as if it could be in Paris.

2 *Old and New* 7 p.m.

Only 10 minutes from downtown Charlottesville, the **Clifton Inn** (1296 Clifton Inn Drive; 434-971-1800; thecliftoninn.com; $$$$) sits amid rolling hills and pasture land. Virginia's inns have embarked on a culinary arms race, and the Clifton has kept up. Its restaurant, inside a white-pillared *Gone With the Wind*-style Southern mansion, offers a design-your-own tasting menu featuring local ingredients. Reservations are essential. For a more casual dinner, eat in Charlottesville at **C & O** (515 East Water Street; 434-971-7044; candorestaurant.com; $$-$$$), a 110-year-old building that originally served as a railroad stop. Sit in the mezzanine, a candlelit room as dark and narrow as a mine shaft, and order dishes like local organic lamb or house-made chorizo with braised collard greens and purple potato frites.

OPPOSITE Monticello, Thomas Jefferson's home and a conspicuous example of his architectural prowess.

RIGHT The restaurant at the *Gone with the Wind*-style Clifton Inn is worth the drive out of town.

SATURDAY

3 *The Morning Tour* 8 a.m.

A quiet Saturday morning is a good time to see Jefferson's Academical Village, the central buildings he designed at the University of Virginia. Pick up coffee at **Mudhouse** on the Main Street mall (213 Main Street; 434-984-6833; mudhouse.com), and walk onto the Grounds (Mr. Jefferson never used the word "campus," and neither does anyone else in Charlottesville). Begin at the **Rotunda** (tours, 434-924-7969; virginia.edu/rotunda), inspired by the Pantheon in Rome, which sits at the north end of the 225-foot-long Lawn. Flanking the Lawn are the Pavilions, where esteemed professors live, and dorm rooms occupied by high-achieving final-year

students ("senior" isn't a word here, either). The charming gardens behind the Pavilions, divided by undulating serpentine walls, are the professors' backyards but are open to the public.

4 *Outback* 10 a.m.

For a fascinating detour little known by outsiders, visit the university's **Kluge-Ruhe Aboriginal Art Collection.** John W. Kluge, a billionaire businessman, built perhaps the largest collection of aboriginal art outside Australia and then donated it to the University of Virginia. The free guided tour, every Saturday at 10:30 a.m., is essential to understanding these stark and sometimes inscrutable works of art (400 Worrell Drive, Peter Jefferson Place; 434-244-0234; virginia.edu/kluge-ruhe).

5 *Colonial Fried Chicken* Noon

Let the lady in the bonnet and the big skirt corral you into the lunch line at **Michie Tavern**, an inn that dates back to 1784 (683 Thomas Jefferson Parkway; 434-977-1234; michietavern.com; $$$). Let more women in bonnets pile fried chicken, black-eyed peas, stewed tomatoes, and cornbread onto your pewter-style plate; then eat at a wooden table by the hearth. Once you accept full tourist status, the food is very tasty.

6 *The Back of the Nickel* 1 p.m.

Tours of historical sites are rarely billed as exciting, but Jefferson's home, **Monticello** (434-984-9800; monticello.org), actually causes goose bumps. Jefferson designed the house to invoke classical ideals of reason, proportion, and balance, and sited it on a rise ("Monticello" is from the Italian for "small hill") for a view of distant mountains. After your introduction at the new visitor center, opened in 2009, enter the house and note the elk antlers in the entrance hall, courtesy of Lewis and Clark, and the private library that once housed 6,700 books. Guides point out Jefferson's design innovations, including a dumbwaiter hidden in a fireplace, and offer insight into the unsung lives of the slaves who kept everything going. Monticello lost its spot on the back of the nickel coin for a brief period a few years ago, but Eric Cantor, a Virginia representative and influential House Republican, ushered through legislation to guarantee that after 2006 it would be back to stay.

7 *Country Roads* 5 p.m.

Drive back toward Charlottesville and turn northeast on Route 20 to Barboursville. The drive, through an area called the **Southwest Mountains Rural Historic District**, winds up and down through green farmland sitting in the shadow of the Southwest range. Keep your eyes out for historical marker signs; the area also boasts a rich trove of African-American history (nps.gov/history/nr/travel/journey/sou.htm).

8 *Dining Amid the Ruins* 7 p.m.

There's more of Jefferson (didn't this man ever sleep?) to be seen at the Barboursville Vineyard,

ABOVE Comestibles at Feast, a stop on the oak-lined downtown mall near the University of Virginia.

BELOW Tasting at Barboursville Vineyard. The winery has a notable restaurant and a Jefferson-designed building.

where you should have made reservations well before now for dinner at the **Palladio Restaurant** (17655 Winery Road, Barboursville; 540-832-7848; barboursvillewine.net; $$$$). Jefferson designed the main building at the vineyard, which dates to 1814. There was a fire in the late 1880s, but you can see the ruins of his design. The restaurant features Northern Italian cooking as well as locally inspired dishes like quail with corn cakes.

9 *Miller Time* 10 p.m.

Every college town needs a few decent bars for grungy bands to play in, but in Charlottesville you wind up later seeing those bands on MTV. The Dave Matthews Band had its start here back when Matthews tended bar at **Miller's** (109 West Main Street; 434-971-8511; millersdowntown.com). He moved on, but Miller's, a converted drugstore that retains the trappings of an old-time apothecary, is still there. Get there before the college crowd packs the place.

SUNDAY

10 *Take a Hike* 10 a.m.

Drive west for 30 minutes on Interstate 64 to **Shenandoah National Park** (Exit 99). By mid-morning the early mist will have lifted. Follow signs to Skyline Drive and the Blue Ridge Parkway. For a vigorous hike, start at the Humpback Gap parking area, six miles south of the Blue Ridge Parkway's northern end. Follow the Appalachian Trail a half-mile south to a challenging spur trail that leads to a breathtaking view of the Shenandoah Valley.

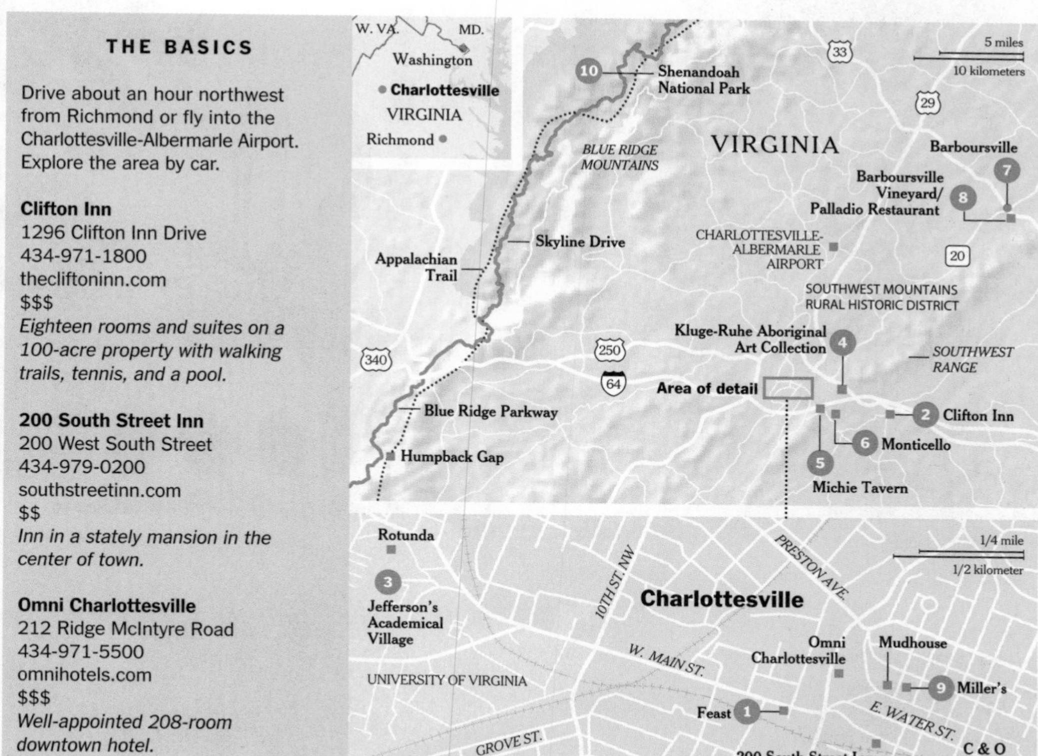

THE BASICS

Drive about an hour northwest from Richmond or fly into the Charlottesville-Albermarle Airport. Explore the area by car.

Clifton Inn
1296 Clifton Inn Drive
434-971-1800
thecliftoninn.com
$$$
Eighteen rooms and suites on a 100-acre property with walking trails, tennis, and a pool.

200 South Street Inn
200 West South Street
434-979-0200
southstreetinn.com
$$
Inn in a stately mansion in the center of town.

Omni Charlottesville
212 Ridge McIntyre Road
434-971-5500
omnihotels.com
$$$
Well-appointed 208-room downtown hotel.

Raleigh-Durham

Tell North Carolinians you're heading to the Raleigh-Durham area, locally called the Research Triangle or just the Triangle, and they will probably ask, "Which school are you visiting?" Yet the close-knit cities of Raleigh, Durham, and Chapel Hill, North Carolina, are marked by more than college bars and basketball fans. Visitors not bound for Duke (Durham), the University of North Carolina (Chapel Hill), or North Carolina State (Raleigh) come to see buzz-worthy bands, dine on food from painstaking chefs, and explore outdoor art. From its biscuits to its boutiques, the Triangle occupies a happy place between slow-paced Southern charm and urban cool.

— BY J. J. GOODE AND INGRID K. WILLIAMS

FRIDAY

1 *Art Inside Out* 2 p.m.

The collection at the **North Carolina Museum of Art** (2110 Blue Ridge Road, Raleigh; 919-839-6262; ncartmuseum.org) is on the small side by major museum standards, and that size has its advantages. The lack of tour bus crowds means unfettered access to the museum's Old Masters and contemporary heavyweights like Anselm Kiefer. The real treat is the adjacent Museum Park, more than 164 acres of open fields and woodlands punctuated by environmental art like Cloud Chamber, a stone hut that acts as a camera obscura with a small hole in the roof projecting inverted, otherworldly images of slowly swaying trees on the floor and walls.

2 *New Wares* 4 p.m.

New restaurants, shops, and galleries have transformed Raleigh's once declining **Warehouse District** (raleighwarehousedistrict.com), several blocks of old red-brick buildings a short stroll from the North Carolina Capitol Building (which is easily spotted because of its dome). Check out the exhibitions at the contemporary art museum **CAM Raleigh** (409 West Martin Street; 919-513-0946; camraleigh.org), and then drop in at **Designbox** (307 West Martin Street; 919-834-3552; designbox.us), where several working artists and craftsmen display and sell their work. At **Videri Chocolate Factory** (327 West Davie Street; 919-755-5053; viderichocolatefactory.com), you can watch the signature product being made before buying some to take home. There's more visible craftsmanship at the **Curatory at the Raleigh Denim Workshop** (319 West Martin Street; 919-917-8969; thecuratory.com), where you can see workers at vintage sewing machines and buy the company's high-end blue jeans as well as jewelry, accessories, and other well-made clothing.

OPPOSITE The neo-Gothic Duke Chapel, a symbol of both Duke University and Durham.

RIGHT University of North Carolina basketball fans.

3 *Going for the Whole Hog* 6 p.m.

Small towns and back roads, not cities, are usually thought to have a monopoly on great barbecue. What makes **The Pit** (328 West Davie Street, Raleigh; 919-890-4500; thepit-raleigh.com; $) a striking exception is the masterly practice here of the eastern North Carolina art form of whole hog cooking. Instead of trekking 100 miles to porcine capitals like Ayden and Lexington, you can dig into pilgrimage-worthy chopped or pulled pork—made from pigs purchased from family farms and cooked for 10 to 14 hours over coals and hickory or oak. Your chopped barbecued pork plate comes with two sides and greaseless hush puppies.

4 *Night at the Theater* 8 p.m.

Raleigh is not only the state's political capital, but its cultural capital as well, home of the North Carolina Symphony, North Carolina Ballet, and Theatre Raleigh. To find a performance, check

the schedule of the **Duke Energy Center for the Performing Arts** (2 East South Street; 919-996-8700; dukeenergycenterraleigh.com). Or drive to Durham for an event at the sparkling glass **Durham Performing Arts Center** (123 Vivian Street; 919-688-3722; dpacnc.com). You might catch a show right off Broadway or a concert—performers have included Smokey Robinson, Diana Krall, and B. B. King.

SATURDAY

5 *Campus Gothic* 9 a.m.

The **Duke University** campus (duke.edu) is the quintessential collegiate setting, with grassy quads and lovely neo-Gothic buildings lorded over by the 210-foot spire of the stately stone Duke Chapel, which despite its modest name is an American version of a richly decorated European cathedral. Nearby are the **Sarah P. Duke Gardens** (420 Anderson Street, Durham; 919-684-3698; hr.duke.edu/dukegardens), 55 meticulously maintained acres bursting with diverse flora. Stroll along the circuitous walking paths that curl around the gorgeous gardens' grassy slopes and placid ponds, keeping an eye out for the majestic resident great blue heron. From the gardens, it's not far to the **Nasher Museum of Art** (2001 Campus Drive; 919-684-5135; nasher.duke.edu), a cluster of modern, monolithic structures that hosts impressive exhibitions.

6 *Fuel for Shoppers* 1 p.m.

Get ready for an afternoon of shopping with a Mexican lunch at **Taqueria La Vaquita** (2700 Chapel Hill Road, Durham; 919-402-0209; lavaquitanc.com; $). It's an unassuming freestanding structure with a plastic cow on its roof, but the tacos are house-made corn tortillas topped with exceptional barbacoa de res (slow-cooked beef) or carnitas (braised-then-fried pork). Then head downtown to **Brightleaf Square** (Main and Gregson Streets; historicbrightleaf.com), where shops occupy former tobacco warehouses. Spend some time at **Vert & Vogue** (919-251-8537; vertandvogue.com), where trendy brands like A.L.C. share space with local labels, and browse at **Wentworth Rare Books & Prints** (919-688-5311; wentworthleggettbooks.com). The nearby **LabourLove Gallery** (807 East Main Street; 919-373-4451; labourlove.com) shows paintings, photography, and other diverse projects from local artists.

7 *Southern Comforts* 5 p.m.

If crispy fried chicken atop pillowy waffles weren't decadent enough, at **Dame's Chicken & Waffles** (317 West Main Street, Durham; 919-682-9235; dameschickenwaffles.com; $) every plate comes with a flavored butter "shmear" and a side. Order the Quilted Buttercup (fried chicken, sweet potato waffles, and a maple-pecan shmear), and do not skip a side of the heavenly Triple Mac and Cheese.

8 *Root for the Home Team* 7 p.m.

The Triangle is college basketball country, home to two of the winningest teams—Duke and North Carolina—and some of the most rabid fans in college sports history. But soon after the madness of March, the more tranquil fans of local baseball stream into the **Durham Bulls Athletic Park** (409 Blackwell Street, Durham; 919-687-6500; dbulls.com). The Bulls, founded in 1902 as the Tobacconists, still offer professional baseball at bargain prices.

9 *Big Bands* 10 p.m.

Nirvana played at the **Cat's Cradle** (300 East Main Street, Carrboro; 919-967-9053; catscradle.com) for the first time in pre-*Nevermind* 1990 to about 100 people. A year later Pearl Jam played to three times as many, filling just half the standing-room-only space. Today the Cradle, just a mile from downtown Chapel Hill, hosts acts you may be hearing more about tomorrow for low ticket prices that seem more like yesterday.

SUNDAY

10 *Drive-Thru Biscuits* 10 a.m.

There are several places in Chapel Hill that serve a distinguished Southern breakfast for an easy-to-swallow price. Diners linger over gravy-smothered pork chops and eggs at **Mama Dip's** (408 West

Rosemary Street, Chapel Hill; 919-942-5837) and peerless shrimp and grits at **Crook's Corner** (610 West Franklin Street, Chapel Hill; 919-929-7643; crookscorner.com). But for a morning meal on the go that's equally unforgettable, roll up to the drive-through window at **Sunrise Biscuit Kitchen** (1305 East Franklin Street, Chapel Hill; 919-933-1324; $), where the iced tea is tooth-achingly sweet and the main course is fluffy, buttery, and filled with salty country ham or crisp fried chicken.

11 *Kitchen Outfitters* 11 a.m.

Find some take-home gifts for your family chef, or yourself, at **Southern Season** (201 South Estes Drive, Chapel Hill; southernseason.com), a culinary superstore with all kinds of fresh foods and kitchen gadgets that has become an institution in Chapel Hill and beyond. You may have to battle hordes of other shoppers to get to those tempting imported pastas, Carolina wines, or Christmas-tree-shaped butter knives, but winding through the crowded aisles is half the fun.

OPPOSITE A fresh batch at Sunrise Biscuit Kitchen.

ABOVE Museum Park is 164 acres of woodland, grassy fields, and outdoor artworks adjacent to the North Carolina Museum of Art in Raleigh.

THE BASICS

The Triangle is easily accessible on interstate highways. Or fly into Raleigh-Durham International Airport and rent a car.

Umstead Hotel and Spa
5 SAS Campus Drive, Cary
866-877-4141
theumstead.com
$$$-$$$$
About 15 minutes from downtown Raleigh, with pool and spa.

Arrowhead Inn
106 Mason Road, Durham
919-477-8430
arrowheadinn.com
$$
Rooms, garden cottage, and log cabin amid lawns and magnolia trees.

Carolina Inn
211 Pittsboro Street, Chapel Hill
919-933-2001
carolinainn.com
$$
Southern grandeur on the University of North Carolina campus.

Durham
Sarah P. Duke Gardens
5 Duke University
CAMPUS DR.
Nasher Museum of Art
MAIN ST.
Vert & Vogue
Brightleaf Square/ Wentworth Rare Books & Prints
Dame's Chicken & Waffles 7
Durham Performing Arts Center
CHAPEL HILL RD.
Durham Bulls Athletic Park 8
LabourLove Gallery
1/2 mile
1 kilometer
VA.
Durham
Raleigh
NORTH CAROLINA
S. C.
Arrowhead Inn
85
Taqueria La Vaquita 6
Durham
Sunrise Biscuit Kitchen
11 Southern Season
Chapel Hill
RALEIGH-DURHAM INTERNATIONAL AIRPORT
40
Umstead Hotel and Spa
Cary
1 North Carolina Museum of Art/ Museum Park
Raleigh
540
264
1
NORTH CAROLINA
5 miles
20 kilometers
Raleigh
401
North Carolina Capitol Building
N. DAWSON ST.
W. MORGAN ST.
CAM Raleigh
Curatory at the Raleigh Denim Workshop
Designbox
E. MARTIN ST.
3 The Pit
E. DAVIE ST.
Videri Chocolate Factory
2 Warehouse District
70
Duke Energy Center for the Performing Arts
W. SOUTH ST.
4
1/4 mile
1/2 kilometer
Chapel Hill
Mama Dip's 10
W. ROSMARY ST.
W. FRANKLIN ST.
9 Cat's Cradle
Crook's Corner
Carolina Inn
1/2 mile
1 kilometer

Charleston

Charleston, South Carolina, is known for its magnolia-tinged Southern atmosphere, for its hospitality as grand as the stucco homes that line the fabled Battery, for its surrounding beaches, and increasingly for its updated Low Country cooking. With some of the country's most aggressive historic preservation, it maintains streets lined with Colonial and antebellum mansions. Tours give visitors a glimpse of the lives and language of the African-American people who built the Gullah culture nearby. But a newer and younger Charleston asserts itself, too—in galleries, shops, restaurants, and boutique bakeries. Charleston is also an appropriate destination for the December holidays: it was the home of Joel Roberts Poinsett, an ambassador to Mexico in the 1820s who brought home the red-and-green plant now identified with Christmas and called the poinsettia. —BY SHAILA DEWAN AND JEANNIE RALSTON

FRIDAY

1 *Meeting Lucinda* 3 p.m.

Embracing the past doesn't always mean being honest about it, but Charleston acknowledges both sides of its history. The four-block **Gateway Walk** shares hidden beauty, taking visitors through quiet gardens and past lovely old churches. Enter it from Church Street across from St. Philip's Episcopal Church, and follow the plaques. A couple of blocks away, a darker past is remembered at the **Old Slave Mart Museum** (6 Chalmers Street; 843-958-6467; nps.gov/history/nr/travel/charleston), in a pre-Civil War slave market building where the first sale, in 1856, was a 20-year-old woman named Lucinda. Out of the city center on Johns Island, Charleston honors botanical longevity in the form of the **Angel Oak** (3688 Angel Oak Road, Johns Island), a tree thought to be three or four centuries old that is so large it could whomp 10 Hogwarts willows.

2 *Up on the Roof* 6 p.m.

Because Charleston is a peninsula with views in most every direction, it's no wonder that rooftop bars are the rage. The perfect perch is the bar at the **Market Pavilion Hotel** (225 East Bay Street; 843-723-0500; marketpavilion.com). It's spacious, with a gleaming year-round pool, and offers a panorama of the harbor. The bar menu is dominated by "M" drinks: imaginative takes on mojitos, martinis, and margaritas.

3 *Low Country Upscale* 8 p.m.

This city of 122,000 is home to a concentration of refined dining that leaves absolutely no excuse for ending up at a fried-filet-and-hushpuppy joint. The king-daddy of contemporary Charleston dining is **Husk** (76 Queen Street; 843-577-2500; huskrestaurant.com; $$$), which turns out dishes like sassafras-glazed pork ribs and duck lacquered with honey and local benne (sesame) seeds. Other restaurants have followed in its footsteps. One of them is **Two Boroughs Larder** (186 Coming Street; 843-637-3722; twoboroughslarder.com; $$$), which serves small plates of astonishingly fresh ingredients in a stripped-down space and has retro pantry items for sale.

SATURDAY

4 *Sweetgrass and Crepes* 9 a.m.

The old South finds new takes at the **Charleston Farmers Market** in Marion Square (843-724-7305; charlestonarts.sc), where you may find pickled watermelon rind or jam and can buy fresh crepes for breakfast. When you've had enough of the market throngs, move on to King Street, long the stylish epicenter of Charleston. On and around upper King,

OPPOSITE Guided kayaking tours take paddlers into the marshy terrain of South Carolina's Lowcountry.

BELOW Alluette Jones-Smalls at Alluette's Café.

north of Marion Square, chic shops and high-concept restaurants coexist with fading emporiums like **Read Brothers** (593 King Street; 843-723-7276; readbrothers.com), established in 1912, which sells a baffling assortment of audio equipment, fabrics, and odds and ends. Pick up a handy one-page guide to parking and neighborhood restaurants at **Blue Bicycle Books** (420 King Street; 843-722-2666; bluebicyclebooks.com).

5 *Who's Got Soul?* Noon

At **Alluette's Café** (80 A Reid Street; 843-577-6929; alluettes.com; $$), Alluette Jones specializes in what she calls "holistic soul food." That means no pork — almost heresy in Southern kitchens — and a focus on vegetables from nearby organic farms. The results, from spicy fish stew to subtle and creamy lima bean soup, are just as flavorful as traditional Low Country food. The many grace notes here include homemade ketchup (secret ingredient: ginger) and iced tea with a dash of pineapple juice.

6 *Under the Bridge* 2 p.m.

You have to go over the two-mile-long **Ravenel Bridge**, the star of the Charleston skyline, to get under it. Across the Cooper River from downtown, drive to **Mount Pleasant Memorial Waterfront Park** (71 Harry M. Hallman Boulevard, Mount Pleasant; mountpleasantrecreation.com), which extends outward on a pier below the impressive suspension structure of the bridge. After experiencing its unique perspective on the bridge, stop at the **Sweetgrass Cultural Arts Pavilion** near the parking lot. Many places sell traditional sweetgrass baskets, made from an indigenous waterfront plant and originally used in winnowing rice on local plantations; here you can watch them being woven and see a handsome museum display that explains the tradition.

7 *Tidal Creek and Pluff Mud* 5 p.m.

Shem Creek in Mount Pleasant is a main harbor for local shrimpers, which means that you'll see sturdy trawlers, draped with netting, chugging in to anchor. Along the boardwalk, you'll find locals trying their luck with fishing rods, seabirds squawking from pylons, and — if it's low tide — crabs scurrying through the pluff mud, as the oozy muck of Low Country tidal flats is called. Follow up with a drink at the Cabana Bar at the **Water's Edge** restaurant (1407 Shrimp Boat Lane, Mount Pleasant; waters-edge-restaurant.com).

8 *Misnomer Cafe* 6:30 p.m.

Who names a restaurant "**The Ordinary**"? Maybe someone who wants reviewers to use the phrase, "It's anything but." Because that's all that can be said about the experience inside a 1927 bank building. (Yes, some British inns that served food were once called ordinaries, but still.) The high-ceilinged interior with arched windows feels like a temple to seafood and Southern-ness. In front of the old bank vault is the raw bar, piled high with a variety of clams, oysters, and crabs. From one night's menu, the pickled shrimp was a masterpiece and the swordfish schnitzel was, yes, extraordinary (544 King Street; 843-414-7060; eattheordinary.com; $$$).

9 *Georgian Encore* 8 p.m.

When the **Dock Street Theatre** (135 Church Street) opened in 1736, the first production had a name only a pre-Revolutionary could love: *The Recruiting Officer*. Luckily, theatrical works with more cheerful names have taken over since it reopened with all its Georgian splendor restored. Said to be the first building in America built to be a

theater, the Dock hosts the Spoleto Festival, the city's artistic crown jewel, in May and June (spoletousa.org) and Charleston Stage (charlestonstage.com), which presents musicals and popular fare the rest of the year.

SUNDAY

10 *Gardens and Gators* 11 a.m.
Ever since Pat Conroy's novel *Prince of Tides*, Charleston has been known for its mossy Low Country terrain as much as for its picturesque history. At **Middleton Place** plantation (4300 Ashley River Road; 843-556-6020; middletonplace.org), one of several plantations within easy reach of downtown, you can get a close-up view of the marsh—or, in winter, of a primeval cypress swamp—on a guided kayak tour; you might see alligators, bald eagles, or river otters. Tours meet at the **Inn at Middleton Place** (4290 Ashley River Road; 843-628-2879; theinnatmiddletonplace.com). After your paddle, take in domesticated nature on the plantation grounds, billed as the oldest landscaped garden in the country.

OPPOSITE ABOVE This 19th century house, an example of cherished local architecture, is the home of Husk, a restaurant known for contemporary cooking.

OPPOSITE BELOW Fishing in Mount Pleasant, across the Cooper River from downtown.

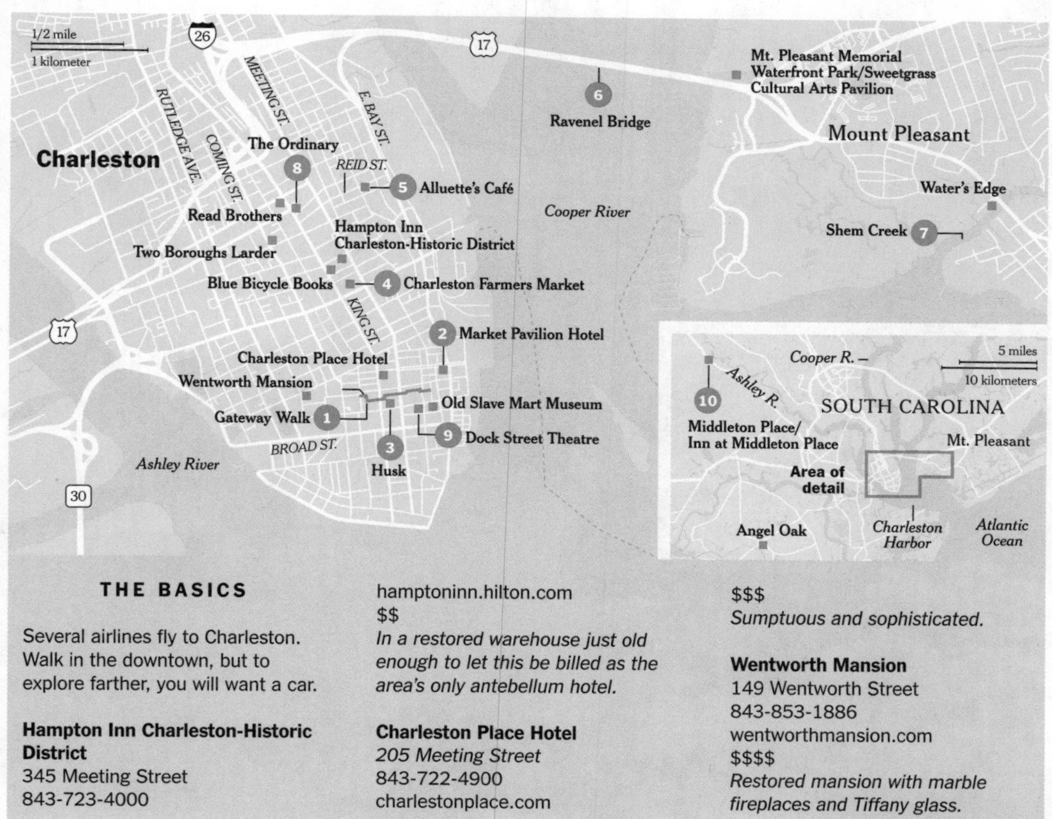

THE BASICS

Several airlines fly to Charleston. Walk in the downtown, but to explore farther, you will want a car.

Hampton Inn Charleston-Historic District
345 Meeting Street
843-723-4000
hamptoninn.hilton.com
$$
In a restored warehouse just old enough to let this be billed as the area's only antebellum hotel.

Charleston Place Hotel
205 Meeting Street
843-722-4900
charlestonplace.com
$$$
Sumptuous and sophisticated.

Wentworth Mansion
149 Wentworth Street
843-853-1886
wentworthmansion.com
$$$$
Restored mansion with marble fireplaces and Tiffany glass.

Savannah

Certain things about Savannah never change—it remains one of America's loveliest cities, organized around a grid of 21 squares, where children play, couples wed, and in the evenings lone saxophonists deliver a jazz soundtrack. Live oaks shade the squares; shops and cafes occupy stately old houses; ships still arrive on the Savannah River. But Savannah also has an appetite for the new. A growing emphasis on art has brought both a major expansion of the South's oldest art museum and a lively contemporary scene energized by students and instructors at the booming Savannah College of Art and Design. Civic boosters (thinking technology as well as art) are even trying to reposition the region as Georgia's Creative Coast. And then there is change of another kind: restoration. Before iron-clad protection of the historic district was established, Savannah lost three of its 24 squares to developers. Now one of the oldest, Ellis Square, long dominated by a parking lot, has been brought back with restored buildings on its edges and a statue of Savannah's favorite son, the songwriter Johnny Mercer, in its bright new center. — BY SHAILA DEWAN

FRIDAY

1 *Good and Evil* 3:30 p.m.

You're in the heart of the gracious South, so embrace every cliché from the frilly to the Gothic, with some eccentric characters for good measure. Begin with a tour of the splendid **Mercer Williams House** on Monterey Square (430 Whitaker Street; 912-236-6352; mercerhouse.com). It was built in the 1860s for Johnny Mercer's great-grandfather and restored by Jim Williams, the antiques dealer memorialized in a now-classic book, *Midnight in the Garden of Good and Evil*. The stern guide won't dwell on the three murder trials of Williams, who was acquitted, and guests aren't allowed on the second floor, which is still a residence. But the guide will offer plenty of detail about the formal courtyard, the nap-ready veranda, the Continental rococo, and the Edwardian Murano glass.

2 *Georgia on Your Plate* 7 p.m.

Dress up a bit (no flip-flops) for the froufrou milieu of **Elizabeth on 37th** (105 East 37th Street; 912-236-5547; elizabethon37th.net; $$$), a Low Country restaurant housed in an early-20th-century mansion where the décor may be prissy but the food is anything but. Expect a seafood-rich menu and what is arguably Savannah's quintessential dining experience. Look for Georgia shrimp, local sea bass, or a pecan crust on the rack of lamb. For a splurge, order the seven-course tasting menu.

3 *Creepy Cocktails* 9 p.m.

The city of Savannah began peacefully enough, with a friendship between Tomochichi, the chief of the Yamacraw tribe, and James Oglethorpe, leader of the British settlers who founded the city in 1733. But then came war, yellow fever, hurricanes, and fires, not to mention pirates and curses—making the city seem, at least to the builders digging around, like one big graveyard. Savannah has turned that sordid history to its advantage: about 30 ghost tours are offered in the city, including a haunted pub crawl. Only one, though, picks you up at your hotel in an open-top hearse, **Hearse Tours** (912-695-1578; hearseghosttours.com). In addition to recounting some of Savannah's most notorious murders, suicides, and deathbed tales, your joke-telling guide might share personal paranormal theories, make everyone scream in unison to spook passersby, or stop for cocktails at favorite haunts. (It's legal to take your julep for a stroll.)

OPPOSITE Savannah, Georgia, in the heart of the gracious South, carefully preserves the elegant houses lining its central grid of oak-shaded squares.

BELOW The ornate cast-iron fountain in Forsyth Park.

SATURDAY

4 *Up-and-Coming* 10 a.m.

Venture out of the historic district to the up-and-coming area called Starland, filled with galleries and studios. Start at **Fresh Exhibition** (2427 De Soto Avenue; 912-335-8204; desotorow.org), a non-profit gallery run by current and recent art students, where exhibitions might feature adventurous drawings and collages, doll lamps, or contemporary illustration. Next, make your way up to **Maldoror's** (2418 De Soto Avenue; 912-443-5355; maldorors.com; $), a frame shop with the aura of a Victorian curio cabinet and a print collection to match. Rounding the corner, you'll come to **Back in the Day** (2403 Bull Street; 912-495-9292; backinthedaybakery.com), an old-fashioned bakery that inspires fervent loyalty among locals. Pick up one of the sandwiches, like the Madras curry chicken on ciabatta, and maybe a cupcake, to take with you for lunch.

5 *Picnic with the Dead* Noon

Few cemeteries are more stately and picnic-perfect than **Bonaventure Cemetery** (330 Bonaventure Road), with its 250-year-old live oaks draped with Spanish moss as if perpetually decorated for Halloween. The cemetery, where Conrad Aiken, Johnny Mercer, and other notable residents are buried, looks out over the Intracoastal Waterway and is a gathering spot for anglers as well as mourners. Find a quiet spot to ponder fate and eat your lunch.

6 *Old Streets, New Museum* 2 p.m.

The battle took years and matched two unlikely adversaries: the **Telfair Museum of Art**, the oldest art museum in the South, which wanted to expand, and the powerful Savannah Historic District Board

ABOVE Elizabeth on 37th, a restaurant with Lowcountry cuisine, serves up seafood-rich dishes in a palatial neoclassical-style villa built in 1900.

BELOW Hearse Tours takes visitors to the haunts of Savannah's thriving population of ghosts.

of Review. The result, after intense haggling, was a light-filled building that is as trim as a yacht and has won accolades for its architect, Moshe Safdie. The addition, the **Jepson Center for the Arts** (207 West York Street; 912-790-8800; telfair.org), preserved Savannah's cherished street grid by dividing the structure into two and joining it with two glass bridges while giving the museum much-needed space. The original 19th-century museum (Telfair Academy, 121 Barnard Street) is home to *The Bird Girl*, the now-famous statue that adorns the cover of *Midnight in the Garden*; she was relocated, like a federal witness, from Bonaventure Cemetery for her protection. The museum also operates tours of the nearly 200-year-old **Owens-Thomas House** (124 Abercorn Street). A combination ticket covers all three.

7 *School Fair* 5 p.m.

Shopping in Savannah is increasingly sophisticated, with recent additions like an imposing Marc by Marc Jacobs store on the rapidly gentrifying Broughton Street. But the most interesting retail is at **shopSCAD**, a boutique that sells the creations of the students, faculty, alumni, and staff of the Savannah College of Art and Design (340 Bull Street; 912-525-5180; shopscadonline.com). There is fine art — drawings, paintings, photography, and prints — as well as decorative and wearable items like hand-dyed ties by Jen Swearington and a pendant lamp by Christopher Moulder.

8 *Crab Heaven* 7:30 p.m.

Forget about crab cakes, stuffed soft shells, or crabmeat au gratin. Crab is most rewarding when it is pure and unadulterated, served in a pile on newspaper with a can of beer and a blunt instrument for whacking at the shell. That, plus some boiled potatoes and corn, is what you will find at **Desposito's** (3501 Merye Street, Thunderbolt; 912-897-9963; $$), an unadorned shack in a onetime fishing village on the outskirts of town. This is not dining; this is working, but the sweet morsels are better than any payday.

9 *Drinking In the Scene* 9:30 p.m.

Many of Savannah's finest bars close early — often when the owners feel like it — so don't wait to start on your drink-by-drink tour. Begin at the **American Legion Post 135**, south of Forsyth Park (1108 Bull Street; 912-233-9277; alpost135.com), a surprisingly shimmery, mirrored space where the clientele is a mix of age and vocation. Proceed to the **Crystal Beer Parlor** (301 West Jones Street; 912-349-1000; crystalbeerparlor.com). On the outside, it's as

ABOVE The no-frills, low-priced Thunderbird Inn plays up its retro ambience.

anonymous as a speakeasy, which it was, but inside, its high-backed booths and colorful hanging lamps are more ice cream than booze. A full menu is available. Wind up at **Planters Tavern** (23 Abercorn Street; 912-232-4286), a noisy, low-ceilinged bar in the basement of the high-dollar Olde Pink House, a dignified restaurant in a 1771 house. With a fireplace on either end of the room, live music, and boisterous locals, it's the place to be.

SUNDAY

10 *Church's Chicken* 11 a.m.

Church and food go together in the South, and they do so especially well at the **Masada Café** (2301 West Bay Street; 912-236-9499), a buffet annex to the United House of Prayer for All People. The church has several locations in Savannah; this one is a mission of sorts, catering to the poor, but the inexpensive, revolving buffet of soul food classics like fried chicken and macaroni and cheese has gained a following among food critics and locals. Get there at 11 a.m. for the Sunday service, where the music and rhythmic hand-clapping surely share some DNA with the "ring shouts" of the Gullah-Geechee people, descendants of slaves who once lived on the nearby barrier islands.

OPPOSITE Learning about art at the Jepson Center.

THE BASICS

Fly to the Savannah / Hilton Head International Airport and take a shuttle into Savannah. The historic district is easily traversed by foot. A cab or a car may be necessary for other destinations.

Mansion on Forsyth Park
700 Drayton Street
912-238-5158
mansiononforsythpark.com
$$$
A lavish 1888 home eccentrically decorated with garish paintings and an antique hat collection.

Andaz Savannah
14 Barnard Street
912-233-2116
savannah.andaz.hyatt.com
$$$
Hip boutique hotel overlooking Ellis Square.

Thunderbird Inn
611 West Oglethorpe Avenue
912-232-2661
thethunderbirdinn.com
$$
A no-frills motel refurbished with a vintage flair.

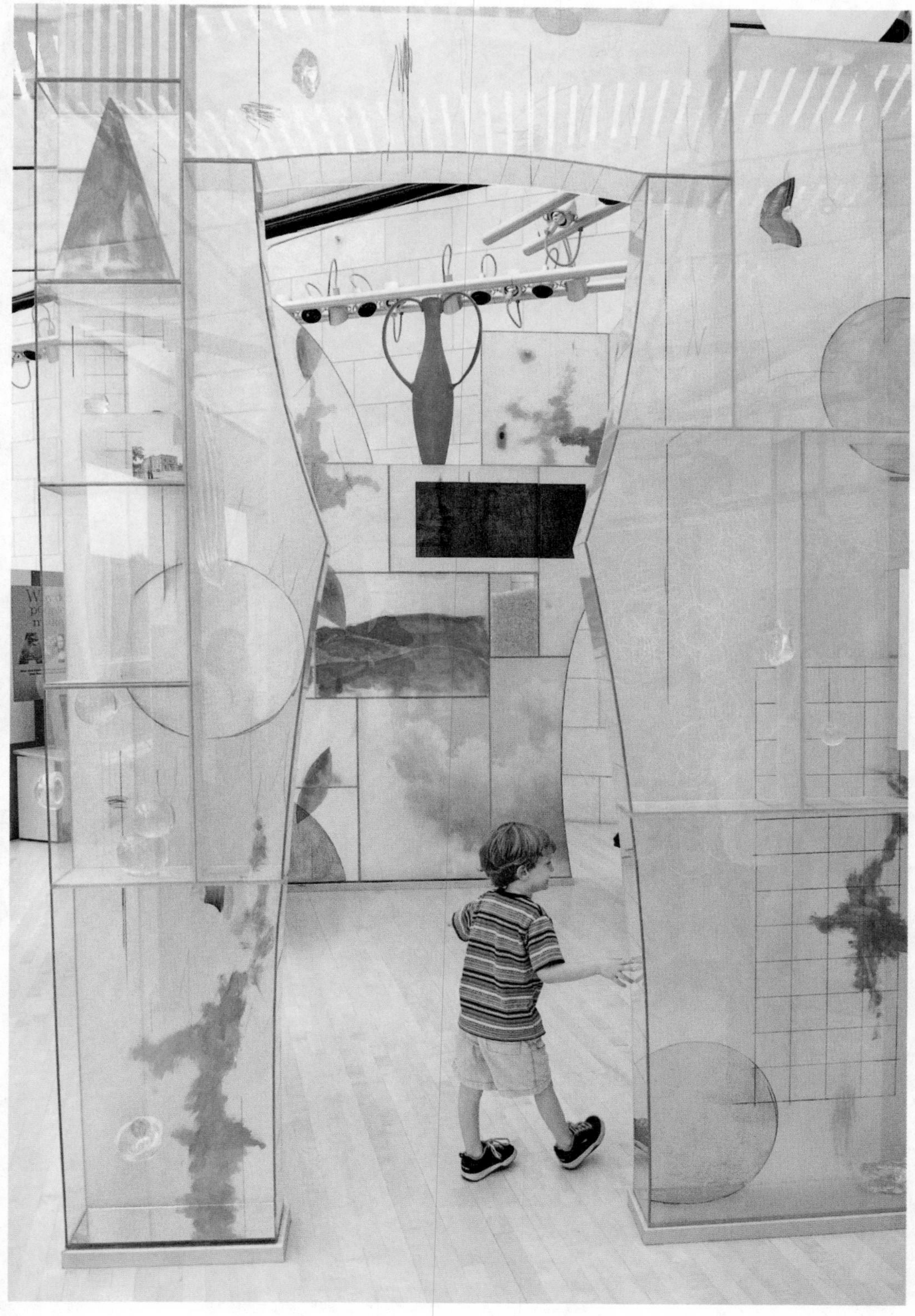

St. Simons Island

The Golden Isles, the barrier islands of Georgia's coast, meld two worlds: the sunny beaches and lollygag pace of island life and the stately Spanish moss-draped grace of the South with antebellum graveyards and ruined plantations. St. Simons, about equidistant between Jacksonville and Savannah, in particular is a literary haunt, home of writers' conferences and a favorite location of authors including Tina McElroy Ansa, whose popular black heroine, Lena McPherson, can see ghosts. Hidden amid the island's resorts and golf courses are remnants of the time when the only residents were Gullah-Geechee people, rice-tenders descended from slaves who speak their own blend of African languages and English. St. Simons, where oak trees turn avenues into tunnels of green, is the hub of the barrier islands, with about 13,000 residents and a bustling strip of restaurants and shops called the Village. — BY SHAILA DEWAN

FRIDAY

1 *On the Pier* 3 p.m.

Start at the **St. Simons Bait & Tackle** shop (121 Mallery Street; 912-634-1888), where you can try for a greeting from the African gray parrot, Mr. Byrd (who has his own Facebook page), and rent fishing poles. Walk outside to the pier to try for anything from sheepshead to flounder, or just dangle the line in the water and daydream. A short stroll takes you to the **St. Simons Island Lighthouse**, built in 1872 after Confederates destroyed the original. It is a quaint white structure with a 360-degree observation deck overlooking St. Simons Sound and the mainland. And it gives you some exercise before you embark on a series of buttery, greasy, delicious Southern meals (912-638-4666; saintsimonslighthouse.org; arrive before 4:30 if you want to climb the tower).

2 *Crab Stew and a Beer* 5:30 p.m.

Head north on scenic Highway 17 to experience a true Georgia tradition, the seafood shack. **Hunter's Café** ($) is on a dirt road amid the marinas—or, as they are called here, fish camps—of Shellman Bluff, about a 30-minute drive toward Savannah. There's no street address; for directions, call 912-832-5771 or check the online map at hunterscafe.com. The diners at the next table are likely to be fishermen just returned from a day in the salt marshes. To the basic shack formula of bright lighting and linoleum floors, Hunter's has added a full bar and a screened porch overlooking the Broro River, but it maintains the customary disdain for any decoration not furnished by a taxidermist. Have the crab stew and fluffy oniony hushpuppies.

3 *Tree Spirits* 9 p.m.

Back on St. Simons, in the commercial district known as the Village, look for the green and yellow awning of **Murphy's Tavern** (415 Mallery Street; 912-638-8966), a favorite haunt of shrimpers, summer residents, and townies. Order a beer, pick someone out, and suggest a game of pool. Outside, look for the face of a "tree spirit" carved into a huge old oak tree. A handful of these spirits, sculptures by Keith Jennings, are on public sites scattered around St. Simons; more are hidden away on private property.

SATURDAY

4 *The Breakfast Rush* 9 a.m.

Sit on the front patio and feast on the seafood omelet or the butter pecan French toast at the **4th**

OPPOSITE The Avenue of Oaks at Sea Island resort.

RIGHT A "tree spirit" sculpture by Keith Jennings.

of May Cafe (321 Mallery Street; 912-638-5444; 4thofmay.net; $), a popular Village restaurant named after the common birthday of the three original owners (two were twins). You're early, so you should beat the rush of retirees, young couples, families, tourists, and regulars who descend like gulls for breakfast.

5 *The Little Island* 10:30 a.m.

If you doze off when you hear the phrase "bird-watcher's paradise," just forget about the bird part and catch the boat to **Little St. Simons Island**, a private retreat where you can spend the day lying on the beach and touring the near-pristine live oak and magnolia forest. Two of the resort's main buildings are an old hunting lodge and a stunning cottage made of tabby, a stuccolike material of lime and oyster shells. Family owned, the resort is also family style, which means help yourself to towels, sunscreen, bug spray, and the beer set out in coolers on the porch. Most of the island has been left virtually untouched, and it is possible in one day to observe river otter, dolphins, the endangered greenfly orchid, and bald eagles, as well as roseate spoonbills and a host of other birds. The beach is littered with sand dollars and conch. A day trip is about $100 a person and includes lunch, transportation to and from the island, a naturalist-guided tour, and time at the beach. You'll leave from the Hampton River Club Marina (1000 Hampton Point Drive on St. Simons) at 10:30 and will be back by 4:30. Reservations are required (the Lodge on Little St. Simons Island; 912-638-7472; littlessi.com).

6 *Alligator Hazard* 5:30 p.m.

Back on the big island, there's still time for nine holes of golf at the **King and Prince Golf Course** (100 Tabbystone; 912-634-0255; hamptonclub.com), a course that makes full use of the starkly beautiful marsh landscape. Ask to play 10 through 18; four of these holes are on little marsh islands connected by bridges. You'll putt surrounded by a sea of golden grasses that even non-golfers will appreciate. One hole is near an island with a resident alligator.

ABOVE Christ Church, built by a lumber magnate mourning the death of his wife on their honeymoon.

RIGHT The King and Prince Golf Course, where you might see an alligator eyeing the golfers.

7 *Upscale Seafood* 8 p.m.

Settle in for drinks and a leisurely dinner at one of the fancy restaurants like **Halyards**, featuring Southern seafood dishes (55 Cinema Lane; 912-638-9100; halyardsrestaurant.com; $$-$$$), or the more traditional **Georgia Sea Grill** (310 Mallery Street; 912-638-1197; georgiaseagrill.com; $$-$$$).

SUNDAY

8 *Church with a Past* 10 a.m.

It has history, it has literary significance, it has a tragic love story. But the thing to notice at Christ Church, Frederica, built in 1884 by a lumber magnate mourning the death of his wife on their honeymoon, is the thick, lambent lawn, one of the great unnoticed triumphs of Southern horticulture. **Christ Church, Frederica** (6329 Frederica Road; christchurchfrederica.org; 912-638-8683), was a setting in a novel by Eugenia Price, who is buried in the graveyard there. The oldest grave dates to

ST. SIMONS
ISLAND
BAIT & TACKLE
ST. SIMONS
BAIT & TACKLE
COFFEE

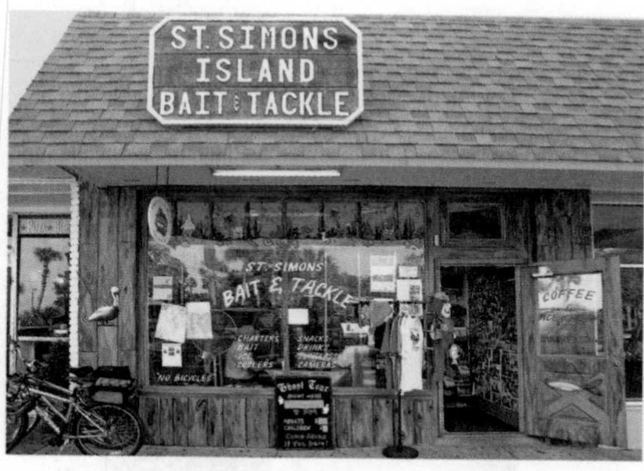

1803. Across the street is a wooded garden dedicated to Charles and John Wesley, who preached on St. Simons in the 1730s as Anglicans; they later returned to England and founded Methodism.

9 *Bicycle-Friendly* 11:30 a.m.

The exclusive **Lodge at Sea Island** (100 Retreat Avenue; 912-638-3611; seaisland.com) is off limits to all but guests and members. But if you go by bike you may be able to sneak a peek of its grounds and the ruins of Retreat Plantation's hospital, where slaves were treated. You'll also experience the island's bicycle-friendly avenues, lined with tremendous 150-year-old oaks. Rent a bike at **Ocean Motion** (1300 Ocean Boulevard; 912-638-5225), head south following the road around the tip of the island, and make a left on Frederica Road to reach the Avenue of Oaks, which leads to the guard house of the Lodge before it loops back to Frederica Road. You can ask to see the ruins just inside the grounds. If you're ambitious, venture onto the Torras Causeway, which leads to the mainland and has a bike path.

ABOVE Rent a fishing pole and drop in a line.

THE BASICS

Fly into Savannah/Hilton Head International Airport or Jacksonville International Airport. Rent a car for the 90-minute drive from either airport, and then use it to stay mobile.

King and Prince Beach & Golf Resort
201 Arnold Road
912-638-3631
kingandprince.com
$$$-$$$$
A sprawling 75-year-old full-service resort with guest rooms, villas, and cabanas.

The Lodge at Sea Island Resorts
100 Retreat Avenue
912-634-4300
seaisland.com
$$$$
Close to golf courses; 24-hour butler service.

Ocean Inn & Suites
599 Beachview Drive
912-634-2122
oceaninnsuites.com
$-$$
Within walking distance of the Village and the lighthouse.

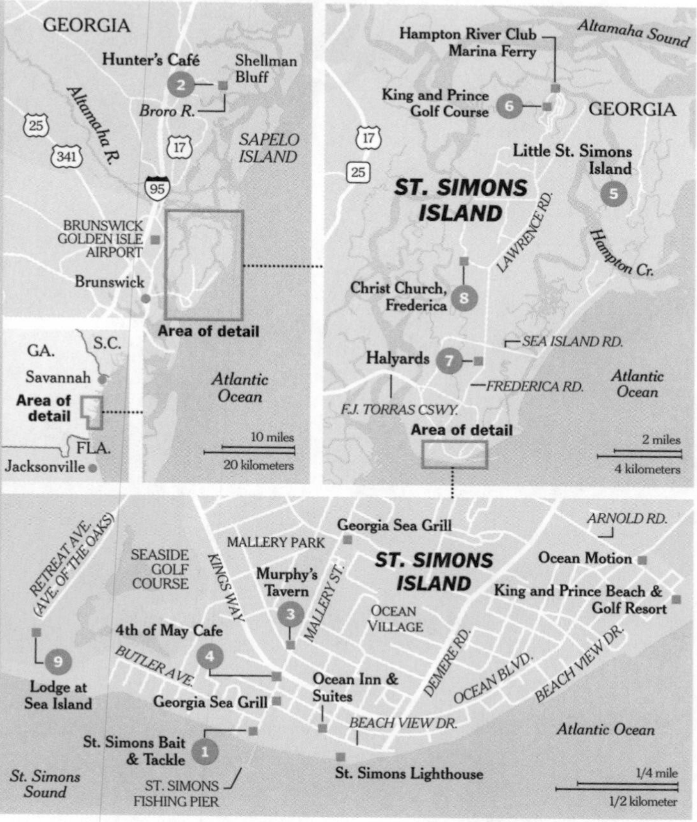
GEORGIA
Hunter's Café
Shellman Bluff
Broro R.
Altamaha R.
25
341
17
95
SAPELO ISLAND
BRUNSWICK GOLDEN ISLE AIRPORT
Brunswick
Area of detail
GA.
S.C.
Savannah
Area of detail
FLA.
Jacksonville
Atlantic Ocean
10 miles
20 kilometers
Hampton River Club Marina Ferry
Altamaha Sound
King and Prince Golf Course
GEORGIA
Little St. Simons Island
ST. SIMONS ISLAND
LAWRENCE RD.
Hampton Cr.
Christ Church, Frederica
SEA ISLAND RD.
Halyards
FREDERICA RD.
Atlantic Ocean
F.J. TORRAS CSWY.
Area of detail
2 miles
4 kilometers
Georgia Sea Grill
ARNOLD RD.
MALLERY PARK
ST. SIMONS ISLAND
Ocean Motion
RETREAT AVE. (AVE. OF THE OAKS)
SEASIDE GOLF COURSE
KINGS WAY
Murphy's Tavern
MALLERY ST.
OCEAN VILLAGE
King and Prince Beach & Golf Resort
4th of May Cafe
BUTLER AVE.
DEMERE RD.
OCEAN BLVD.
BEACH VIEW DR.
Lodge at Sea Island
Georgia Sea Grill
Ocean Inn & Suites
BEACH VIEW DR.
Atlantic Ocean
St. Simons Bait & Tackle
St. Simons Sound
ST. SIMONS FISHING PIER
St. Simons Lighthouse
1/4 mile
1/2 kilometer

Orlando

People who live in the Orlando area will tell you that there is life here beyond the theme parks, gator farms, and citrus groves. You can't go far without stumbling upon a picturesque lake, and the area abounds with small regional museums like the Zora Neale Hurston National Museum of Fine Arts in nearby Eatonville. Downtown, the new Amway Center, home of the Orlando Magic, has given a boost to the nightlife district on Church Street. And Orlando's many neighborhoods are home to lounge acts, bars, vintage fast-food joints, and brick-paved streets. — BY SHAILA DEWAN

FRIDAY

1 *Plunge In* 1 p.m.

Wakeboarding is to water skiing what snowboarding is to downhill skiing — in other words, the extreme version of the sport — and Orlando likes to call itself the "wakeboarding capital of the world." At the **Orlando Watersports Complex** (8615 Florida Rock Road; 407-251-3100; orlandowatersports.com), a beginner's cable tow, anchored to poles in the lake, pulls you and your wakeboard around at 17 miles per hour. The patient instructor will give you pointers, and you can watch some of the sport's best-known hot-doggers navigate the ramps and slides.

2 *High Design* 3 p.m.

Just a few miles from downtown Orlando, Winter Park — considered part of the greater Orlando area — is famous for the brick-paved streets of chichi chocolatiers and its boutiques along Park Avenue. But across the railroad tracks near Hannibal Square, there's a bent toward high design. Amid the newer shops and restaurants, you can find **Rifle Paper Co.** (558 West New England Avenue, Suite 150; 407-622-7679; riflepaperco.com), the fashionable Orlando-based stationer, and the studio and storefront where **Makr Carry Goods** churns out its minimalist leather bags and iPod cases (444 West New England Avenue, Suite 102; 407-284-0192; makr.com). For a taste of local history, visit the **Hannibal Square Heritage Center** (642 West New England Avenue; 407-539-2680; hannibalsquareheritagecenter.org), where a collection of photographs and oral histories document the area's early role as a Reconstruction-era community for freed slaves.

OPPOSITE Wakeboarding on the advanced cable tow at the Orlando Watersports Complex.

RIGHT The strip-mall location may be uninspiring, but dinner at the Ravenous Pig in Winter Park is worth the trip.

3 *Dress Up, Dress Down* 7 p.m.

From the outside, the **Ravenous Pig** (1234 North Orange Avenue, Winter Park; 407-628-2333; theravenouspig.com; $$$) looks like your average strip-mall restaurant. But with attention to detail like house-made sour mix at the bar and much-in-demand cheese biscuits, James and Julie Petrakis have made this one of Orlando's most popular gathering spots. The menu, like the restaurant, is dress-up/dress-down, with bar fare like mussels and fries dusted with fennel pollen or more dignified entrees like dry-aged strip steak with wild mushroom bread pudding. Reserve a table or hover in the bar.

4 *Lounge Act* 10 p.m.

If the **Red Fox Lounge** (110 South Orlando Avenue, Winter Park; 407-647-1166) were an amusement park, it might be called ToupeeWorld. This stuck-in-amber hotel bar in a Best Western hotel appeals to a broad cross-section of Orlando, from retirees to young professionals to a drinking club whose members wear identical captain's hats. The main draw is the consummate lounge act. Mark Wayne and Lorna Lambey deliver silky, singalong versions of "Sweet Caroline," "Hava Nagila," and other golden oldies.

SATURDAY

5 *Tiffany Extravaganza* 10 a.m.

Louis Comfort Tiffany's masterpiece was Laurelton Hall, his estate on Long Island, which featured a wisteria blossom window over 30 feet long and a terrace whose columns were crowned in glass daffodils. When the house burned in 1957, Jeanette and Hugh McKean, from Winter Park, rescued those pieces and many more, adding them to what would become the most comprehensive collection of Tiffany glass, jewelry, and ceramics in the world. The collection, including a chapel with a stunning peacock mosaic that was made for the Chicago World's Fair in 1893, is housed in the **Morse Museum of American Art** (445 North Park Avenue, Winter Park; 407-645-5311; morsemuseum.org), where a new wing allows the largest Laurelton Hall pieces, including the daffodil terrace, to be on permanent display.

6 *A Fast-Food Original* Noon

Devotees of American fast food in all its glory will not want to miss the roast beef sandwiches and cherry milkshakes at **Beefy King**, a lunchtime standby for more than four decades (424 North Bumby Avenue; 407-894-2241; beefyking.com; $). Perch on the old-fashioned swivel chairs and admire the vintage logo of a snorting steer, also available on hot pink T-shirts.

7 *Pontoon Tour* 3 p.m.

Orlando is not quite an American Venice, but it does have about 100 lakes, many connected by narrow canals. Despite the alligators, the lakes are prime real estate, and at **Lake Osceola**, you can board a pontoon boat and take an hourlong cruise (**Scenic Boat Tour;** 312 East Morse Boulevard; 407-644-4056; scenicboattours.com) that will provide glimpses of Spanish colonial-style mansions, azalea gardens, stately Rollins College, and moss-laden cypresses. The ride is billed as Florida's longest continuously running tourist attraction, though you are likely to find plenty of locals aboard. The guide will entertain you with celebrity anecdotes, a smattering of history, and a reasonably small number of cheesy jokes. Tours leave on the hour.

8 *Cultural Fusion* 6 p.m.

The city of theme parks does have a studious side, as evidenced in a blossoming neighborhood called College Park, where the streets have names like Harvard and Vassar and where Jack Kerouac wrote *Dharma Bums*. The main commercial drag, Edgewater Drive, is chockablock with local favorites like **K Restaurant** (1710 Edgewater Drive; 407-872-2332; kwinebar.com; $$), where the servers'

ABOVE The Morse Museum of American Art.

habit of asking for and using your name makes you feel like a regular. With an appetizer of crispy pig's ear on a salad with peanuts and cilantro, the chef gives a nod to Vietnamese flavors that abound in Orlando. At **Infusion Tea** (1600 Edgewater Drive; 407-999-5255; infusionorlando.com; $), choose from dozens of loose teas like Organic Monkey-Picked Oolong to go along with chocolate-coated Cheerios or a cupcake. Or you can choose among the scarves, vintage aprons, and jewelry at the attached artists' collective.

9 *Crafty Brews* 9 p.m.

Craft beers have proliferated in Orlando. The lively restaurant and bar **Cask & Larder** (565 West Fairbanks Avenue, Winter Park; 321-280-4200; caskandlarder.com) has a menu of rotating ales brewed in a glassed room so customers can watch the process. This place also offers beers paired with Southern-influenced cuisine like fish fry with okra and hush puppies or chicken and biscuits. **Orlando Brewing** (1301 Atlanta Avenue, Orlando; 407-872-1117; orlandobrewing.com), which bills itself as a U.S.D.A.-certified organic brewery, operates in a 7,000-square-foot space where bluegrass and country bands play on weekends.

SUNDAY

10 *Sweet Potato Hash* 11 a.m.

You never know what will turn up on the improvised brunch menu — a slip of notebook paper with a ballpoint scrawl — at **Stardust Video and Coffee** (1842 East Winter Park Road, 407-623-3393; stardustvideoandcoffee.wordpress.com; $), a hub for

ABOVE Wally's, a stop on the dive-bar circuit.

BELOW A Winter Park canal, part of the Orlando area's abundant supply of lakes and connecting waterways.

Orlando's artistic types. Zucchini pancakes, maybe, or vegan sweet potato hash with eggs and (real) bacon. You're also likely to find art installations, an old-fashioned photo booth, and a slew of obscure videos and DVDs on the shelves at the far end of this sunny, airy space. There is a full bar for the performances, screenings, and lectures that unfold here in the later hours.

11 *Fool's Gold, Real Finds* Noon

Flea markets can offer too many tube socks and T-shirts, while antiques markets can be entirely too stuffy. **Renningers Twin Markets** in Mount Dora (20651 Highway 441; 352-383-3141; renningers.com), about a 30-minute drive from downtown, puts the thrill back in the hunt. Just past the main entrance, you can turn right and head to a vast antiques barn crammed with treasures like meticulously constructed wooden model ships and 19th-century quilts. Or you can turn left for the flea and farmers' market, where home-grown orchids and leather motorcycle chaps compete for attention. Behind that, there is a field where curio dealers set up tables with all manner of bona fide junk, fool's gold, and the occasional real finds that make it clear why so many thrift aficionados make road trips to Florida.

OPPOSITE The Morse Museum of American Art displays an extensive collection of works by Louis Comfort Tiffany.

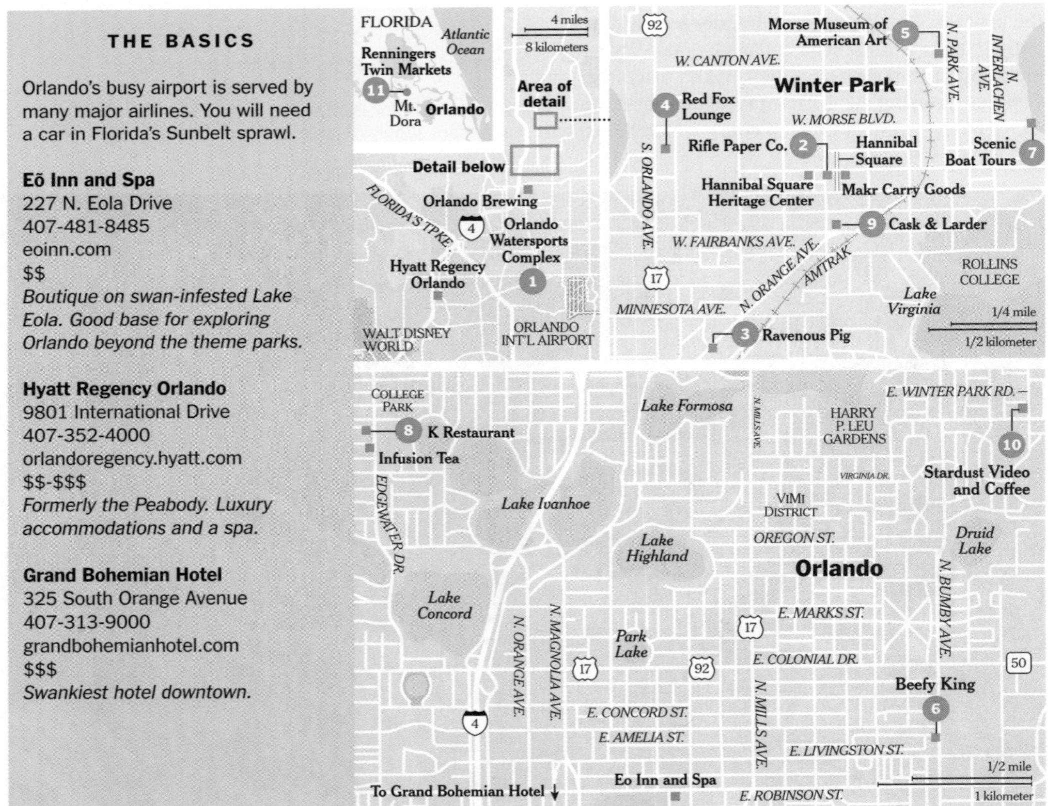

THE BASICS

Orlando's busy airport is served by many major airlines. You will need a car in Florida's Sunbelt sprawl.

Eõ Inn and Spa
227 N. Eola Drive
407-481-8485
eoinn.com
$$
Boutique on swan-infested Lake Eola. Good base for exploring Orlando beyond the theme parks.

Hyatt Regency Orlando
9801 International Drive
407-352-4000
orlandoregency.hyatt.com
$$-$$$
Formerly the Peabody. Luxury accommodations and a spa.

Grand Bohemian Hotel
325 South Orange Avenue
407-313-9000
grandbohemianhotel.com
$$$
Swankiest hotel downtown.

AGENA
9
UNITED STATES
NASA
553
UNITED STATES
19

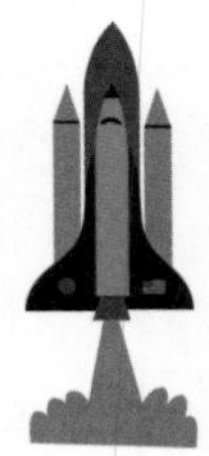

Cape Canaveral

The glory days of the space program, when regular flights to the moon left from Cape Canaveral, are far in the past, but NASA still has a presence, the local area code is still 321, and the Kennedy Space Center remains the conservator of proud national memories. In other ways, this part of Florida is still coming into its own. Cocoa Beach, just south on the long stretch of barrier sand and islands off the state's central Atlantic coast, has been thoroughly discovered, though it still feels almost unspoiled in comparison to the condo-towered shores of South Florida. Canaveral has emerged as a busy cruise port. And there's more to see, from citrus groves and wild protected seashores to one of the country's best surf shops. Feeling hungry? You can dine on fine French cuisine or fresh Florida seafood —or just head to a local souvenir shop for some freeze-dried ice cream, an astronaut favorite.

— BY CHARLES PASSY

FRIDAY

1 *Ocean Outreach* 6 p.m.

The lovably scruffy side of an older Florida reveals itself at the **Cocoa Beach Pier** (401 Meade Avenue, Cocoa Beach; cocoabeachpier.com), a 44-year-old hangout that stretches some 800 feet into the Atlantic Ocean. You come here to drink, dine, or fish—the pier is dotted with stores, bars, and restaurants, both indoors and outdoors—or just take in the expansive view. The pier scene really hops during the Friday-night Boardwalk Bash, when bands perform. Enjoy a cold one and some bar fare (wings, burgers, fish and chips) at **Marlins Good Times Bar & Grill** (321-783-7549) while listening to the music.

2 *Hang 10, 24/7* 8 p.m.

Who doesn't feel the need to go surfboard shopping on a Friday night? O.K., so maybe you're not ready to plunk down $1,000 to ride the waves in style, but the selections at the justly famous flagship **Ron Jon Surf Shop** (4151 North Atlantic Avenue, Cocoa Beach; 321-799-8888; ronjonsurfshop.com) go beyond boards and surfing gear. The two-story, 52,000-square-foot store, which is open 24 hours a day—and claims to be visited by more than two million people annually—also sells beachwear, shot glasses, Polynesian kitsch, and other "why did I buy that?" items. A spirit of endless hooky pervades, as evidenced by the T-shirt for sale that says, "I was on summer vacation for 20 years."

SATURDAY

3 *Breakfast Cubano* 8 a.m.

While Cuban food is most associated with Miami and environs, the Canaveral area can lay claim to one of the state's best spots—**Roberto's Little Havana Restaurant** (26 North Orlando Avenue, Cocoa Beach; 321-784-1868; robertoslittlehavana.com; $). It's a downtown Cocoa Beach favorite serving all the Cuban classics, from palomilla steak to fried yucca to flan. But at breakfast time, it's the place to be for an egg-bacon-cheese sandwich, served on soft Cuban bread. Good Cuban coffee, too.

4 *Citrus Stop* 9:30 a.m.

You're a few miles from the Indian River fruit area that is one of Florida's legendary spots for citrus groves. So you'll have to stop for some liquid

OPPOSITE Space Age relics at the Kennedy Space Center. American Astronauts left from this sprawling complex on trips to the moon.

RIGHT Partying comes with a view at the Cocoa Beach Pier, which juts 800 feet out into the Atlantic.

sunshine. **Policicchio Groves** (5780 North Courtenay Parkway Route 3, Merritt Island; 321-452-4866; juicycitrus.com), a family enterprise nearly nine decades old, has an assortment of oranges and grapefruits; the varieties change each month during the winter and the spring-to-early-summer growing seasons. Everything is freshly picked; the groves are across the road. The store will help you pack and ship the bounty.

5 *A Space Odyssey* 10:30 a.m.

Go north on Route 3 and left on NASA Parkway (Route 405) for the **Kennedy Space Center Visitor Complex** (321-449-4444; kennedyspacecenter.com). The complex may vaguely resemble one of Florida's theme parks at first, and the ticket prices suggest something of the kind. But very soon it becomes much more inspiring. Start with a walk through the Rocket Garden, an open-air space that features awe-inspiring Redstone, Atlas, and Titan rockets that date from the days of the Mercury and Gemini missions; you can also squeeze into replicas of the capsules the astronauts used. But that's the appetizer to the space center's main course — a roughly three-hour bus tour that gives you a sense of how big the center truly is (some 140,000 acres, including the surrounding wildlife refuge). Along the way, you'll pass the Vehicle Assembly Building — a structure so cavernous that clouds are said to have formed inside it. The tour's most jaw-dropping stop is the Apollo/Saturn V Center, a huge hangar that contains an actual Saturn V rocket. Take time to look at the individual exhibits about the Apollo program, all presented with extraordinary detail.

6 *Close Encounter* 2:45 p.m.

Now that you've gotten yourself acquainted (or reacquainted) with the space program, it's time to meet a real astronaut. The center's Astronaut Encounter affords an opportunity to do just that. Veterans of the space program, mostly from the shuttle era, give daily 30-minute presentations about their experiences and field questions from the audience. Want a little more face time? For an extra fee, you can sign up for lunch with an astronaut. You can also get an idea of the astronaut experience for yourself with hands-on simulators, or slip into fantasy at the Angry Birds Space Encounter.

7 *Astronaut Memorial* 3:30 p.m.

About two dozen astronauts have died in their attempts to slip "the surly bonds of earth," as the World War II pilot John Gillespie Magee Jr. put it in a poem quoted by President Reagan after the 1986 Challenger disaster. Those men and women are remembered at the center's simple, stark Space Mirror Memorial — a black granite surface in which the names are inscribed. When the light is at the right angle, the names seem to float in space.

8 *Au Côte d'Espace* 7 p.m.

The Cape Canaveral area may not be a citadel of fine dining, but **Café Margaux** (220 Brevard Avenue, Cocoa; 321-639-8343; cafemargaux.com; $$$) is an exception to the rule. This quaint restaurant, set in the tree-lined Cocoa Village district, is proudly French, with a few nods elsewhere. The wine list places equal emphasis on New and Old World vintages.

SUNDAY

9 *Natural Habitat* 10 a.m.

It takes a lot of surrounding land to keep the Kennedy Space Center's launch sites properly isolated. Much of that acreage is encompassed

within the buffer zone that is the **Merritt Island National Wildlife Refuge** (321-861-0667; fws.gov/merrittisland), a huge, mostly untouched tract that is home to migratory birds and bald eagles. Begin your journey by picking up a map at one of the kiosks near the entrances to the refuge (the small visitor's center may be closed if you're in the wrong season), and then head to the gloriously remote beaches, which are part of the separately managed **Canaveral National Seashore** (321-267-1110; nps.gov/cana). Conclude with a visit to the refuge's Black Point Wildlife Drive — a seven-mile loop that allows you to get close to wildlife, including alligators and egrets, without leaving your car.

10 *In the Realm of the Shrimp* 1 p.m.

The family-owned **Dixie Crossroads Seafood Restaurant** (1475 Garden Street, Titusville; 321-268-5000; dixiecrossroads.com; $$-$$$) is mostly about shrimp. It has its own fleet of about 10 full-time commercial shrimpers, which provide the restaurant with its lobsterlike rock shrimp and more firmly textured Royal Red shrimp, among other Florida varieties. (Once you try these, you'll find it hard to go back to garden-variety frozen shrimp.) The shrimp can be served broiled, fried, or steamed. But before you dig in, you'll get to enjoy the corn fritter starters included with every meal. The bustling setting is also a hoot — part Old Florida (wildlife murals and a fish pond), part pure kitsch. You can pose outside with Mr. and Mrs. Rock — cartoonish statues of a rock shrimp family.

OPPOSITE ABOVE Sunrise surfing at the pier.

OPPOSITE BELOW Oranges for the buying at Policicchio Groves. Florida's famous Indian River citrus-growing region is just inland from Cape Canaveral.

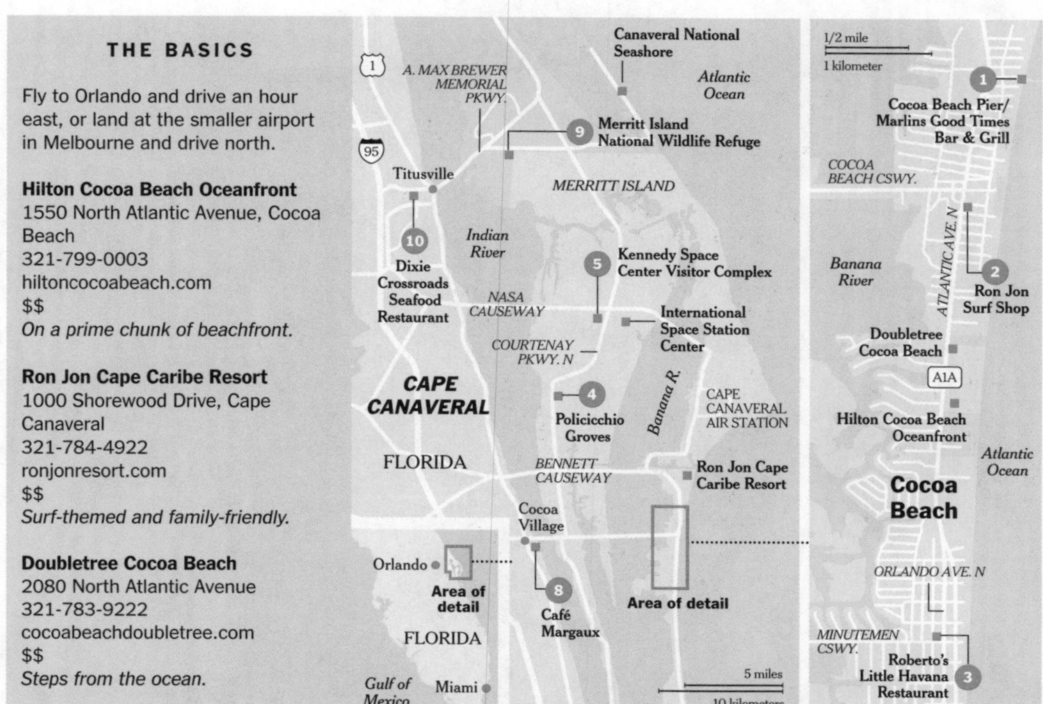

THE BASICS

Fly to Orlando and drive an hour east, or land at the smaller airport in Melbourne and drive north.

Hilton Cocoa Beach Oceanfront
1550 North Atlantic Avenue, Cocoa Beach
321-799-0003
hiltoncocoabeach.com
$$
On a prime chunk of beachfront.

Ron Jon Cape Caribe Resort
1000 Shorewood Drive, Cape Canaveral
321-784-4922
ronjonresort.com
$$
Surf-themed and family-friendly.

Doubletree Cocoa Beach
2080 North Atlantic Avenue
321-783-9222
cocoabeachdoubletree.com
$$
Steps from the ocean.

Palm Beach

The tiny island of Palm Beach, on Florida's southeast coast, boasts some of the country's dreamiest estates, where the staff lives better than many Americans, cashmere sweaters in trademark pastel greens and pinks go for $800, and Rolls-Royces show up at the supermarket with regularity. Some Palm Beachers had to tighten their Gucci belts in the wake of the Bernard Madoff scandal; he selected many of his victims at the local golf club. But judging by the perfectly clipped hedges that envelop the manicured mansions, most residents may be doing with less, but not much less, in a town where more is never quite enough.
— BY GERALDINE FABRIKANT

FRIDAY

1 *The Big Gape* 4 p.m.

Big money means big house, so rent a nice convertible and stare. For envy-inducing views of these winter palaces, drive south along **South Ocean Boulevard** for about six miles starting at Barton Avenue. Even those obsessed with privacy relish their ocean views (why pay millions for beachfront if you can't enjoy it?), which means the gates and hedges along these mansions are slightly lower than elsewhere in town. You can catch a glimpse of the Mar-a-Lago Club, Donald Trump's former residence and now a private club he owns.

2 *Grande Dame* 6:30 p.m.

For a sunset cocktail, glide into the **Breakers Hotel** (1 South County Road; 561-655-6611; thebreakers.com), originally built in 1896. So central is its location that the hotel has been rebuilt twice after fires destroyed it. The Seafood Bar has delightful views of the sea. If you prefer upholstered opulence, head for the Tapestry Bar with its two Flemish tapestries and a grand bar built using a mantel from Caxton Hall in London.

3 *Diner's Club* 8:30 p.m.

Palm Beach dining runs from supremely pretentious to casually simple. Many restaurants survive over decades, and because Palm Beach is a small town, where the same cast shows up frequently, they have the feel of private clubs. The **Palm Beach Grill** (340 Royal Poinciana Way; 561-835-1077; palmbeachgrill.com; $$$) is a darkly wooded, dimly lighted social fixture that is a favorite of the author James Patterson and almost everyone else. If the mobbed dining room is for the island's old guard, the bar seems to attract newcomers: snowbirds deciding whether to move south, city types longing for a slower, more glamorous life, and locals who want to have fun. Don't miss American classics like spare ribs and ice cream sundaes. Book before you fly.

SATURDAY

4 *Empty Beaches* 8 a.m.

Park on **South Ocean Boulevard** and take a long, languorous walk on the beach. The beaches here are flat, wide, clean, and wonderful in the early morning when there are not many people around.

5 *Early Snowbirds* 9 a.m.

This may be a party town, but it wakes up early. A clutch of restaurants along Royal Poinciana Way are busy by 8:30 a.m., with diners sitting outside and savoring the sunshine and breakfast. **Testa's Palm Beach Restaurant** (221 Royal Poinciana Way; 561-832-0992; testasrestaurants.com; $$), a sprawling, relaxed space, serves blueberry, pecan, and bran pancakes. Around the corner is **Green's Pharmacy** (151 North County Road; 561-832-4443; $$), which

OPPOSITE The lobby at the Breakers, the iconic Palm Beach hotel where the wealthy have long come to be pampered.

BELOW For drive-by glimpses of the waterfront mansions, head out along South Ocean Boulevard.

offers breakfast at an old-fashioned lunch counter. Afterward, pick up candy buttons and other long-forgotten stuff.

6 *History Class* 10:30 a.m.

For an authentic sense of Palm Beach in its early days, drop by the **Flagler Museum** (1 Whitehall Way; 561-655-2833; flaglermuseum.us). It was once the home of Henry Morrison Flagler, one of the founders of Standard Oil and the man who brought the railroad to southern Florida. He spent millions in 1902 to build the 55-room house that became a hotel and finally a museum. The decoration is lavish: gilded furniture and ceilings, marble pillars and fireplaces, golden bed curtains. One of the items on display is Flagler's private railway car.

7 *Retail Strut* Noon

On Worth Avenue, where every brand that you've seen in *Vogue* has a storefront, the real fun is the crowd: women in green cashmere sweaters walking dogs in matching outfits; elderly gents with bow ties and blazers. But the true gems — Cartier aside — are the smaller, lesser-known stores that have survived by wit and originality. **Maryanna Suzanna** (313 Worth Avenue; 561-833-0204) carries colorful jewelry by Monies and the Italian designer Angela Caputi — some earrings are under $50. Across the street, **Sherry Frankel's Melangerie** (256 Worth Avenue; 561-655-1996) will custom-embroider anything and sells amusing plastic watches for $68. And nearby is **Il Sandalo** (240 Worth Avenue; 561-805-8674; ilsandalo.com), where the shoemaker Hernan Garcia makes custom sandals starting at around $200. For lunch, head to **Ta-boo** (221 Worth Avenue; 561-835-3500; tabooerestaurant.com; $$$), with its British colonial décor, where women swathed in white linen and wearing enormous straw hats pick carefully at the chopped chef's salad.

ABOVE Palm Beach feels exclusive, but the beach is public. Walk it in the early morning, when few people are out.

8 *Gilt Trip* 3:30 p.m.

It's a challenge to fill those sprawling estates with furniture, but there are armies of antiques merchants poised to try. Antiques enthusiasts should go all the way south to Southern Boulevard for some notably good prospecting. Start at the emporium of the elegant French dealer **Cedric Dupont** (3415 South Dixie Highway; 561-835-1319; cedricdupontantiques.com), and then go on to **The Elephant's Foot** (3800 South Dixie Highway; 561-832-0170; theelephantsfootantiques.com), which has a range of English, French, and Oriental antiques at varying prices. For a resale find, try **Circa Who** (531 Northwood Road; 561-655-5224; circawho.com), which has faux bamboo and Old Florida furniture.

9 *Mediterranean Flavor* 8 p.m.

For a casual dinner in the heart of town, head to **Cucina Dell'Arte** (257 Royal Poinciana Way; 561-655-0770; cucinadellarte.com; $$$), which is popular with a younger crowd and is open until 3 a.m. It is decorated in the earth tones and mustards and peaches typical of the Mediterranean and seems to be busy all day with families, couples, and groups of friends. You can eat outdoors and watch the crowds go by.

10 *Party Time* 10:30 p.m.

There are plenty of multi-carat jewels in Palm Beach, but they are generally worn at private parties.

The night life for visitors is casual. Stop in for a drink at the very pretty **Brazilian Court Hotel** (301 Australian Avenue; 561-655-7740; thebraziliancourt.com). You might try a Bikini Martini, with Sagatiba cachaça and passion fruit purée. On Saturdays a small band or D.J. plays in the lobby until 1 a.m., attracting a preppy crowd. Or head across the bridge to **Blue Martini** (CityPlace, 550 South Rosemary Avenue, West Palm Beach; 561-835-8601; bluemartinilounge.com) in a trendy shopping mall, where you can sip a martini and hear the music pour out of B. B. King's Blues Club next door.

SUNDAY

11 *Hit the Trail* 10 a.m.

A flat and easy bike trail hugs the Intracoastal Waterway, which skirts the west side of Palm Beach, and offers fantastic views of the Marina in West Palm Beach. Rent a bike at **Palm Beach Bicycle Trail Shop** (223 Sunrise Avenue; 561-659-4583; palmbeachbicycle.com), which has multispeed bikes. If biking is not your thing, you can jog the route.

ABOVE The Blue Martini in West Palm Beach, the humbler sister town across the Intracoastal Waterway.

THE BASICS

Fly to Palm Beach International Airport and rent a car.

The Breakers
1 South County Road
561-655-6611
thebreakers.com
$$$$
A 550-room stunner directly on the beach.

The Chesterfield
363 Cocoanut Row
561-659-5800
chesterfieldpb.com
$$$$
Elegantly appointed boutique hotel in walking distance of Worth Avenue.

Marriott West Palm Beach
1001 Okeechobee Boulevard
561-833-1234
marriott.com
$$$
A reliable choice just outside of town in West Palm Beach.

Fort Lauderdale

Fort Lauderdale continues to mature beyond its spring-break days, with posh resorts now rising along the beach. Meanwhile, Las Olas Boulevard, the lively commercial strip that links the beach to downtown, has welcomed an array of new boutiques and restaurants. Sure, a smattering of raucous bars still dot the beach, and the rowdy clubgoers of Himmarshee Village can be three deep in the middle of the week. But at the end of a sunny, water-logged day, this Florida resort town offers a sophisticated evening that doesn't involve neon bikinis and syrupy daiquiris. — BY GERALDINE FABRIKANT

FRIDAY

1 *Seaside Dusk* 5 p.m.

There are a slew of beachfront restaurants and bars in Fort Lauderdale where you can have a drink, watch the clouds roll over the ocean, soak up the sea air, and catch the parade of sun-soaked tourists in beachwear and residents going home in suits and ties. One of the more welcoming spots is the relatively quiet **H2O Café** (101 South Fort Lauderdale Beach Boulevard; 954-414-1024; h2ocafe.net), which occupies part of an Art Deco building dating to 1937.

2 *Waterfront Wahoo* 7 p.m.

Fort Lauderdale's dining scene is alive and well inland as well as on the water. The **Bimini Boatyard Bar and Grill** (1555 Southeast 17th Street; 954-525-7400; biminiboatyard.com; $$) evokes a New England-style boathouse with its crisp blue and white décor, enormous cathedral ceiling, gleaming oak floors, and portal-style windows. An outdoor bar facing a marina brings in a nautical mix of young and old who dine on fresh seafood like wood-grilled wahoo and yellowtail snapper.

3 *Nice and Cool* 9 p.m.

For a cool nightcap, slide over to **Blue Jean Blues** (3320 Northeast 33rd Street; 954-306-6330; bluejeanblues.net), where you can sit at the bar and listen to live jazz and blues bands. The club has a tiny stage and a dance floor, and the music can go from jazz to Caribbean depending on the evening.

SATURDAY

4 *Dawn Patrol* 8 a.m.

Take an early morning stroll along the wide, white beach. It is open to joggers, walkers, and swimmers and is surprisingly clean. For a leafier, more secluded adventure that is a favorite with resident runners and walkers, try the two-mile loop through the woods in the **Hugh Taylor Birch State Park** (954-468-2791; floridastateparks.org/hughtaylorbirch). Its entrance is only steps from the beach at the intersection of A1A and Sunrise Boulevard. If you're not a jogger, take a drive through anyway.

5 *Sunny Nosh* 10 a.m.

Finish off the jog at the beachside **Ritz-Carlton** (1 North Fort Lauderdale Beach Boulevard; 954-465-2300; ritzcarlton.com/fortlauderdale). The Ritz-Carlton Hotel Company bought the former St. Regis and put its own stamp on the property. For a relaxed breakfast (served until 11 a.m.), either indoors or out, go to **Via Luna** ($$$), the hotel's restaurant, where you can choose your fare from a buffet with omelets, smoked salmon, cereals, and fruit.

6 *Eccentric Estate* 1 p.m.

Bonnet House (900 North Birch Road; 954-563-5393; bonnethouse.org) was the vacation

OPPOSITE Fort Lauderdale's sun-kissed beach.

RIGHT The International Swimming Hall of Fame. Among the curious facts to learn inside: Leonardo da Vinci and Benjamin Franklin both experimented with swim fins.

home of the artists and art patrons Frederic Bartlett and his wife, Evelyn, whose first husband was the grandson and namesake of the founder of Eli Lilly and Company. They created an eccentric, brightly painted retreat, now a museum — more Caribbean mansion than Florida estate — near a swamp where alligators thrived. Window bars protected the house from the panthers that once roamed the estate and the monkeys that still live there.

7 *Cruising the Pier* 3:30 p.m.

If you want to go a bit off the beaten track, drive up Route A1A to Commercial Boulevard and hang out on **Anglin's Pier**. There is a little shopping area for swim gear, and you can rent a fishing pole. Or just sit and have a coffee.

8 *Crabs or Pizza* 7 p.m.

One trendy restaurant is **Truluck's**, at the Galleria Mall (2584A East Sunrise Boulevard; 954-396-5656; trulucks.com; $$$$). An elegant room with dark woods and red leather upholstery, it adds a bit of glamour to the popular mall and has a busy bar where a piano player entertains all evening. It has a surf-and-turf menu but is perhaps best known for stone crabs. For lighter fare, try **D'Angelo** (4215 North Federal Highway, Oakland Park; 954-561-7300; pizzadangelo.com; $), a modern Tuscan-style restaurant. It attracts a fashion-aware young crowd with its meatball tapas and Napoletana pizzas.

9 *Mall Party* 9 p.m.

It may not be spring break, but you would never know, looking at the huge crowds at the **Blue Martini**, at the Galleria Mall (2432 East Sunrise Boulevard; 954-653-2583; bluemartinilounge.com). But the patrons are decidedly more upscale. By 8 p.m. when the band is playing, the bar is packed with young professionals and snow birds, schmoozing and dancing. A newer place is **SoLita Las Olas** (1032 East Las Olas; 954-357-2616; solitalasolas.com), which has a lively bar. Fort Lauderdale also has a booming gay night-life scene; one spot to try is the ever-popular **Georgie's Alibi** (2266 Wilton Drive; 954-565-2526; georgiesalibi.com).

SUNDAY

10 *Southern Comfort* 11 a.m.

The **Pelican Grand Beach Resort** (2000 North Ocean Boulevard; 954-568-9431; pelicanbeach.com) offers a Sunday brunch with eggs Benedict, rice pilaf, bloody marys, and mimosas. The plantation-style restaurant overlooks the beach, with a big veranda with white wicker tables and rocking chairs that catch the sea breezes.

11 *Super Swimmers* 12:30 p.m.

Water enthusiasts should stop in at the **International Swimming Hall of Fame** (One Hall of Fame Drive; 954-462-6536; ishof.org). Did you know that both Leonardo da Vinci and Benjamin Franklin

ABOVE The Bonnet House museum was the vacation home of the artists Frederic and Evelyn Bartlett in the days when panthers roamed the nearby swamps.

BELOW Morning exercise on the sand. Fort Lauderdale's expansive beach has plenty of room for joggers, early-bird swimmers, and martial artists.

experimented with swim fins? Or that Polynesian swimmers used palm leaves tied to their feet? Those and other nuggets of swimming trivia are lovingly conveyed at this sleek white building on the Intracoastal Waterway.

12 *Las Olas Stroll* 2 p.m.

In an era when shopping in new cities can remind you of every mall back home, Fort Lauderdale has kept its streak of independence: nothing fancy but fun. East Las Olas Boulevard has a rash of one-off stores; one is **KumBaYa** (No. 1012; 954-768-9004; kumbayashop.com), which carries colorful T-shirts and straw bags. If you want to take edible gifts home or you can't resist them yourself, drop in at **Kilwin's**, an ice cream, chocolate, and fudge shop (No. 809; 954-523-8338; kilwins.com). Its motto is "Life is uncertain. Eat dessert first." Ponder that over a bag of caramel corn as you explore the rest of the shops.

ABOVE The elegant dining room at Truluck's, a glamorous local dinner spot known for steaks and seafood, especially its stone crab.

THE BASICS

The Fort Lauderdale International Airport is served by multiple airlines.

You will need a car if you plan to spend any time away from the beach.

Pelican Grand Beach Resort
2000 North Ocean Boulevard
954-568-9431
pelicanbeach.com
$$-$$$
156 rooms, directly on the beach.

Ritz-Carlton
1 North Fort Lauderdale Beach Boulevard
954-465-2300
ritzcarlton.com/fortlauderdale
$$$-$$$$
192 rooms, full-service spa and wine room with more than 5,000 bottles.

W Fort Lauderdale
401 North Fort Lauderdale Beach Boulevard
954-414-8200
wfortlauderdalehotel.com
$$$-$$$$
Sleekly modern, with spa and two pools.

1 mile
2 kilometers
Fort Lauderdale
COMMERCIAL BLVD.
NE 50TH ST.
D'Angelo
Anglin's Pier 7
N. FEDERAL HWY.
A1A
1
N. ANDREWS AVE.
NE SIXTH AVE.
NE 33RD ST.
E. OAKLAND PARK BLVD.
95
3 Blue Jean Blues
Georgie's Alibi
WILTON DR.
Pelican Grand Beach Resort 10
NW 15TH AVE.
NW NINTH AVE.
Truluck's 8
Blue Martini 9
4 Hugh Taylor Birch State Park
E. SUNRISE HWY.
Galleria Mall
Bonnet House 6
N. FEDERAL HWY.
W Fort Lauderdale
NW SIXTH ST.
W. BROWARD BLVD.
Area of detail
E. LAS OLAS BLVD.
Area of detail
KumBaYa 12
Kilwin's
E. LAS OLAS BLVD.
SoLita Las Olas
SE 17TH ST.
2 Bimini Boatyard Bar and Grill
FLORIDA
Lake Okeechobee
West Palm Beach
Fort Lauderdale
Miami
Atlantic Ocean
N. FT. LAUDERDALE BEACH BLVD.
Ritz-Carlton/ Via Luna 5
H20 Café 1
S. FT. LAUDERDALE BEACH BLVD.
A1A
11 International Swimming Hall of Fame

LIBERTY OF THE SEAS
prince

South Beach Miami

A weekend in South Beach ought to begin not with "What to pack?" but rather with "What to pursue?" Do you long for the South Beach of painted-on dresses, frozen margaritas, and electric neon? The South Beach of slick new hotels and restaurants? Or the South Beach of yesteryear, of pastel Art Deco buildings, museums, and monuments? Perhaps you simply crave the beach? Miami can be whatever you want it to be—laid back, decked out, gay, straight, a family vacation, a singles' playground—which is precisely what makes it such an effortless getaway. In this dreamland at the southern tip of Miami Beach, you get to choose your own adventure. All you need is sunscreen. — BY STEPHANIE ROSENBLOOM

FRIDAY

1 *Fill the Spare Suitcase* 4 p.m.

South Beach is a breeze to tour by foot or on a bicycle (rentals at DecoBike.com), and one of the easiest places to begin is **Lincoln Road**. Retailers high and low line this wide outdoor pedestrian shopping and eating zone between Alton Road and Washington Avenue. You can pick up South Beach essentials like crystal-embellished Havaianas flip-flops and sarongs in tropical hues. You'll also find coffee shops, ice cream parlors, art galleries, bars, clubs, and retail chains like Anthropologie, Madewell, and Kiehl's. Designer brand names dot the surrounding streets. In other words: pack light.

2 *Spectator Sport* 7 p.m.

For some, nothing beats the absurdity of drinking a frozen margarita the size of a noodle bowl stuffed with two upside-down bottles of Corona beer (yes, people do this) at one of the outdoor tables lining the sidewalk on Ocean Drive. This touristy beachside stretch of restaurants doesn't offer the finest cuisine, though what the area lacks in culinary flavor it makes up for with flavor of a different sort—an endless parade of creatively dressed (or undressed) revelers enjoying the breeze coming off the ocean. More refined restaurants are on Lincoln Road. For some of the best outdoor gawking there, head over to **SushiSamba** (600 Lincoln Road; 305-673-5337; sushisamba.com; $$-$$$) and take in the unofficial fashion show with an irresistible plate of rock shrimp tempura and specialty rolls like the Ezo (salmon, asparagus, onion, chives, sesame, tempura flakes, and wasabi mayonnaise).

3 *Symphony on the Wall* 8 p.m.

South Beach has many soundtracks, but few musical institutions here are as beloved as the **New World Symphony** (500 17th Street; 305-673-3330; nws.edu), an orchestral academy founded by the conductor Michael Tilson Thomas. You won't find it hard to locate the symphony's home—it was designed by Frank Gehry. Some concerts are even free to the public and shown via "live Wallcast" on a 7,000-square-foot projection wall adjacent to the New World Center. (For other sorts of music and theatrical productions, there's also the Art Deco-style Colony Theatre.)

4 *Hotel Crawl* 10 p.m.

After dark, when the sun-kissed passersby are but shadows, it's time for another walk on Ocean Drive, this time to check out the Art Deco hotels, like Colony, Boulevard, and Starlite, illuminated in neon blue, pink, and red. Stop by **Hotel Victor** (1144 Ocean Drive; 305-779-8700; hotelvictorsouthbeach.com), next to the mansion once owned by the designer Gianni Versace. Sit at a sidewalk table with a glass

OPPOSITE A cruise ship glides past South Pointe, the southern tip of South Beach.

RIGHT The view of South Beach, with the ocean in the background, from Juvia, an indoor-outdoor restaurant and bar.

of wine and enjoy live music on the hotel's porch. For a little flash and glamour, stroll to Collins Avenue to tour the lobbies and bars of classic Miami hotels like the Delano, the Stork Club, and the Fontainebleau.

SATURDAY

5 *Art Deco Town* 10 a.m.

Miami's sizeable Art Deco district has hundreds of buildings from the 1920s through the 1940s, many of them prime examples of the era's favorite architectural style. Think pastel hues and architecture evocative of ships. The **Art Deco Welcome Center** (1001 Ocean Drive; 305-672-2014; mdpl.org) offers guided 10:30 a.m. tours that include stops at hotels, restaurants, and other commercial buildings. If you'd prefer to go on your own, rent an audio tour at the center. Either way, make a reservation in advance.

6 *Pop Over for Brunch* Noon

Extend your trip back in time with brunch at the **Betsy Hotel** (1440 Ocean Drive; 305-531-6100; thebetsyhotel.com), a renovated structure that captures an old-fashioned charm that flappers could appreciate. Have brunch in the lobby restaurant, **BLT Steak** (305-673-0044; bltsteak.com; $$$). As you consume a BLT popover or the blueberry pancakes with orange-blossom-water syrup, scan the crowd, an interesting mix of the wealthy and established with the young and scantily dressed.

7 *Sun, Surf, Sand* 1 p.m.

The afternoon is for relaxing amid miles of white sand. The free public sands generally defined as South Beach stretch from Ocean Drive and 5th Street to 21st Street and Collins Avenue. **Lummus**

ABOVE Palms and atmosphere at the Betsy Hotel, a good place for brunch. The Betsy has been renovated, but with a charm that flappers could appreciate.

LEFT The fountain in front of the Colony Theater, one of the favorites in South Beach's cherished collection of preserved Art Deco buildings.

Park (Ocean Drive between 5th and 15th Streets) has beach volleyball courts and a playground, while **South Pointe Park** (1 Washington Avenue) has interactive water features and an observation deck. Bring a deli picnic or, if you want a scene (music, money, pretty young things), seek a restaurant in one of the newer hotels, like **SLS South Beach** (1701 Collins Avenue; 305-674-1701; slshotels.com), where **Hyde Beach** ($$$) serves high-end burgers and tuna ceviche.

8 *Indoor Art* 4 p.m.

South Beach is home to the **Bass Museum of Art** (2100 Collins Avenue; 305-673-7530; bassmuseum.org), with paintings and sculpture spanning 500 years of European art history. Among the artists represented are Rubens, Rembrandt, Botticelli, and Domenico Ghirlandaio. Art lovers who have time to venture beyond South Beach will also want to explore the dozens of galleries, bars, and antiques stores in the **Wynwood Arts District** of Miami; it's a short cab ride away.

9 *Moon View* 9 p.m.

Venture away from kitschy Ocean Drive for a different view of the city from the penthouse of **Juvia** (1111 Lincoln Road; 305-763-8272; juviamiami.com; $$$$), a 10,000-square-foot indoor-outdoor restaurant and bar. The restaurant serves Japanese, French, and Peruvian food as varied as salmon nashi and roasted chicken vadouvan, but the view is the real showstopper. Juvia won a James Beard award for restaurant design and graphics. From its roof, the moon over Miami can seem almost close enough to touch.

BELOW Early morning beach yoga. A vacation here can work for everyone from fitness addicts to big spenders.

SUNDAY

10 *Oceanfront Workout* 10 a.m.

There are few places in South Beach better designed for a workout than the 17th Street Beachwalk, where runners and people on a variety of wheels—in-line skates, bicycles, Segways—swish by (seriously, be careful). Should you wish to join them, you'll have no problem spotting one of the beachside rental companies. For a quieter, more leisurely workout, take a walk through the **Miami Beach Botanical Garden** (2000 Convention Center Drive; 305-673-7256; mbgarden.org), which is stocked with tropical and subtropical plants: orchids, bromeliads, flowering trees, and, of course, palms.

11 *Taste of the Mediterranean* 12:30 p.m.

Don't leave South Beach without wandering over to **Española Way**, a short stretch north of 14th Street between Washington and Pennsylvania Avenues with Spanish colonial architecture as reinterpreted in 1925. Swing by for a casual meal, a savory snack (margaritas and chips hit the spot), or some ice cream. The streets, inspired by Mediterranean villages in Spain and France and once a destination for gamblers like Al Capone, are a cleaner, sleepier, more international version of New York's Little Italy—minus the karaoke and cannoli.

ABOVE The newly refurbished South Pointe Park.

OPPOSITE SoundScape park, near the New World Symphony.

THE BASICS

South Beach, the trendiest stretch of Miami Beach, is best navigated by walking and taking taxis.

James Royal Palm
1545 Collins Avenue
305-604-5700
jameshotels.com/miami
$$$$
Art Deco with hallmarks and adding a bevy of modern amenities.

Gale South Beach
1690 Collins Avenue
305-673-0199
galehotel.com
$$$
Built in 1941 and stylishly redone.

The Fontainebleau
4441 Collins Avenue
305-538-2000
fontainebleau.com
$$$$
Recapturing former glory after a $1 billion renovation.

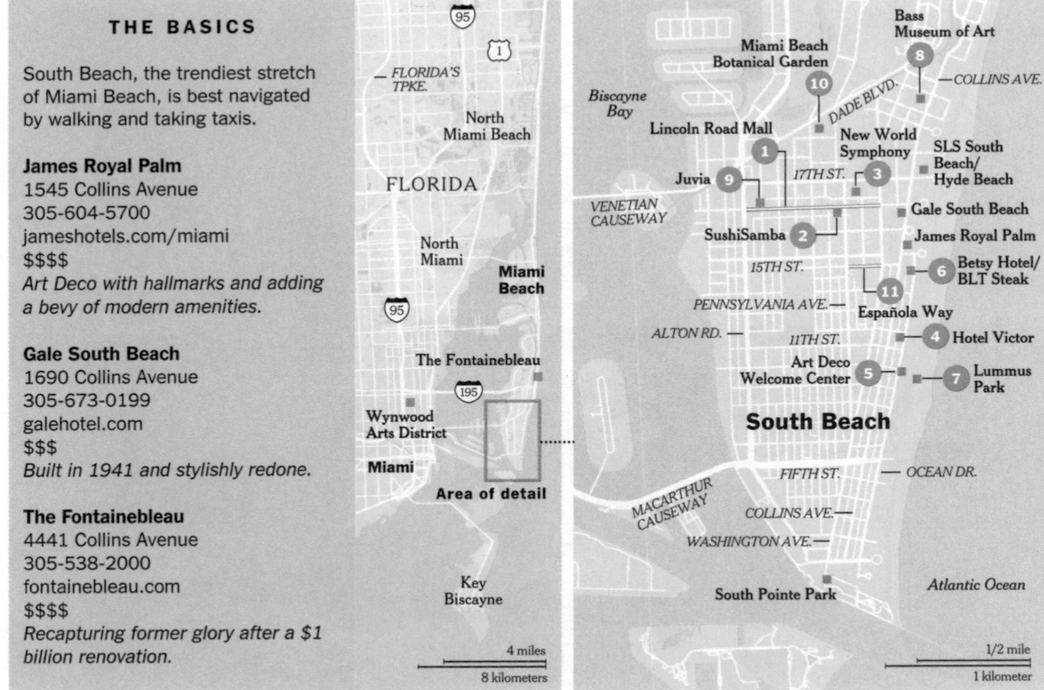

The Everglades

Not quite the brackish swamp that many imagine it to be, the vast south Florida wetland known as the Everglades is actually a clear, wide, shallow river that flows like molasses. And living within its million-plus acres are 200 types of fish, 350 species of birds, and 120 different kinds of trees, just for starters, all less than an hour south of Miami. Of course, to see the iridescent-winged purple gallinule, breaching bottlenose dolphins, and still alligators soaking in the sun, you have to be willing to stop and slow down, moving as languidly as the River of Grass itself. Luckily, the availability of ranger programs and self-guided tours means you needn't be an expert hiker or kayaker to get below the surface of this beautiful, tangled landscape. — BY BETH GREENFIELD

FRIDAY

1 *Under the Boardwalk* 2 p.m.

To hang with more creatures than you can count, head into the **Everglades National Park**'s main **Ernest F. Coe** entrance (305-242-7700; nps.gov/ever/planyourvisit/visitorcenters.htm), near Homestead. You'll find winding boardwalks like the Anhinga Trail, named for the majestic water bird that stands with wings stretched wide to dry its black and white feathers in the sun. A stroll is likely to reveal several anhingas, plus green and tri-colored herons, red-bellied turtles, double-crested cormorants, and many alligators. Don't miss the striking Pa-hay-okee Overlook, a short and steep walkway that juts out over a dreamily endless field of billowing, wheat-colored sawgrass.

2 *Pleasure Cruise* 4:45 p.m.

Pick up maps at the Coe entrance and then head deeper west in the park to the **Flamingo Visitor Center** (239-695-2945), where a small, quiet tour boat (evergladesnationalparkboattoursflamingo.com) whisks passengers from the close wetlands of the park out into the glimmering, airy expanse of Florida Bay. In just under two hours, you'll get a narrated tour, glimpses of elegant water birds (perhaps the great white heron or roseate spoonbill), and a glorious, multicolored sunset over the water.

3 *Search for Tamale* 7:30 p.m.

There's nothing much going on in Homestead, the scruffy town that borders the park's eastern entrance, but a small collection of Mexican restaurants serving tasty fare on North Krome Avenue ensures that you'll at least be well fed. **Casita Tejas** (27 North Krome Avenue, Homestead; 305-248-8224; casitatejas.com; $) offers authentic dishes like beef gorditas, chicken tamales, and chile rellenos in a homey, festive atmosphere.

SATURDAY

4 *Fruit Basket* 8 a.m.

Start your morning off with a thick, fresh-fruit milkshake at **Robert Is Here** (19200 Southwest 344th Street, Homestead; 305-246-1592; robertishere.com), a family-run farm stand offering papayas, star fruits, kumquats, guavas, sapodillas, mameys, and other tropical treats among heaps of fresh oranges and grapefruits.

5 *In the Loop* 10 a.m.

Along the northern rim of the national park you will find the **Shark Valley** entrance (Route 41, Tamiami Trail; 305-221-8455), where a paved loop is traversable by foot, bicycle, or guided tram ride and is often host

OPPOSITE Big Cypress National Preserve.

RIGHT Boardwalks in the swamps of Everglades National Park are vantage points for seeing alligators, turtles, and a multicolored profusion of water-loving birds.

to sleepy crocs or gators. (The Everglades is the only place in the world where alligators, which live in fresh water, and saltwater crocodiles live side by side.) The two-hour tram ride, led by a naturalist, is the best option for coping with the heat and the mosquitoes, which peak here between June and October. It will pause halfway through to let you climb to the top of a 45-foot-high observation deck affording 20-mile wilderness views in all directions.

6 *Swamp Things* 1 p.m.

Just north of the Everglades National Park is the **Big Cypress National Preserve** (nps.gov/bicy)—a tract that narrowly escaped being developed as Miami's international airport in the 1970s. And within its borders lies a novel opportunity for those who prefer to explore this region on foot: ranger-led swamp hikes that set off from the **Oasis Visitor Center** (52105 Tamiami Trail East, Ochopee). "From the highway, all you see is brown and green," a ranger, Corinne Fenner, said as she led people into the thigh-deep waters of cypress-tree stands. "It's nice to get out into the prairie and notice all the colors." And the hues you'll see are certainly magical: the butter yellow of the Everglades daisy, bright violet of nettle-leaf velvetberry flowers, electric lime of freshwater sponges, and deep scarlet of a red-bellied woodpecker. The water itself—which collects in a sandy peat and limestone basin, helping silvery bald cypress trees thrive—looks shockingly clear and feels deliciously cool soaking through jeans and sneakers.

BELOW Take a ranger-led hike in water that looks surprisingly clean and feels deliciously cool on a hot day.

7 *Drive-Thru Wilderness* 3:30 p.m.

A Big Cypress driving tour, north of the Gulf Coast canoe launch on the gravel Turner River Road, offers various close-up encounters with wildlife. Along the scenic 17-mile route, you're sure to rub elbows with creeping turtles, nesting ospreys, and clusters of the alligators that like to float lazily in the narrow creeks here, leaving nothing but steely eyes and snouts above water.

8 *Stuffed Animals, Stuffed Belly* 6 p.m.

Not for the faint of heart when it comes to pushing carnivorous limits, the **Rod and Gun Club**, in the small fishing village of Everglades City (200 West Broadway; 239-695-2100; evergladesrodandgun.com; $$), is a handsome, historic riverside inn where you can unwind from your full day of touring with a hearty dinner. Swamp and Turf (steak and frogs' legs) and gator nuggets are among the menu items. Afterward, have a cocktail in the cozy lounge, where you can shoot pool under the eerie double gaze of a gator skin and deer head, both mounted on the wall.

SUNDAY

9 *Paddle Your Own Canoe* 10 a.m.

The southwest edge of the park sits at the precipice of glistening Chokoloskee Bay and the Ten Thousand Islands area—a pristine region of mangroves and sandy keys mostly reachable only by boat via the 99-mile Wilderness Waterway canoe and kayak trail. While experienced paddlers can plunge right into a days-long journey, camping on raised "chickee" platforms or sand spits along the way, beginners are best off joining one of the many shorter, organized trips on more navigable creeks, like the one led weekly by national park naturalists, leaving from the park's **Gulf Coast Visitor Center** (815 Oyster Bar Lane, Everglades

City). "I never get tired of this area," a naturalist, Brian Ettling, said during one such four-hour journey, leading canoeists single file beneath a cathedral of arching mangrove branches. He excitedly pointed out blue herons, jumping mullet fish, and skittish tree crabs. He gave lessons on the hunting habits of swooping turkey vultures, which have a sense of smell rivaling a bloodhound's, and on the hip attributes of screechy red-shouldered hawks: "They're like the local punk rockers. They eat lizards and scream."

10 *Caught on Film* 3 p.m.

On your way back east along the Tamiami Trail, be sure to stop and visit the **Big Cypress Gallery** (52388 Tamiami Trail, Ochopee; 239-695-2428; clydebutcher.com). Here the photographer Clyde Butcher's large-format, black and white landscapes perfectly capture the romantic essence of this swampland and put your own fresh experiences into striking artistic perspective. Butcher also provides naturalist-led swamp walks on his 13 acres within the Big Cypress National Preserve.

ABOVE Wild beauty at sunset in the Big Cypress National Preserve.

THE BASICS

Everglades National Park's Homestead entrance is a 40-minute drive from Miami International Airport. Plan to tour by car. Maps are online at nps.gov/ever and nps.gov/bicy.

Hampton Inn & Suites
2855 Northeast 9th Street, Homestead
305-257-7000
hamptoninn.hilton.com
$$
One in a cluster of chain motels in Homestead and Florida City.

Rod and Gun Club
200 West Broadway, Everglades City
239-695-2100
evergladesrodandgun.com
$$
Cocktail lounge, riverfront dining, and a big front porch.

Ivey House
107 East Camellia Street, Everglades City
239-695-3299
iveyhouse.com
$$
Basic, motel-like, and friendly, with a screened-in pool.

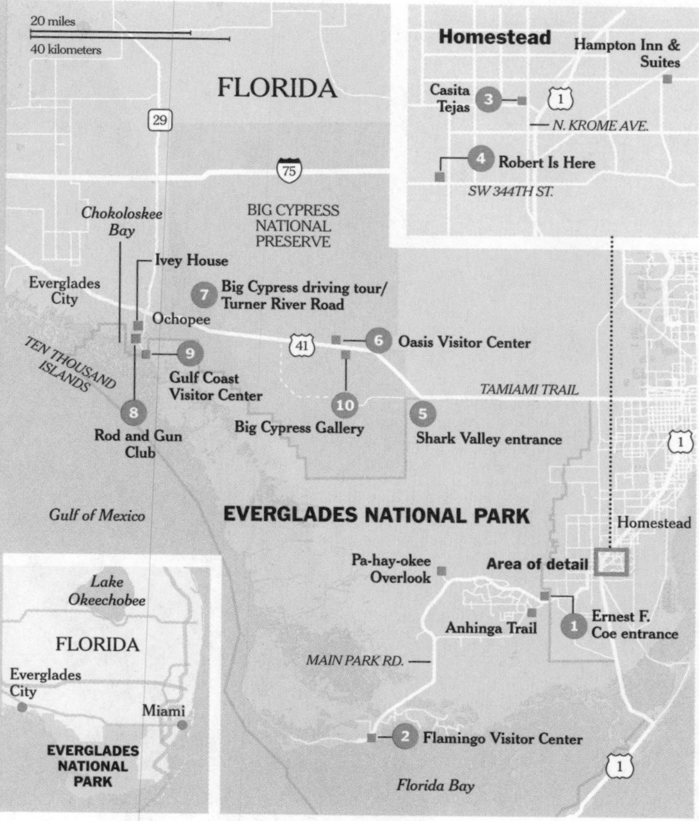

20 miles
40 kilometers
FLORIDA
29
75
BIG CYPRESS NATIONAL PRESERVE
Chokoloskee Bay
Ivey House
Everglades City
7 Big Cypress driving tour/ Turner River Road
Ochopee
41
6 Oasis Visitor Center
TEN THOUSAND ISLANDS
9 Gulf Coast Visitor Center
TAMIAMI TRAIL
10 Big Cypress Gallery
5 Shark Valley entrance
8 Rod and Gun Club
Gulf of Mexico
EVERGLADES NATIONAL PARK
Homestead
Pa-hay-okee Overlook
Area of detail
Anhinga Trail
1 Ernest F. Coe entrance
MAIN PARK RD.
2 Flamingo Visitor Center
Florida Bay
1
Homestead
Hampton Inn & Suites
Casita Tejas 3
N. KROME AVE.
4 Robert Is Here
SW 344TH ST.
Lake Okeechobee
FLORIDA
Everglades City
Miami
EVERGLADES NATIONAL PARK

Key West

Key West, haven to artists and writers, chefs and hippies, is somehow more Caribbean than Floridian. The independent-spirited transplants who inhabit it work hard to keep it that way. One-speed bicycles weave their way through colorful village streets crammed with almost as many chickens as cars. Happy hour blends into dinner. And everything is shaped by the ocean, from the fish market-driven menus and the nautical-inspired art to the dawn gatherings of sunrise worshipers and the tipplers' goodbye waves at sunset. Be careful or you might just catch what islanders call "Keys disease"—a sudden desire to cut ties with home and move there.
— BY SARAH WILDMAN

FRIDAY

1 *Two Wheels Are Enough* 4 p.m.

As any self-respecting bohemian local knows, the best way to get around Key West is on a bicycle. Bike rental businesses offer drop-off service to many hotels. Two reliable companies are **Eaton Bikes** (830 Eaton Street; 305-294-8188; eatonbikes.com) and **We-Cycle** (5160 Overseas Highway; U.S. 1; 305-292-3336; wecyclekw.com). Orient yourself by biking over to the **Truman Annex**, a palm-lined oasis of calm made up of two-story whitewashed buildings that surrounds the **Little White House** (111 Front Street; 305-294-9911; trumanlittlewhitehouse.com), where Harry Truman spent working vacations.

2 *Cleanse the Palate* 8 p.m.

Key West chefs pride themselves on a culinary philosophy of simple cooking and fresh ingredients. A perfect example is the **Flaming Buoy Filet Co.** (1100 Packer Street; 305-295-7970; theflamingbuoy.com; $$), a nouveau seafood restaurant owned and run by two Cincinnati transplants, Fred Isch and his partner, Scot Forste. The 10 rustic wood tables are hand-painted in orange and yellow; the lights are low and the crowd amiable. This is home-cooking, island style, with dishes like black bean soup swirled with Cheddar cheese, sour cream, and cilantro or the fresh catch of the day served with a broccoli cake and tasty mashed potatoes.

3 *Observe the Customs* 10 p.m.

Contrary to popular belief, people in Key West are not drunk all the time. But let's just say it's late, and you have some catching up to do. **Finnegan's Wake** (320 Grinnell Street; 305-293-0222; keywestirish.com) is the kind of split-personality bar you dream about. Though it hugs a quiet corner of Old Town, inside you'll find live music and frothy pints. Out back is even better—a secluded backyard pub where you're almost guaranteed a seat while the band plays in the distance. If you're looking to hit a drag show—and the ever-popular **Aqua** (711 Duval Street; 305-294-0555; aquakeywest.com) is packed—check out the lively and less crowded cabaret at **801 Bourbon Bar** (801 Duval Street; 305-294-4737; 801bourbon.com).

SATURDAY

4 *Salute the Sun* 8:15 a.m.

Every morning, a dozen spiritual seekers—an eclectic mix including tattooed artists and elementary-school teachers—assemble at Fort Zachary Taylor State Park for **Yoga on the Beach** (305-296-7352; yogaonbeach.com). Nancy Curran and Don Bartolone,

OPPOSITE The Seven Mile Bridge on the highway to Key West.

RIGHT Some of the finds at Bésame Mucho, one of multiple shopping options around town.

yogis from Massachusetts, teach energetic vinyasa-style yoga in a clearing of pines facing the sea. The drop-in fee includes state park entrance, muslin drop cloths, and yoga mats.

5 *Imports at Breakfast* 11 a.m.

An island of transplants offers plenty to sample from the world over. Craving France? Stop at **La Crêperie Key West** (300 Petronia Street; 305-517-6799; lacreperiekeywest.com; $$), where Yolande Findlay and Sylvie Le Nouail, both Brittany born, serve crepes in an open kitchen. Start with a savory crepe like ratatouille and then move on to something sweet like red velvet with dark Belgian chocolate, strawberries, and English custard. If you feel more like New York, try **Sarabeth's** (530 Simonton Street; 305-293-8181; sarabethskeywest.com; $), a branch of a popular Manhattan brunch spot.

6 *Island Style* 1 p.m.

Just because islanders pride themselves on being casual, do not assume they don't want to look great. **Bésame Mucho** (315 Petronia Street; 305-294-1928; besamemucho.net) is an Old-World general store packed with everything from Belgian linen to Dr. Hauschka skin care, to delicate baubles like tiny beaded pyrite necklaces. Across the street is **Wanderlust kw** (310 Petronia Street; 305-509-7065; wanderlustkw.com), stocked with well-priced dresses and whimsical watercolors of Key West houses by local artists. Browse nearby blocks for other entertaining shops as well.

7 *Drinks at Sunset* 5 p.m.

Skip the hustle of Mallory Square and work your way through the white-tablecloth dining room to **Louie's Backyard Afterdeck Bar** (700 Waddell Avenue; 305-294-1061; louiesbackyard.com), where a large wood-planked patio faces the ocean and the setting sun. A gregarious crowd of artists and New England snowbirds gathers daily. It's like an outdoor Cheers.

8 *Dining on the Duval* 7 p.m.

Since opening in 2002, the restaurant **Nine One Five** (915 Duval Street; 305-296-0669; 915duval.com; $$$) has gotten high marks for its Asian-inspired seafood and ambience — a large white porch that's great for people-watching. Later the owner, Stuart Kemp, turned the second floor into the Point5 lounge, serving drinks and smaller bites like grilled snapper tacos and stick-to-your-ribs mac and cheese to a younger crowd.

9 *Mix It Up* 9 p.m.

While Key West night life has long been synonymous with boozy karaoke and mediocre margaritas, watering holes like the tiny **Orchid Bar** (1004 Duval Street; 305-296-9915; orchidkeyinn.com)

are quietly moving in a more sophisticated direction. Bartenders there take mixology seriously. Try the St.-Germain 75, with Hendrick's Gin, St.-Germain, fresh lemon juice, and Champagne. This Deco-cool sliver of a space overlooks an illuminated pool and draws a mellow crew.

SUNDAY

10 *Seaworthy Pursuits* Noon

With all the shopping and eating, it is easy to forget why you're really here: to get off the street and onto the water. **Lazy Dog** (5114 Overseas Highway; 305-295-9898; lazydog.com) offers two- and four-hour kayaking or two-hour paddleboard tours through crystal-clear coastal waters and into the deep green waterways of the gnarled mangrove forests. Or if you're just looking to dip a toe in the sea, bike over to Clarence S. Higgs Memorial Beach, a strip of sand by the genial beach bar restaurant **Salute!** (1000 Atlantic Boulevard; 305-292-1117; saluteonthebeach.com), rent a beach chair, and kick back.

OPPOSITE ABOVE A Key West sunset. Many of the growing population of islanders moved in after succumbing to what they call "Keys disease," a visitor's sudden desire to stay for good.

OPPOSITE BELOW Touring by bicycle with Lloyd's Tropical Bike.

THE BASICS

Fly into Key West airport, take a fast ferry from Miami, or drive United States Route 1 through the Florida Keys. In town, rent a bicycle.

Gardens Hotel
526 Angela Street
305-294-2661
gardenshotel.com
$$-$$$$
Seventeen suites spread across an acre of tropical gardens, steps from everything but as quiet as a country inn.

Alexander's Guest House
1118 Fleming Street
305-294-9919
alexanderskeywest.com
$$-$$$
Stylish bed-and-breakfast that attracts a primarily gay and lesbian crowd.

Casa Marina
1500 Reynolds Avenue
888-303-5717
casamarinaresort.com
$$$-$$$$
A Waldorf-Astoria property.

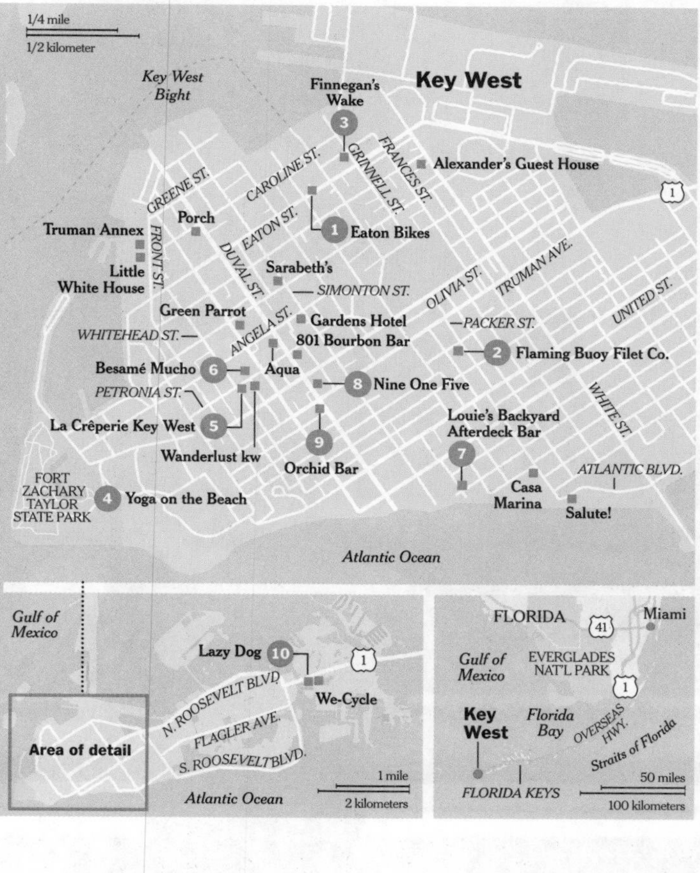

Sarasota

Where else can one spend the morning reveling in the beauty of works by Peter Paul Rubens, Frans Hals, and Botticelli and the afternoon lolling on a powdery white sand beach? That is the lure of Sarasota, the city perched on the Gulf of Mexico where John and Mable Ringling, the circus impresario and his wife, set the stage for a vibrant cultural life after buying land in 1911. Not only did John Ringling create the John and Mable Ringling Museum of Art, but he brought the Ringling Brothers and Barnum & Bailey Circus to winter in Sarasota. His elephants even hauled timber for the John Ringling Causeway, which links the mainland to Lido Key. Nature, which initially attracted the Ringlings and other wealthy Midwesterners, provides its own set of pleasures beyond the beaches: whether it's fishing, watching manatees and sea turtles, or strolling past orchids and mangroves in an expansive botanical garden. For more civilized diversions, there is an abundance of restaurants and shops, and even an opera and an orchestra. — BY GERALDINE FABRIKANT

FRIDAY

1 *First Look* 4 p.m.

Sarasotans are serious about happy hour, when drink prices often drop to half-price Monday through Friday. Enjoy the vista and the good value at **Marina Jack** (2 Marina Plaza; 941-365-4232; marinajacks.com) on the marina between downtown Sarasota and St. Armands Circle. Take in the expansive view of Bird Key as you sip a Southern Peach Tea, made with vodka, lemonade, and iced tea. Music lovers will enjoy the live band that plays every afternoon. On the quieter outdoor deck, you can admire the yachts in the harbor.

2 *Fried Green Tomatoes* 8 p.m.

Whether you have dinner in one of the series of rooms with dark parquet wood floors, a profusion of plants, and smoky emerald green walls covered with art, or eat upstairs in the more casual dining room and bar, don't pass up appetizers like the fried green tomato fusion (panko- and cornmeal-crusted green tomatoes pan-fried with sweet chili sauce) at **Euphemia Haye** (5540 Gulf of Mexico Drive; 941-383-3633; euphemiahaye.com; $$$). Then splurge on roast duckling filled with bread crumb stuffing and topped with a tangy fruit sauce. The lush dessert menu includes Key lime pie.

SATURDAY

3 *A Taste of France* 8:30 a.m.

Arrive early for chocolate croissants or cheese-and-ham crepes at **C'est la Vie** (1553 Main Street; 941-906-9575; cestlaviesarasota.com; $); locals often line up for breakfast at this Provence-style cafe. Then beat the crowd to Sarasota's loveliest beach, **Siesta Beach** on Siesta Key (948 Beach Road; simplysiestakey.com/beaches.htm); later in the day, its wide expanse of soft-as-cotton sand gets clogged with families and a parade of beachgoers, both old and young. In 2011 Siesta Beach was designated America's best beach by Stephen Leatherman, a professor and director of the Laboratory for Coastal Research at Florida International University; its sand is 99 percent quartz crystal and stays white in part because it does not need replenishment from darker sands dredged from the seabed.

4 *Waterside Lunch* 12:30 p.m.

For buckets of peel-and-eat shrimp, or blackened grouper sandwiches with a chipotle tortilla, locals love the **Old Salty Dog** (1601 Ken Thompson Parkway;

OPPOSITE A painting by Peter Paul Rubens on view at the John and Mable Ringling Museum of Art.

BELOW The koi pond is an extra at the Marie Selby Botanical Garden. The main attraction is exotic plants.

941-388-4311; theoldsaltydog.com; $$) on Sarasota Bay. You can smell the sea and watch the Longboat Key Pass Bridge open periodically for boats heading out into the Gulf of Mexico. The original owners were English and wanted to create a publike atmosphere; today, you can still order fish 'n' chips.

5 *Manatees and More* 2 p.m.

Hugh and Buffett, two placid manatees each weighing well over 1,000 pounds, were raised in captivity at the **Mote Marine Laboratory and Aquarium** (1600 Ken Thompson Parkway; 941-388-4441; mote.org). Watch them smush their noses against the glass or consume a few of the approximately 75 heads of romaine lettuce that the pair devour each day. Or gape at Shelley and Montego (two loggerhead sea turtles), sharks, toadfish, convict cichlid fish, and hundreds of other kinds of marine life. You're sure to pick up some stray facts—for instance, did you know that dolphins get arthritis?

6 *Seashells and Cover-Ups* 4:30 p.m.

Don't miss St. Armands Circle, where you'll find coffee shops, formal restaurants, and a wide range of shops. If you need protection from the sun, **Island Pursuit** (355-357 St. Armands Circle; 941-388-4515; islandpursuit.com) has casual wear for men and Scala cotton hats and multicolored bathing suit cover-ups for women; **FantaSea** (378 St. Armands Circle; 941-388-3031; fantaseashells.com) stocks seashell night lights and towels decorated with mermaids.

7 *Martini Time* 5 p.m.

Head downtown and sit under the umbrellas at **Mattison's City Grille** (1 North Lemon Avenue; 941-330-0440; mattisons.com), where you can order a Blue Lion Martini. The cocktail hour is cooler and plusher indoors at the **Bar at Hyde Park Prime Steakhouse** (35 South Lemon Avenue; 941-366-7788; hydeparkrestaurants.com) where you can drop into a deep velveteen sofa or sit at the bar and order a martini.

8 *Mediterranean Medley* 7 p.m.

The chef Dylan Elhajoui came to the United States from Morocco more than two decades ago, and at his colorful 24-table restaurant **Mozaic** (1377 Main Street; 941-951-6272; mozaicsarasota.com; $$) in downtown Sarasota, he combines Moroccan and Southern European cuisine. Choose an appetizer like fricassee of escargot and shiitake mushrooms with white wine; for a main course you might try a tangy tagine of chicken breast and artichoke with couscous. After dinner, check out the **Jack Dusty** bar at the Ritz-Carlton (1111 Ritz-Carlton Drive; 941-309-2000; ritzcarlton.com); its heavy wood paneling and upholstered sofas don't intimidate the casual crowd that shows up for drinks like the toasted almond martini, with amaretto, Kahlúa, half-and-half, and a cherry garnish.

SUNDAY

9 *Hash and Hot Sauce* 9:30 a.m.

With its brightly painted walls and paisley-print booths, the **Blue Dolphin** (470 John Ringling Boulevard; 941-388-3566; bluedolphincafe.com; $$) is the funky Florida version of a coffee shop. The corned beef hash topped with two eggs is popular, as are the six versions of hot sauce on each table. "Some people even put it on pancakes and some just pour a spoonful and eat it straight," one waitress said.

10 *The Ringling Legacy* 11 a.m.

The **John and Mable Ringling Museum of Art** (5401 Bay Shore Boulevard; 941-359-5700; ringling.org) reflects John Ringling's dual passions: Baroque art

and the circus. His collection, which includes five paintings by Rubens, as well as works by Botticelli and Hals, is housed in a mansion resembling an Italian villa and overlooking Sarasota Bay. The **Circus Museum**, also on the property, has its own share of wonders, including a car from the Pullman train in which John and Mable traveled. There is also a version of the circus in miniature, with figurines of more than 900 animals.

11 *Opulent Orchids* 1 p.m.

Situated on Sarasota Bay, the **Marie Selby Botanical Garden** (811 South Palm Avenue; 941-366-5731; selby.org) has a profusion of orchids and other plants. Here you might learn that twigs from the neem tree were used to fight tooth decay and that its extracts helped cure athlete's foot, and that leaves from the seagrape, a plant native to Florida and Central and South America, may have been used for writing paper by early Spaniards in Mexico.

OPPOSITE ABOVE The Old Salty Dog serves buckets of peel-and-eat shrimp along with its close-up view of Sarasota Bay.

OPPOSITE BELOW Seagulls and friend at Siesta Beach.

ABOVE Cafe dining downtown at C'est la Vie.

THE BASICS

Fly into the airport at Sarasota or the much larger Tampa airport, which is about an hour's drive away.

Ritz-Carlton
1111 Ritz Carlton Drive
941-309-2000
ritzcarlton.com
$$$
The toniest hotel in town. Includes a nearby beach club with dining on the water and a luxurious golf club; its bar is popular with locals.

Hilton Longboat Key
4711 Gulf of Mexico Drive
941-383-2451
hiltonhotels.com
$$
Ideal setting right on the Longboat Key beach.

Hotel Ranola
118 Indian Place
941-951-0111
hotelranola.com
$$
Groovier and cheaper in-town lodging.

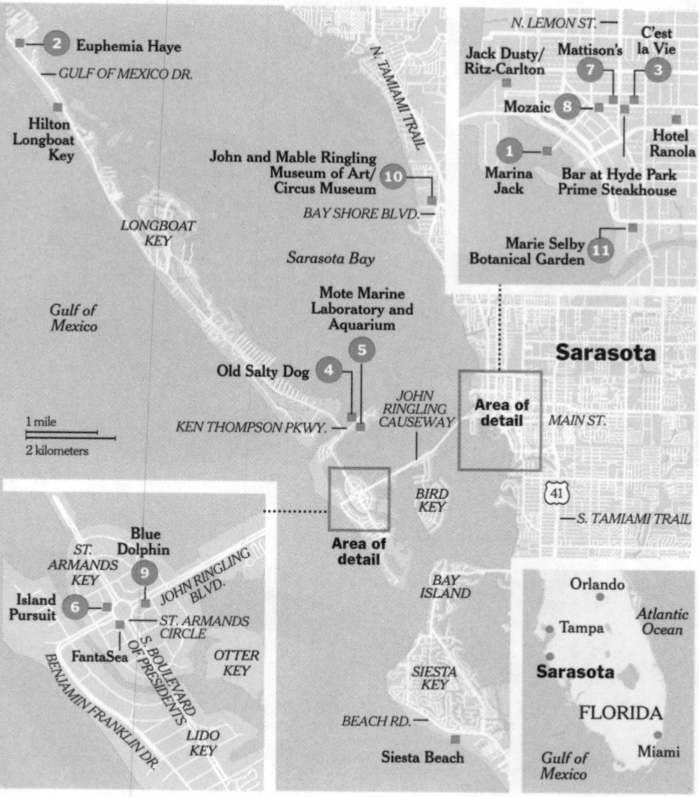

Featuring the World's Largest Painting
"The Battle of Atlanta"
Celebrating Our Centennial Year
CYCLORAMA
PLEASE
KEEP OFF

Atlanta

First, don't call it Hotlanta anymore. It's the ATL, the code for the teeming airport that is a fitting emblem for a city so transient it barely recognizes itself, where more than half the adult population is from somewhere else, and where every urban fad, from underground parking to savory ice cream, is embraced. A corporate stronghold, a Southern belle, and a hip-hop capital, Atlanta has wrestled with identity confusion, trying out several slogans in the past few years, from a hip-hop-accompanied "Every Day Is an Opening Day" to a blander "City Lights, Southern Nights." Major civic investments like a grandiose $220 million aquarium, a significant expansion of the High Museum of Art by the architect Renzo Piano, and the purchase of the papers of the Rev. Dr. Martin Luther King Jr. add up to a high tide of enthusiasm, even in a city where optimism is liberally indulged. — BY SHAILA DEWAN

FRIDAY

1 *Rail Trail* 4 p.m.

When railroads ruled American transportation and commerce, Atlanta played a central role, and part of the legacy of its railroad supremacy in the South is miles of old tracks and lines. Over the next 20 years, the city plans to add 1,300 acres of parks and green spaces, public transit, and trails along this necklace, increasing its green space by nearly 40 percent. The **Eastside Trail**, one of the first legs of this new network, is a two-mile corridor already bustling with joggers, bikers, and strollers. Join the amiable crowd ambling and pedaling past pine and sassafras trees.

2 *Tastes of the Town* 7 p.m.

Few places can be said to be definitively Atlantan, but the **Colonnade** (1879 Cheshire Bridge Road NE; 404-874-5642; colonnadeatl.com; $) is one: a meat-and-three restaurant with a full bar (rare) and a sizable gay clientele (more rare). The resulting mix is spectacular: black fingernails, Sansabelt trousers, birthday tiaras, Hawaiian shirts, all in a buzzing carpeted dining room with efficiently friendly waiters. When it comes to ordering, stick to the classics: a bloody mary to start, fried chicken with yeasty dinner rolls straight from the school cafeteria, and the day's pie.

3 *Where Heads Spin* 9 p.m.

At the **Sun Dial**, the revolving bar atop the Westin hotel (210 Peachtree Street; 404-589-7506; sundialrestaurant.com), young Atlantans come for the throwback cool. Sip an Atlanta Hurricane (it's in the colada-daiquiri family and arrives in a souvenir glass) or a chocolate martini as you orient yourself with a glittery panoramic view of downtown, the Georgia Dome, CNN's headquarters, and the Georgia Aquarium.

4 *On a Roll* 11:30 p.m.

Roller-skating is an integral part of hip-hop culture in Atlanta, which is home to OutKast, Usher, and Young Jeezy, among other stars. Beyoncé had her 21st birthday party at the Cascade roller rink here, and Dallas Austin paid homage to the flawless moves of skate dancers in his film *The ATL*. On Friday nights, the virtuosos descend on **Golden Glide** (2750 Wesley Chapel Road in Decatur, tucked behind a shopping strip; 404-288-7773; atlantafamilyfuncenters.com) for adult skate, where posses practice their smooth moves until the wee hours. If you haven't been

OPPOSITE The Atlanta Cyclorama and Civil War Museum. Inside is a panoramic painting of the Battle of Atlanta.

RIGHT The railroads have largely gone, but their old tracks and lines are being converted into urban trails.

practicing, skate inside the green line for your own safety. Or just stay on the sideline and gawk.

SATURDAY

5 *Robust Start* 11:30 a.m.

You had a late night, so take your time getting to **Watershed** (1820 Peachtree Road; 404-378-4900; watershedrestaurant.com; $$), an airy Southern restaurant. Reservations are recommended, and child-tolerance is required, but the chicken hash with griddle cakes and poached eggs is worth the bother.

6 *A Little Shopping* 1:30 p.m.

In the affluent **Buckhead** area, hotels and skyscrapers have edged out some mansions and period commercial buildings, but if you look, you can still get a glimpse of old Atlanta. This is also the city's most established area for shopping. Designer brands and familiar chain stores are clustered in the malls **Lenox Square** (3393 Peachtree Road Northeast; lenoxsquare.com) and **Phipps Plaza** (3500 Peachtree Road Northeast; phippsplaza.com). At the **Peachtree Battle Shopping Center** (2385 Peachtree Road Northeast), the locally owned stores include **Richards Variety Store** (richardsvarietystore.com), a throwback to the five-and-dime that invites extended browsing.

7 *War on Canvas* 3:30 p.m.

When Gen. John A. Logan was considering a run for vice president in the 1880s, he commissioned a political ad in the form of a giant painting of the Battle of Atlanta, in which he had for a time commanded the Army of the Tennessee for the Union. The work, billed as the world's largest oil painting, is now housed in **Grant Park**, in a circular room not unlike a planetarium, and viewed from a rotating bank of seats (**Atlanta Cyclorama and Civil War Museum**; 800 Cherokee Avenue; 404-658-7625; atlantacyclorama.org). The taped narration will catch you up on your Civil War history. Leave time to see the exhibit on the Great Locomotive Chase, a slapstick adventure involving hand cars, cut wires, and engines traveling in reverse.

8 *Spreading the Sopchoppy* 6 p.m.

A city where a treasured chef's departure can be front-page news, Atlanta has more than its share of fine restaurants, many of them cavernous, overdesigned colonizations of old industrial buildings. Smaller and friendlier is **Restaurant Eugene** (2277

ABOVE AND OPPOSITE The Martin Luther King Jr. National Historic Site includes King's tomb and exhibits recalling his leadership in the struggle to end racial segregation in the South. Other stops are his boyhood home and the Ebenezer Baptist Church he served as pastor.

Peachtree Road; 404-355-0321; restauranteugene.com; $$$), where the staff shares its passions readily and the menu can read like a Southern safari: foie gras on French toast with Sopchoppy brand molasses from Florida; A & J Farms squash blossoms with Anson Mills's grits and Sweetgrass Dairy goat cheese.

9 *Culture and Cars* 8 p.m.

If you like theater, opera, ballet, or Broadway shows, check the schedules at the **Woodruff Arts Center** (1280 Peachtree Street NE; 404-733-4200; woodruffcenter.org) and the **Fox Theatre** (660 Peachtree Street NE; 404-881-2100; foxtheatre.org). Atlanta is one of the South's primary culture centers. For something more downmarket, drive out to the **Starlight Six Drive-In** (2000 Moreland Avenue SE; 404-627-5786; starlightdrivein.com) for Southern-culture-on-the-skids charm, retro with a hint of rockabilly. Sometimes used for campy evenings of B-movies and bands, the rest of the time this is just a straight-up, steamy-windowed cinematic experience in a hummocky parking lot.

SUNDAY

10 *Pancakes and Quiet Neighbors* 10 a.m.

The gruff proprietor of **Ria's Bluebird** (421 Memorial Drive SE; 404-521-3737; riasbluebird.com; $) has the word "hate" tattooed on the nape of her neck. But local residents give her nothing but love, lining up, pleasantly sleep-tousled, on weekend mornings for what some customers say are the world's best pancakes. The light-filled storefront is just right if you feel the need to keep your sunglasses on in the morning; the floor is made from wooden wall paneling, creating the illusion of an old barroom. The restaurant is across the street from

Atlanta's oldest and loveliest cemetery, **Oakland Cemetery** (248 Oakland Avenue SE; 404-688-2107; oaklandcemetery.com), where Margaret Mitchell, author of *Gone with the Wind*; 25 mayors; and thousands of unidentified Confederate soldiers are buried. In warm weather, guided tours are available on Sunday afternoons.

11 *The King Legacy* 11 a.m.

At the **Martin Luther King Jr. National Historic Site** (450 Auburn Avenue NE; 404-331-5190; nps.gov/malu), you can take a tour of the house where King was born (501 Auburn Avenue NE; reserve in advance) and, at the visitor center, see his life retraced in photos, print, film, video, and art. If you get an earlier start, you might want to stop by the new Ebenezer Baptist Church, adjacent to the visitor center, for a service. The historic **Old Ebenezer Baptist Church**, where King, his father, and his grandfather preached, is across the street (407 Auburn Avenue NE), no longer used for services but open to view. Inside, in the quiet sanctuary where King's inspiring words once echoed, visitors may find their emotions running high.

OPPOSITE An elaborate mausoleum at Oakland Cemetery. A burial ground for generations of Atlantans, the cemetery holds the graves of Confederate soldiers, 25 Atlanta mayors, and Margaret Mitchell, the author of *Gone With the Wind*.

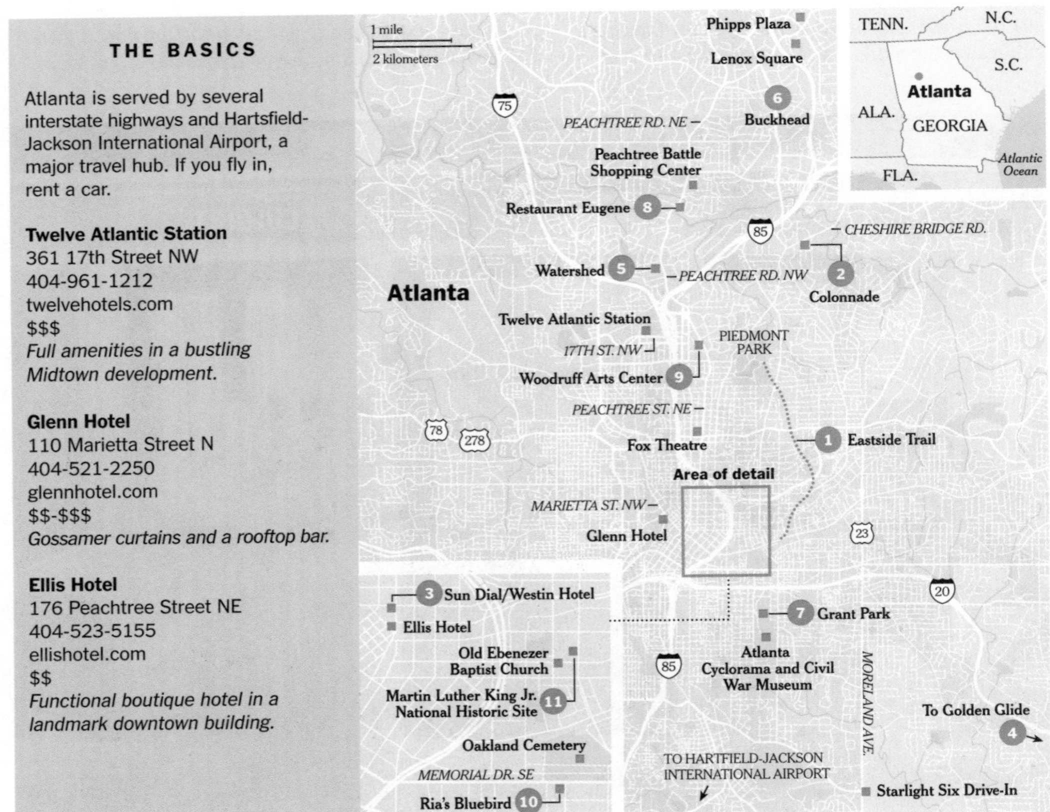

THE BASICS

Atlanta is served by several interstate highways and Hartsfield-Jackson International Airport, a major travel hub. If you fly in, rent a car.

Twelve Atlantic Station
361 17th Street NW
404-961-1212
twelvehotels.com
$$$
Full amenities in a bustling Midtown development.

Glenn Hotel
110 Marietta Street N
404-521-2250
glennhotel.com
$$-$$$
Gossamer curtains and a rooftop bar.

Ellis Hotel
176 Peachtree Street NE
404-523-5155
ellishotel.com
$$
Functional boutique hotel in a landmark downtown building.

RICHARDS

Asheville

Whether it's culture, the great outdoors, or homegrown food and beer, Asheville, North Carolina, takes its pleasures seriously. Playgrounds are equipped with rock-climbing walls. Bumper stickers exhort the locals to buy local. The town is proud of Biltmore, the outsize Vanderbilt mansion, but funds are also being raised for a distinctly more modern kind of museum tracing the intersection of science and music and named for Bob Moog, the synthesizer pioneer, who lived in Asheville. All this connoisseurship unfolds against the backdrop of the seriously beautiful Blue Ridge Mountains, and close to the Blue Ridge Parkway, one of the country's most beautiful roads. — BY SHAILA DEWAN

FRIDAY

1 *Secret (Edible) Garden* 3 p.m.

A small amphitheater, an interactive fountain, and public sculpture adorn the newly redone **Pack Square Park** (packsquarepark.org) at the pink Art Deco-style city hall. But a quick walk away is another, almost secret, park that embodies the scruffy, idealistic side of Asheville: **George Washington Carver Edible Park**. There, the public can graze on apples, chestnuts, and other delectables. To find it, take the outdoor stairway behind Pack's Tavern, go left on Marjorie Street, and cross the pedestrian bridge by the corner of Marjorie and Davidson.

2 *Chai Time* 5 p.m.

Asheville residents love their Indian food, and they are particularly taken with a bright cafe called **Chai Pani** (22 Battery Park Avenue; 828-254-4003; chaipani.net; $) for its fresh, cilantro-strewn takes on Indian street food. For a late-afternoon snack, pop in for a nimbu pani, or salty limeade, and bhel puri, a snack of puffed rice and chickpea noodles in fresh tamarind chutney.

3 *Downtown Drumming* 7 p.m.

There may be 10 onlookers for every drummer at the long-running Friday-night drum circle in triangular **Pritchard Park** (College Street and Patton Avenue) — and there are plenty of drummers. The congas, doumbeks, tambourines, and cowbells provide an ecstatic soundtrack for families, college couples, and dreadlocked nomads. The drum circle is the throbbing heart of downtown, a district of shops, bars, buskers, and street magicians that springs into action as the weekend begins.

4 *Microbrew and a Movie* 9 p.m.

In recent years, Asheville has come to rival Portland, Oregon, as a center for craft beer, and the city has claimed to have more microbreweries per capita — from places like **Green Man Brewery** (greenmanbrewery.com) with its cask-conditioned beers, to the hip **Wedge Brewing Company** (wedgebrewing.com) in the River Arts District. You can try a few on an **Asheville Brews Cruise** tour (brewscruise.com), or linger at the student-friendly **Asheville Pizza and Brewing Company** (675 Merrimon Avenue; 828-254-1281; ashevillebrewing.com), which has a bar, arcade, and cut-rate movie theater. Settle down in front of the large screen with a pint of Rocket Girl or Ninja Porter and a quite respectable pizza (toppings may include Spam, as well as smoked Gouda and artichoke hearts).

SATURDAY

5 *Wood-Fired Breakfast* 9 a.m.

The East-West fusion and wholesome rusticity in **Farm and Sparrow**'s wood-fired pastries seem to sum up Asheville. The croissants stuffed with kimchi and an open-faced pear, Gorgonzola,

OPPOSITE A class at Black Mountain Yoga.

BELOW Working artists cluster at Curve Studios.

and bee pollen confection are made at the bakery (farmandsparrow.com) in nearby Candler, N.C., and are available at some of Asheville's tailgate markets, a kind of hyper-local version of a farmers' market. The **North Asheville Tailgate Market** (828-776-6286; northashevilletailgatemarket.org), held in a parking lot on the campus of the University of North Carolina at Asheville, is where you'll also find locally made kombucha from Buchi, trout dip from the Sunburst Trout Company, and fresh goat cheese with lavender from Three Graces Dairy.

6 *Mountain Stretch* 10:30 a.m.

Like any bohemian resort worth its coarse-ground Himalayan salt, Asheville has its share of healing arts. Find spa treatments, colonics, and "affordable acupuncture" at the **Thrifty Taoist** in the town of Black Mountain (106 Black Mountain Avenue; 828-713-9185), about 15 minutes from downtown. **Black Mountain Yoga** offers one-on-one yoga therapy sessions with Martia Rachman and her husband, Brad, a naturopath (116 Montreat; 828-669-2939; blackmountainyoga.com). While you perform stretches and poses, one of the Rachmans will identify problem areas and massage and manipulate stubborn muscles. An hour later, a looser, more relaxed you will emerge from their clutches.

7 *Artists' Utopia* Noon

Short-lived but enormously influential, **Black Mountain College** (blackmountaincollege.org) was evidence of Asheville's pull on the unconventionally creative. John Cage, Merce Cunningham, Buckminster Fuller, and Josef Albers were among the teachers at this oft-re-examined intellectual utopia that closed, after a quarter-century, in the late 1950s. The campus at Lake Eden (375 Lake Eden Road, Black Mountain) is now a Christian boys' camp, but when it is not in session you can still inspect the Bauhaus-inspired main campus building and fading murals by Jean Charlot. Modern-day artists cluster at **Curve Studios** in Asheville's River Arts District (6, 9, and 12 Riverside Drive; 828-388-3526; curvestudiosnc.com). Look here for beautifully crafted pottery, a North Carolina specialty.

ABOVE The Friday drum circle at Pritchard Park draws families, college couples, and dreadlocked nomads.

8 *Treetop Zip* 2 p.m.

Leaf peeping is a serious sport in Asheville—hence the weekly "fall color report" from the local visitor's bureau (exploreasheville.com). Experience the local treetops, whatever the season, from a whole new angle on the three-and-a-half-hour zipline course at **Navitat Canopy Adventures**, about 20 minutes north of town (242 Poverty Branch Road, Barnardsville; 828-626-3700; navitat.com). Wearing a hard hat, you'll be strapped in and hooked up with a series of reassuring clicks for each of the 10 zips, the longest at 1,100 feet. They take you from chestnut oaks to tulip poplars, soaring over valleys with a bird's-eye view that will remind you, once again, of the Blue Ridge bedrock of Asheville's eternal appeal.

9 *Toast to Literature* 6 p.m.

The **Battery Park Book Exchange and Champagne Bar** (Grove Arcade, 1 Page Avenue; 828-252-0020; batteryparkbookexchange.com) is not a place to find shabby paperbacks. Instead, think Civil War histories, first editions of works by 20th-century writers like Eudora Welty and Sylvia Plath, acres of gardening and art hardbacks, and a glass of fizzy Heidsieck & Co. Monopole. The Mission-style sofas and leather armchairs in book-lined alcoves bring the cozy nook idea to a new level.

10 *Gastro-Dive* 8 p.m.

What are truffles, steak tartare, and imported oysters doing in a cinderblock dive bar amid the cool haunts of West Asheville? One bite of dinner at the **Admiral** (400 Haywood Road; 828-252-2541; theadmiralnc.com), and such questions subside into flavor combinations like balsamic pears with honey cap mushrooms or foie gras with Nutella. Late on Saturday nights, the tables are cleared away for a crowded and sweaty dance party.

SUNDAY

11 *That Old-Time One Percent* 10 a.m.

Back when a million was real money, George Washington Vanderbilt, who had several of them, built the largest private home in the country, **Biltmore** (1 Lodge Street; 828-225-1333; biltmore.com). A 250-room French Renaissance chateau, it's still decorated with paintings by the likes of Whistler, John Singer Sargent, and Raphael. A mere 8,000 acres remain from the original estate, but the mountain views are gorgeous, and the formal landscape design is by Frederick Law Olmsted. This is Asheville's biggest tourist attraction, but the place is so huge it swallows crowds easily.

THE BASICS

Several airlines fly to Asheville. Rent a car at the airport.

Hotel Indigo
151 Haywood Street
828-239-0239
hotelindigo.com
$$
Contemporary design near the action at the Grove Arcade, with a locavore restaurant, iPad rentals, and fitness center.

The Grove Park Inn
290 Macon Avenue
828-252-2711
groveparkinn.com
$$$
Patronized by a long line of presidents and celebrities.

Inn on the Biltmore Estate
1 Antler Road
828-225-1600
biltmore.com/stay
$$$$
The plushest place around, on the 8,000-acre Biltmore estate.

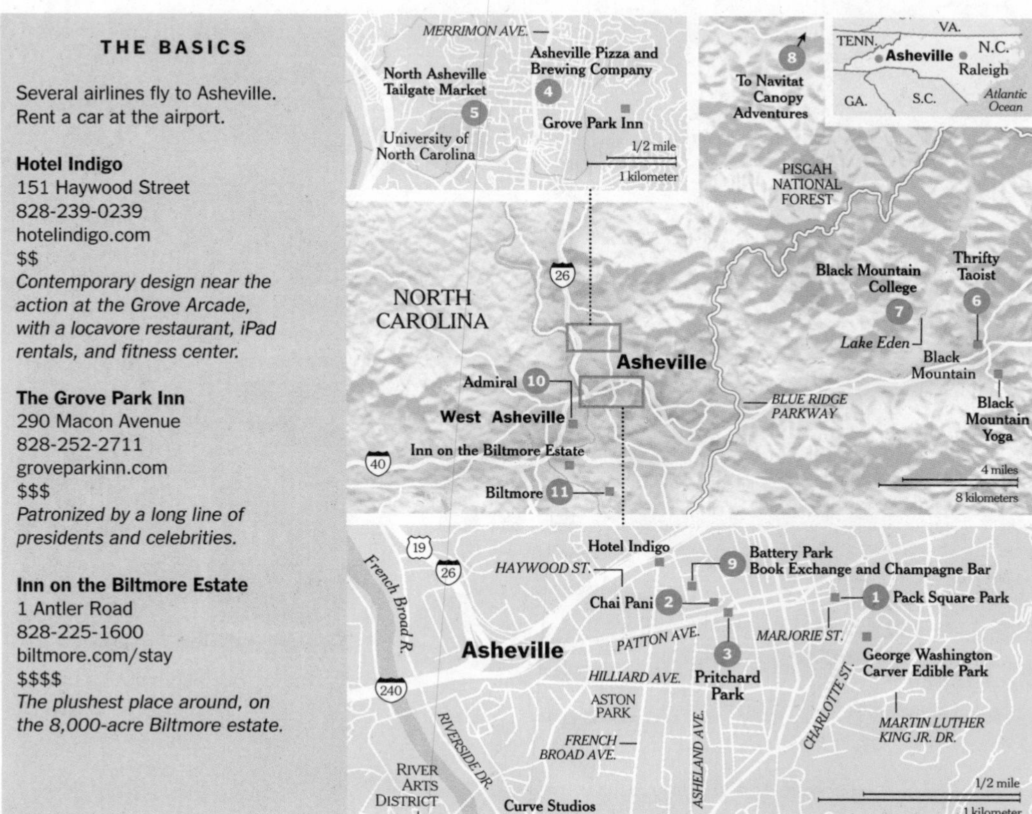

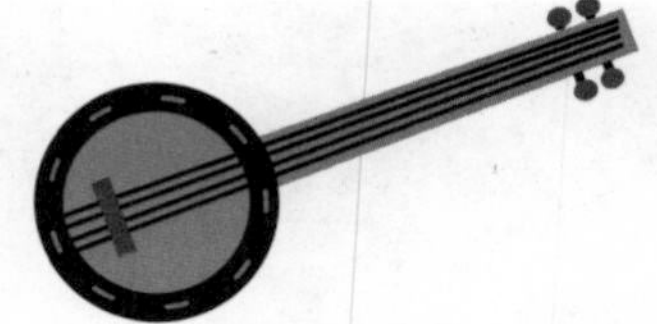

Knoxville

Knoxville, Tennessee, is sometimes called "the couch" by people who live there. It is a place too unassuming to shout about but too comfortable to leave. The city, the third largest in Tennessee behind Nashville and Memphis, is also referred to as Knoxpatch, Knoxvegas, and for those prone to irony and finger pistols, K-town, baby. The truth is, Knoxville, a college town cheerfully ensconced in the foothills of the Great Smoky Mountains and banked against the Tennessee River, has an intrinsically lazy, soulful air about it. The geography is soft, green, and rolling. The climate is gentle, breezy, and bright. Locals tend to be not just friendly—a given in most Southern towns—but chilled out, too. This is not the Old South of magnolias and seersucker so much as a modern Appalachia of roots music, locavore food, folk art, and hillbilly pride. Or, as yet another city moniker aptly puts it, "Austin without the hype." — BY ALLISON GLOCK

FRIDAY

1 *Cultivated Bluegrass* Noon

Knoxville is known for its music—Dolly Parton was discovered here, Hank Williams stopped here on his last road trip, and most locals know their way around a banjo. The listener-supported station **WDVX-FM**, multiple winner of the national title Bluegrass Station of the Year, hosts the Monday-through-Saturday *Blue Plate Special* show, offering free live music from noon to 1 p.m. (301 South Gay Street; 865-544-1029; wdvx.com). Guests have ranged from Béla Fleck and Ricky Skaggs to the Gypsy jazz band Ameranouche and homegrown Appalachian talent. Bring a bag lunch or pick up an ice-cold cola and some snacks from the old-fashioned mercantile **Mast General Store** (402 South Gay Street; 865-546-1336; mastgeneralstore.com) and take a seat for some down-home music in an unusually intimate setting.

OPPOSITE Sequoyah Hills Park has 87 acres of land with trails for walking, running, and biking, as well as free boat access to the Tennessee River.

RIGHT The Sunsphere, built for a 1982 world's fair, rises above the city. From its observation deck, views extend out to the surrounding countryside.

2 *Mountain View* 2 p.m.

Take the elevator to the top of the **Sunsphere** (810 Clinch Avenue; 865-251-6860), an architectural leftover from the 1982 World's Fair and a parody victim of *The Simpsons*. A 600-ton, 266-foot steel truss topped with a 74-foot gold ball, it looks like a Titleist on steroids, but it offers the best views of the city and the mountains just beyond.

3 *In Another Sphere* 3 p.m.

The **Women's Basketball Hall of Fame** (700 Hall of Fame Drive; 865-633-9000; wbhof.com) is the home of the world's largest basketball—30 feet tall, 10 tons, no Sunsphere, but still—and myriad artifacts of early women's basketball from throughout the world, including an original 1901 rulebook. Of course, there are bounteous tributes to Pat Summit, the head coach emeritus of the hometown University of Tennessee Lady Vols, who has the most victories in Division 1 basketball history.

4 *Meats and Sweets* 7 p.m.

Litton's (2803 Essary Road; 865-687-8788; littonburgers.com; $) is a bit off the beaten path, which doesn't keep it from being standing room only virtually every lunch and dinner. Started in a small back room, the diner-style restaurant, meat market, and bakery has sprawled to fill a warehouse's worth of space. Known for its burgers and desserts, Litton's is not the place to come if cholesterol is a preoccupation. Go for the Thunder Road burger (pimento cheese, sautéed onions, and jalapeño with fries) and a slice of red velvet cake. Lines are long, but pews are

available while you wait. Just be sure to sign in on the chalkboard.

SATURDAY

5 *Pioneer Spirit* 10 a.m.

A 20-minute drive outside Knoxville will take you to the **Museum of Appalachia** (2819 Andersonville Highway, Clinton; 865-494-7680; museumofappalachia.org). Born of the historian John Rice Irwin's love for the mountain people of Tennessee, the museum encompasses truckloads of Appalachian pioneer artifacts and folk art as well as actual cabins, churches, and outbuildings that were carefully moved from their original locations and reassembled on its expansive grounds. Live music can be heard almost every day thanks to the Porch Musicians Project, Irwin's effort to expose all guests to "authentic old-time music" and preserve America's aural history. Lunch is available in the cafe. Order the fresh-fried pinto beans and cornbread.

6 *Let Them Eat Cupcakes* 4 p.m.

Sure, cupcake mania has shown up everywhere. But nowhere is it more deserved than at **MagPies** (846 North Central Street; 865-673-0471; magpiescakes.com), a place whose motto is "all butter all the time." The baker, proprietress, and adequate accordion player Peggy Hambright specializes in "super deluxe flavors" that change every month. (Examples: Chocolate Guinness Stout, Key lime pie, and blackberry buttermilk.) A dozen minis or a six-pack of regulars, the usual units of purchase, may seem like a lot to buy at once, but don't plan on any leftovers.

7 *Square Deal* 5 p.m.

Take in the scene around **Market Square**, a cheek-by-jowl assortment of cafes, boutiques, galleries, and pubs. Stores worth some exploration include **Reruns Consignment Boutique** (521 Union Avenue; 865-525-9525; rerunsboutique.com) for bargain-priced designer finds and **Bliss** (24 Market Square; 865-329-8868; shopinbliss.com), an everything-but-the-kitchen-sink gift emporium offering apparel, furniture, frames, and flatware. As the afternoon wears down, restaurants, many with outdoor seating, begin to fill up. Most evenings find amateur pickers and singers performing in the square, lending the whole space the feeling of a giant impromptu party.

8 *Say Tomato* 7 p.m.

The nexus for all things hip and happening in town, the vegan-friendly **Tomato Head** (12 Market Square; 865-637-4067; thetomatohead.com; $$), is the place to go for epicurean pizza and unparalleled people watching. The founder, chef, and local foodie icon Mahasti Vafaie makes everything you eat there, including the breads, buns, and salad dressings. Order the No. 8 (pesto-based pizza with Roma tomato and roasted portobello), the Greek salad (heavy on the kalamata olives), and a glass of wine. Sit outside if you can, where your table overlooks the whole of Market Square.

9 *Ale Power* 10 p.m.

Amid the Market Square madness sits the **Preservation Pub** (28 Market Square; 865-524-2224; preservationpub.com), a narrow slip of a bar that manages to squeeze quite a few folks and even more beer choices into its cozy confines. There are 20-plus strong ale selections alone (try the Stone Arrogant Bastard or the Orkney Skull Splitter) but know that the bartenders keep an eye on the number of strong ales you down, so as to avoid chaos spilling onto the square — unless it is live music night. Then all bets are off.

OPPOSITE ABOVE Inside the restored Tennessee Theatre in the Market Square area, the heart of downtown.

OPPOSITE BELOW A performance at Blue Plate Special, a radio show that hosts country stars and homegrown talent.

BELOW A mural of a London Street in the Crown & Goose English-style pub, where brunch can include Stilton cheese.

SUNDAY

10 *Green Acres* 9 a.m.

Jog, walk, bike, or paddle at **Sequoyah Hills Park** (1400 Cherokee Boulevard; ci.knoxville.tn.us/parks/sequoyah.asp), an 87-acre sprawl of green lawns, flowering trees, dog paths, and picnic spots on the Tennessee River. Water access is easy, as is parking. For a longer hike, the **Ijams Nature Center** (2915 Island Home Avenue; 865-577-4717; ijams.org), a 160-acre park and wildlife sanctuary, is a 10-minute drive from downtown.

ABOVE One of the preserved historic buildings moved to the grounds of the Museum of Appalachia, a treasure trove of pioneer artifacts and folk art.

OPPOSITE The exterior of the Crown & Goose. Repurposed and renovated old buildings are an important element of the city's downtown revival.

11 *English Eaten Here* Noon

The **Crown & Goose** gastropub (123 South Central Street; 865-524-2100; thecrownandgoose.com; $$) serves a hearty brunch along with whatever soccer match happens to be on TV that day. Sidle up to the huge 19th-century-style bar and sample the eggs Benedict with fried green tomatoes or the Belgian waffles dipped in cider batter and loaded with sweet cream cheese, maple syrup, and fresh fruit. Traditional English fare is also on offer, from a cheese board that includes Stilton to the requisite fish and chips.

Knoxville
500 feet
1/4 kilometer
40
N. BROADWAY
11 Crown & Goose
S. CENTRAL ST.
1 WDVX-FM
W. SUMMIT HILL DR.
Mast General Store
9 Preservation Pub
Bliss
Market Square
8 Tomato Head
7 Reruns Consignment Boutique
Hotel St. Oliver
HALL OF FAME DR.
W. CHURCH AVE.
2 Sunsphere
CLINCH AVE.
Hilton Knoxville
S. GAY ST.
3 Women's Basketball Hall of Fame
WHITE AVE.
Four Points by Sheraton Knoxville Cumberland House
HENLEY ST.
W. MAIN ST.
NEYLAND DR.
Tennessee River

5 To Museum of Appalachia
4 Litton's
2 miles
4 kilometers
640
275
75
40
6 MagPies
Knoxville
Tennessee River
Area of detail
10 Sequoyah Hills Park
CHEROKEE BLVD.
KY.
VA.
Nashville
Knoxville
TENNESSEE
N.C.
GA.
S.C.
ALA.
Atlanta

THE BASICS

Fly in and rent a car.

Hotel St. Oliver
407 Union Avenue
865-521-0050
stoliverhotel.com
$$
Historic inn off Market Square.

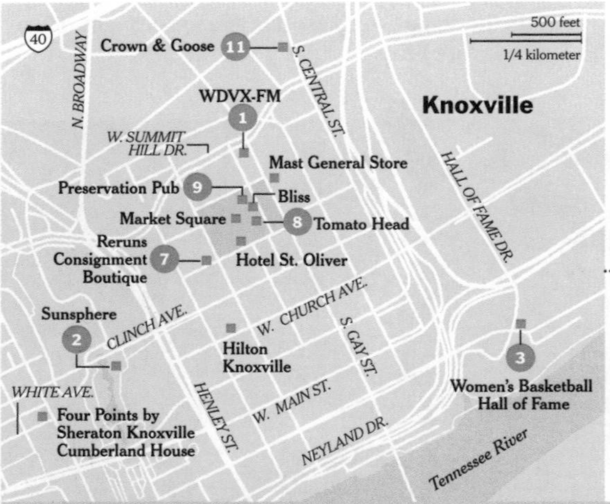

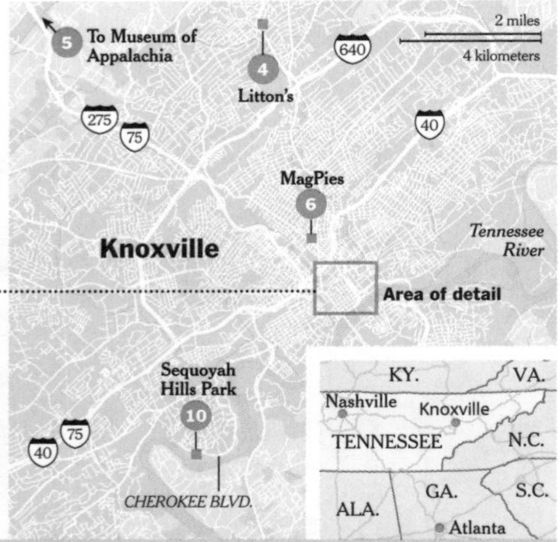

Four Points by Sheraton Knoxville Cumberland House
1109 White Avenue
865-971-4663
starwoodhotels.com/fourpoints/knoxville
$$
Close to the University of Tennessee campus.

Hilton Knoxville
501 West Church Avenue
865-523-2300
hilton.com
$$
Standard Hilton amenities.

The Crown & Goose
your local
gastropub
Lounge

Lexington

Miles of low fences line the winding, two-lane roads of the Bluegrass Country around Lexington, Kentucky, and enclose its rolling green horse farms, where magnificent thoroughbreds rest near pristinely painted barns. Now and again, the fences break for a leafy lane leading to an age-old bourbon distillery with doors open for a tour and a tipple. Then they lead away to a quaint 19th-century town, a quintessential country inn, or a serene Shaker village. These magical fences, made of wood or of stones stacked long ago by slaves and Scots-Irish settlers, take you back in time and away in space. But you'll be brought back soon enough by Kentucky's modern hosts serving up Southern charm and distinctly American food and drink. — BY TAYLOR HOLLIDAY

FRIDAY

1 *Horse Fixation* 1:45 p.m.

Lexington, a leisurely university city with preserved antebellum houses, calls itself the horse capital of the world. On thousands of acres of nearby farms, pampered horses graze on the local bluegrass, so called because it blooms a purplish blue. Dip into the horse world at **Kentucky Horse Park** (4089 Iron Works Parkway; 859-233-4303; kyhorsepark.com). It may seem at first like merely a giant horsy theme park, but the horse trailers in the parking lot attest to its importance for competitions as well. There are displays on the history of the horse, paeans to winners like Man o' War and Cigar, and a Parade of Breeds (catch it at 2 p.m.). Horse shows and races are frequent — you might catch a steeplechase. And in June, musicians arrive from far and wide for a festival of bluegrass music.

2 *Chefs of the Country* 7 p.m.

Northwest of Lexington, Route 62 cuts a path through lush countryside to charming little Midway, a railroad town of about 1,600 people where trains still run right down the middle of the main street. A gem of a restaurant, the **Holly Hill Inn** (426 North Winter Street, Midway; 859-846-4732; hollyhillinn.com; $$$), awaits you down a nearby lane, in a house dating to 1839. Ouita Michel, the chef, and her husband, Chris, the sommelier, both graduates of the Culinary Institute of America, serve a four-course prix fixe dinner. Choices on the changing menus have included spoonbread souffle, pork roast with figs and dates, and tile fish with Kentucky red rice.

OPPOSITE White rail fences mark the rolling green fields of a horse farm in Kentucky Bluegrass Country.

SATURDAY

3 *Brake for Bourbon* 10 a.m.

The land around Lexington grows more than thoroughbreds. West of the city, you're in bourbon country. Several distillers have banded together to create what they call the Bourbon Trail, so spend a day learning why their product is such a source of Kentucky pride. Stop first in Versailles (pronounce it "ver-SALES"), where the stately limestone **Woodford Reserve** (7855 McCracken Pike; 859-879-1812; woodfordreserve.com) is nestled deep among farms with cupola-topped stables and miles of black-painted board fences. The only product made here is the small-batch Woodford Reserve, but visitors come by the thousands, and you'll see the entire bourbon-making process from mash to bottle. Inhale the smells of whiskey and old wood, and sip a sample.

RIGHT Woodford Reserve, one of the Kentucky bourbon distilleries where a tour is capped with a sip of the whiskey.

4 *Whiskey Saga* Noon

Bardstown, a city of about 10,000 in the heart of bourbon territory, honors its debt to spirits at the **Oscar Getz Museum of Whiskey History** (114 North Fifth Street; 502-348-2999; whiskeymuseum.com). In the 1790s, Scotch-Irish distillers fleeing George Washington's whiskey tax and the quelling of the subsequent Whiskey Rebellion landed in an area of Virginia then called Bourbon County, which now covers several counties of northeastern Kentucky. They found perfect conditions for their trade, partly because of a layer of limestone that filters iron from the local water, and bourbon whiskey was born. In the museum, examine local artifacts including authentic moonshine stills.

5 *Vary the Stimuli* 1 p.m.

Make a temporary switch from booze to caffeine at **Java Joint** (126 North 3rd Street, Bardstown; 502-350-0883; $), where you can grab a quick lunch of sandwiches, soup, or salad along with the signature cup of flavorful coffee.

6 *Dip Your Own* 2 p.m.

Meander about 15 miles south on Route 49 to tiny Loretto and enter the red-shuttered, brown-clapboard buildings of **Maker's Mark** (3350 Burks Springs Road; 270-865-2099; makersmark.com). The oldest bourbon distillery in the country, dating to 1805, it is well schooled in the rules of bourbon: the mash must be at least 51 percent corn, barrels for aging must be new and made of charred white oak, alcohol must be at prescribed strengths in the years-long process of transforming grain into whiskey. The tour here shows you the cooker, mash fermentation, the still, aging rackhouses, and hand-bottling. You can dip a finger into a vat of bubbling, fermenting mash to get a taste (like sweetened cereal gone sour), and you can even hand-dip your own souvenir bottle in the trademark red wax.

7 *Jim Beam's Place* 4 p.m.

Drive back north to Bardstown and take Route 245 west to Clermont, the home of **Jim Beam** (526 Happy Hollow Road; 502-543-9877; jimbeam.com), the biggest of the bourbon distillers. Jim Beam doesn't have an extensive tour, but you'll get a good tasting. And from the porch of the Beam family's whitewashed mansion on the hill, you have a perfect view of the vapor-spewing, multibuilding factory, which has turned out millions of bottles of bourbon.

8 *Kentucky Comfort Food* 6 p.m.

For real Kentucky skillet-fried chicken, take a table at **Kurtz** (418 East Stephen Foster Avenue, Bardstown; 502-348-8964; bardstownparkview.com/dining.htm; $$), which has been satisfying hungry Kentuckians since 1937. The chicken is superb and

the fixings are traditional — mashed potatoes, cornbread, green beans with Kentucky ham. For dessert, ask for the biscuit pudding with bourbon sauce.

9 *Bourbons by the Dozen* 8 p.m.

When you're finished with the day's driving and ready to relax, sample the atmosphere and the libations at a bourbon bar, where knowledgeable bartenders serve Kentucky's favorite drink in dozens of varieties. In Bardstown, there's a classic of the genre at **Old Talbott Tavern** (107 West Stephen Foster Avenue; 502-348-3494; talbotts.com). In Lexington, try **Bluegrass Tavern** (115 Cheapside; 859-389-6664).

SUNDAY

10 *Thoroughbreds at Home* 9 a.m.

Taking tourists to the horse farms is a Lexington specialty — the local convention and visitors bureau publishes a list of tour companies and private guides (visitlex.com/idea/horse-farms.php). One good choice is a trip with the women of **Horse Farm Tours** (859-268-2906; horsefarmtours.com), who point out historical buildings in downtown Lexington on the way to a sampling of farms. If decadently luxurious stables and a 10-bedroom mansion at one farm are a reminder that thoroughbreds are a rich person's hobby, the wholesome young broodmare manager at the next farm, attending to the mares and their wobbly, week-old foals, is proof of how intense the horse-and-human relationship can be. At the stud farm, it's all about bloodlines and breeding techniques. You'll also be whisked to the best seats in the ivy-covered limestone viewing stand at Keeneland, Lexington's

OPPOSITE Oak barrels at Woodford Reserve. On the tour, you'll see the bourbon-making process from mash to bottle.

TOP Green countryside near Loretto, on one of the winding side roads to explore near Lexington.

ABOVE Whiskey makers migrated to this part of Kentucky, then known as Bourbon County, Virginia, around 1800. Some of their tools are displayed at Maker's Mark distillery.

renowned race track — to see, perhaps, some horses in training.

11 *Plain or Crispy* 1 p.m.

Drive south from Lexington, and pick your version of local history. Route 68, through undulating hills and forested bluffs, will take you to **Shaker Village of Pleasant Hill** (3501 Lexington Road, Harrodsburg; 859-734-5411; shakervillageky.org), a home of the plain-living 19th-century Shaker sect. Wander around 34 restored buildings and stay for dinner in the restaurant. If you prefer more populist fare, head south on Interstate 75, exit at the Cumberland Gap Parkway, Route 25E, and turn right onto 25W to get to the **Harland Sanders Cafe and Museum** (688 Highway 25W, Corbin; corbin-ky.gov/index.php/visitor/sanders-cafe), located in the restaurant where the renowned Colonel Sanders cooked a lot of chickens before becoming world-famous. You can still savor his 11 herbs and spices at the KFC cafe.

ABOVE Maker's Mark, in Loretto, finishes off its bourbon bottles with signature red wax.

OPPOSITE A warehouse at the Jim Beam distillery.

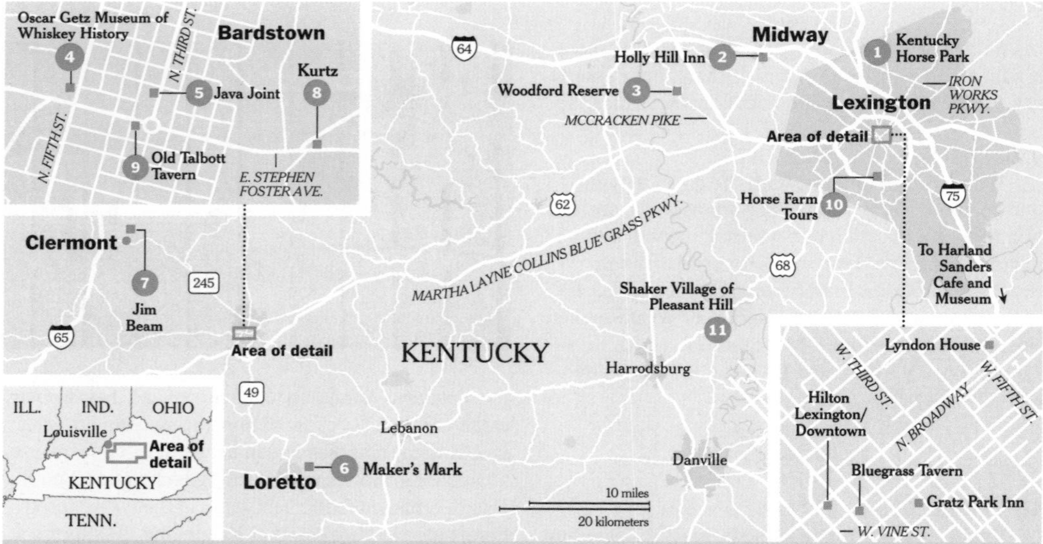

Oscar Getz Museum of Whiskey History 4
Bardstown
N. THIRD ST.
Kurtz 8
5 Java Joint
N. FIFTH ST.
9 Old Talbott Tavern
E. STEPHEN FOSTER AVE.
Clermont
7 Jim Beam
245
65
Area of detail
ILL. IND. OHIO
Louisville
Area of detail
KENTUCKY
TENN.
49
64
Midway
Holly Hill Inn 2
1 Kentucky Horse Park
Woodford Reserve 3
MCCRACKEN PIKE
IRON WORKS PKWY.
Lexington
Area of detail
62
Horse Farm Tours 10
75
MARTHA LAYNE COLLINS BLUE GRASS PKWY.
68
To Harland Sanders Cafe and Museum
Shaker Village of Pleasant Hill 11
KENTUCKY
Harrodsburg
Lebanon
Danville
Loretto
6 Maker's Mark
10 miles
20 kilometers
Lyndon House
W. THIRD ST.
W. FIFTH ST.
N. BROADWAY
Hilton Lexington/ Downtown
Bluegrass Tavern
Gratz Park Inn
W. VINE ST.

THE BASICS

Blue Grass Airport in Lexington is served by several airlines and rental car companies.

Gratz Park Inn
120 West Second Street
859-231-1777
gratzparkinn.com
$$
An attractive 1906 brick building in the Gratz Park Historic District.

Hilton Lexington/Downtown
369 West Vine Street
859-231-9000
lexingtondowntownhotel.com
$$
Recently renovated; good downtown location.

Lyndon House
507 North Broadway
859-420-2683
lyndonhouse.com
$$
An 1883 mansion converted to a bed and breakfast.

JIM BEAM
10,000,000 BARRELS
THE STUFF INSIDE MATTERS MOST.
FEBRUARY 8, 2005

1875
2008

Louisville

Every May, Louisville, Kentucky, bolts into the public eye for 120 seconds—the time it takes to run the Kentucky Derby. But there is more to this courtly city on the Ohio River than the Derby. The last decade has seen a cultural and civic blooming, with new galleries, restaurants, and performance spaces taking their place alongside the city's already robust roster of seductions. Entire neighborhoods—Butchertown, for instance, and East Market—have been reimagined as engines of cultural and culinary expression. Regardless of the changes, Derby City retains its easy charm—a glass of fine bourbon and good conversation aren't hard to find. And for the record, it's pronounced "LOU-uh-vull."
— BY MICHAEL WASHBURN

FRIDAY

1 *Getting Acquainted* 6 p.m.

More than 45 different watering holes line the roughly two miles of the Bardstown Road-Baxter Avenue corridor, from elegant restaurants to sticky-floored dives. Sandwiched among them are cafes and galleries specializing in regional ceramics and woodwork, and shops selling vintage clothing and jewelry, musical instruments, and Louisville-themed curiosities. Stop in at the **Holy Grale** (1034 Bardstown Road; 502-459-9939; holygralelouisville.com). Located in a century-old church, this dark, snug tavern with a polished bar running its length offers a selection of fine beers, including rare drafts. The menu of small plates, with selections from poutine to kale salad, lists suggested beer pairings.

2 *Bootleggers and Grits* 8:30 p.m.

Jack Fry's (1007 Bardstown Road; 502-452-9244; jackfrys.com; $$$) opened in 1933 as a haven for bootleggers and bookies and has remained a popular dining spot, with its classic Old South atmosphere and original décor. A collection of 1930s-era photographs—including shots of the 1937 flood that devastated downtown Louisville and prompted development in the eastern, now more affluent, sections of town—adorns the walls, and a discreet jazz trio performs in the corner. These days the restaurant focuses on subtle reinventions of Southern staples: shrimp and grits with red-eye gravy and country ham, for example, or lamb chops in a rosemary natural jus with shiitakes and thyme.

3 *Night Music* 10:30 p.m.

From Will Oldham and Slint to My Morning Jacket, Louisville performers have sent their music echoing around the world. Even if you're not lucky enough to catch Oldham or MMJ in one of their local appearances, you can always find something to spirit you away. **Zanzabar** (2100 South Preston Street; 502-635-9227; zanzabarlouisville.com) offers cheap whiskey for you to sip at its horseshoe-shaped bar while you catch one of the city's (or country's) comers on its intimate stage. Closing time here—and almost everywhere in Louisville—is 4 a.m.

SATURDAY

4 *Art and Comfort Food* 10 a.m.

The East Market District, dubbed NuLu (new Louisville), is perhaps the best of the city's revitalization projects, offering antiques stores, boutiques, and galleries. The **Zephyr Gallery** (610 East Market Street; 502-585-5646; zephyrgallery.org) and **Swanson Reed Contemporary** (638 East Market Street; 502-589-5466; swansonreedgallery.com) show the work of regional and national artists. The **Paul Paletti Gallery** (713 East Market Street; 502-589-9254; paulpalettigallery.com) displays photography. Before exploring too far, visit **Hillbilly Tea** (120 South First Street; 502-587-7350; hillbillytea.com; $$) for the Hillbilly Benedict (ham and eggs on a biscuit) or herb scrambled eggs with steak or a pancake. The gettin's good, and the locals know it, so be patient.

5 *Float Like a Butterfly* 11 a.m.

Louisville's greatest son is the greatest: Muhammad Ali. The **Muhammad Ali Center** (144 North Sixth Street; 502-584-9254; alicenter.org) celebrates his singular talent as a fighter and his post-retirement humanitarian efforts, but the curators pulled no punches with the history. Sure, you can try the speed bag, but not before you're immersed in multimedia presentations that contextualize Ali's career within the civil rights struggle. The Ali Center

OPPOSITE On the track at the Kentucky Derby.

is part of **Museum Row** (museumrowonmain.com), an eclectic confederation of museums and galleries devoted to science, blown glass art, Louisville Slugger baseball bats, historical artifacts (including armor worn by English knights), and more.

6 *Riders Up!* 1:30 p.m.

Churchill Downs (700 Central Avenue; 502-636-4400; churchilldowns.com) demands a visit even if you're not here for the Derby—especially if you're not here for the Derby. During other races in the spring meet, which runs for several months, a spot on Millionaire's Row costing Diddy and his ilk $68,000 on Derby Day will set you back only $20 when you walk among the mortals; don't worry, the ponies charge just as hard. Adjacent to the Downs, the **Kentucky Derby Museum** (704 Central Avenue; 502-637-7097; derbymuseum.org), open all year, offers an overview of the Run for the Roses and hosts several track tours, including one of the "backside," home to 1,400 thoroughbreds during racing season. After leaving the Downs, visit **Wagner's Pharmacy** (3113 South Fourth Street; 502-375-3800; wagnerspharmacy.com), fabled hangout of grooms, jockeys, and sportswriters. Barely changed since 1922, Wagner's lunch counter displays fading photos of legends—two- and four-legged—from Derby history.

7 *Whiskey Row* 6 p.m.

Doc Crows (127 West Main Street; 502-587-1626; doccrows.com; $$) occupies the former Bonnie Bros. distillery, one of Louisville's collection of cast-iron-facade buildings in an area called Whiskey Row. Take a seat in the back room of this 1880s-era gem and enjoy oysters on the half shell with bourbon mignonette or Carolina-style pulled pork.

8 *Broadway on the Ohio* 8 p.m.

Home of the annual spring Humana Festival of New American Plays, one of the nation's foremost new-works festivals, **Actors Theatre of Louisville** (316 West Main Street; 502-584-1205; actorstheatre.org) not only provides a rigorous testing ground for new talent, but shows well-acted plays for most of the year. The festival introduced Pulitzer Prize-winning plays including *Dinner With Friends* and *Crimes of the Heart* and has sent an impressive cadre of graduates on to Broadway. If nothing at Actors Theatre strikes your fancy, check out the **Kentucky Center for the Arts** (501 West Main Street; 502-562-0100; kentuckycenter.org), which hosts touring productions as well as performances by the Louisville Orchestra and the Louisville Ballet.

9 *Borne Back Ceaselessly* 10:30 p.m.

The college crowd and some of their elders party at Louisville's overwrought, underthought **Fourth Street Live**, an urban mall featuring clubs, bars, and places like T.G.I. Fridays and a Hard Rock Cafe. Take a few steps from that chaos, however, and discover the wonderfully worn **Old Seelbach Bar** (500 Fourth Street; 502-585-3200; seelbachhilton.com). It's rumored that when F. Scott Fitzgerald was a young military officer stationed in Louisville, he would while away the hours at this stately lounge directly off the Seelbach Hotel's grand lobby. Fitzgerald gave the hotel itself a cameo in the *The Great Gatsby*,

ABOVE Reliving the Derby at the Kentucky Derby Museum. The museum offers films, memorabilia, and several tours of the track and areas where horses are stabled.

OPPOSITE The Moonshine Breakfast at Hillbilly Tea.

but he didn't highlight the bar in his masterpiece, preferring to keep the best for himself. At least that's how the local story goes. Whatever the reason, it's better this way.

SUNDAY

10 *A Walk in the Park* 10 a.m.

Wake up with a jolt from the local favorite **Heine Brothers' Coffee** (1295 Bardstown Road; 502-456-5108; heinebroscoffee.com). This location shares a passageway with one of the last great bookstores, **Carmichael's** (1295 Bardstown Road; 502-456-6950; carmichaelsbookstore.com). Feel free to amble back and forth while you prepare for **Cherokee Park**. Opened in 1892, Cherokee was one of Frederick Law Olmsted's last and wildest creations—think Prospect Park in the foothills of Appalachia. Park near Hogan's Fountain and you can explore the nearly 400 acres of trails, hills, and meadows.

11 *Cave Hill* 1 p.m.

Colonel Harland Sanders lies alongside local luminaries like George Rogers Clark, the city's founder, at **Cave Hill Cemetery** (701 Baxter Avenue; 502-451-5630; cavehillcemetery.com), a lush Victorian-era graveyard that offers, unsurprisingly, a peaceful respite amid the bustle of the Highlands neighborhood. Before leaving, go native and leave a spork or a packet of ketchup at the Colonel's Doric-columned grave site, a memorial to his fried chicken fame.

THE BASICS

Fly into Louisville International Airport or drive into town on interstate highways 64, 65, or 71.

You will need a car to get around.

21C Museum Hotel
700 West Main Street
502-217-6300
21chotel.com
$$$
A highly rated hotel-art gallery with 9,000 square feet of exhibition space.

The Brown Hotel
335 West Broadway
502-583-1234
brownhotel.com
$$
Grand old hotel open since 1923.

The Seelbach-Hilton
500 Fourth Street
502-585-3200
seelbachhilton.com
$$$$
A Louisville classic.

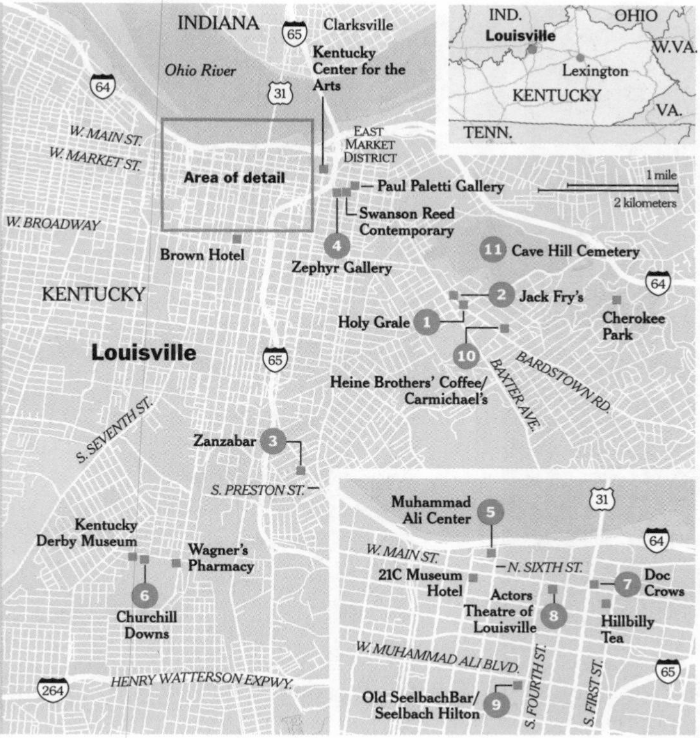

INDIANA
Clarksville
Ohio River
Kentucky Center for the Arts
W. MAIN ST.
W. MARKET ST.
EAST MARKET DISTRICT
Area of detail
Paul Paletti Gallery
Swanson Reed Contemporary
W. BROADWAY
Brown Hotel
4 Zephyr Gallery
11 Cave Hill Cemetery
2 Jack Fry's
KENTUCKY
Holy Grale 1
Cherokee Park
Louisville
10 Heine Brothers' Coffee/ Carmichael's
BARDSTOWN RD.
BAXTER AVE.
S. SEVENTH ST.
Zanzabar 3
S. PRESTON ST.
Kentucky Derby Museum
Wagner's Pharmacy
6 Churchill Downs
HENRY WATTERSON EXPWY.
IND.
OHIO
Louisville
W.VA.
Lexington
KENTUCKY
VA.
TENN.
1 mile
2 kilometers
Muhammad Ali Center 5
W. MAIN ST.
N. SIXTH ST.
21C Museum Hotel
Actors Theatre of Louisville 8
7 Doc Crows
Hillbilly Tea
W. MUHAMMAD ALI BLVD.
Old Seelbach Bar/ Seelbach Hilton 9
S. FOURTH ST.
S. FIRST ST.

1897 CONFEDERATE GALLERY
RYMAN
AUDITORIUM

Nashville

Nashville, Tennessee, isn't nicknamed Music City for nothing. Singers, songwriters, and pickers — not to mention their toe-tapping admirers — have been pouring in for decades. This is where country music lives and breathes, but Nashville is a big tent for good music, nurturing generations of musicians playing rock and alt-country, R & B, and even jazz and classical. While it revels in its country roots, there's a new beat in once-sleepy neighborhoods like East Nashville and 12 South that thrive with lively bars, stylish restaurants, and a young, eclectic crop of music makers, churning out everything from bluegrass to punkabilly.
— BY KEITH MULVIHILL AND TAYLOR HOLLIDAY

FRIDAY

1 *Get the Picture* 4 p.m.

For an introduction to downtown, traditionally country music central, stroll along the Cumberland River and over the Shelby Avenue bridge, where the view is superb. Head uptown along Broadway, and turn on Fifth Avenue South to find **Hatch Show Print** (224 Fifth Avenue South; 615-256-2805; hatchshowprint.com), in business since 1879. A letterpress print shop and gallery, it displays and sells handmade copies of gems like "Dolly Parton and Her Family Traveling Band" and "In Person: B.B. King." The **Ernest Tubb Record Shop** (417 Broadway; 615-255-7503; etrecordshop.com), where the original honky-tonk hero once broadcast his midnight radio jamboree, carries almost every classic country and bluegrass recording available. And close by is the Ryman Auditorium, the original Grand Ole Opry stage.

2 *Tennessee Italian* 7 p.m.

Nashville has undergone a culinary renaissance, and **City House** (1222 Fourth Avenue North; 615-736-5838; cityhousenashville.com; $$), in a historic district called Germantown, is a part of the new wave. When chefs aren't working and musicians have some money to spend, they come to this former sculptor's studio tucked into a residential side street for pizza topped with house-made belly ham, oregano, and chiles; and trout with peanuts, raisins, and parsley. Tandy Wilson, the owner, describes himself as "an old redneck from Tennessee" but cooks as if he had been raised in Italy.

3 *Do the Grapevine* 9:30 p.m.

In the mid-1990s, *The Wildhorse Saloon Dance Show* on the Nashville Network inspired legions of viewers to learn the Boot Scootin' Boogie and the Watermelon Crawl. Today, the sprawling **Wildhorse Saloon** (120 Second Avenue North; 615-902-8200; wildhorsesaloon.com) continues to draw eager crowds. That there are more flip-flops than cowboy boots is a tad disheartening, but the enthusiasm for line dancing doesn't appear to have waned. You don't know how to do a grapevine? No problem. Check the schedule and arrive early for a lesson when an instructor walks everyone through the steps. You'll be kick-ball-change-stomp stomping like a pro.

SATURDAY

4 *Music Box* 10:30 a.m.

Hundreds of country hits were recorded at **Studio B** (1611 Roy Acuff Place), a drab cinderblock building in the historic Music Row district, where RCA legends like Elvis, Roy Orbison, and Dolly Parton sang their hearts out. The unglamorous space looks largely unchanged from when it was shuttered in 1977. Many visiting music fans haven't even heard of the studio let alone realize that it's one of the last vestiges of country music's golden years. The **Country Music Hall of Fame** (222 Fifth Avenue South; 615-416-2001; countrymusichalloffame.org) offers hourlong tours of

OPPOSITE The Ryman Auditorium downtown.

RIGHT Hometown pride in a downtown mural.

the studio. Piano players may be invited to tickle the ivories of the original Steinway grand piano.

5 *Fire Bird* 1 p.m.

"You can't handle it," a woman at **Prince's Hot Chicken Shack** (123 Ewing Drive; 615-226-9442; $) told one group of newbies who tried to order the "medium" spicy fried chicken. This long-revered spot serves four variations of hot chicken, a unique Nashville dish: mild, medium, hot, and extra hot. Order at your peril. The moist flesh is marinated and enveloped in a spicy rub before it's fried, so the hotness runs deep. The savory hellfire is the draw—that, and the terrific sides of baked beans, coleslaw, and oh-so-sweet chess pie.

ABOVE The Beaux Arts lobby of the century-old Hermitage Hotel in downtown Nashville.

BELOW A Roy Orbison guitar sculpture outside Studio B, an important stop on any country music pilgrimage.

6 *Popsicles and Fringe* 2 p.m.

Cool off your first-degree burn at **Las Paletas Gourmet Popsicles** (2911 12th Avenue South; 615-386-2101), a small storefront that makes popsicles from fresh fruit and vegetables like honeydew, avocado, or hibiscus. Known simply as 12 South, 12th Avenue South is a trendy, tree-lined neighborhood packed with boutiques, cafes, and bars. You'll also find **Katy K Designs** (2407 12th Avenue South; 615-297-4242; katyk.com), a vintage clothing shop that specializes in country western wear from Johnny Cash black to Dollyesque showstoppers. For an early, casual dinner, hop over to East Nashville, another trendy neighborhood, to **Pharmacy Burger Parlor and Beer Garden** (731 McFerrin Avenue; 615-712-9517; thepharmacynashville.com; $). On a busy day here, hundreds of hamburgers are ground from Tennessee beef and served on soft potato rolls.

7 *Opryland or Not* 7 p.m.

If country is calling, you'll find the sometimes corny, sometimes brilliant, but always endearing Grand Ole Opry most weekends several miles from

downtown at **Opryland** (2804 Opryland Drive; 615-871-6779; opry.com). Country legends, has-beens, stars, and wannabes all show up for this broadcast, the world's longest-running radio show. If you want more adventurous live music, stay in East Nashville for the **Family Wash** (2038 Greenwood Avenue; 615-226-6070; familywash.com; $), where alt-country, alt-rock, and alt-folk acts start at 9 p.m.

8 *Southern Comfort* 11 p.m.

If your ears need a rest, grab a stool at the **Patterson House** (1711 Division Street; 615-636-7724; thepattersonnashville.com), a trendy mahogany-lined bar. Its creative libations have included a bacon-infused old-fashioned and the Juliet and Romeo, made with gin, rosewater, angostura bitters, mint, and a sliver of cucumber. Dark wood and dim chandeliers make for a seductive backdrop.

SUNDAY

9 *Alt-Brunch* 9 a.m.

The menu may not list Southern good-ole-boy favorites, but there's nothing persnickety about **Marché Artisan Foods** (1000 Main Street; 615-262-1111; marcheartisanfoods.com; $$) in East Nashville, a bistro and market that fills a former boat showroom. The space has a homey vibe thanks to enticing display cases filled with baked goods, and a few family-size wooden tables. Standouts include the quiche with sausage and provolone.

10 *Horsey Set* 11 a.m.

Relive Nashville's antebellum days at **Belle Meade Plantation** (5025 Harding Pike; 615-356-0501; bellemeadeplantation.com), a 30-acre estate six miles from downtown. The centerpiece is a grand Greek-revival mansion completed in 1853, with a labyrinth

ABOVE The antebellum mansion at Belle Meade Plantation, six miles outside of Nashville.

BELOW Hatch Show Print, a prominent maker of country music posters for generations.

of colorful rooms. In its heyday, the plantation was one of the most prosperous and successful thoroughbred farms around. Portraits of muscular stallions grace the walls. On the grounds are a posh carriage house, sobering slave quarters, and an 18th-century log cabin.

11 *A Writer's Choices* 2 p.m.

Parnassus Books (3900 Hillsboro Pike; 615-953-2243; parnassusbooks.net) was the author Ann Patchett's reply to the closing of one too many local bookstores. Stocked with a selection of books chosen to match a literary sensibility, it's a good Nashville stop for any book lover. If you're lucky, you may catch a visit by a nationally known author; among those who have come for book signings or other events are Doris Kearns Goodwin, Pat Conroy, and Elizabeth Gilbert.

ABOVE Pastries for sale at Marché Artisan Foods, a bakery and bistro in East Nashville.

OPPOSITE Dolly Parton, Elvis Presley, and Roy Orbison all sang their hearts out for recordings made in Studio B, in the historic Music Row district.

THE BASICS

Several carriers serve the Nashville airport, a 15-minute drive from downtown.

If you're not driving your own car, rent one.

Hermitage Hotel
231 Sixth Avenue North
615-244-3121
thehermitagehotel.com
$$$
An updated Nashville classic with a romantic Beaux-Arts lobby.

Hutton Hotel
1808 West End Avenue
615-340-9333
huttonhotel.com
$$
New, centrally located, smoke-free, and eco-friendly.

Union Station Hotel
1001 Broadway
615-726-1001
unionstationhotelnashville.com
$$
Ultramodern rooms in a former train station.

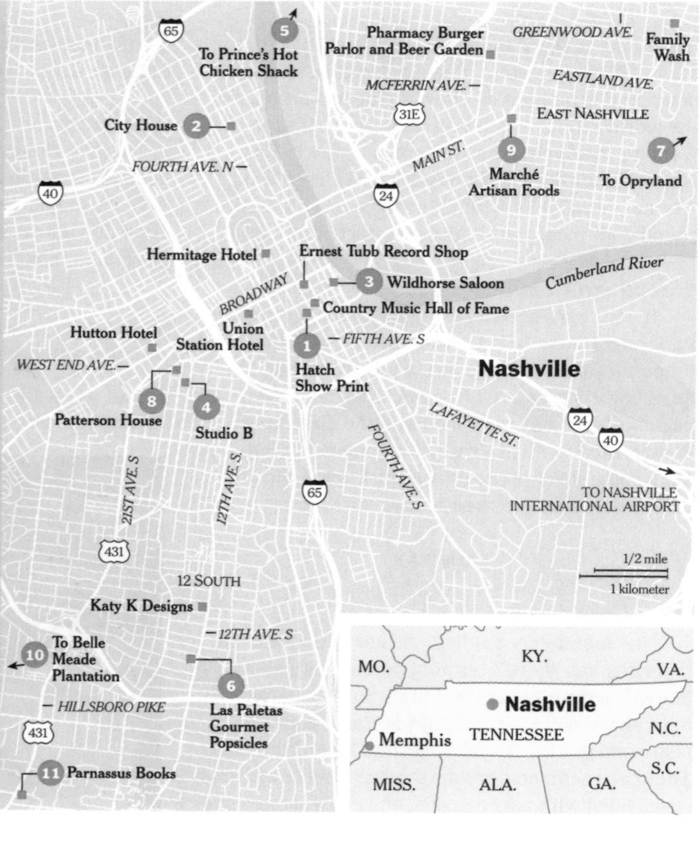

65
5 To Prince's Hot Chicken Shack
Pharmacy Burger Parlor and Beer Garden
GREENWOOD AVE.
Family Wash
EASTLAND AVE.
MCFERRIN AVE.
31E
EAST NASHVILLE
2 City House
MAIN ST.
9 Marché Artisan Foods
7 To Opryland
FOURTH AVE. N
40
24
Hermitage Hotel
Ernest Tubb Record Shop
3 Wildhorse Saloon
Cumberland River
BROADWAY
Country Music Hall of Fame
Union Station Hotel
Hutton Hotel
1 Hatch Show Print
FIFTH AVE. S
WEST END AVE.
Nashville
8 Patterson House
4 Studio B
LAFAYETTE ST.
FOURTH AVE. S
21ST AVE. S
12TH AVE. S
65
24
40
TO NASHVILLE INTERNATIONAL AIRPORT
431
12 SOUTH
1/2 mile
1 kilometer
Katy K Designs
12TH AVE. S
10 To Belle Meade Plantation
6 Las Paletas Gourmet Popsicles
HILLSBORO PIKE
431
11 Parnassus Books
MO.
KY.
VA.
Nashville
Memphis
TENNESSEE
N.C.
S.C.
MISS.
ALA.
GA.

STEINWAY & SONS

Memphis

You've worn Memphis's cotton, moved to its rhythm, sung its blues. Elvis Presley found his sound in this bluff city; B.B. King took his name, the Beale Street Blues Boy, from its 1940s entertainment district. "Home of the blues," the city now likes to trumpet. "Birthplace of rock 'n' roll." But these cultural revolutions, and the African-American milieu that spawned them, got no respect until Elvis died in 1977 and the city was inundated by grieving fans spending green money. Soon, Memphis began the urban-renewed version of Beale Street—its answer to Bourbon Street, sans the nudie shows—which over the years has become more like frat row. But deep blues do still exist in Memphis. You just have to dig deep to find them. —BY ROBERT GORDON

FRIDAY

1 *Three Little Words* 3 p.m.

Discussions about Memphis barbecue, even among friends, can lead to fisticuffs. Stop at **Payne's** (1762 Lamar Avenue; 901-272-1523; $) on your way in from the airport. It's a former service station, cavernous and spare. In Memphis, barbecue means pork shoulder, pulled from the bone or chopped and served with hot sauce or mild, with a dollop of cole slaw on top. The slaw is essential, as the perfect sandwich—i.e., Payne's—is a matter not only of taste but also of texture. "One chopped hot," you say at the counter, and three little words have never meant so much. The meat is succulent and tender; the mustardy slaw seeps into the tangy sauce. Don't worry. The sandwich isn't big enough to spoil dinner.

2 *It Came from Memphis* 5 p.m.

As Elvis would assure us, the world does indeed look great from inside a '55 Cadillac. See for yourself on Tad Pierson's three-hour **Greatest Hits** tour (901-527-8870; americandreamsafari.com; $200 for a party of one to five people). He picks you up—usually at the Peabody Hotel (149 Union Avenue), although other arrangements may be made—in his refurbished Caddy and shows you the opulence and poverty of the city and its famous recording studios: Sun, home to Howling Wolf and Elvis; Stax, where Booker T. and the MG's backed Otis Redding; Hi, where Al Green recorded his sultry hits. In the entrepreneurial spirit of the city that brought you Holiday Inns and self-serve supermarkets, Mr. Pierson also peddles his Memphis Mary, a bloody mary mix with barbecue sauce. Get you some.

3 *You Said You Was High Class* 8:30 p.m.

There's a lot of grease in your future, so tonight it's dine fancy. **Mollie Fontaine** (679 Adams Avenue; 901-524-1886; molliefontainelounge.com; $$-$$$), a stylish bar and restaurant, fills two floors of a Victorian house where the soul songwriter Dan Penn—"Do Right Woman," "Cry Like a Baby"—once had his studio. Songs still float in the air, and patrons are as likely as the local greats—Di Anne Price included—to be playing them on the bar's piano. The menu of small plates mingles eclectic selections like lamb souvlaki and Spanish-style garlic shrimp with upscaled versions of sliders and fish fry.

4 *Nothin' but the Blues* 10:30 p.m.

It would be easy to hit Beale Street (if you do go, look for the soul performers James Govan or FreeWorld), but you came to Memphis for deep blues. Drive to **Wild Bill's** (1580 Vollintine Avenue; 901-726-5473), a storefront juke joint in a crumbling shopping strip. The room is deep and narrow, with snapshots of revelers tacked to the walls. Beer is served in quarts on long community tables, and when the dance floor fills up, folks shake it in the aisles. The band evolves and revolves; these players have backed Albert King and B.B. King, played world tours and dirt-floor hovels, and they'll transport you back in time, a real good time.

SATURDAY

5 *Hot Water Cornbread* 9:30 a.m.

Ease in with a Memphis Mary in your room before facing the harsh sun outside. Then hop on the Main Street Trolley (matatransit.com), jumping off at Market Avenue to duck into **Alcenia's** (317 North Main Street; 901-523-0200; alcenias.com; $). B.J.—Alcenia's daughter—hugs everyone, and she usually serves hot water cornbread while you wait for your food.

OPPOSITE Beale Street now courts a party crowd, but deep blues still exist in Memphis.

You can't make a bad choice: options include salmon croquettes, dense pancakes, and sublime fried green tomatoes. Service can be slow, but this morning you're probably not moving too fast anyway. If you're staying out east, **Bryant's Biscuits** (3965 Summer Avenue; 901-324-7494; bryantsmemphis.com) is worth the wait in line. Flaky and hot biscuits, fresh home-cookin' lunch.

6 *Soul, Man* 11 a.m.

Last night you lived the music, today you'll learn it. The headset tour at the **Memphis Rock 'n' Soul Museum** (191 Beale Street, in the FedExForum; 901-205-2533; memphisrocknsoul.org) includes original interviews and great music, evoking Memphis as a crossroads that bred new ideas and sounds. Look for an exhibit about Sputnik Monroe, a white wrestler who used his black fan base to integrate the city auditorium in the '50s. Then drive to the **Stax Museum of American Soul Music** (926 East McLemore Avenue; 901-946-2535; staxmuseum.com), an institution of a completely different nature—it has a dance floor, you dig? Stax was a studio and record label from 1957 to 1975, home of Isaac Hayes, Sam & Dave, the Staple Singers, and Albert King. There are more short, fun films than you can absorb in one visit, and you'll exit (into the gift shop) snapping your fingers.

7 *Memphis Soul Stew* 3 p.m.

You're hungry, you're in Soulsville USA—time for some soul food. The **Four Way** (998 Mississippi Boulevard; 901-507-1519; fourwaymemphis.com; $) has been serving heaping portions for decades. The tender catfish is salted to perfection and fried in a crispy crust; the fried chicken is among the best in the South. Even if you're full, leaving without tasting the lemon meringue pie would be a tragedy.

8 *Find the Vinyl* 4:30 p.m.

There's good record hunting in Memphis—blues, rock 'n' roll, soul, indies. Start at **Goner Records** (2152 Young Avenue; 901-722-0095; goner-records.com) or nearby **Shangri-La Records** (1916 Madison Avenue; 901-274-1916; shangri.com). Both double as indie labels and have achieved national attention with regional artists, including the late garage rocker Jay Reatard, Harlan T. Bobo, and the Grifters. At Goner, look for the mini-shrine to Elvis impersonators. **Audiomania** (1698 Madison Avenue; 901-278-1166) has a deeper jazz and soul collection.

9 *Rollin' on the River* 6 p.m.

Park anywhere on Front Street downtown and take a few steps to the **Riverwalk**, a footpath carved into the bluffs along the Mississippi River. Evenings don't always cool down, but the whiff of magnolia and the sight of a tug pushing a massive load upstream will inspire the Huck Finn in anyone. During May weekends, Memphians throng the riverbank for events—a music festival, a barbecue contest, a symphony (memphisinmay.org).

10 *Night of Many Sounds* 9 p.m.

The cocktail is the concoction at the **Cove** (2559 Broad Avenue; 901-730-0719; thecovememphis.com). Disappear into an overstuffed leatherette booth and float away on the Blue Steel—tequila, just enough curacao to make it glow, and a lemon twist. Catch upcoming locals and some of the better indie bands here, or drift not far to the **Hi-Tone Café** (412-414 North Cleveland Street; 901-278-8663; hitonememphis.com), where higher-profile acts perform. The Hi-Tone is in the location of the former dojo where Elvis got his black belt; there's a photo over the bar. If you want a D.J. who's as likely to

play Rufus Thomas as the latest dance hit, sail back downtown to **Paula and Raiford's Disco** (14 South 2nd Steet; 901-521-2494; paularaifords.com), and put on your b-b-boogie shoes.

SUNDAY

11 *Love, Happiness, Breakfast* 10 a.m.

The soul food on the menu at the **Rev. Al Green's Full Gospel Tabernacle Church** (787 Hale Road; algreenmusic.com/fullgospeltabernacle.html) is purely of the intangible kind. Even though he has a rejuvenated pop career, the reverend makes it home for more Sundays than he misses. He's as likely to break out into "Take Me to the River" as a psalm. Visitors are welcome, appropriate dress encouraged. Services start at 11:15, but first grab a sweet-potato-pancake breakfast with eggs and grits at the **Arcade Restaurant** (540 South Main Street; 901-526-5757; arcaderestaurant.com; $), across from the train station. In Jim Jarmusch's film *Mystery Train*, Elvis reappears at the Arcade. Keep your eyes open.

OPPOSITE ABOVE The Rock 'n' Soul Museum evokes Memphis as a crossroads that bred new ideas and sounds.

OPPOSITE BELOW Drinks in the piano bar at Mollie Fontaine, a stylish spot occupying two floors of a Victorian house where the soul songwriter Dan Penn once had his studio.

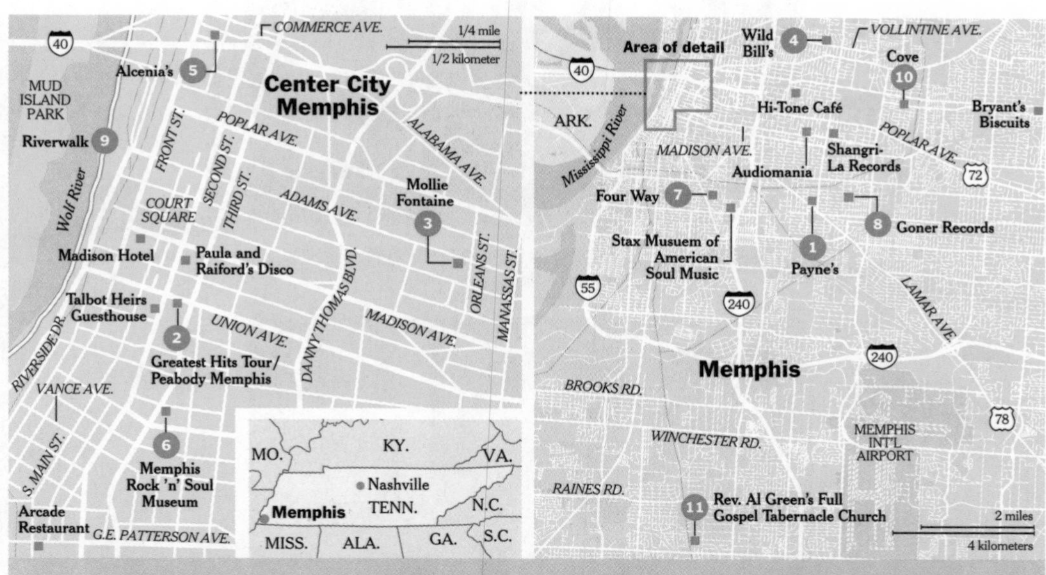

THE BASICS

Memphis International Airport is served by major airlines. About the only transportation worse than taxis in Memphis is the bus service. Rent a car.

The Peabody Memphis
149 Union Avenue
901-529-4000
peabodymemphis.com
$$$
Refurbished grand old downtown hotel, dripping with tradition and known for its resident ducks.

The Talbot Heirs Guesthouse
99 South Second Street
901-527-9772
talbotheirs.com
$$-$$$
One of Memphis's best secrets.

Madison Hotel
79 Madison Avenue
901-333-1200
madisonhotelmemphis.com
$$$
Lots of character.

Jackson

When movie crews descended on Jackson in 2010 to film The Help, *based on Kathryn Stockett's novel about the city's maids in the 1960s, it didn't take much to recreate the scenes necessary for cinematic time travel. Local loyalty has assured the survival of mom-and-pop stores like Brent's Drugs, where you can still sit at the counter and order a chocolate malt. Time rewinds as you savor a dish of peach cobbler at one of the city's beloved dining spots. The city's population of fewer than 200,000 still gives it the familiarity of a big country town, and Mississippians' old-fashioned charm is no rumor. But much has changed as well. Today Jackson calls itself the City with Soul, and top-notch restaurants and music venues mixing many genres have joined soul-food restaurants to create a relaxed marriage of old and new.* — BY LAURA TILLMAN

FRIDAY

1 *A Writer's Refuge* 3 p.m.

A stroll through the rolling hills of the historic Belhaven neighborhood is the perfect introduction to Jackson's laid-back mood. Join the couples power-walking past bungalow-style houses, parks, and front-yard vegetable gardens; and make your way to **Eudora Welty House** (1119 Pinehurst Street; 601-353-7762; eudorawelty.org), the preserved home of the Pulitzer Prize-winning author, who died in 2001. Born in Jackson, Welty lived here most of her life and made Mississippi her subject. You can tour the house, which is arranged to look as it did in the 1980s, when she was still writing and the couches, coffee tables, and chairs were stacked high with books. Outside again, take a lap around the campus of **Belhaven University** (1500 Peachtree Street; belhaven.edu) and breathe in the scent of magnolia.

2 *Living History* 4 p.m.

When Mississippi's "new" **Capitol** building (the first had architectural flaws and still stands a few blocks away) opened in 1903, electricity was an uncommon luxury in this state. That may be why the architect, Theodore Link, installed over 4,700 decorative light bulbs throughout the Beaux Arts-style building (400 High Street; 601-359-3114). On the night of the grand opening, 20,000 spectators gathered in the pouring rain outside the brightly illuminated building. The stories associated with the Capitol provide a candid portrait of the state's history, and you can learn about more of them in a self-guided tour (or come earlier in the day for a free guided tour). The Confederate battle emblem still occupies a corner of the state's banner, and the face of the Choctaw Indian Theresa Whitecloud is at the top of the Senate rotunda.

3 *Sophisticated Southern* 7 p.m.

Jackson's historic downtown is primarily a place of business, active in the daytime, but a few ambitious restaurants are now challenging the after-dark quiet. One impressive entrant is **Parlor Market** (115 West Capitol Street; 601-360-0090; parlormarket.com; $$), which serves playful interpretations of classic Southern fare. One memorable entree on the frequently changing menu combined lamb ragout with squid ink cavatelli, lady peas, preserved lemon, pickled chilies, and mint.

4 *Honky Tonk* 9 p.m.

Head over to **Hal and Mal's** (200 Commerce Street; 601-948-0888; halandmals.com), a bar and

OPPOSITE Over 4,700 light bulbs decorate the Mississippi State Capitol, built when electricity was still a luxury.

BELOW Canned goods at the Jackson Farmer's Market.

restaurant not far from Parlor Market. Started by a pair of brothers, Hal and Malcolm White, it has been bringing blues, jazz, and country bands to Jackson since 1985. Pictures of past acts plaster the walls, along with musicians' signatures. The bar keeps regional beers on draft.

SATURDAY

5 *A Venerable Survivor* 9 a.m.

Farish Street was the center of African-American life in Jackson during the Jim Crow era, but in recent decades the street has nearly emptied out. The **Big Apple Inn** (509 North Farish Street; 601-354-9371; $), which opened more than 70 years ago, is one of a handful of businesses to survive the exodus. The limited menu includes smoked sausage sandwiches and pig ear sandwiches. For breakfast, ask the cook to add an egg. Medgar Evers, the Jackson civil rights activist who in 1963 was shot in his driveway by a white supremacist, had a small office above the Big Apple Inn when he was a field officer for the N.A.A.C.P. He held meetings here with Freedom Riders, one of whom was the owner's mother. Little seems to have changed inside the restaurant since those days. A gleaming soda vending machine nods to the present, and after you taste the homemade hot sauce, you'll be grateful for this allowance.

6 *Taste of the Country* 10 a.m.

The **Jackson Farmer's Market**, held on Saturdays at the Mississippi Fairgrounds (929 High Street; 601-354-6573), is a taste of the rest of this largely rural state. Try the hand-churned goat's milk ice cream, and buy some Mississippi-made soap, cutting boards, and cornmeal to take home.

ABOVE Preparations at the Big Apple Inn, a 70-year-old restaurant. The menu is limited, and the specialties of the house include pig ear sandwiches.

7 *Mississippi Greats* Noon

Lemuria Books (4465 I-55 North; 601-366-7619; lemuriabooks.com), a Jackson institution, has changed locations a few times since it opened in the 1970s. Don't be put off by its current site, in a shopping complex next to the highway. Once you step inside the cozy store, pick out a book, and sink into one of the plush, timeworn couches, you'll begin to feel Lemuria's magic. There are sections on everything Southern, from cooking to gardening, literature to religion. Lemuria also has a room of rare, signed books; seeing William Faulkner's signature on a limited-edition print is humbling.

8 *Fondren Finds* 3:30 p.m.

In Fondren, Jackson's hub of creative, locally owned businesses, the more you look, the more you find. At **Sneaky Beans** (2914 North State Street; 601-487-6349), a good place to stop for a cup of coffee or a craft beer, posters advertise concerts and events around town. Check out **Morning Bell Records & Studios** (622 Duling Avenue; 769-233-7468; morningbellrecords.com) and **Brent's Drugs** (655 Duling Avenue; 601-366-3427), the throwback luncheonette that served as a setting in *The Help*. Next explore the shops inside the mixed-use building **Fondren Corner** (2906 North State Street) for clothing, jewelry, and gifts. Leave some time to sit on the patio at **Babalu** (622 Duling Avenue; 601-366-5757; babalums.com) and sip a Cat 5—similar to a mojito, but with Mississippi-made Cathead Vodka instead of rum.

9 *At the Drive-In* 7 p.m.

Walker's Drive-In (3016 North State Street; walkersdrivein.com) isn't really a drive-in. It's a beloved restaurant, considered by many to serve the best meals in Jackson, and it manages to make retro diner décor elegant. At lunch, patrons crowd the booths for the redfish sandwiches, sweet potato fries, and salads. During dinner, the menu changes entirely, with entrees like lamb with curry-tzatziki sauce and appetizers like fried oysters with warm Brie and apple slaw.

10 *Going Underground* 9 p.m.

Underground 119 (119 South President Street; 601-352-2322; underground119.com) brings together

the best of Jackson, with music of all genres and a diverse crowd. Tom Ramsey, the chef, who left a career as an investment banker and lobbyist to follow his dream, frequently makes the rounds to ensure everyone's having a good time.

SUNDAY

11 *Sweet Tea* 1:30 p.m.

Eating at **Two Sisters' Kitchen** (707 North Congress Street; 601-353-1180) feels a little like coming home, and only in part because it's inside an old house. The restaurant was named for the sisters of the owner, Diann Irving Alford, and they still provide some of the recipes. Take a plate and fill it at the buffet with comforting Southern standards like collard greens, fried chicken, black-eyed peas, macaroni and cheese, biscuits, and fried okra. Sit down inside the house or out on the patio, where there's often live music. It's an easy way to get a helping of all things Southern, and the servers are as sweet as the tea.

ABOVE At Walker's Drive-In, where the food is some of the finest in Jackson, the décor is retro and so is the name. It isn't a drive-in and has an elegant look.

THE BASICS

Jackson is accessible by air or road. Once in town, you will want a car to get around.

Fairview Inn
734 Fairview Street
601-948-3429
fairviewinn.com
$$
A 1908 Colonial Revival mansion in the Belhaven neighborhood.

Hilton Garden Inn Jackson Downtown
235 West Capitol Street
601-353-5464
hilton.com
$
A modern incarnation of the renovated King Edward Hotel.

Old Capitol Inn
226 North State Street
601-359-9000
oldcapitolinn.com
$
In a converted Y.W.C.A. building. Rooms and suites have Mississippi themes, like Elvis Sleeps and Faulkner's Flat.

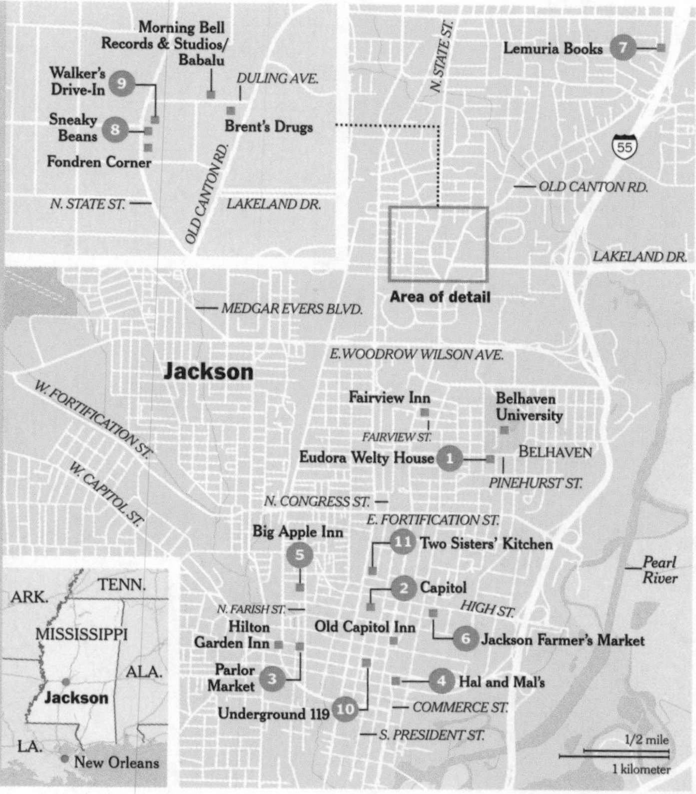

Morning Bell Records & Studios/ Babalu
Walker's Drive-In 9
Sneaky Beans 8
Fondren Corner
Brent's Drugs
DULING AVE.
N. STATE ST.
OLD CANTON RD.
LAKELAND DR.
Lemuria Books 7
55
OLD CANTON RD.
LAKELAND DR.
Area of detail
MEDGAR EVERS BLVD.
E. WOODROW WILSON AVE.
Jackson
W. FORTIFICATION ST.
W. CAPITOL ST.
Fairview Inn
Belhaven University
FAIRVIEW ST.
Eudora Welty House 1
BELHAVEN
PINEHURST ST.
N. CONGRESS ST.
E. FORTIFICATION ST.
Big Apple Inn 5
11 Two Sisters' Kitchen
2 Capitol
Pearl River
HIGH ST.
N. FARISH ST.
Hilton Garden Inn
Old Capitol Inn
6 Jackson Farmer's Market
Parlor Market 3
4 Hal and Mal's
Underground 119 10
COMMERCE ST.
S. PRESIDENT ST.
1/2 mile
1 kilometer
ARK.
TENN.
MISSISSIPPI
ALA.
Jackson
LA.
New Orleans

Birmingham

In the golden days of rail travel, a sign proclaiming "Welcome to Birmingham, the Magic City" greeted passengers arriving at Terminal Station. Although the station is only a memory today, Alabama's largest city still retains a special ability to surprise the uninitiated —particularly for modern visitors who arrive with collective memories of the city's violent civil rights past. That past is certainly memorialized, but the city has plenty more to offer: enticing takes on Southern cuisine, a nationally acclaimed motorsports park, and upscale shopping opportunities.

— BY JIM NOLES

FRIDAY

1 *Standing Tall* 4 p.m.

In 1871, Birmingham was incorporated at the strategic juncture of two rail lines where local deposits of iron and coal would nurture the young city's iron furnaces. The founders' vision was so successful that when the city's Commerce Club was invited to dispatch a symbol of Birmingham to the 1904 World's Fair, it commissioned a cast-iron statue of **Vulcan**, the Roman god of the forge. Today, the impressive statue (1701 Valley View Drive; 205-933-1409; visitvulcan.com) stands in a park atop Red Mountain, offering an unmatched vista of Birmingham's downtown skyline to those who go up to visit it—and providing residents of downtown Homewood, south of the mountain, with a view of Vulcan's massive bare rump.

2 *Not Your Grandma's Grits* 6 p.m.

Highlands Bar & Grill (2011 11th Avenue South; 205-939-1400; highlandsbarandgrill.com; $$$), recognized by the James Beard Foundation as one of the country's best restaurants, owes its reputation to chef and owner Frank Stitt, who deftly combines fresh, rural ingredients and French-inspired technique. The restaurant's stone-ground baked grits, accented with Smoky Mountain-raised country ham, mushrooms, thyme, and Parmesan, have been a local favorite for years. Call ahead for a reservation, but arrive early for a drink at the bar, where fresh oysters on the half-shell whet appetites for entrees like farm-raised lamb with fresh mint and sweet peas.

3 *All Work and All Play* 9 p.m.

The brainchild of Alan Hunter, one of MTV's original V.J.'s, **WorkPlay** (500 23rd Street South; 205-879-4773; workplay.com) is an entertainment complex that includes a live-music venue, a bar packed with a 20-something crowd, a professional sound stage, and even a suite of offices for creative professional types, all on the edge of Birmingham's warehouse district. The bar usually clears out when the live music starts next door, courtesy of acts ranging from the singer-songwriter Neko Case to the Southern rockers the Zac Brown Band. Intimacy is part of the appeal: a mere arm's length separates the musicians from the audience. Check WorkPlay's Web site for scheduled acts and to purchase tickets.

SATURDAY

4 *Continental's Breakfast* 8 a.m.

Just over the crest of Red Mountain, **Continental Bakery** (1909 Cahaba Road; 205-870-5584; chezlulu.us) greets arrivals to English Village, a small commercial district on the edge of the affluent suburb of Mountain Brook. Order inside the narrow shop, where display cases lined with fresh baguettes, bread, and pastries conjure the ambience of Dijon rather than Dixie. Outside, claim a seat at a sidewalk table, pet a neighbor's dog, and enjoy a butter croissant.

OPPOSITE Vulcan, cast in iron, stands atop Red Mountain. The iron and steel industry built Birmingham.

RIGHT An after-work crowd at Highlands Bar & Grill.

5 *It Takes a Village* 10 a.m.

Just down the hill from English Village, Mountain Brook Village holds tony shops befitting the area's origins as a forested suburban refuge from the soot-spewing smokestacks of early industrial Birmingham. At **Table Matters** (2402 Montevallo Road; 205-879-0125; table-matters.com), shoppers brush shoulders as they search for gifts ranging from William Yeoward crystal to the Good Earth Pottery produced by the Mississippi craftsman Richie Watts. Nearby at **Etc. Jewelry and Accessories** (2726 Cahaba Road; 205-871-6747; shopetcjewelry.com), husbands seek surreptitious guidance on the latest jewelry from the designer Diane Cotton or handbags from Proenza Schouler.

6 *Good Golly Miss Myra* 12:30 p.m.

In any travel article discussing Alabama, you'd expect a reference to barbecue. Here it is. Although every Birmingham resident has a favorite, **Miss Myra's Pit Bar-B-Q** (3278 Cahaba Heights Road; 205-967-6004; $) makes any aficionado's short list. The lunch crowd is steady, even into the early afternoon, as fragrant smoke wafts across the parking lot from the wide brick chimney. Inside, the décor of this former convenience store is mostly a celebration of the past glory of the Crimson Tide; a display of porcelain pigs donated by loyal customers offers its own homage to the restaurant's most delectable offerings. Pork and rib sandwiches and plates are available, of course, but Myra Grissom's signature white sauce (a concoction of mayo, pepper, and vinegar) works particularly well on her chicken.

7 *A Monument to Injustice* 2 p.m.

Two very different museums offer equally compelling glimpses of Birmingham—one of its past, the other of its future. Across the street from the historic **Sixteenth Street Baptist Church,** site of the infamous bombing that killed four girls in 1963, the **Birmingham Civil Rights Institute** (520 16th Street North; 205-328-9696; bcri.org) tells the story of the civil rights movement in Alabama and beyond and provides a somber reminder of how far the city and the nation have come in five decades. The church itself, still serving a downtown congregation, offers tours Tuesday through Friday, and, by appointment only, on Saturdays (205-251-9402; 16thstreetbaptist.org).

8 *Need for Speed* 4 p.m.

Twenty minutes east of town, in the rolling hills along the Cahaba River, the **Barber Vintage Motorsports Museum** (6030 Barber Motorsports Parkway; 205-699-7275; barbermuseum.org) hints at how Birmingham's future reputation might be cast. The museum claims the largest motorcycle collection in North America (more than 900 bikes in total) in an airy five-story display that feels as much like an art museum as a motor pool. The **Barber Motorsports Park** (barbermotorsports.com) is adjacent to the museum. Its creator, George Barber, refers to its immaculately groomed grounds as "the Augusta of racetracks."

9 *Front Row Seats* 6 p.m.

Despite his restaurant's name, Chris Hastings, the chef and owner of the **Hot and Hot Fish Club** (2180 11th Court South; 205-933-5474; hotandhotfishclub.com; $$$), quickly recommended the pork-belly appetizer. "It will set your mind free," he said. The dish combined a melt-in-your-mouth fattiness with just the right

amount of crispy skin. "I get my pork from Henry Fudge, up in north Alabama," Hastings added. "The man's a pig genius." Apparently so. Hastings reserved similar enthusiasm for his simple grilled fish, on this particular visit a pompano that just the day before had been swimming in the Gulf of Mexico. It was served whole on a bed of couscous. Reservations are suggested, as are seats at the chef's counter, where conversation with fellow patrons flows naturally.

SUNDAY

10 *Brunch at the Park* 11 a.m.

Little Savannah (3811 Clairmont Avenue; 205-591-1119;littlesavannah.com; $$), on the edge of the historic Forest Park neighborhood, calls itself a "quaint neighborhood Southern Bistro" —an apt description. Orders of the cranberry-pecan cream cheese-filled French toast and the crab cake with bacon, creamed spinach, and a poached egg threatened to disrupt the peace one Sunday with a lively debate on which selection was better. Reservations recommended.

OPPOSITE ABOVE Half art museum, half motor pool, the Barber Vintage Motorsports Museum has 900 bikes.

OPPOSITE BELOW The Birmingham Civil Rights Institute is a reminder of how far the city has come since the infamous church bombing that killed four girls in 1963.

THE BASICS

Major carriers serve the Birmingham airport. Once you're there, you'll need a car for touring.

The Tutwiler Hotel
2021 Park Place North
205-322-2100
thetutwilerhotel.com
$$
A Hampton Inn property with early-20th-century historical ambience.

The Westin Birmingham
2221 Richard Arrington Jr. Boulevard
205-307-3600
westinbirmingham.com
$$
Centrally located, recently built, attractive rooms.

Renaissance Ross Bridge Golf Resort & Spa
4000 Grand Avenue, Hoover
205-916-7677
rossbridgeresort.com
$$$
Out of town, with a golf course on Alabama's Robert Trent Jones Golf Trail.

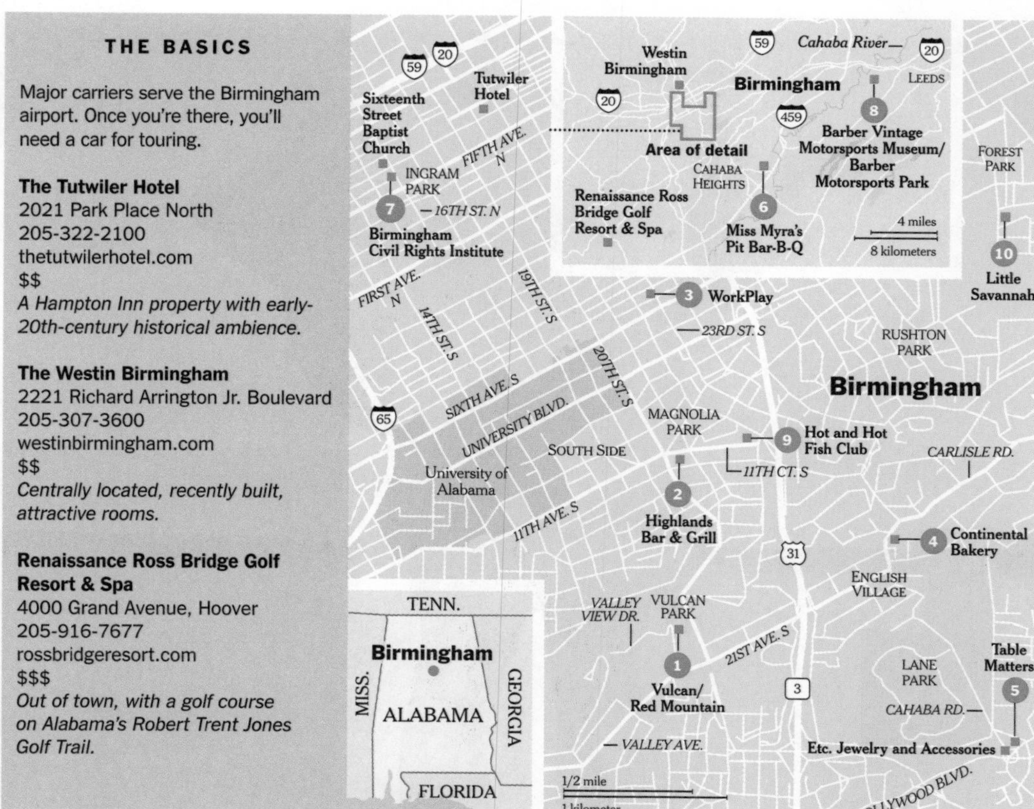

CITY AVDITORIVM

Montgomery

When the United Daughters of the Confederacy organized a Montgomery branch in 1896, its members named their chapter "Cradle of the Confederacy." A century later, veterans of the civil rights movement began referring to Alabama, and its capital, Montgomery, in particular, as the "birthplace of the civil rights movement." Now this city at a gooseneck bend in the Alabama River delivers on both claims. After a spate of museum building and downtown redevelopment, it also attracts cultural tourists. But the transition has not wiped clean the contradictions. Drive south of downtown and, in the shadow of the Martin Luther King Jr. Expressway (Interstate 85), you will pass a sign for Taraland Learning Center. It's just a few blocks west of the intersection of Jefferson Davis and Rosa L. Parks Avenues.
— BY JOHN T. EDGE

FRIDAY

1 *Learning About Hank* 4 p.m.

Hank Williams, who was born near Garland, Alabama, is Montgomery's favorite musical son. And the best place to get a bead on the man who, before his death at the age of 29 in 1953, wrote and recorded standards like "I'll Never Get Out of This World Alive," is the storefront **Hank Williams Museum** (118 Commerce Street; 334-262-3600; thehankwilliamsmuseum.net). View the baby blue Cadillac in which Williams died and artifacts like a selection of toothpicks pulled from one of his suits, a lime-fringed black shirt custom-made by Nudie's Rodeo Tailors, and the saddle he used for riding his horse, Hi-Life.

2 *Alabama Riverside* 8 p.m.

Call for directions to the **Capitol Oyster Bar** at the Montgomery Marina (617 Shady Street; 334-239-8958; capitoloysterbar.com; $), and you're still likely to get lost. But a short trek across a web of freight tracks and through the city's industrial areas brings you to the ideal time-worn perch for a sunset beer. Below are the slips of sailboats and cabin cruisers. In the distance, barges ply the Alabama River. Stay for a casual dinner. The menu is simple (fried seafood platters, steak, cheeseburgers), but the setting is lulling and there may be some music.

3 *Jazz Underground* 11 p.m.

Keep the evening going at **Sous La Terre Downtown Underground** (82 Commerce Street; 334-265-2069; souslaterre.com), a private club set, true to its moniker, in a windowless basement. It usually opens around 11 p.m. and springs to life after midnight when a jazz piano player, Henry Pugh, takes the stage. Guests must apply for membership to enter, but you won't find that much of a barrier. The crowd is friendly and the jazz is the real thing.

SATURDAY

4 *Curbside Eating* 9 a.m.

Open since 1927, the **Montgomery Curb Market** (1004 Madison Avenue; 334-263-6445; montgomeryal.gov/index.aspx?page=648) is an open-air shebang lighted by dangling bulbs and topped by a metal roof. In addition to produce, you'll find a heady array of baked goods. Hungry? Look for homemade sausage and cheese biscuits, fried peach pies, and miniature sweet potato pies.

5 *Old South* 10 a.m.

Dexter Avenue is only six blocks long, but it's the spine of a route from the site of Jefferson Davis's inauguration to the bus stop where Rosa Parks boarded for her fateful journey. Start an Old South morning atop Goat Hill, at the **Alabama State Capitol** (600 Dexter Avenue; 334-242-3935;

OPPOSITE A bronze Hank Williams strums downtown.

RIGHT The Cross Garden, one man's roadside obsession.

sos.state.al.us/OfficeOfSoS/CapitolTours.aspx), which is ringed by statuary and monuments that honor, among others, Dr. J. Marion Sims, who is called the father of modern gynecology. From the portico, where Davis took his oath as president of the Confederacy in 1861, George Wallace proclaimed in 1963, "Segregation now, segregation tomorrow, segregation forever." On the northern lawn rises a white marble memorial to the Confederacy. Detour one street south of Dexter Avenue and you stand in front of the **First White House of the Confederacy** (644 Washington Avenue; 334-242-1861; firstwhitehouse.org), the modest—and now musty—Italianate two-story building that Davis and his family called home in the aftermath of secession. The gift shop sells books and souvenirs including reproduction Confederate money.

6 *All American* Noon

Take a lunch break from history at **Chris' Hot Dogs** (138 Dexter Avenue; 334-265-6850; chrishotdogs.com), which has been selling the timeless American snack since 1917. The dogs come mustard-slathered and drenched in chili sauce. Snag a stool at the worn linoleum counter where some locals say Hank Williams sat and scribbled lyrics.

7 *New South* 12:30 p.m.

Advance to the 20th century, starting at the **Dexter Avenue King Memorial Baptist Church** (454 Dexter Avenue; 334-263-3970; dexterkingmemorial.org), where Martin Luther King Jr. rose to fame as leader of the Montgomery Improvement Association. The church stands out in red brick amid the white masonry of state government buildings. Founded by former slaves in 1877, it remains a place of worship and also gives tours in which docents explain the history. One comment about Vernon Johns, King's predecessor: "If he had led the movement, we'd all be dead—he wasn't one to turn the other cheek." Next, stop at the **Civil Rights Memorial** (400 Washington Avenue; splcenter.org/civil-rights-memorial), designed by Maya Lin and commissioned by the Southern Poverty Law Center, the group that bankrupted the United Klans of America. Water emerges from the core of a circular granite table, washing over the names of martyrs of the civil rights movement in what might be interpreted as absolution of the South's sins. The **Rosa L. Parks Library and Museum** (252 Montgomery Street; 334-241-8615; http://www.troy.edu/rosaparks/), at the spot where in 1955 Parks refused to give up her seat on a bus to a white passenger, has multimedia displays and uses special effects to take visitors on a simulated bus ride back in time.

8 *Pull the Trigger* 7 p.m.

A shotgun restaurant with a bar on the side and a trophy-size blue marlin arcing across the back wall, **Jubilee Seafood** (1057 Woodley Road; 334-262-6224; jubileeseafoodrestaurant.com; $$-$$$) serves up dishes like pecan-topped snapper and grilled sea bass with mushrooms and crabmeat. The Key lime pie is a comely whorl of citrus and meringue.

SUNDAY

9 *Brimstone in the Pines* 9 a.m.

Drive about 12 miles north on I-65 and a few miles west on Highway 82 toward Prattville, and take a left on Autauga County Road 86, also called Indian Hills Road. At a bend in the two-lane

blacktop, the **Cross Garden** erupts. Constructed as a testimony of Christian faith by W.C. Rice, who died in 2004, this folk art environment, set amid gullies rife with castoff appliances, warns, by way of hundreds of painted crosses, "Hell Is Hot, Hot, Hot!" and recalls Flannery O'Connor's observation that the South was a "Christ-haunted" place.

10 *Country-Fried Brunch* 10:45 a.m.

Wend back into town for an experience closer to the heavenly side. **Martin's Restaurant** (1796 Carter Hill Road; 334-265-1767; martinsrestaurant.org; $$) has been frying chickens and baking coconut meringue pies since 1940. It also does right by collard greens, candied yams, and string beans. But the best is the simplest: corn muffins crisp and steaming with sweet corn flavor. Plan to arrive soon after they open at 10:45, or you'll spend your Sunday morning in line with the crowds that flock from nearby churches.

OPPOSITE ABOVE The Rosa Parks bus replica.

OPPOSITE BELOW The Civil Rights Monument.

ABOVE The Alabama State Capitol.

THE BASICS

Montgomery Regional Airport is served by commuter airlines.

You will want a car for touring.

Renaissance Montgomery Hotel & Spa
201 Tallapoosa Street
334-481-5000
marriott.com
$$
At the downtown Convention Center. Rooftop pool and 9,000-square-foot spa.

Hampton Inn & Suites Montgomery-Downtown
100 Commerce Street
334-265-1010
hamptoninn.hilton.com
$$
Nicely executed renovation of a historic downtown hotel built in 1928.

Red Bluff Cottage
551 Clay Street
334-264-0056
redbluffcottage.com
$$
Five-room B&B that's almost too darned quaint.

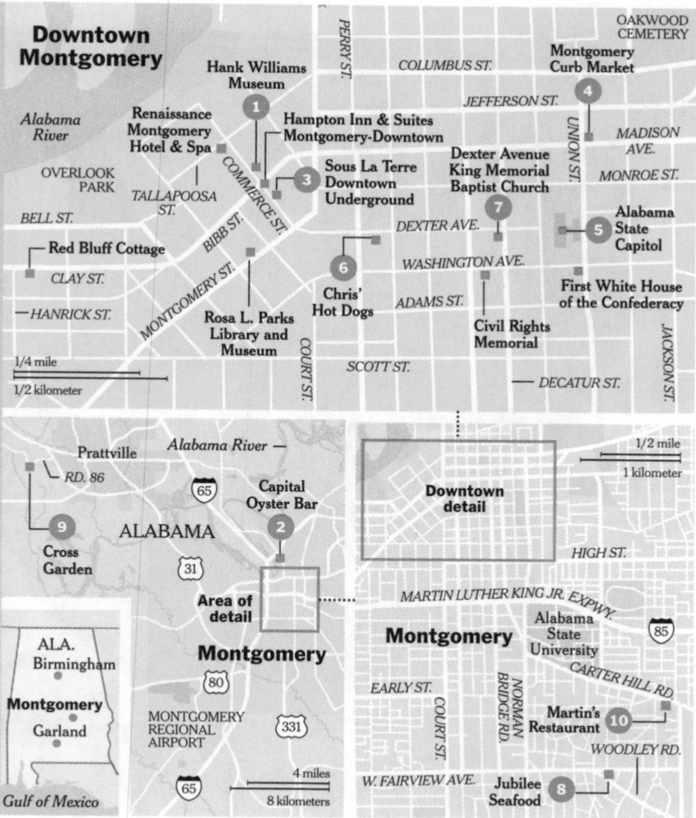

New Orleans

The weekend here begins midday on Friday when the smartly dressed lunch crowd descends upon Galatoire's restaurant in the French Quarter and, well armed with cocktails, starts its long assault on the afternoon. But a strong case could be made for the weekend starting off on Wednesday night when the Treme Brass Band settles in at the Candlelight Lounge. That is only in normal time, anyway. The season leading up to Mardi Gras fuses into one long weekend, as the streets around the city begin filling up with floats, and the living rooms of New Orleanians become littered with feathers, glue, and the makings of costumes. This is how they do it in New Orleans, a city that was four-fifths underwater after the infamous Hurricane Katrina and has survived to take up the countless parades and festivals that are part of its life. —BY CAMPBELL ROBERTSON

FRIDAY

1 *Cocktail Hour* 5 p.m.

In a city blossoming with craft-cocktail bars, best begin with a classic. The **French 75 Bar** (813 Bienville Street; 504-523-5433; arnaudsrestaurant.com/french-75) is a side chapel to **Arnaud's**, one of the old French Quarter dining palaces. The bar can get smoky, but that's part of its French colonial charm, along with the animal print upholstery and tuxedoed bar staff. Order a Sazerac, or let the bartender stir up something of his own design.

2 *No Diets* 7 p.m.

For a scenic if unhurried ride uptown, take the streetcar past the mansions and live oaks to the end of St. Charles Avenue. There is good food here. For classic south Louisiana cuisine, including a justly celebrated roast duck, head to **Brigtsen's** (723 Dante Street; 504-861-7610; brigtsens.com; $$$), situated in a homey Victorian cottage. Or for a more casual meal, cross the street to **Dante's Kitchen** (736 Dante Street; 504-861-3121; danteskitchen.com; $$), which begins dinner with spoon bread so good you want to eat it with a ladle. A walk of a few blocks is worth it for **Boucherie** (8115 Jeannette Street; 504-862-5514; boucherie-nola.com; $$), a Southern-flavored bistro that began its life as a food truck. Start off with the boudin balls and end with—this is real—Krispy Kreme bread pudding.

3 *Decisions* 10 p.m.

Stuffed and standing at the corner of Oak Street and South Carrollton Avenue, you have a choice. If you're in the mood for refined, you can go to **Oak** (8118 Oak Street; 504-302-1485; oaknola.com), a glossy wine bar, and conclude the evening all civilized-like with a crisp riesling. If you're restless, walk to the **Maple Leaf Bar** (8316 Oak Street; 504-866-9359; mapleleafbar.com) and join the crowd already dancing to the Dirty Dozen Brass Band or whoever is on the bill. And if you're game, turn around and head to **Snake and Jake's Christmas Club Lounge** (7612 Oak Street; 504-861-2802; snakeandjakes.com), strike up a conversation with the person sitting next to you, and see where the night goes.

SATURDAY

4 *City of the Dead* 10 a.m.

New Orleans is known for its cemeteries, built largely above ground in part because the water

OPPOSITE The French Quarter, the heart of old New Orleans and still its atmospheric center.

RIGHT Snake and Jake's Christmas Club Lounge, where the locals stay up late and the conversation is convivial.

table lurks only a few feet below. The variety runs from the eerily beautiful tombs of Creole grandees to a small plot on the grounds of a former plantation outside town where one of Adolf Hitler's horses is said to be buried. The best place to start looking is just outside the French Quarter in **St. Louis Cemetery No. 1** (1300 St. Louis Street), the oldest existing cemetery in the city. Explore on your own, or take a tour (501 Basin Street; 504-525-3377; saveourcemeteries.org) and study the tombs of mayors, gamblers, jazz musicians, and heroes of the War of 1812, as well as the graves of Paul Morphy, one of the greatest chess players of the 19th century; Marie Laveau, the voodoo priestess; and, potentially, Nicolas Cage, who financed the construction of a rather odd-looking pyramidal tomb presumably for his future use.

5 *Use a Fork* Noon

There's no SUBstitute for a real New Orleans po'boy, or so the bumper sticker goes, and whether your taste runs to gravy-doused roast beef or barbecued shrimp, the one at **Liuzza's by the Track** (1518 North Lopez; 504-218-7888; $$) is so overstuffed that it verges on a stew. Still, the buckboard bacon melt sandwich at **Cochon Butcher** (930 Tchoupitoulas Street; 504-588-7675; cochonbutcher.com; $$) makes for a pretty good stand-in.

ABOVE The Social Aid and Pleasure Clubs play at funerals and parade through town on Sunday afternoons.

6 *The Lower Ninth* 2 p.m.

The destruction wrought by Katrina and the subsequent flooding go far beyond the famous Lower Ninth Ward, but it is also true that the wonders of the Lower Ninth Ward go far beyond the floodwaters. There is the pastel origami of the "Brad Pitt houses," Fats Domino's black-and-yellow mini-mansion, the beguiling steamboat houses on Egania Street, and the little museum behind Ronald Lewis's house at 1317 Tupelo Street. Call Lewis ahead (504-957-2678), and he'll arrange a visit to the House of Dance and Feathers, his private collection dedicated to the Mardi Gras Indian, the still vibrant but century-plus-old tradition wherein black New Orleanians create ornate suits and parade the streets. If you have a car, you can hire a guide from lowernine.org, a nonprofit rebuilding group (504-344-4884); all the proceeds go to their work in the neighborhood. But you can also explore on a bicycle tour with **Ninth Ward Rebirth Bike Tours** (504-338-3603; ninthwardrebirthbiketours.com).

7 *Punks and Pinots* 7 p.m.

If the night is breezy and it is not too late, head over to **Bacchanal** (600 Poland Avenue; 504-948-9111;

bacchanalwine.com; $$), order a bottle of whatever they suggest, and take a seat in the courtyard under lights strung among the mulberry and oleander trees. It will only grow more crowded, which is why you should come on the early side (especially if there are a few of you). But once you've established a beachhead, there is live jazz and there is very good food, including bacon-wrapped dates and a cheese plate that you create yourself. Oh, and what the heck, maybe another bottle.

8 *Music Town* 10 p.m.

Frenchmen Street on Saturday night is like a big radio dial: you can just pop in and out of the bars and hear something different at each one. A swing band is most likely on stage at the **Spotted Cat** (623 Frenchmen Street; 504-258-3135; spottedcatmusicclub.com); over at **d.b.a.**, John Boutté may be well into a Saturday night gig (618 Frenchmen Street; 504-942-3731; dbabars.com/dbano); a chanteuse is giving way to a jazz trio at the **Three Muses** (536 Frenchmen Street; 504-252-4801; thethreemuses.com); and at the little Japanese tavern **Yuki Izakaya** (525 Frenchmen Street; 504-943-1122), Norbert Slama, the virtuosic blind French accordionist, is playing torch songs over the sake and yakitori.

ABOVE Make a Sunday morning visit to St. Augustine Catholic Church, where the choir is always good and sometimes there is the bonus of a jazz Mass.

RIGHT The exterior of St. Augustine's, built in 1842. The church has been integrated from the start, when black and white Catholics competed to buy up pews.

SUNDAY

9 *Down in the Treme* 10 a.m.

Shortly before **St. Augustine Catholic Church** (1210 Governor Nicholls Street; 504-525-5934; staugustinecatholicchurch-neworleans.org) was dedicated in 1842, white and black Catholics in the area began battling to see who could buy up the most pews. When the "War of the Pews" ended, the

congregation was a mix of free blacks, whites, and slaves, possibly the most integrated in the country. The church is known for its jazz Masses throughout the year, but any given Sunday the choir and the church's history make it worth a visit.

10 *Stepping Out* Noon

The boundary between parade and spectator in New Orleans is always a blurry one, especially when the second line comes down the street. Every Sunday from the fall through spring, neighborhood associations known as Social Aid and Pleasure Clubs, formed long ago as insurance and financial assistance pools, take turns putting on parades. The brass band and the club's dancers march out front, followed by everyone else—the "second line." That is, when you go, you will be in the second line. The parades usually last a few hours, and you can hop in at any point. Check the Web site of radio station WWOZ (wwoz.org/new-orleans-community/inthestreet) for the route.

ABOVE Kermit Ruffins, a jazz trumpeter and singer, is a local favorite. Music is plentiful here; check the listings to see where the top acts are playing.

OPPOSITE Above-ground graves at St. Louis Cemetery No. 1. Tour here to see tombs of mayors, gamblers, jazz musicians, and heroes of the War of 1812.

Mississippi River
OAK ST.
DANTE ST.
Boucherie
Maple Leaf Bar
3
Oak
Dante's Kitchen
2
Brigsten's
S. CARROLLTON AVE.
Snake and Jake's Christmas Club Lounge
N. LOPEZ
5
Liuzza's by the Track
10
FRANKLIN AVE.
1 mile
2 kilometers
EGANIA ST.
POLAND AVE.
Bacchanal
7
6
Ninth Ward Rebirth Bike Tours
BAYWATER
Area of detail
BIENVILLE ST.
CANAL ST.
10
90
PONTCHARTRAIN EXPWY.
1
French 75 Bar
New Orleans
Area of detail
TCHOUPITOULAS ST.
S. CLAIBORNE AVE.
Cochon Butcher
MAGAZINE ST.
90
Terrell House
BROADWAY
AUDUBON PARK
JEFFERSON AVE.
ST. CHARLES AVE.
St Augustine Catholic Church
GOV. NICHOLLS ST.
FRENCHMEN ST.
d.b.a
8
Spotted Cat
9
N. RAMPART ST.
Royal Street Inn
Yuki Izayaka
ST. LOUIS ST.
FRENCH QUARTER
Three Muses
4
St. Louis Cemetery No. 1
Mississippi River
ROYAL ST.
Arnaud's
Hotel Monteleone

THE BASICS

Fly into Louis Armstrong New Orleans International Airport. In town, travel on foot and by streetcar.

Hotel Monteleone
214 Royal Street
504-523-3341
hotelmonteleone.com
$$
The 600-room grande dame of French Quarter hotels.

Royal Street Inn
1431 Royal Street
504-948-7499
royalstreetinn.com
$
Attached to the always-jumping R bar and described as a "bed and beverage."

MINTKEN

MIDWEST
& GREAT LAKES

356 WINNIPEG

352 Duluth

444 the Black Hills

348 MINNEAPOLIS St. Paul

MILWAUK
3

the Niobrara River Valley

438

416 DES MOINES

Oak Park
338

OMAHA

434

410 Iowa's Mississippi river

328 Chicago Neighborhoo

424 Oklahoma City

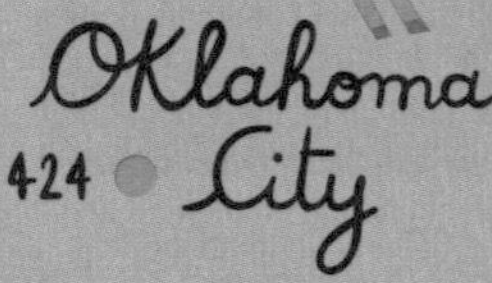

430 Kansas City

420 St. Louis

Toronto for Hipsters
376
TORONTO 370
Ann Arbor
360
380
Niagara Falls
Chicago by Water
DETROIT
364
384
398
Buffalo
Cleveland
CHICAGO
PITTSBURGH
390
ndianapolis
406
Cincinnati
402
394
the Laurel Highlands

TOWER SELF PARK
TOWER SELF PARK

Chicago

All cities have their ups and downs, but Chicago has learned to play to its strengths, adding parks, architectural crowd pleasers, and public art. A solid base of good urban design and buildings gave the city a lot to build from — this is a place where adventurous architecture was already a tradition, despite the inevitable overlay of urban decay. But now Chicago is going forward, too. A raft of improvements in the last decade or so have left it fortified by both 19th- and 20th-century public spaces brimming with 21st-century attractions. — BY FRED A. BERNSTEIN

FRIDAY

1 *Loop the Loop* 3 p.m.

Even if you've been there in the past, a good place to start in Chicago is at the **Chicago Architecture Foundation** (224 South Michigan Avenue; 312-922-3432; caf.architecture.org). The guided downtown walking tour orients newbies to the late 19th- and early 20th-century buildings that first gave Chicago its reputation as a center of great architecture, and several other walking tours will help give you a feeling for the city. If you already know what to look for, get reacquainted with a ride on the "L," the elevated railway that defines the Loop (transitchicago.com). Get on the brown, orange, or pink line — it doesn't matter which color, as long as you sit in the first car by the front-view window — and ride around the two-square-mile area. You'll see Bertrand Goldberg's spectacular **Marina City**, with a design inspired by corncobs; the **Trump International Hotel and Tower**; Frank Gehry's **Pritzker Pavilion** band shell; and Louis Sullivan's **Auditorium Building**, now part of Roosevelt University.

2 *Gilded Fare* 8 p.m.

A number of good midprice but high-style restaurants have opened in Chicago in the past few years. A favorite is **Gilt Bar** (230 West Kinzie Street; 312-464-9544; giltbarchicago.com; $$), a casual restaurant that isn't casual about its cooking. The menu features New American dishes like blackened cauliflower with capers and ricotta gnocchi with sage and brown butter. After dinner, head downstairs for a drink at the Library, a cozy basement bar and restaurant lined with bookshelves and decorated in red velvet, golden lighting, and dark wood.

3 *Choose Your Bubbly* 11 p.m.

There are so many clubs on Ontario Street, just north of the Loop, that it's sometimes known as Red Bull Row. For something unusual, try **Pops for Champagne** (601 North State Street at Ohio; 312-266-7677; popsforchampagne.com), a sleek, upscale lounge with a roundish bar and some 200 bubbly selections. Footage of spring fashion shows — Derek Lam, Luca Luca, BCBG — streams across screens, and European lounge music wafts from the speakers as smartly dressed men and women laugh beneath dim lights. Or head to the Uptown neighborhood, to **Big Chicks** (5024 North Sheridan Road; 773-728-5511; bigchicks.com), a gay bar that welcomes everyone.

SATURDAY

4 *Eggs Plus* 9 a.m.

Couldn't get to dinner at Frontera Grill, the nouvelle Mexican restaurant owned by the celebrity chef Rick Bayless? No worries. Just head over to **Xoco** (449 North Clark Street; 312-661-1434; rickbayless.com;

OPPOSITE Chicago's urban canyons and the Willis Tower, formerly the Sears Tower.

RIGHT The view down from the Willis Tower Skydeck.

$), another Bayless restaurant. Breakfast is served till 10 a.m.; expect a line after 8:30. Favorites include scrambled egg empanada with poblano chili, and an open-face torta with soft poached egg, salsa, cheese, cilantro, and black beans.

5 *Off-Label Strip* 11 a.m.

The Magnificent Mile area is filled with flagships (Gucci, Vuitton—you know the list). But there are still some independent stores you won't find at your hometown mall. **Ikram** (15 East Huron Street; 312-587-1000; ikram.com) is the stylish boutique that counts Michelle Obama among its customers, with fashion-forward labels like Martin Margiela. East Oak Street has a couple of cool shops, including **Colletti Gallery** (No. 49; 312-664-6767; collettigallery.com), which has a gorgeous selection of Art Deco and Art Nouveau furniture and objets.

ABOVE The Girl and the Goat, Chef Stephanie Izard's restaurant on Randolph Street just west of downtown.

BELOW Aqua, a new addition to Chicago's skyscraper collection, was designed by Jeanne Gang.

6 *Grand Piano* 1 p.m.

Chicago knows how to mix neoclassical architecture with contemporary design, and no place in town does it better than the **Art Institute of Chicago** (111 South Michigan Avenue; 312-443-3600; artic.edu). Its celebrated Modern Wing, designed by Renzo Piano, is a luminous space containing a magnificent set of galleries for 1900-1950 European art (Picasso, Giacometti, and Klee are among the big names) and a capacious room for the museum's design collection. Arrive in time for lunch and check out **Terzo Piano**, the stunning rooftop restaurant with views of the Pritzker Pavilion in Millennium Park across the street.

7 *Bridges to Tomorrow* 4 p.m.

From the museum, walk over the pedestrian bridge, also designed by Piano, to **Millennium Park**, which is best known for the big, reflective *Cloud Gate* sculpture (known to locals as the Bean) and the newer Crown Fountain, a combination of video, fountain, and sculpture. At the south end of the park is the **Lurie Garden**, which is magical during the summer and works in the winter as well, when colorful blooms are replaced by the captivating shapes of downy seed heads and silver panicles. Then, take Millennium Park's serpentine Frank Gehry-designed BP Bridge to the edge of **Maggie Daley Park** to see the latest stage in the evolution of Chicago's front yard.

8 *Livestock Menu* 7 p.m.

Chicago was once the meatpacking capital of the world, and it still knows what to do with meat. Take **Girl & the Goat** (809 West Randolph Street; 312-492-6262; girlandthegoat.com; $$), a much-blogged-about restaurant where the *Top Chef* winner Stephanie Izard takes livestock parts seriously. The often-updated menu has included the likes of lamb ribs with grilled avocado and pistachio piccata, and braised beef tongue with masa and beef vinaigrette. But you don't have to be a carnivore. If you are vegetarian, there is something for you, too—perhaps chickpeas three ways, and for dessert, potato fritters with lemon poached eggplant and Greek yogurt. The soaring dining room, designed by the Chicago design firm 555 International, is warm and modern, with exposed beams, walls of charred cedar, and a large open kitchen.

9 *Funny Bone* 10 p.m.

You won't find big names at the **The Comedy Bar** (157 West Ontario Street; 773-387-8412; comedybarchicago.com). But a hit-or-miss roster of itinerant comedians will be looking for laughs, including some who heckle the audience in language

BELOW The Pritzker Pavilion and its Frank Gehry-designed band shell, in Millennium Park.

that Grandma would not consider polite. There's more comedy at **UP** (230 West North Avenue; 312-662-4562; upcomedyclub.com) in the Old Town neighborhood, roughly two miles north of the Loop. UP is the Second City improv group's foray into standup.

SUNDAY

10 *Wheels Up* 10 a.m.

At Millennium Park, rent bikes from **Bike and Roll** (312-729-1000; bikechicago.com) for a ride up the shore of Lake Michigan. You'll pass Navy Pier, skyscrapers by Mies van der Rohe, and hundreds of beach volleyball courts that make this the Malibu of the Midwest on summer and fall weekends. Along the way, you'll see Lincoln Park, with a pavilion by the Chicago architect Jeanne Gang — another example of how the city is updating its open spaces.

ABOVE Cloud Gate, signature sculpture of Millennium Park.

OPPOSITE One way to see great Chicago architecture is to ride the "L," the elevated railway that defines the Loop. Just pay your fare and look out the window.

THE BASICS

From O'Hare International Airport to the Loop, take the L's Blue Line, about a 40-minute ride. From Midway International Airport, use the Orange Line, about a 30-minute journey.

Langham Chicago
330 North Wabash Avenue
312-923-9988
chicago.langhamhotels.com
$$$$
In the former IBM Building designed by Mies van der Rohe.

Hotel Allegro
171 West Randolph Street
312-236-0123
allegrochicago.com
$$
A 483-room hotel in the bold style of Kimpton hotels.

Wit Hotel
201 North State Street
312-467-0200
thewithotel.com
$$
Chic hotel with a popular rooftop bar.

Chicago
To Big Chicks
Colletti Gallery
1/2 mile
1 kilometer
W. OAK ST.
N. STATE ST.
N. MICHIGAN AVE.
N. CLARK ST.
Ikram 5
North Branch Chicago River
E. HURON ST.
The Comedy Bar 9
Xoco 4
3 Pops for Champagne
E. OHIO ST.
W. ILLINOIS ST.
Langham Chicago
W. KINZIE ST.
Trump International Hotel and Tower
94
90
Gilt Bar/ The Library 2
Marina City
Chicago River
Hotel Allegro
Wit Hotel
10 Bike and Roll
W. RANDOLPH ST.
Pritzker Pavilion
Maggie Daley Park
8 Girl & the Goat
Millennium Park 7
Lurie Garden
Chicago Architecture Foundation 1
6
Art Institute of Chicago/ Terzo Piano
WIS.
MICH.
IOWA
Chicago
ILLINOIS
IND.
St. Louis
MO.
KY.
Auditorium Building/ Roosevelt University
GRANT PARK
Lake Michigan
S. WELLS ST.
S. CLARK ST.
S. STATE ST.
S. MICHIGAN AVE.
W. ROOSEVELT RD.

Chicago Neighborhoods

The notion that Chicago is a city of neighborhoods seems silly and obvious at first. Aren't all cities? But a weekend here, wandering the nooks far from the tourists swarming Navy Pier near downtown or ogling the masterpieces at the Art Institute of Chicago, explains the distinction. Cross a single street, from one neighborhood into the next, and you will often find a suddenly changed style of architecture, a distinct language on the signs and, in the street, an utterly different feel. Sadly, a single getaway weekend will never allow enough time to make your way through the vast patchwork of Chicago's neighborhoods. But there is time enough to explore a few, and enough to come away understanding why this is, indeed, a city of neighborhoods. — BY MONICA DAVEY

FRIDAY

1 *The Glamour! The Art!* 3 p.m.

The Magnificent Mile, just north of the Loop along Michigan Avenue, is a neighborhood too full of the city's most glamorous, high-end shops to feel like a neighborhood at all. But in the blur of sales and shopping bags, the **Museum of Contemporary Art** (220 East Chicago Avenue; 312-280-2660; mcachicago.org) makes the Magnificent Mile worth seeing, even for those who hate to shop.

2 *Go West* 5 p.m.

Due west of downtown, the West Loop neighborhood and its surroundings, once distinguished by meat-packing companies, have been transformed into a place of lofts and galleries. **City Winery** (1200 West Randolph Street; 312-733-9463; citywinery.com/chicago) combines a live music venue, a winery, and a restaurant. The Harpo Studios building at 1058 West Washington Boulevard, where Oprah Winfrey built her empire, is worth a glance as you pass. Venture on into Ukrainian Village to **Old Lviv** (2228 West Chicago Avenue; 773-772-7250; $), a small, out-of-the-way spot, for authentic borscht and pirogi. Or dine at nearby **Ruxbin** (851 North Ashland; 312-624-8509; ruxbinchicago.com; $$), an unpretentious B.Y.O.B. restaurant serving surprisingly elegant dishes. Its owner, Edward Kim, mixes Asian flavors with Midwestern ingredients in dishes like a delicious seafood bourride with white beans, fennel, sake, sun-dried tomato, fines herbes, and lemon aioli.

3 *Night People* 10 p.m.

The **Public Chicago** hotel (1301 North State Parkway; 312-787-3700; publichotels.com/chicago), which opened in the Gold Coast neighborhood along Lake Michigan after a redesign by Ian Schrager, was formerly the Ambassador East, famous as a location in Alfred Hitchcock's *North by Northwest*. Stop in for a drink at its Pump Room restaurant, once a celebrity favorite and now transformed into a sleek space with neutral décor and spherical lights, a cocktail mixologist, and music.

SATURDAY

4 *Head North* 10 a.m.

Lakeview, north of downtown, is a neighborhood of young people, not far from Wrigley Field and the struggling but always popular Cubs, Lake Michigan, and a million places to shop. If coffee is your passion, seek out **Bow Truss** (2934 North Broadway; 773-857-1361; bowtruss.com), a single-minded coffee roaster. Find a more substantial brunch at **Southport**

OPPOSITE Performers at Constellation on the North Side.

RIGHT The Pump Room in the Public Chicago hotel.

Grocery and Cafe (3552 North Southport Avenue; 773-665-0100; southportgrocery.com; $$), where you might choose pancakes made with bread pudding or French toast stuffed with apples, white Cheddar cheese, and streusel.

5 *To Sweden and Beyond* Noon

It's a short hop to Andersonville, traditionally the Swedish quarter. It's booming now with families, a substantial gay population, restaurants that serve diverse cuisine, and the kinds of shops that sell vintage housewares. The Swedish Bakery and the Swedish American Museum Center seem surrounded and joined by arrivals from other places. At the **Hopleaf Bar** (5148 North Clark Street; 773-334-9851; hopleaf.com; $$), pause to choose a sampling from nearly 300 beers, many of them Belgian, and munch on moules frites.

6 *Check Your Chakras* 2 p.m.

The dress code in Wicker Park is flannel and denim, and fine old buildings mix with an upscale bohemian cachet. Milwaukee Avenue is dotted with stylish boutiques and cafes. If chakra crystals are your thing, stop by **Ruby Room** (1743 West Division; 773-235-2323; rubyroom.com), a haute New Age spa, salon, and inn where you might measure your electromagnetic field or attend a meditation class. At the **Filter Cafe** (1373 North Milwaukee Avenue; 773-904-7819), a coffee house furnished with a jumble of well-used coffee tables and sofas, you can chill with a mix of people in their 20s and 30s, most of them eating silently while they read or clack on their Macs.

7 *Under the Eagle's Eye* 5 p.m.

Logan Square is a remnant of Chicago's late-19th-century beautification movement, with broad boulevards and grand turn-of-the-20th-century mansions. After a long decline, it has picked up again in recent years, but its still affordable rents, an alternative to now pricey Wicker Park and Bucktown, make it a magnet for creative types running everything from hip hair salons to an international film series. A statue of an eagle by Evelyn Longman stands where two of the grandest boulevards meet, and nearby, **Longman & Eagle** (2657 North Kedzie Avenue; 773-276-7110; longmanandeagle.com; $$) serves refined pub food to a friendly clientele. It doesn't take reservations, so be prepared to wait.

8 *Show Time* 9 p.m.

For an intriguing take on up-to-the-minute music, seek out **Constellation** (3111 North Western Avenue; constellation-chicago.com), a venue opened in Roscoe Village by the drummer, composer, and Pitchfork Music Festival producer Mike Reed. With influences as varied as Duke Ellington and John Cage, it defines its mission as promoting "forward-thinking" jazz, improvisation, and contemporary classical music. For entertainment in a nostalgic setting, see a movie at the **Music Box** (3733 North Southport Avenue; 773-871-6604; musicboxtheatre.com), a grand old Lakeview neighborhood theater (complete with an organ) that opened in 1929 and shows an eclectic mix, from cutting-edge independent films to old, comforting classics.

SUNDAY

9 *Get Thee to the Fernery* 9 a.m.

Craving peace and quiet? Start the morning in the fern room at the **Garfield Park Conservatory** (300 North Central Park Avenue; 312-746-5100; garfield-conservatory.org), an exquisite building opened in 1908 on the Far West Side. A Green Line L train or cab will carry you through tougher-looking neighborhoods to within a few steps of the conservatory. Once inside, a waft of warm, humid air and the smell of plants will greet you. Relax and breathe.

10 *Southern Exposures* 11 a.m.

Head south to the Pilsen neighborhood, which once was mainly home to Bohemians, Irish, and Germans and is now one of the city's largest Mexican-American communities. Start with a cup of coffee or Mexican hot chocolate and a vegetarian brunch at **Cafe Jumping Bean** (1439 West 18th Street; 312-455-0019; $). Then wander past bakeries and art galleries a few blocks toward the **National Museum of Mexican Art** (1852 West 19th Street; 312-738-1503;

nationalmuseumofmexicanart.org), which has made a name for itself both with its fine art displays and with its exhibitions that confront political and cultural issues. Nearby at the **Maxwell Street Market** (800 S. Desplaines Street; maxwellstreetmarket.us), Latin music blares and shoppers browse a four-block stretch of stalls.

11 *Obama Country* Noon

South of downtown is Hyde Park, home to the University of Chicago and the stellar **Museum of Science and Industry** (5700 Lake Shore Drive; msichicago.org), with its trademark U-505 submarine, baby chick hatchery, and model train with 1,400 feet of track. It's easy to see why Barack and Michelle Obama settled in this leafy neighborhood. Their house, on South Greenwood Avenue between 50th and 51st Streets, is nearly invisible behind Secret Service barricades. But the streets are great for walking, and the university's beautifully landscaped campus is worth exploring for an afternoon.

OPPOSITE A seller at the Maxwell Street Market.

ABOVE Relaxing at Cafe Jumping Bean in Pilsen.

THE BASICS

The best ways to get around Chicago are by L train, by bus, and by foot, reserving cabs for late nights or lazy moments.

Public Chicago
1301 North State Parkway
312-787-3700
publichotels.com
$$
Ian Schrager-designed overhaul of the Ambassador East, a 1926 landmark; elegant despite stripped-down amenities.

Wicker Park Inn
1329 North Wicker Park Avenue
773-486-2743
wickerparkinn.com
$$
Attractive bed-and-breakfast in Wicker Park.

The James
55 East Ontario Street
312-337-1000
jameshotels.com/chicago
$$$
High-design boutique hotel on the Near North Side.

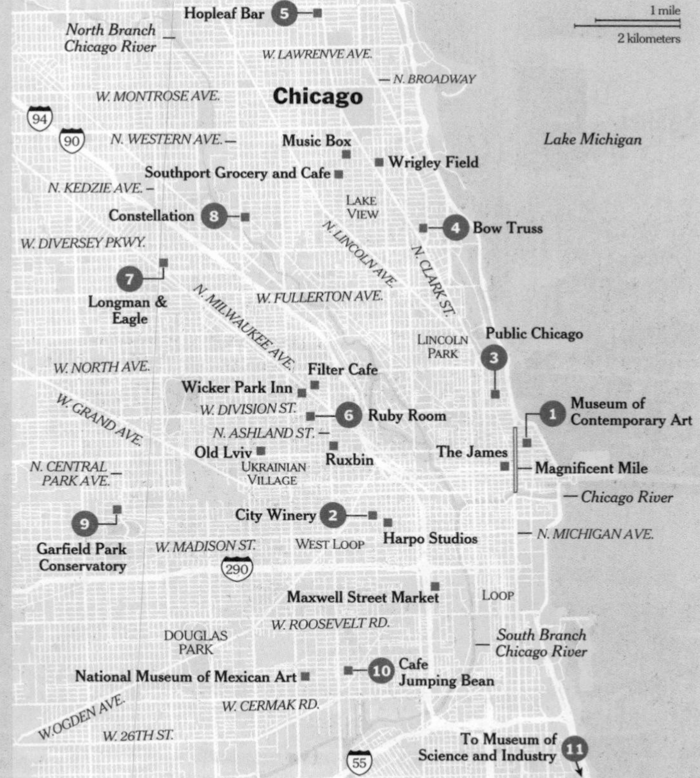

Chicago by Water

Expensive water-view condos and gleaming commercial towers line the Chicago River in downtown Chicago, close to its connection to Lake Michigan. Long ago the river was a polluted dumping ground, but now kayakers ply its waters and tour boats glide along as guides explain some of the wealth of interesting architecture on the banks. For an intimate, easygoing exploration of the river, with stops to look deeper at some of what's close by on land, create your own tour by water taxi. From late spring through fall, two taxi companies operate on the river, running distinct, though partly overlapping, routes. One ventures out into Lake Michigan. The boats operate like buses, following scheduled routes that take you to standard tourist stops. Hop on and off at will, and see the heart of the city from a different point of view.
— BY RUSSELL WORKING

FRIDAY

1 *Know Your River* 3 p.m.

Get your bearings at the **Michigan Avenue Bridge**. Stop on the pedestrian walkway, gaze down the river into the heart of the city and then back the other way toward Lake Michigan. You may spot a water taxi—yellow for Chicago Water Taxi or blue for Shoreline. Inside the ornately decorated stone tower at the southwest corner of the bridge is the **McCormick Tribune Bridgehouse & Chicago River Museum** (376 North Michigan Avenue; 312-977-0227; bridgehousemuseum.org), where you can see the inner workings of a drawbridge and learn about river history, including the arrival of Jean Baptiste Point du-Sable, a black French pioneer, in the 1780s. At the north end of the bridge, duck down to the lower level and find the **Billy Goat Tavern** (430 North Michigan Avenue; 312-222-1525; billygoattavern.com), a reporters' watering hole for generations and the inspiration for the *Saturday Night Live* "cheeseburger" sketches with John Belushi as the single-minded counter man.

2 *Down by the Docks* 4 p.m.

Still at the bridge's north end, walk down to water level to see where the taxis leave. For **Chicago Water Taxi** (400 North Michigan Avenue; 312-337-1446; chicagowatertaxi.com for routes and prices), go down the stairs by the **Wrigley Building** and follow the signs to the taxi dock. For **Shoreline Water** Taxi (401 North Michigan Avenue; 312-222-9328; shorelinesightseeing.com/watertaxis), take the steps down on the northeast side of the bridge. There's no reason to take a water taxi anywhere today, but if you'd like to have the names and histories to go with some of the buildings you'll see on your taxi tour tomorrow, one option is to cross the bridge, walk down the steps on the southern side, and find the dock for the **Chicago Architecture Foundation**'s 90-minute architecture cruise. (To minimize waiting, buy tickets in advance; check caf.architecture.org or go to the foundation's shop at 224 South Michigan Avenue.) It's a pleasant, breezy introduction to the heart of the city. Another way to prepare is with a guidebook; a good one is Jennifer Marjorie Bosch's *View From the River: The Chicago Architecture Foundation River Cruise* (Pomegranate Communications).

3 *Mellow Out* 8 p.m.

Relax and plan your strategy for tomorrow over drinks and dinner at **State and Lake** (201 North State Street; 312-239-9400; stateandlakechicago.com; $$), a restaurant that's at least as much about the beverages as the food. The dining choices include comfort food specials, sandwiches and salads, and entrees like steak frites or angel hair pasta and shrimp. Linger over one of the wines or a draft or bottled beer.

SATURDAY

4 *Squint at the Corncobs* 9 a.m.

Return to the Michigan Avenue dock and catch a Chicago Water Taxi headed west. Out on the river, glide along for a while, squinting upward at the skyscrapers in the morning light. There are dozens of landmarks, including the **Marina City** towers at 300 North State Street, designed to resemble corncobs; the sprawling **Merchandise Mart** at North Wells Street, built in 1930; and the **Civic Opera House** on North Wacker Drive, constructed in the Art Deco armchair form and nicknamed Insull's Throne after the tycoon who commissioned it.

OPPOSITE The Merchandise Mart, built in 1930, hulks over the Chicago River, a highway for water taxis.

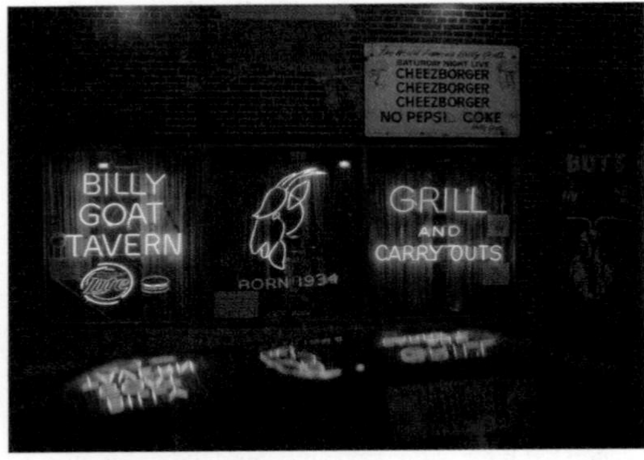

5 *Waterside* 10 a.m.

Get off at the LaSalle/Clark Street stop and walk across the river on the Clark Street bridge to find the new **Riverwalk** (explorechicago.org). Explore for a while, passing outdoor cafes and kiosks that thrive in the summer season. You're also close here to the area around State and Randolph Streets that is home to several major theaters and the Joffrey Ballet.

6 *Brunch Umbrellas* Noon

A pleasant place for brunch is the **Bridge House Tavern** (321 North Clark Street, river level; 312-644-0283; bridgehousetavern.com; $$), where tables under red umbrellas are lined up close to the river's edge and yachts pull up to dock for lunch. There's also indoor seating, but the river is the real draw here, so why not stay close? (The people watching is good, too.) Check the menu for the crab cakes Benedict. When you're ready to venture out again, return to the LaSalle/Clark Street stop to pick up another taxi and continue west on the river.

7 *Do Look Down* 1:30 p.m.

After the river bends south, alight at the spot near the **Willis Tower** (233 South Wacker Drive; willistower.com), once known as the Sears Tower, where both taxi lines stop. Ride the elevator to the Skydeck (theskydeck.com). Take the dare — venture out onto one of the glass-floored retractable bays to join the other sightseers scaring themselves silly by staring 1,353 feet straight down at the street. Across the river is Union Station, a cavernous rail terminal. Its Beaux-Arts Great Hall has been featured in several films, including *The Untouchables*.

8 *Chinatown* 3:30 p.m.

Continue south on the Chicago Water Taxi to **Ping Tom Memorial Park** (named for a Chinese-American civic leader), and proceed on foot under an ornate gate into **Chinatown**, where you'll find hole-in-the-wall restaurants and stores selling barrels of ginseng or aquariums full of live frogs. Stop in at the one-room **Dr. Sun Yat-Sen Museum** (2245 South Wentworth Avenue, third floor; 312-842-5462; open until 5 p.m.), dedicated to the revolutionary who played a leading role in overthrowing the Qing Dynasty — the last of the Chinese emperors — in 1911. The photos inside include some from Sun's visit to Chicago at around that time. At **Chinatown Square**, an outdoor mall just south of the park, you'll find stores selling green tea and Chinese cookies. For an early dinner, take a short walk to **Yan Bang Cai** (228 West Cermak Road; 312-842-7818; yanbangcaichicago.com; $), which serves the food of Sichuan province.

9 *Honky-Tonk Bard* 7 p.m.

There's enough going on at the **Navy Pier** (navypier.com) to keep you busy all weekend. Reach it from the Michigan Avenue dock of the Shoreline Water Taxi. (And as you debark, take note of the schedule; you don't want to miss the last taxi back.) The pier is 50 acres of parks, promenades, restaurants, carnival-like stalls, and souvenir shops, with fireworks on summer Saturday nights. There's also an indoor garden, a stained-glass museum, and the **Chicago Shakespeare Theater** (800 East Grand Avenue; 312-595-5600; chicagoshakes.com), where you might find local fare in addition to the serious drama. A few years ago Second City's *Rod Blagojevich Superstar* had a successful run at the theater, including an appearance by Blagojevich himself, although he was still smarting from the scandal that cost him the Illinois governorship. He recited lines from *Henry V* and invited the cast for dinner, adding, "We'll be serving tarantulas."

SUNDAY

10 *Feeding the Spirit* 10 a.m.

From either Michigan Avenue or the LaSalle/Clark stop, it's a short walk to the **House of Blues** (329 North Dearborn Street; 312-923-2000; houseofblues.com; $$$), where the Sunday-morning Gospel Brunch includes a buffet with blackened catfish, jambalaya, fried chicken, and omelets,

OPPOSITE ABOVE The Billy Goat Tavern, open since 1934.

OPPOSITE BELOW Aboard the Shoreline Water Taxi.

ABOVE The view from the Chicago River up at the Clark Street Bridge.

along with exhilarating African-American worship and music.

11 *Lakeside Dinosaurs* Noon

For a nice ride out into Lake Michigan, take the Shoreline taxi to the Navy Pier, change boats, and go to the lakeside museum campus that is home to the **Field Museum**, **Shedd Aquarium**, and **Adler Planetarium.** All are worth serious time, but for generations of children, the must-see has been the Field's dinosaur skeletons, including a Tyrannosaurus rex found in South Dakota in 1990 and nicknamed Sue.

ABOVE The Shedd Aquarium and the Adler Planetarium at Grant Park, on Lake Michigan. Get there from downtown on the Shoreline Water Taxi. Both Shoreline and Chicago Water Taxis cater to commuters and tourists alike.

OPPOSITE Marina City, two corncob-shaped towers.

THE BASICS

The Chicago River, in the heart of downtown, is the north and west boundary of the Loop. When you're not on a water taxi, take the "L" (that's "El" to some) or land-bound cabs.

Fairmont Chicago Millennium Park
200 North Columbus Drive
312-565-8000
fairmont.com/chicago
$$
Recently renovated; a short walk to the Michigan Avenue bridge.

Radisson Blu Aqua Hotel Chicago
221 North Columbus Drive
312-565-5258
radissonblu.com/aquahotel-chicago
$$
Upscale version of a Radisson in a prime spot — where the Chicago River meets Lake Michigan.

Hotel Sax
333 North Dearborn Street
312-245-0333
hotelsaxchicago.com
$$
Stylish hotel beneath Marina City towers.

N. WELLS ST.
N. LASALLE DR.
N. CLARK ST.
N. DEARBORN ST.
N. STATE ST.
41
N. MICHIGAN AVE.
1/2 mile
1 kilometer
Chicago Water Taxi
2
Billy Goat Tavern
Shoreline Water Taxi
Chicago Shakespeare Theater
9
Navy Pier
Area of detail below
Marina City 4
Radisson Blu Aqua Hotel Chicago
Fairmont Chicago Millennium Park
1
McCormick Tribune Bridgehouse & Chicago River Museum
Civic Opera House
3
State and Lake
S. WACKER DR.
E. JACKSON DR.
Chicago Architecture Foundation
Lake Michigan
W. CONGRESS PKWY.
7
Willis Tower/ Skydeck
S. LAKE SHORE DR.
Chicago River
Shedd Aquarium
Adler Planetarium
W. ROOSEVELT RD.
Field Museum 11
Chicago
S. MICHIGAN AVE.
Ping Tom Memorial Park
8
W. 18 TH ST.
CHINATOWN
Yan Bang Cai
W. CERMAK RD.
Dr. Sun Yat-Sen Museum
S. WENTWORTH AVE.
N. DEARBORN ST.
N. CLARK ST.
N. STATE ST.
Merchandise Mart
Hotel Sax
Bridge House Tavern 6
House of Blues 10
Riverwalk 5

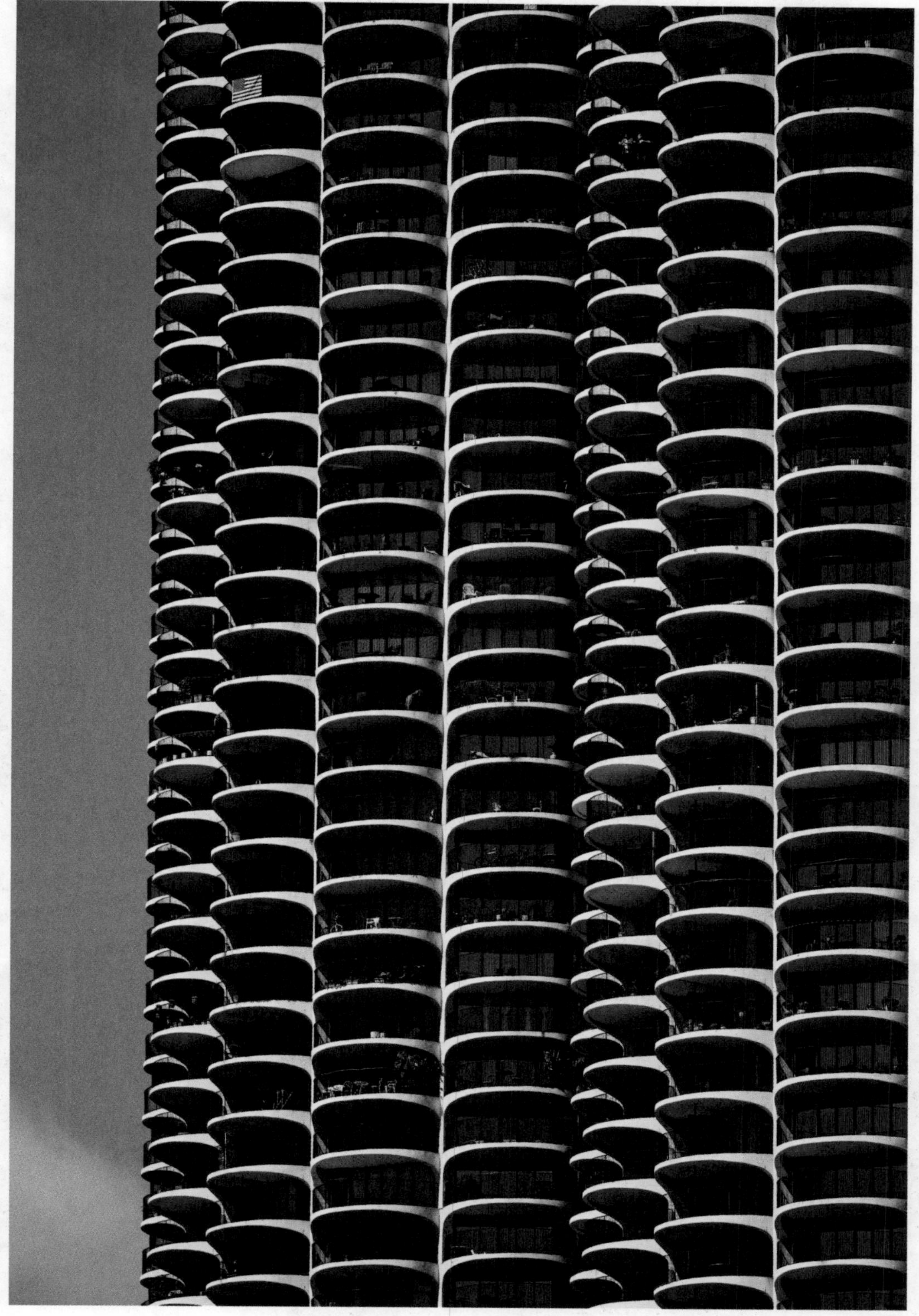

Oak Park

On most weekends, people from all over the world can be seen walking slowly down the streets of Oak Park, Illinois, clutching their maps, guidebooks, audio-tour wands, and cameras. Spotting a celebrity—a house designed by Frank Lloyd Wright—they stop, stare, and snap photographs. Then they move on to the next Wright house wedged amid the historic district's attractive but conventional Victorians. Oak Park, which is the location not only of the home and studio where Wright spent his early career, but of the world's largest collection of his buildings (25), has long attracted design pilgrims. In a weekend there, you will also find galleries, shops, restaurants, and the painstakingly restored childhood home of Ernest Hemingway. And a few miles away in the Hyde Park section of Chicago, another Wright house awaits, one of the master's most renowned.

— BY BETSY RUBINER

FRIDAY

1 *The Son Also Rises* 3 p.m.

Ernest Hemingway was born in Oak Park in 1899 and lived here through high school. Whether Hemingway ever actually described the town as a place of "broad lawns and narrow minds" is in dispute. But you can get a feel for his genteel origins at the **Ernest Hemingway Birthplace Home** (339 North Oak Park Avenue; 708-445-3071; ehfop.org). Just south, at the companion **Ernest Hemingway Museum** (200 North Oak Park Avenue), you can see Hemingway's high school report card (he did well in commercial law, not so well in geometry) and teenage scribblings.

2 *Shop Downtown* 4:30 p.m.

In Oak Park's downtown, there's good shopping on the 100 block of North Marion Street, a former pedestrian mall remade into a vehicle- and pedestrian-friendly street. Check out **Sugarcup Trading** (No. 110; 708-524-5336; sugarcuptrading.com), which sells recycled and eco-friendly children's toys, clothes, and gear; **Sugar Fixé Pâtisserie** (No. 119; 708-948-7720; sugarfixe.com), a French pastry shop whose almond croissants and macaroons have won beaucoup praise; **Scratch 'n Sniff** (No. 120; 708-725-3043; scratchnsniff.biz) specializing in gifts for dogs, cats, and humans; and **Takara** (No. 123; 708-445-7511; shoptakara.com), a boutique with the inviting slogan "Real women. Real sizes. Real fashion."

3 *The Cheese Course* 6:30 p.m.

Marion Street Cheese Market (100 South Marion Street; 708-725-7200; marionstreetcheesemarket.com) not only sells artisan and farmstead cheese and charcuterie from far and near, but serves them in various selections, or "flights." The market's bistro also offers a full dinner menu. If the weather is nice, grab a table outside on the patio. Dinner offerings vary by season; a sample autumn menu included beef tartare, mac 'n' cheese with a Mornay sauce made of Midwest cheeses, and chicken glazed with Ohio maple syrup.

4 *Reading Up* 8 p.m.

Bone up for a weekend of Frank Lloyd Wright immersion with some selections from the **Book Table** (1045 Lake Street; 708-386-9800; booktable.net), which stocks several titles on the master in its pleasant, book-filled store. Wright's profoundly original and seminal architecture is what assures his continuing fame, but when he was alive, his flamboyant personality garnered more attention. As you pick up some books of your own, you can go serious, with scholarly architectural criticism; local, focusing on Wright in Oak Park; or gossipy, digging into recent books on

OPPOSITE AND BELOW The sanctuary of Unity Temple and the exterior of the Frank Lloyd Wright Home and Studio. Wright designed both structures, and several others in town, during his years as an Oak Park resident.

the architect's sometimes messy, sometimes tragic private life.

SATURDAY

5 *The Main Attraction* 10:30 a.m.

Before Frank Lloyd Wright built homes for clients, he field-tested many of his design principles in the house he built for his first wife and their six children. Wright built a compact dark-wood and light-brick New England Shingle-style home in 1889, and in 1898 he added the eye-catching studio addition where he developed his Prairie style. Walking through his rooms during the guided interior tour of what is now the **Frank Lloyd Wright Home and Studio** (951 Chicago Avenue; 708-848-1976; gowright.org), you experience his ideas about space, light, and shelter. You'll also see his signature touches — the art glass, the central hearth, the intimate spaces tucked within the open plan. During a guided walking tour (exteriors only) of other Wright-designed homes nearby, you'll see how his ideas evolved. Arrive early or buy advance tickets online — tours often fill quickly.

6 *On the Avenue* 1:30 p.m.

For over a century, the intersection of Oak Park Avenue and Lake Street has been a lively retail area known by locals as "the Avenue." Stop for lunch at **Winberie's** (151 North Oak Park Avenue; 708-386-2600; winberies.com; $$) in a 1905 Prairie-style commercial building in Scoville Square. It's a bistro with large picture windows, exposed brick walls, and shiny white-and-black tile floors, and it serves a broad selection of sandwiches, salads, and pastas.

7 *The Jewel Box* 3 p.m.

Sitting sternly, almost bunkerlike, on a busy downtown street, **Unity Temple** (875 Lake Street; 708-383-8873; unitytemple.org) is one of Wright's most influential buildings and is still home to its original Unitarian Universalist congregation. The building resembles three giant children's blocks made of poured concrete. A guided tour leads you through a low, dark cloister and into a stunning high-ceilinged sanctuary filled with light filtered through art-glass windows. The intimate, minutely detailed interior is profoundly calming. Wright called it his "little jewel box."

8 *Try the Thai* 7 p.m.

Rangsan Sutcharit, who once cooked at Arun's, a superb Thai restaurant in Chicago, now cooks simpler and less expensive but still delicious Thai food, combining fresh ingredients and pungent spices, at **Amarind's** (6822 West North Avenue, Chicago; 773-889-9999; amarinds.com; $). It's in a small brick castle-like building on an easy-to-miss corner just over Oak Park's northern border with Chicago. Don't miss the Golden Cup appetizer, delicate flower-shaped pastry cups filled with corn, shrimp, sweet peas, and shiitake mushrooms. The signature entree is spinach noodles with shrimp and crab in a chili sauce.

9 *Roots Music* 9:30 p.m.

A weathered club inside a green wood-frame building, **FitzGerald's** (6615 West Roosevelt Road, Berwyn; 708-788-2118; fitzgeraldsnightclub.com) still looks and feels like a 1920s roadhouse. But it sits back slightly on a commercial strip in Berwyn, just south of Oak Park. One of the best places in the Chicago area to hear live roots music, FitzGerald's has long been host to impressive national and local musicians who play everything from Chicago blues to R&B, jazz, rock,

ABOVE Ernest Hemingway's genteel childhood home.

BELOW Spring in an Oak Park city park.

and alternative country. Bands play on a simple raised stage for a beer-in-hand crowd gathered on the scuffed wooden dance floor.

SUNDAY

10 *Going Organic* 9 a.m.

The buzz about **Buzz Café** (905 South Lombard Avenue; 708-524-2899; thebuzzcafe.com; $) is that it's a community-minded gathering spot with plenty of organic and vegetarian choices. Paintings and drawings by local artists cover the green and purple walls, artists sketch at tables while sitting on brightly painted second-hand chairs, and children and reading groups curl up on comfy sofas in the back. Sunday brunch includes eggs and sausage, pancakes, waffles, and wraps.

11 *Chicago Prairie* 11 a.m.

Wright's Oak Park houses show the development of his style in his first decades as an architect, culminating in his signature Prairie houses. To see the Prairie house in full flower and on a scale that only his wealthiest clients could afford, journey to the Hyde Park neighborhood of Chicago to tour his **Robie House** (5757 South Woodlawn Avenue, Chicago; 312-994-4000; gowright.org). This is a masterpiece, one of the clearest examples anywhere of a building that is fully, from top to bottom and inside and out, an integrated and harmonious work of art.

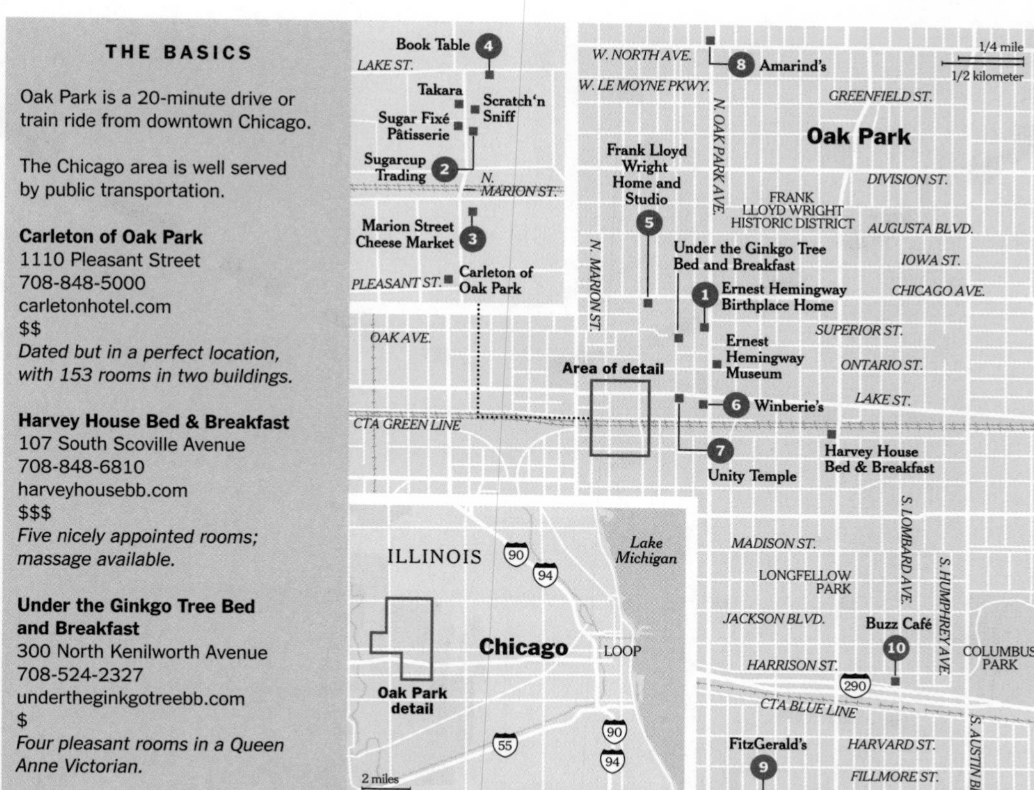

THE BASICS

Oak Park is a 20-minute drive or train ride from downtown Chicago.

The Chicago area is well served by public transportation.

Carleton of Oak Park
1110 Pleasant Street
708-848-5000
carletonhotel.com
$$
Dated but in a perfect location, with 153 rooms in two buildings.

Harvey House Bed & Breakfast
107 South Scoville Avenue
708-848-6810
harveyhousebb.com
$$$
Five nicely appointed rooms; massage available.

Under the Ginkgo Tree Bed and Breakfast
300 North Kenilworth Avenue
708-524-2327
undertheginkgotreebb.com
$
Four pleasant rooms in a Queen Anne Victorian.

Milwaukee

There's plenty about modern-day Milwaukee, Wisconsin, that would be unrecognizable to Laverne and Shirley from Happy Days *and their own spinoff sitcom, both set here in the '50s and '60s. Oh, the area still appreciates its beer and bratwurst: delis carry a mind-boggling variety of sausage, and bars are known to have 50-plus brands of brew. But Milwaukee also has 95 miles of bike lanes, parks lacing the shores of Lake Michigan, and a revitalized riverfront where sophisticated shops coexist with remnants of an industrial past. Modern Milwaukee is defined less by the Rust Belt than by its lively downtown and a signature museum so architecturally striking that it competes for attention with the art it holds.* — MAURA J. CASEY

FRIDAY

1 *Hog Heaven* 4 p.m.

Roar on over to the **Harley-Davidson Museum** (400 West Canal Street; 877-436-8738; h-dmuseum.com), which celebrates the 1903 birth of the signature product of Milwaukee residents William Harley and Arthur Davidson. The motorcycles on display include the first two Harley-Davidson models from 1903 and 1905, a 1920 Sport model marketed to women, and the 1932 Servi-Car used for commercial deliveries and credited with keeping the company solvent during the Great Depression. Harley-Davidson has been setting aside at least one motorcycle every year since 1915, and the resulting collection tells the story of a machine, America, and the open road in the 20th century—an absorbing tale whether or not you ride.

2 *Snake Chasers* 6 p.m.

There's more to Milwaukee than beer, but beer undeniably helped build the city. At one point in the 19th century, 150 breweries flourished here, some established by German immigrants whose names were Pabst, Miller, and Schlitz. So to better appreciate all that history and perhaps take a sip yourself, tour the **Lakefront Brewery** (1872 North Commerce Street; 414-372-8800; lakefrontbrewery.com), housed in a century-old former utility building with soaring, 30-foot-high ceilings. You'll learn about how beer is made and taste a few of Lakefront's winning brews, including the Snake Chaser, an Irish-style stout made in honor of St. Patrick's Day. The guides are very funny, so for the laughs alone, it's worth the trip.

3 *Slavic Feast* 8 p.m.

For authentic Eastern European flavors, you can't do better than **Three Brothers Bar and Restaurant** (2414 South St. Clair Street; 414-481-7530; $$), a Milwaukee institution that has been serving Serbian cuisine since 1954. Where else could you order roast suckling pig with rice and vegetables, served with home-pickled cabbage? Or a chicken paprikash followed by an incredibly light seven-layer walnut torte? The dining room has the unpretentious feel of a neighborhood tavern.

SATURDAY

4 *A Ward Updated* 10 a.m.

Many cities have warehouse districts that have become revitalized; Milwaukee has the **Historic Third Ward** (historicthirdward.org), made up of the blocks between the Milwaukee River and Jackson Street. A century ago, this was a manufacturing center. Now it is a magnet for shoppers, with old brick warehouses converted into boutiques and restaurants. For distinctive fashions, search no farther than **Five Hearts Boutique** (153 North Milwaukee Street; 414-727-4622; shopfivehearts.com). And for an eclectic

OPPOSITE Inside the Quadracci Pavilion, designed by Santiago Calatrava, at the Milwaukee Art Museum.

RIGHT Lake Michigan and the Milwaukee skyline.

and international array of home furnishings and artifacts, linger in **Embelezar** (241 North Broadway; 414-224-7644), whose name is Portuguese for, fittingly enough, "to embellish and adorn."

5 *Sausage and Cheese* Noon

Before finding a spot to hang out in one of the city's lovely waterfront parks, pack a picnic on Old World Third Street, the center of German life in 19th-century Milwaukee. The **Wisconsin Cheese Mart** (215 West Highland Avenue; 414-272-3544; wisconsincheesemart.com), which opened in 1938, sells hundreds of varieties of cheese. A few doors down is **Usingers** (1030 North Old World Third Street; 414-272-9100; usinger.com), sausage makers since 1880. There are 70 varieties, including a lean summer sausage.

6 *Spreading Wings* 2 p.m.

The **Milwaukee Art Museum** (700 North Art Museum Drive; 414-224-3200; mam.org) may have opened in 1888, but the eye-catching Quadracci Pavilion, designed by Santiago Calatrava and opened in 2001, has become a symbol of modern Milwaukee. With its movable wings expanded to their full, 217-foot span, the building looks either like a large white bird landing on Lake Michigan or the tail of a white whale emerging from the water. There's art, too: extensive collections of folk, central European and Germanic, and post-1960 contemporary.

7 *What Is the Fonz Reading?* 5 p.m.

While you're in the waterfront area, walk a couple of blocks to the west side of the Wells Street Bridge for a look at the **Bronzie Fonzie**, a life-size statue of the Fonz, the iconic television character from *Happy Days*. It's a favorite spot for a photograph, so smile and remember: two thumbs up for the camera. Then

ABOVE The Harley-Davidson Museum.

LEFT Up and Under Pub, a home of the blues.

OPPOSITE BELOW Updated tradition at the Lakefront Brewery.

while away some time at the **Boswell Book Company** (2559 North Downer Avenue; 414-332-1181; boswell.indiebound.com), a sprawling shop that has long hours, a huge Wisconsin section, and readings by nationally known authors.

8 *Third Coast Custard* 7 p.m.

The "Third Coast," a term not always familiar along the Atlantic and Pacific shores, refers in the Midwest to the coasts of the Great Lakes — the United States alone has 5,000 miles of shoreline along them. The airy restaurant **Blue Jacket** (135 East National Avenue; bluejacketbar.com; $$) plays up the theme with the slogan "Live the Third Coast" and offers seasonal, locally sourced dishes. Depending on the day's menu, you might find whitefish from Lake Superior or smelt, a Great Lakes staple, presented as batter-fried snacks, as well as locally produced liquors. For a dessert that's pure Milwaukee, drive out to **Leon's** (3131 South 27th Street; 414-383-1784; leonsfrozencustard.us), which has been serving its decadently rich frozen custard since 1942 and is said to have been the inspiration for Arnold's in *Happy Days*.

9 *Blues in the Night* 9:30 p.m.

East Brady Street, which stretches for about eight blocks from Lake Michigan to the Milwaukee River, was a hippie hangout in the 1960s. Today, its well-preserved buildings and 19th-century Victorian homes are a backdrop to one of the city's liveliest neighborhoods. During the day, boutiques and small stores draw shoppers. At night, restaurants and bars keep the street lively. A good spot for music is the **Up and Under Pub** (1216 East Brady Street; theupandunderpub.com), which proclaims itself the blues capital of Milwaukee. With high ceilings, an antique bar and a couple of dozen beers on tap, it offers live blues, rock, and reggae until 2 a.m. If you'd rather avoid alcohol, **Rochambo Coffee and**

Tea House down the street (1317 East Brady Street; 414-291-0095; rochambo.com) offers dozens of teas and stays open until midnight.

SUNDAY

10 *Lakeside Brunch* 10 a.m.

The Knick (1030 East Juneau Avenue; 414-272-0011; theknickrestaurant.com; $$) is busy and breezy on Sunday mornings, with an outdoor patio near Lake Michigan overlooking Veterans Park. For a memorable breakfast, try the crab hash, a mixture of crabmeat, onions, and hash browns topped with two eggs, or the banana pecan pancakes, dripping with whiskey butter and served with maple syrup.

11 *Wisconsin Tropics* 1 p.m.

Rain or shine, the **Mitchell Park Horticultural Conservatory** (524 South Layton Boulevard; 414-257-5611; countyparks.com) offers perennial respite. Affectionately known as the Domes, the conservatory is housed in three 85-foot-high, beehive-shaped buildings with different climates: the Floral Dome has more than 150 floral displays; the Arid Dome mimics the desert, with an oasis-like pool surrounded by cactuses; and the Tropical Dome has 1,200 rain-forest plants, tropical birds flying overhead, and a 30-foot waterfall.

OPPOSITE Green space along the waterfront.

THE BASICS

Fly to the Milwaukee airport and rent a car or drive two hours north from Chicago.

Pfister Hotel
424 East Wisconsin Avenue
414-273-8222
thepfisterhotel.com
$$$
A throwback to Victorian elegance within walking distance of the waterfront.

Iron Horse Hotel
500 West Florida Street
414-374-4766
theironhorsehotel.com
$$$-$$$$
Recent transformation of a 100-year-old warehouse.

Hotel Metro
411 East Mason Street
414-272-1937
hotelmetro.com
$$$
Serenely chic boutique hotel.

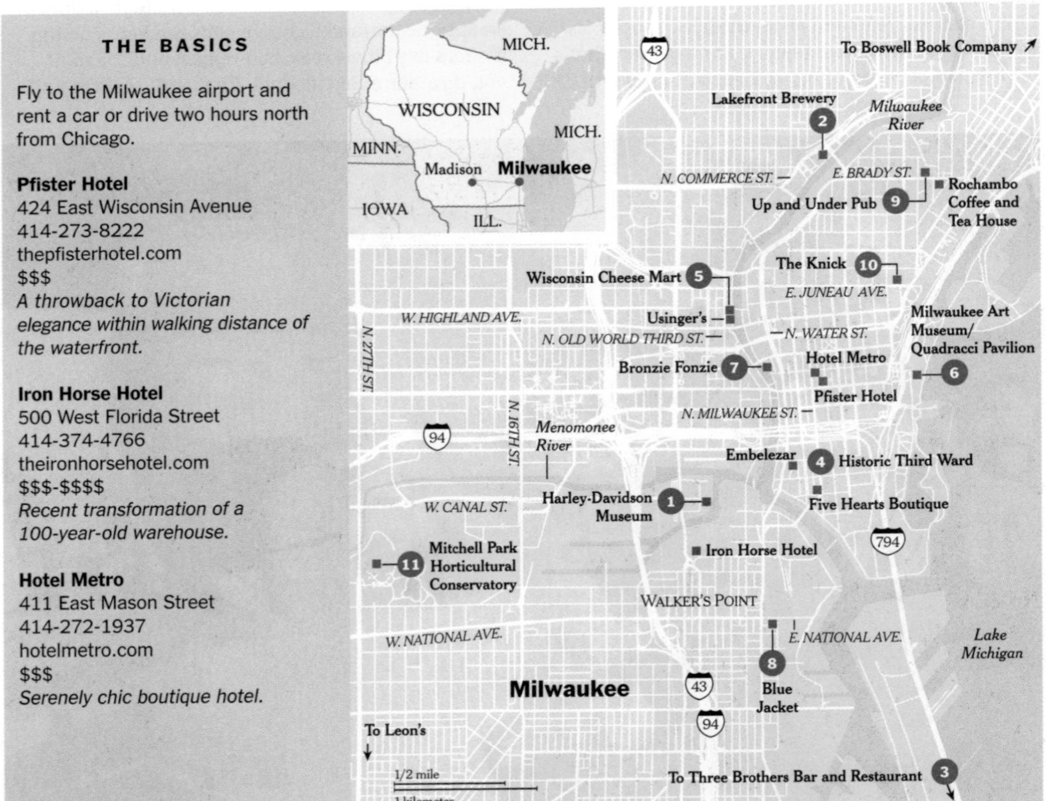

usbank
usbank
Northwestern Mutual

Minneapolis-St. Paul

Minnesotans take pride in their humility, but make an exception when it comes to showing folks around. And they have a lot to show. There is a depth of cultural amenities to Minneapolis and its not-so-twin city St. Paul that will surprise a first-time visitor. And please remember, when they ask you at the coffee shop, "How you doing, today?" they really want to know.
— BY DAVID CARR

FRIDAY

1 *By the Falls of Minnehaha* 5 p.m.

On a hot summer day, there is convenient and diverting respite at **Minnehaha Park** (4801 South Minnehaha Park Drive; 612-230-6400; minneapolisparks.org). Don't go there expecting Niagara; rather, you'll find a quaint urban park with both landscaped, and wild elements, a surprisingly good seafood restaurant (the Sea Salt Eatery; seasalteatery.wordpress.com), and, of course, the 53-foot Falls of Minnehaha that Henry Wadsworth Longfellow wrote about in *The Song of Hiawatha*. Now, Longfellow never actually saw the falls—he was inspired by the writing of others—but why put such a fine point on it?

2 *Intermission with a View* 7 p.m.

Many cities in the middle of the country chirp reflexively about their "great theater," but Minneapolis lives up to its rhetoric with strong independent companies. Among them is the **Guthrie Theater** (818 South Second Street; 612-377-2224; guthrietheater.org), a first-rate repertory theater with a recently built facility featuring a cantilevered bridge to nowhere. Step out and you can see all the way to the city's industrial northeast. Inside, you can take in a well-acted play.

3 *To the Warehouses* 8 p.m.

People are of two minds about Minneapolis's warehouse district. There are those who live for the street-filling frolic of a Friday night, and many who would drive miles to avoid it. A point for the former is the **112 Eatery** (112 North Third Street; 612-343-7696; 112eatery.com; $$), where you can avoid the mob by going to the upstairs bar for the tagliatelle with foie gras meatballs. Afterward, liquid diversions can commence. Start at the **Monte Carlo** (219 Third Avenue North; 612-333-5900; montecarlomn.com). Lawyers, politicos, and media types congregate here amid a mind-boggling, and potentially mind-bending, array of alcohol. Move on to **Lee's Liquor Lounge** (101 Glenwood Avenue; 612-338-9491; leesliquorlounge.com), just west of downtown, where Trailer Trash may be playing. You can face-plant at the nearby and artful Chambers hotel, or just have a nightcap on the rooftop then cab back to your own hotel.

SATURDAY

4 *You Going to Eat That?* 10 a.m.

Tell room service to keep it quiet when they deliver coffee. Or if you are feeling ambitious, go to **Al's Breakfast** in Dinkytown (413 14th Avenue Southeast; 612-331-9991), hard by the east-bank campus of the University of Minnesota. Wait against the wall for one of 14 stools while eyeing the food of the patron whose stool you are coveting. Minnesota is a friendly place, but don't ask for a bite of his blueberry pancakes. Order the hash browns and forswear ever eating so-called home fries again.

OPPOSITE AND RIGHT The Walker Art Center, devoted to modern and contemporary art, and Claes Oldenburg's *Spoonbridge and Cherry* in its sculpture garden.

5 *Necklace of Blue* 11:30 a.m.

So many lakes right in the city, but which one is for you? If you wear socks with sandals and think walking is a sport, **Lake Harriet** is for you. If you are prone to nudity and like swimming at night, then it's **Hidden Beach at Cedar Lake**. The rest of us can go to **Lake Calhoun**. Wheels of any kind, most commonly rollerblades, take you around it, but why not go to the boathouse and rent a canoe (wheelfunrentals.com)? Avoid the sailboats and windsurfers by paddling under the bridge into Lake of the Isles, which is sort of swampy to walk around, but lovely from the water.

6 *Spoon Feeding* 2:30 p.m.

The **Walker Art Center** (1750 Hennepin Avenue; 612-375-7600; walkerart.org) has one of the best contemporary art collections between the coasts, but why not stay outside for a little artist-designed mini-golf? At the sculpture garden, one might be tempted to climb into the giant spoon by Claes Oldenburg and Coosje van Bruggen. Don't. Motion detectors were installed after locals decided to memorialize their love with nocturnal visits. **Café Lurcat** (1624 Harmon Place; 612-486-5500; cafelurcat.com; $$), across the walking bridge, has excellent small plates.

7 *Ambulatory Retail* 4:30 p.m.

Shopping in Minnesota is usually reductively assigned to the Mall of America, but there is a strollable necklace of stores along Grand Avenue in St. Paul where down-home and style make nice. **Bibelot** (No. 1082; 651-222-0321; bibelotshops.com) has been featuring cool local stuff for four decades, and **Cooks of Crocus Hill** (No. 877; 651-228-1333; cooksofcrocushill.com) is the foodie perennial that just won't quit. If you get hungry or thirsty, you can always walk into **Dixie's on Grand** (No. 695; 651-222-7345; dixiesongrand.com) for some Southern-inspired fare.

8 *The North Star* 7 p.m.

As in many urban areas, the ineffable epicenter of cool migrates on a schedule known only to a select few. In Minneapolis, the indigenous tribe of artists, musicians, and wannabes have forsaken Uptown for Northeast, where trendy restaurants and bars have taken root. **Brasa Rotisserie** (600 East Hennepin Avenue; 612-379-3030; brasa.us) is a new-ish favorite where precious food localism comes without a dear price. Another is **331 Club** (331 13th Avenue Northeast; 612-331-1746; 331club.com), with a neighborhood vibe even a visitor can't miss. Yes, you should try the Hot Polack, a mix of jalapeños, kraut, and bratwurst. And anyone who knows Minneapolis will ask if you visited **Nye's Polonaise Room** (112 East Hennepin Avenue; 612-379-2021; nyespolonaise.com) to sample its wondrously cheesy piano bar and slamming polka.

9 *Here Comes a Regular* 11 p.m.

The Replacements may not drink anymore at the **CC Club** (2600 Lyndale Avenue South; 612-874-7226;

ABOVE The Guthrie Theater in Minneapolis.

RIGHT Kitchenware at Cooks of Crocus Hill, one of the stores that make for good shopping on Grand Avenue.

OPPOSITE So many lakes in Minneapolis — which to choose on a summer day? This beach lover picked Lake Calhoun.

ccclubuptown.com). And Tom Arnold was 86'ed for the last time a while ago. But the venerable club remains a nexus for the city's down and dirty rock scene. Plus, there's a killer juke box and no live music to try to talk over.

SUNDAY

10 *Over the River* 9 a.m.

Head over the river and check out St. Paul's **City Hall** (15 Kellogg Boulevard West; stpaul.gov), where *Vision of Peace*, a 60-ton onyx statue, towers over a lobby done in black Zigzag Moderne. And try to grab a booth at **Mickey's Diner** (36 Seventh Street West; 651-222-5633; mickeysdiningcar.com).

11 *A Historic Visit* Noon

History museums in fairly young places like Minnesota can be dreary, but not so at the **Minnesota History Center** (345 Kellogg Boulevard West, St. Paul; 651-259-3000; mnhs.org/historycenter). Get some metaphorical manure on your boots by visiting the Grainland/Boxcar exhibit. After all the eating you've done, it's worth finding out what happens inside those big elevators that tower over middle America. The hokey charms of so-called Minnesota Nice loom large.

THE BASICS

Take light rail or drive from the airport to downtown. There are cabs, but you will want a car to get beyond downtown.

Le Méridien Chambers Minneapolis
901 Hennepin Avenue
612-767-6900
lemeridienchambers.com
$$-$$$
Gorgeous, beautifully designed hotel with good food, lovely rooms, and a wonderful lounge.

The Depot Renaissance Hotel
225 Third Avenue South
612-375-1700
thedepotminneapolis.com
$$
Retrofitted in the historic Depot.

hotel340
340 Cedar Street, St. Paul
651-280-4120
hotel340.com
$$
Comfortable modern rooms in a lavishly detailed 1917 landmark building.

Duluth

Believe it. Minnesota bakes in the summer. And when temperatures hit the 90s, many Minnesotans head for Duluth, a city on the westernmost tip of Lake Superior that is cooled to comfort by lakeshore breezes. Built into bluffs overlooking this largest of the Great Lakes, Duluth was shaped by its long role as the port gateway to Minnesota's Iron Range (although many outside Minnesota know it best as the childhood home of Bob Dylan). Bed-and-breakfasts and museums now occupy spacious Victorian mansions built by mining and lumber barons. And Canal Park, once an abandoned warehouse district, is a vibrant waterfront area of shops, bars, and restaurants. — BY PAT BORZI

FRIDAY

1 *Lakefront Ramble* 5 p.m.

Acquaint yourself with **Canal Park** and the harbor by strolling the **Lakewalk**, a three-mile path along the Lake Superior shore. Whether you go the whole way or only part of it, rest your feet and enjoy the view from the courtyard deck of the **Fitger's Brewery Complex** (600 East Superior Street; fitgers.com), a mile from Canal Park. A big brewery from 1859 until 1972, Fitger's was converted into shops, nightclubs, restaurants, and a luxury hotel and now houses a microbrewery, **Fitger's Brewhouse** (218-279-2739). Have a drink and watch the hulking ore boats inch in and out of the harbor. Too tired to walk back? Hop the **Port Town Trolley** (duluthtransit.com), which serves Canal Park and the downtown hotels until about 7 p.m. in summer.

2 *What, No Ping?* 7 p.m.

They use real wooden bats in the Northwoods League, whose 12 teams are made up of top-level players from colleges around the United States and Canada. The Duluth Huskies play at cozy **Wade Municipal Stadium** (101 North 35th Avenue West; 218-786-9909; duluthhuskies2.com), a Works Progress Administration relic that opened in 1941. Tickets are cheap, and families have a great time.

3 *Ironman Gelato* 10 p.m.

Sometimes the iron ore didn't make it out of Duluth, and one relic of those days is **Clyde Iron Works** (2920 West Michigan Street; 218-727-1150; clydeparkduluth.com), once a foundry complex that turned out heavy equipment for logging and construction. Today it's a cavernous space that holds a restaurant, bakery, and events hall. Catch some live music, a late dinner, and drinks. Or at least dig into a homemade baked dessert or gelato.

SATURDAY

4 *Breakfast at Mom's* 10 a.m.

Few places in Duluth do breakfast as well as the **Amazing Grace Bakery Café** (394 South Lake Avenue; 218-723-0075; amazinggraceduluth.com; $), in the basement of the **DeWitt-Seitz Marketplace** in Canal Park. The funky interior is a hoot. If your mother ever had plastic tablecloths with designs of oranges, apples, and peaches on them, she'd love this place. Try French toast, muffins, or scones.

5 *Crime Scene* 11:30 a.m.

Of all the captains of industry who once called Duluth home, Chester A. Congdon was one of the richest. **Glensheen** (3300 London Road; 218-726-8910; glensheen.org), his baronial 39-room lakefront mansion on almost eight acres, was completed in

OPPOSITE Glensheen, a baronial mansion on the Lake Superior waterfront, belonged to Chester A. Congdon, one of Duluth's captains of industry. If your tour guide doesn't bring it up, ask about the double murder committed at the estate in 1977.

BELOW The former Fitger's Brewery Complex now holds shops, restaurants, a hotel, and a microbrewery.

1908. The basic tour of the main house's lower floors takes about an hour. An expanded tour includes the Arts and Crafts collection on the third floor. At one time tour guides were discouraged from discussing the double murder committed at the estate in 1977. An intruder smothered the 83-year-old heiress to the Congdon family fortune with a pink satin pillow and beat her night nurse to death with a candlestick holder. Most guides now mention the crime, but you may not hear about it unless you ask.

6 *A View from the Wall* 2 p.m.

Grandma's Saloon & Grill (522 Lake Avenue South; 218-727-4192; grandmasrestaurants.com/retail.htm) is a popular Canal Park destination. Its deck overlooks the century-old Aerial Lift Bridge, where the roadway rises in one piece to let ore and grain boats pass. But it's more fun to grab a single-scoop waffle cone at **Grandma's Ice Cream Boxcar**, the grill's ice cream and soda stand across the parking lot, and join the crowd along the canal wall and watch these huge vessels go by. Wave to the deckhands—they'll wave back—but don't be the one who jumps when the ship sounds its horn.

7 *The Iron Boats* 3:30 p.m.

The doomed ore freighter *Edmund Fitzgerald*, sunk in a storm on Lake Superior in 1975 and immortalized in song by Gordon Lightfoot, departed from Superior, Wisconsin, across the harbor from Duluth. To get a sense of proportion, tour the immense *William A. Irvin*, a 610-foot retired laker that is 110 feet shorter than the Fitzgerald. The flagship of U.S. Steel's Great Lakes Fleet from 1938 to 1978, the ***Irvin*** (350 Harbor Drive; 218-722-7876; decc.org) is named for the former U.S. Steel president who occasionally sailed on it himself. The tour takes you through the engine room, the immense hold that could handle up to 14,000 tons of iron ore and coal, and the officers' and crew's quarters. Note the contrast of the stark crew's rooms with the stunning walnut-paneled staterooms for big-shot passengers.

8 *Millionaire Cuisine* 7 p.m.

The name trades on Duluth's reputation around 1900 as the United States city with the most millionaires per capita, but with fare like Workingman's Pot Roast and the Bankrupt Burger (not to mention the worthless stock certificates decorating the bathroom), **Tycoons Alehouse and Eatery** (132 East Superior Street; 218-623-1889; duluthtycoons.com; $$) plays the wealth theme mostly for laughs. The product of a $2.3 million restoration of the old City Hall, built in 1889, Tycoons features glittering chandeliers and plush armchairs along with the roast chicken and local beer. There's live music on a small stage, and downstairs in the subbasement, a speakeasy-style bar.

SUNDAY

9 *On the Rails* 10 a.m.

Hop the trolley to the Depot, also known as the **Lake Superior Railroad Museum** (506 West Michigan Street; 218-727-8025; lsrm.org), and relive Duluth's rich railroad history. Beneath the former Union Depot, which in its heyday handled seven railroads and up to

ABOVE The Lake Superior Railroad Museum has an extensive collection of old locomotives and train cars.

OPPOSITE Take the Lakewalk from Canal Park to reach Fitger's, a landmark impossible to miss.

50 trains a day, lies one of the country's most extensive collections of old locomotives, coaches, and other equipment. The admission price also gets you into the rest of the St. Louis County Heritage and Arts Center, which includes a children's museum and a gallery.

10 *Just an Embryo* Noon

The **Electric Fetus** (12 East Superior Street; 218-722-9970; electricfetus/Venue/10092.com) is a record shop as eccentric as its name suggests. If you absolutely have to get your toddler a Dead Kennedys T-shirt, this is the place to find it. The original Fetus opened in Minneapolis in 1968, and in many ways this branch remains stuck in time: for starters, the store smells like incense. The Fetus is known for offering CDs across every genre, and even if you don't buy anything on your way out of town, you should get a laugh out of looking at the buttons and head-shop merchandise.

THE BASICS

Fly into Duluth International Airport or drive two and a half hours from Minneapolis. You will need a car to venture beyond downtown and Canal Park.

South Pier Inn on the Canal
701 South Lake Avenue
218-786-9007
southpierinn.com
$$-$$$
Water views near the lift bridge on the Duluth Harbor canal.

Suites Hotel at Waterfront Plaza
325 Lake Avenue South
218-727-4663
thesuitesduluth.com
$$
Former home of Marshall-Wells, once billed as the world's largest hardware distributor.

Fitger's Inn
600 East Superior Street
218-722-8826
fitgers.com
$$
Has the feel of a grand old Western hotel, with 19th-century furnishings and an ornate cashier's cage.

1 mile
2 kilometers
Glensheen 5
MINNESOTA
61
Area of detail
Duluth
Clyde Iron Works 3
South Pier Inn on the Canal
CANAL PARK
Lake Superior
2 Wade Municipal Stadium
Superior
WISCONSIN
CANADA
MINN.
N.D.
Lake Superior
Duluth
WIS.
Minneapolis
St. Paul
S.D.
IOWA
1/4 mile
1/2 kilometer
Fitger's Brewery Complex/ Fitger's Brewhouse/ Fitger's Inn
N. THIRD AVE. E.
E. FIRST ST.
E. SUPERIOR ST.
N. FIRST AVE. E.
8 Tycoons Alehouse and Eatery
10 Electric Fetus
Lake Superior
Duluth
35
1 Lakewalk
Suites Hotel at Waterfront Plaza
Port Town Trolley
William A. Irvin 7
CANAL PARK
Amazing Grace Bakery Café/ DeWitt-Seitz Marketplace 4
E. BUCHANAN ST.
Grandma's Saloon & Grill 6
Grandma's Ice Cream Boxcar
Lake Superior Railroad Museum 9
St. Louis County Heritage and Arts Center
HARBOR DR.
LAKE AVE. S.
AERIAL LIFT BRIDGE

Winnipeg

Once known as "the Chicago of the North," Winnipeg (population 780,000) is a smaller version of the Windy City, with similar broad avenues, century-old architecture, and indie-style art and music. Winnipeg is geographically isolated (it's a thousand miles in either direction to the next large city), so it's a place that has learned how to generate its own entertainment. There are four distinct seasons, all arriving with exclamation marks. (If Winnipeg were portrayed in a stage play, the weather would be one of the main characters.) Culture is the city's principal export industry, and Burton Cummings, Carol Shields, Guy Maddin, the Guess Who, Bachman-Turner Overdrive, Neil Young, the Royal Winnipeg Ballet, and countless painters, writers, and actors have grown up out of its cracked sidewalks.

— BY JAKE MACDONALD

FRIDAY

1 *Straight to the Heart* 3 p.m.

Winnipeg was shaped by its rivers, and the two main waterways, the Red River and the Assiniboine, meet in the heart of the city. At the confluence, called the Forks, you'll find a village of restored warehouse buildings, cobblestone avenues, busking musicians, charcoal grills, restaurants, and little shops purveying exotic clothes and handicrafts. For a tour of the city by boat, check out the **M.S. River Rouge** (112-1 Forks Market Road; 204-774-7009; msrouge.com) and **Splash Dash Tours** (204-783-6633; splashdash.ca). Splash Dash also operates water taxis that stop every 15 minutes at each of 11 "bus stops" along the river—a great way to explore the city's neighborhoods.

2 *Five-Course Feast* 7 p.m.

Like the converging rivers outside the window, delectable flavors from around the world swirl together at **Sydney's at the Forks** (1 Forks Market Road No. 215; 204-942-6075; sydneysattheforks.com; $$$), with gourmet influences from Asia, France, and Italy. Although it's a high-end dining room with ancient brick walls and a crackling fireplace, Sydney's offers good value for what it serves: dinners made up of five elegant courses. On a warm night, ask to be seated on the patio, which affords a grand view of the waterfront.

3 *River Shimmer* 9 p.m.

At the Forks a paved riverwalk winds off along the waterfront in either direction. Colored lanterns and city lights swim on the water on a summer night, and boats cruise past in the darkness. It's a bucolic and safe inner-city stroll, populated with skaters, lovers, and families. Some of biggest catfish on the continent live in this river, and here and there you'll see anglers sitting on the bank, waiting for a tug.

SATURDAY

4 *First, the Flapjacks* 8:30 a.m.

Seek out the **Original Pancake House** (1 Forks Market Road; 204-947-5077; originalpancakehouse.ca; $$), a local institution founded over half a century ago. Great coffee comes from a bottomless vat, and lovely morning light pours through all-glass walls. The pride of the house is the oven-baked apple pancake topped with cinnamon-sugar glaze, with sausages on the side.

5 *Sailors and Fur Traders* 10 a.m.

Three centuries ago, much of the interior of North America was governed by a private corporation, its currency being the "MB" (Made Beaver) and its fortified headquarters at trading posts along Hudson Bay and the river network to the south. The Hudson's Bay Company, established in 1670 and soon rich on the fur trade, is still the oldest corporation in North America, and its Fort Garry eventually grew into the city of Winnipeg. At the **Manitoba Museum** (190 Rupert Avenue; 204-956-2830; manitobamuseum.ca), the company gets its due and the early history of the continent comes to life. Visitors can enter a gallery that recreates the English port of Deptford, circa 1668, and climb aboard a seaworthy replica of the *HMS Nonsuch*, the sailing ship that conducted the first trading voyage to North America. In other galleries, aboriginal families make camp in the woods, and an immense polar bear pads across snow under the Northern Lights.

OPPOSITE The skyline of Winnipeg, the metropolis of the Canadian heartland.

6 *Lunch With the Bears* 1 p.m.

A short drive or bus ride takes you to **Assiniboine Park** (55 Pavilion Crescent; 204-927-6000; assiniboinepark.ca), a vast estate of lawn, ponds, and forest with a conservatory, a miniature steam train, and a zoo. Before exploring the grounds, stop at the **Tundra Grill** (204-927-8060; $$) and have lunch while watching polar bears through a 150-foot-wide wall of windows. Later, before you leave the park, find the statue of a soldier and a bear cub near the entrance and take the time to learn the story behind it. A young lieutenant heading off to World War I in 1914 adopted a black bear cub and named it for his hometown — Winnipeg, or Winnie for short. It became his unit's mascot, and in 1919 he donated it to the London Zoo. It was a popular attraction, and a boy named Christopher Robin named his teddy bear after it. You can guess the rest: the boy's father was A.A. Milne, and the bear was immortalized as Winnie the Pooh.

7 *Date Night* 7:30 p.m.

There are a couple of sushi restaurants in town more expensive than **Blufish** (179 Bannatyne Avenue; 204-779-9888; blufish.ca; $$), but this is the place that locals regard as the ultimate in delicate Japanese cuisine. Small and elegant, it is quiet enough for intimate conversation, and the exquisite tidbits of sashimi, ben roll, and tuna tataki awaken the nerve endings like Sonny Rollins playing the sax. Winnipeg males seeking to impress their dates reserve Table One.

8 *Action After Dark* 9:30 p.m.

You're in the heart of the Exchange District, a neighborhood of historical buildings, art galleries, and offbeat boutiques. A few blocks west of Blufish is the **Old Market Square**, an open-air park with live world music and thronging crowds on warm nights. Across the street is the **King's Head** (120 King Street; 204-957-7710; kingshead.ca), a loud, crowded pub with designer beers on tap, a good supply of pool tables, and a rowdy Celtic dance band doing its best to blow the roof off.

SUNDAY

9 *Brunch at the Fort* 10 a.m.

The **Fort Garry Hotel** (222 Broadway; 204-942-8251; fortgarryhotel.com), Winnipeg's grandest and oldest, puts on a magnificent brunch every Sunday

ABOVE Autumn on the Assiniboine Riverwalk. Winnipeg is a city of rivers, and the Forks, where the Assiniboine meets the Red, is a favorite playground.

OPPOSITE ABOVE "The Great Buffalo Hunt," a diorama at the Manitoba Museum in Winnipeg.

morning. The building is an outstanding example of the "neo chateau" style of architecture that was established in New York at the Plaza Hotel and spread across Canada with a chain of palatial railway hotels. The Fort Garry has a ghost, of course, who seldom comes for breakfast but is occasionally spotted in the hallways.

10 *Rebellion Gone Wrong* 11 a.m.

Right behind the hotel are the remains of the fort where Louis Riel, a leader in the French-descended Métis community, hatched a plan to rebel against the Canadian government of 1870 and start a new nation. Riel apparently agreed with the old revolutionary dictum that you have to break a few eggs to make an omelet, and ordered the death of a local loudmouth named Thomas Scott. By some accounts, the firing squad was drunk and the execution was a messy affair with the not-quite-dead Scott shouting from inside his coffin. Is Thomas Scott the hotel ghost? Is he still upset at Louis Riel?

11 *The French Quarter* Noon

Immediately east of the Forks is the **Esplanade Riel**, a futuristic-looking pedestrian cable bridge that crosses the river and leads into Winnipeg's **French Quarter**, the home of the largest Canadian French population outside Quebec. Its citizens are proudly francophone, and the shops and cafes have a French flavor. Visit the nearby cemetery and the grave of Louis Riel (tourismeriel.com), who was eventually charged with treason and hanged but is now celebrated as the Father of Manitoba.

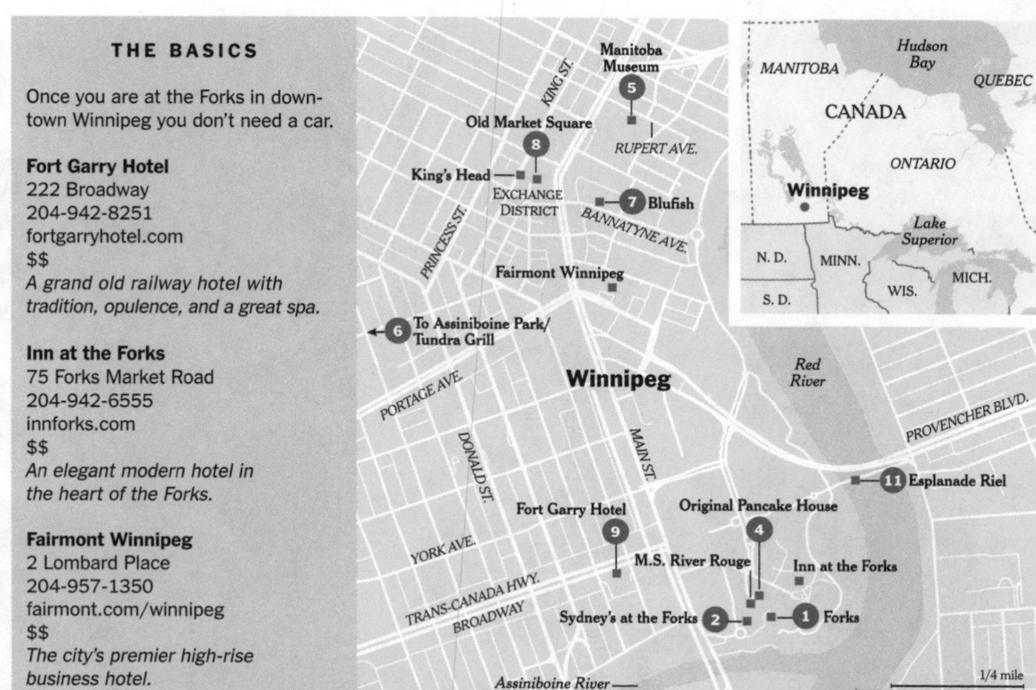

THE BASICS

Once you are at the Forks in downtown Winnipeg you don't need a car.

Fort Garry Hotel
222 Broadway
204-942-8251
fortgarryhotel.com
$$
A grand old railway hotel with tradition, opulence, and a great spa.

Inn at the Forks
75 Forks Market Road
204-942-6555
innforks.com
$$
An elegant modern hotel in the heart of the Forks.

Fairmont Winnipeg
2 Lombard Place
204-957-1350
fairmont.com/winnipeg
$$
The city's premier high-rise business hotel.

GO
M

Ann Arbor

It is not just the football season throngs of University of Michigan students dressed in maize and blue singing "Hail to the Victors" that make Ann Arbor the ultimate college town. Nor is it Michigan Stadium, with the largest attendance in the country (114,000 at some games), and renovated to the tune of $226 million. Rather it is the urban sophistication of this town—with its mix of restaurants, bars, boutiques, art-house movie theaters, and world-class art museums—that keeps many University of Michigan alumni from leaving long after they have graduated. For travelers, the sheer energy and the abundance of cultural opportunities, from classical dance performances to bluegrass concerts, makes a visit here a good time to get into the college spirit, even if it's not football season.

— BY JENNIFER CONLIN

FRIDAY

1 *Old-Time Shopping* 2 p.m.

Start your weekend in **Nickels Arcade**, an elegant glass-covered atrium that opened in 1918 and still houses businesses dating back 90 years. **Van Boven Clothing** (326 South State Street; 734-665-7228; vanboven.com) is a men's clothier that has long catered to well-dressed fraternity boys. The intimate **Comet Coffee** (16 Nickels Arcade; 734-222-0579) brews with beans grown from Ethiopia to El Salvador, one cup at a time. Then cross State Street to **Moe Sport Shop** (711 North University Avenue; 734-668-6915; moesportshops.com) to suit up as a Michigan fan. "U of M" apparel has been sold here since 1915, and you'll find such items as T-shirts and temporary "M" face tattoos.

2 *Student Scene* 3 p.m.

The **Diag**, as the open space on the central campus is called, is a leafy oasis intersected by sidewalks connecting academic buildings. Relax on a bench and take in the student scene, featuring everything from charity bucket drives to Ultimate Frisbee games. Just don't step on the brass inlaid "M" in front of the Harlan Hatcher Graduate Library—lore has it that freshmen who step on it will earn an F on their first exam. Then visit the architecturally stunning **Michigan Law School quadrangle** (625 South State Street), which could easily stand in for Harry Potter's Hogwarts, as could the library's Reading Room, with its vaulted ceilings, oak wainscoting, and stained glass windows.

3 *New Nostalgia* 5 p.m.

Between the Law School and the Ross School of Business you'll find **Dominick's** (812 Monroe Street; 734-662-5414), which has been serving students and the area's aging hippie population ever since the '60s, when the town was at the forefront of the Vietnam War protest movement. Though its picnic tables and booths are increasingly filled with entrepreneurs and M.B.A. candidates, everyone seems to enjoy the sangria served in jam jars on the patio. But avoid the temptation to eat here; instead head to **Mark's Carts** (markscartsannarbor.com)—a jumble of inexpensive ethnic food carts in a cozy courtyard on Washington Street between First and Ashley Streets, where, on Friday evenings, you can eat paella or tangy Thai slaw while listening to jazz, folk, and rock performers.

4 *Cool Culture* 8 p.m.

The University Musical Society (ums.org) offers a range of dance, theater, and musical productions performed at places that include the Hill Auditorium, with its superb acoustics, and the small but elegant Lydia Mendelssohn Theater. But it is the **Ark** (316 South Main Street; 734-761-1818; theark.org), one of North America's oldest nonprofit acoustic music clubs, that

OPPOSITE In football season, Michigan Stadium reverberates with cheering, roaring, and the school fight song.

RIGHT The Lunch Room, a vegan option at Mark's Carts.

has developed an international reputation, not just for preserving American music (folk and bluegrass, in particular), but also for showcasing world music from Africa, the Caribbean, and elsewhere.

SATURDAY

5 *Sunny Side Up* 9 a.m.

Beat the crowds at **Angelo's** (1100 Catherine; 734-761-8996; angelosa2.com; $), where thick slices of raisin toast are second only to the pumpkin pancakes. Work off the calories with a brisk walk to the **Farmers' Market** (315 Detroit Street; 734-794-6255). Browse your way through stalls stocked with local products from fruit-flavored syrups (rhubarb, peach, cantaloupe) to wooden bird houses.

6 *Patience and Pumpernickel* Noon

Don't be put off by the line outside **Zingerman's** deli (422 Detroit Street; 734-663-3354; zingermansdeli.com; $$). Waiting is part of the experience. The friendly servers hand out nibbles of fresh bread, cheese, and brownies while you decide which of the 99 sandwiches you want (most popular: Zingerman's Reuben on Jewish rye). Or cross the street to **Monahan's Seafood Market** (407 North Fifth Avenue; 734-662-5118; monahansseafood.com; $) for an oyster po' boy or fresh chowder.

7 *Fun in the Big House* 1 p.m.

Kickoff time varies between noon and 4 p.m., depending on the college football broadcast schedule. Don't show up at the **Big House**, as the stadium is called, ticketless. Buying seats in advance (mgoblue.com) is a must. Though alcohol is not allowed, there is plenty of spirit in the cheering of "Let's Go Blue" and the tunes played by the Michigan Marching Band. If you're here on one of the 45 or so weekends each year when there's no football game, don't despair. Find out how well Ann Arbor fits its name by checking out the trees, both native and exotic, in an afternoon ramble around **Nichols Arboretum** (1610 Washington Heights; 734-647-7600; lsa.umich.edu/mbg). It's a 123-acre site with panoramic views and a path along the winding Huron River.

8 *Cocktail Crawl* 5 p.m.

Whether Michigan has won or lost, students hit the bars. Avoid South University and State Street (student hubs) and head to the more civilized **Ann Street** (the place Bob Seger, who grew up in Ann Arbor, is actually singing about in the song "Mainstreet"). With dozens of night spots, it's easy to find a martini or microbrew; one favorite is **Palio** (347 South Main; 734-930-6156; palioannarbor.com), where postgame parties erupt on the rooftop bar.

9 *The Global Gourmet* 7 p.m.

If it's ethnic food you crave, try **Pacific Rim** (114 West Liberty Street; 734-662-9303; pacificrimbykana.com; $$$), whose pan-Asian menu may include a delicate tuna tartare or pan-seared quinoa-crusted scallops. Head to **Logan** (115 West Washington Street; 734-327-2312; logan-restaurant.com; $$$) for dishes like Gruyère custard with caramelized onions and tomatoes or wild boar Bolognese. If you want a quick bite, **Frita Batidos** (117 West Washington Street; 734-761-2882; fritabatidos.com; $) serves Cuban specialties like fritas, spicy burgers of chorizo, black bean, white fish, beef, or turkey on a soft brioche. Batidos, fresh fruit shakes, are made with sweetened milk and crushed ice—with rum an optional addition.

10 *Wild at Dark* 9 p.m.

Housed in an old brewery, the **Cavern Club** (210 South First Street; 734-913-8890; cavernclubannarbor.com) attracts some of the biggest bands and D.J.'s from metro Detroit. Or you may prefer an evening at the **Michigan Theater** (603 East Liberty Street; 734-668-8463; michtheater.org). Opened in 1928 as a vaudeville and silent movie palace, it now offers live entertainment (the Ann

ABOVE Saturday breakfast at Angelo's involves coffee, eggs, and thick slices of raisin toast.

OPPOSITE It's not all football at the University of Michigan. Serious reading takes place in this law school library.

Arbor Symphony performs here regularly), as well as independent films. Night owls will appreciate the Saturday midnight shows of cult classics like *The Rocky Horror Picture Show* at the nearby **State Theater**, an Art Deco cinema built in 1942 (233 South State Street; 734-761-8667; michtheater.org/state).

SUNDAY

11 *Feed Body and Soul* 10:30 a.m.

Café Zola (112 West Washington Street; 734-769-2020; cafezola.com; $$) offers an eclectic menu that borrows from French, Italian, and Turkish cuisines—the crepes are both savory and sweet, and Turkish eggs are made with feta, spinach, tomato, olives, and cucumber. Next, experience another kind of eclecticism at the **University of Michigan Museum of Art** (525 South State Street; 734-764-0395; umma.umich.edu). With more than 18,000 works—European, African, Asian, American, and Middle Eastern—it has something for everyone. For a different museum experience, cross the street to the **Kelsey Museum of Archaeology** (No. 434; 734-764-9304; lsa.umich.edu/kelsey), which holds thousands of ancient finds from the Mediterranean and Middle East.

THE BASICS

Ann Arbor is 45 miles west of Detroit and 35 miles north of the Ohio state line. Fly to the Detroit airport and take a cab to Ann Arbor, where you can explore on foot.

The Bell Tower
300 South Thayer Street
734-769-3010
belltowerhotel.com
$$
A charming hotel located right on campus and close to downtown.

The Inn at the League
911 North University Avenue
734-764-3177
uunions.umich.edu/league/inn
$$
A true campus experience, with wonderful views of the grounds, several dining spots, and a garden.

Dahlmann Campus Inn
615 East Huron Street
734-769-2200
campusinn.com
$$$
Conveniently located close to the university and downtown.

Marriott

Detroit

Eminem celebrated Detroit, Michigan, in a slick Super Bowl commercial. Glenn Beck denigrated it by comparing it to Hiroshima. To visit Detroit these days is to experience both ends of that spectrum — a once great metropolis worn down by decades of corruption and economic woes, and a city fueled by newfound hope and enthusiasm as it painstakingly rebuilds itself. Edgy cafes and shops cater to young artists and professionals moving into downtown loft spaces. Established restaurants, museums, and musical venues recapture the storied past. You may have to work a little to find the best of Detroit, but it's worth it.
— BY JENNIFER CONLIN

FRIDAY

1 *Groove Time* 2 p.m.

Get into the beat of Detroit immediately with a visit to the **Motown Historical Museum** (2648 West Grand Boulevard; 313-875-2264; motownmuseum.com), where the tour guides are nearly as entertaining as the artists who first recorded their songs here at Berry Gordy Jr.'s recording studio, Hitsville USA, in the early 1960s. The memorabilia ranges from Marvelettes album covers to the Jackson Five's psychedelic bell bottoms. You can't help but sing the tunes of Marvin Gaye, Stevie Wonder, Diana Ross, Smokey Robinson, the Four Tops, and the Temptations as you wander into Studio A, where it all began.

2 *French Flavor* 5 p.m.

Though it is easy to forget this city's French colonial roots, at **Good Girls Go to Paris Crepes** (15 East Kirby Street; 313-664-0490; goodgirlsgotopariscrepes.com; $), Le Détroit feels alive and well in a setting of dark red walls and classic French movie posters. Try a Celeste (Brie, dried cranberries, and roast beef) or a Claire (chicken, broccoli, and Cotswold cheese), and leave room for an ooh-la-la dessert crepe. After dinner, stroll over to the elegant **Detroit Institute of Arts** (5200 Woodward Avenue; 313-833-7900; dia.org), which stays open until 10 p.m. on Fridays. The museum's remarkable collection has been threatened as the city grappled with bankruptcy, but see what you can while it is available. There are works by Picasso and van Gogh, but the don't-miss is Diego Rivera's *Detroit Industry* fresco cycle from the 1930s.

3 *Cool Cat Cafe* 10 p.m.

Don't let the abandoned buildings or strip joint across the street keep you from **Café D'Mongo's** (1439 Griswold Street; cafedmongos.com), a wonderfully eccentric speakeasy that feels more like a private party than a bustling bar. The owner, Larry Mongo, is like a funky Mr. Rogers who knows everyone in the neighborhood and beyond, from the young "creative class" that frequents his establishment to the glamorous 60-something women sipping dark cocktails at the bar. Live jazz and country music play on alternating Friday nights. Café D'Mongo's is open only on Fridays and occasionally, if the owner feels like it, the last Saturday of each month.

SATURDAY

4 *To Market* 8 a.m.

The six-block **Eastern Market** (2934 Russell Street; 313-833-9300; detroiteasternmarket.com), founded in 1891, is home to Detroit foodies with more than 250 vendors selling everything from fruits and vegetables to Michigan maple syrup and artisanal breads. This is also a great area for antiques and

OPPOSITE The GM Renaissance Center downtown.

RIGHT Hitsville USA, now the Motown Historical Museum. Wander into Studio A, where it all began for the likes of Marvin Gaye, Stevie Wonder, and Diana Ross.

bric-a-brac. Try **Marketplace Antiques Gallery** (2047 Gratiot Avenue; 313-567-8250) or **Eastern Market Antiques** (2530 Market Street; 313-259-0600). And if you have not sufficiently grazed your way through the market, stop at the **Russell St. Deli** (2465 Russell Street; 313-567-2900; russellstreetdeli.com; $) for breakfast. The delicious raisin bread French toast is even better slathered with toasted pecans or fresh fruit.

5 *T Man* 10 a.m.

While Detroit has no shortage of historic homes and museums honoring the car industry, the **Model T Automotive Heritage Complex** (461 Piquette Avenue; 313-872-8759; tplex.org), the birthplace of the Model T Ford, stands out. This was Henry Ford's first factory, and it appears much as it did when it opened in 1904. See various fully restored Model T's and visit the "secret experimental room" where Ford invented the car that would take motoring to the masses.

6 *Fire Up Your Belly* Noon

Located in Corktown, across the street from one of the saddest yet most historic landmarks in Detroit — the now abandoned Michigan Central Station — **Slows Bar B Q** (2138 Michigan Avenue; 313-962-9828; slowsbarbq.com; $$) is single-handedly revitalizing this area of the city with its baby back ribs, pulled pork, beef brisket, and chicken wings, as well as its charitable donations to local shelters, hospitals, and schools. Inside, the place is comfortable, with salvaged lumber, exposed brick walls, and a wrap-around bar. Outside, there may be a line, but Slows makes it worth taking a place at the end. What's more, waiting gives you a chance to dream up interesting development ideas for the haunting rail building in the distance.

7 *A Matinee Moment* 2 p.m.

The one thing not missing in this city is theaters — and they are housed in pristinely restored historic buildings. While away the afternoon with a performance in one of their classy interiors. On

one weekend, matinee choices included a comedy at the intimate **Gem Theatre** (333 Madison Avenue; 313-963-9800; gemtheatre.com), a dance troupe at the breathtakingly renovated **Detroit Opera House** (1526 Broadway; 313-237-7464; michiganopera.org), a Broadway musical at the **Fisher Theatre** (3011 West Grand Boulevard; 313-872-1000; broadwayindetroit.com), a children's show at the former movie palace the **Fox Theatre** (2211 Woodward Avenue; 313-471-3200; olympiaentertainment.com), and a concert at **Music Hall** (350 Madison Avenue; 313-887-8500; musichall.org).

8 *Cheap and Cheerful* 6 p.m.

By far the best happy hour deal in town, and the crowds prove it, is at **Roast**, a modern brasserie on the ground floor of the newly renovated Westin Book Cadillac Detroit (1128 Washington Boulevard; 313-961-2500; roastdetroit.com; $). Sidle up to the polished bar, settle onto a comfortable padded stool, and start ordering. You'll find beer, wine, and cocktails, and the bar food includes burgers, macaroni and cheese, and huge paper cones of hot fries.

9 *Jazz It Up* 9 p.m.

Cliff Bell's (2030 Park Avenue; 313-961-2543; cliffbells.com; $$) is one of the oldest and most famous supper clubs in Detroit (it originally opened in 1935), and after years of meticulous renovations, it is once again the place to be on a weekend night. Amid its Art Deco features, vaulted ceilings, mahogany bar, and mirrored walls, to say nothing of the sounds of the jazz ensembles performing each night, entering Cliff Bell's is like walking into a Fred Astaire film. With a cocktail menu divided into two categories — Martinis (Dirty Detroit Martini, Gypsy Kiss) and Swizzlers (the Cliff Bell, Cumberland Cup) — food could easily be forgotten, but should not be. The menu ranges from filet mignon to shrimp and grits.

SUNDAY

10 *Art After Porridge* 11 a.m.

Spend some time amid the venturesome works at the **Museum of Contemporary Art Detroit** (4454 Woodward Avenue; 313-832-6622; mocadetroit.org), which is housed in a former auto dealership. Exhibits explore emerging ideas in the contemporary art

OPPOSITE ABOVE A survivor from 1911 at the Model T Automotive Heritage Complex, the birthplace of the Model T Ford. The building was Henry Ford's first factory and appears much as it did when it opened in 1904.

OPPOSITE BELOW Good Girls Go to Paris Crepes.

ABOVE The Detroit Opera House.

world, and the museum's store attracts students from the neighboring College for Creative Studies.

11 *Potter's Paradise* Noon

Truly unique to Detroit is **Pewabic Pottery** (10125 East Jefferson Avenue; 313-626-2000; pewabic.org), founded by ceramicist Mary Stratton during the Arts and Crafts movement in 1903. A National Historic Landmark, the building is now a production facility, museum, and educational center with a store where eager fans, including Martha Stewart, still flock to buy its tiles and vessel ware in unique glazes. Take home a classic Pewabic tile, perhaps an acorn or a dragonfly.

ABOVE The Museum of Contemporary Art Detroit explores emerging art in a former auto dealership.

OPPOSITE The Italian Garden Room at the elegantly restored Book Cadillac Hotel, now a Westin.

THE BASICS

Detroit's airport receives flights from around the world. Walk and use taxis, which are cheap and plentiful.

Westin Book Cadillac Detroit
1114 Washington Boulevard
313-442-1600
bookcadillacwestin.com
$$
Landmark hotel built in 1924 and reopened in 2009 after a $200 million renovation.

Inn on Ferry Street
84 East Ferry Street
313-871-6000
innonferrystreetdetroit.com
$$
Four historic homes and two carriage houses connected as a charming inn.

Detroit Marriott at the Renaissance Center
400 Renaissance Drive
313-568-8000
marriott.com
$$
A 1,298-room skyscraper hotel at General Motors headquarters.

Fisher Theatre
5 Model T Automotive Heritage Complex
W. GRAND BLVD.
PIQUETTE AVE.
1 Motown Historical Museum
E. FERRY ST.
Good Girls Go to Paris Crepes 2
Inn on Ferry Street
Detroit Institute of Arts
94
Museum of Contemporary Art Detroit 10
75
Marketplace Antiques Gallery
W. WARREN AVE.
TRUMBULL AVE.
CASS AVE.
WOODWARD AVE.
10
Eastern Market 4
Eastern Market Antiques
GRAND RIVER AVE.
Detroit
PARK AVE.
Russell St. Deli
GRATIOT AVE.
Gem Theatre 7
MARTIN LUTHER KING JR. BLVD.
Fox Theatre
Cliff Bell's 9
Music Hall
Detroit Opera House
Slows Bar B Q 6
75
Café D'Mongo's 3
WASHINGTON BLVD.
To Pewabic Pottery 11
MICHIGAN AVE.
12
Roast/ Westin Book Cadillac Detroit 8
96
Detroit Marriott at the Renaissance Center
10
W. FRONT ST.
1/2 mile
1 kilometer
Detroit River
MICH.
CANADA
Lake Huron
WIS.
MICHIGAN
Lake Michigan
Lansing
ILL.
Detroit
Lake Erie
IND.
OHIO

HUNCH

Toronto

After half a century of immigration from virtually every country, Toronto has realized its promise as a vibrant picture postcard of world culture. Cafes, clubs, restaurants, theaters, museums, and galleries are everywhere, and instead of making a summer exodus to cottage country, Torontonians these days are just as likely to stay in their city during the warm weather. Which is not to say that the buttoned-up poise coded deep in the town's DNA is completely gone — many places retain the 1950s veneer of Toronto the Good while adding the sound and tempo of T.O. today. You might want to visit before the latter completely consumes the former.

— BY DAVE BIDINI AND SARAH WILDMAN

FRIDAY

1 *Kensington Blend* 3 p.m.

The **Kensington Market** (kensington-market.ca) is a joyful collision of secondhand-clothing shops, fishmongers, cafes, cheese merchants, folksingers, and garage bands that spans its neighborhood's history from early Jewish hub to Portuguese quarter to Chinatown to Vietnamese neighborhood. Punks, Rastafarians, students, and shopkeepers sit shoulder to shoulder in the market's myriad bars and cafes, whatever the hour. After your tour around the market, wander into **Bellevue Park**. The gorgeous Byzantine Revival building at its edge is the Kiever Synagogue (25 Bellevue Avenue), built in 1927 by Ukrainian Jews.

2 *In the English Style* 6 p.m.

The chef Ben Heaton serves food for up-to-date Anglophiles at the **Grove** (1214 Dundas Street West; 416-588-2299; thegroveto.com; $$$). One evening at the dinner hour, parts of the menu read classically English — "Beef, carrots, horseradish, barley," for example — but without those descriptions, a diner would be hard-pressed to categorize them as anything but delicious and well prepared. That beef dish, for instance, was a contrasting duo of pleasantly chewy hanger steak and tender stout-braised beef cheek. The desserts included Eton mess, a traditional English "pudding" that incorporates meringue, custard, and fruit.

OPPOSITE Toronto's changing skyline is still dominated by the CN Tower. Day or night, there's a great wraparound view from the observation deck.

RIGHT A ferry to the Toronto Islands, a short hop from the city in Toronto Harbor.

3 *Laugh Factory* 8 p.m.

Come armed with pre-purchased tickets to see a show at **Second City** (51 Mercer Street; 416-343-0011; secondcity.com), the comedy theater that has sent famous alumni to Hollywood and *Saturday Night Live*. Over the decades, Second City Toronto (a sister of the equally renowned original company in Chicago) has spawned the careers of Mike Myers, John Candy, Dan Aykroyd, Gilda Radner, Andrea Martin, and Martin Short and has provided the city's most consistent, and most consistently funny, entertainment. If you'd rather hear music, stay in Kensington and go later to **Graffiti's Bar & Grill** (170 Baldwin Street; 416-506-6699) or **Last Temptation** (12 Kensington Avenue; 416-599-2551), long staples of Kensington Market's music and nightlife.

SATURDAY

4 *Art of the Angle* 10 a.m.

The **Royal Ontario Museum** (100 Queens Park; 416-586-8000; rom.on.ca), devoted to natural history and human culture, is a perennial crowd pleaser, and it makes a stunning mark on the landscape with its sharp-angled addition designed by Daniel Libeskind. Playing off the museum's vast mineral

collection, he designed the glass structure to look like mineral crystals (an immense heap of quartz, as one critic described it) and named it the Crystal. You won't see this whole museum in a short visit, but you can get acquainted with a small percentage of its five million artifacts.

5 *Diner on the Park* Noon

The sprawling **Trinity Bellwoods Park**, between Queen Street West and Dundas Street West, is filled with well-dressed locals, dogs, children, and yoga practitioners. Take a breather here, and grab a quick lunch at the **Swan Restaurant** (892 Queen Street West; 416-532-0452; $) at its edge. The Swan has 1950s décor and high-diner cuisine to melt the heart.

6 *The Gehry Contribution* 1 p.m.

Toronto has impressive architecture by the likes of Ludwig Mies van der Rohe, Santiago Calatrava, and Thom Mayne. But work by its favorite son, Frank Gehry, was missing until 2008, when the **Art Gallery of Ontario** (317 Dundas Street West; 416-979-6648; ago.net) reopened with a bold renovation by Gehry, who grew up just blocks from the century-old museum. He wrapped the original Beaux-Arts structure in sheets of billowing glass and swaths of Douglas fir, and added a spiraling wood staircase that pierces the glass roof to a contemporary-art wing. It was a stunning homecoming for an architect credited with helping other cities flourish, and it is an uplifting setting for viewing works by contemporary art stars like David Altmejd, Stephen Andrews, Murray Favro, Janice Kerbel, and Suzy Lake.

7 *It's All About the Game* 3:30 p.m.

For all its culture and nightlife, Toronto is still largely about hockey, and that requires a visit to the **Hockey Hall of Fame** (30 Yonge Street; 416-360-7765; hhof.com). The hall, situated partly in an old bank building, is full of great interactive exhibits for children and, for the hockey pilgrim, hallowed

ABOVE Daniel Libeskind's sharp-edged museum addition.

LEFT Chinatown, part of Toronto's lively ethnic mix.

skates, sticks, and sweaters (or, as they say in the United States, jerseys). But the great hall, with its glimmering, glass-encased National Hockey League trophies — including, when it's not on tour, the Stanley Cup itself — is perhaps the most beautifully meditative spot in all the city.

8 *Grown-up Dinner* 7 p.m.

Try on a slice of besuited old Toronto at the **Harbour Sixty Steakhouse** (60 Harbour Street; 416-777-2111; harboursixty.com; $$$$). The proper meal here is long and detailed, starting with the Seafood Tower appetizer and moving on to the steak of your choice, with appropriate wines and a rich dessert involving liqueurs, cream, and chocolate sauce. The restaurant's quarters were elegantly carved from the old lakeside Toronto Harbour Commission building. It's near other landmarks like the Rogers Centre (formerly SkyDome), home of the Blue Jays, and the CN Tower, at 1,815 feet North America's tallest.

9 *The Space Ship* 9:30 p.m.

Since you're this close to Toronto's most prominent landmark, you may as well go there. Tear yourself away from dinner early enough to allow for an elevator ride up to the **CN Tower**'s observation decks (301 Front Street West; 416-360-8500; cntower.ca). You'll be rewarded with a glittering nighttime view of the city's lighted skyscrapers and the Lake Ontario waterfront. If you're looking for real Canadian icons, there's also another one around here.

ABOVE AND BELOW A bagel lineup and fish by the heap, both at the crowded, sprawling Kensington Market. Shops and cafes here are packed tight and open late.

It's a short hop for a beer at **Wayne Gretzky's** restaurant (99 Blue Jays Way; 416-979-7825; gretzky's.com), where memorabilia of Gretzky's hockey career are in ample evidence. Gretzky's is underrated as a place to eat and drink, and among the popular appetizers on the menu are Grandma Gretzky's pirogi, said to be the favorite of the Great One himself.

SUNDAY

10 *Island Getaway* 10 a.m.

Make your way by taxi or streetcar to the **Toronto Islands ferry docks** at the foot of Bay Street at Queen's Quay (416-392-8193; torontoislandferryfinder.com). The islands, connected by small bridges, are a four-mile-long car-free harbor paradise, close enough to downtown to be reached on moving sidewalks in a new underwater pedestrian tunnel connecting to the small Billy Bishop Airport. A self-contained community of 600 people has thrived on the islands since the late 19th century, and it is the place where, in 1914, Babe Ruth hit his first professional home run. For visitors, walking the islands amid the cool lake breezes can be a day's reverie. You can rent a canoe or a bike, lie on a beach, visit the **Centreville Amusement Park** (Centre Island; 416-203-0405; centreisland.ca), and on many Sundays, find a concert or a festival.

OPPOSITE Cityscapes at the Art Gallery of Ontario.

THE BASICS

Toronto Pearson International Airport is about 25 minutes west of downtown by taxi or bus.

Thompson Toronto
550 Wellington Street West
416-640-7778
thompsonhotels.com
$$$
Sleek and cosmopolitan, particularly for those whose trip includes a bit of see-and-be-seen.

Hotel Ocho
195 Spadina Avenue
416-593-0885
hotelocho.com
$$
Chinatown textile factory from 1902; designed by local cutting-edge Design38.

The Hazelton Hotel
118 Yorkville Avenue
416-963-6300
thehazeltonhotel.com
$$$$
Luxury, fine amenities, and arresting style. Favored by visiting celebrities.

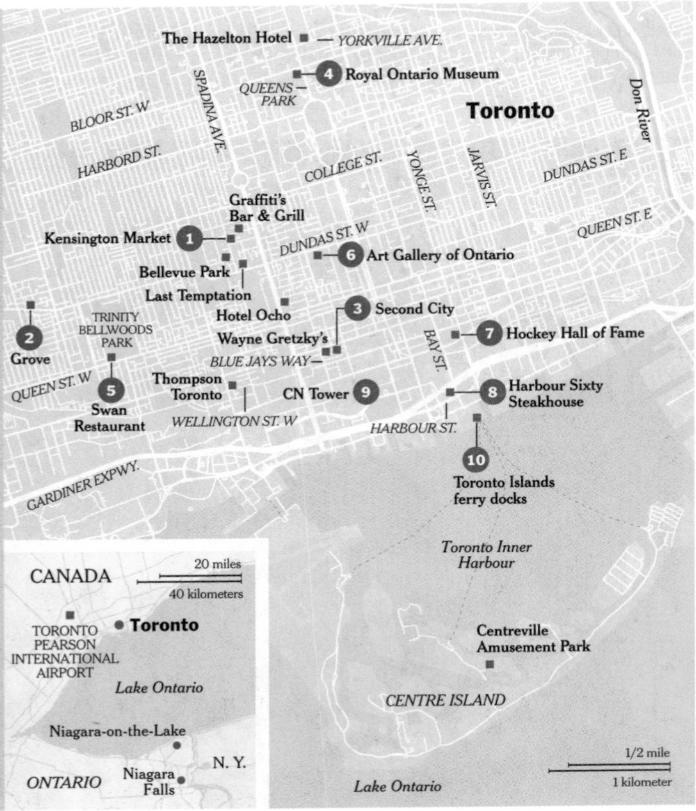

ART GALLERY OF ONTARIO
AGO
PICASSO
PAINTER,
SCULPTOR,
REBEL,
GENIUS.
PICASSO
FEAST
YOUR EYES,
DELIGHT
YOUR
TASTEBUDS.
FRANK
FRANK

CES
(416) 231-4788
TANGERINE
SALON
PARKING
PEDESTRIAN
X
STOP FOR
PEDESTRIANS

Toronto for Hipsters

Toronto's art and design scenes are thriving, and not just on the red carpets of the Toronto International Film Festival, held every September. Firmly established as the country's financial capital, the city is also its continually self-renewing cultural capital, seemingly limitless in its urbanity and diversity. Industrial zones have been reborn into gallery districts, dark alleys now lead to designer studios, and young innovators colonize new neighborhoods as soon as the old ones take on the taint of too much comfortable prosperity.

— BY DENNY LEE

FRIDAY

1 *West Enders* 3 p.m.

Toronto's cool scene seems to migrate west along Queen Street West every few years. It started out at Yonge Street, with punk rockers and art students pouring into sweaty clubs. Then, when mainstream stores like the Gap moved in, the scenesters fled west, past Bathurst Street, to a district now called **West Queen West** (westqueenwest.ca), where old appliance stores are still being carved into rough-hewn galleries and hunter-chic boutiques. Start your stroll along Toronto's art mile at Bathurst Street and go west. One of the more established among several raw spaces that showcase young Canadian artists is **Paul Petro Contemporary Art** (980 Queen Street West; 416-979-7874; paulpetro.com). Others are clustered steps away.

2 *Art Central* 4 p.m.

The anchor of this artistic cluster is the **Museum of Contemporary Canadian Art** (952 Queen Street West; 416-395-0067; mocca.ca), an airy warehouse-style gallery excellent for large-form photography and video projections. MOCCA collects works from a long list of Canadian artists, and its international exhibitions include recent works from around the world. The art tends to be challenging, well curated, and fun.

3 *Hip Tacos* 8 p.m.

For a taste of hipsterdom, put on a T-shirt and flannel shirt and squeeze into **Grand Electric** (1330 Queen Street West; 416-627-3459; grandelectricbar.com; $$). If the line is long, leave your name and stroll around a bit until you get a text announcing that seats are ready for you. The theme is Mexican, and the come-on is "tacos and bourbon seven days a week." Tacos are interesting, with flavors like scrapple and crispy caulfilower, and you don't have to have bourbon. Drinks run from Mexican beers to margaritas and Jesus Juice (gin, black cherry, soda).

4 *Trend North* 10:30 p.m.

Let the frat boys have College Street. And West Queen West has been overrun lately with 905ers, slang for out-of-towners with suburban area codes. The cool kids, it seems, are now migrating north along Ossington Avenue. Bookending the district are **Sweaty Betty's** (13 Ossington Avenue; 416-535-6861), a hole-in-the-wall with a brash jukebox, and **Communist's Daughter** (1149 Dundas Street West; 647-435-0103), an understated lounge. A trendy bar crawl is emerging in between, tucked among old Portuguese bakeries and kitchen supply stores.

SATURDAY

5 *Eggs and Egg Chairs* 10:30 a.m.

Brunch is serious business in this town, and discerning eaters are making their way to Leslieville, a once grimy neighborhood in East Toronto now packed with smart-looking cafes and midcentury-modern stores. Get your morning eggs at **Table 17**

OPPOSITE In a city of neighborhoods, one that's up and coming is Roncesvalles Village.

BELOW Brick row houses in Little Portugal.

(782 Queen Street East; 416-519-1851; table17.ca; $$), a country-style French bistro. Afterward, look over well-priced and well-curated antiques shops like **Machine Age Modern** (1000 Queen Street East; 416-461-3588; machineagemodern.com), which carries teak dining tables, George Nelson clocks, and other vintage modern treasures.

6 *O Calcutta* 1 p.m.

This is a city of minority neighborhoods, from the souvlaki joints in Greektown to the rainbow-hued windows of Gay Village. There are even two Chinatowns. But for color and spice, hop a taxi to Little India. The hilltop district spans just six blocks along Gerrard Street East, but it's jammed with more than a hundred stores and restaurants. Sparkly silks are piled high at **Chandan Fashion** (No. 1439; 416-462-0277; chandanfashion.ca). **Dubai Jewellers** (No. 1407; 416-465-1200) has a dazzling assortment of Indian-designed gold pieces. And for a midday snack, **Udupi Palace** (No. 1460; 416-405-8189; udupipalace.ca) is a bright restaurant that makes delicious dosas, chaats, and other South Indian treats.

7 *Made in Canada* 4 p.m.

Local fashion is disappointing, even in West Queen West. A handsome exception is **Klaxon Howl** (behind 706 Queen Street West; 647-436-6628; klaxonhowl.com), a homegrown men's label that blends vintage military gear with its own rugged work shirts, selvage denim jeans, and waxed cotton jackets. The design scene, on the other hand, is flourishing. For clever housewares, take a slight detour to **Made** (867 Dundas Street West; 416-607-6384; madedesign.ca), a gallery store that represents young product designers with a fresh and playful eye.

8 *Tofu and Pork Loin* 8 p.m.

Amid the explosion of new restaurants in Queen Street West, most serve excellent food and trend toward a rustic-hipster design, with filament lights and hardwood floors. One avant-garde example is **Ursa** (924 Queen Street West; 416-536-8963; ursa-restaurant.com; $$), where the tofu is made on site and the modern Canadian locavore cuisine includes dishes like whey-brined Niagara pork loin with kale, lentils, and sunchoke purée. It's served in a dining room with dark stained wood and sexy intimacy.

9 *Get Wiggy* 11 p.m.

O.K., College Street is not all bad, especially if you're single and in your mid-20s to 30s. A place to start is the unimaginatively named **College Street Bar** (No. 574; 416-533-2417; collegestreetbar.com). The dim space has brick walls, a woodsy patio, and a refreshing microbrew that draws a good-looking crowd of Web designers and writer types. Afterward, you can catch the 1 a.m. drag show at **El Convento Rico** (No. 750; 416-588-7800; elconventorico.com), a low-rent, high-octane club that attracts an exuberant mix of bachelorettes in plastic tiaras and muscular men with high voices.

SUNDAY

10 *Dim Sum Luxe* 11 a.m.

For inventive dim sum you won't find anywhere else, make a beeline for **Lai Wah Heen** (on the second floor of the Doubletree Hotel at 108 Chestnut Street; 416-977-9899; doubletree3.hilton.com; $$$), a

white-tablecloth restaurant. Expect fanciful creations like crab dumplings that resemble purple crabs and tofu paired with truffles and mushroom.

11 *Rendezvous with Roncey* 1 p.m.

Another area with newfound casual-hip cachet is Roncesvalles (fondly called Roncey), a west-end traditionally Polish enclave that now attracts youthful artistic types with its relatively low real estate prices and small-town-in-the-city feeling. Stroll Roncesvalles Avenue and drop in at places like **Sweetpea's** (No. 163; 416-537-3700; sweetpeablooms.ca) for stylish decorative objects and floral pieces; **Fresh Collective** (No. 401; 647-352-7123; freshcollective.com), which sells clothing by local designers; and **Defina** (No. 321; 416-534-4414; pizzeriadefina.com; $), where the pizzas are both well priced and artful, with combinations like steak and chanterelles or tomato sauce with wild boar meatballs.

OPPOSITE ABOVE An urban street scene in Toronto.

OPPOSITE BELOW Behind the counter at Sweetpeas, which sells stylish floral pieces and decorative objects.

ABOVE Inside Klaxon Howl, one of the original fashion stores in West Queen West.

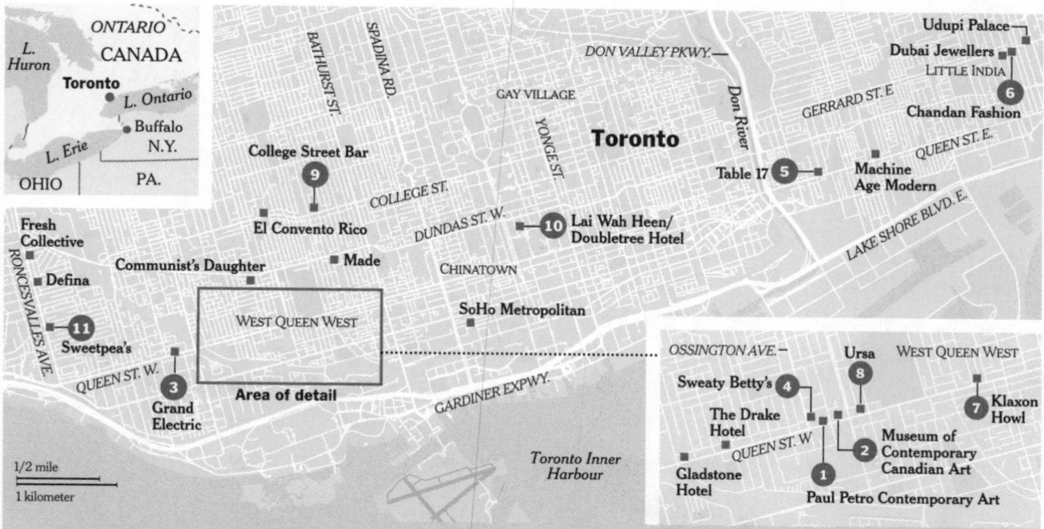

ONTARIO
CANADA
L. Huron
Toronto
L. Ontario
Buffalo
N.Y.
L. Erie
OHIO
PA.

BATHURST ST.
SPADINA RD.
DON VALLEY PKWY.
GAY VILLAGE
YONGE ST.
Don River
Toronto
GERRARD ST. E
Udupi Palace
Dubai Jewellers
LITTLE INDIA
6 Chandan Fashion
College Street Bar
9
5 Table 17
Machine Age Modern
QUEEN ST. E.
COLLEGE ST.
El Convento Rico
DUNDAS ST. W.
10 Lai Wah Heen/ Doubletree Hotel
LAKE SHORE BLVD. E.
Fresh Collective
RONCESVALLES AVE.
Defina
Communist's Daughter
Made
CHINATOWN
WEST QUEEN WEST
SoHo Metropolitan
11 Sweetpea's
QUEEN ST. W.
3 Grand Electric
Area of detail
GARDINER EXPWY.
1/2 mile
1 kilometer
Toronto Inner Harbour
OSSINGTON AVE.
Ursa
8
WEST QUEEN WEST
4 Sweaty Betty's
The Drake Hotel
7 Klaxon Howl
QUEEN ST. W
2 Museum of Contemporary Canadian Art
Gladstone Hotel
1 Paul Petro Contemporary Art

THE BASICS

Toronto receives flights from all over the world. In town, take taxis or use the network of streetcars, subways, and buses.

The Drake Hotel
1150 Queen Street West
416-531-5042
thedrakehotel.ca
$$
Evokes a luxury yacht.

Gladstone Hotel
1214 Queen Street West
416-531-4635
gladstonehotel.com
$$
Boutique hotel in a renovated Victorian. The bar is a popular gay-and-arts-scene hangout.

SoHo Metropolitan
318 Wellington Street West
416-599-8800
metropolitan.com/soho
$$$
Stylish boutique hotel in the heart of the city.

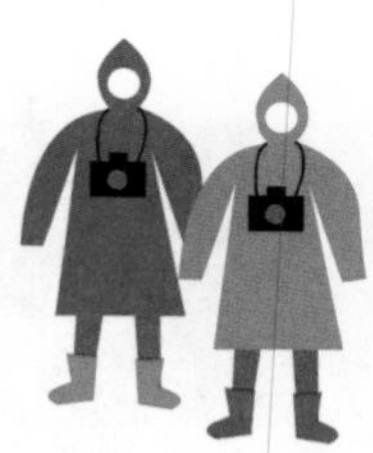

Niagara Falls

To grasp the might of Niagara Falls, you have to see and feel it close up, with the spray hitting your face and the thunder of the water drowning out all other sound. Niagara is not by any particular statistic the largest waterfall in the world, but there is a good case to be made that it is the most impressive. The falls are very tall, very wide, and gracefully shaped. They drop in a single long descent and run year round with a massive, unimaginable volume. They are majestic and beautiful. They are also international, shared by the United States and Canada. Niagara Falls, Ontario, has the wide-angle vista and more commercial attractions; Niagara Falls, New York, has a close-up view of the roaring Niagara River and a more natural feeling. The border is easy to cross, especially on foot, so why limit yourself to one side or the other? Hop back and forth to get the best of both Niagaras.

— BY BARBARA IRELAND

FRIDAY

1 *Feet Across the Border* 5 p.m.

Cars sometimes line up for hours to cross the international border at the **Rainbow Bridge**, a few hundred yards downriver from the falls. But on the walkway it's a breeze—a 10-minute stroll for 50 cents in American or Canadian currency (niagarafallsbridges.com). Customs agents at each end are pedestrian-friendly, though you must have your passport. If you're staying on the American side, make your first crossing now. If your hotel is in Canada, wait until tomorrow. Either way, this is one of the most scenic saunters you will ever take.

2 *Brinkmanship* 6 p.m.

Push into the crowds on the riverfront walkway in Canada and see the whole geological spectacle at once. The imposing cascade on the left, 850 feet wide, is the **American Falls**. The supercharged one on the right, nearly half a mile wide, is the **Horseshoe Falls**, often called the Canadian Falls even though the international border actually runs through it. Stop at the Horseshoe brink and wait your turn to be doused at the rail by spray from thousands of tons of water plunging down every second. Impressed? This thundering mass is only half of the river's natural flow. The other 50 percent (75 percent in the off-season) is channeled away underground to hydroelectric plants.

OPPOSITE Niagara Falls State Park offers jaw-dropping up-close views of both the American and Canadian Falls.

3 *Wine and Bacon* 7 p.m.

From the terrace at **Edgewaters Tap & Grill** (6345 Niagara Parkway; 905-356-2217; niagaraparks.com/dining; $$), the tourist hordes below seem far away. Relax and sample one of the Niagara Region wines, like the Inniskillin Riesling. For a casual dinner, try a hearty sandwich made with the high-quality Canadian bacon hard to find south of the border. Afterward, explore shady **Queen Victoria Park**, where gracious landscaping reflects the English style.

4 *Over the Top* 9 p.m.

You want to hate **Clifton Hill**, a garish strip of funhouses, glow-in-the-dark miniature-golf palaces, 4-D theaters, wax museums, and noisy bars. But tackiness on this level cries out to be experienced. So watch a multinational crowd shovel tickets into blinking game machines at the Great Canadian Midway. Observe the story-high monster chomping a hamburger atop the House of Frankenstein. Shop for maple candy and a moose puppet. And climb aboard the **SkyWheel** Ferris wheel (4950 Clifton Hill; cliftonhill.com) for five vertiginous revolutions and a view of the colored lights projected nightly on the falls. (Oh right, there are waterfalls here. Remember?)

SATURDAY

5 *The Central Park* 10 a.m.

Frederick Law Olmsted and Frederic Church were among the 19th-century champions of a radical idea, public parks at Niagara Falls, erasing a clutter of factories and tourist traps (at some locations, visitors had paid to see the falls through a peephole in a fence). The Free Niagara movement succeeded on both sides of the border, and on the American side Olmsted designed landscapes at the crest of both waterfalls and on Goat Island, which separates them. Explore the woods and walkways of the resulting **Niagara Falls State Park** (716-278-1796; niagarafallsstatepark.com) to find what remains

of the essential experience of Niagara. For an enticing mix of quiet glades and furious rapids, venture out on the tiny **Three Sisters Islands** above the thunderous Horseshoe.

6 *Wings Optional* 1 p.m.

Buffalo chicken wings were invented just 20 miles away, and the menu at the **Top of the Falls** restaurant (in the state park; 716-278-0337; $$) won't let you forget it. Partake or not; alternatives include salads, burgers, and wraps. Every table has a falls view.

7 *Why the Waterfall?* 2 p.m.

You'll hunt in vain on both sides of the river for a straightforward geological explanation of Niagara Falls. At the **Niagara Gorge Discovery Center** in the state park, look selectively at the displays and ask questions to tease out the basic facts. What's falling is the water of the Great Lakes. The falls are on the move upriver, naturally receding as much as 6 feet a year. There's a giant whirlpool where they took a sharp turn 40 centuries ago. (A Canadian attempt at explaining Niagara, a film called *Niagara's Fury*, niagarasfury.com, is entertaining for children but also not especially informative, mixing cartoon stereotypes with snippets of textbook language.) Outside the Discovery Center, a trail heads toward the deep Niagara Gorge, where hikers get within a few feet of the largest standing waves in North America. Don't bring the kayak: these rapids are Level 6.

8 *The Close-up* 3 p.m.

Many of the contrived attractions at Niagara Falls are overhyped and disappointing. But the **Maid of the Mist** tour boats (maidofthemist.com) have been thrilling customers since 1846. Chug out to the base of the Horseshoe on one of these sturdy craft, struggle to look up 170 feet to the top through the torrents, and you'll grasp the power of what brought you here. At the end of the ride, you can hang on to your flimsy slicker and take a wet but exhilarating hike to the base of the American Falls. You'll no longer find the *Maid* in Canada, as the Hornblower Niagara Cruises (905-642-4272; niagarafallstourism.com/play/attractions) have taken over the *Maid*'s old home turf, but the thrill is the same on either boat.

9 *Culinary Canada* 7 p.m.

AG, the soothing, stylish restaurant in the **Sterling Inn & Spa** (5195 Magdalen Street, Niagara Falls, Ontario; 289-292-0000; sterlingniagara.com; $$$), serves imaginative dishes using seasonal Canadian ingredients, paired with local wines. One summer menu included basil-and-potato-encrusted Lake Huron trout and pork tenderloin stuffed with macerated Niagara fruit. The desserts are good, too, but if you're not up for one, you can get by on the eye candy of the red, white, and crystal dining room.

SUNDAY

10 *Vineyards Haven* 10 a.m.

Leave the falls behind and drive north along the river in Canada on the lovely **Niagara Parkway**. Beyond placid Queenston, where an American attack was turned back in the War of 1812, the Niagara turns tame, and wineries, peach orchards, manor-like houses, and an inviting bicycle path line the road. The tasting rooms pour chardonnays, pinot noirs, and the regional specialty, ice wine. At **Inniskillin** (on the Parkway at Line 3; 905-468-9910; inniskillin.com), tours and signboards explain grape-friendly local conditions. **Reif Estate** (15608 Niagara Parkway; 905-468-9463; reifwinery.com) has a gimmicky but pleasant Wine Sensory Garden. **Peller Estates** (just off the parkway at 290 John Street West; peller.com) pairs its vintages with a posh restaurant. Between the reds and whites, stop in at the **Kurtz Orchards Gourmet Marketplace** (16006 Niagara Parkway; 905-468-2937; kurtzorchards.com), where you can munch enough free samples of breads, tapenades, jams, cheeses, and nut butters to take you all the way to dinner.

OPPOSITE ABOVE Slickers are essential equipment for exploring the Cave of the Winds at the American Falls.

THE BASICS

By car, Niagara Falls is eight hours from New York City, 90 minutes from Toronto, and 45 minutes from the Buffalo Niagara airport. At the falls, walk and take trolleys and people movers. For exploring, drive a car.

Sterling Inn & Spa
5195 Magdalen Street, Niagara Falls, Ontario
877-783-7772
sterlingniagara.com
$$$
A boutique-hotel oasis at the edge of the tourist maelstrom.

Doubletree Fallsview Resort & Spa
6039 Fallsview Boulevard, Niagara Falls, Ontario
905-358-3817
niagarafallsdoubletree.com
$$
On a hill overlooking the falls.

The Giacomo
222 First Street, Niagara Falls, New York
716-299-0200
thegiacomo.com
$$$
Renovated Art Deco building.

ELLICOTT·SQUARE

Buffalo

Prospering where East Coast railroads met Great Lakes cargo, Buffalo, New York, was a rich city around 1900, the same era when dynamic innovators were transforming American architecture. Wealth and vision came together in works by Frank Lloyd Wright, Louis Sullivan, H. H. Richardson, Frederick Law Olmsted, Eliel and Eero Saarinen, and more—arrayed amid blocks of Victorian houses and lavish mansions. When industry eventually collapsed, a shaken and considerably poorer Buffalo slowly realized it had a legacy. Now the city is eager to show off its remarkable architectural collection. Visit in the months when Buffalo gets a glorious payback for its snowy winters with some of the best summer weather in the country.

— BY BARBARA IRELAND

FRIDAY

1 *Lake to River* 2 p.m.

At **Erie Basin Marina** (329 Erie Street), a popular spot with sailors, joggers, and just about everyone else, climb the small observation tower for a view of grain elevators (a Buffalo invention), an 1833 lighthouse, and the final expanse of Lake Erie as it narrows to become the Niagara River. The trees a couple of miles across the water are in Canada—British troops came across to burn Buffalo in the War of 1812, but all is now forgiven. Have a drink and a snack on the patio at **Templeton Landing** (2 Templeton Terrace; 716-852-7337; templetonlanding.com; $$) or at **Liberty Hound** (1 Naval Park Cove; 716-845-9173; libertyhoundbuffalo.com; $$), and continue your waterfront walk at **Canalside** (canalsidebuffalo.com), a newly developed park at the nearby terminus of the original Erie Canal.

2 *She's the Babe* 4 p.m.

Architectural preservation has achieved the status of a local religion, and the singer Ani DiFranco, a Buffalo native, made a creative contribution with **Babeville** (341 Delaware Avenue; 716-852-3835; babevillebuffalo.com), an 1876 red sandstone church adapted into a public event space and the headquarters of her Righteous Babe Records. To get there, drive north on Delaware Avenue past the massive Art Deco City Hall and the McKinley Monument, a marble apology to the president who was assassinated in Buffalo in 1901. Inside Babeville, look over the current show at **Hallwalls** (716-854-1694; hallwalls.org), a contemporary art gallery.

3 *The Temple of Wings* 8 p.m.

Take a table at the **Anchor Bar** (1047 Main Street; 716-886-8920; anchorbar.com; $), where the fame of Buffalo chicken wings began, for a plate of the spicy originals and the tale of their invention by a resourceful cook. Add a salad and some Canadian beer, and stay for live jazz. Another nightlife option is **Mike A's** (391 Washington Street; 716-253-6453; mikealafayette.com), an Art Deco-style cocktail bar in the Lafayette Hotel.

SATURDAY

4 *Sullivan and Friends* 9:45 a.m.

You'll get a quick course in 19th-century American architecture in a downtown walking tour with **Preservation Buffalo Niagara** (617 Main Street; 716-852-3300; buffalotours.org). Louis Sullivan's 1895 **Guaranty Building** (28 Church Street), a floral fantasia of intricately molded terra cotta enclosing a steel skeleton, stands across a narrow street from **St. Paul's Cathedral** (128 Pearl Street), designed by Richard Upjohn, the architect of New York City's Trinity Church. Nearby, the Gothic Revival **Erie Community College** (121 Ellicott Street) was built in lavish style as a federal building when the city's friends included President Grover Cleveland, a former Buffalo mayor and briefly the town hangman. Daniel Burnham's elaborate **Ellicott Square Building** (295 Main Street) has been carefully preserved—from the Medusa heads peering out from its roof line perimeter to its refined interior atrium—by its current owner, Carl Paladino, who is better known for his boisterous 2010 campaign for governor of New York. A recent restoration returned former glory to the **Hotel Lafayette** (391 Washington Street), designed in 1902 by Louise Bethune, the first professionally recognized American female architect.

OPPOSITE Daniel Burnham's Ellicott Square Building, one of Buffalo's many architectural gems.

5 *Olmsted Next Door* Noon

Have a panini at the cafe in the **Albright-Knox Art Gallery** (1285 Elmwood Avenue; 716-882-8700; albrightknox.org) and then take a quick look around, concentrating on mid-20th-century paintings, where the collection is particularly strong. Seymour H. Knox, a Buffalo banker and heir to part of the F. W. Woolworth fortune, was an early patron of Abstract Expressionists like Willem de Kooning, Mark Rothko, and, especially, Clyfford Still, and he gave the gallery hundreds of their works. Look out from the back portico, past the caryatids sculptured by Augustus Saint-Gaudens, at a view of 350-acre Delaware Park, the "central park" of an extensive system of parks and connecting parkways designed for Buffalo by Frederick Law Olmsted.

ABOVE A 19th-century grain elevator and a 21st-century marina in the Buffalo harbor.

BELOW The permanent collection at the Albright-Knox Art Gallery includes hundreds of Abstract Expressionist works.

6 *Wright Writ Large* 2 p.m.

Frank Lloyd Wright liked nothing more than an open checkbook to work with, and when he designed a home in 1904 for Darwin Martin, a Buffalo businessman, in effect he had one. The result was the **Martin House Complex** (125 Jewett Parkway; 716-856-3858; darwinmartinhouse.org) — a sprawling 15,000-square-foot Prairie-style house filled with art glass and Wright-designed furniture, two smaller houses on the same property, a conservatory, stables, gardens, and a 100-foot-long pergola. A $50 million restoration has brought it back from long neglect and added an ethereally transparent visitor center designed by Toshiko Mori. Tour the complex, a stunningly beautiful and intricate work of art, and hear the stories. Martin became a lifelong friend and lent Wright tens of thousands of dollars (which were not repaid). Wright's obsession with detail extended to designing a dress for Mrs. Martin to wear in the house, but he resisted giving her a closet.

7 *A Little Richardson* 4 p.m.

Back on Elmwood Avenue, drive south, past the **Burchfield-Penney Art Center** (burchfieldpenney.org), a gallery with a collection of eye-poppingly original paintings by the mystically inclined Charles Burchfield. Turn onto Forest Avenue and look behind a graceful screen of trees (another Olmsted landscape) for the majestic towers of the **H.H. Richardson Complex**, a former mental hospital that is now being restored for more mainstream uses. It was one of Richardson's earliest and largest buildings in the style now known as Richardsonian Romanesque.

8 *Retail Break* 4:30 p.m.

Shops are sprinkled along Elmwood Avenue from Bidwell Parkway to West Ferry Street. Browse through jewelry, clothing, handcrafted curios, and books. Then, if you're not yet tired of National Historic Landmarks, drive a few blocks to the 1940 **Kleinhans Music Hall** (3 Symphony Circle), where Eliel and Eero Saarinen married upswept lines and near-perfect acoustics. Its carefully shaped wooden interior walls were "as warm as the wood in my violin," Isaac Stern once told an audience there.

ABOVE A sailboat heads out toward the open waters of Lake Erie from the Erie Basin Marina. The waterfront has been redeveloped for residences and recreation.

RIGHT Kleinhans Music Hall, designed by Eliel and Eero Saarinen, delivers near-perfect acoustics for a busy program of classical music performances.

9 *The French Style* 8 p.m.

Rue Franklin (341 Franklin Street; 716-852-4416; ruefranklin.com; $$$), whose reputation as Buffalo's best restaurant is rarely challenged, serves French wines and updated French food, including a popular prix fixe dinner, in a building that feels a bit like a cozy French country cottage. Reserve a table on the quiet back terrace.

SUNDAY

10 *Early to Betty's* 9 a.m.

The scones and coffee are great at **Betty's** (370 Virginia Street; 716-362-0633; bettysbuffalo.com; $), but there's more for breakfast, including spinach potato pancakes with bacon or scrambled tofu hash, served in a setting of brick walls and changing work by local artists. Get there early to beat the crowd.

11 *Wright on the Lake* 11:30 a.m.

It's a leisurely drive south along Lake Erie to **Graycliff** (6472 Old Lake Shore Road, Derby; 716-947-9217; graycliffestate.org), the summer house that Frank Lloyd Wright designed in the 1920s for Darwin Martin. The house and its lakeside setting are inspiring, but the story ends sadly here. Martin lost his fortune in the Great Depression, and his family eventually sold or abandoned all of their Wright-designed properties. Remarking on Martin's death in 1935, Wright said he had lost "my best friend."

ABOVE A shop at the restored Hotel Lafayette.

OPPOSITE Part of Frederick Law Olmsted's parkway design.

THE BASICS

Fly into Buffalo Niagara International Airport or drive 100 miles from Toronto or 400 miles from New York City. A car is necessary.

The Mansion
414 Delaware Avenue
716-886-3300
mansionondelaware.com
$$$
Luxurious 28-room hotel in an elegant oversized house built in 1869.

Hyatt Regency Buffalo
300 Pearl Street
716-856-1234
buffalo.hyatt.com
$$
Built in and around a 1923 office building.

The Hotel Lafayette
391 Washington Street
716-853-1505
$$
thehotellafayette.com
Restored landmark hotel designed by Louise Bethune, America's first fully recognized female architect.

1/2 mile
1 kilometer
Martin House Complex 6
JEWETT PKWY.
Albright-Knox Art Gallery 5
7 Burchfield-Penney Art Center
198
H.H. Richardson Complex
FOREST AVE.
Buffalo
Niagara River
190
LAFAYETTE AVE.
RICHMOND AVE.
ELMWOOD AVE.
W. FERRY ST.
CANADA
NEW YORK
DELAWARE AVE.
PEARL ST.
Kleinhans Music Hall 8
NIAGARA ST.
PORTER AVE.
E. NORTH ST.
MAIN ST.
3 Anchor Bar
33
JEFFERSON AVE.
VIRGINIA ST.
Betty's 10
The Mansion
9 Rue Franklin
Babeville/Hallwalls 2
4 Preservation Buffalo Niagara
PEARL ST.
Hyatt Regency Buffalo
Templeton Landing
Erie Basin Marina 1
Area of detail
Lake Erie
Liberty Hound
Canalside
CANADA
20 miles
40 kilometers
Toronto
Lake Ontario
Niagara Falls
ONTARIO
Buffalo
11 Graycliff
Lake Erie
Derby
NEW YORK
90
Guaranty Building
Mike A's/ Hotel Lafayette
St. Paul's Cathedral
Ellicott Square Building
Erie Community College

Pittsburgh

Pittsburgh has undergone a striking renaissance from a down-and-out smokestack town to a gleaming cultural oasis known for educational and technical prowess. There are great restaurants, excellent shopping, breakthrough galleries, and prestigious museums. The convergence of three rivers and surrounding green hills make a surprisingly pretty urban setting, and with abandoned steel mills long since torn down, more of the natural beauty of this part of Pennsylvania has emerged. If the Pirates are in town, head to the waterfront ballpark. Besides seeing the game, you'll have an excuse to explore downtown and take in the river views.

— BY JEFF SCHLEGEL

FRIDAY

1 *Gridiron and Steel* 4 p.m.

Get to know what makes the city tick at the **Senator John Heinz History Center** (1212 Smallman Street; 412-454-6000; pghhistory.org), which chronicles past and present glories from United States Steel to the Pittsburgh Steelers. This is actually a twofer: the main museum is devoted to everything from the Heinz food empire to the city's polyglot population. The upper two floors are occupied by the Western Pennsylvania Sports Museum.

2 *Waterfall Dining* 7 p.m.

The martini menu changes almost as often as the seasonal specials at **Soba** (5847 Ellsworth Avenue; 412-362-5656; sobapa.com; $$$), a pan-Asian restaurant with a Victorian exterior and a Zen-like interior that features a two-story wall of cascading water. Scan the menu for dishes like lobster maki and seafood and tandoori-grilled salmon. The wine list is extensive, and the vibe is upscale and trendy, but not in an overbearing way. If you arrive early, grab a special martini, perhaps made with ginger-infused vodka, on the rooftop deck.

3 *Brillo Pad* 10 p.m.

Brillobox (4104 Penn Avenue; 412-621-4900; brillobox.net) feels like an arty bar in New York's East Village — little wonder, considering the 30-something artist couple who own it are former New Yorkers. They came back home to Pittsburgh, they said, to contribute to the city's growing arts scene, and if the name of their establishment reminds you of Andy Warhol, you're on the right track. Pittsburgh is Warhol's hometown, and the Andy Warhol Museum Downtown holds 12,000 of his works. Brillobox catches some of his adventurous spirit with art-film screenings, spoken-word performances, and live music held upstairs in a room decked out in velvet wallpaper and murals. But you can just hang loose in the downstairs bar with its atmospheric red lights and an eclectic jukebox that has Goldfrapp, Patsy Cline, and Snoop Dogg.

SATURDAY

4 *Nosh 'n' Stroll* 10:30 a.m.

By night, the formerly industrial **Strip District** is filled with partygoers bouncing between bars and clubs. But on Saturday mornings, the parallel thoroughfares of Penn Avenue and Smallman Street (roughly between 16th and 26th Streets) are turned into a sprawling outdoor market with international food kiosks that serve Middle Eastern kebabs, Italian sausages, and Greek baklava. Shop for produce, clothing, and vintage knickknacks as accordionists and mariachi bands provide a festive soundtrack.

OPPOSITE The Mattress Factory on the North Side, home to room-size installations from artists like Yayoi Kusama.

BELOW The Duquesne Incline, a funicular first opened in 1877, takes passengers to Mount Washington for a view of the city.

Take a breather with a cup of coffee and a mele, a fruit-filled pastry, at **La Prima Espresso Bar** (205 21st Street; 412-281-1922; laprima.com), where the old men sitting at the outdoor tables look like they've been sipping espresso and playing cards for eternity.

5 *No Beds Here* 1 p.m.

If you haven't already been there, don't miss the **Andy Warhol Museum** (117 Sandusky Street; 412-237-8300; warhol.org). For more radical contemporary art, beat a new path in the Mexican War Streets neighborhood to the **Mattress Factory** (505 Jacksonia Street; 412-231-3169; mattress.org). Housed in a former mattress factory, the museum is dedicated to room-size art installations.

6 *Hard-to-Find Items* 3 p.m.

Some of the city's funkiest shopping can be found in the **16:62 Design Zone** (1662designzone.com), which spans the Strip District and Lawrenceville neighborhoods. It has more than 100 locally owned shops that focus on design, home décor, contemporary art, clothing, and architecture. Among the more interesting is the nonprofit **Society for Contemporary Craft** (2100 Smallman Street; 412-261-7003; contemporarycraft.org), a gallery and store that showcases handmade crafts like jewelry by national and local artists

7 *Grab the Camera* 6 p.m.

The best views of Pittsburgh are from Mount Washington, and the best way to get there—or at least the most fun—is up the **Duquesne Incline** (1197 West Carson Street; 412-381-1665; duquesneincline.org). One of two surviving hillside cable cars from the 1870s, it takes three minutes to climb 800 feet to Grandview Avenue. There's a neat little history museum at the top that has old newspaper clippings, but the real spectacle is the view of downtown Pittsburgh, where the Allegheny and Monongahela Rivers meet to form the Ohio.

8 *City Under Glass* 7 p.m.

While you're up there, Grandview Avenue is also home to a cliff-hugging restaurant row. For amazing seafood to go with the river views, make reservations for the **Monterey Bay Fish Grotto** (1411 Grandview Avenue; 412-481-4414; montereybayfishgrotto.com; $$$). This tri-level restaurant sits atop a 10-story apartment building. Jackets aren't required, but nice clothes are apropos. Fresh fish is flown in daily, and the menu changes often. On one visit the specials included a charcoal-grilled Atlantic salmon with fresh peppered strawberries in a red-wine sauce.

9 *Off-Downtown Theater* 9 p.m.

Generally regarded as Pittsburgh's most innovative theater company, the **City Theatre** (1300 Bingham Street; 412-431-2489; citytheatrecompany.org) does challenging plays that aren't likely to be staged in the downtown cultural district. Housed in a pair of former churches, it has both a 272-seat mainstage and a more intimate 110-seat theater. After the show, stop in at **Dee's Cafe** (1314 East Carson Street; 412-431-1314; deescafe.com), a comfortable, jam-packed dive that is part of what by some counts is the country's longest continuous stretch of bars.

SUNDAY

10 *Brunch and Bric-a-Brac* 11 a.m.

One of the city's more unusual brunch spots is the **Zenith** (86 South 26th Street; 412-481-4833; zenithpgh.com; $-$$), a combination art gallery,

vintage clothing store, antiques shop, and vegetarian restaurant. For those who can't stomach tofu, brunch includes traditional staples like eggs, pancakes, and French toast. It gets busy, so to avoid the line, get there before it opens at 11.

11 *Brain Food* 12:30 p.m.

The Oakland district teems with intellectual energy from the University of Pittsburgh, Carnegie Mellon University, and several museums. Start out at the Nationality Rooms at the **Cathedral of Learning** (4200 Fifth Avenue; 412-624-6000; nationalityrooms.pitt.edu), a 42-story Gothic-style tower on the Pittsburgh campus with 27 classrooms, each devoted to a different nationality. Then head over to the renowned **Carnegie Museum of Art** (412-622-3131; cmoa.org) and **Carnegie Museum of Natural History** (carnegiemnh.org), both at 4400 Forbes Avenue, for Degas and dinosaurs. Before leaving, pick up a handy walking tour of Oakland and public art in the neighborhood.

OPPOSITE ABOVE The unassuming exterior of the Andy Warhol Museum on Sandusky Street. Warhol was from Pittsburgh, and the museum holds thousands of his works. Those on display are spread over six floors of gallery space.

OPPOSITE BELOW A table with a view out over the city at the Monterey Bay Fish Grotto, a dining spot on the Grandview restaurant row.

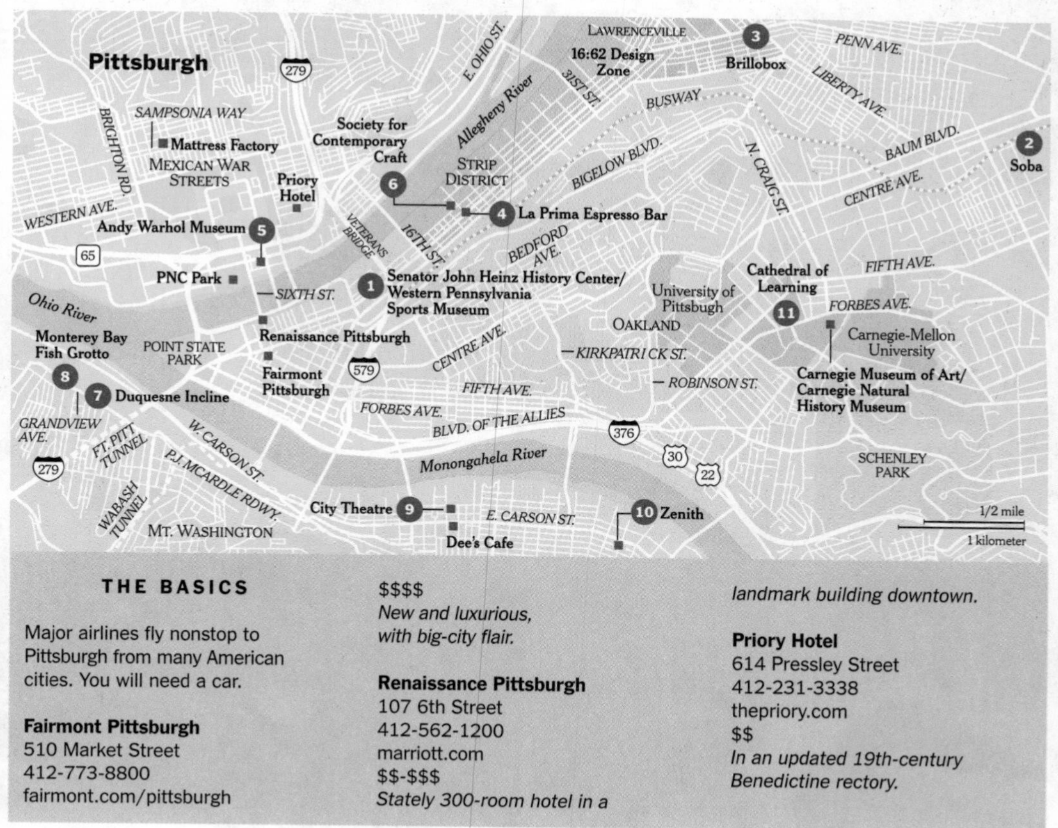

THE BASICS

Major airlines fly nonstop to Pittsburgh from many American cities. You will need a car.

Fairmont Pittsburgh
510 Market Street
412-773-8800
fairmont.com/pittsburgh
$$$$
New and luxurious, with big-city flair.

Renaissance Pittsburgh
107 6th Street
412-562-1200
marriott.com
$$-$$$
Stately 300-room hotel in a landmark building downtown.

Priory Hotel
614 Pressley Street
412-231-3338
thepriory.com
$$
In an updated 19th-century Benedictine rectory.

The Laurel Highlands

In the Laurel Highlands of southwestern Pennsylvania, cornfields undulate between forested slopes and rivers spill downward in a rush of whitewater, luring fishermen and rafters. These green hills gave Frank Lloyd Wright the setting for Fallingwater, his cantilevered masterpiece of a house set over a swiftly flowing creek. Nearby, another client hired Wright to design Kentuck Knob, a quirky counterpart. And a bit north in Acme, a Wright ranch house saved from demolition in Illinois arrived in pieces, completing the setting for a Wrightian weekend. Balancing the architectural immersion with a little history and some outdoor adventures creates a memorable experience under the shiny leaves of the mountain laurel.

— BY BETHANY SCHNEIDER AND BARBARA IRELAND

FRIDAY

1 *A Matter of Necessity* 4 p.m.

Everybody has to start somewhere, and George Washington's first battlefield command was in 1754 at what is now **Fort Necessity National Battlefield** (off Route 40 in Farmington; 724-329-5805; nps.gov/fone). The reconstruction of the fort that Washington's forces threw together in their moment of necessity (they were about to be attacked) is terrifying in its meagerness. Sure enough, the French and their Indian allies made mincemeat of the British led by Colonel Washington, then just 22. But other victories came later, and the French and Indian War made Washington's reputation. Rangers evoke the feel of combat in the era when these highlands were virgin forest, delivering dramatic lines like "Half King, Washington's Indian ally, washed his hands in the brains of the French commander."

2 *Dinner Downtown* 7 p.m.

Wash your own hands in something more appropriate as you tidy up for dinner. Find it in the old town center of Uniontown at **Caileigh's** (105 East Fayette Street; 724-437-9463; caileighs.com; $$). Uniontown was home to coal and steel barons in the boomtown days of this part of Pennsylvania, and Caileigh's occupies one of the era's mansions. As you settle in for dishes like spiced duck or seared grouper topped with Puerto Rican crab, chat with your waiter about General George C. Marshall, father of the Marshall Plan and Uniontown's favorite son.

SATURDAY

3 *The Masterwork* 8:15 a.m.

Arrive in plenty of time for your in-depth tour at **Fallingwater** (1491 Mill Run Road, Mill Run; 724-329-8501; fallingwater.org; tours must be purchased several weeks in advance). You're up early, but it's worth it; this tour, longer than the basic version, allows more time inside the house and more leisure to absorb the complexity of its construction. Projecting airily over a waterfall on Bear Run Creek, its platforms mimicking the striations of the local rock, the house still looks as strikingly original and eerily perfect for its setting as it did when it was completed in 1939. Instantly famous, it resuscitated the faltering career of its creator, Frank Lloyd Wright, who was then 72. No matter how many times you've seen it, Fallingwater is breathtaking. On one bright May day, a middle-aged visitor from Scotland, dressed in a blue anorak, stood with tears flowing down his cheeks at his first sight of it. The guide assured him this was normal.

OPPOSITE Frank Lloyd Wright's Fallingwater, the famed masterwork cantilevered over a waterfall in the woods of the Laurel Highlands.

RIGHT The Cucumber Falls at Ohiopyle State Park.

4 *Lingering for Lunch* Noon

Fallingwater's inviting grounds, not to mention various vantage points for your perfect photo, will keep you busy until lunchtime, so stay for a sandwich at the cafe. The shopping is good, too. At the Fallingwater Museum Store, even the souvenir mugs are classy.

5 *A Bike in the Forest* 1 p.m.

In Confluence, a tiny, charming town wedged between the tines of three converging rivers, you'll find the gateway to the most beautiful 11 miles of the 150-mile **Great Allegheny Passage** rail trail (atatrail.org), following an old railroad bed. Rent a mountain bike or a recumbent (easy on the body if you're not a regular cyclist) from one of the village outfitters, and glide through the dreamy woodland of **Ohiopyle State Park** (dcnr.state.pa.us/stateparks/findapark/ohiopyle/).

6 *Nature's Water Park* 3 p.m.

Cool down in daredevil style at the **Natural Waterslides**, still in the park, just south of Ohiopyle on Route 381. Sit in the stream, and it barrels you across smooth rocks and through a curving sluice, producing an adrenaline rush and maybe a few bruises. Dry off by **Cucumber Falls** around the corner on Route 2019, a bridal veil that splashes into a pool the pale green and rusty red of a glass of Pimm's. When you feel refreshed, cycle back to Confluence and drop off your bike.

7 *Going Usonian* 7:30 p.m.

Make your way over hill and dale to secluded **Polymath Park** (187 Evergreen Lane, Acme; 877-833-7829; polymathpark.com), a quiet, tree-shaded resort whose intriguing business plan centers on architectural preservation. You made your dinner reservations here long ago, so take a little time now to explore the shaded drives and find the **Duncan House**, one of the modest houses that Frank Lloyd Wright designed for the middle class and christened Usonians. Rescued from its original site in Illinois, where it was threatened with teardown, it was moved to Pennsylvania in thousands of numbered pieces and, after some cliffhanger misadventures, painstakingly reassembled here. The house is vastly more modest than the tour de force of Fallingwater, but it bears the unmistakable marks of Wright's ingenuity. It is available for short-term rentals, so be respectful of the tenants who may be inside and view it from a distance. (Unless, of course, you are the lucky tenant this weekend yourself, in which case you are already well into a uniquely memorable experience.) Wind along the other drives to find three more houses, designed by Wright apprentices and also available as lodging.

8 *Food of the Polymaths* 8 p.m.

The fare runs to entrees like pecan-crusted brook trout and wood-fired filet mignon at **Tree Tops Restaurant** (877-833-7829; $$-$$$) on the Polymath Park grounds. Soak in the atmosphere and share the evening with the other Wright groupies who will have found their way to this quiet spot. If the night is right, you can exchange some stories.

SUNDAY

9 *His Lordship's Getaway* 10 a.m.

Kentuck Knob (723 Kentuck Road, Chalk Hill; 724-329-1901; kentuckknob.com), in another wooded

OPPOSITE ABOVE AND RIGHT Wright's Duncan House, reassembled in Polymath Park after facing destruction on its original site in Lisle, Illinois, is available for short-term stays.

OPPOSITE BELOW A swivel gun demonstration at Fort Necessity National Battlefield, where Colonel George Washington lost a battle at age 22.

setting, represents the middle ground of your Wright weekend: less renowned than the spectacular Fallingwater, but far more impressive than the Duncan House. A stone-and-cypress hexagon with a balcony ending in a stone prow, it is full of eccentric angles and unexpected viewpoints that add up to the usual Wrightian mastery. Wright designed it as a hillside home for a local ice cream magnate, but the current owner is a British lord who not only lets the public traipse through but also displays his collectibles, from Claes Oldenburg sculptures to bullets from Custer's Last Stand. Take the tour and then take your time on the grounds.

10 *Tuck It In* 1 p.m.

Locals praise the food at the **Out of the Fire Cafe** (3784 State Route 31, Donegal; 724-593-4200; outofthefirecafe.com; $$), and it's a good spot for a substantial Sunday dinner: an apple-stuffed pork chop with garlic potatoes, perhaps, or pan-seared Scottish salmon with sweet potato and roasted corn hash. Tuck it away, and it should get you all the way back home.

THE BASICS

The Laurel Highlands are southeast of Pittsburgh. The country roads can be confusing. Arm yourself with maps, a GPS unit, and a cellphone.

The Duncan House
187 Evergreen Lane, Acme
877-833-7829
polymathpark.com
$$$$
Designed by Frank Lloyd Wright. Stay overnight and pretend he built it just for you.

Summit Inn Resort
101 Skyline Drive, Farmington
724-438-8594
summitinnresort.com
$$
Porch rockers and mountain views.

Hampton Inn Uniontown
698 West Main Street, Uniontown
724-430-1000
hamptoninn.com
$$
One of several chain options.

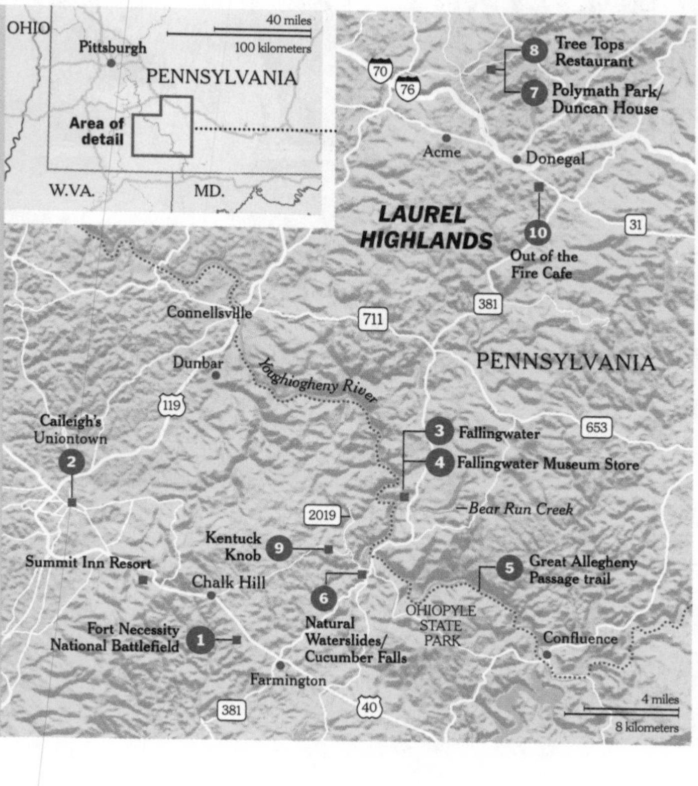

Cleveland

"You Gotta Be Tough" was a popular T-shirt slogan worn by Clevelanders during the 1970s, a grim period marked by industrial decline, large-scale population flight, and an urban environment so toxic that the Cuyahoga River actually caught on fire. These days it still helps to be at least a little tough; a fiercely blue-collar ethos endures in this part of Ohio. But instead of abandoning the city, local entrepreneurs and bohemian dreamers alike are sinking roots; opening a wave of funky boutiques, offbeat art galleries, and sophisticated restaurants; and injecting fresh life into previously rusted-out spaces. Spend the weekend and catch the vibrant spirit. — BRETT SOKOL

FRIDAY

1 *Hello, Cleveland!* 3 p.m.

Staring at platform shoes worn by Keith Moon or at Elvis Presley's white jumpsuit hardly evokes the visceral excitement of rock music, let alone its rich history, but the **Rock and Roll Hall of Fame and Museum** (751 Erieside Avenue; 216-781-7625; rockhall.com) has a wealth of interactive exhibits in addition to its displays of the goofier fashion choices of rock stardom. There's a fascinating look at the genre's initial 1950s heyday, as well as the hysteria that greeted it — preachers and politicians warning of everything from incipient Communist subversion to wanton sexuality.

2 *Iron Chef, Polish Comfort* 7 p.m.

Cleveland's restaurant of popular distinction is **Lolita** (900 Literary Road; 216-771-5652; lolitarestaurant.com; $$$), where the owner, *Iron Chef America* regular Michael Symon, offers creative spins on Mediterranean favorites like duck prosciutto pizza and crispy chicken livers with polenta, wild mushrooms, and pancetta. (Reservations are recommended.) More traditional comfort food is at **Sokolowski's University Inn** (1201 University Road; 216-771-9236; sokolowskis.com; $), beloved stop for classic Polish dishes since 1923. Even if you're unswayed by Anthony Bourdain's description of the smoked kielbasa as "artery busting" (from him, a compliment), at least swing by for the view from the parking lot — a panorama encompassing Cleveland old and new, from the stadiums dotting the downtown skyline to the smoking factories and oddly beautiful slag heaps on the riverside below.

3 *Classic Cocktails* 10 p.m.

Discerning drinkers head for the **Velvet Tango Room** (2095 Columbus Road; 216-241-8869; velvettangoroom.com), inside a one-time Prohibition-era speakeasy and seemingly little changed: the bitters are house-made, and the bartenders pride themselves on effortlessly mixing a perfect Bourbon Daisy or Rangpur Gimlet. Yes, as their menu explains, you can order a chocolate-tini — "But we die a little bit every time."

SATURDAY

4 *Farm-Fresh* 10 a.m.

Start your day at the **West Side Market** (1979 West 25th Street; 216-664-3387; westsidemarket.com), where many of the city's chefs go to stock their own kitchens. Browse over stalls where 100 vendors sell meat, cheese, fruit, vegetables, and baked goods, or just pull up a chair at **Crêpes De Luxe**'s counter (crepesdeluxe.com; $) for a savory Montréal (filled with smoked brisket and Emmental cheese) or the Elvis homage Le Roi (bananas, peanut butter, and chocolate).

OPPOSITE The Cleveland Museum of Art in the culture-saturated University Circle district.

RIGHT At the Velvet Tango Room, the bitters are house-made and the cocktails are precisely mixed.

5 *From Steel to Stylish* Noon

The steelworkers who once filled the Tremont neighborhood's low-slung houses and ornately topped churches have largely vanished. A new breed of resident has moved in along with a wealth of upscale restaurants, galleries, and artisanal shops. Inside **Lilly Handmade Chocolates** (761 Starkweather Avenue; 216-771-3333; lillytremont.com), you can join the throngs practically drooling over the mounds of freshly made truffles. Or grab a glass at the wine bar inside **Visible Voice Books** (1023 Kenilworth Avenue; 216-961-0084; visiblevoicebooks.com), which features scores of small-press titles, many by local authors.

6 *Some Still Like Canvas* 3 p.m.

For more than 20 years the **William Busta Gallery** (2731 Prospect Avenue; 216-298-9071; williambustagallery.com) has remained a conceptual-art-free zone—video installations included. "With video, it takes 15 minutes to see how bad somebody really is," said Mr. Busta, the gallery's owner. "With painting, you can spot talent right away." And that's predominantly what he exhibits, with a focus on exciting homegrown figures like Don Harvey and Matthew Kolodziej. In the nearby Warehouse District, **Shaheen Modern & Contemporary Art** (740 West Superior Avenue, Suite 101; 216-830-8888; shaheengallery.com) casts a wider geographic net with solo exhibits from New York-based artists.

7 *Paris on Lake Erie* 6 p.m.

A much talked-about spot is **L'Albatros** (11401 Bellflower Road; 216-791-7880; albatrosbrasserie.com; $$), run by the chef Zachary Bruell. Set inside a 19th-century carriage house on the campus of Case Western Reserve University, this inviting brasserie serves impeccably executed French specialties like chicken liver and foie gras mousseline, a niçoise salad, and cassoulet.

8 *Ballroom Blitz* 8 p.m.

The polka bands are long gone from the **Beachland Ballroom** (15711 Waterloo Road; 216-383-1124;beachlandballroom.com), replaced by an eclectic mix of rock groups. But by running a place that's as much a clubhouse as a concert venue, the co-owners Cindy Barber and Mark Leddy have retained plenty of this former Croatian social hall's old-school character. Beachland books national bands and favorite local acts. Leddy, formerly an antiques dealer, still hunts down finds for the This Way Out Vintage Shoppe in the basement.

SUNDAY

9 *Vegan and Carnivore* 9 a.m.

One of the few restaurants in town where requesting the vegan option won't elicit a raised eyebrow, **Tommy's** (1824 Coventry Road; 216-321-7757; tommyscoventry.com; $) has been serving tofu since 1972, when the surrounding Coventry Village, in Cleveland Heights, was a hippie oasis. The bloom is off that countercultural rose, but the delicious falafel and thick milkshakes endure. For breakfast, there are plenty of carnivore options along with the tofu scramble.

ABOVE The Rock and Roll Hall of Fame, repository of John Lennon's "Sgt. Pepper" suit and Michael Jackson's glove.

OPPOSITE Home cooks and chefs both stock their kitchens at the West Side Market, a good stop for Saturday morning.

10 *Free Impressionists* 11 a.m.

For decades, the University Circle district has housed many of the city's cultural jewels, including Severance Hall, the majestic Georgian residence of the Cleveland Orchestra, and the Cleveland Institute of Art Cinematheque, one of the country's best repertory movie theaters. At the **Cleveland Museum of Art** (11150 East Boulevard; 216-421-7340; clevelandart.org), already famed for its collection of Old Masters and kid-friendly armor, the opening of the Rafael Viñoly-designed East Wing has put the spotlight on more modern fare, including Impressionist paintings. A special inducement: admission to the museum's permanent collections is free. Nearby, the **Museum of Contemporary Art Cleveland** (11400 Euclid Avenue; 216-421-8671; mocacleveland.org) has a stunning new home designed by the Iranian-born London architect Farshid Moussavi.

THE BASICS

Several major airlines have frequent flights to Cleveland. A light rail system connects the airport with downtown and University Circle. A car is needed for reaching most other neighborhoods.

The Glidden House
1901 Ford Drive
866-812-4537
gliddenhouse.com
$$
Quaint rooms in a 1910 mansion on the Case Western Reserve University campus.

Renaissance Cleveland Hotel
24 Public Square
216-696-5600
marriott.com
$$-$$$
A renovated elegant downtown classic, now a Marriott property.

Aloft Cleveland Downtown
1111 West 10th Street
216-400-6469
aloftclevelanddowntown.com
$$
Bright, colorful, and contemporary.

Lake Erie
1 Rock and Roll Hall of Fame and Museum
1/2 mile
1 kilometer
ERIESIDE AVE.
LAKESIDE AVE.
ST. CLAIR AVE.
SUPERIOR AVE.
Cleveland
20
Aloft Cleveland Downtown
EUCLID AVE.
PROSPECT AVE.
PUBLIC SQUARE
6 William Busta Gallery
CARNEGIE AVE.
Shaheen Modern and Contemporary Art
Renaissance Cleveland Hotel
90
COMMUNITY COLLEGE AVE.
6
20
2
COLUMBUS RD.
Cuyahoga R.
LORAIN AVE.
77
W. 25TH ST.
Sokolowski's University Inn
UNIVERSITY RD.
LITERARY RD.
MICH.
Cleveland
PA.
INDIANA
OHIO
KY.
W.VA.
West Side Market 4
Velvet Tango Room 3
Visible Voice Books
2 Lolita
TREMONT
10
KENILWORTH AVE.
Lilly Handmade Chocolates 5
4 miles
8 kilometers
Beachland Ballroom 8
EUCLID AVE.
Museum of Contemporary Art Cleveland
Cleveland Heights
Lake Erie
9 Tommy's
University Circle
L'Albatros 7
EAST BLVD.
Glidden House
Cleveland Museum of Art 10
BELLFLOWER RD.
E. 105TH ST.
Case Western Reserve University
Severance Hall
90
Cleveland
Cuyahoga R.
422
FAIRVIEW PARK
71
CLEVELAND HOPKINS INTERNATIONAL AIRPORT
77
OHIO

Cincinnati

With the quiet momentum of a work in progress, Cincinnati, Ohio, is finding an artsy swagger, infused with a casual combination of Midwest and Southern charm. The city center, for decades rich with cultural and performing arts venues, now offers a renovated Fountain Square area and a gleaming new baseball stadium with views of the Ohio River. Transformations are taking place in surrounding areas and across the river in the neighboring Kentucky cities of Newport and Covington — with cool music venues, funky shopping outlets, and smart culinary options. While it looks to the future, the city also honors its historic role in the antislavery movement with its National Underground Railroad Freedom Center. — BY KASSIE BRACKEN

FRIDAY

1 *Tranquility and Eternity* 4 p.m.

A graveyard may not be the most obvious place to start a trip, but **Spring Grove Cemetery and Arboretum** (4521 Spring Grove Avenue; 513-681-7526; springgrove.org) is not your average resting place. The arboretum, designed in 1845 as a place for botanical experiments, features 1,200 types of plants artfully arranged around mausoleums and tranquil ponds. Roman- and Greek-inspired monuments bear the names of many of Cincinnati's most prominent families, including the Procters and the Gambles, whose business, begun in the 1830s, still dominates the city. Admission and parking are free, and the office provides printed guides and information about the plant collection.

2 *Where Hipsters Roam* 6 p.m.

The Northside district has blossomed into a casually hip destination for shopping and night life, particularly along Hamilton Avenue. Vinyl gets ample real estate at **Shake It Records** (4156 Hamilton Avenue; 513-591-0123; shakeitrecords.com), a music store specializing in independent labels; if you can't find a title among the 40,000 they carry, the owners will track it down for you. For a bite, locals swear by **Melt Eclectic Deli** (4165 Hamilton Avenue; 513-681-6358; meltcincy.com; $), a quirky restaurant friendly to vegans and carnivores alike. Order the Joan of Arc sandwich, with blue cheese and caramelized onions atop roast beef, or the hummus-laden Helen of Troy, and retreat to the patio.

3 *Local Bands, Local Beer* 9 p.m.

Saunter next door to find 20-somethings in skinny jeans mingling with 30-somethings in flip-flops at **Northside Tavern** (4163 Hamilton Avenue; 513-542-3603; northsidetav.com/cinci), a prime spot for live music. Sip a pint of Cincinnati's own Christian Moerlein beer and listen to jazz, blues, and acoustic rock acts in the intimate front bar. Or head to the back room, where the best local bands take the larger stage. Wind down with a crowd heavy with artists and musicians at the **Comet** (4579 Hamilton Avenue; 513-541-8900; cometbar.com), a noirish dive bar with an impossibly cool selection on its jukebox and top-notch burritos to satisfy any late-night cravings.

SATURDAY

4 *The Aerobic Arabesque* 9:30 a.m.

The fiberglass pigs in tutus that greet you outside the **Cincinnati Ballet** (1555 Central Parkway; 513-621-5219) might indicate otherwise, but don't be fooled: the Ballet's Open Adult Division program (cballet.org/academy/adult) is a great place to get lean. Start your Saturday with a beginning ballet class (90 minutes, under $20), as a company member steers novices through basic movements. More experienced dancers might try the one-hour Rhythm

OPPOSITE The John A. Roebling Suspension Bridge over the Ohio River connects Cincinnati to its Kentucky suburbs.

RIGHT The revitalized Over-the-Rhine neighborhood.

and Motion class, which combines hip-hop, modern, and African dance. Regulars know the moves, so pick a spot in the back and prepare to sweat.

5 *A Bridge to Brunch* 11:30 a.m.

If John Roebling's Suspension Bridge looks familiar, you might be thinking of his more famous design in New York. (Cincinnati's version opened in 1867, almost two decades before the Brooklyn Bridge.) It's a pedestrian-friendly span over the Ohio River, providing terrific views of the skyline. Cross into Covington, Kentucky, and walk a few blocks to the **Keystone Bar & Grill** (313 Greenup Street; 859-261-6777; keystonebar.com; $-$$), where alcohol-fueled partying gives way to brunch on weekend mornings. You'll be well fueled for the walk back.

6 *Tracing a Legacy* 2 p.m.

The **National Underground Railroad Freedom Center** (50 East Freedom Way; 513-333-7500; freedomcenter.org) is a dynamic testament to Cincinnati's place in the antislavery movement. Multimedia presentations, art displays, and interactive timelines trace the history of the global slave trade as well as 21st-century human trafficking. Leave time for the genealogy center, where volunteers assist individuals with detailed family searches.

7 *Sin City, Updated* 5 p.m.

For decades, Cincinnatians scoffed at their Kentucky neighbors, but that has been changing in the last few years, especially with the revitalization of Newport, a waterfront and historic housing district. Stroll to **York St. Café** (738 York Street, entrance on Eighth Street; 859-261-9675; yorkstonline.com; $$), an 1880s-era apothecary transformed into a three-story restaurant, music, and art space, where wood shelves are stocked with kitschy memorabilia. Browse a bit before scanning the menu for bistro fare like a Mediterranean board (an array of shareable appetizers) or a delicate fresh halibut with spinach and artichoke. Leave room for the excellent homemade desserts, including the strawberry buttermilk cake.

8 *Stage to Stage* 7 p.m.

Cincinnati Playhouse in the Park (962 Mount Adams Circle; 513-421-3888; cincyplay.com), which has been producing plays for five decades, offers splendid vistas of Mount Adams and a solid theatergoing experience. A lesser-known but equally engaging option can be found at the **University of Cincinnati College-Conservatory of Music** (Corry Boulevard; 513-556-4183; ccm.uc.edu/theatre). Students dreaming of Lincoln Center perform in full-scale productions of serious drama and opera. Check the online calendar for show times and locations.

9 *Ballroom Bliss* 10 p.m.

Head back to Newport's Third Street and its bars and clubs. A standout, **Southgate House Revival**, is set in a big converted church (111 East Sixth Street, Newport; 859-431-2201; southgatehouse.com) with stained glass and multiple spaces for several acts to play on the same date. On a typical Saturday night, music fans of all ages and sensibilities roam among its multiple stages and bars.

SUNDAY

10 *Neighborhood Reborn* 11 a.m.

As the epicenter of 19th-century German immigrant society, the neighborhood known as Over-the-Rhine once teemed with breweries, theaters, and social halls. Though it fell into disrepair and

parts remain rough around the edges, an $80 million revitalization effort has slowly brought back visitors. Walk down Main Street between 12th and 15th Streets to find local artists' galleries and the **Iris BookCafe** (1331 Main Street; 513-381-2665; irisbookcafe.com), a serene rare-book shop with an outdoor sculpture garden. A few blocks away, Vine Street between Central Parkway and 13th Street offers new boutiques including the craft shop **MiCA 12/v** (1201 Vine Street; 513-421-3500; shopmica.com), which specializes in contemporary designers.

11 *Designs to Take Home* 1 p.m.

Before heading home, find inspiring décor at **HighStreet** (1401 Reading Road; 513-723-1901; highstreetcincinnati.com), a spacious and sleek design store. The owners have carefully composed a cosmopolitan mix of textiles, clothing, and jewelry by New York and London designers as well as local artists, showcased in a creatively appointed space. A free cup of red flower tea makes it all the more inviting.

OPPOSITE ABOVE Spring Grove Cemetery and Arboretum.

OPPOSITE BELOW Northside, an area for shopping and night life.

ABOVE The National Underground Railroad Freedom Center. Cincinnati was a stop for many who escaped slavery.

THE BASICS

Fly into Cincinnati/Northern Kentucky International Airport, a 25-minute drive from downtown. A rental car is recommended.

Hilton Cincinnati Netherland Plaza
35 West Fifth Street
513-421-9100
hilton.com
$$
561 renovated rooms in a landmark building, the Art Deco Carew Tower.

The Westin Cincinnati
21 East Fifth Street
513-621-7700
starwoodhotels.com
$$
Downtown with views of Fountain Square from many rooms.

Cincinnatian Hotel
601 Vine Street
513-381-3000
cincinnatianhotel.com
$$
Updated rooms in a classic hotel dating to 1882.

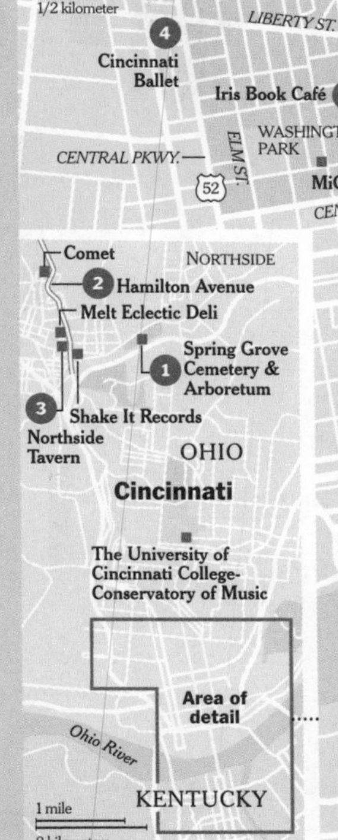

OneAmerica
OLD NATIONAL

Indianapolis

Indianapolis, Indiana's capital city, may be best known outside the state for sports—professional basketball and football teams, the headquarters of the National Collegiate Athletic Association, and, of course, the Indianapolis Motor Speedway, home of the Indy 500. But there's much more—a new sculpture park, a downtown canal walk, a library dedicated to Kurt Vonnegut, and the multiethnic influences of thriving populations of recent immigrants. It's all mixed in with the old Indianapolis standbys of hearty Midwestern food and Hoosier hospitality and charm. — BY JOHN HOLL

FRIDAY

1 *A Cocktail with That Scotch* 6:30 p.m.

Start with a drink downtown at one of the city's oldest restaurants, **St. Elmo Steak House** (127 South Illinois Street; 317-635-0636; stelmos.com; $$$), where for more than a century patrons have sidled up to the tiger oak bar—first used in the 1893 Chicago World's Fair—for martinis and single malts. Settle in under the gaze of the Indiana celebrities whose photos adorn the walls (David Letterman, Larry Bird) and try St. Elmo's not-for-the-faint-of-heart signature dish: the shrimp cocktail. The jumbo shrimp are served smothered in horseradish cocktail sauce made every hour to ensure freshness and a proper sinus assault. If you can see through the tears in your eyes, you'll probably notice one of the tuxedoed bartenders having a quiet chuckle at your expense.

2 *New Indiana* 7 p.m.

While downtown has been rejuvenating itself with new development, areas out toward the suburbs have been transformed by immigration, with Pakistanis, Salvadorans, Burmese, and an assortment of other groups mingling comfortably. To see a bit of what this melting pot has brought to Indianapolis dining, drive a few miles to **Abyssinia** (5352 West 38th Street, in the Honey Creek Plaza; 317-299-0608; $), an Ethiopian restaurant decorated with Haile Selassie portraits and Ethiopia tourism posters. The authentic, well-cooked cuisine incorporates lots of lentils as well as goat in berbere sauce, house-made injera bread, and sambusas, the Ethiopian version of samosas. The place draws Africans, Indians, vegans, and plenty of longtime Indianans who like a culinary adventure.

OPPOSITE The Canal Walk in downtown Indianapolis.

3 *Blues and Bands* 10:30 p.m.

Indianapolis has had a blues scene for generations, and it's still alive and kickin' at the **Slippery Noodle Inn** (372 South Meridian Street; 317-631-6974; slipperynoodle.com). Housed in a two-story building constructed as a bar and roadhouse around 1850, the Noodle attracts a lively crowd (including, back in the day, the Dillinger Gang) and nationally known blues musicians like Country Joe McDonald and Ronnie Earl. But it's the local bands that make the place rock, so hoist a pint of the Indiana-brewed Upland IPA and groove on the dance floor to the thumping bass.

SATURDAY

4 *Monumental Efforts* 10 a.m.

Start a walking tour in the heart of downtown at the neoclassical **Soldiers and Sailors Monument** (1 Monument Circle; 317-232-7615), a 284-foot-tall obelisk dating back to 1902. Look over the Civil War museum in the base and then take the elevator or brave the 330 stairs to the top. Back on the ground, it's a short walk down West Market Street to the **Indiana Statehouse**, a suitably domed and columned structure built in 1888. A few blocks north is the **Freemasons' Scottish Rite Cathedral** (650 North Meridian Street; 317-262-3110; aasr-indy.org), actually a meeting hall, not a church. It's a tour de force of ornate decoration with a 212-foot tower, 54 bells, a 2,500-pound gilded bronze chandelier, cavernous oak-paneled halls, and stained-glass windows. If it's open (Monday through Friday and the third Saturday of each month), take an hourlong guided tour.

5 *Duckpins* Noon

Order a salad to keep it light at the **Smokehouse on Shelby** (317-685-1959; $) in the 1928 **Fountain Square Theatre Building** (1105 Prospect Street; fountainsquareindy.com), so that you can follow up with a chocolate malt or a strawberry soda from the restored 1950s soda fountain, rescued from a defunct

Woolworth's. Then rent a lane and some shoes at one of the two duckpin bowling alleys in the building. The one upstairs still uses the original 1930s equipment. Downstairs has '50s-vintage bowling.

6 *Bless You, Mr. Vonnegut* 1:30 p.m.

Growing up in Indianapolis, Kurt Vonnegut absorbed an Indiana world-view that informed many of his novels, even when the references to Midwestern virtues and values were ironic. Indianapolis acknowledges its famous literary son at the **Kurt Vonnegut Memorial Library** (340 North Senate Avenue; 317-652-1954; vonnegutlibrary.org), which displays mementoes including his typewriter, his World War II Purple Heart, and rejection letters sent to him by editors in the days before he became famous. The library also has a collection of books, articles, films, and papers, and it sponsors readings and other literary events

7 *White River Junction* 3 p.m.

Stroll along the canal and through the green spaces of **White River State Park** (801 West Washington Street; 317-233-2434; inwhiteriver.wrsp.in.gov) on the city's west side. You can take your pick of several museums and the Indianapolis Zoo, but a more unusual destination here is the headquarters of the National Collegiate Athletic Association. The **N.C.A.A. Hall of Champions** (317-916-4255; ncaahallofchampions.org) has displays on 23 men's and women's sports, a theater showing memorable college sports moments, and interactive simulators that take you on a virtual trip into a game.

8 *Hoosier Heartland* 6 p.m.

For a real taste of Hoosier country (Indianans wear the Hoosier nickname proudly), grab some hors d'oeuvres and a bottle of wine and drive about 40 minutes northeast of the city, past farmland and cornfields, till you come to **Bonge's Tavern** (9830 West 280 North, Perkinsville; 765-734-1625; bongestavern.com; $$), a country roadhouse that opened in 1934. The restaurant does not take reservations for fewer than 10 people, so arrive early and be ready to wait 90 minutes or more. Part of the Bonge's experience is chatting with other patrons while sitting on rocking chairs on the enclosed porch, maybe sharing some of the wine and snacks you so thoughtfully brought. Once inside, order the Perkinsville Pork, a juicy, pounded-flat, parmesan-crusted loin that is worth waiting for.

9 *Basketball Bar* 10 p.m.

High school basketball is practically a religion in Indiana, and there is no more famous team than the 1954 squad from small Milan High School. It won the statewide championship on a final shot by Bobby Plump, who quickly became a folk hero. The story formed the basis for the 1986 film *Hoosiers*. Today, Plump and his family operate a bar, **Plump's Last Shot** (6416 Cornell Avenue; 317-257-5867; plumpslastshot.com), a hoops-memorabilia-filled hangout in the Broad Ripple neighborhood and the perfect place to catch a game on TV. Sports-mad as Indianapolis may be, however, it also has a healthy respect for the arts. When the **Indianapolis Symphony Orchestra** (indianapolissymphony.org) was threatened financially, the owners of the Colts and the Pacers, the city's two pro teams, were major donors to a successful fund drive to save it.

SUNDAY

10 *Sculpture Hike* 9 a.m.

Explore and play amid 100 acres of outdoor art at the **Virginia B. Fairbanks Art & Nature Park** (4000

Michigan Road; 317-923-1331; imamuseum.org/visit/100acres), adjoining the Indianapolis Museum of Art. Aside from large, lighthearted, and interactive artworks (there's no "no-touch" rule here), the park satisfies a Sunday morning wanderer's wants with woods, grass, wetlands, and a lake.

11 *Start Your Engines* Noon

Naturally you want to get a look at the **Indianapolis Motor Speedway** (4790 West 16th Street; 317-492-6784; indianapolismotorspeedway.com), home of the Indianapolis 500. The **Hall of Fame Museum** within the racetrack grounds displays vintage race cars, trophies, and more than two dozen cars that won the race, including the very first winner (in 1911), a Marmon Wasp. The narrated bus ride around the fabled oval may be the closest you ever come to racing in the old Brickyard, but unfortunately the driver never gets above 30 miles an hour. You will get up-close views of the famed racing pagoda, Gasoline Alley, and the last remaining strip of the track's original brick surface, 36 inches wide, which now serves as the start/finish line.

OPPOSITE ABOVE The first winner of the Indianapolis 500, on display at the Indianapolis Motor Speedway.

OPPOSITE BELOW Take the dare and order the super-spicy horseradish shrimp cocktail at the century-old St. Elmo Steak House.

THE BASICS

Fly into the Indianapolis airport or drive about three hours south from Chicago. For getting around in the city, you will need a car.

The Alexander
333 South Delaware Street
317-624-8200
thealexander.com
$$
Stylish new hotel; part of CityWay, a downtown residential, retail, and office development.

Conrad Indianapolis
50 West Washington Street
317-713-5000
conradindianapolis.com
$$
Luxurious outpost of the Hilton chain.

JW Marriott Indianapolis
10 South West Street
317-860-5800
jwindy.com
$$$
A 34-story swoosh of Indianapolis Colts-blue glass.

OLD NAVY 2007

Iowa's Mississippi River

"For 60 years the foreign tourist has steamed up and down the river between St. Louis and New Orleans... believing he had seen all of the river that was worth seeing or that had anything to see," Mark Twain lamented in Life on the Mississippi. *The visitors were missing an "amazing region" to the north, he wrote. They were missing "extraordinary sunsets" and "enchanting scenery." They were missing Iowa. Today, tourists do find Iowa's Mississippi riverfront, thanks partly to modern confections like riverboat casinos and a water park resort, but much of this shore still feels undiscovered. Set out for a weekend car trip on quiet back roads, and you'll find the real life of the Mississippi amid green hilltops and fields, in small villages and busy cities, and on the wide river itself.*
— BY BETSY RUBINER

FRIDAY

1 *Skimming the River* 4 p.m.

Start your Mississippi River explorations in Davenport, about 1,775 miles upstream from the Gulf of Mexico. With no flood wall (though there are perennial arguments about whether to build one), downtown Davenport has a feeling of intimacy with the river, and you can get even closer on the **Channel Cat Water Taxi** (foot of Mound Street at the river; 309-788-3360; qcchannelcat.com), a small ferry with several stops. From its benches you may see blocks-long grain barges, speedboats, 19th-century riverbank mansions, and egrets on small wooded islands.

2 *Field of Dreams* 7 p.m.

One of the best points to enjoy Davenport's unusual eye-level river view is **Modern Woodmen Park** (209 South Gaines Street; 563-322-6348; riverbandits.com), the riverfront minor-league baseball field. If the River Bandits are playing at home, have some hot dogs or cheese steak as you take in a game. (There's also a tiki bar.) The park has a small cornfield where, when the stalks are high enough, the Bandits emerge at game time like the ghostly players in *Field of Dreams*, which was filmed in Iowa. If it's not a game night, seek a more substantial dinner at **Front Street Brewery** (208 East River Drive; 563-322-1569; frontstreetbrew.com; $). Look on the menu for walleye, a favorite Midwestern native fish.

OPPOSITE Success in the form of a smallmouth bass, pulled from the Mississippi at McGregor.

RIGHT Rolling farmland along Highway 52 between Bellevue and St. Donatus.

SATURDAY

3 *A River Still Traveled* 10 a.m.

Drive down to the levee at **Le Claire** to see a nicely preserved example of the craft used for traveling the river in Twain's day. The *Lone Star* is an 1860s sternwheel steamboat in dry dock at the **Buffalo Bill Museum** (199 North Front Street; 563-289-5580; buffalobillmuseumleclaire.com). Nearby, S.U.V.'s towing today's pleasure boats pull up to a launching ramp, disgorging day trippers toting kids, coolers, and life jackets. After the families have sped off, you may see them again, picnicking on an island. A block from the river, along Cody Road—named, as is the museum, for Le Claire's favorite son, William Cody—inviting shops and restaurants rejuvenate old brick storefronts.

4 *From the Heights* Noon

You're passing some of the world's most expensive farmland—fertile valley acreage conveniently close to river transportation on the grain barges—as you head north on Routes 67 and 52 to Bellevue. The town lives up to its name with sweeping views from the high bluffs at **Bellevue State Park** (24668 Highway 52; 563-872-4019; iowadnr.gov). A display in the park's

nature center recalls an early industry in these river towns: making buttons from mussel shells. In the pretty riverside downtown, check out the pizza at **2nd Street Station** (116 South 2nd Street; 563-872-5410) and stop for a look at **Lock and Dam No. 12** (Route 52 at Franklin Street). Locks are a common feature on the Upper Mississippi, where tugs push as many as 15 barges at a time, carrying as much freight as 870 tractor trailers or a 225-car train.

5 *Luxembourgers* 2:30 p.m.

Stop for a quick glance around tiny **St. Donatus**, where one of America's rarer ethnic groups, immigrants from Luxembourg, arrived in the 1800s and built limestone and stucco buildings. For some classic Iowa landscape, walk up the Way of the Cross path behind the Catholic church and look across the valley at patches of hay and corn quilting the hills. You may smell hogs. Or is it cattle?

6 *Gawk at the Gar* 3 p.m.

Spend some time in **Dubuque**, Davenport's rival Iowa river city. At the **National Mississippi River Museum and Aquarium** (350 East Third Street; 563-557-9545; rivermuseum.com), a Smithsonian affiliate, huge blue catfish, gar, and paddlefish swim in a 30,000-gallon tank; a boardwalk goes through reclaimed wetlands inhabited by herons and bald eagles; and a model shows havoc caused by a 1965 flood. Downtown, Dubuque feels like an old factory town, with Victorian mansions (several converted into inns), brick row houses flush to the street, and many a church and corner tap. Ride the **Fenelon Place Elevator** (512 Fenelon Place; dbq.com/fenplco), a funicular that makes a steep climb to a bluff top where Wisconsin and Illinois are visible across the river.

7 *American Pie* 6 p.m.

Follow Highway 52 and the County Route C9Y, the Balltown Road, through a peaceful valley up and up onto a ridge with views worthy of a painting by Grant Wood (an Iowan): wide open sky, a lone pheasant in a field, alternating rows of crops, grazing cows, and tidy farms with stone houses, weathered red barns, and blue silos. Your goal is **Balltown**, which has about 75 residents and one famous restaurant, **Breitbach's** (563 Balltown Road, Route C9Y; 563-552-2220; breitbachscountrydining.com; $-$$). It has been open since 1852 and is justly famed for its fried chicken, barbecued ribs, and fresh pie.

ABOVE Lock and Dam No. 12 spanning the river at Bellevue.

OPPOSITE ABOVE The Fenelon Place Elevator in Dubuque climbs a steep bluff to a panoramic river view.

OPPOSITE BELOW Riverside baseball in Davenport.

SUNDAY

8 *A "T" Too Far* 10 a.m.

Forty miles north of Dubuque, Highway 52 brings you to the river at **Guttenberg**, a lovely town settled by German immigrants in the 1840s and named after the inventor of moveable type, Johannes Gutenberg. (Word has it that an early typographical error accounts for the extra T.) Admire the downtown's well-preserved pre-Civil War-era limestone buildings and stroll at mile-long **Ingleside Park**. A few miles farther on, stop at **McGregor**, where boaters hang out by the marina and locals eat bratwurst and drink beer on riverview restaurant decks. McGregor is also the home of the **River Junction Trade Company** (312 Main Street, McGregor; 866-259-9172; riverjunction.com; open Monday to Saturday), which makes reproductions of Old West gear, sometimes selling to Hollywood production companies.

9 *Pike's Other Peak* 11 a.m.

Even if you're getting weary of river panoramas, stop at **Pikes Peak State Park** (32264 Pikes Peak Road, McGregor; 563-873-2341; iowadnr.gov) to see one from the highest bluff on the Mississippi. Like Pikes Peak in Colorado, this spot is named for the explorer Zebulon Pike. Scouting for federal fort locations in 1805, Pike thought this peak was an ideal spot, and although the fort ended up across the river in Wisconsin, you can understand his reasoning. Look out at a swirl of green forested islands and mud-brown river pools. To the north, suspension bridges connect to Wisconsin. To the south, the Wisconsin River empties out at the place where in 1673 the

explorers Jacques Marquette and Louis Jolliet first saw the Mississippi.

10 *Mound Builders* 1 p.m.

At **Effigy Mounds National Monument** (151 Highway 76, Harpers Ferry; 563-873-3491; nps.gov/efmo), 2,526 acres of grounds are dotted with mysterious prehistoric burial and ceremonial mounds, some as old as 2,500 years. The Indians of the Upper Midwest built large numbers of mounds shaped like animals, most often bears and birds that lived along the Mississippi. Why they were built and who was meant to see them — since the best views are from the sky — remains unknown. Take the two-mile Fire Point Trail up a 360-foot bluff, through forests and past mounds. At the top, a clearing reveals a Mississippi that seems wild — with forested banks and islands, a soupy marsh, and hawks soaring above a bluff — until out of nowhere a speedboat zips by, breaking the silence.

ABOVE A houseboat anchored near McGregor.

OPPOSITE Downtown McGregor, a promising stop for Mississippi River souvenir hunters.

THE BASICS

The Mississippi River is a three-hour drive west from Chicago. The Quad City International Airport serves Davenport.

Hotel Blackhawk
200 East 3rd Street, Davenport
563-322-5000
hotelblackhawk.com
$$
Stylishly decorated landmark hotel, reopened in 2010 after extensive renovation.

Hotel Julien Dubuque
200 Main Street, Dubuque
563-556-4200
hoteljuliendubuque.com
$$
Boutique décor, pool, and spa in a hotel with history back to Abraham Lincoln's day.

The Landing
703 South River Park Drive, Guttenberg
563-252-1615
thelanding615.com
$
Rooms and suites in a renovated stone riverfront warehouse.

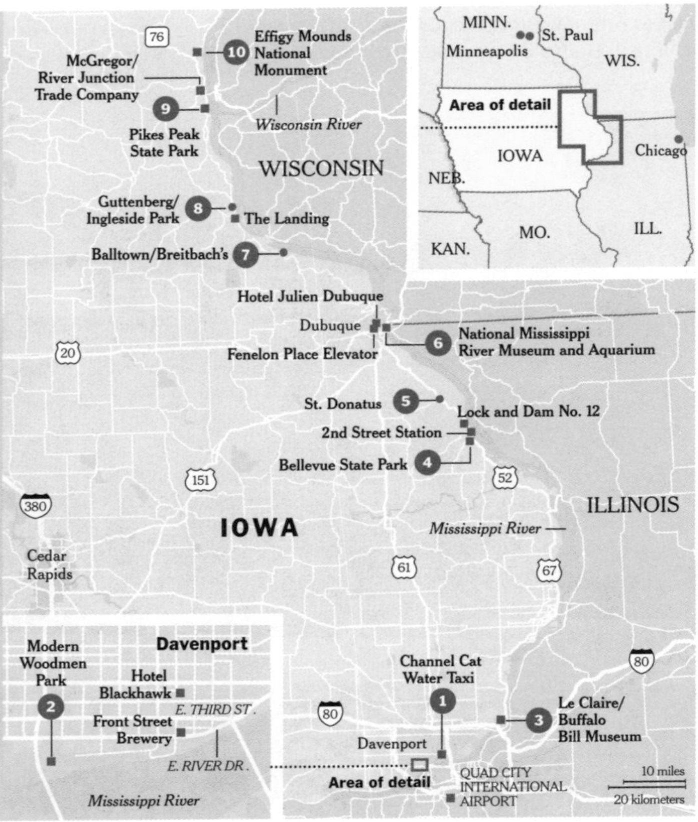

76
10 Effigy Mounds National Monument
McGregor/River Junction Trade Company
9 Pikes Peak State Park
Wisconsin River
WISCONSIN
8 Guttenberg/Ingleside Park
The Landing
7 Balltown/Breitbach's
Hotel Julien Dubuque
Dubuque
Fenelon Place Elevator
6 National Mississippi River Museum and Aquarium
20
5 St. Donatus
Lock and Dam No. 12
2nd Street Station
4 Bellevue State Park
151
52
380
IOWA
ILLINOIS
Mississippi River
Cedar Rapids
61
67
MINN.
St. Paul
Minneapolis
WIS.
Area of detail
IOWA
NEB.
Chicago
MO.
ILL.
KAN.
Davenport
Modern Woodmen Park
2
Hotel Blackhawk
E. THIRD ST.
Front Street Brewery
E. RIVER DR.
Mississippi River
80
1 Channel Cat Water Taxi
80
3 Le Claire/Buffalo Bill Museum
Davenport
Area of detail
QUAD CITY INTERNATIONAL AIRPORT
10 miles
20 kilometers

DiAMOND
JOE
TRADING
LLC
ANTIQUES
ANTIQUES
GIFTS
FOLK ART

Des Moines

In Iowa's landscape of small towns and farms, Des Moines is the Big City — the state's capital; its business, civic, and cultural hub; and an evolving center of urban pleasures. Well-designed new buildings and a popular sculpture park have revitalized the downtown, theaters and galleries are thriving, and the refurbished East Village area is crowded with restaurants, coffeehouses, shops, and clubs. Des Moines is starting to stay up late. Still, the countryside never feels far away, in miles or in mind-set. And for 10 days every August, there's the Iowa State Fair, renowned for its blue-ribbon agricultural exhibits, butter sculptures, and pork chops on a stick. — BY BETSY RUBINER

FRIDAY

1 *Sculpture on the Lawn* 3 p.m.

Drivers entering Des Moines from the west once sped past a motley collection of worn-out buildings and abandoned auto dealerships, but that vista has been replaced by a five-block landscape of green parkland, meant to be enjoyed on foot. There are curving pathways, benches, and thick grass, but what makes this park outstanding are two dozen contemporary sculptures — by Willem de Kooning, Louise Bourgeois, Richard Serra, and Sol Lewitt, among others — arranged on an undulating lawn. The **John and Mary Pappajohn Sculpture Park** (between Locust Street and Grand Avenue, 13th and 15th Streets; desmoinesartcenter.org; cellphone tour 515-657-8264), named for the venture capitalist and his wife who donated the sculptures, covers two formerly dreary blocks. Two arresting pieces: *Nomade*, by the Spanish sculptor Jaume Plensa, a 27-foot-tall hollow human form made of a latticework of white steel letters, and *Glass Colour Circle* by the Berlin-based Olafur Eliasson, a walk-in structure made of 23 nine-foot-tall, 1,200-pound glass panels in various colors, illuminated by lantern light that casts a hazy rainbow.

2 *Transformed Core* 5 p.m.

The park is at the front door of the striking **Des Moines Central Library**, designed by the London architect David Chipperfield. A two-story, 110,000-square-foot building, it is sheathed in glass reinforced by copper mesh that gives it a beguiling glow and makes it a warm anchor to downtown. In the downtown core, many in the dense assortment of office buildings are linked by sheltering sky walks, especially welcome in winter. Along the Des Moines River, a 1.2-mile loop called the **Principal Riverwalk** incorporates gardens, more sculpture, pedestrian bridges, and an outdoor ice rink, **Brenton Skating Plaza** (520 Robert D. Ray Drive; 515-284-1000; brentonplaza.com). Downriver is **Principal Park**, a handsome Triple A ballpark surrounded by old buildings converted into condominiums.

3 *Center Stage* 7 p.m.

An ornate Masonic temple built in 1913 was in danger of being torn down before it was taken over by a local real estate developer, Harry Bookey, who converted it into the **Temple for Performing Arts** (1011 Locust Street; 515-246-2300; templeforperformingarts.com), a recital hall with a richly decorated grand hall and a theater hosting plays and performances. **Centro** (1003 Locust Street; 515-248-1780; centrodesmoines.com; $$),

OPPOSITE A photo opportunity beneath *T8*, by Mark di Suvero, at the John and Mary Pappajohn Sculpture Park.

BELOW Bread for sale at La Mie, a bakery and restaurant. Quiches, sandwiches, and tartines are on the lunch menu.

the bustling ground-floor restaurant, is an enduring symbol of the re-energized downtown. Centro expresses its "Italian urban" theme in choices like lobster ravioli, chicken saltimbocca, and tofu gnocchi, and it has an appealing drinks menu and wine list. Stroll the nearby blocks of the **Court Avenue Entertainment District** for more night life.

SATURDAY

4 *Farm Fresh* 9 a.m.

On Saturday mornings from May to October, the **Downtown Farmers Market** (desmoinesfarmersmarket.com) takes over a chunk of downtown around the intersection of Fourth and Court Avenues. There are spring morels, rhubarb, and asparagus; summer tomatoes, sweet corn, and raspberries; fall apples, squash, and pumpkins; plus a mishmash of ethnic foods (Salvadoran, Indian, Laotian, Afghan) and specialty items (Mennonite pies, elk jerky, buffalo bologna). Don't miss the Dutch Letters — S-shaped pastries filled with almond paste. If you're here on a day when there's no market, take a tour of the **Iowa State Capitol** (515-281-5591; legis.iowa.gov/resources/tourCapitol), one of the country's most beautiful state capitol buildings. Its gilded dome rises grandly over downtown, and inside are marble and carved wood, mosaics, paintings, and other ornate decoration.

5 *Artful Inside and Out* 10:30 a.m.

In 1948 Eliel Saarinen's flat-roofed stone building appeared; in 1968 I.M. Pei's heavy geometric concrete addition; in 1985 Richard Meier's towering wing, clad in white porcelain-coated metal panels. Combined, they make up the **Des Moines Art Center** (4700 Grand Avenue; 515-277-4405; desmoinesartcenter.org), west of downtown. It's a showcase for contemporary art as well as architecture, with works by Edward Hopper, John Singer Sargent, Louise Bourgeois, Carl Milles, Maya Lin, and Andy Goldsworthy.

ABOVE The dome of the Iowa State Capitol rises grandly over downtown Des Moines. Inside, tour guides point out details of the ornate interior decoration.

OPPOSITE ABOVE Transacting business on a Saturday morning at the Downtown Farmers Market.

6 *Iowa Patisserie* 1 p.m.

La Mie (841 42nd Street; 515-255-1625; lamiebakery.com; $), in a commercial strip on the edge of an old residential neighborhood, specializes in breads (baguette, foccacia, olive ciabatta, rye) and pastries (tarts, macarons, cheesecakes, cookies). It's also the right stop for a classy brunch or lunch (quiche, tartines, sandwiches), with tables and booths beyond the pastry counter.

7 *The Village* 2 p.m.

A once-dying neighborhood east of the Des Moines River, at the foot of the Capitol's golden dome, was reborn as the **East Village**, drawing new, young residents and sprinkled with stylish restaurants, boutiques, galleries, and specialty shops. Do not miss **Sticks** (510 East Locust Street; 515-282-0844; sticksgallery.com), which sells one-of-a-kind hand-painted wood furniture that's made in Des Moines. Stop at **Gong Fu Tea** (414 East Sixth Street; 515-288-3388; gongfu-tea.com), a tranquil Asian-inspired teahouse. **Raygun** (400 East Locust Street; 515-288-1323; raygunsite.com) sells cheeky, Iowacentric T-shirts including one aimed at one of the state's famed college towns with the message "Iowa City: All our creativity went into this name."

8 *Dine Beneath the Doors* 8 p.m.

Alba (524 East Sixth Street; 515-244-0261; albadsm.com; $$), an East Village favorite, serves contemporary American food in a minimalist space decorated with colorful paintings and a motley collection of wood-paneled doors hanging from the ceiling. The menu changes often; typical entrees are pan-roasted chicken breast, herb-rubbed hanger steak, and paella. After dinner, stop off at **Wooly's** (504 East Locust Street; 515-244-0550; woolysdm.com), for live music performed in a former Woolworth's store.

SUNDAY

9 *Down on the Farms* 10 a.m.

Experience the evolution of Iowa farming by touring **Living History Farms** (2600 111th Street; Urbandale; 515-278-5286; lhf.org), an open-air museum in a suburb west of the city. A trail connects three period farms that look, feel, and smell like the real McCoy, with authentic crops and livestock as well as interpreters demonstrating chores. The Ioway Indian Farm (circa 1700) has bark lodges and lush gardens of corn, beans, and squash. The 30-acre 1850 Pioneer Farm has a plain log house and hard-working oxen. The 40-acre 1900 farm has a pretty white frame house and the next stage of animal muscle—draft horses.

10 *A Prescription for Ice Cream* Noon

Hidden inside **Bauder Pharmacy** (3802 Ingersoll Avenue; 515-255-1124; bauderpharmacy.com) is an old-fashioned soda fountain serving its own delicious ice cream. Bauder's has tinted medicine bottles behind the prescription counter and turtle sundaes served in glass dishes at a counter with upholstered stools high enough for your legs to dangle. But it isn't a self-conscious throwback—it just hasn't changed much since it opened here in 1925.

THE BASICS

Downtown Des Moines is about 10 minutes by taxi from Des Moines International Airport

Renaissance Savery Hotel
401 Locust Street
515-244-2151
marriott.com
$$
Renovated hotel, originally opened in 1919, in a Georgian Revival building.

Des Moines Marriott Downtown
700 Grand Avenue
515-245-5500
marriott.com
$$
Pool, downtown location, and flashy City Center Lounge.

Suites of 800 Locust Street
800 Locust Street
515-288-5800
800locust.com
$$
Luxury hotel with spa; near the sculpture park.

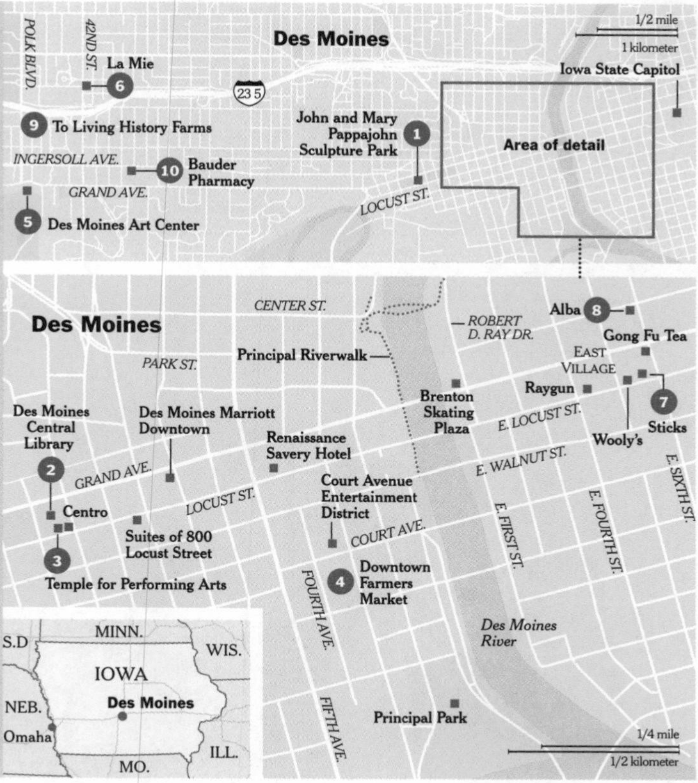

us bank

St. Louis

St. Louis, Missouri, is more than just a Gateway to the West. It's a lively destination in its own right, full of inviting neighborhoods, some coming out of a long decline and revitalized by public art, varied night life, and restaurants that draw on the bounty of surrounding farmland and rivers. The famous arch, of course, is still there, along with plenty of 19th-century architecture and an eye-opening amount of green space. Add to that a mix of Midwestern sensibility and Southern charm, and you've got plenty of reason to stay a while. — BY DAN SALTZSTEIN

FRIDAY

1 *Out in the Open* 4 p.m.

The new jewel of downtown St. Louis is **Citygarden** (citygardenstl.org), a sculpture park the city opened in 2009, framed by the old courthouse on one side and the Gateway Arch on the other. The oversize public art, by boldface-name artists like Mark di Suvero and Keith Haring, is terrific, but the real genius of the garden's layout is that it reflects the landscape of the St. Louis area: an arcing wall of local limestone, for instance, echoes the bends of the Mississippi and Missouri Rivers, which join just north of town.

2 *Up in the Sky* 6 p.m.

If you've never been to the top of the 630-foot **Gateway Arch** (gatewayarch.com), the four-minute ride up in a uniquely designed tram system is a must. And even if you have, it's worth reminding yourself that yes, that water down there is the Mississippi River, and that city spreading out beyond it is where a lot of optimistic Easterners slogged their first miles into the west. Eero Saarinen designed the arch, made of stainless steel, and it was completed in 1965. Besides providing a helicopter-height view, it's an elegantly simple artwork that endures.

3 *Soulard Soul* 8 p.m.

Historic Soulard (pronounced SOO-lard) is one of those neighborhoods experiencing a renaissance thanks in part to several new quality restaurants. **Franco** (1535 South Eighth Street; 314-436-2500; eatatfranco.com; $$), an industrial-chic bistro next to the locally famous Soulard farmers' market, serves soulful takes on French bistro fare, like country-fried frogs' legs in a red wine gravy and grilled Missouri rainbow trout in a crayfish and Cognac cream sauce.

4 *Analog Underground* 10 p.m.

Jazz and blues are part of the St. Louis legacy, and one of the best places to hear the tradition play on is **BB's Jazz, Blues, and Soups** (700 South Broadway; 314-436-5222; bbsjazzbluessoups.com), a club in an old brick building a few blocks from the river and the Gateway Arch. In addition to the music, you'll find a variety of beers. And yes, there really is soup, and its house-made goodness is a point of pride.

SATURDAY

5 *Cupcakes and Blooms* 9 a.m.

In the leafy neighborhood of Shaw, stately architecture mixes with hip spots like **SweetArt** (2203 South 39th Street; 314-771-4278; sweetartstl.com), a mom-and-pop bakery where you can eat a virtuous vegan breakfast topped off by a light-as-air cupcake. Shaw is named for Henry Shaw, a botanist and philanthropist whose crowning achievement is the

OPPOSITE St. Louis's signature, the Gateway Arch designed by Eero Saarinen. Take the tram to the top, and you'll be riding up 630 feet on an elegant work of art.

BELOW The Missouri Botanical Garden.

Missouri Botanical Garden (4344 Shaw Boulevard; 314-577-5100; mobot.org). Founded in 1859, it is billed as the oldest continuously operating botanical garden in the nation. It covers an impressive 79 acres and includes a large Japanese garden and Henry Shaw's 1850 estate home, as well as his (slightly creepy) mausoleum.

6 *Taste of Memphis* 1 p.m.

St. Louis-style ribs are found on menus across the country, but it's a Memphis-style joint (think slow-smoked meats, easy on the sauce) that seems to be the consensus favorite for barbecue in town. Just survey the best-of awards that decorate the walls at **Pappy's Smokehouse** (3106 Olive Street; 314-535-4340; pappyssmokehouse.com; $-$$). Crowds line up for heaping plates of meat and sides, served in an unassuming space (while you wait, take a peek at the smoker parked out back on a side street). The ribs and pulled pork are pretty good, but the winners might be the sides — bright and tangy slaw and deep-fried corn on the cob.

7 *Green Day* 3 p.m.

St. Louis boasts 105 city-run parks, but none rivals **Forest Park** (stlouis.missouri.org/citygov/parks/forestpark), which covers more than 1,200 acres smack in the heart of the city. It opened in 1876, but it was the 1904 World's Fair that made it a world-class public space, spawning comely buildings like the Palace of Fine Art, which now houses the Saint Louis Art Museum. The Jewel Box, a towering, contemporary-looking greenhouse, dates back to 1936 but was renovated in the early 2000s. For an overview, rent a bike from the park visitor's center at 5595 Grand Drive (914-367-7275) and just meander.

8 *Midwest Bounty* 8 p.m.

Locavore fever has hit St. Louis. Leading the pack may be **Local Harvest Cafe and Catering** (3137 Morgan Ford Road; 314-772-8815; localharvestcafe.com; $$$), a mellow spot in the Tower Grove neighborhood that's a spinoff of an organic grocery store across the street. A chalkboard menu lists all the local products featured that day, including items like honey and peanut butter. On Saturday nights the chef creates a four-course menu based on what's fresh at the farms and markets that morning. One menu included a light vegetarian cassoulet with beer pairings from local producers like Tin Mill Brewery.

9 *Royale Treatment* 10 p.m.

Tower Grove is also home to a handful of fine watering holes, including the **Royale** (3132 South Kingshighway Boulevard; 314-772-3600; theroyale.com), where an Art Deco-style bar of blond wood and glass is accompanied by old photos of political leaders (John F. Kennedy, Martin Luther King Jr., the late Missouri governor Mel Carnahan). But it's the extensive cocktail list, with drinks named after city neighborhoods (like the Carondelet Sazerac), and a backyard patio that keep the aficionados coming. There's plenty of craft beer, too.

SUNDAY

10 *The Home Team* 10 a.m.

Take a number for one of the small, worn wooden tables at **Winslow's Home** (7211 Delmar Boulevard;

BELOW In the impressive and sprawling Forest Park, the Palace of Fine Art, a leftover from the 1904 world's fair, now houses the Saint Louis Art Museum.

314-725-7559; winslowshome.com; $). It's more than just a pleasant place for brunch and espresso; it doubles as a general store that carries groceries, dry goods, books, and kitchen items like stainless steel olive oil dispensers. Have a hearty breakfast and then take time to browse.

11 *Art Class* Noon

Washington University gets high marks for its academics. But the campus, with its rolling green hills and grand halls, is also home to terrific contemporary art. See its collection at the **Mildred Lane Kemper Art Museum** (1 Brookings Drive; 314-935-4523; kemperartmuseum.wustl.edu). Designed by the Pritzker Prize-winning architect Fumihiko Maki, it's charmingly cramped and vaguely organized by theme — so you'll find a Jackson Pollock cheek by jowl with a 19th-century portrait of Daniel Boone. You'll also find ambitious contemporary art exhibitions curated by Wash U faculty. Like much of St. Louis, the Kemper may not be flashy, but it's full of gems.

OPPOSITE ABOVE Oversize public art finds space at Citygarden, a downtown sculpture park.

ABOVE The extensive cocktail list at the Royale in the Tower Grove area features drinks — the Carondelet Sazerac, for one — that are named after city neighborhoods.

THE BASICS

Lambert International Airport is served by major airlines. For getting around in town, it's best to have a car.

Moonrise Hotel
6177 Delmar Boulevard
314-721-1111
moonrisehotel.com
$$
Pleasant boutique vibe and a central location.

Four Seasons St. Louis
999 North 2nd Street
314-881-5800
fourseasons.com/stlouis
$$$-$$$$
Part of a striking riverside complex that also includes a casino.

St. Louis Union Station Marriott
1820 Market Street
314-621-5262
stlunionstationhotel.com
$$
In the grand old downtown railroad station.

MILLER JACKSON COMPANY
HOOTERS
BCM

Oklahoma City

It shouldn't take more than a day for the song—who doesn't know that song?—to clear your head. Yes, a constant wind does seem to come sweepin' down the plain (more accurately, the red-dirt prairie). But amid the grand urban projects, gleaming museums, and air of new sophistication in today's Oklahoma City, the only folks yelling "Ayipioeeay" are likely to be visitors. Hints of what's behind the revitalization pop up everywhere: oil rigs, even on the State Capitol grounds. Even so, newcomers to town might wonder at first where they are. A generally flat cityscape, friendly hellos, and Chicago-style downtown architecture suggest the Midwest. Jazz, blues bars, and barbecue joints speak of the South. But the wide vistas and the American Indian shops (Oklahoma has 38 sovereign tribes), pickups, and cowboy hats tell another story: this is the West.

— BY FINN-OLAF JONES

FRIDAY

1 *Bricks and Bronzes* 4 p.m.

The Oklahoma River waterfront has come alive since 1999, when a canal was completed to attract visitors. In the lively Bricktown district, old warehouses now hold restaurants, clubs, and shops. Catch the bold spirit by checking out the **Centennial Land Run Monument** (Centennial Avenue; okc.gov/landrun), an eye-popping, larger-than-life-size commemoration of the great Land Run of 1889, when 10,000 people rushed into town on a single day. Its series of ultra-realistic bronze statues, by the sculptor Paul Moore, shows pioneers, horses, and wagons caught in motion as they charge into the fray and ford a river. Together, they make up one of the largest freestanding bronze sculptures in the world. Nearby, duck inside for a look at some of the 300 banjos in the **American Banjo Museum** (9 East Sheridan Avenue; 405-604-2793; americanbanjomuseum.com), ranging from lavishly decorated Jazz Age beauties to replicas of slaves' homemade instruments.

OPPOSITE Taxi boats on the canal in Bricktown, a happening Oklahoma City neighborhood.

RIGHT Oil has been good to Oklahoma, and derricks appear all over town, even on the grounds of the State Capitol.

2 *Wasabi on the Range* 7 p.m.

If you're in the mood for steak, you will never have far to look in Oklahoma City. But even if you're not, have dinner at the **Mantel Wine Bar & Bistro** (201 East Sheridan Avenue; 405-236-8040; themantelokc.com; $$). The menu honors the regional theme with several beef entrees, but also offers interesting alternatives like duck breast with cranberry port wine sauce or wasabi-encrusted tuna.

3 *You'll Never Bowl Alone* 9 p.m.

Check out the night life in Bricktown, where taxi boats ferry merrymakers to the teeming homegrown jazz and blues joints. One of the livelier spots is **RedPin** (200 South Oklahoma Avenue; 405-702-8880; bowlredpin.com), a 10-lane bowling alley masquerading as a nightclub. Rent some hip-looking high-top bowling shoes, grab a beer or a pomegranate martini, and bowl the night away.

SATURDAY

4 *Feed Your Inner Cowboy* 11 a.m.

South of the river, the century-old Oklahoma National Stockyards are still used for enormous cattle auctions several times a week, but there's another kind of show one block farther up at **Cattlemen's Steakhouse** (1309 South Agnew Avenue;

405-236-0416; cattlemensrestaurant.com; $$). Long lines form for lunch and dinner (no reservations taken), so try breakfast. "Usually it's just the old-timers that want this," a waitress said when one out-of-towner succumbed to curiosity and ordered the calf brains. For the record, it looks like oatmeal, has a slight livery aftertaste, and isn't half bad. But wash it down with a couple of mugs of hot coffee and a plate of eggs and magnificently aged and tenderized steak.

5 *Dress Your Inner Cowboy* 12:30 p.m.

Cross the street to **Langston's Western Wear** (2224 Exchange Avenue; 405-235-9536; langstons.com) for your dungarees and boots, and then wander into the **National Saddlery Company** (1400 South Agnew Avenue; 405-239-2104; nationalsaddlery.com) for a hand-tooled saddle—prices run from about $1,500 for a base model to $30,000 for a masterpiece with silver trimmings. Down the street, **Shorty's Caboy Hattery** (1206 South Agnew Avenue; 405-232-4287; shortyshattery.com) will supply you with a custom-made cattleman's hat described by Mike Nunn, who manned the counter one day, as "the only hat that will stay on your head in Oklahoma wind." On the next block, **Oklahoma Native Art and Jewelry** (1316 South Agnew Avenue; 405-604-9800) carries a broad variety of items from Oklahoma's tribes. White pottery pieces with horse hairs burned onto their surfaces in Jackson Pollock-like swirling patterns are made by the store's owner, Yolanda White Antelope. Her son, Mario Badillo, creates silver jewelry.

6 *Where the West Is Found* 2 p.m.

James Earle Fraser's famous 18-foot statue of an American Indian slumped on his horse, *The End of the Trail*, greets you in the lobby of the **National Cowboy and Western Heritage Museum** (1700 Northeast 63rd Street; 405-478-2250; nationalcowboymuseum.org). Beware. You may think you can cover it in a couple of hours, but a whole day could be too little to reach the end of this trail. Exhibits in tentlike pavilions around a central courtyard cover everything about cowboys from their roots in Africa and England to how they operate on contemporary corporate ranches. Examine a replica of a turn-of-the-century cattle town; guns including John Wayne's impressive personal arsenal; and Western art including works by Frederic Remington, Albert Bierstadt, and Charles M. Russell.

7 *Cosmopolitans* 7 p.m.

The city's new economy has attracted a whole new class of settler, business types from world financial capitals, usually male and accompanied by stylish spouses. Find them—and a pre-dinner cocktail—in

ABOVE The memorial to victims of the 1995 bombing.

the noirish-cool **Lobby Bar** (4322 North Western Avenue; 405-604-4650; willrogerslobbybar.com) in the newly renovated Will Rogers Theatre, which looms over an affluent corridor of North Western Avenue. The street continues up to Tara-sized mansions dotting Nichols Hills, on the way passing establishments like **French Cowgirl** (4514 North Western Avenue; 405-604-4696), which sells tooled cellphone holders to match your saddle. For dinner, drive a few blocks to the **Coach House** (6437 Avondale Drive; 405-842-1000; thecoachhouseokc.com; $$-$$$), where the name of many an entree includes words borrowed from the French.

8 *Dances With Bulls* 10 p.m.

Find friends fast at **Cowboys OKC**, formerly Club Rodeo (2301 South Meridian Avenue; 405-686-1191; cowboysokc.com). Modern cowgirls and cowboys of every age group and shape can be found hootin' and hollerin' at this acre-sized honky-tonk south of downtown near the airport. Fellow carousers will help you figure out the dance moves to go with

ABOVE Shorty's Caboy Hattery. The cattleman's hat, they'll tell you at Shorty's, is the only kind that will stay on your head in an Oklahoma wind.

BELOW A view of downtown Oklahoma City from the fountain in front of City Hall.

country sounds. The mood may turn real cowpokey when dance-floor lights go dark to be replaced by spotlights on a tennis-court-sized rodeo ring, where revelers migrate with their beers to watch hopefuls try to hang onto bucking bulls for longer than eight seconds. The loudest cheers have been known to go to the orneriest bulls.

SUNDAY

9 *The Memorial* 10 a.m.

All longtime residents of Oklahoma City seem to know exactly where they were at 9:02 a.m. on April 19, 1995, when Timothy McVeigh detonated an explosives-filled truck beneath the Alfred P. Murrah Federal Building, killing 168 people and damaging 312 surrounding buildings. At the **Oklahoma City National Memorial** (620 North Harvey Avenue; 405-235-3313; oklahomacitynationalmemorial.org) that now covers the site, a gently flowing reflecting pool and two massive gates preside over 168 empty bronze chairs—one for each victim, the 19 smaller ones denoting children. Absorb the quiet, and the message.

10 *Under Glass* 11 a.m.

The **Oklahoma City Museum of Art** (415 Couch Drive; 405-236-3100; okcmoa.com) boasts the world's most comprehensive collection of glass sculptures by Dale Chihuly, starting with the 55-foot-tall centerpiece at the front door. Savor the mesmerizing play of light, color, and fantastic shapes, a fitting goodbye to a town that never seems shy about grabbing your attention.

OPPOSITE *The End of the Trail*, by James Earle Fraser, at the National Cowboy and Western Heritage Museum.

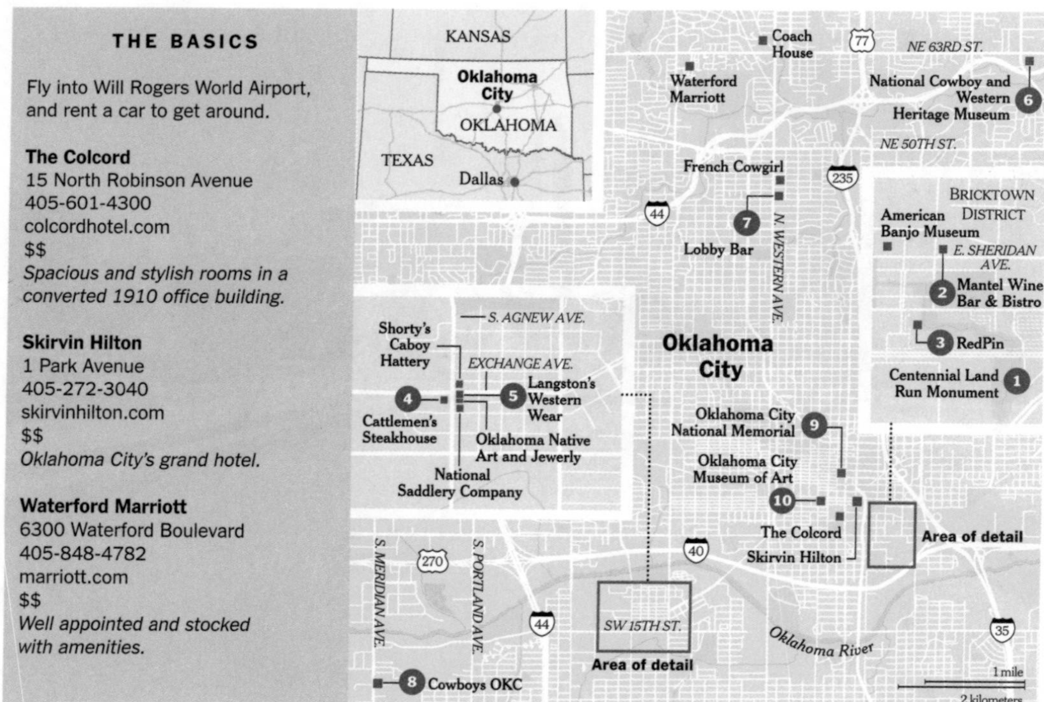

THE BASICS

Fly into Will Rogers World Airport, and rent a car to get around.

The Colcord
15 North Robinson Avenue
405-601-4300
colcordhotel.com
$$
Spacious and stylish rooms in a converted 1910 office building.

Skirvin Hilton
1 Park Avenue
405-272-3040
skirvinhilton.com
$$
Oklahoma City's grand hotel.

Waterford Marriott
6300 Waterford Boulevard
405-848-4782
marriott.com
$$
Well appointed and stocked with amenities.

WESTERN
AUTO
TRADERS ON GRAND

Kansas City

Kansas City, Missouri, is known for its barbecue, bebop, and easy-does-it Midwestern charm. Still a jazz mecca, the place where Charlie Parker, Lester Young, and Count Basie all got their start, it also has a newer and broader cultural richness. A decade-long effort to revitalize the downtown includes construction of the Kauffman Center for the Performing Arts, giving a sleek new home to the symphony, opera, and ballet. Yet while this metropolis on the Missouri River is no backwater, don't expect high polish. The city's best asset may be the unvarnished grit traceable all the way back to its days as the jumping-off point to the West on the Santa Fe Trail. — BY CHARLY WILDER

FRIDAY

1 *Crossroads Redefined* 2 p.m.

Industrial stagnation and suburban exodus in the 1960s left the Crossroads neighborhood nearly deserted. But now it is the **Crossroads Arts District** (kccrossroads.org), home to fashionable lofts in buildings like the former Western Auto offices, and to some 70 galleries. A pioneering mainstay is **Sherry Leedy Contemporary Art** (2004 Baltimore Avenue; 816-221-2626; sherryleedy.com). The **Belger Arts Center** (2100 Walnut Street; 816-474-3250; belgerartscenter.org), the project of a local family foundation, has varying exhibitions that have included 3D and 4D works. If it's the first Friday of the month, many galleries hold open houses until about 9 p.m.

2 *Sauce It Up* 6 p.m.

Debates over the best barbecue rouse as much passion here as religion or politics. Some swear by the old guard like Gates Bar-B-Q (gatesbbq.com) and Arthur Bryant's (arthurbryantsbbq.com), both of which have multiple branches. Others make the quick trip across the state line into Kansas City, Kansas, to a relative newcomer, **Oklahoma Joe's** (3002 West 47th Avenue; 913-722-3366; oklahomajoesbbq.com; $). It serves pulled pork and beef brisket piled high on white bread, in a sauce that may just be the perfect amalgam of sweet, smoke, and vinegar.

OPPOSITE Kansas City's Crossroads district.

3 *Under the Safdie Domes* 8 p.m.

Arts lovers in Kansas City raised the funds to build the $326 million **Kauffman Center for the Performing Arts** (1601 Broadway; 816-994-7200; kauffmancenter.org), designed by Moshe Safdie, which opened in 2011. Placido Domingo, Itzhak Perlman, and the jazz artist Diana Krall performed on opening night, and the building quickly won rave reviews from architecture critics, music critics, and the people of Kansas City. Its two clamshell domes hold an 1,800-seat theater for the city's ballet and opera companies and a 1,600-seat concert hall for the symphony orchestra. It's a rare Friday night when there's nothing going on here. Check the schedule in advance, and enjoy the performance.

SATURDAY

4 *Park Life* 10 a.m.

Kansas City is said to have more fountains than any other city except Rome. (This is difficult to prove, but with about 200 of them, it certainly has a good claim.) One of the loveliest can be found at **Jacob L. Loose Park** (51st Street and Wornall Road), a Civil War site, where the Laura Conyers Smith Fountain, made of Italian stone, is encircled by thousands of roses in some 150 varieties. The park is popular with picnicking families and bongo-playing teenagers on furlough from the suburbs.

5 *Contemporary Greens* Noon

If last night's barbecue has you yearning for a salad, head to **Café Sebastienne**, an airy, glass-covered restaurant at the **Kemper Museum of Contemporary Art** (4420 Warwick Boulevard; 816-561-7740; kemperart.org/cafe; $$). Seasonal greens come with cucumber, red onion, grape tomatoes, sheep's milk cheese, and grilled pita. After lunch, pop inside for a quick look at the Kemper's small but diverse collection of modern and contemporary works by artists like Dale Chihuly and Louise Bourgeois, whose gigantic iron spider sculpture looms over the front lawn.

6 *Art in a Cube* 1:30 p.m.

In 2007, the **Nelson-Atkins Museum of Art** (4525 Oak Street; 816-751-1278; nelson-atkins.org) was thrust into the national spotlight when it

opened a new wing designed by Steven Holl. The Bloch Building — which holds contemporary art, photography, and special exhibitions — consists of five translucent glass blocks that create what Nicolai Ouroussoff, the architecture critic of *The New York Times*, described as "a work of haunting power." The museum's suite of American Indian galleries shows an assemblage of about 200 works from more than 68 tribes.

7 *18th Street Couture* 4 p.m.

The Crossroads cultural awakening extends beyond art and into fashion. Three boutiques carrying the work of up-and-coming designers occupy a former film storage unit on West 18th Street. Peregrine Honig and Danielle Meister hand-pick lingerie and swimwear to carry at their shop, **Birdies** (116 West 18th Street; 816-842-2473; birdiespanties.com). **Peggy Noland** (124 West 18th Street; 816-221-7652; peggynoland.com) sells creations on the border of art and fashion in a shop that has often changed décor, at one time resembling the interior of a cloud, at another time covered floor-to-ceiling with stuffed animals.

8 *Midwest Tapas* 7 p.m.

Stay in the Crossroads to sample modern Mediterranean-style tapas at **Extra Virgin** (1900 Main Street; 816-842-2205; extravirginkc.com; $$-$$$), whose chef and owner is Kansas City's culinary titan, Michael Smith. The fare is more playful and adventurous than in his formal restaurant (called simply Michael Smith) next door. And if the loud, euro-chic décor, replete with a floor-to-ceiling *La Dolce Vita* mural, seems to be trying a little too hard, the crowd of unbuttoned professionals enjoying inspired dishes like crispy pork belly with green romesco and chickpea fries doesn't seem to mind. The menu is diverse, as is the wine list.

9 *'Round Midnight* 10 p.m.

The flashy new **Kansas City Power and Light District** (1100 Walnut Street; powerandlightdistrict.com) offers a wide range of bars, restaurants, and clubs, but it can feel like an open-air fraternity party. When midnight strikes, head to the **Mutual Musicians Foundation** (1823 Highland Avenue; 816-471-5212; mutualmusiciansfoundation.org). The legendary haunt opened in 1917, and public jam sessions are held every Saturday until dawn. For a small cover, you can catch impromptu sets by some of the city's undiscovered musicians in the same room where Charlie Parker had a cymbal thrown at him in 1937.

SUNDAY

10 *Viva Brunch* 10 a.m.

As any resident will tell you, Mexican food is a big deal here. Look for an inventive take on it at **Port**

Fonda (4141 Pennsylvania Avenue; 816-216-6462; portfondakc.com; $$). For brunch, the originality translates into eggs with chorizo, borracho beans, pico de gallo, and fresh corn tortillas, or Huevos Benedictos — poached eggs, biscuits, pork belly tomatillo-chile jam, and hollandaise.

11 *Homage to the Greats* 11 a.m.

The **American Jazz Museum** and **Negro Leagues Baseball Museum** (1616 East 18th Street; 816-474-8463 and 816-221-1920; americanjazzmuseum.com and nlbm.com) share a building in the 18th and Vine Historic District, once the heart of the city's African-American shopping area. The jazz museum, with listening stations to bring the music to life, pays tribute to legendary jazz stars including Charlie Parker, Louis Armstrong, Duke Ellington, and Ella Fitzgerald. The baseball museum is dedicated to the leagues where black stars like Satchel Paige, Josh Gibson, and Kansas City's own Buck O'Neil played until the integration of Major League Baseball in 1947. It was in Kansas City in 1920 that the first of them, the National Negro League, was founded.

OPPOSITE ABOVE The translucent glass Bloch Building, designed by Stephen Holl, at the Nelson-Atkins Museum of Art. The building is the museum's contemporary wing.

OPPOSITE BELOW Sample modern Mediterranean-style tapas at Extra Virgin, owned by the Kansas City chef Michael Smith.

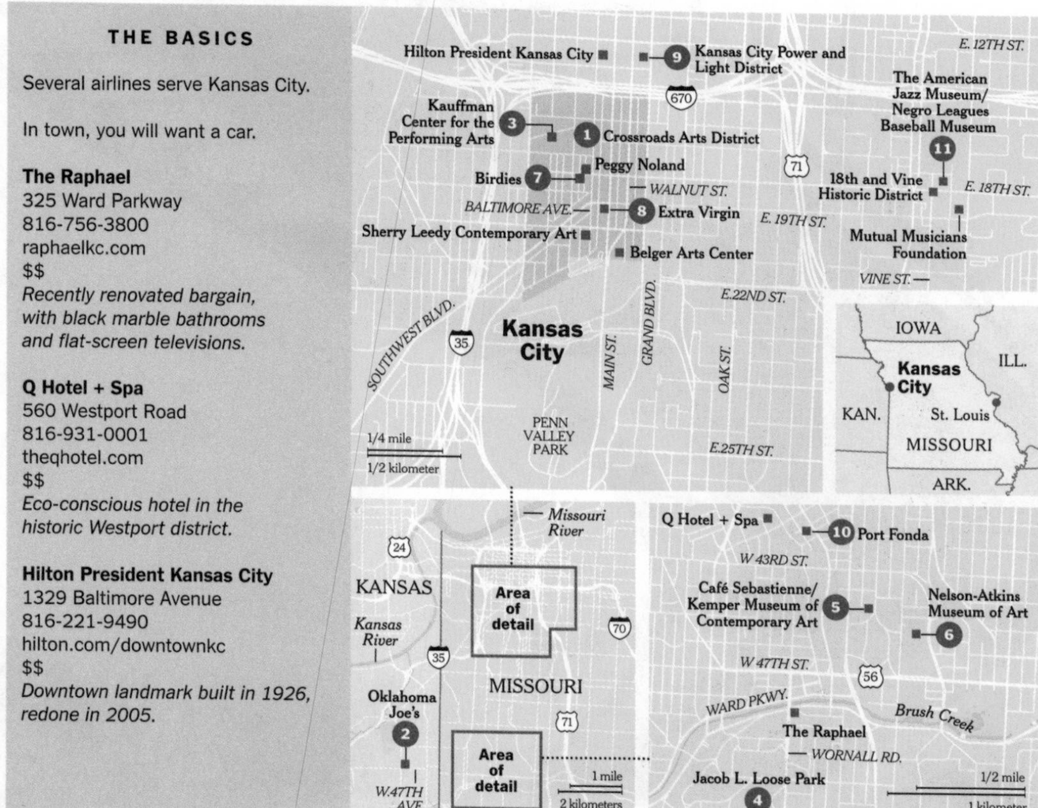

THE BASICS

Several airlines serve Kansas City.

In town, you will want a car.

The Raphael
325 Ward Parkway
816-756-3800
raphaelkc.com
$$
Recently renovated bargain, with black marble bathrooms and flat-screen televisions.

Q Hotel + Spa
560 Westport Road
816-931-0001
theqhotel.com
$$
Eco-conscious hotel in the historic Westport district.

Hilton President Kansas City
1329 Baltimore Avenue
816-221-9490
hilton.com/downtownkc
$$
Downtown landmark built in 1926, redone in 2005.

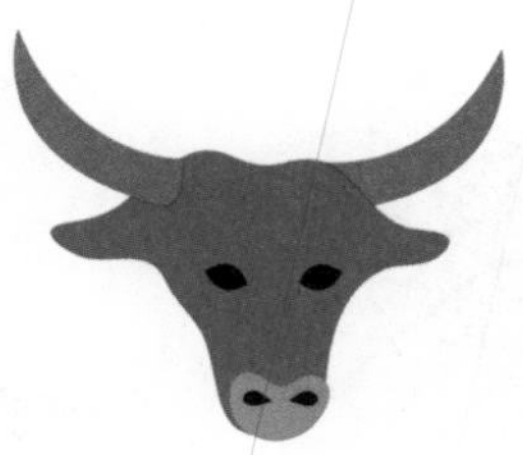

Omaha

As the birthplace of both Warren Buffett and TV dinners, Omaha is a pragmatic, come-as-you-are sort of place — but one with a hip cultural swagger it has earned. With a steady stream of musicians, visual artists, designers, and chefs opting to stay and create here (or seeking refuge from the high rents of Brooklyn, Chicago, or the Bay Area), Omaha has become known for something other than its steaks: it is fertile creative ground. This growth has burnished the reputation of a city with already well-regarded museums, gardens, and zoo. Pedestrian-friendly downtown development has led to a revitalized riverfront, a concert hall, a convention center, and a ballpark hosting the annual College World Series. There's even a one-stop hipster district anchored by Saddle Creek Records, the indie-rock exporter of the "Omaha sound." Of course, in places like the Old Market, visitors can still glimpse the distinctly American mix of the Old West and the Old World that makes Omaha feel like part hearty frontier town and part arty downtown. — BY ANNA BAHNEY

FRIDAY

1 *The Mighty Mo* 4 p.m.

Stroll along the Missouri River, once a vital waterway for the native Omaha tribe. The **Lewis and Clark Landing** (345 Riverfront Drive; 402-444-5900; cityofomaha.org/parks), a 23-acre park with walking trails along the river, marks the site where the historic expedition landed in 1804. Less than a half-mile north is the graceful **Bob Kerrey Pedestrian Bridge** (705 Riverfront Drive; 402-444-5900), a 15-foot-wide footbridge spanning the Missouri. Walkers can cross into Iowa and then return to Nebraska, following the river trails south to **Heartland of America Park** (800 Douglas Street) and the **Gene Leahy Mall** (1302 Farnam), both of which border the Old Market.

2 *The Old Is New* 5 p.m.

The vibrant brick streets of the **Old Market** are lined with buildings bearing the fading advertisements for rugs, fruit, and stoves — goods these late-19th-century brick buildings once warehoused. Now they are bustling with galleries, bars, boutiques, and sidewalk cafes. Slip into **La Buvette** (511 South 11th Street; 402-344-8627; labuvetteomaha.com) for some Old World gastronomy, selecting from among 800 wines, 30 cheeses, and fresh breads. Saunter through shops selling books, music, jewelry, clothing, and art. A dozen galleries are located in the Old Market, a couple of them in the **Passageway**, a grotto-like hideaway of spots tucked into balconies and archways.

3 *Unfussy Feast* 8 p.m.

The **Grey Plume** (220 South 31st Avenue; 402-763-4447; thegreyplume.com; $$), in the revitalized Midtown neighborhood, has impressed diners with an exquisite farm-to-table, fine-dining experience that is neither precious nor pretentious. Everything here has a story — the floorboards are from a barn, the peaches were preserved last summer, the rabbit comes from a farm near Lincoln. The chef, Clayton Chapman, a prodigal native who returned to Omaha via Chicago and France, turns out some of Omaha's finest food — a bright steelhead trout with crème fraiche spätzle, for example, or tender Wagyu beef with maitake mushroom and parsnip.

OPPOSITE The sinuous Bob Kerrey Pedestrian Bridge crosses the Missouri River to Iowa

RIGHT Downtown and the riverfront.

4 *Scotch Honor* 10 p.m.

Drop by the homey **Dundee Dell** (5007 Underwood Avenue; 402-553-9501; dundeedell.com), an unassuming yet formidable bar in the residential neighborhood of Dundee. What seems like an ordinary pub slinging fried pickles and fish and chips beneath large-screen TVs is also known for one of the largest collections of single-malt Scotch whiskies in the world. The Scotch menu, which lists more than 700 single malts and includes two maps of Scotland, runs 15 pages. Beer drinkers may have to do their homework, too: a dozen kinds are on tap and hundreds of varieties are in bottles.

SATURDAY

5 *Sit a Spell* 9 a.m.

Take your appetite to **Big Mama's Kitchen** (3223 North 45th Street; 402-455-6262; bigmamaskitchen.com; $), where Patricia Barron (a.k.a. Big Mama) serves it old school in what is actually an old school. Big Mama's gained local fame for the oven-fried chicken and sweet-potato-pie ice cream served at lunch and dinner, but it turns out made-from-scratch classics for breakfast, too, like biscuits and gravy, breakfast casseroles, buttermilk pancakes, and pork chop with eggs.

6 *Wild Kingdom* 10 a.m.

Prepare for adventure at Omaha's **Henry Doorly Zoo and Aquarium** (3701 South 10th Street; 402-733-8401; omahazoo.com). Meander over suspension bridges and along trails in the Lied Jungle, an eight-story-high indoor habitat amid lush trees and waterfalls, where three-toed sloths hang and pygmy hippos waddle. In the aquarium, walk the ocean floor in a transparent 70-foot-long tunnel as sharks (in 900,000 gallons of water) dart above your head. Then explore the Desert Dome, the bat caves, and the butterfly habitat, and take in an IMAX film.

7 *All Aboard* 1 p.m.

Transport yourself to bygone days when the country traveled by train at the **Durham Museum** (801 South 10th Street; 402-444-5071; durhammuseum.org), housed in the former Omaha Union Station, a stunning 1931 Art Deco jewel. The museum has history and science exhibitions including trains, but the real delight is wandering the station. The 160-foot-long hall is crowned with ornate ceilings that soar 65 feet above the rose and yellow patterned terrazzo floor. Take it in over a hot dog or sandwich from the lunch counter at the Soda Fountain—and don't forget the thick chocolate malt or cherry phosphate.

8 *Future Perfect* 3 p.m.

Since the 1980s, **Bemis Center for Contemporary Arts** (724 South 12th Street; 402-341-7130; bemiscenter.org) has supported contemporary artists from around the world through residencies in Omaha. The center mounts exhibitions of contemporary work by both established and emerging artists. Whatever is on, chances are you've never seen anything like it.

9 *Have What Jack Had* 8 p.m.

Johnny's Cafe (4702 South 27th Street; 402-731-4774; johnnyscafe.com; $$) appeared in the film *About Schmidt*, starring Jack Nicholson and directed by Omaha's native bard of Midwestern middle-class mediocrity, Alexander Payne.

ABOVE Inside the Desert Dome, one of many habitats to explore at the Henry Doorly Zoo and Aquarium.

RIGHT Civic pride in a wall mural.

Nicholson's character sat at the right end of the bar after excusing himself from his own retirement party in the banquet room. But this steakhouse was a favorite long before he bellied up. Opened in 1922 by Frank Kawa, whose family still runs it, the place served meat where it could not get any fresher: right next to the stockyards. The stockyards closed in 1999, but the delicious steaks are still hand-cut and aged on site.

10 *Do NoDo* 9 p.m.

When the growing indie-music label Saddle Creek Records needed both new offices and a viable rock club, the young music execs made a pragmatic decision to build their own. The resulting club is **Slowdown** (729 North 14th Street; 402-345-7569; theslowdown.com), a sleek but chill lounge, bar, and performance space owned by Saddle Creek that is now an anchor of North Downtown, or NoDo. **Film Streams** (1340 Mike Fahey Street; 402-933-0259; filmstreams.org), a nonprofit cinema, shows first-run and repertory films, and nearby are a coffee house and design, bike, and apparel shops.

SUNDAY

11 *Native Nature* 10 a.m.

Wander the gardens, fields, and trails at **Lauritzen Gardens** (100 Bancroft Street; 402-346-4002; lauritzengardens.org). Situated on 100 acres high on the bluffs overlooking the Missouri River, the garden offers more than 15 seasonal or themed plots, from English gardens to woodland walks. Pause among the native wildflowers in the serene Song of the Lark Meadow, named after Willa Cather's story of the same name, to see if you can hear the call of a meadowlark.

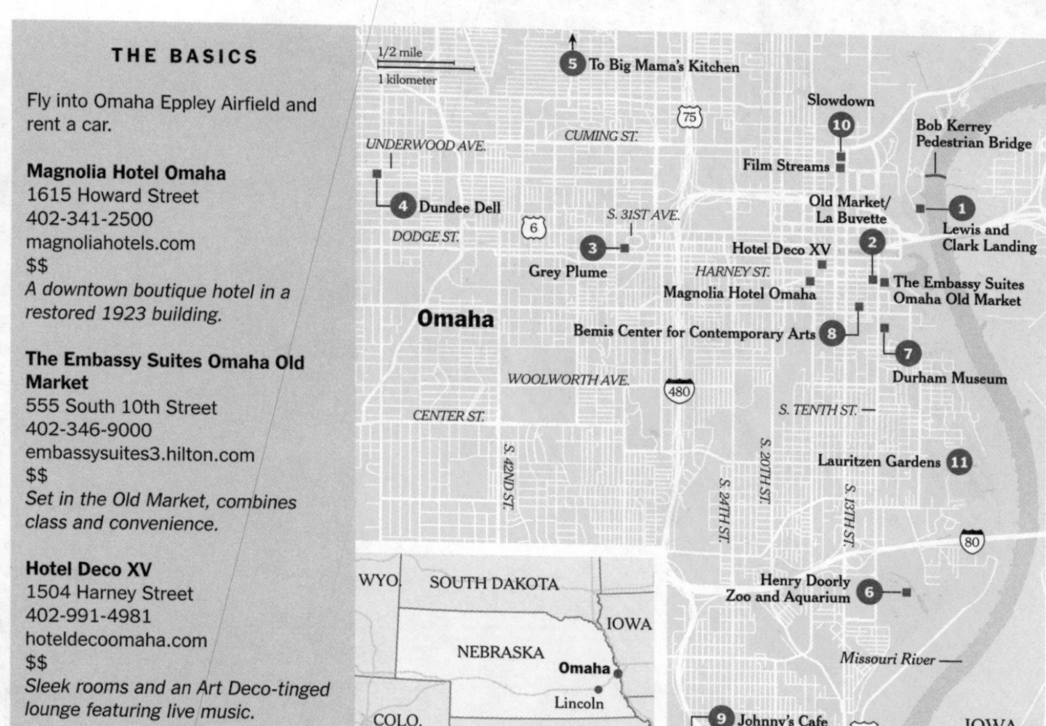

The Niobrara River Valley

To the uninitiated, Nebraska conjures a certain image: a treeless prairie steamrolled pancake-flat, stretching to the horizon. But tucked in a north-central patch of the state is the Niobrara River Valley, filled with a surprising collection of conifers and hardwoods, 200-foot sandstone bluffs, and spring-fed waterfalls. The Niobrara starts in eastern Wyoming and flows across Nebraska for more than 400 miles, emptying into the Missouri River. Seventy-six miles, starting just east of Valentine, are designated as national scenic river (nps.gov/niob). The rapids are mostly riffles, and the water is knee-deep in most spots, inviting a journey by canoe. And although a good float on the river is the center of your trip, there is more to see on land nearby. — BY HELEN OLSSON

FRIDAY

1 *Spurs and Saddles* 2 p.m.

In Valentine (population 2,820), red hearts are painted on the sidewalks and ranchers in cowboy hats roll down Main Street in dusty pickups. Browse the jeans, chaps, hats, ropes, and saddles at **Young's Western Wear** (143 North Main Street; 402-376-1281; discountwesternwear.com), purveyor of all things cowboy. The store has 5,000 pairs of cowboy boots, in snakeskin, elephant, stingray, ostrich, and—if you must—cow leather. Take time to stop by your float-trip outfitter to make sure your reservations are in order for tomorrow. A handful of outfitters in Valentine rent canoes, kayaks, and giant inner tubes and can shuttle you or your car from point to point. One is **Little Outlaw** (1005 East Highway 20; 402-376-1822; outlawcanoe.com). If you canoe or kayak, you can run 22 miles from the Fort Niobrara Refuge to Rocky Ford in a day. A lazy float in a tube takes twice as long, so tubers might get only as far as Smith Falls by day's end.

2 *Under the Waterfall* 3:30 p.m.

Drive 23 miles south on Highway 97 through the Sandhills, past grazing cattle, massive spools of rolled hay, and spinning windmills, to **Snake River Falls**. (This Snake River is a tributary of the Niobrara.) Descend the trail through sumac and yucca to the base and crawl behind the 54-foot-wide falls to marvel at the gushing torrent inches away. Look for the cliff swallows' mud nests clinging to the limestone cliffs around the falls.

3 *Caribbean Meets Prairie* 5:30 p.m.

Three miles down Highway 97 is **Merritt Reservoir** (402-376-3320; outdoornebraska.ne.gov/parks.asp), a deep emerald lake rimmed by white sand beaches. Bury your toes in the warm sugar sand and look for the tiny tracks of sand toads. Anglers pull walleyes, crappies, and wide-mouth bass from the depths, and jet skiers trace arcs on the surface. When you're ready for dinner, find your way to the **Merritt Trading Post and Resort** (402-376-3437; merritttradingpost.com), the only development at the lake, and its **Water's Edge** restaurant (402-376-1878; $$). Or stop for beef tenderloin or fresh walleye at the **Prairie Club** (402-376-1361; theprairieclub.com), a swanky golf course and country club 15 miles north of the reservoir on Highway 97.

4 *Yes, It's the Milky Way* 9 p.m.

Because of its remote location, the **Merritt Reservoir** is a prime spot for stargazing. "On a clear

OPPOSITE Floating on the Niobrara near Valentine, Nebraska.

RIGHT An elk in the Valentine National Wildlife Refuge.

moonless night, no kidding, it's so bright the Milky Way casts a shadow," said John Bauer, owner of the Merritt Trading Post and Reservoir. In late July or early August, amateur astronomers gather here for the annual Nebraska Star Party. They camp on the beach and crane their necks staring into the cosmos. If you're camping at the reservoir, you can gaze until sunrise. Otherwise, get back on the road by 10 or so and let the stars light your way back to Valentine.

SATURDAY

5 *Downriver With a Paddle* 9 a.m.

Grab sandwiches from Henderson's IGA or Scotty's Ranchland, Valentine's local grocers. (There's also a Subway in town.) Meet your outfitter at Cornell Bridge in the **Fort Niobrara National Wildlife Refuge**. Whatever your craft of choice—canoe, kayak, or inner tube—this is where you'll put in and float away on the shallow Niobrara. Over the eons, the Niobrara (pronounced nigh-oh-BRAH-rah) has cut more than 400 feet through a series of rock formations, pinkish-red, chalky white, and gray. Drifting in it is not unlike floating through an enormous block of Neopolitan ice cream. Beach your craft whenever you like and go for a swim or take a walk on shore. On the banks, wade through cold streams and search for small waterfalls tucked in side canyons. A recent National Park Service study found more than 230 falls, most only a few feet high, tumbling into the river along a 35-mile stretch in this part of the Niobrara.

6 *In the Mist* Noon

Twelve miles down river, just past Allen Bridge, watch for signs along the riverbank for **Smith Falls State Park**. Stop to eat the picnic lunch you packed this morning. Stretch your legs with a short hike to the Smith Falls, Nebraska's tallest. Follow the trail across the steel truss Verdigre Bridge and up a winding boardwalk to the falls, where water plunges 63 feet over a bell-shaped rock. Surrounded by moss and mist, red cedar and bur oak, you'd be surprised to find that just a quick hike will take you to the dry, windswept Sandhills Prairie. The cool, moist environment in the river valley not only nurtures these familiar trees, but has preserved ancient species, like the giant paper birch that died out in the rest of Nebraska as the climate grew hotter and drier thousands of years ago. Animal life thrives here too: turkey vultures ride the thermals, sandpipers perch on sandbars, dragonflies dart above the water's surface.

ABOVE Stars, trailing across the sky in a time-lapse photograph, at the Merritt Reservoir, a lake south of Valentine. The remote reservoir is a prime stargazing spot.

OPPOSITE Sunset at the Merritt Reservoir.

7 *Floating Party Zone* 1:30 p.m.

By now, you are probably passing flotillas of summertime tubers from Iowa, Missouri, Kansas, and Nebraska—young things in bikinis and shorts, broiling in the sun and imbibing mightily. As bald eagles soar overhead, hip-hop may be thumping from boom boxes. Stuart Schneider, a park ranger, patrolled the river one late summer day, passing out mesh bags for empties. "On a busy Saturday, we can get 3,000 people," he said. "My favorite time on the river is the fall," he added. "The water is clear, there are no bugs, and the leaves can be spectacular." And, of course, the students are back in school.

8 *Time to Take Out* 4:30 p.m.

Having paddled 22 miles, you can take out at **Rocky Ford**, where your outfitter will retrieve you and your canoe and shuttle you back to your car. Beyond Rocky Ford, there are Class III and IV rapids. Unless you have a death wish, exit here.

9 *Meat Eater's Paradise* 7 p.m.

Back in Valentine, reward yourself with a big aged Nebraska steak at **Jordan's** (404 East Highway 20; 402-376-1255; jordansfinedining.com; $$). You're in cattle country after all. (Thursdays are livestock auction day in Valentine, where the buyers sit 10 deep on bleachers.) Of course, there isn't a menu in town that doesn't have chicken-fried steak. Jordan's is no exception.

SUNDAY

10 *Fuel Up* 10 a.m.

Have breakfast in Valentine at the **Bunkhouse Restaurant & Saloon** (109 East Highway 20; 402-376-1609; $). Under various names and owners, the Bunkhouse building has been serving grub since the 1940s. Slide into a booth and load up with a sirloin steak and eggs (when in Rome, you know…) or a stack of Joe's pancakes. Try a side order of Indian

fry bread with powdered sugar or honey. Rest assured the window you gaze out won't have the unseemly imprint of Valentine's infamous "Butt Bandit." The man who, for more than a year, left greasy prints of his nether regions on the windows of Valentine businesses was arrested in 2008.

11 *Birder's Paradise* 11 a.m.

Twenty miles south of Valentine, you'll find the **Valentine National Wildlife Refuge** (fws.gov/valentine). Where the Ogallala Aquifer nears the surface, bright blue lakes and marshes sparkle like jewels in the green grass. Hundreds of bird species have been sighted here: sharp-tailed grouse, blue-winged teal, long-billed curlews. Just beyond the park's main headquarters, a trail mowed through the grass rises up to a rusting fire tower. From that perch, gaze at the Sandhills, which spread out like a turbulent sea in a hundred shades of green, blue, and gold. It's time to reflect that the only pancake you've seen in Nebraska came with syrup and a generous pat of butter.

ABOVE A view of West Long Lake in the Valentine National Wildlife Refuge.

OPPOSITE At Snake River Falls, near the Merritt Reservoir, adventurers can climb behind the cascade. This Snake River is a tributary of the Niobrara.

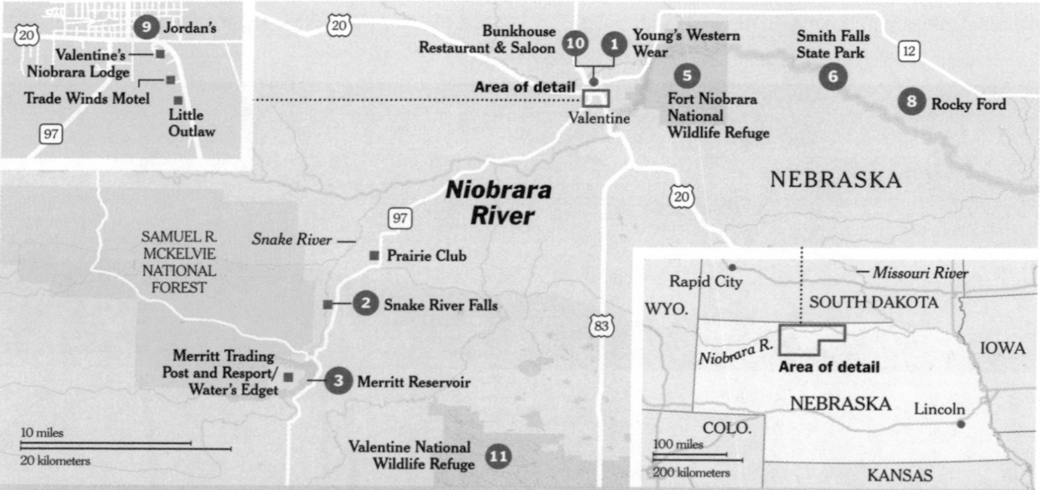

20
9 Jordan's
Valentine's Niobrara Lodge
Trade Winds Motel
Little Outlaw
97
20
Bunkhouse Restaurant & Saloon 10
1 Young's Western Wear
Area of detail
Valentine
5 Fort Niobrara National Wildlife Refuge
Smith Falls State Park 6
12
8 Rocky Ford
NEBRASKA
Niobrara River
97
20
SAMUEL R. MCKELVIE NATIONAL FOREST
Snake River
Prairie Club
2 Snake River Falls
83
Merritt Trading Post and Resport/ Water's Edget
3 Merritt Reservoir
10 miles
20 kilometers
Valentine National Wildlife Refuge 11
Rapid City
Missouri River
WYO.
SOUTH DAKOTA
Niobrara R.
Area of detail
IOWA
NEBRASKA
Lincoln
COLO.
100 miles
200 kilometers
KANSAS

THE BASICS

Valentine is a three-and-a-half-hour drive from Rapid City, South Dakota. Canoe, kayak, or tube on the river and drive nearby.

Trade Winds Motel
East Highway 20, Valentine
402-376-1600
tradewindslodge.com
$
Locally owned, retro, and tidy.

Merritt Trading Post and Resort
Highway 97, 26 miles south of Valentine
402-376-3437
merritttradingpost.com
$
Cabins and campsites, catering to the fishing crowd at the Merritt Reservoir.

Valentine's Niobrara Lodge
803 East Highway 20
402-376-3000
valentinesniobraralodge.com
$$
Cozy but modern.

The Black Hills

Everything may, as they say, be big in Texas, but everything is positively monumental in the southwest corner of South Dakota, in and around the Black Hills. The caves are unusually cavernous, the badlands especially bad; the archaeological sites turn up mammoths. Giant faces gaze from more than one mountain. Drive through this sometimes hilly, sometimes flat, sometimes grassy, sometimes downright lunar landscape, and it will seem that every crossroad has a sign pointing to an outsize attraction, a national monument, or some other officially remembered site. — BY PAUL SCHNEIDER

FRIDAY

1 *Old Men of the Mountain* 2 p.m.

Begin at **Mount Rushmore National Memorial** (1300 Highway 244, Keystone; 605-574-3171; nps.gov/moru). Never mind that Teddy Roosevelt doesn't altogether fit in the group, or that the former republican solemnity of the place has been woefully squandered by the addition of imperial arches and triumphal gewgaws at the entrance. And never mind if you are re-enacting a childhood visit to the place. A visit to Abe and the boys is a fitting start to your zigzagging tour through country where communal gawking and commemoration are de rigueur.

2 *Would Crazy Horse Approve?* 4 p.m.

Just outside Custer, appropriately, is the **Crazy Horse Memorial** (12151 Avenue of the Chiefs, Crazy Horse; 605-673-4681; crazyhorsememorial.org), which when completed, its builders say, will be the largest sculpture on the planet. All of the presidential men on Rushmore would fit on the head of Crazy Horse, an Oglala Lakota chief, which has gradually been emerging from a granite mountain since 1948. The memorial already has what must be one of the world's largest interpretive centers, with all of the requisite snack and souvenir opportunities. The nonprofit, family-run place is somehow unnerving, as much a monument to monument makers and monument marketers as to the man who, with Sitting Bull, defeated George Armstrong Custer at the Little Bighorn. What Crazy Horse, who never permitted a photograph of himself to be taken, would have thought of laser shows projected on his graven image is anybody's guess, but Buffalo Bill Cody would have eaten it up.

3 *Comfort Food* 6 p.m.

Drive into **Hot Springs** and take a quick walk around its eye-catching downtown of carved pink sandstone buildings. Yes, there really are hot springs here, once visited as healing waters and today marketed more as a theme park for children (evansplunge.com). As evening deepens, find your way to the **Vault** (329 North River Street; 605-745-3342; thehotspringsvault.com; $), in one of those fine old buildings—this one dating from 1905—for pub food and beer or soda.

SATURDAY

4 *Platters and Provisions* 8 a.m.

You're setting out for a long day of exploring, so have a hearty breakfast at **Dale's Family Restaurant** (745 Battle Mountain Avenue, Hot

OPPOSITE The face of Crazy Horse, an Oglala Lakota chief, at the Crazy Horse Memorial, which has been gradually emerging from a granite mountain since 1948.

RIGHT Sunset falls on Badlands National Park, an arid wilderness of singular beauty.

Springs; 605-745-3028; $), where you can expect hefty portions, standard eggs-and-bacon fare, and a cheerful local crowd. For lighter fare and muffins to go, try **Fall River Bakery** (407 North River Street; 605-745-6190; $). Be sure to pick up water, as well as snacks, before leaving town. When hunger strikes again, you may be far from the nearest restaurant.

5 *Boys Will Be Boys* 9 a.m.

Even nature seems to be in the business of turning out stone memorials to fallen behemoths. On the southern outskirts of Hot Springs, a mass grave for mammoths is slowly emerging from an ancient sink hole called the **Mammoth Site** (1800 U.S. 18 Bypass, Hot Springs; 605-745-6017; mammothsite.com). The effect is intensely sculptural: a mass of femurs and fibulas, skulls and tusks, backbones and pelvises, some just beginning to show in bas relief, some nearly freed from the surrounding matrix, some displayed behind glass. A few other animals have turned up in the hole, but it's mostly mammoths that ventured in and couldn't get out. And of those, nearly all seem to have been young males, the population most inclined, some mammoth experts have theorized, to risk-taking behavior.

6 *The Underground* 11 a.m.

Crystal lovers may prefer nearby Jewel Cave National Monument, which is one of the world's largest cavern systems, but **Wind Cave National Park** (visitor center on Route 285, 11 miles north of Hot Springs; 605-745-4600; nps.gov/wica) is only marginally less labyrinthine, with 134 miles of mapped passages. It is also where Crazy Horse and his fellow Lakota believed a trickster spirit first convinced humans into coming above ground sometime back at the beginning of the world, which seems more in keeping with the monumental theme. Take along a jacket (it's chilly down there), and choose the tour that descends through the natural entrance rather than the elevator.

7 *Slow Roads* 2 p.m.

Take your time for an afternoon meander through some of the most beautiful parts of the Black Hills. Travel north on Route 87 through **Custer State Park** (605-255-4464; custerstatepark.info), where there's a celebrated herd of buffalo. (For help finding them, ask at the park entrance.) Turn right, toward Keystone, on Route 16A, which will take you through an improbable number of hairpin turns and one-lane tunnels in turreted mountains. For more of the same, check out the more crowded Route 87, the renowned **Needles Highway**. Either way, when you re-emerge, make your way north to Rapid City.

8 *Beef and a Nice Red* 8 p.m.

Cattle ranching country is close by, and at the **Delmonico Grill** (609 Main Street, Rapid City; 605-791-1664; delmonicogrill.biz; $$$), beef is the specialty. Order the classics, like straightforward New York strip and filet mignon, or something more unusual, like ribeye with poblano chiles, crimini mushrooms, caramelized onions, and poblano cream sauce. (Cattle consumption is not required: the menu also includes some seafood and

ABOVE The famous sculptures of the Mount Rushmore National Memorial. The heads of the four presidents are 60 feet high, with 20-foot noses.

pasta.) The wine list is extensive, with California heavily represented.

SUNDAY

9 *Not So Bad* 9 a.m.

The baddest parts of **Badlands National Park**—desiccated, vaguely Martian landscapes formed by erosion—aren't the whole story. Find an alternative on the **Sage Creek Rim Road** (in a convertible if you were smart enough to rent one), which overlooks rolling grasslands that stretch to the horizon. To get to it, leave I-90 at Exit 131, drive south on Route 240, which loops west just before the town called Interior, and turn left at the sign a few miles past the Pinnacles Overlook. Stop at the Sage Creek primitive campground, where you can just walk off into the wide-open wilderness in whatever direction suits your fancy, following buffalo trails and creek beds.

10 *Cold War Firepower* 1:30 p.m.

At the **Minuteman Missile National Historic Site** (605-433-5552; nps.gov/mimi), you can peer into an open silo containing one of the missiles that the United States once had ready for launch to the Soviet Union. It's difficult even to absorb the startling fact that the single bomb that armed this missile had two-thirds of the power of all the weapons expended in World War II. If you want to visit the launch control room, a fortified bunker, show up early; tickets are in demand.

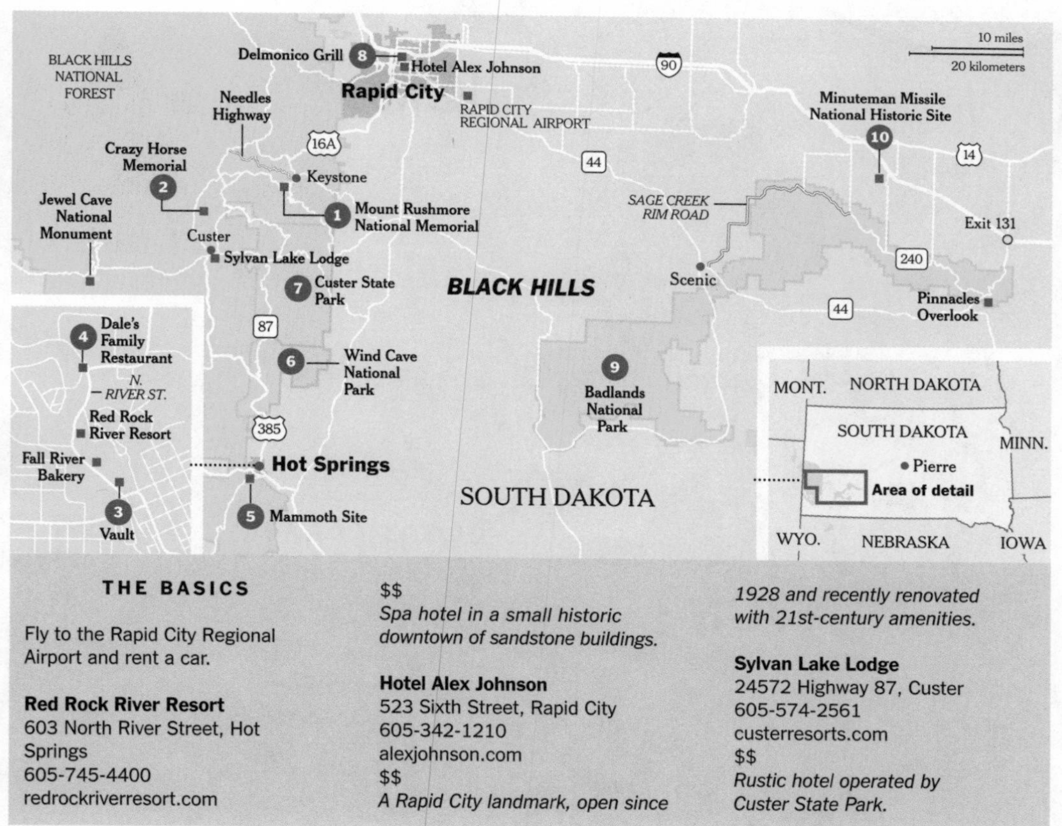

THE BASICS

Fly to the Rapid City Regional Airport and rent a car.

Red Rock River Resort
603 North River Street, Hot Springs
605-745-4400
redrockriverresort.com
$$
Spa hotel in a small historic downtown of sandstone buildings.

Hotel Alex Johnson
523 Sixth Street, Rapid City
605-342-1210
alexjohnson.com
$$
A Rapid City landmark, open since 1928 and recently renovated with 21st-century amenities.

Sylvan Lake Lodge
24572 Highway 87, Custer
605-574-2561
custerresorts.com
$$
Rustic hotel operated by Custer State Park.

504 Banff
500 CALGARY
496
Boise
JACKSON HOLE
508
512
The Tetons
Salt lake City
488
492 PARK CITY
Aspen 524
WELCOME TO Fabulous
LAS VEGAS
476
482 MOAB
532
TELLURIDE
470 the Grand Canyon
464
SEDONA
SCOTTSDALE
456
Albuquerqu
54
450
phoenix
tucson
460

SOUTHWEST
& ROCKY MOUNTAINS

Steamboat Springs

516 Denver

0 AIL

536 Santa Fe

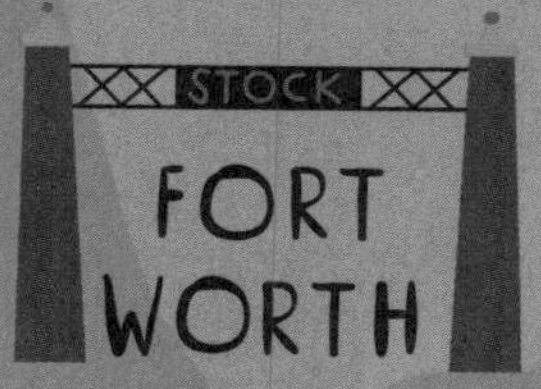

568

574 Dallas

546 El Paso

Texas Hill Country
554

AUSTIN

558

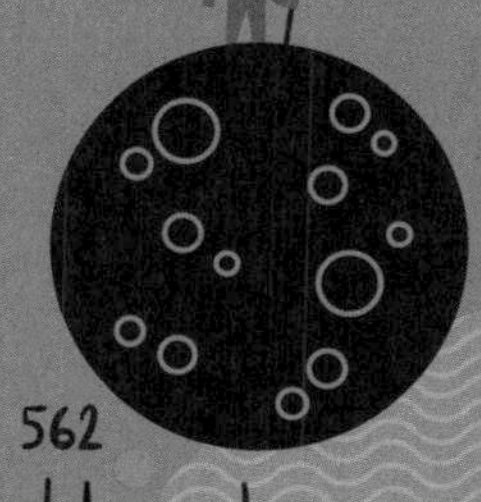

562 Houston

550 SAN ANTONIO

Phoenix

With one of the fastest growth rates in the United States, Phoenix, Arizona, seemed to come out of nowhere to rank in the first years of the 21st century as the nation's fifth-largest city. Although the go-go trend came to a crashing halt when the housing bubble collapsed in 2008 and 2009, the city never lost its appeal, and the housing market rebounded. The southern Arizona heat makes it an inferno in the summer, but the other nine months of the year are gorgeous and sunny. That means that three-fourths of the time, Phoenix, with its resorts, restaurants, contemporary shops, Southwest culture, and desert and mountain landscape, is perfect for exploring.
— BY RANDAL C. ARCHIBOLD AND AMY SILVERMAN

FRIDAY

1 *One Man's Castle* 3 p.m.

All sorts of people, some of them rich and famous, once flocked to Phoenix for health reasons, at least before smog became a big problem. But perhaps none was stranger than Boyce Luther Gulley, an architect from Seattle, who arrived in 1930 to recover from tuberculosis and, while he was at it, built a "castle" largely from found objects. The **Mystery Castle** (800 East Mineral Road; 602-268-1581; mymysterycastle.com), a trippy monument to Gulley's imagination, is adorned with all sorts of stuff, including tree branches for chairs, crooked windows, and Indian artifacts.

2 *Tacos and Mariachi* 6 p.m.

The border is just three hours away by car and more than a third of the city's residents are Latino, so Mexican food rules. Phoenicians argue over the best restaurants, but it is hard to top **Garcia's Las Avenidas** (2212 North 35th Avenue; 602-272-5584; garciasmexicanfood.com; $), a family-run place known for its traditional menu and cavernous setting. A mariachi band often drifts from table to table, belting out ballads. No, the menu is not daring, but the plates come heaping with home-style favorites like tacos and enchiladas that won't damage the wallet. The juicy carnitas de puerco are worth a try.

3 *Hollywood in Phoenix* 8 p.m.

The juggernaut of downtown construction in the frenetic days of the real estate boom — projects included a convention center expansion, a hotel, and condominiums — spared a few jewels, including the historic **Hotel San Carlos** (202 North Central Avenue). Hollywood stars like Mae West and Marilyn Monroe stayed in this 1928 Italian Renaissance-style landmark, which still exudes an air of European refinement. Walk inside for a look around, and then move on to the **Crescent Ballroom** (308 North 2nd Avenue; 602-716-2222; crescentphx.com), where you can have a drink and listen to live bands.

SATURDAY

4 *Up Close at Camelback* 8 a.m.

Camelback Mountain sits in the middle of metropolitan Phoenix, and the Echo Canyon Trail in the **Echo Canyon Recreation Area** (phoenix.org/top-ten/hikes-in-the-phoenix-area/) is its most renowned hike. Locals call it the Scenic Stairmaster, and they'll warn you that this is no dawdle — the hike is 1.2 miles, and about 1,200 feet up, one way. On a clear day, you can see the Salt River Pima-Maricopa Indian Community to the east and Piestewa Peak (formerly known as Squaw Peak) to the west. You might also see cottontail rabbits,

OPPOSITE Saguaros at the Desert Botanical Garden, an oasis of towering cacti, aromatic flowers, and verdant plants in the middle of the urban grid.

RIGHT Phoenix sprawls out in the desert below a lookout point in South Mountain Park.

rattlesnakes, coyotes — and unfortunate hikers who didn't bring enough water (prepare yourself with a large bottle). For more child-friendly hiking, try some of the many miles of trails at **South Mountain Park** (phoenixasap.com/south-mountain-park.html), which at 16,000 acres is sometimes called the world's largest municipal park.

5 *Hiker's Reward* 11 a.m.

Gaze up at the mountain you just conquered from a patio table at **La Grande Orange Grocery** (4410 North 40th Street; 602-840-7777; lagrandeorangegrocery.com; $). You'll fit in at this little fine-foods market and cafe whether you've showered post-hike or not. Look on the menu for the Jersey Girl Omelet made with pastrami and roasted potatoes. Or go vegetarian — there are plenty of good choices.

6 *Hiker's Rejuvenation* Noon

Step into the lobby of the **Arizona Biltmore Resort & Spa** (2400 East Missouri Avenue; 602-955-6600; arizonabiltmore.com) to appreciate the Frank Lloyd Wright-inspired architecture fully. Even on the hottest day, you'll instantly feel cooled by the structure of Biltmore Block, precast concrete blocks that make up the high-ceilinged main building. The Biltmore welcomes nonguests at its spa, so wrap yourself in a thick terry robe and head to a treatment room. (Reservations recommended.) Shopaholics may want to stick around afterward to seek out **Biltmore Fashion Park** (2502 East Camelback Road; 602-955-8400; shopbiltmore.com), a largely open-air mall stocked with high-end stores.

7 *Art Spaces* 2 p.m.

A cluster of galleries, boutiques, and restaurants in rehabilitated bungalows and old commercial buildings along once-forlorn Roosevelt Street have

ABOVE Seclusion at the Royal Palms Resort.

LEFT Camelback Mountain rises up beyond the cactus at the Desert Botanical Garden.

led to the area's christening as **CenPho**, the central Phoenix art district. Examine the local and regional contemporary art at **Modified Arts** (407 East Roosevelt Street; 602-462-5516; modifiedarts.org) and adventurous pieces at **eye lounge** (419 East Roosevelt Street; 602-430-1490; eyelounge.com). Take a look at **monOrchid** (214 East Roosevelt Street; 602-253-0339; monorchid.com), which does double duty as an art space and a wedding venue. And walk around the corner to the front of **MADE Art Boutique** (922 North Fifth Street; 602-256-6233; madephx.com), which carries books, ceramics, craft items, and jewelry.

8 *The Original Residents* 3:30 p.m.

American Indian culture runs deep here, with several active tribes and reservations in the region. Just about all of them have contributed displays or materials to the **Heard Museum** (2301 North Central Avenue; 602-252-8848; heard.org), renowned for its collection of Native American art. The museum shop is also a great place to buy gifts.

9 *Steak and the Fixings* 7 p.m.

Phoenicians love a good steak as much as the next westerner, and since 1955, many in search of a chunk of beef and a bottle of wine have flocked to **Durant's** (2611 North Central Avenue; 602-264-5967; durantsaz.com; $$$). The steaks come in several cuts, from Delmonico and strip to the "humble T-bone," and the rest of the menu hits all the familiar notes: shrimp cocktail, oysters Rockefeller, stuffed baked potatoes, surf and turf. The place is well stocked with regular customers, but you may not be the only newcomer dropping in.

BELOW A pool at the Arizona Biltmore Resort & Spa. You don't have to be a hotel guest to use the spa, so schedule a treatment after a morning of hiking.

10 *Remember Alice?* 10 p.m.

For a drink and a few helpings of eccentricity, drop in at **Alice Cooperstown** (101 East Jackson Street; 602-253-7337; alicecooperstown.com), named after the shock rocker and Phoenix resident Alice Cooper. You may find a live band or a boxing match, and the servers wear "Alice eyes" makeup. Need we say more?

ABOVE Alice Cooperstown, named for a favorite son.

OPPOSITE The Hotel San Carlos, built in 1928.

SUNDAY

11 *Urban Desert* 10 a.m.

Driving through central Phoenix, you're more likely to see imported pine trees than saguaros, the giant native cactuses. The **Desert Botanical Garden** (1201 North Galvin Parkway; 480-941-1225; dbg.org) is the perfect place to get your dose of desert life without ever leaving a brick pathway. Spread across 50 acres in Papago Park, the garden is an oasis of towering cacti, aromatic flowers, and surprisingly verdant plants in the middle of the urban grid.

THE BASICS

Phoenix, 350 miles east of Los Angeles, is served by multiple airlines.

On the ground, a car is essential.

Royal Palms Resort
5200 East Camelback Road
602-840-3610
royalpalmshotel.com
$$$
Palms, gardens, and fountains help create a feeling of seclusion amid the Phoenix sprawl.

Arizona Biltmore Resort and Spa
2400 East Missouri Avenue
602-955-6600
arizonabiltmore.com
$$$$
Eight swimming pools, a golf course, and well-reviewed restaurants.

Sheraton Phoenix Downtown
340 North Third Street
602-262-2500
sheratonphoenixdowntown.com
$$$
A 31-story, 1,000-room tower that opened in 2008.

Phoenix
La Grande Orange Grocery 5
E. THUNDERBIRD RD.
N. SEVENTH ST.
51
PHOENIX MOUNTAINS PRESERVE
17
E. NORTHERN AVE.
W. GLENDALE AVE.
Arizona Biltmore Resort and Spa 6
Biltmore Fashion Park
Echo Canyon Recreation Area
ECHO CANYON PARK
4 Camelback Mountain
Royal Palms Resort
Scottsdale
Durant's 9
E. INDIAN SCHOOL RD.
60
16TH ST.
24TH ST.
48TH ST.
E. THOMAS RD.
Heard Museum 8
PAPAGO PARK
RED MOUNTAIN FWY.
10
11 Desert Botanical Garden
2 Garcia's Las Avenidas
Area of detail
10 Alice Cooperstown
Salt River
W. SOUTHERN AVE.
Mystery Castle 1
E. BASELINE RD.
SOUTH MOUNTAIN PARK
NEV.
ARIZONA
CALIF.
Phoenix
Tucson
N.M.
MEXICO
2 miles
4 kilometers
monOrchid
eye lounge
CENPHO
Modified Arts 7
MADE Art Boutique
N. CENTRAL AVE.
Downtown Phoenix
Crescent Ballroom
Sheraton Phoenix Downtown
3 Hotel San Carlos

Hotel
SAN CARLOS
Hotel San Carlos
SILVER SPOON CAFE

Scottsdale

It might be tempting a curse from the golf gods to enter the Scottsdale city limits without a set of clubs. But it's easy to spend a full weekend here far from the fairways. Just east of Phoenix, Scottsdale was once home to the Hohokam Indians; the town was founded in the 1880s by Winfield Scott, an Army chaplain who bought land to farm sweet potatoes. Today, Scottsdale is associated less with farming than with Frank Lloyd Wright, massage therapists, affluent second-home owners, and posh resorts. Wright's influence can be seen in much of the city's architecture as well as in his own Arizona headquarters, Taliesin West. Golf, if you wish. Or eat, explore, and then float in an infinity pool, contemplating your next cocktail.

— BY JENNIFER STEINHAUER

FRIDAY

1 *Enchilada Central* 7:30 p.m.

Much of Scottsdale may look as if it sprang up yesterday, but there are a few vestiges here and there of an earlier era. **Los Olivos** (7328 East Second Street; 480-946-2256; losolivosrestaurant.com; $), one of the oldest restaurants in the original area known now as Old Town, is still family run and has a personality all its own; the building itself looks like a piece of folk art, with a sculpture of a Mayan head rising from the roof. Inside, there's a lively central dining and bar area and a Blue Room that risks aquamarine overload. The food is solid Tex-Mex.

2 *Exotic Vintages* 10 p.m.

Kazimierz World Wine Bar (7137 East Stetson Drive; 480-946-3004; kazbar.net), known as the Kaz Bar, has all the trappings of hipness — no sign over the door (which is in the back), sofas, and a crowd of varying ages and sexual orientations. There are wines from dozens of nations available — yes, this is the place to find that elusive Thracian Valley merlot from Bulgaria. Expect live music or a D.J., too. Cavelike and dimly lit, Kaz Bar makes for good people watching.

SATURDAY

3 *A Plan over Pancakes* 9 a.m.

The coffee is strong and the banana buttermilk pancakes are yummy at **Cafe ZuZu** in the Hotel Valley Ho (6850 East Main Street; 480-248-2000; hotelvalleyho.com; $). Sit in the supermodern chairs or comfy booths and plot potential misadventures.

4 *Desert Produce* 11 a.m.

For a sense of how irrigation can make a desert bloom, mingle with the locals shopping at the **Old Town Farmers Market** (Brown Avenue and 1st Street; arizonafarmersmarkets.com). Along with the Arizona oranges and vegetables, expect a variety of other artisan and homemade products vying for your attention: apricot walnut bread, vegan desserts, barbecue sauce, bee pollen, cherry pepper relish, organic cider, tamales, hot doughnuts, and more.

5 *Taste of the East* 1 p.m.

While you are in the neighborhood, do as the local residents do and hit **Malee's Thai Bistro** (7131 East Main Street; 480-947-6042; maleesthaibistro.com; $), a softly lighted room that muffles the sun-drenched action outside. The best bets are the tofu spinach

OPPOSITE Splashing in the open-air waterfall at the Willow Stream Spa in the Fairmont Scottsdale Princess. Scottsdale resorts cater to an affluent clientele.

RIGHT The Old Town Farmers' Market, where local growers show off the variety of plants and produce that a well watered desert can provide.

pot stickers, Evil Jungle Princess (a pile of chicken doused in coconut cream with mushrooms and fresh mint), and the reliable pad Thai.

6 *A Bit of the Old West* 2 p.m.

Stay in Old Town for a stroll and a little browsing. There are scores of galleries displaying everything from works of the masters to American Indian jewelry to large contemporary paintings by local artists. You'll also find questionable Western-themed statuary, store names with puns (Coyo-T's), and the obligatory wind chimes and dried chili peppers lilting and listing in the breeze. Check out **Mexican Imports** (3933 North Brown Avenue; 480-945-6476) for all the South of the Border kitsch you've always wanted. Of interest nearby is **Guidon Books** (7109 East Main Street; 480-945-8811; guidon.com), which specializes in out-of-print Western Americana and Civil War volumes.

7 *Boot Up* 3:30 p.m.

For western wear—especially boots—the traditional stop in Scottsdale is **Saba's** (sabas.com), which has two stores in Old Town, nearly across the street from each other. For the complete look, you'll have to visit both. The one at 7254 Main Street (480-949-7404) sells only boots; the one at 3965 Brown Avenue (480-947-7664) has clothing and hats.

8 *There's Always the Rub* 5 p.m.

The ways to get pummeled, peeled, and rubbed in Scottsdale are endless, and there seems to be an almost Constitutional obligation to submit. From the shoulder rubs at the most commonplace hair salons to the aquatic watsu massage at the gorgeous **Sanctuary Camelback Mountain Resort & Spa** (5700 East McDonald Drive; 480-948-2100; sanctuaryoncamelback.com), there is something for every (reasonably generous) budget. Right in the middle is the **VH Spa for Vitality and Health** at the Hotel Valley Ho (hotelvalleyho.com), where the Back, Neck, Shoulders massage was heaven.

9 *Serenity, Inside and Out* 7 p.m.

Start dinner right at **Elements** (at the Sanctuary resort; elementsrestaurant.com; $$$) by angling for just the right seat on the patio at the Jade Bar, where you can watch the sunset while eavesdropping on first-daters as you munch on wasabi-covered peanuts. This moment is best paired with an Asian pear cucumber and ginger martini or a glass of sparkling rose. You will want to ask for a window booth inside the restaurant, where the chef cooks up seasonal

fare as you take in Paradise Valley. The view is really the main course, but there have been some standout offerings on the changing menu, like grilled salmon, carrot and millet pot stickers, or a diabolical banana fluffernutter sundae. The Zen-like setting with stone and fireplaces is serene.

SUNDAY

10 *The Architect's Place* 10:30 a.m.

Do not miss **Taliesin West**, the international headquarters for the Frank Lloyd Wright Foundation and the winter campus for the Frank Lloyd Wright School of Architecture (12621 Frank Lloyd Wright Boulevard; 480-860-2700; franklloydwright.org). Troubled by poor health, Wright took up half-year residence in this 600-acre "camp" in 1937, and the complex was built by apprentices. Take the 90-minute tour, which takes you through the living quarters, working areas, and outdoor spaces that incorporate indigenous materials and organic forms. Then there's all that Asian art.

OPPOSITE ABOVE Taliesin West, built by Frank Lloyd Wright as a community of architects and apprentices. Its low-slung buildings on 540 acres of desert attract 120,000 visitors a year for tours.

OPPOSITE BELOW Year-round Arizona sunshine makes for steady activity at outdoor pools, like this one at the Fairmont.

THE BASICS

Many airlines serve Phoenix Sky Harbor Airport. Arizona sprawl demands a car.

Saguaro Scottsdale
4000 North Drinkwater Boulevard
480-308-1100
thesaguaro.com
$$
An urban resort in the suburban desert, with a pool-party scene, boutique spa, and Distrito, a destination restaurant.

Fairmont Scottsdale Princess
7575 East Princess Drive
480-585-4848
fairmont.com/scottsdale
$$$$
Golf courses, pools, tennis, and a waterfall in the lavish spa.

Hotel Valley Ho
6850 East Main Street
866-882-4484
hotelvalleyho.com
$$$
Inviting and chic renovated mid-20th-century hotel.

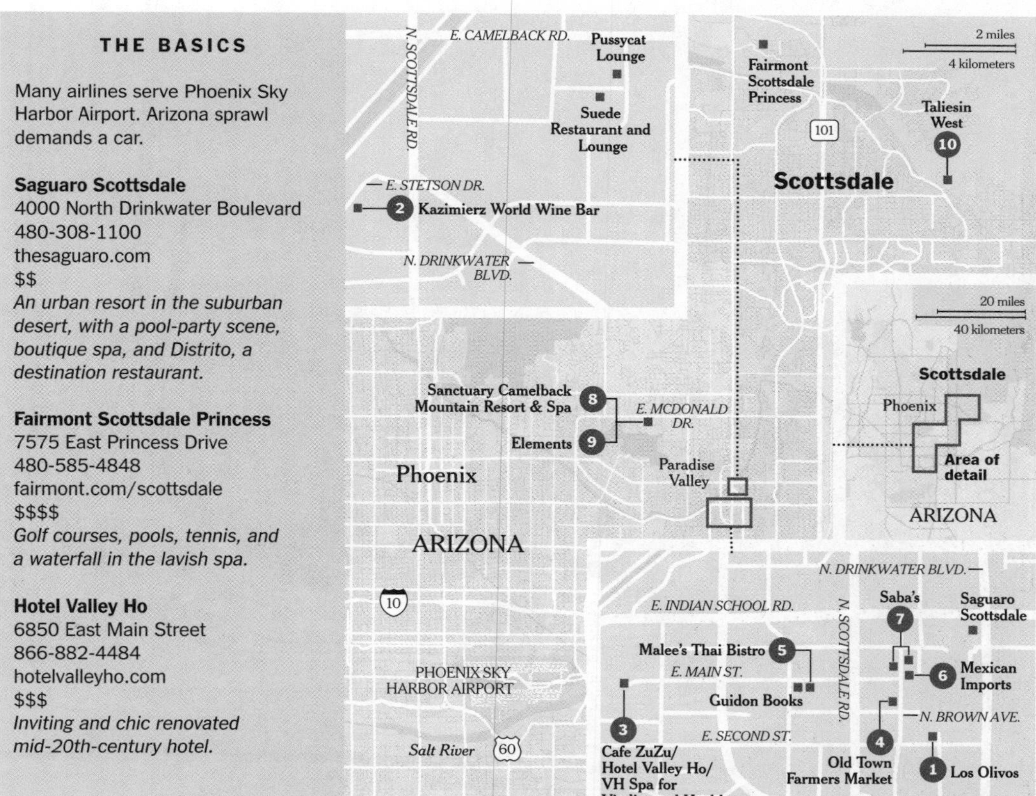

Tucson

Tucson, Arizona, has worked hard to shed its reputation as a tanning salon for retirees and snowbirds. To complement its natural beauty—a national park in its midst and mountains on four sides—the city has poured hundreds of millions of dollars into its downtown. In lieu of adding strip malls and high-rises, older buildings were saved and retooled as movie houses and museums. And with a deep-rooted Hispanic community, tides of Mexican immigrants, and students from the University of Arizona who never left after graduation, the city has a youthful and multicultural glow. — RICHARD B. WOODWARD

FRIDAY

1 *Jet Age Graveyard* 4 p.m.

Tucson's bone-dry climate is easy on all kinds of metal bodies. The city is a hunting ground for used-car buyers as well as home to one of the world's largest airplane graveyards. A sample of the 4,000 or so stranded military and civilian aircraft can be viewed by driving along the fence on Kolb Road by the Davis-Monthan Air Force Base. For a closer look, the **Pima Air & Space Museum** (6000 East Valencia Road; 520-574-0462; pimaair.org) offers tours with frighteningly knowledgeable guides who can run down all the specs on the SR-71 "Blackbird" spy plane.

2 *Hear That Whistle Blow* 6 p.m.

The Southern Pacific railroad reached Tucson in 1880, and the moaning whistle of freight and passenger trains can still be heard day and night. For a front-row seat to the passing leviathans, head to **Maynard's Market and Kitchen** (400 North Toole Avenue; 520-545-0577; maynardsmarkettucson.com; $$). Less than 50 feet from the tracks, this dark and handsome former depot attracts an upscale crowd that comes for the extensive choice of wines (from the store next door) and the reasonably priced menu. Meat eaters enjoy the 14-ounce dry-aged New York strip, and vegetarians the roast garlic and wild mushroom stone-baked pizza. But just as inviting are the sights and sounds of the rattling plates and glasses.

3 *Tucson Nights* 8 p.m.

Tucson has a jumping band scene on weekends, a sleepier one the other five days. On warm nights, the noise of music pumps through the open doors of restaurants and bars along Congress Street. The center of the action is often the historic **Rialto Theater** (318 East Congress Street; 520-740-1000; rialtotheatre.com). A nonprofit showcase vital to downtown's renewal, it books major acts but has no stylistic agenda.

SATURDAY

4 *Roadrunner* 9 a.m.

When the summer sun isn't blazing, Tucsonians head outdoors. A prime destination is the **Saguaro National Park** (3693 South Old Spanish Trail; 520-733-5155; nps.gov/sagu), which embraces the city on two sides. To walk among fields of multi-armed cactus giants, drive west about a half-hour along a snaking road. Look for an unmarked parking lot a few hundred feet beyond the Arizona-Sonora Desert Museum. This is the start of the **King Canyon Trail** (saguaronationalpark.com/favorite-trails.html), put in by the Civilian Conservation Corps in the 1930s and the path for a refreshing morning hike. A covered picnic area is at mile 0.9. Fitter types can proceed 2.6 miles to Wasson Peak, the highest point in the Tucson Mountains.

OPPOSITE Saguaro National Park, a favorite Tucson playground when the summer sun isn't blazing.

RIGHT Terror remembered: a cold war artifact, the top of a missile, at the Titan Missile Museum outside Tucson.

5 *Modern Mexican* Noon

Tucson thinks highly of its Mexican restaurants, and one place that it can justly be proud of is **Cafe Poca Cosa** (110 East Pennington Street; 520-622-6400; cafepocacosatucson.com; $$$). Don't be put off by its location (in an ugly office building) or the décor (a vain attempt to import some glam L.A. style). The place has attracted national attention for a novel take on Mexican cuisine, which emphasizes fresh and regional. Try the daily sampler (El Plato Poca Cosa) of three dishes chosen by the chef. Expect an exotic mole and perhaps a zinger like a vegetarian tamale with pineapple salsa. Dinner reservations are essential for weekends.

6 *Picture This* 1:30 p.m.

One of the most impressive collections of 20th-century North American photographs can be found at the **Center for Creative Photography** (1030 North Olive Road; 520-621-7970; creativephotography.org), in a hard-to-find building on the University of Arizona campus. Containing the archives of Ansel Adams, Edward Weston, Garry Winogrand, W. Eugene Smith, and more than 40 other eminent photographers, it also runs a first-rate exhibition program.

7 *The Buy and Buy* 3:30 p.m.

Phoenix-style shopping has arrived at **La Encantada**, a mall in the foothills of the Santa Catalinas, with Tiffany and Louis Vuitton (2905 East Skyline Drive, at Campbell Avenue; 520-615-2561; laencantadashoppingcenter.com). North of downtown at the **Plaza Palomino** (2970 North Swan Road), local merchants carry more idiosyncratic items like funky handmade jewelry and crafts.

8 *Eyes on the Desert Sky* 5 p.m.

The surrounding mountains are heavenly for stargazing. The **Kitt Peak National Observatory** (Tohono O'odham Reservation; 520-318-8726; noao.edu), about 90 minutes southwest of the city and 6,900 feet above sea level, says it has more optical research telescopes than anywhere in the world. Aside from serving professional astronomers, it also has generous offerings for amateurs. One of these, the Nightly Observing Program, begins an hour before sunset and lasts four hours. An expert will show you how to use star charts and identify constellations and will give you a peek through one of the mammoth instruments. (Dinner is a deli sandwich; remember to wear warm clothing.) Reserving a month in advance is recommended, but you may get lucky and find an opening the same day.

9 *More Cosmos* 11 p.m.

For a nightcap, head to the boisterous **Club Congress** (on the ground floor of the Hotel Congress, 311 East Congress Street; 520-622-8848; hotelcongress.com/club), a nightclub with five different bar areas. The beats of live bands often send crowds of dancers spilling out into the lobby of the hotel. Finish the night at **Plush** (340 East 6th Street; 520-798-1298; plushtucson.com), where the acts are less polished but the drinks are almost as cheap and just as strong.

SUNDAY

10 *Early Bird* 9 a.m.

The **Epic Cafe** (745 North Fourth Avenue; 520-624-6844; $) is a happening spot at almost any

ABOVE The control room at the Titan Missile Museum.

BELOW The Kitt Peak National Observatory. For nighttime stargazing, reserve well in advance.

hour. This neighborhood hub on the corner of University Boulevard is open from 6 a.m. to midnight and serves an eclectic menu of sandwiches, sweets, and drinks to a clientele of laptop-toting would-be intellectuals and dog owners who jam the sidewalk tables. Grab a cup of the excellent coffee and a vegan seed cookie. If it tastes like delicious bird food, that's because it is.

11 *Missile America* 10 a.m.

For a terrifying yet educational reminder of the cold war, drive about 30 minutes south of downtown on Interstate 19 to the **Titan Missile Museum** (1580 West Duval Mine Road, Sahuarita; 520-625-7736; titanmissilemuseum.org). The nuclear silo housed a single intercontinental ballistic missile equipped with a warhead 700 times more powerful than the Hiroshima bomb. The museum tour lasts an hour. Much of it is underground, behind eight-foot-thick blast walls, and it ends with a peek at the 103-foot weapon, with its warhead removed.

ABOVE At Maynard's Market and Kitchen, in a former depot, glasses rattle as trains go by less than 50 feet away.

THE BASICS

Fly to Tucson, or for often-cheaper rates, land in Phoenix and drive two hours.

A car is essential for touring.

Ritz-Carlton, Dove Mountain
15000 North Secret Springs Drive
520-572-3000
ritzcarlton.com/dovemountain
$$$$
Upscale hotel with a Jack Nicklaus golf course and a luxurious spa.

Arizona Inn
2200 East Elm Street
520-325-1541
arizonainn.com
$$$
The granddaddy of Tucson luxury hotels and still family-owned.

Best Western Royal Sun Inn & Suites
1015 North Stone Avenue
520-622-8871
bwroyalsun.com
$$
A good choice for budget travelers.

Ritz-Carlton Dove Mountain
77
SANTA CATALINA MTNS.
10
E. SKYLINE DR.
La Encantada 7
Saguaro National Park
WASSON PEAK
4
KING CANYON TRAIL
TUCSON MTS.
Arizona-Sonora Desert Museum
Tucson
Plaza Palomino
Arizona Inn
Area of detail
Davis-Monthan Air Force Base
86
KOLB RD.
8
To Kitt Peak National Observatory
Pima Air & Space Museum 1
ARIZONA
19
S. NOGALES HWY.
Titan Missile Museum 11
W. DUVAL MINE RD.
5 miles
10 kilometers
NEV.
UTAH
COLO.
Las Vegas
Flagstaff
CALIF.
ARIZONA
N.M.
Phoenix
Tucson
200 miles
400 kilometers
MEXICO
Best Western Royal Inn and Suites
Center for Creative Photography 6
N. STONE AVE.
N. SIXTH AVE.
E. UNIVERSITY BLVD.
10
University of Arizona
Epic Cafe
Plush
E. SIXTH ST.
Cafe Poca Cosa
5
2 Maynard's Market and Kitchen
3 Rialto Theater
E. CONGRESS ST.
E. BROADWAY BLVD.
9 Club Congress/ Hotel Congress

Sedona

Ask five people to sum up Sedona, Arizona, and you'll probably get five wildly different responses. Art lovers enthuse over the galleries specializing in Southwestern tableaus. Shopaholics rave about boutiques selling Western duds and American Indian jewelry. Pessimists rue the rash of T-shirt shops, while enlightenment-seekers wax spiritual about the "vortexes." And outdoor enthusiasts rhapsodize about hiking among red rock spires and ancient Indian ruins. All of this is great news for visitors, who can sample it all in a quirky city that some call the most beautiful place in the United States.
— BY KERIDWEN CORNELIUS

FRIDAY

1 *Red Rock Rover* 4 p.m.

Sedona's cinematic red rocks have been zipping across your windshield like scenes from a Hollywood western as you've driven toward town. Now it's your turn to ride off into the sunset. Turn up Airport Road to Airport Saddleback — you want the tiny parking lot on the left, not the chockablock Airport Vista farther up the road. Slip on hiking boots and hit the **Airport Loop Trail** for close encounters with the towering crimson sandstones: Bell Rock, Courthouse Butte, Coffee Pot Rock, and the Cockscombe. It's a 90-minute ramble, but if your energy flags, just turn back and scramble up Overlook Point, a good spot to watch paprika-red sunsets.

2 *Shopping for Dinner* 7 p.m.

It's hard to find authentic Southwestern food in Sedona, but there are good restaurants. One is **René at Tlaquepaque** (336 State Route 179; 928-282-9255; rene-sedona.com; $$$), where the dishes are mainstream — filet mignon, rack of lamb, duck with wild rice — but the quality is reliable. It's in the **Tlaquepaque Arts & Crafts Village** (tlaq.com), a Spanish-colonial-style shopping arcade with fountains and muscular sycamores. The shops and galleries are worth a look. Peek in the window of Kuivato Glass Gallery, which sells glass sculptures and jewelry.

3 *Wine by the Fire* 9:30 p.m.

Sedona isn't known for its night life. Most bars, in fact, shut down at 10 p.m. For a little art to go with your nightcap, swing by **Hundred Rox** inside the **Amara Resort and Spa** (310 North Highway 89A; 928-340-8900; amararesort.com). Sample a cocktail or a boutique shiraz from a 200-strong wine list as you examine a collection of paintings and sculptures culled from local galleries. The outdoor fire pit is just as picturesque.

SATURDAY

4 *Break an Egg* 9 a.m.

Kick-start your day in classic Sedona fashion with breakfast at the **Coffee Pot Restaurant** (2050 West Highway 89A; 928-282-6626; coffeepotsedona.com; $), which serves 101 "famous" omelets. Locals and tourists pack this kitschy joint, so you may have to browse the gift shop for jewelry and coffee mugs while waiting for a table. But once you're seated, the friendly waitresses are swift and might even leave the coffeepot on your table for convenient refills. Overwhelmed by the omelet choices? Try the hearty huevos rancheros, smothered in green chili. If you have kids, dare them to order the peanut butter, jelly, and banana omelet.

OPPOSITE The red sandstone rocks of Sedona.

BELOW The Chapel of the Holy Cross sits atop one of Sedona's famous vortexes, revered as sites of psychic energy.

5 *Southwest Inspiration* 10 a.m.

Galleries dot the city. The biggest of them is **Exposures International** (561 State Route 179; 928-282-1125; exposuresfineart.com), a sprawling space overflowing with paintings, sculpture, jewelry, and more. Check out Bill Worrell's prehistoric-art-inspired sculptures. Other interesting galleries can be found at **Hozho Center**, including **Lanning Gallery** (431 State Route 179; 928-282-6865; lanninggallery.com), which specializes in contemporary art. To learn more about the local art scene, visit the **Sedona Arts Center** (15 Art Barn Road; 928-282-3865; sedonaartscenter.com), a nonprofit gallery that holds exhibits and poetry readings.

ABOVE Rust-colored cliffs, shaded by oxidation of their iron-laced stone, tower above Enchantment Resort.

BELOW Earth Wisdom tours explore local history, geology, American Indian culture, and vortexes.

OPPOSITE Oak Creek, the gentle stream running through the valley that cradles Sedona.

6 *A Creek Runs Through It* 1 p.m.

Sedona is cradled in a fragrant riparian valley through which Oak Creek gently runs. Weather permitting, dine creekside at **L'Auberge de Sedona** (301 L'Auberge Lane; 928-282-1667; lauberge.com; $$$), a contemporary American restaurant with a stone patio perched at the water's edge. Indulge in grilled salmon or a tenderloin salad. Cottonwoods rustle, the creek burbles, and ducks waddle between the linen-draped tables.

7 *Spirited Away* 2:30 p.m.

You can't get far in Sedona without hearing about the vortexes, places where the earth supposedly radiates psychic energy. Believers claim that they induce everything from heightened energy to tear-inducing spiritual enlightenment. Whether you're a skeptic or a believer, a guided tour of the vortexes by **Earth Wisdom Jeep Tours** (293 North Highway 89A; 928-282-4714; earthwisdomjeeptours.com) is definitely scenic. If vortexes aren't your thing, go anyway. This tour also explores the area's history, geology, and American Indian culture, and there are other tours to choose from. You'll learn how the rocks became rust-colored: add a dash of iron, let it oxidize for several million years and voilà!

8 *Cactus on the Rocks* 6 p.m.

A prickly pear margarita — made from a local cactus — is the must-drink cocktail in Sedona, and one of the best spots to try it is the terrace at **Tii Gavo** at **Enchantment Resort** (525 Boynton Canyon Road; 928-282-2900; enchantmentresort.com). Tii Gavo means gathering place in the Havasupai Indian language, and in this restaurant well-heeled spa-lovers rub elbows with hikers fresh off the trail. Afterward, move inside to the **Che-Ah-Chi** (928-282-2900; $$$; reservations required for nonguests). With its American Indian pottery and views of Boynton Canyon, this restaurant is well known to Sedona's celebrity visitors. The wine list is extensive and far-ranging, but consider one of the local Echo Canyon reds.

9 *A Galaxy Far, Far Away* 9:30 p.m.

Thanks to strict ordinances on light pollution, the dark skies over Sedona are ideal for stargazing (or U.F.O. spotting). Take a cosmic journey with **Evening Sky Tours** (928-203-0006; eveningskytours.com). You'll be led by an astronomer who can point out those elusive constellations as well as an eyeful of spiral galaxies and the rings of Saturn.

SUNDAY

10 *Rock Your World* 6 a.m.

Soar over Sedona valley in a hot-air balloon at sunrise for jaw-dropping views of rose-tinted buttes. **Northern Light Balloon Expeditions** (928-282-2274; northernlightballoon.com) offers three- to four-hour trips that include a Champagne breakfast picnic in

a remote spot (about $200). If you prefer to stay earthbound, pack your own picnic and set out on the 3.6-mile **Broken Arrow Trail**. A Red Rock Day Pass (redrockcountry.org/redrock; $5) allows entry to a number of natural areas and is available at most hotels and many stores. Hike along red rocks stained with desert varnish, weave through cypress forests, and climb up a doughlike outcropping for commanding views of Casner Canyon.

ABOVE Inside Tlaquepaque Arts & Crafts Village, a Spanish-colonial-style shopping arcade.

OPPOSITE Poolside at the Enchantment Resort.

11 *Morning Spiritual* 10 a.m.

Peek inside the **Chapel of the Holy Cross** (780 Chapel Road; 928-282-4069; chapeloftheholycross.com), a modernist icon that looks like a concrete spaceship jutting out of the craggy boulders. Designed in 1932 by Marguerite Brunswig Staude (but not built until 1956), the chapel is sandwiched between soaring concrete walls that bookend a gigantic glass window with a 90-foot-tall cross. Prayer services are held on Monday evenings, so don't worry about interrupting when you make your visit this morning. This spot affords spectacular photo ops and another chance to have a psychic moment. The chapel sits on—you guessed it—a vortex.

THE BASICS

Fly to Phoenix, rent a car, and drive north for about two hours.

Enchantment Resort
525 Boynton Canyon Road
928-282-2900
enchantmentresort.com
$$$
Adobe casitas, nature walks, a Native American culture program, and star gazing.

L'Auberge de Sedona
301 L'Auberge Lane
928-282-1661
lauberge.com
$$$$
Blends log cabin style with a touch of France.

Lantern Light Inn
3085 West State Route 89A
928-282-3419
lanternlightinn.com
$$
Attractive bed-and-breakfast with fireplaces, fountains, and patios.

The Grand Canyon

More than a mile deep at its most majestic, the Grand Canyon can still drop the most jaded of jaws. The sun sparkling across the exposed rock, the delicate curl of the Colorado River, the birds chirping in the pinyon pines — and then a bus grinds past you on a hunt for the best postcards in the park. Yes, the Grand Canyon is big in every way, including the category of tourist trap. Over four million people visit this remote corner of Arizona each year, and the experience can be a bit death-by-gift-shop if you don't plan ahead — a necessity even if crowds and kitsch are your thing. During peak season, May through September, hotel rooms sell out months in advance, ditto for those mule rides, and certain rafting trips can be a year-long wait or more. Ah, wilderness!
— BY BROOKS BARNES

FRIDAY

1 *The Main Event* 5 p.m.

Save the best for last? Not on this trip. After driving the 81 miles from Flagstaff, Arizona, the destination where most air travelers land, head to **El Tovar Hotel** (Grand Canyon Village; 928-638-2631, extension 6380; grandcanyonlodges.com). The historic lodge, purposely built at such an angle that guests must leave their rooms to see more than a glimpse of the splendor, features one of the easiest access points to the canyon rim. Stretch your legs with a walk along the eastern portion of the 13-mile **Rim Trail**, which may leave you out of breath at 7,000 feet above sea level. Resist the temptation to go off the trail; park officials say about one person a year falls and dies and others are injured.

2 *Eat Hearty, Folks* 7:30 p.m.

El Tovar may look familiar — the exterior of the hotel had a cameo in *Vacation*, the 1983 road-trip movie. Clark Griswold, a.k.a. Chevy Chase, pulls up in his pea-green station wagon and robs the front desk. He should have at least eaten dinner first. The restaurant at El Tovar (928-638-2631, extension 6432; $$$) is by far the best in the area. As twin fireplaces blaze, relax with an Arizona Sunrise (orange juice, tequila, and grenadine) and take in the wall-mounted Hopi and Navajo weavings. For dinner, start with a house salad or roasted corn chowder and then choose something wilderness-appropriate (buffalo ribeye? venison chops? rainbow trout?) for the main course.

3 *Star Struck* 10 p.m.

If dinner got a bit pricey, take comfort in a free show afterward. Because there is so little pollution here — the nearest large cities, Phoenix and Las Vegas, are both 200 miles or more away — the night sky is crowded with stars. Pick up one of the free constellation-finder brochures in the lobby of El Tovar and gaze away. Bonus points for anybody who can spot the Lesser Watersnake.

SATURDAY

4 *Sunrise Sonata* 5 a.m.

The canyon's multiple layers of exposed rock are glorious in the morning light; download the soundtrack to *2001: A Space Odyssey* as a dawn complement — the combination heightens the experience even further. Take a morning run or walk along the Rim Trail heading west, and keep your eyes peeled for woodpeckers making their morning

OPPOSITE Looking into the canyon from the Rim Trail.

RIGHT The lobby at the Bright Angel Lodge.

rounds. Don't bother trying to make it to Hermit's Rest, a 1914 stone building named for a 19th-century French-Canadian prospector who had a roughly built homestead in the area. These days, it's — you guessed it — a gift shop and snack bar.

5 *Hop On* 10 a.m.

Those famous mules? Ride one if you want to — and can take more time than you may be willing to spend on a weekend trip here — but be aware that they walk scary narrow ledges and come with a daunting list of rules. (Reads one brochure: "Each rider must not weigh more than 200 pounds, fully dressed, and, yes, we do weigh everyone!") An alternative is to tour the canyon aboard an Eco-Star helicopter, an energy-efficient model built with extra viewing windows. There are several tour companies that offer flights; one with a newish fleet and friendly service is **Maverick Helicopters** (Grand Canyon National Airport on Highway 64; 928-638-2622; maverickhelicopter.com/canyon.php). The tours are personal — seven passengers maximum — and are priced according to the length of the trip. (None are cheap.) Ask the pilot to point out the Tower of Ra, a soaring butte named for the Egyptian sun god.

6 *Pack a Picnic* Noon

The nearest town and the location of the heliport, Tusayan, Arizona, is a disappointing collection of fast-food restaurants, motels, and souvenir shops. Get out of Dodge and pick up lunch at the deli counter tucked inside the general store at **Market Plaza** (located a mile or two inside the park gates; 928-638-2262). It's nothing fancy — pastrami sandwiches and the like — but it will at least save you from an order of junk food.

7 *Desert View* 1 p.m.

Hitting the **Desert View Watchtower** (26 miles past Market Plaza on Highway 64 East; scienceviews.com/parks/watchtower.html) at midday will keep you clear of the throngs that assemble here for sunrise and sunset. From the historic tower, constructed in 1932, you can see the Painted Desert, a broad area of badlands where wind and rain have exposed stratified layers of minerals, which glow in hues of violet, red, and gold. Park rangers give daily talks about the area's cultural history.

8 *Play Archaeologist* 3 p.m.

Outdoorsy types will want to do another hike — more power to them. For those who have had enough of the canyon for one day, another of this area's cultural treasures still waits to be explored.

ABOVE The Wukoki Pueblo at the Wupatki National Monument near Flagstaff.

About 800 years ago, **Wupatki Pueblo National Monument** (about 34 miles north of Flagstaff on Highway 89; 928-679-2365; nps.gov/wupa) was a flourishing home base for the Sinagua, Kayenta Anasazi, and Cohonina peoples. The remnants of 100 rooms remain, including a space that archaeologists identified as a ball court similar to those found in other sites left by pre-Columbian cultures.

9 *Who Screams?* 5:30 p.m.

If heights aren't your thing, you can relax now: you've made it through the hard parts of touring the Grand Canyon. Regroup after the drive back to the Grand Canyon National Park with ice cream on the patio at **Bright Angel Lodge** (about two blocks west of El Tovar; 928-638-2631; grandcanyonlodges.com), which features an old-fashioned soda fountain. There are multiple ice cream flavors to choose from, plus other fountain specialties — try a strawberry milkshake. Inside the lodge, a rustic motel, is a newsstand, one of the few in the park.

10 *Dinner and a Dance* 7 p.m.

Apart from the dining room at El Tovar, Grand Canyon food can be alarmingly bad. But walk inside the Bright Angel Lodge and give the **Arizona Room** ($$) a whirl. The dishes are a mouthful in name — chili-crusted, pan-seared wild salmon with fresh melon salsa and pinyon black bean rice pilaf, for example — if not exactly in quality. After dinner, hang out around the stone fireplace in the lobby. With any luck, you will catch one of the randomly presented Hopi dancing demonstrations.

BELOW The Desert View Watchtower, built in 1932.

SUNDAY

11 *Wild Side* 10 a.m.

Kaibab National Forest, 1.6 million acres of ponderosa pine that surrounds the Grand Canyon, is a destination on its own for nature lovers and camping enthusiasts. After saying goodbye to the world's most famous hole in the ground, stop on the way back to Flagstaff to explore the **Kendrick Park Watchable Wildlife Trail** (Highway 180, about 20 miles north of Flagstaff; wildlifeviewingareas.com). Elk, badgers, western bluebirds, and red-tailed hawks are relatively easy to see, along with short-horned lizards and a variety of other forest creatures. The Grand Canyon area is also home to scorpions, tarantulas, rattlesnakes, and Gila monsters — but those are (mostly) confined to the canyon itself.

ABOVE A Navajo hoop dancer performing in costume at the canyon's South Rim.

OPPOSITE Mule trains take tourists bumping down into the canyon along the Bright Angel Trail. Other sightseeing options include helicopter rides and rigorous hikes.

THE BASICS

Fly to Flagstaff, Arizona, and rent a car at the airport.

El Tovar Hotel
Off Village Loop in Grand Canyon Village
303-297-2757
grandcanyonlodges.com/lodging/el-tovar/
$$
By far the most upscale lodging in the area; centrally located and recently renovated.

Bright Angel Lodge & Cabins
Near El Tovar
303-297-2757
grandcanyonlodges.com/lodging/bright-angel/
$$
A cabin-style motel built in the 1930s that is bare bones but surprisingly comfortable.

Red Feather Lodge
106 North Highway 64
928-638-2414
redfeatherlodge.com
$$
As good a motel as any of the many in the Tusayan area.

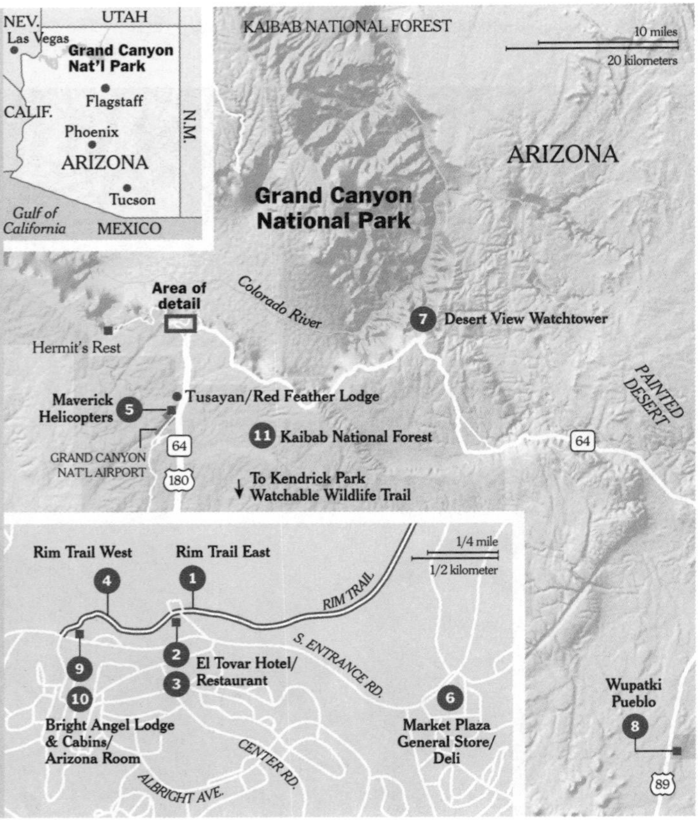

NEV.
UTAH
Las Vegas
Grand Canyon Nat'l Park
Flagstaff
CALIF.
N.M.
Phoenix
ARIZONA
Tucson
Gulf of California
MEXICO
KAIBAB NATIONAL FOREST
10 miles
20 kilometers
ARIZONA
Grand Canyon National Park
Colorado River
Area of detail
Hermit's Rest
7 Desert View Watchtower
PAINTED DESERT
Maverick Helicopters 5
Tusayan/Red Feather Lodge
11 Kaibab National Forest
GRAND CANYON NAT'L AIRPORT
64
180
To Kendrick Park Watchable Wildlife Trail
Rim Trail West 4
Rim Trail East 1
1/4 mile
1/2 kilometer
RIM TRAIL
S. ENTRANCE RD.
2 El Tovar Hotel/
3 Restaurant
9
10 Bright Angel Lodge & Cabins/ Arizona Room
6 Market Plaza General Store/ Deli
CENTER RD.
ALBRIGHT AVE.
Wupatki Pueblo 8
89

COSMOPOLITAN
Aria
ZARKANA
planet hollywood
ph
BELLAGIO
O
Mlife
Paris

Las Vegas

From a tourism perspective, Las Vegas is ever the chameleon. New restaurants, shows, clubs, and hotels are constantly reinventing Sin City with the aim of getting repeaters back to the tables. Big construction projects are always underway; the competition even extends to two dueling Ferris wheels. But lately, projects have moved away from kitschy copies of foreign landmarks like an Egyptian pyramid in favor of celebrating Las Vegas's own swinging style, and there are even Vegas-compatible museums downtown. — BY ELAINE GLUSAC

FRIDAY

1 *Buy or Browse* 3 p.m.

Las Vegas shops make up a parade of high-end global brands designed to tempt high rollers. The **Crystals at the CityCenter** mall (3720 Las Vegas Boulevard South; crystalsatcitycenter.com) exemplifies the mode with swimsuits from Eres, clothing from Stella McCartney, and accessories from Porsche Design. But the center, with sharp and soaring angles, designed by the architect Daniel Libeskind to resemble a quartz crystal, has an artistic side, too. Pick up a free CityCenter Fine Art walking tour brochure from the concierge at Aria or Vdara, the two neighboring resorts, for a self-guided tour of the public art collection in and around the building, including a sculpture by Henry Moore; *Big Edge*, a stack of boats wired in a web, by the artist Nancy Rubins; and several ice pillars that slowly melt each day, only to be refrozen each night, from the designers of the Bellagio fountains.

2 *Haute Perch* 6 p.m.

Since Wolfgang Puck arrived in 1992, celebrity chefs have flocked to the Strip. But most local observers agree that the food scene didn't really improve until the French guys arrived — the chefs Joël Robuchon and Guy Savoy, principally. Their namesake restaurants remain bastions of formality, but **L'Atelier de Joël Robuchon** (3799 Las Vegas Boulevard South; 702-891-7358; mgmgrand.com; $$$$), the 33-seat à la carte restaurant next door to Joël Robuchon in the MGM Grand, offers a more affordable meal and relaxed setting. Reserve a seat at the black granite bar to watch the chefs prepare dishes like quail stuffed with foie gras or steak tartare with frites.

3 *Circus Circuit* 9:30 p.m.

Move over, showgirls. The pervasive **Cirque du Soleil** performances — at several different hotels — and the mammoth ads everywhere make Cirque something like the Starbucks of the entertainment circuit here. Its Vegas extravaganzas have included shows based on the lives and music of Michael Jackson and the Beatles; the saga of a magical ringmaster visiting a haunted theater with trapeze artists, jump ropers, and strongmen; and the adult-themed "Absinthe," with circus acts, some nudity, and lots of risqué humor. Tickets for all of the Cirque shows are available at cirquedusoleil.com.

SATURDAY

4 *Downward Dolphin* 8:30 a.m.

Las Vegas is a multitasking kind of town. It's only fitting, then, that while you practice yoga, you should

OPPOSITE The Las Vegas Strip, where ostentation can never be overdone.

ABOVE A performance of Cirque du Soleil's Beatles-based show at the Mirage.

be able to watch dolphins. That's the combination offered in the hourlong **Yoga Among the Dolphins** at the Mirage Las Vegas (3400 Las Vegas Boulevard South; mirage.com). Students adopt yoga poses in a subterranean room with glass windows looking into the dolphin pools in Siegfried & Roy's Secret Garden and Dolphin Habitat. Curious bottlenose dolphins peer through the glass at you while you hold your Warrior I position.

5 *All That Glows* 11 a.m.

Before the Strip's Eiffel Tower replica and pseudo Manhattan skyline, Las Vegas marketed itself via neon signs. The **Neon Museum** (770 Las Vegas Boulevard North; 702-387-6366; neonmuseum.org) celebrates the showy signage in a collection of more than 150 pieces, most still vibrant though not operational in their resting place in the outdoor "Neon Boneyard." Casino castoffs include signs from the Golden Nugget, Binion's, and the defunct Stardust and Moulin Rouge; a bright yellow duck that once advertised a used car lot; and a "Free Aspirin & Tender Sympathies" sign that was used to market a gas station. Book an hourlong guided tour; visitors are not allowed to wander here on their own.

6 *Made Men* 12:30 p.m.

The **Mob Museum** (300 East Stewart; 702-229-2734; themobmuseum.org) covers a more notorious aspect of Las Vegas history. Occupying a 1933 former federal courthouse and post office where one of the anti-Mafia Kefauver Committee hearings was held, the Mob Museum lays out the history of organized crime across America with interactive exhibits, including the chance to simulate firing your own Tommy gun. Eventually it narrows its focus to Las Vegas, where a number of crime syndicates funneled their energies after legal

ABOVE AND LEFT The Crystals at CityCenter, designed by Daniel Libeskind to resemble a quartz crystal, takes the shopping mall to a new level in flamboyant Las Vegas style. Inside are shops including Tiffany's and Prada; a public art collection; and a Wolfgang Puck pizzeria.

crackdowns elsewhere. The tour through the three-story building thoughtfully offers the squeamish a chance to opt out of some of the more graphic galleries, featuring photos of mob hits, and winds up in a theater screening a documentary on Hollywood's fascination with gangsters.

7 *Go Fish* 2 p.m.

Estiatorio Milos (3708 Las Vegas Boulevard South; 702-698-7930; milos.ca/restaurants/las-vegas; $$$), a spinoff of the Greek seafood-focused restaurants run by the chef Costas Spiliadis in Montreal, New York, and other cities, is a mandatory midday stop, serving a three-course prix fixe lunch that manages to be relatively healthy in a town that equates fine dining with excess. Appetizer/entree/dessert combinations include dishes like a Greek mezze plate, grilled whole bass, and walnut cake. You'll eat well and still be ambulatory for the next stop.

8 *Dip or Strip* 4 p.m.

Poolside clubs known as day clubs have become the afternoon indulgence du jour at hotels up and down the Strip, primarily patronized by the trim and toned under-30 set. At the **Aria Resort & Casino Las Vegas**, you can party with the bikini-clad, water-gun-armed crowds at the adults-only **Liquid Club & Lounge** (3730 Las Vegas Boulevard South; 702-588-5656; liquidpoollv.com). Or, for a quieter experience, seek serenity in the 81,000-square-foot **Spa & Salon at Aria** (aria.com), which has 62 treatment rooms, heated stone beds, a salt room, a steam room, a sauna, and an outdoor pool.

9 *Omakase Hour* 8 p.m.

The chef Nobu Matsuhisa and partners have their own hotel-within-a-hotel in a separate tower at Caesars Palace Hotel & Casino. Anchoring the Nobu Hotel just off the Caesars casino floor is the largest branch yet of **Nobu** restaurants (3570 Las Vegas Boulevard South; 702-785-6677; nobucaesarspalace.com/restaurants.html; $$$$). Cushion-like fixtures that hang above the dining room like U.F.O.'s emit flattering light. The vast menu encompasses tiradito (Peruvian raw fish salad) and ceviche, wagyu steaks and brick-oven-baked chicken, skewered meats and, of course, sushi.

10 *Club House* 10 p.m.

There are limitless places to party in Las Vegas. For drinks overlooking the dancing fountains at the Bellagio resort, **Hyde** (3600 South Las Vegas Boulevard South; hydebellagio.com), designed in sleek style, morphs from sunset cocktail calm to

ABOVE Blackjack tables at the Cosmopolitan. Gambling is still at the heart of it all.

late-night bash. **Hakkasan Las Vegas Restaurant and Nightclub** in the MGM Grand (3799 Las Vegas Boulevard South; hakkasanlv.com) sprawls over five levels of nightclubs and dancing.

SUNDAY

11 *Muscle Bound* 10:30 a.m.

In the city that sells itself on wish fulfillment, the American Muscle Car Driving Experience is a perfect fit. The company **World Class Driving** (4055 Dean Martin Drive; 877-597-6403; worldclassdriving.com/muscle/drive-muscle-cars-las-vegas) stables classic car models, like Mustangs and Dodge Challengers, designed to appeal to your inner teenager. Traveling as a caravan, drivers can take the cars to the **Red Rock Canyon National Conservation Area** (State Road 159; redrockcanyonlv.org), 23 miles west of the Strip, for 30- or 50-mile drives. The posted speed limit is 50 m.p.h., but the director of operations, Darren Strahl, said, "We put the 'what happens in Vegas stays in Vegas' rule in effect."

ABOVE The Neon Museum celebrates a Las Vegas cliché, the bright, brash signs that light the nighttime on the Strip. In its collection are castoffs from casinos and oddities like a yellow duck that once advertised a used-car lot.

OPPOSITE A downsized Eiffel Tower and Arc de Triomphe at the Paris Las Vegas hotel. Gleaming in front is a desert extravagance, the Bellagio's pond.

THE BASICS

Las Vegas is a four-hour drive from Los Angeles. Its airport is served by the major airlines. Along the Strip, walk or use taxis, buses, and the monorail. Elsewhere, drive a car.

The Cosmopolitan
3708 Las Vegas Boulevard South
702-698-7000
cosmopolitanlasvegas.com
$$$
In a multibillion-dollar development, with hotel interiors designed by David Rockwell.

Aria Resort and Casino
3730 Las Vegas Boulevard South, in CityCenter
702-590-7111
aria.com
$$$
In CityCenter, with 4,000 rooms and every amenity (some with extra fees).

SPRING MOUNTAIN RD.
Yoga Among the Dolphins/ Mirage Las Vegas 4
15
DEAN MARTIN DR.
9 Nobu/ Caesars Palace Hotel & Casino
11 World Class Driving
FLAMINGO RD.
Hyde/ Bellagio 10
Las Vegas
7 Estiatorio Milos/ The Cosmopolitan
Liquid Club & Lounge/ Spa & Salon at Aria 8
1 Crystals at CityCenter
HARMON AVE.
PARADISE RD.
Aria Resort & Casino
LAS VEGAS BLVD. S.
2 L'Atelier de Joël Robuchon/ MGM Grand/ Hakkasan Las Vegas Restaurant and Nightclub
TROPICANA AVE.
604
1/4 mile
1/2 kilometer
Luxor
MCCARRAN INTERNATIONAL AIRPORT
Red Rock Canyon National Conservation Area
Neon Museum 5
Mob Museum 6
Las Vegas
NEVADA
215
Area of detail
4 miles
8 kilometers
ORE. IDAHO
NEVADA UTAH
Las Vegas
CALIF. ARIZ.

Moab

It's hard not to become a dime-store philosopher in Moab. With its dipping green valleys and great red rocks piercing the wide blue sky, this tiny town in southeastern Utah can be a heady study in perspective. One minute you're sipping coffee on Main Street, tucked safely between the wild, barren Canyonlands National Park and the magnificent stony surrealism of Arches National Park. A short drive later, you're thousands of dizzying feet above civilization, the wind whipping you senseless. The startling beauty of this terrain is enough to leave even the most seasoned traveler frozen in the sand, blinking in disbelief. — BY CINDY PRICE

FRIDAY

1 *A Delicate Balance* 3 p.m.

You can look at a million photos of the **Delicate Arch** (and you will), but nothing prepares you for the real deal. At **Arches National Park** (Highway 191; 435-719-2299; nps.gov/arch), take the mile-and-a-half hike up steep, uneven slick rock to hit the landmark just before sunset (bring a flashlight and plenty of water). The massive arch doesn't come into view until the last second, and when it does, it is unforgettable. It's perched on the brink of an enormous sandstone bowl, and you can edge your way around and stand beneath it for a picture, but be forewarned—though the ground there is wider than a big-city sidewalk, the combination of steep dropoff, gusty wind, and gleaming sun makes for a dizzying few seconds.

2 *The Barroom Floor* 8 p.m.

It's no Las Vegas, but Moab knows how to kick it. Swing by **La Hacienda** (574 North Main Street; 435-259-6319; moablahacienda.com; $), a townie favorite, for tasty fried fish tacos. Then hit **World Famous Woody's Tavern** (221 South Main Street; 435-259-3550; woodystavernmoab.com), where everyone from local hipsters to vacationing Dutch couples pull on cold drafts. Some say the floor is painted red to cover up bloodstains from brawls, but don't be put off—aside from foosball, Woody's is fairly docile these days.

SATURDAY

3 *Rough Riders* 8:30 a.m.

There are gentler ways to take in the lay of the land, but some scenic tours are just too tame. At the **Moab Adventure Center** (225 South Main Street; 435-259-7019; moabadventurecenter.com), you can book a Hummer Safari—a guide does the driving—that will take you in and out of rock canyons and up rough and steep sandstone hills (don't think about what it's going to be like coming down). Moab is also popular with mountain bikers—if that's your thing, check out **Moab Cyclery** (391 Main Street; 435-259-7423; moabcyclery.com) or another local bike outfitter for rentals and day trips.

4 *Old School* 12:30 p.m.

In a town where scenery looms large, it's easy to drive past the unassuming **Milt's Stop & Eat** (356 South 400 East; 435-259-7424; miltsstopandeat.com; $). But this little diner, which has been doling out fresh chili and shakes since 1954, comes through where it counts. Pull up to the counter and order a mouthwatering double bacon cheeseburger. It's a greasy-spoon chef-d'oeuvre, with aged-beef patties and thick slices of smoked bacon. A creamy chocolate malt will have you cursing the advent of frozen yogurt.

OPPOSITE The Delicate Arch, perched on the brink of an enormous sandstone bowl at Arches National Park.

RIGHT After a uranium mining bust in the 1980s, Moab reinvented itself as an outdoor recreation spot.

5 *Hole Sweet Hole* 1:30 p.m.

In 1945, Albert Christensen built his wife, Gladys, the home of their dreams—in the middle of a rock. Part kitsch memorial, part love story, **Hole N'' the Rock** (11037 South Highway 191; 435-686-2250; theholeintherock.com) is surely a tourist trap, but a heartwarming one. Even the steady drone of a gum-smacking tour guide can't dispel the sheer marvel of this 5,000-square-foot testament to one man's obsession. It took Albert 12 years to hand-drill the place, and Gladys another eight to give it a woman's touch. Each room is lovingly decorated with knick knacks or Albert's taxidermy. Outside, wander over to the inexplicable but equally delightful petting zoo filled with llamas, emus, and wallabies.

ABOVE Main Street and its rugged backdrop.

BELOW Heading for a cold draft at Woody's Tavern.

OPPOSITE ABOVE A heartwarming tourist trap.

OPPOSITE BELOW A sunset over Moab.

6 *Main Street* 3:30 p.m.

Like most small towns with attitude, Moab has a main street that's pretty darn cute. Start your walk with an iced coffee and a fresh slice of quiche at **EklectiCafé** (352 North Main Street; 435-259-6896; $). For a quick lesson on local topography, check out the area relief map at the **Museum of Moab** (118 East Center Street; 435-259-7985; moabmuseum.org). The artifacts on display include dinosaur bones and tracks, ancient pottery, mining tools, and a proud pioneer's piano—all part of the Moab story.

7 *World's Biggest Stage Set* 6 p.m.

Head out of town, hang a right at Scenic Byway 128, drive 18 miles, and take a right on La Sal Mountain Road toward Castle Valley. The pretty, winding route leads to **Castle Rock**—a dead ringer for Disney's Big Thunder Mountain Railroad and the star of old Chevrolet commercials. Turn around at Castleton Tower and drop into **Red Cliffs Lodge** (Mile Post 14, Highway 128; 435-259-2002; redcliffslodge.com) for a free wine tasting at the **Castle Creek Winery**. Afterward, check out the **Movie Museum** in the basement—a small homage to the many films shot in Moab, including *Rio Grande* and *Indiana Jones and the Last Crusade*.

8 *Local Brew* 8 p.m.

You've tasted the wine. Now sample the ale. The **Moab Brewery** (686 South Main Street; 435-259-6333; themoabbrewery.com; $) has a variety of hearty brews, plus its own homemade root beer. The dinner menu has plenty of beef and chicken, including barbecue, balanced by a cheese-heavy "Very Veggie" section and a promise that the frying is done in zero-trans-fat oil.

SUNDAY

9 *Dawn on the Cliffs* 7 a.m.

There are few reasons to endorse waking up at 7 on a Sunday, but a sunrise at Dead Horse Point passes the test. Hit the **Wicked Brew Drive Thru** (132 North Main Street; 435-259-0021; wickedbrewmoab.com) for an espresso-laced eye opener, and then take the winding drive up Route 313 to the 2,000-foot vantage point at **Dead Horse Point State Park** (435-259-2614;

utah.com/stateparks/dead_horse.htm). Watch the sun break over the vast, beautiful Canyonlands. To the west, look for Shafer Trail, the dusty road where Thelma and Louise sealed their fate in the 1991 Ridley Scott film.

10 *Rapid Observations* 10:30 a.m.

In the '70s, before Moab became known as the mountain-biking capital of the world, whitewater rafting was the big buzz. **Red River Adventures** (1140 South Main Street; 435-259-4046; redriveradventures.com) offers trips that take it easy through Class II and III rapids, and others that go for Class IV. If you'd rather try a different form of sightseeing, the company also offers rock climbing and horseback trips.

ABOVE Scenery looms large for Moab, tucked between Canyonlands and Arches National Parks.

OPPOSITE Cycling along Scenic Byway 128 outside of town. The local terrain is legendary among mountain bikers, and outfitters in Moab will provide bicycles and gear.

THE BASICS

Fly to Salt Lake City, rent a car, and drive 235 scenic miles southeast to Moab.

Sunflower Hill Inn
185 North 300 East
435-259-2974
sunflowerhill.com
$$
Lovely restored inn with 12 rooms.

Gonzo Inn
100 West 200 South
435-259-2515
gonzoinn.com
$$
Colorful retro-style hotel.

Red Cliffs Lodge
Mile Post 14, Highway 128
435-259-2002
redcliffslodge.com
$$-$$$
Overlooking the Colorado River 20 minutes out of town.

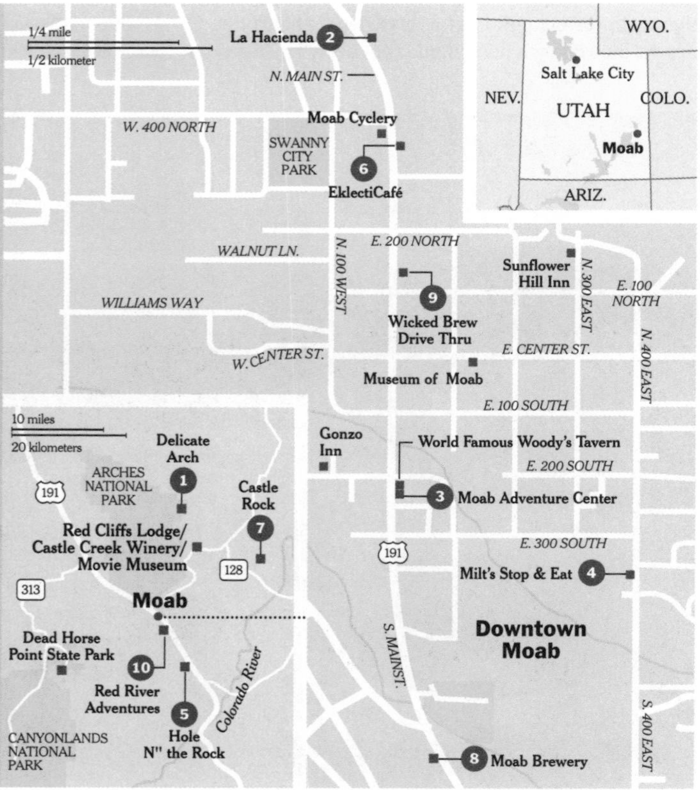

Docent Check-in

Salt Lake City

Sprawling and rapidly growing, Salt Lake City, Utah, is more complicated and cosmopolitan than most outsiders know. It's also more beautiful. Situated directly below the towering Wasatch Front, the city has a spectacular natural backdrop, beautiful 1900s neighborhoods, and one of the nation's most inviting college campuses at the University of Utah. Salt Lake City is still the headquarters of the Mormon Church and the place to go to see Mormon monuments. But it also has a rejuvenated downtown, a bold new natural history museum, interesting restaurants, and an open-door stance toward refugees and immigrants that has brought a variety of newcomers to town.

— BY JAIME GILLIN AND CHRISTOPHER SOLOMON

FRIDAY

1 *City Structure* 4 p.m.

Chart your own downtown tour. The **Main Library** (210 East 400 South; 801-524-8200; slcpl.lib.ut.us), which was an early and influential venture in the city center revitalization, is a curving glass structure designed by the architect Moshe Safdie. Step inside. There are fireplaces on every floor and a rooftop garden with views of the city and the Wasatch Mountains. Downtown has bloomed with new businesses, including shops and galleries, but the single biggest catalyst of change is **City Creek Center** (50 South Main Street; shopcitycreekcenter.com), a sprawling, 23-acre development with residential towers, office space, and a shopping mall, all financed by an arm of the Mormon Church. A handsome monument to consumption, the mall has more than 100 stores, including the likes of Tiffany, Nordstrom, and Coach. There are also Las Vegas-like fountains (music! jets of flame!), a retractable glass roof that closes in inclement weather, and a river that runs through it (O.K., a stream, the reimagined City Creek) with actual trout.

2 *Hungry in Utah* 7 p.m.

There's been an explosion of places to eat in downtown Salt Lake. Ryan Lowder, the local chef and owner, who had worked in the Jean-Georges Vongerichten and Mario Batali empires in Manhattan, opened the **Copper Onion** (111 East Broadway; 801-355-3282; thecopperonion.com; $$), which serves American food with what he calls "a pretty decent Mediterranean influence" and lots of house-made ingredients, from the noodles in the popular beef stroganoff to some cheeses. Lowder's second restaurant, **Plum Alley** (111 East Broadway; 801-355-0543; plumalley.com; $), named for a now-vanished street that was once part of a thriving Chinatown, is "white guys cookin' Asian food," Lowder said wryly. Look for ramen with house-made noodles and a bone broth or locally raised beef with coconut milk curry and bean sprouts.

3 *Open City* 9 p.m.

Since local liquor laws loosened in 2009, night spots have proliferated. **The Red Door** (57 West 200 South; 801-363-6030; behindthereddoor.com) has dim lighting, a great martini list, and kitschy revolution décor—yes, that's a Che Guevara mural on the wall. **Squatters Pub Brewery** (147 West Broadway; 801-363-2739; squatters.com) is one of several microbreweries now operating downtown.

SATURDAY

4 *Botanical Bliss* 9 a.m.

The **Red Butte Garden** (300 Wakara Way; 801-585-0556; redbuttegarden.org), nestled in the Wasatch foothills above the University of Utah campus, has a rose garden, 3.5 miles of walking trails,

OPPOSITE The Moshe Safdie-designed Public Library.

BELOW The University of Utah's Red Butte Garden and Arboretum has 3.5 miles of walking trails.

and morning yoga in the Fragrance Garden. For a wake-up hike, ask the front desk for directions to the Living Room, a lookout point named for the flat orange rocks that resemble couches. Sit back and absorb the expansive views of the valley, mountains, and the Great Salt Lake.

5 *Skulls and Moccasins* 11 a.m.

A state with such tremendous natural assets deserves a museum of natural history fit to contain it. Now it has one—the **Natural History Museum of Utah** at the Rio Tinto Center (301 Wakara Way; 801-581-6927; nhmu.utah.edu), next to Red Butte Garden. Sheathed in copper and designed to blend with the mountainside, the dramatic building houses 10 galleries of fearsome skulls, ancient moccasins, and interactive displays. Ramps let you see eye-to-eye with giant monsters in the dinosaur hall. And continuing research isn't far away here: visitors stare through glass windows and watch scientists cleaning dinosaur bones. Outside, there's a view of downtown, in the flat land below, and the big Utah sky.

6 *Diverse Palate* 2 p.m.

Salt Lake City has growing contingents of Latinos, Pacific Islanders (particularly Samoan and Tongan), and refugees from Tibet, Bosnia, and Somalia. One place to taste this kind of imported flavor is **Himalayan Kitchen** (360 South State Street; 801-328-2077; himalayankitchen.com; $$), a down-home dining room with turmeric-yellow walls and red tablecloth tables, where you might find Nepali goat curry or Himalayan momos, steamed chicken dumplings served with sesame seed sauce. For Middle Eastern food, go to **Mazza** (912 East 900 South; 801-521-4572; mazzacafe.com; $$), the second location of an established Salt Lake City original.

7 *A Taste of Marmalade* 3 p.m.

Branch out into some different neighborhoods. To see more of the city as it once was, wander the **Marmalade Historic District**, home to many original pioneer homes from the 19th century, or go on a walking tour with the **Utah Heritage Foundation** (801-533-0858; utahheritagefoundation.com). In the mini-neighborhood called **15th and 15th** (1500 East and 1500 South), get a sense of the city's gracious middle-class residential districts dating from the mid-20th century. Stop in at the charming **King's English Bookshop** (1511 South 1500 East; 801-484-9100; kingsenglish.com), a creaky old house filled with books and cozy reading nooks.

8 *Italian Hour* 7 p.m.

Salt Lake City has plenty of appealing Italian restaurants, but the most romantic may be **Fresco Italian Cafe** (1513 South 1500 East; 801-486-1300; frescoitaliancafe.com; $$), an intimate 14-table restaurant next to the King's English Bookshop. The menu is small but spot-on, with simple northern Italian dishes with a twist. The butternut squash ravioli, for example, was served with a splash of reduced apple cider and micro-planed hazelnuts. There's a roaring fire, candlelight, and, in the summer, dining on the brick patio. A roomier restaurant for good Italian food is **Caffe Molise** (55 West 100 South; 801-364-8833; caffemolise.com; $$). Its location around the corner from Abravanel Hall, home of the Utah Symphony, makes it a favorite destination for music lovers.

9 *Live From Utah* 9 p.m.

As the only sizable city between Denver and Northern California, Salt Lake City gets many touring bands passing through. Hear established and up-and-coming acts at places like the **Urban Lounge** (241

South 500 East; 801-746-0557; theurbanloungeslc.com) and **Kilby Court** (741 South Kilby Court; 801-364-3538; kilbycourt.com). If you want to make your own sweet music, stop by **Keys on Main** (242 South Main Street; 801-363-3638; keysonmain.com), a piano bar where the audience sings along.

SUNDAY

10 *Voices on High* 9 a.m.

Almost every Sunday morning the 360 volunteer members of the Mormon Tabernacle Choir sing at the **Mormon Tabernacle** in Temple Square (801-240-4150; mormontabernaclechoir.org). The egg-shaped hall, with its 150-foot roof span, is an acoustical marvel, and the nearly 12,000-pipe organ is among the largest in the world. You can join the live audience at the concert broadcast from 9:30 to 10 a.m., but you need to be in your seat by 9:15. Afterward, drop in at one of the Temple Square visitors' centers (visittemplesquare.com) and then take a look around. The square is 35 acres, the epicenter of the Mormon Church, and its monumental scale is a spectacle in itself.

OPPOSITE ABOVE A light rail trolley system runs through downtown past Temple Square and Mormon monuments.

OPPOSITE BELOW A congenial stop for readers is the King's English Bookshop, in an old house with cozy nooks.

THE BASICS

From Salt Lake City International Airport, the TRAX light-rail line (rideuta.com) will take you into the heart of the city in about 20 minutes.

Grand America Hotel
555 South Main Street
801-258-6000
grandamerica.com
$$
Lives up to its name with afternoon tea and 775 palatial rooms with Italian marble bathrooms.

The Inn on the Hill
225 North State Street
801-328-1466
inn-on-the-hill.com
$$
Twelve guest rooms in a 1909 English-style manor with Tiffany windows.

Hotel Monaco
15 West 200 South
801-595-0000
monaco-saltlakecity.com
$$
Downtown, with 225 whimsical rooms.

SALT LAKE 2002

Park City

To ski or not to ski. That's the luxurious question in Park City, Utah, the rare ski resort that offers lively diversions on and off the slopes. Historic Main Street still evokes a silver mining town, with local delis mixed in among upscale restaurants and fashion boutiques. And thanks to constant refinements, the powdery slopes remain a favorite of hard-core ski bums—not to mention the United States Ski Team, which calls Park City home—and the fur-trimmed celebrities who invade during the Sundance Film Festival. But the town's greatest asset may be location: Park City is 30 minutes from Salt Lake City and a short hop to several of the most popular slopes in the Rockies.

— BY DENNY LEE

FRIDAY

1 *Foraging on Main* 4:30 p.m.

As dusk shrouds the Wasatch Range, the Old West-style storefronts of Main Street light up with the hubbub of shoppers and après-skiers. Wedged among the ski shops and real estate windows are some stylish shops. **Flight Boutique** (545 Main Street; 435-604-0806; flightclothing.blogspot.com) carries such brands as Elizabeth & James and Theory. Another fashionable spot is **Cake Boutique** (511 Main Street; 435-649-1256; shopcakeboutique.com), which carries brands like Rag & Bone. If you'd rather skip the shopping and sample local culture, go to the **Kimball Art Center** (638 Park Avenue; 435-649-8882; kimballartcenter.org), the region's nonprofit arts anchor, which is housed in a historic stable.

2 *Dining Camp* 6 p.m.

The buttermilk fried chicken is free-range, organic, and, in all likelihood, raised in Utah. Yes, hipster fare has arrived in Park City, and it comes at a steep price at **Talisker on Main** (515 Main Street; 435-658-5479; taliskeronmain.com; $$$), a fine but casual restaurant that ranks among the town's best. Clever dishes might include lobster hush puppies and short rib shepherd's pie. The décor also invokes whimsy. With its tin ceilings and checkerboard floors, the cozy dining room feels like an English clubhouse squeezed inside an ice cream parlor. Service is crisp yet relaxed, and the dress code embraces both fur coats and wool beanies.

3 *Show Time* 8 p.m.

Channel Sundance's glamour at the **Egyptian Theatre** (328 Main Street; 435-649-9371; egyptiantheatrecompany.org), the pharaoh-themed landmark in the middle of town. When the 1926 theater isn't used for red-carpet premieres, it features concerts, comedy acts, and other live performances. Check its Web site for coming shows. For a more cinematic experience, the **Park City Film Series** (1255 Park Avenue; 435-615-8291; parkcityfilmseries.com) offers a stellar lineup of indie films at the Park City Library Building.

SATURDAY

4 *Town Lift* 9 a.m.

One of the underappreciated things about Park City is that the entire town is practically ski in/ski out. A triple lift on Main Street whisks riders to the **Park City Mountain Resort** (parkcitymountain.com), so if you're staying in town, there's no need for parking or shuttles. There are 3,300 acres of terrain to cover, so it's a good idea to check the morning's grooming reports before clicking in. Warm up on the Crescent and King Con mountain zones before tackling the black diamonds.

5 *Dine In/Ski Out* 1 p.m.

The town lift goes both ways, so if you're hankering for more than just burgers and pizzas, skip the

OPPOSITE The bobsled run at the Utah Olympic Park.

BELOW A marquee for the Sundance Film Festival.

slopeside cafeterias and ski into town for a more civilized lunch. For upscale fare in a dress-down setting, waddle over to **Zoom** (660 Main Street; 435-649-9108; zoomparkcity.com; $$). Opened by Robert Redford in a former train depot, Zoom offers refined American fare like braised lamb shank and fish tacos. After lunch, just hop back onto the lift. Trails can get packed along the lower runs, so work your way to the right side of the trail map.

6 *Getting Steamed* 5 p.m.

After an exhausting day of skiing, there's nothing like soaking half-naked with a bunch of tipsy strangers. That's the idea, anyway, at **Haven**, the rooftop bar at the **Sky Lodge**, Park City's hippest hotel (201 Heber Avenue; 435-658-2500; theskylodge.com). The hotel opens its large outdoor hot tub, which looks out onto the Wasatch Range, to nonguests; black terry robes are provided. The fancy, cocktail-free version of this concept is found at **Spa Montage** in Deer Valley (9100 Marsac Avenue; 435-604-1300; spamontage.com), a Roman-style wellness center with steaming whirlpools, volcanic saunas, massage services, and a quiet room for a little nap.

7 *Western Beef* 8 p.m.

As Utah's first distillery since Prohibition, the **High West Distillery and Saloon** (703 Park Avenue; 435-649-8300; highwest.com; $$) gets high marks for its small-batch whiskeys and vodkas. But it also gets props for its Western-inspired menu, which includes nouveau cowboy fare like dry-aged bison with a porcini sauce and pan-seared trout. Try the tasting menu, which pairs a five-course dinner with individual whiskeys. Another option, for those seeking a more club-like atmosphere, is **Silver** (508 Main Street; 435-940-1000; silverrestaurant.com; $$), a three-story restaurant that draws the martini set with sleek décor, D.J. booths, and a young-at-heart mood.

8 *Rough and Tumble* 10 p.m.

The brothels and casinos are long gone, but party seekers won't have any trouble finding a bar stool or a dance floor to keep the night going. An old reliable is the **No Name Saloon** (447 Main Street; 435-649-6667; nonamesaloon.net), a packed and friendly spot with the motto "Helping People Forget Their Names Since 1903." For a younger singles crowd, follow the cologne trail to **Downstairs** (625 Main Street; 435-226-5340; downstairspc.com), a throbbing disco partly owned by Danny Masterson, the curly-haired actor from *That '70s Show*. Expect bottle service,

ABOVE Main Street is achingly picturesque but can also be jammed with smoking S.U.V.'s.

BELOW On the mountain after a confectioner's sifting of Utah's famous light snow.

waitresses who dance on tables, and guys who fist-pump to rap music.

SUNDAY

9 *Go for the Gold* 9:30 a.m.

See how the pros do it. Built for the 2002 Winter Olympics, the vertiginous **Utah Olympic Park** (3419 Olympic Parkway; 435-658-4200; olyparks.com) remains an active training center for Olympic-class skiers. Call ahead to see if anyone is barreling down the K120 Nordic ski jump. Or catch some air yourself: the park offers Sunday ski clinics for intermediate skiers. Speed demons, however, will gravitate toward another sport: the Comet Bobsled. The mile-long track offers 80-mile-per-hour speeds and up to five G's of force. Those with heart problems may want to stand on the sidelines.

10 *Grander Canyons* Noon

If you have time to ski only one other resort, point your tips toward **Canyons** (canyonsresort.com), just north of Park City. The resort has undergone huge upgrades in recent years, and now counts 4,000 acres of terrain — so wide that it had trouble fitting it all on a trail map. Start at the Orange Bubble lift, a covered, heated chairlift that feels like riding inside a pair of toasty ski goggles. At the summit lookout, direct your gaze at Iron Mountain, one of the newest peaks. To ski there, connect the trails that lead to the left side of the map. It's a veritable winter wonderland.

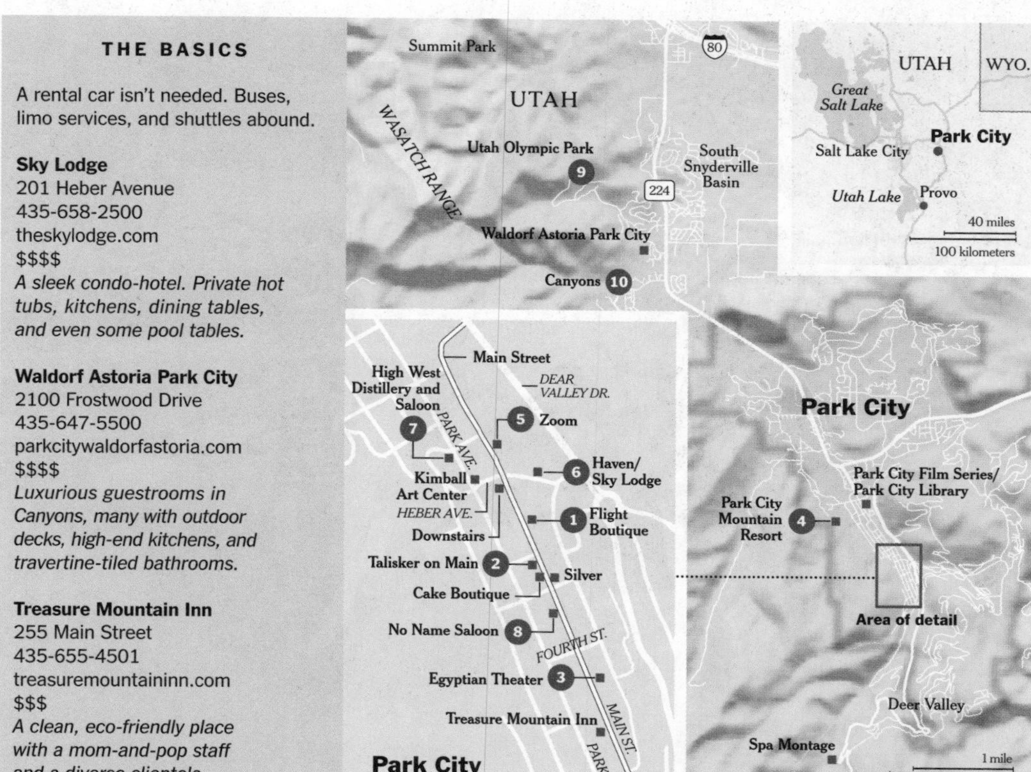

THE BASICS

A rental car isn't needed. Buses, limo services, and shuttles abound.

Sky Lodge
201 Heber Avenue
435-658-2500
theskylodge.com
$$$$
A sleek condo-hotel. Private hot tubs, kitchens, dining tables, and even some pool tables.

Waldorf Astoria Park City
2100 Frostwood Drive
435-647-5500
parkcitywaldorfastoria.com
$$$$
Luxurious guestrooms in Canyons, many with outdoor decks, high-end kitchens, and travertine-tiled bathrooms.

Treasure Mountain Inn
255 Main Street
435-655-4501
treasuremountaininn.com
$$$
A clean, eco-friendly place with a mom-and-pop staff and a diverse clientele.

Boise

Boise, Idaho, once ruled by the bait-and-bullet crowd, has embraced the Lycra lifestyle. Sitting at the junction of the arid plateau of the high desert and the western foothills of the Rocky Mountains, Boise, Idaho's capital, offers all the outdoor advantages of more ballyhooed Western towns but with less ballyhoo. Boise may have a population of more than 200,000, but it is still a mining and farming town at heart, and it attracts active professionals and young families who will tell you that theirs is a great hometown—just don't let too many people know. They wouldn't want those trailheads or hot springs to get too crowded. A rejuvenated downtown and a budding arts community mean that after a day of rafting on the Payette River, mountain biking in the foothills, or carving at Bogus Basin Ski Resort you don't have to turn in once the sun fades behind the Snake River.
— BY MATTHEW PREUSCH

FRIDAY

1 *The Idaho Story* 4 p.m.

It's best to educate before you recreate, so check out the pioneer days reconstructions and Lewis and Clark artifacts at the **Idaho Historical Museum** (610 North Julia Davis Drive; 208-334-2120; history.idaho.gov) in **Julia Davis Park**. From there, walk down the **Boise River Greenbelt** (parks.cityofboise.org), a much-loved and gloriously scenic corridor of parks and trails snug against the Boise River. It stretches for 23 miles, but you won't be going that far tonight.

2 *Big Game* 7 p.m.

Emerge at the **Cottonwood Grille** (913 West River Street; 208-333-9800; cottonwoodgrille.com; $$) to reward yourself with drinks and dinner. Have a cocktail or a glass of wine on the patio overlooking the river and, of course, cottonwoods. Check out the game menu. This is your chance to try elk sirloin, bison with cabernet sauce, or grilled pheasant. If you're feeling more conventional, there's always the pasta or Idaho trout.

OPPOSITE Rafting on the South Fork of the Payette River north of Boise.

RIGHT Join the Boiseans browsing amid carrots and lettuces near the Capitol dome at the Capital City Public Market.

SATURDAY

3 *Breakfast Builders* 8 a.m.

Put your name on the list at **Goldy's Breakfast Bistro** (108 South Capitol Boulevard; 208-345-4100; goldysbreakfastbistro.com; $$) and stroll two blocks north to the domed Capitol to contemplate the statue of Governor Frank Steunenberg. He was killed in 1905 by a bomb planted near his garden gate; the perpetrators were enraged by his rough handling of labor uprisings in upstate mines. But don't let that assassination ruin your appetite. Return to Goldy's and examine the menu to see which elements of the build-your-own breakfast you'd like to have with your scrambled eggs. Red flannel hash? Black beans? Salmon cake? Blueberry pancake? Be creative.

4 *Bumper Crop* 10 a.m.

Join stroller-pushing Boiseans gathered near the Capitol dome at the **Capital City Public Market** (280 North 8th Street; capitalcitypublicmarket.com). Browse amid the lettuces—not to mention the fruit, flowers, desserts, and art glass—and reflect that Idaho grows more than potatoes.

5 *Basque Brawn* 11 a.m.

A century ago, Basque shepherds tended flocks in the grassy foothills around Boise. Today the mayor and many other prominent Idahoans claim Basque heritage. Learn about aspects of the Basques' culture,

including their love of a stirring strongman competition, at the **Basque Museum and Cultural Center** (611 Grove Street; 208-343-2671; basquemuseum.com). Don't drop the theme when you leave the museum in search of lunch. Grab a table at **Bar Gernika Basque Pub & Eatery** (202 South Capitol Boulevard; 208-344-2175; bargernika.com; $). The lamb grinder is a safe bet, but for something more spirited, brave the beef tongue in tomato and pepper sauce. Wash it down with Basque cider.

6 *Rapid Transit* 1:30 p.m.

Join the weekend exodus of pickups hauling A.T.V.'s and Subarus bearing bikes as they head over the brown foothills of the Boise Front to outdoor adventure. Drive 45 minutes north to Horseshoe Bend and hook up with **Cascade Raft and Kayaking** (7050 Highway 55; 208-793-2221; cascaderaft.com) for a half-day raft trip through Class III and IV rapids on the Lower South Fork of the Payette River. There's also a milder trip with Class II and III rapids. If even that seems like whiter water than you're up for, stay in town, buy an inner tube, and join lazy locals floating down the relatively placid Boise River for six miles between **Barber Park** (4049 Eckert Road) and **Ann Morrison Park** (1000 Americana Boulevard). Avoid the river if the water is high.

ABOVE Downtown and the Boise Mountains.

OPPOSITE Hikers, runners, and cyclists share the 130 miles of paths in the Ridge to Rivers trail system.

7 *How about a Potato-tini?* 7 p.m.

Swap your swimsuit for town wear and find an outdoor table on the pedestrian plaza outside the overtly cosmopolitan **Red Feather Lounge** (246 North 8th Street; 208-429-6340; bcrfl.com/redfeather/; $$), where the focus is on post-classic cocktails like a Tangerine Rangoon: Plymouth gin, fresh tangerine juice, and homemade pomegranate grenadine. Pair that with pan-roasted halibut or potato confit pizza, and you might forget that you're in laid-back Boise. That is, until you spot the guy in running shorts and a fanny pack sitting at the bar.

8 *Bard by the Boise* 8 p.m.

Borrow a blanket from your hotel and find a spot on the lawn at the **Idaho Shakespeare Festival**, overlooking the Boise River east of town (5657 Warm Springs Avenue; 208-336-9221; idahoshakespeare.org), which runs June to September. It features productions of Shakespeare as well as more contemporary works at an outdoor amphitheater. As the sun sets and the stars come out, you might start to think that Boise's status as one of the most isolated metro areas in the lower 48 states is not a bad thing.

SUNDAY

9 *Pedal for Your Coffee* 9 a.m.

Head to **Idaho Mountain Touring** (1310 West Main Street; 208-336-3854; idahomountaintouring.com), rent a full-suspension mountain bike, and head north on 13th Street to Hyde Park, a neighborhood of bungalows and tree-lined streets. Park your bike with the others in front of **Java Hyde Park** (1612 North 13th Street; 208-345-4777) and make your way past the dogs tied up outside to order your favorite caffeinated creation.

10 *Up, Down, Repeat* 10 a.m.

Fortified, and perhaps jittery, remount your rented ride and pedal a few blocks farther up 13th Street to **Camel's Back Park** (1200 West Heron Street). Look for the trailhead east of the tennis courts, one of many entrances to the Ridge to Rivers trail system (ridgetorivers.org), a single- and double-track network that covers 80,000 acres between the Boise Ridge and Boise River. Climb the Red Cliffs Trail to open vistas of the Treasure Valley below, then loop back down on the rollicking Lower Hulls Gulch Trail. Repeat as necessary.

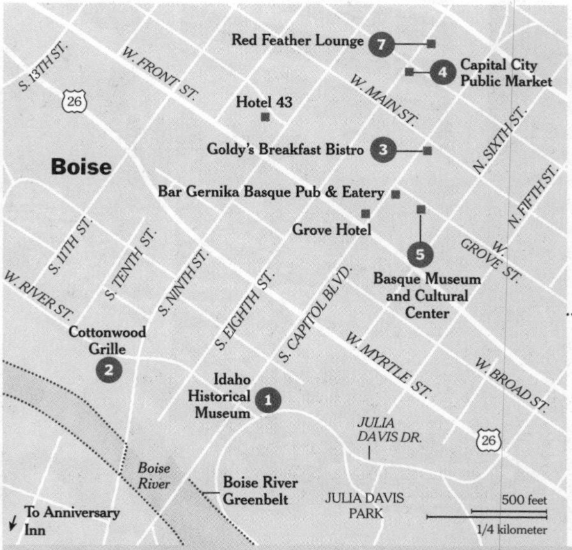

Red Feather Lounge 7
4 Capital City Public Market
Hotel 43
Goldy's Breakfast Bistro 3
Bar Gernika Basque Pub & Eatery
Grove Hotel
5 Basque Museum and Cultural Center
Cottonwood Grille 2
Idaho Historical Museum 1
Boise
S. 13TH ST.
W. FRONT ST.
W. MAIN ST.
N. SIXTH ST.
N. FIFTH ST.
W. GROVE ST.
S. 11TH ST.
S. TENTH ST.
S. NINTH ST.
S. EIGHTH ST.
S. CAPITOL BLVD.
W. MYRTLE ST.
W. BROAD ST.
W. RIVER ST.
26
JULIA DAVIS DR.
Boise River
Boise River Greenbelt
JULIA DAVIS PARK
To Anniversary Inn
500 feet
1/4 kilometer

6 To Cascade Raft and Kayaking
Camel's Back Park 10
Java Hyde Park
9 Idaho Mountain Touring
Area of detail
Ann Morrison Park
Boise
IDAHO
BOISE RIDGE
Boise River
Idaho Shakespeare Festival 8
Barber Park
2 miles
4 kilometers

ORE.
MONT.
Payette R.
Boise
IDAHO
NEV.
UTAH

THE BASICS

Boise is 431 miles from Portland, Oregon. Major airlines serve its airport. Two wheels are good for some adventures; for others, you need four.

Hotel 43
981 Grove Street
208-342-4622
hotel43.com
$$
Boutique hotel downtown with views of the city and the foothills.

The Grove Hotel
245 South Capitol Boulevard
208-333-8000
grovehotelboise.com
$$
Near the Capitol.

The Anniversary Inn
1575 South Lusk Avenue
208-387-4900
anniversaryinn.com
$$
Every room themed, from Romeo and Juliet to Biker Roadhouse.

Calgary

There was a time, not so many years ago, when the only reasons most tourists would bother venturing into Calgary was for the famous Stampede, a two-week rodeo festival in July, or in winter for a Flames hockey game. But this rugged city in central Alberta is undergoing an energetic revitalization brought on by the long-running oil boom, and its population has increased by tens of thousands every year for well over a decade, bringing the number of residents to more than a million. For visitors, all this activity means a revived downtown core with restaurants whose chefs — and prices — could vie with those in Toronto or Montreal; spruced-up outlying neighborhoods; and urban boutique hotels. But perhaps most surprising is that the Heart of the New West, as Calgary is billing itself these days, is becoming known as a center of culture, with sophisticated museums and diverse options for music and live theater. — BY SUSAN CATTO

FRIDAY

1 *Sandstone Downtown* 3 p.m.

Founded in the 19th century as an outpost of the Northwest Mounted Police, Calgary soon found prosperity based on sandstone quarries, and the honey-hued sandstone buildings lining the **Stephen Avenue Walk**, a pedestrian mall between First Street Southwest and Sixth Street Southwest, date from the late 1880s. Today the street is a brick pedestrian strip filled with shops and restaurants, a good place to get acquainted with the city and start your weekend.

2 *Cocktails and Petroleum* 5 p.m.

At the fashionable **Metropolitan Grill** (317 Seventh Avenue Southwest; 403-263-5432; themet.ca) at the top of Stephen Avenue's sandstone row, mingle with casually dressed young professionals meeting for after-work drinks. Listen for shop talk about the petroleum business. Many of the patrons are probably recent arrivals from someplace else, drawn by the ongoing oil boom. Oil was discovered in this area in 1914, and a boom-bust cycle repeated itself in the 1920s, 1950s, and 1980s. During busts, the city hollowed out; during booms, it was the Houston of Canada, complete with cowboy hats and swagger. The current upswing seems likely to last a while. Calgary is home to Canada's biggest oil and gas companies and the administrative headquarters of the oil sands extraction projects centered 470 miles north in Fort McMurray, Alberta.

3 *Steak Special* 7 p.m.

Calgary is not only Canada's energy capital, but its beef capital, too, surrounded by grasslands perfect for grazing cattle. While you're here, you have to have at least one steak dinner. There are plenty of steakhouses to choose from, including the well-regarded **Belvedere** (107 Eighth Avenue Southwest; 403-265-9595: thebelvedere.ca: $$$) and **Saltlik** (101 Eighth Avenue Southwest; 403-537-1160; saltlik.com; $$$). But you'll find steak from Alberta beef at most fine-dining restaurants in town.

4 *Your Kind of Sound* 10 p.m.

Visitors to Calgary can easily fill their nights with music. Live bands play in bars around town; **Wine-Ohs** (811 First Street Southwest; 403-263-1650), formerly called the Beat Niq Jazz & Social Club, has live jazz shows most nights; and the **Calgary Philharmonic Orchestra** (cpo-live.com) maintains a busy schedule.

OPPOSITE Skating in the sunshine at the Olympic Plaza.

RIGHT The Kensington Riverside Inn, a boutique hotel.

SATURDAY

5 *Blackfoot Country* 10 a.m.

The **Glenbow Museum** (130 Ninth Avenue Southeast; 403-268-4100; glenbow.org) is both art gallery and history museum, emphasizing the history of Alberta, including display areas dedicated to the province's original inhabitants, the Blackfoot Indians. The Glenbow also has an incongruous but beautiful collection of early Asian sculpture. The museum shop, which carries jewelry, carvings, and beadwork, has a fine collection of books on Blackfoot history and culture.

6 *Going Upscale* Noon

As condominiums spring up along the Bow River, neighborhoods on the edge of downtown are becoming destinations, too. **Kensington**, just over the Louise Bridge, is prime shopping and strolling territory, geared to a population prosperous enough to afford neighborhood restaurants that serve entrees like lobster lasagna but young enough to desire a bit of bohemia. Lunch is easy to find in a pub or bistro, and the array of stores includes **Livingstone and Cavell Extraordinary Toys** (1124 Kensington Road Northwest; 403-270-4165; extraordinarytoys.com), which, though small, lives up to its name, and a shop of the favorite local chocolatier **Bernard Callebaut** (1123 Kensington Road Northwest; 403-283-5550; bernardcallebaut.com).

7 *Riverside Park* 2 p.m.

Calgary, though sprawling, lives day to day in a beautiful setting on the high plains along the Bow and Elbow Rivers, with the snowy Canadian Rockies off in the distance. The best way to get in touch with the city's natural side is along 130 miles of bikeways and pathways that line Calgary's rivers, meander through parks, and crisscross the city. A good place to start is **Prince's Island Park** (First Avenue and Fourth Street Southwest; 403-268-2489; calgary.ca/CSPS/Parks), which runs along the Bow River and is the scene of festivals and open-air theater in summer. Despite the views of downtown on one side and Kensington on the other, the park isn't too urban — signs warn visitors to give a wide berth to coyotes. In 2013, the rivers showed their aggressive side in massive flooding, but the city soon recovered.

8 *Dinner in Red* 6:30 p.m.

Inglewood, often cited as the next Kensington, is an increasingly upscale district with blocks of antique stores, home furnishing shops, and quirky boutiques. It's also the home of **Rouge** (1240 Eighth Avenue Southeast; 403-531-2767; rougecalgary.com; $$$-$$$$), a romantic high-end French restaurant in a red Victorian-era house surrounded by a lawn and trees. On the menu, expect Canadian beef, lamb, and probably elk, and fish from Canadian waters. For a splurge, order the chef's tasting menu with wine pairings.

9 *Theater Town* 8 p.m.

The downtown **Epcor Centre for the Performing Arts** (225 Eighth Avenue Southeast; 403-294-7455; epcorcentre.org) houses — with style — several theater groups. Theatre Calgary has presented professional productions since 1968. Downstage and One Yellow Rabbit tend toward the provocative. Alberta Theatre Projects presents an annual festival of new Canadian plays.

ABOVE The Calgary skyline at dusk.

BELOW Mountain biking at Canada Olympic Park.

SUNDAY

10 *Your Inner Olympian* 10 a.m.

How about trying the luge, biking down a mountain, and riding a zip line off a ski jump, all in one place? A legacy of the 1988 Calgary Winter Games, the **Canada Olympic Park** (88 Canada Olympic Road Southwest; 403-247-5452; winsport.ca), 15 minutes west of downtown, has a high thrill quotient, including rides on a luge track. The Skyline, a zip line, shoots harnessed passengers from the top of the ski-jump tower. Chairlifts are turned over to mountain bikers, while milder adventure options include mini-golf, a climbing wall, and a bungee trampoline.

11 *Jurassic Side Trip* Noon

Alberta's badlands are home to Canada's biggest dinosaur finds, so if you have budding paleontologists in your family, consider driving 80 miles northeast to the **Royal Tyrrell Museum** (Highway 838, Midland Provincial Park, Drumheller; 403-823-7707; tyrrellmuseum.com). You'll find more than 40 dinosaur skeletons and galleries devoted to the excavation of fossils and long-extinct underwater creatures. In Drumheller, murals of dinosaurs decorate downtown buildings, and at the end of Main Street you'll find an 86-foot-high fiberglass Tyrannosaurus rex (four times bigger than life size). Climb 106 stairs up into the beast's mouth for a panoramic view of the Canadian Badlands.

THE BASICS

A car will come in handy, but Calgary is small enough to enjoy on foot much of the time.

Hôtel Le Germain Calgary
899 Centre Street Southwest
403-264-8990
germaincalgary.com
$$
Calgary outpost of a Quebec City-based chain of stylish boutique hotels.

Hotel Arts
119 12th Avenue Southwest
403-266-4611
hotelarts.ca
$$
Art installations in the lobby and minimalist chic bedrooms.

Kensington Riverside Inn
1126 Memorial Drive Northwest
403-228-4442
kensingtonriversideinn.com
$$
Just across the Bow River from downtown.

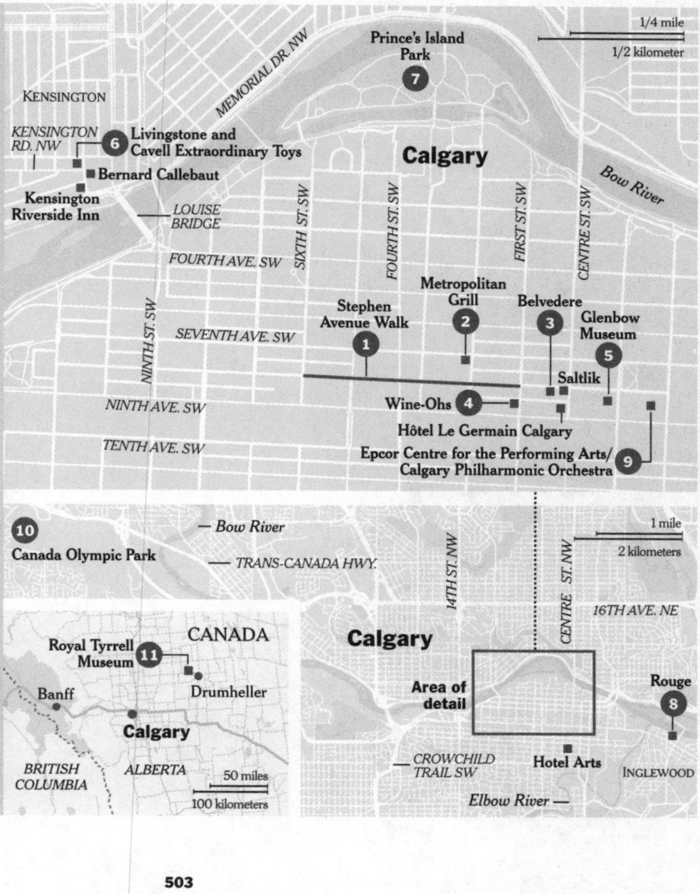

Banff

There are higher towns in the Canadian Rockies, but Banff in almost any season feels about as close to heaven as one can get. In winter, the S.U.V.'s rolling into town are loaded with skiing and snowboarding gear; in the warmer seasons, this is a place to get close to the wilderness by bike, on horseback, or, best of all, on foot. The glacier-fed rivers and lakes are an electrifying aqua-tinted blue, and the breathtaking mountain scenery is highlighted by the dark boughs of matchstick-straight lodgepole pines. When you've seen enough snowy peaks and waterfalls for the day, sample Banff's other side: grand hotels, fine restaurants, shopping, and spas. And thanks in part to the Banff Centre for the Arts, the town has a cultural life that few resort towns enjoy.

—BY BRUCE HEADLAM AND BARBARA IRELAND

FRIDAY

1 *First Steps* 3:30 p.m.

Pick up maps and hiking advice from the knowledgeable and cheerful staff at the **Banff Visitor Centre** (224 Banff Avenue; 403-762-1550; pc.gc.ca/pn-np/ab/banff/contact.aspx), and then warm up your hiking muscles with a walk along rugged **Lake Minnewanka**, nicknamed the Devil's Lake for the creature that is supposed to live in its cold waters. Drive north out of Banff for 15 minutes, following the signs to the lake, and then park near the launch of Lake Minnewanka Boat Tours. Follow the path along the west side of the lake, then take the trail to the bridge at Cascade River. Drink in the mountain scenery while looking out for bighorn sheep along the shore and listening for the howls of distant wolves. If the Lake Minnewanka trail is closed (as it sometimes is when bears are active), stay in Banff and walk the serene **Fenland Trail** (off Mount Norquay Road; friendsofbanff.com/blog/hike/fenland-trail) through sun-dappled woods.

2 *Western Gourmet* 8 p.m.

If you're not easily intimidated by graduate-level cuisine and encyclopedic wine lists, take Mountain Avenue to the **Eden** restaurant in the **Rimrock Resort Hotel** (866-288-8063; banffeden.com; $$$$). In its well-appointed dining rooms overlooking the town, Eden offers tasting menus with multiple courses that incorporate Canadian ingredients into French-style cooking. The attentive waiters—more like consultants, really—walk you through each course, and the sommelier will match your meal with a bottle from the restaurant's vast cellar. Those who prefer their food and surroundings a little rougher (and prices a little lower) can try **Grizzly House** (207 Banff Avenue; 403-762-4055; banffgrizzlyhouse.com; $$$$), a Western-kitsch restaurant where you can cook your own combination of exotic game (buffalo, rattlesnake, ostrich) over hot rocks at your table.

SATURDAY

3 *Day Breaks* 8 a.m.

Early morning—before the tour buses are herded into town—is the quietest time of day in Banff, so get up early and take a leisurely walk to breakfast at **Melissa's Missteak** (218 Lynx Street; 403-762-5511; melissasmissteak.com; $$). The crowd will already be assembling in Melissa's big main room, which looks like the inside of an especially large log cabin. The Swiss apple pancake may not be authentically Western, but it's a great way to start the day.

4 *Happy Trails* 9:30 a.m.

Walk south on Banff Avenue, turn left just before the downtown bridge, and find the paved walking

OPPOSITE Moraine Lake in Banff National Park.

BELOW Have a drink and a casual dinner, or in season get your hockey fix, at the Elk & Oarsman.

trail marked **Bow Falls**. The trail follows the Bow River past the falls (a favorite site for wedding photographs) and then briefly joins with a paved road before descending into the Bow Valley. The trail will carry you through the deep forest, then up a moderately steep incline to Tunnel Mountain. The path forks in places, but there is no need to have a Robert Frost moment: all the trails converge eventually. Follow Tunnel Mountain Road east to the Banff Hoodoos, free-standing pillars that have separated from the mountain's side. After walking back to town on Tunnel Mountain Road, get a grand perspective on the **Banff Gondola** (403-762-2523; explorerockies.com/banff-gondola). Drive to the base station, take the eight-minute ride to the upper terminal and then follow the Vista Trail up to Sanson Peak. Admire the views from all sides.

5 *Soak It Up* Noon

Time to ease your sore muscles. Follow the signs from the gondola parking lot to the historic **Banff Upper Hot Springs** (403-762-1515; hotsprings.ca) and slip into one of the 105-degree outdoor pools, fed by naturally heated spring water. Lie back and enjoy the spectacular mountain scenery.

6 *Afternoon Tea* 2 p.m.

Afternoon tea, a splendid British tradition, has never looked quite so splendid as it does at the **Fairmont Banff Springs** hotel, the magnificent former railroad lodge known locally as the castle. Tea is served every afternoon in the Rundle Lounge. Sit back in the overstuffed chairs with a pot of the hotel's own blend, some scones, pastries, and, of course, cucumber sandwiches, and enjoy the serene view of the Bow Valley. The hotel recommends booking in advance (405 Spray Avenue; 403-762-2211; fairmont.com/banff-springs; $$$) for a window seat, but every table has its rewards. Allow yourself a few extra minutes to poke around the hotel's nooks, especially the baronial dining halls (you may see the place settings going in for a wedding dinner) and exquisite wine bars, and to pick up a package of tea from the hotel's pantry shop.

7 *Mountain Shopping* 4 p.m.

If you're short on workout clothes and cold-weather wear, Banff is the place to stock up. Several stores sell clothing and gear for the outdoor sports that this town so loves; even the local Gap honors the fleece-and-Lycra theme. Budget some serious time to investigate **Monod Sports** (129 Banff Avenue; 403-762-4571; monodsports.com), which has been catering to fans of the Canadian Rockies since 1949. Its four floors are stocked with clothing and supplies from parkas and biking shorts to fly-fishing rods and ice axes.

8 *Elk on the Lawn* 6 p.m.

Wander toward the **Banff Centre** (107 Tunnel Mountain Drive; 403-762-6301; banffcentre.ca), watching for the giant elk that gather on the grounds year-round. In addition to holding book, film, and television festivals, the center puts on challenging music and opera performances by visiting artists. Try the box office (in the Eric Harvie Theatre; open late the day of performances) for last-minute tickets.

9 *Elk on the Plate* 8 p.m.

Find sustenance and conviviality at **Elk & Oarsman** (119 Banff Avenue, second floor;

403-762-4616; elkandoarsman.com; $$), a pub with a wood-beamed ceiling where everyone seems to gather. Seth Rogen look-alikes swill the crisp house lager, and triathletes are quick to crack a smile and start a conversation. Try the elk burgers, Tuscan-sausage pizzas, or chicken wings, and stick around for live music.

SUNDAY

10 *The Spring That Started It All* 9:30 a.m.

On a winter visit, you would be taking today to go to Lake Louise for some skating or skiing. But on a summer trip, rent a bicycle (there are several rental spots around this mountain bike-crazy town) and pedal south to the end of Cave Avenue to the **Cave and Basin National Historic Site** (311 Cave Avenue; 403-762-1566; pc.gc.ca/eng/progs/lhn-nhs/index.aspx), the hot spring cave that first drew tourists to Banff more than 100 years ago. Take the tour, and see the original cave entrance. Then go back outside and continue on the 4.5-mile trail along the Bow River until you get to the bike racks at the last point before you're required to continue on foot. Climb the trail to the **Sundance Canyon**, a magical glen with a cascading stream falling next to your upward path.

OPPOSITE Banff is an all-weather resort, with year-round beauty and seasonal sports.

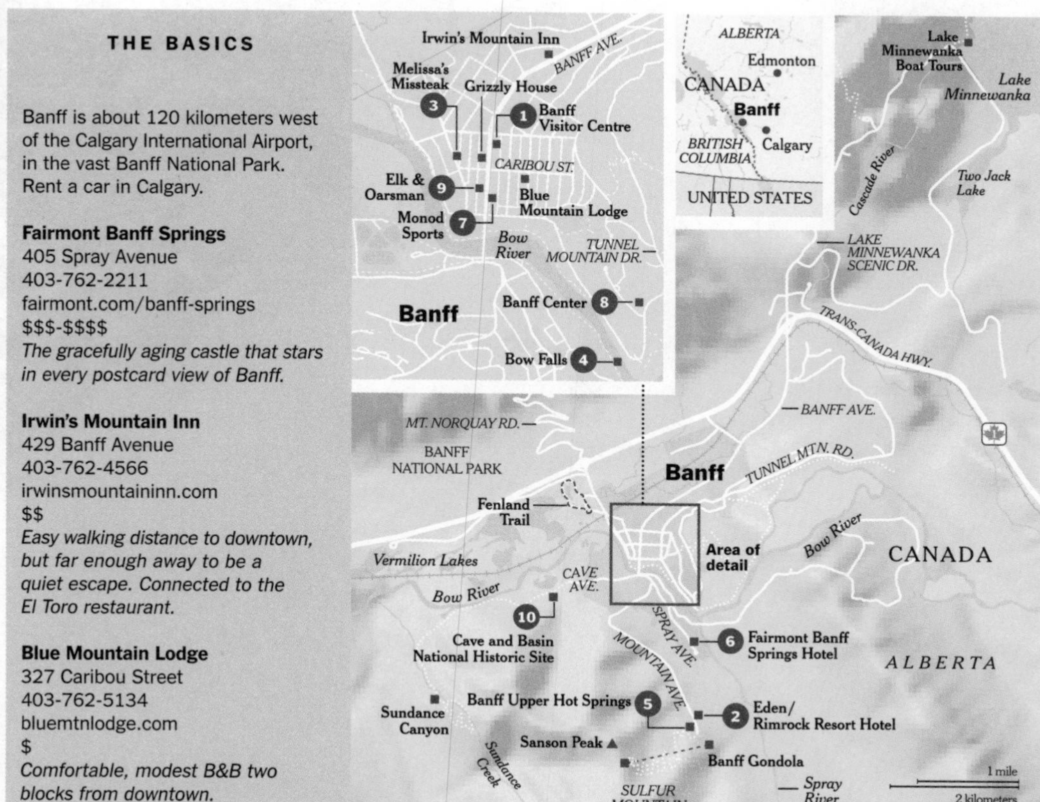

THE BASICS

Banff is about 120 kilometers west of the Calgary International Airport, in the vast Banff National Park. Rent a car in Calgary.

Fairmont Banff Springs
405 Spray Avenue
403-762-2211
fairmont.com/banff-springs
$$$-$$$$
The gracefully aging castle that stars in every postcard view of Banff.

Irwin's Mountain Inn
429 Banff Avenue
403-762-4566
irwinsmountaininn.com
$$
Easy walking distance to downtown, but far enough away to be a quiet escape. Connected to the El Toro restaurant.

Blue Mountain Lodge
327 Caribou Street
403-762-5134
bluemtnlodge.com
$
Comfortable, modest B&B two blocks from downtown.

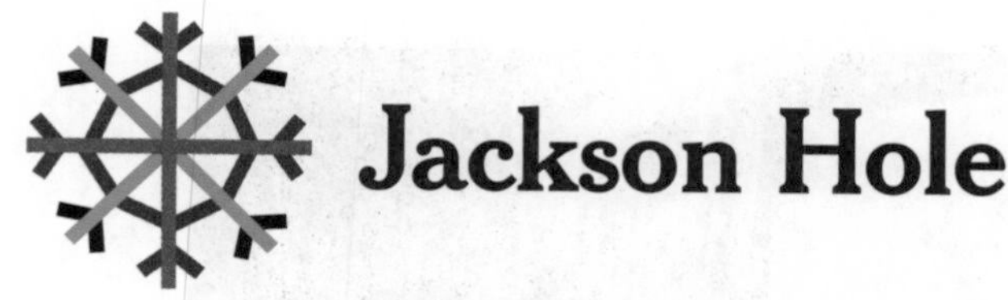

Jackson Hole

When the first mountain men crossed into Jackson Hole from the Yellowstone Park area, they were flabbergasted by its epic beauty. Before them lay a flat plain fenced in by snow-clad peaks soaring a mile up from the valley floor. That beauty is still here, but in winter, it is not the only lure. This is powder country — the valley's microclimate produces considerable precipitation within a generally dry climate — and those conditions combine with the favorable tilt of the mountain slopes to create excellent skiing and boarding. Add to that a recent five-year overhaul of Jackson Hole Ski Resort's lift system and the resort's luxurious modern facilities, plus the proximity of the valley town of Jackson, and it's easy to see why Jackson Hole has almost a cult following among skiers.

— BY FINN-OLAF JONES AND TOM PRICE

FRIDAY

1 *The Local Mountain* 3 p.m.

While the big ski resort that drew you here closes at 4 p.m., you can still get in a little skiing this afternoon at the more intimate **Snow King Mountain** (400 East Snow King Avenue, Jackson; 307-733-5200; snowkingmountain.com), which stays open until 7 p.m. thanks to lots of floodlights. Snow King, beloved by locals, almost never has lift lines and charges a bargain rate for night skiing. Exhibition ski run, with its steep, long, unbroken fall line, is where generations of Olympians cut their teeth; beginners and intermediate skiers hit their stride under the Rafferty lift. If you arrive early enough, take a good look around. From the summit here, the view stretches 50 miles to Yellowstone.

2 *Sleigh Ride* 6:30 p.m.

At **Spring Creek Ranch** (1800 Spirit Dance Road; 307-733-8833; springcreekranch.com), which straddles East Gros Ventre Butte, cowhands will pull thick blankets over you for a horse-pulled sleigh ride to the top of the butte. After gaping at what must be one of the best views on the continent, sleigh back down to dinner at the Ranch's **Granary Restaurant** ($$$-$$$$), a popular Friday night destination with live jazz. (The ride and dinner come as a package.) The chef excels at Jackson Hole high-altitude cuisine with dishes like Cajun-spice elk tenderloin and rainbow trout with black truffles — all served at the edge of the butte with the stars twinkling above the Teton Range and moose, mule deer, and elk grazing among the cabins outside.

OPPOSITE A seasoned skier tries out expert terrain at the Jackson Hole Mountain Resort.

RIGHT The town of Jackson seen from Snow King Mountain.

SATURDAY

3 *Breakfast at the Top* 9 a.m.

From the Teton Village, the **Jackson Hole Mountain Resort tram** (tram-formation.com) will whisk you through spectacular scenery up 4,139 feet to the 10,450-foot summit of Rendezvous Mountain. There's been a "big red box" on this mountain since 1966, but the beloved original was retired and replaced by this newer, larger, more streamlined version, which holds 100 people. Once at the top, join the morning ski patrol and eager skiers for waffles — with brown sugar butter or with peanut butter and bacon — in the cozy confines of the seemingly permanently ice-encrusted **Corbet's Cabin** (307-739-2688; jacksonhole.com/on-mountain-dining.html; $). Situated right next to the tram, Corbet's offers convenience along with its delicious options to fuel a day on the slopes.

4 *Skiing the Tetons* 9:30 a.m.

Jackson Hole Mountain Resort (Teton Village; jacksonhole.com) is unlike any other ski mountain. There's that favorable microclimate, and in addition, this side of the valley was created by tectonic tilting, resulting in slopes rising straight out of the prairie like an upended table. The skier's choices range from gentle slopes to cliffs, and from spacious bowls to narrow chutes. The Casper high-speed quad lift opens up the vast intermediate and beginner slopes. For advanced skiers, Corbet's Couloir, Rendezvous Mountain, and the unusually accessible backcountry skiing (they even have testing devices for your personal avalanche gear at the gates) remain legendary.

5 *Slopeside Lunch* 1 p.m.

You may be skiing in some of the best wilderness cowboy country in the world, but that's all the more reason to eat well, even at the top of the slopes. **Couloir** (Top of Bridger Gondola, Teton Village; jacksonhole.com/couloir-restaurant.html; $$$), next to the summit of the Bridger Gondola, is popular for elaborate prix fixe dinners and for weddings on its terrace, which has killer views. You're here at lunchtime, so you might as well sample its confit duck wings, house-cured Reuben sandwiches, or grilled Colorado lamb loin salad for a worthy ski break. The restaurant goes to local sources for its food and even a lot of its beverages. (Yeehaw for oaky, vanilla-ish Wyoming bourbon!)

6 *Change of Pace* 5 p.m.

When it's time for relaxation and a massage to ease those tired muscles, you'll have several spas to choose from. The **Four Seasons Spa** (7680 Granite Loop Road, Teton Village; 307-732-5000; fourseasons.com/jacksonhole) promises altitude-adjusted treatments using local materials like hawthorne berries, sage, willow bark, and smooth stones from the Snake River. The **Snake River Lodge** (7710 Granite Loop Road, Teton Village; 855-342-4712; snakeriverlodge.com) advertises a 17,000-square-foot spa and rooms with mountain views. **Chill Spa** at the Hotel Terra (3335 West Village Drive, Teton Village; 307-201-6065; hotelterrajacksonhole.com) lives up to its name with a heated outdoor infinity pool.

7 *Moose Music* 8 p.m.

Dig into an elk steak, accompanied by a local beer, at the **Mangy Moose Restaurant and Saloon** (Teton Village, Village Road; 307-733-4913; mangymoose.com; $$), which looks almost as self-consciously rustic as its name. Primarily a steakhouse, this place also offers salads, burgers, and truffle fries, and it's a consistent favorite with Jackson Hole insiders. As the evening wears on, the locals crowd in for the live music, which includes national and local acts.

SUNDAY

8 *Swimming With Django* 11 a.m.

The whole valley bubbles with underground thermal activity that makes for exotic swimming holes. Drive out to the tiny town of Kelly, turn right at Gros Ventre Road, and you'll find a small parking lot next to the **Kelly Warm Springs** (intersection of Lower Gros Ventre Road and Gros Ventre Road, Kelly). Steam will be wafting into the valley. Film buffs might recognize the springs from the movie

ABOVE Corbet's Cabin, a cozy restaurant near the top of the Jackson Hole Mountain Resort tram.

BELOW Simon Gudgeon's bronze *Isis*, a work on the sculpture trail at the National Museum of Wildlife Art.

Django Unchained, which was filmed here. It's a stunning scene — wilderness and the towering Tetons. Wade into the 80-degree water and swim with the hundreds of tropical fish that improbably have found their way here — legend has it that this is a favorite spot for locals to dump their aquariums.

9 *Bronze Buffalo* 1 p.m.

A hillside quartzite building designed to resemble a ruined Scottish castle overlooking the plains where herds of elk graze is the setting for **the National Museum of Wildlife Art** (2820 Rungius Road; 307-733-5771; wildlifeart.org). The collection, primarily American and European paintings and sculpture, has objects created as far back as 2500 B.C. If you're prepared for an easy outdoor hike, follow the three-quarter-mile sculpture trail that meanders across the terrain where impressive animal forms like Simon Gudgeon's bronze *Isis* seem to be meditating on the Gros Ventre Range across the valley. The view can also be savored over a lunch of buffalo burgers in the museum's scenic Rising Sage Café ($$).

ABOVE Kelly Warm Springs are good for a winter swim.

THE BASICS

Shuttles take passengers from the airport to locations in Jackson Hole, and buses connect the major spots. But for more freedom to explore, you may want to rent a car.

Teton Mountain Lodge & Spa
3385 Cody Lane, Teton Village
307-734-7111
tetonlodge.com
$$$$
Convenient and family-friendly; close to the tram.

Four Seasons Resort
7680 Granite Loop Road, Teton Village
307-732-5000
fourseasons.com/jacksonhole
$$$$
Luxury ski hotel with all of the expected amenities.

Spring Creek Ranch
1800 Spirit Dance Road, Jackson
307-733-8833
springcreekranch.com
$$
Perched atop a butte rising out of the valley. Amazing views and cabin rooms overlooking the mountains.

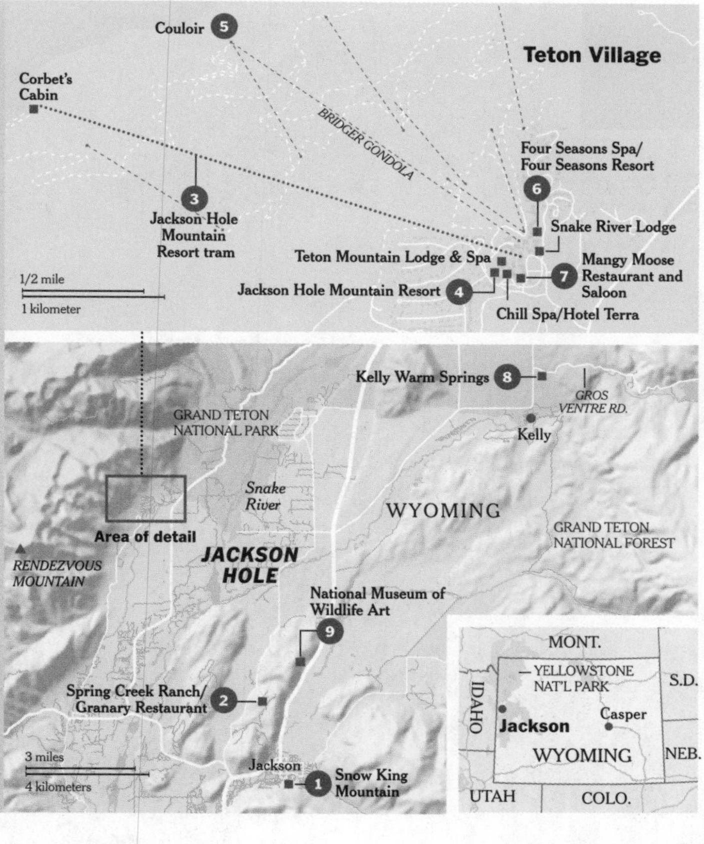

The Tetons

The three iconic peaks of the Tetons—13,770-foot Grand Teton and the mountains flanking it on either side—have been a landmark since the days of the French fur trade and probably for centuries before that. While they once guided long-distance travelers struggling through the Rockies on horseback, today they are a symbol of the beauty of the American West and an invitation to lovers of hiking, fishing, and adventure sports. The town of Jackson, at the edge of Grand Teton National Park, has avoided becoming a sprawling tourist trap thanks to a quirk of geography: hemmed in by public land, it has no room to expand. New money has been drawn to Jackson, but it has added cosmopolitan flair without loss of respect for the town's Old West tradition. — BY TOM PRICE AND FINN-OLAF JONES

FRIDAY

1 *Western Style* 4 p.m.

Get oriented with a ramble around the town square, which is framed by four arches made from elk horns gathered in nearby forests (the animals shed them annually). Then check out some of the nearby shops. If you want to blend in, the local look is "cowpine," and that's what you'll find at **Stio** (10 East Broadway; 307-201-1890; stio.com), which blends elegance with modern insulating technology under its own brand. In Gaslight Alley, at 125 North Cache Street, you can pick up books on local lore at the **Valley Bookstore** (307-733-4533; valleybookstore.com), vintage used cowboy boots at **Bet the Ranch** (307-733-7374; bettheranchJH.com), and glass belt buckles (by designer and owner John Frechette) and bags of candied bacon at **Made** (307-690-7957; madejacksonhole.com).

2 *Log Cabin Gourmet* 7 p.m.

Climb the steps to the **Snake River Grill** (84 East Broadway; 307-733-0557; snakerivergrill.com; $$$-$$$$) and settle down at one of the tables in the log-walled dining room. Its log-cabin-chic décor, extensive wine list, and master chef put Jackson Hole on the culinary map. Warm up with one of the house cocktails, the Honey Badger, a fabulous concoction of Glenfiddich, Amaro Nonino, honey syrup, and lemon, and then it's onward to the kind of fare rarely unloaded from the back of a chuck wagon, including local beef tenderloin with pesto and tomato-bacon jam or house-smoked trout with roasted baby beets and bagel crisps.

3 *Star Bright* 10 p.m.

After dinner, stroll north, toward the **National Elk Refuge**, which abuts town. If the season is right, you may find southbound geese asleep on the grass roof of the visitors center (532 North Cache Street; 307-733-9212; fws.gov/refuge/national_elk_refuge/). But look up higher. Away from the lights and neon, you'll have a striking view of the night sky.

SATURDAY

4 *Preparations* 9 a.m.

For all its worldliness, Jackson is a tiny town of about 9,000 full-time residents, and it's easy to pick up snacks or a meal with a minimum of wandering around. Get your caffeine ration, along with granola or a breakfast sandwich, at **Jackson Hole Coffee Roasters** (50 West Broadway; 307-200-6099;

OPPOSITE A settler's barn remains in a historic district in Grand Teton National Park.

RIGHT Rivers and natural ponds thread through the park and other publicly owned wilderness nearby.

jacksonholeroasters.com). Then take a quick walk around the corner to the **Backcountry Delicatessen** (50 West Deloney Avenue; 307-734-9420; backcountry-deli.com) to pick up food for a picnic later in the day.

5 *And Wear a Helmet* 10 a.m.

Get fitted for a mountain bike rental at **Hoback Sports** (520 West Broadway; 307-733-5335; hobacksports.com), buy a trail map, and start pedaling. Ride east toward the 20-mile Cache Creek-Game Creek loop through the **Bridger Teton National Forest**. Take either the smooth dirt road or the parallel single-track Putt-Putt Trail, winding along a shaded stream. At the Game Creek turnoff, crank up a short steep climb, and you'll be rewarded with a five-mile descent down sage- and aspen-covered hills before connecting with a paved path back to town.

6 *Drive-By Shooting* 2 p.m.

Relax with a behind-the-wheel wander through **Grand Teton National Park** (307-739-3300; nps.gov/grte). Best bet for scenic photos: loop north on Route 191 past the Snake River Overlook, where you can frame the river that carved the valley and the mountains behind it in one shot. Then head south along Teton Park Road past Jenny Lake. On your way back, stop at **Dornan's** in the town of Moose (200 Moose Street; 307-733-2415; dornans.com) for cocktails on the deck, about as close as you can get to the Tetons and still have someone bring you a drink.

7 *Japanese Plus* 7 p.m.

At **the Kitchen** (155 North Glenwood Street; 307-734-1633; kitchenjacksonhole.com; $$$), a Japanese bistro in a casual, contemporary space, you can start with sashimi and move on to veal in a chile-miso broth or an organic burger. The drinks menu has similar mixed influences. There's a wide selection of sakes and 19 different types of tequila.

8 *Two-Stepping* 9 p.m.

Sidle up to a saddle bar stool at the **Million Dollar Cowboy Bar** (25 North Cache Street; 307-733-2207; milliondollarcowboybar.com)—the bucking bronco of Jackson Hole's night life since 1937—for a bottle of the local brew or a fire cider (whiskey, cider, and cinnamon) amid knobbled pine beams and Wild West artifacts, including a stuffed grizzly killed bare-handed by one C. Dale Petersen. Look over the spur collection and 70 years' worth of other accumulated Westernalia. Around the corner, the **Silver Dollar Bar & Grill** (in the Wort Hotel, 50 North Glenwood; worthotel.com) is another cowpoke scene, featuring live fiddling bands and guys in suspenders dancing with tight-jeaned women beneath the curved pink lights of the "Cowboy Deco"-style bar.

SUNDAY

9 *Never Toasted* 8 a.m.

Join the lineup for coffee at **Pearl Street Bagels** (145 West Pearl Avenue; 307-739-1218). Purists, rejoice; even after pranksters nailed a dozen toasters to Pearl Street's pink facade several years ago, it still serves its bagels warm from the oven but always untoasted. And with bagels this fresh and good, it seems a little unfair to quibble.

10 *The Compleat Angler* 10 a.m.

Not every full-service hotel is likely to have a director of fishing, but this is Jackson Hole, and you'll find one at the **Four Seasons Resort** (7680 Granite Loop Road, Teton Village; 307-732-5000; fourseasons.com/jacksonhole). In the resort's handmade wooden dory, he'll take you down one of the secluded braids of the Snake River and offer expert advice on how to reel in some of the Snake's 2,500 fish per mile. You don't have to be a guest, even first-timers are welcome, and it's safe to feel very surprised if you don't land a fish. A day trip will set you back several hundred dollars, and if it's a couple of hundred too many, you can look for a less expensive guide back in town.

OPPOSITE ABOVE Night life beckons in Jackson.

OPPOSITE BELOW Fishing the Snake River. Jackson attracts a well-to-do crowd that loves getting outdoors.

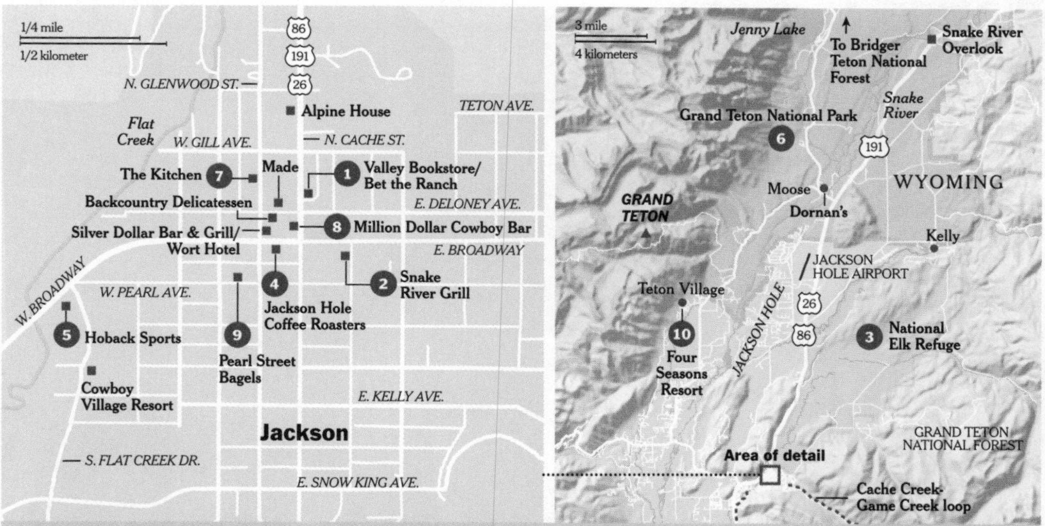

THE BASICS

Arrive at Jackson Hole Airport and rent a car.

Alpine House
285 North Glenwood Street
307-739-1570
alpinehouse.com
$$
An upscale 22-room B&B a few blocks from the town square.

Cowboy Village Resort
120 South Flat Creek Drive
307-733-3121
townsquareinns.com/cowboy-village
$$
Two-room, two-bed cabins with lots of logs and knotty pine.

Wort Hotel
Glenwood and Broadway
307-733-2190
worthotel.com
$$$$
First opened in 1941. Its popular Silver Dollar Bar has 2,000 inlaid silver dollars.

Qwest

Denver

Denver, Colorado, is a city in a constant state of reinvention, expanding its cultural institutions and welcoming new shops and chefs while nurturing the nature-loving, outdoorsy sensibility engendered by the majestic surrounding Rocky Mountains. It is no small point of pride for the energized Mile High City that its increasingly diverse population has been growing, reversing an exodus of families to the suburbs. Visiting some of its recently refurbished attractions, especially the now bustling LoDo district, it's hard to escape the feeling of a modern gold rush.
— BY ERIC WILSON

FRIDAY

1 *Vertical Mile* 1 p.m.

Walk across Civic Center Park to the steps of the imposingly gray state **Capitol**, a dead ringer for the one in Washington except that it's a study in Colorado granite instead of white marble. Ascend the west side to find the spot, around the 13th step, that is exactly 5,280 feet above sea level. The gold marker makes it official: Denver deserves its altitudinal nickname.

2 *Change to Believe In* 2 p.m.

Remember those pennies imprinted with a "D" that you found in your childhood coin-collecting phase? Now is your chance to visit the **Denver Mint** (320 West Colfax Avenue; 303-405-4761; usmint.gov) and see where they came from. You'll get some history along with an explanation of how coins are made, but won't see much of the actual production. Reservations are highly recommended (usmint.gov/mint_tours). Just about everything in your pockets is forbidden, so dress as you would for the airport.

3 *The Urban Outdoors* 4 p.m.

Coloradans are passionate about the outdoors, even in the city. Denver has more than 100 miles of pedestrian and bicycle paths, and you can get to one of the most popular, the **Cherry Creek Path**, right downtown. Hop on the MallRide, a free bus service along 16th Street, at the Civic Center. Hop off at Larimer Street and walk a couple of blocks southwest on Larimer to find the steps down to the creek level. Take the path north, staying alert for occasional glimpses of the snow-capped Rockies, and arrive at **Confluence Park**, where the creek meets the South Platte River. This is the historic center of Denver, the spot where the city had its start. Continue on the path until you've had enough, and then return.

4 *Where's the Beef?* 7 p.m.

There's no getting around Denver's culinary specialty, red meat, the starring attraction at Old West-themed grill joints all over town. Count the Wild West species represented in the form of taxidermy on the walls (or on the menu) of **Buckhorn Exchange**, billed as Denver's oldest restaurant (1000 Osage Street; 303-534-9505; buckhornexchange.com; $$$). Here, steak can be ordered by the pound. For something lighter and more in line with the modern field-to-fork credo, try **Root Down** (1600 West 33rd Avenue; 303-993-4200; rootdowndenver.com; $$$), the kind of place that grows its own herbs and lettuces. There's folk art on the walls, red curry sauce on the mussels, and plenty of potency in the cocktails.

SATURDAY

5 *The Old Glass Ceiling* 10 a.m.

One of Denver's most famous homes belonged to a backwoods social climber who set out in the 1880s to land herself a rich husband and a big house on

OPPOSITE The Denver Art Museum's new Hamilton building, designed by Daniel Libeskind.

BELOW Dinner at Rioja in Larimer Square.

what was then called Pennsylvania Avenue. (Now it's Pennsylvania Street.) Margaret Tobin Brown, later mythologized as Molly Brown, was a suffragette who survived the sinking of the *Titanic* and ran for United States Senate, unsuccessfully, years before women won the right to vote. Certain spurned trailblazers might find solace in a tour of her Victorian mansion (**Molly Brown House Museum**, 1340 Pennsylvania Street; 303-832-4092; mollybrown.org). They might even be inspired to stand on the front porch like Debbie Reynolds in the 1964 *The Unsinkable Molly Brown* and holler, "Pennsylvania Avenue, I'll admit you gave me a nose full of splinters, but it's all good wood from the very best doors!"

6 *For You and Your Walls* 1 p.m.

For boutique shopping, go to Larimer Square, a bona fide downtown shopping district in an area that in the 19th century was filled with saloons and stores catering to gold miners. If you're shopping for art, a wealth of remarkable galleries is concentrated in Lower Downtown (LoDo) and also along Santa Fe Drive. For novices, one of the most accessible is **Artists on Santa Fe** (747 Santa Fe Drive; 303-573-5903; artistsonsantafe.com), a warren of studios where sculptors and painters in residence will personally explain their work. Wander down the street and you'll find many more.

7 *How the West Was Worn* 4 p.m.

Let's say you have an image problem. Some people, misguided as they may be, think you are an elitist. Now, that's nothing that can't be fixed with a little fashion makeover at **Rockmount Ranch Wear** (1626 Wazee Street; 303-629-7777; rockmount.com), a LoDo shop famous in these parts for introducing the snap button to the western shirt, making it easier for cowboys to ride the range or re-enact scenes from *Brokeback Mountain.* (Yep, Jack and Ennis were Rockmount customers.) The store—and an accompanying museum—have the fascinating feel of a ghost town relic, with a lasso-rope logo and dusty displays, but the shirts have modern-day prices.

8 *All That Glitters* 8 p.m.

Night life can be found in LoDo, around where gold was first discovered in Colorado in the 1850s. Now the closest thing to gold around here is more likely to come in a bottle of Cuervo. At **Rioja**, for example, you can precede your pasta or grilled salmon dinner with the likes of the Loca Hot, made with Fresno pepper-infused tequila, plus Agavero (tequila liqueur), orange, and lime (1431 Larimer Street; 303-820-2282; riojadenver.com; $$-$$$). It's a short walk from here to a wine bar, Crú, and a Champagne bar, Corridor 44. Given the intensified effects of alcohol at high altitudes, you might want to head underground to **Lannie's Clocktower Cabaret**, the local singer Lannie Garrett's place in the basement of the D&F Tower (16th Street and Arapahoe Street; 303-293-0075; lannies.com). Be warned: the burlesque shows late on Saturday nights are raunchy.

SUNDAY

9 *Juxtapositions* 10 a.m.

The **Denver Art Museum**'s jutting addition, designed by Daniel Libeskind, looks like an Imperial

ABOVE The Victorian trophy home of the "unsinkable" *Titanic* survivor, Molly Brown.

RIGHT Denver's oldest restaurant, the Buckhorn Exchange.

Cruiser from *Star Wars*, and once you are inside, the vertigo-inducing floor plan will make you long to get your feet back on earth (100 West 14th Avenue; 720-865-5000; denverartmuseum.org). But the museum's juxtaposition of many styles and eras, from the work of contemporary art stars to Native American artifacts, is compelling, and your inner ears will soon adjust.

10 *Horizontal Mile* 1 p.m.

The **Mile High Flea Market** could just as well be named the Mile Wide Flea Market, given that its hundreds of tightly packed, pastel-colored stalls cover 80 acres of pavement (I-76 and 88th Avenue; milehighmarketplace.com). Browse through T-shirts, watermelons, antiques, fishing tackle, jewelry, and as many other kinds of merchandise as you can take. You can also sample delicious street fare, like corn on the cob rolled in a tray of butter, Parmesan, and seasoning salt. And if you're man enough, try a chelada, a stomach-churning brew of Clamato juice and Budweiser.

ABOVE Rotary telephones, part of Root Down's décor.

THE BASICS

Denver International Airport is one of the busiest in the nation, served by several major carriers. If you want to venture far, you'll need a car.

Hotel Teatro
1100 14th Street
303-228-1100
hotelteatro.com
$$$
Boutique hotel across from the Denver Center for Performing Arts.

Brown Palace
321 17th Street
303-297-3111
brownpalace.com
$$
Updated downtown classic in a flatiron-style building, with spa.

Best Western Denver Southwest
3440 South Vance Street, Lakewood
303-989-5500
bestwesterndenver.com
$$
Newly transformed on a paleontology theme, with a replica dinosaur skeleton behind the front desk; located 20 minutes from downtown near fossil-rich Dinosaur Ridge.

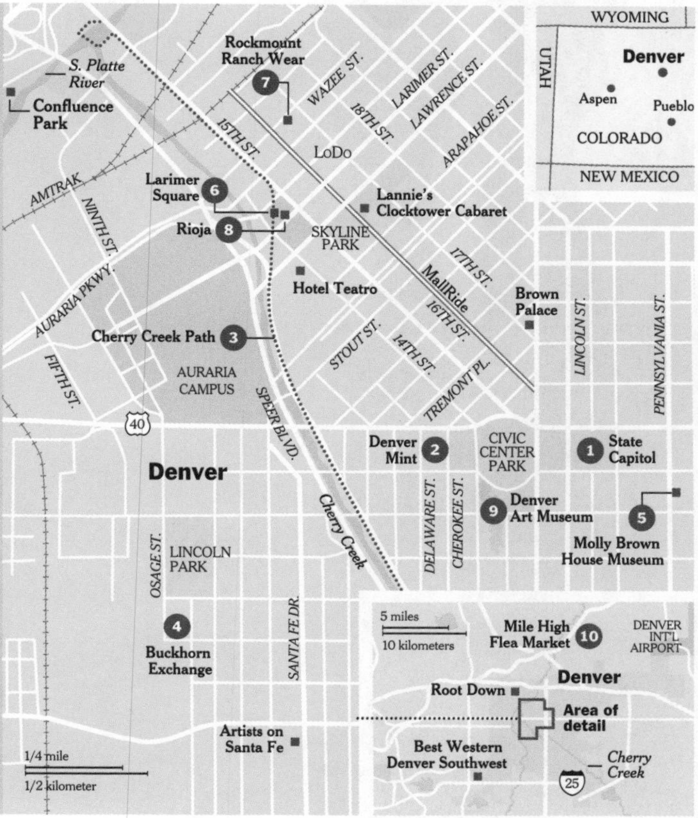

Vail

In the late 1950s, Pete Seibert, who dreamed of building a major ski resort in Colorado, spent seven hours hiking to the top of what is now Vail Mountain. At the crest of the obscure, unpopulated hill, he glimpsed a rare landscape of largely treeless bowls, a vast panorama of seemingly boundless, perfect skiing terrain. Seibert, a former member of the United States ski team, turned to his hiking partner, Earl Eaton, a local uranium prospector, and said, "My God, we've climbed all the way to heaven." The Vail resort opened for the winter of 1962-63, and now, more than 50 years later, the climb up the mountain that took Seibert most of the day is replaced by a seven-and-a-half-minute ascent in a 10-person gondola equipped with heated seats and Wi-Fi access. At 5,289 acres, Vail is one of the nation's largest ski areas, and it attracts 1.7 million people to its slopes per season.

— BY BILL PENNINGTON AND ELAINE GLUSAC

FRIDAY

1 *Bespoke Skiing* 2 p.m.

A skier who hasn't been to Vail lately can feel out of place. Large new hotels tower over old landmarks, pedestrian walkways have replaced ordinary streets, and a new level of pampering is evident everywhere. Many resorts have infused the traditional ski trip with technologically advanced creature comforts and luxuries, but none have embraced the new philosophy more than Vail. When you arrive at your hotel in Vail, you may encounter the ski valet, a service that carries, stores, and delivers your ski gear and boots, so that you can walk unencumbered. There's more. Ski rental companies can now receive your specifications online days before your arrival so the appropriate gear can be waiting for you. If you're a regular guest at the same slopeside condo, the unit can be stocked with your preferred cookies and Scotch.

2 *Nordic at Dusk* 3:30 p.m.

You don't need to be on the slopes to appreciate the Southern Rockies, 10,000-plus-foot-tall peaks that edge narrow Vail Valley, cut by clear mountain streams that flow in winter's deep freeze. While it's still daylight, explore this winter wonderland on cross-country skis. At the **Vail Nordic Center** (1778 Vail Valley Drive; 970-476-8366; vailnordiccenter.com), trails loop across wooden bridges, gentle pine stands, and snow-blanketed golf fairways.

3 *Familiar Territory* 7 p.m.

Weave around the massive Arrabelle, a sparkling Vail-owned hotel and adjacent public square with a skating rink, shops, restaurants, water fountains, and outdoor concert arena. Around a curve and down an alley, escape to Vail's less worldly past at **Garfinkel's** (536 East Lionshead Circle; 970-476-3789 garfsvail.com; $), a holdover from the old days with an unpretentious menu of burgers, pasta, steak, and fried chicken. The beer list is lengthy, and the place is packed with skiers and snowboarders. Other old favorites that have held out against the gentrification are **Bart and Yeti's** (553 East Lionshead Circle; 970-476-2754; bartnyetis.com), an economical and rustic lunch place, and **Vendetta's** (291 Bridge Street; 970-476-5070; vendettasvail.com), a pizza and beer joint that fills up with locals, instructors, and staff just off work.

SATURDAY

4 *Pick a Bowl* 8:30 a.m.

Once on **Vail Mountain**, how you choose to navigate has been transformed by technology. Thanks to social networking, streaming alerts, and the resort's

OPPOSITE Après-ski afterglow in Vail.

RIGHT The Ritz-Carlton Club & Residences, part of the luxurious side of Vail.

own Twitter account, skiers have up-to-the minute updates on which lifts are open and how long the lines are. Still, skiing Vail's legendary back bowls requires a game plan. Aim to catch one of the first lifts to get atop the mountain ridge before everyone else does. Though most of the backside bowls are expert only, intermediate skiers are welcome at China Bowl, a gentler basin with wide-open expanses and panoramic views. Staying ahead of the crowds, push on to Blue Sky Basin, one ridge to the south. Hit the effervescent Champagne Glade before everybody else does.

5 *Unbuckle and Refuel* Noon

Relive your morning conquests at **Two Elk Restaurant** (970-754-4560; $$), Vail's flagship restaurant atop China Bowl. During lunch, skiers from the mountain's front and back sides meet here to unbuckle their boots and loosen their belts. Although the restaurant has 1,200 seats—all bordered by massive timber-framed windows that overlook the Colorado Rockies—plan on getting there before 12:15 p.m. (alternatively, after 1:30 p.m.), or you'll be left standing. Service may be cafeteria style, but the fare is upscale. Dishes one chilly afternoon included chicken posole soup, buffalo chili, and portobello mushroom sandwiches.

6 *Long-Distance Cruising* 1:30 p.m.

Continue conquering the mountain in contrarian fashion, and skiing where the masses aren't. Now that the back bowls are brimming, point your skis toward Vail's front side, carved with many stamina-testing runs. By midafternoon, hit the four-mile-long **Riva Ridge** cruiser, the resort's longest trail.

7 *Muscle Relaxer* 4:30 p.m.

As the sun begins to dip and your muscles begin to tire, make your way to the Lionshead, one of Vail's three base villages, and check into the **RockResorts Spa** at the Arrabelle at Vail Square (675 Lionshead Place; 970-754-7754; arrabelle.rockresorts.com). Relax in the steam room, sauna, and whirlpool. Treatments are mountain-themed: massages with pine-infused oils, body wraps incorporating wildflower essences. Therapists will even treat seriously sore muscles with an ice pack filled with mountain snow.

8 *Wired for Dinner* 7:30 p.m.

Take a quick ride back up the gondola, and a few steps from the top you'll find **The 10th** (base of Look Ma run, mid-Vail; 970-754-1010; the10thvail.com; $$$), where you can savor dishes like hazelnut and ginger buffalo carpaccio and selections from a 2,200-bottle on-site wine cellar. Guests coming off the mountain here can exchange ski boots for slippers before looking over the menu. Just outside the restaurant door, there's evidence of Vail's aggressive adaptation to the wired world. Photographers will take your picture, and using the chip embedded in your lift ticket, send it to friends through the social network of your choice. The same chip can chart and digest every detail of your day: the number of vertical feet skied, trails visited, and your top speed.

SUNDAY

9 *A Walk in the Woods* 9:30 a.m.

In a ski town that lives and breathes sports, Olympic-caliber athletes are the real celebrities. So if

ABOVE Belt buckles at Axel's, one of the Vail shops that can supply ingredients for an upscale cowboy look.

BELOW Skating at Vail Square in Lionshead.

you're planning to go snowshoeing, there's no better guide than Ellen Miller, the first North American woman to reach the summit of Mount Everest from both the north and south sides. Miller teaches a 90-minute Mountain Divas class at the **Vail Athletic Club** (352 East Meadow Drive; 970-476-7960; vailmountainlodge.com), which takes a crunchy cult of triathletes and trail racers on a valley trek through towering aspen forests, past trout-filled streams, and under snowy pine boughs. Unlike skiing, snowshoeing requires no special skills. Beginners, finally, are welcome.

10 *Western Chic* Noon

Like the mountainside chalets that share a modern rustic look — beamed ceilings, cathedral windows, stone decks — so, too, does the local fashion, which could be described as upscale cowboy. Get into the spirit at **Gorsuch** (263 East Gore Creek Drive; 970-476-2294; gorsuch.com), a luxe store with von Trapp-gone-Vail looks for her (crystal-studded cashmere hats), him (Brunello Cucinelli suede jackets), and home (Megeve crystal-etched wineglasses). Nearby is **Axel's** (201 Gore Creek Drive; 970-476-7625; axelsltd.com), which carries shearling coats and vests, alligator and bison belt straps, and Clint Orms belt buckles. For that rugged cowboy swagger, step into **Kemo Sabe** (230 Bridge Street; 970-479-7474; kemosabe.com), known for its handmade Lucchese cowboy boots.

THE BASICS

From Vail/Eagle County Airport, downtown Vail is 35 miles by shuttle (Colorado Mountain Express is the best known service) along I-70. In Vail, a free, efficient bus system seamlessly connects all the village amenities.

Ritz-Carlton Club & Residences
728 West Lionshead Circle
970-477-3700
thevailcollection.com
$$$$
Luxurious accommodations and lavish service in hotel rooms and condominiums.

Westin Riverfront Resort & Spa
126 Riverfront Lane, Avon
970-790-6000
westin.com/riverfrontavon
$$$
A gondola zips guests to Beaver Creek, Vail's sister resort.

The Lodge at Vail
174 East Gore Creek Drive
970-476-5011
lodgeatvail.rockresorts.com
$$$
The best rooms face the ski runs.

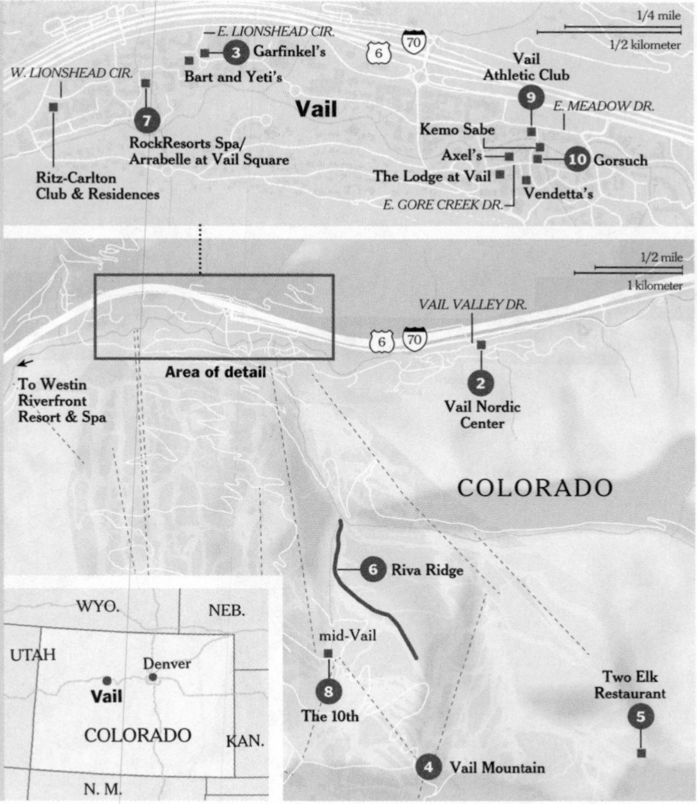

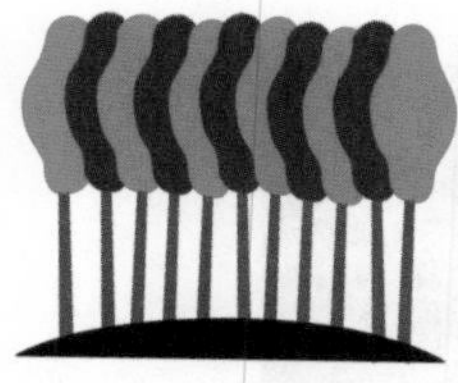

Aspen

At times Aspen, Colorado, verges on parody. Scoring reservations at the restaurant du jour requires the will of a tenacious personal assistant. Lines waiting to hand over black American Express cards for $1,000 Moncler jackets rival the ones for the Silver Queen gondola. Yet behind the mirrored aviator sunglasses is a culture devoted to the mountain's transcendent beauty and perpetual sporting life: skiing, boarding, hiking, snowshoeing, fly-fishing. Aspen is an international playground that remains a small town, one where it doesn't matter how much money you have, it matters how you handle a bump run. — BY MARY BILLARD

FRIDAY

1 *Après Someone Else's Skiing* 5 p.m.

With alpenglow illuminating the Wheeler Opera House (1889) and the Elks Building dome (1891), saunter through this 19th-century Victorian mining town while enjoying the crisp mountain air and window shopping at stores like Fendi (fur flip-flops?). Though you didn't earn it, join the après ski action at the **39 Degrees Lounge** in the **Sky Hotel** (709 East Durant Avenue; 970-925-6760; theskyhotel.com), where a young, windburned crowd gathers by a crackling fire in wool hats to watch Teton Gravity Research movies on flat-screen TVs. The footage of death-defying flips is a perfect way to get revved up. So are the drinks, including the Ménage à Trois, a mixologist's triumph combining vodka, double shots of espresso, and coffee beans.

2 *Chill Over Chili* 7:30 p.m.

In the Roaring Fork Valley, billionaires aspire to be locals. Trade the *Us Weekly* setting for a more traditional down-home scene: the red-and-white-checked tablecloth décor at **Little Annie's Eating House** (517 East Hyman Avenue; 970-925-1098; littleannies.com; $$), an Aspen mainstay since 1972. Thick homemade soups, juicy burgers, and hearty chili are on the menu, as well as fresh trout. Everything goes with Fat Tire or Sunshine beer.

3 *Fresh Musical Tracks* 10 p.m.

Aspen offers a wide variety of night life in a few tightly packed streets, from South American frat-boy types playing pool at **Eric's Bar** (315 East Hyman Avenue; 970-920-1488; sucasaaspen.com), to the fun-fur-wearing Euros at the members-only Caribou Club (caribouclub.com). But for live music go to the **Belly Up Aspen** (450 South Galena Street; 970-544-9800; bellyupaspen.com), formerly the Double Diamond. Ben Harper, the Flaming Lips, Ice-T, Stone Temple Pilots, and Dwight Yoakam have all played this 450-seat club.

SATURDAY

4 *Sunblock, Advil, Small Talk* 8 a.m.

To forestall the slight headache that may come with the high altitude (or a hangover), make a pit stop at **Carl's Pharmacy** (306 East Main Street; 970-925-3273) for a dose of small-town friendliness. Stocked with everything from hand warmers to wine, and open from 9 a.m. to 9 p.m., it is a place to trade gossip and feel at home. Even the out-of-town customers are Mayberry polite. And if you're buying a knee brace or reading glasses, someone will commiserate.

5 *Think About Seizing the Day* 8:30 a.m.

As you wait for the sun to soften up the snow from the overnight freeze, fuel up at **Paradise Bakery** (320 South Galena Street; 970-925-7585; paradisebakery.com). Fresh muffins and something

OPPOSITE Working the moguls at Aspen Highlands, with the Maroon Bells peaks in the background.

BELOW Cloud Nine Bistro, a good spot for lunch, is 100 yards below the Cloud Nine chair.

delicious from the coffee family are ready to be enjoyed while you sit on one of the outside benches facing the mountain. Read *The Aspen Times* and *The Aspen Daily News*, whose slogan is "If you don't want it printed, don't let it happen." Far from being resort boosters, the newspapers report on community concerns like seasonal workers and affordable housing and always have letters to the editor complaining about nearly everything. A town of millionaires shows its hippie heritage by still raging against the machine.

6 *Follow the Sun* 10 a.m.

Start with the legendary Ajax. The east-facing black runs—Walsh's or Kristi or the section called the Dumps—are best in the morning sun. **Bonnie's** (970-544-6252; $-$$) above Lift 3 is a must for lunch. Avoid the crowds by going before noon or after 1:30, and grab a spot on the deck. The staff makes everything from scratch, including the pizza dough. Look for warming choices like chicken artichoke chili pesto pizza and white-bean chili. The strudel is made with apples from a Colorado orchard, and it's best with fresh schlag. While some prefer the reserved seating of the members-only Aspen Mountain Club, there are plenty of captains of industry, Hollywood players, and members of the House of Saud carrying cafeteria trays. After lunch, hit the west-facing Face of Bell when the afternoon sun lights up the bumps and trees.

7 *Après Schussing, Shopping* 4 p.m.

Aspen has been called, and sometimes not so lovingly, Rodeo Drive East. The one global fashion temple to check out is **Prada** (312 South Galena Street; 970-925-7001), not only for its sleek clothes, but also for the shop's rustic-chic modern mountain design of luxurious woods and stone. People frequently ask the name of the architect (Roberto Baciocchi of Arezzo, Italy). Then head to **Performance Ski** (408 South Hunter Street; 970-925-8657), where the co-owner Lee Keating and the latest crop of snowboard dudes will give you honest answers on how those Prada pants actually fit. A very pleasant place to curl up in an old leather club chair is **Explore Booksellers and Bistro** (221 East Main Street; 970-925-5336; explorebooksellers.com), a warren of book-laden rooms, a vegetarian restaurant, and a coffeehouse. For housewares, head to **Amen Wardy Home** (520 East Durant Avenue; 970-920-7700; amenwardy.com). The merchandise is so unusual (whimsical house gifts to fur blankets for a few thousand dollars), that it's worth shipping home.

8 *Spa Decadence* 6 p.m.

To take care of those aching muscles, hobble over to the 15,000-square-foot **Remède Spa** at the **St. Regis Resort** (315 East Dean Street; 970-920-6783; remede.com). It's pricey, but worth it. All treatments end with something that sounds a little zany but is actually relaxing: a stop at a cozy parlor where white-robed spagoers lie on chaise longues and strap on air masks, inhaling oxygen infused with fresh fruit essences. Prosecco and chocolates are also provided.

9 *Did You Reserve Last Month?* 8 p.m.

The ski trails are never that crowded, even during school holidays, but trying to get a table for six at a hot Aspen restaurant is brutal. Two newcomers worth speed-dialing are out-of-towners with Italian cuisine. New York's famed **Il Mulino** (501 East Dean Street; 970-205-1000; ilmulino.com/aspen; $$$-$$$$) has old-school Italian pastas, fresh fish, and flirtatious waiters. Miami export **Casa Tua** (403 South Galena Street;

970-920-7277; $$$-$$$$) goes for a feel of an Italian Alps chalet.

SUNDAY

10 *Morning Tuneup* 8 a.m.

Stretch your muscles with a pre-ski yoga or pilates class at **O2Aspen** (500 West Main Street; 970-925-4002; 02aspen.com), in a beautifully renovated Victorian house. Drop-in classes are about $20. A small boutique has everything from cashmere sweaters in the $500 range to more moderately priced workout wear.

11 *Bragging Rights* 10 a.m.

The cool kids tackle the Highland Bowl. It is not served by any lifts, and it takes anywhere from 20 minutes to an hour to climb 750 feet to its 12,392-foot-high summit with a fearsome 45-degree pitch. The really cool kids do circuits of two or three laps. Slightly tamer is Deep Temerity, a 180-acre bowl that gives expert skiers an additional 1,000-foot drop. Lunch at the aptly named **Cloud Nine Alpine Bistro** (970-544-3063) 100 yards below the Cloud Nine chair, with an old ski-hut feel and views of the Maroon Bells.

OPPOSITE ABOVE Downtown Aspen at dusk.

OPPOSITE BELOW Jogging past a Lamborghini. Glitz and glamour hide the real town of Aspen.

ABOVE At the top of the Aspen Highlands ski area.

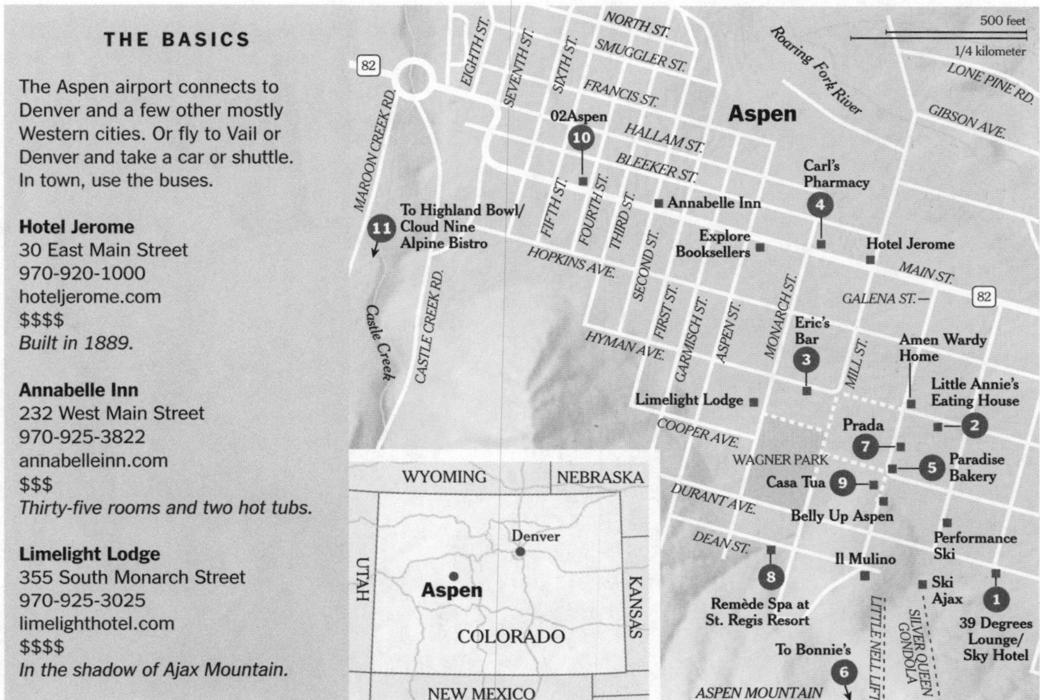

THE BASICS

The Aspen airport connects to Denver and a few other mostly Western cities. Or fly to Vail or Denver and take a car or shuttle. In town, use the buses.

Hotel Jerome
30 East Main Street
970-920-1000
hoteljerome.com
$$$$
Built in 1889.

Annabelle Inn
232 West Main Street
970-925-3822
annabelleinn.com
$$$
Thirty-five rooms and two hot tubs.

Limelight Lodge
355 South Monarch Street
970-925-3025
limelighthotel.com
$$$$
In the shadow of Ajax Mountain.

Steamboat Springs

Steamboat Springs, a town nestled along the Yampa River in northwest Colorado, evokes an era when cattle ranchers roamed the streets and locals preferred Stetsons to ski vests. But in recent years, Steamboat has sought to shed a bit of its family-friendly image as a cowboy theme park by installing après-ski bars, haute cuisine restaurants, and late-night haunts, as well as upscale lodgings, like One Steamboat Place, that can rival anything at Vail or Aspen. The centerpiece of Steamboat's face-lift is a redeveloped promenade at the base of its gondola, with a heated walkway, a musical stage, and a three-tiered ice castle. Families still flock to Steamboat for its dude ranches and hot springs. But after the children are put to bed, downtown comes alive with night life and innovative restaurant cuisine. — BY LIONEL BEEHNER

FRIDAY

1 *John Wayne's Wardrobe* 5 p.m.

To get a sense of Steamboat's Old West ambience, take a stroll down Lincoln Avenue, the main street. It's lined with the usual tourist traps but also has a few surprises, including shops that feel like time capsules of Steamboat's cattle ranching past. A case in point is **F. M. Light & Sons** (830 Lincoln Avenue; 970-879-1822; fmlight.com), which looks as if it hasn't changed since it opened its doors in 1905. The shop sells Stetsons cut from real buffalo fur and fire-engine-red rodeo shirts emblazoned with poker cards. Look for the retail shrine to John Wayne tucked within the store.

2 *Top Chef Steamboat* 6 p.m.

Until recently, fine dining in Steamboat was limited to **Café Diva** (1855 Ski Time Square Drive; 970-871-0508, cafediva.com), whose red velvety interior and refined menu still appeal to well-heeled visitors who dine on its nicely presented entrees of elk and other wild game. Now a new wave of restaurateurs is colonizing Steamboat. A spot that has become popular among locals is **Bistro C.V.** (345 Lincoln Avenue, 970-879-4197; bistrocv.com; $$), which has industrial-chic décor — including a curvilinear ceiling spangled with funky minimalist light fixtures and a blond wood bar — and colorful dishes to match. The chef, Brian Vaughn (the "V" in the restaurant's name), tops his wagyu-beef burgers with foie gras and marinates his chicken in maple syrup.

3 *Ghost Buskers* 8 p.m.

For something a bit more rustic, head to the multilevel saloon **Ghost Ranch Steamboat** (56 Seventh Street; 970-879-9898; ghostranchsteamboat.com), where the Wild West trimmings include animal trophies adorning the walls and old wooden booths that look as if they'd been lifted from the set of *Deadwood*. The spacious dance floor fills up most weekends with a tipsy, all-ages crowd two-stepping to live music.

SATURDAY

4 *Sweet Cinnamon* 8 a.m.

A cinnamon roll arms race breaks out every morning in Steamboat. First, there's **Freshies** (595 South Lincoln Avenue; 970-879-8099;

OPPOSITE Winter warmth at Strawberry Park Hot Springs, in the hills outside of Steamboat Springs. Have a massage here in a heated stone hut, and then gaze up at the stars from one of the steaming-hot mineral baths.

BELOW A cabin at the Home Ranch, 20 minutes from Steamboat, one of several dude ranches close to the town.

freshiessteamboat.com), which serves up gooey cinnamon rolls glazed in melted cream cheese. Then there's **Winona's** (617 Lincoln Avenue; 970-879-2483; winonassteamboat.com), a homey spot whose cinnamon buns literally spill over the plate. For something less sweet or sticky, try **MountainBrew** (427 Oak Street; 970-879-7846), a relaxed cafe with tasty scones and smoothies. Or for something heartier, have a bacon, egg, and cheese sandwich at the **Paramount** (1865 Ski Time Square Drive; 970-879-1170; theparamountcolorado.com; $), an unassuming spot with counter service and a rustic-chic air.

5 *Snow Tires* 10:30 a.m.

For more than 30 years, a cow pasture outside Steamboat has been coated every winter with a quarter-million gallons of water that freezes into a treacherous sheet of ice, the perfect terrain track for the **Bridgestone Winter Driving School** (2300 Mount Werner Circle; 970-879-6104; winterdrive.com), which bills itself as the longest continually running school of its kind in the country. In a yurt, students get a primer on transferring weight, handling slick conditions, and braking on ice. Then they take a test spin on the icy tracks with two hours of training in a fleet of Lexus S.U.V.'s and sedans.

6 *Dudes on Skis* 2:30 p.m.

A handful of dude ranches ring Steamboat Springs, and several of them are winter wonderlands for cross-country skiers. Whether you prefer open meadows blanketed in snow or winding paths through the aspen woods, the area boasts some of Colorado's best trails. Though most ranch trails are closed to nonguests, one exception, if you don't mind the one-hour drive, is **Latigo Ranch** (201 County Road 1911, Kremmling; 970-724-9008; latigotrails.com), which grooms over 65 kilometers of backcountry trails with sweeping views of the Continental Divide. In town, the **Howelsen Hill Ski Area** (845 Howelsen Parkway; 970-879-8499) has over 20 kilometers of groomed paths.

7 *Starlit Dip* 5 p.m.

Strawberry Park Hot Springs (44200 County Road 36, 970-879-0342; strawberryhotsprings.com) is a secluded retreat nestled in the hills just outside of town. Cold and hot natural plunge pools carved along a ridge draw couples as well as groups of loud kids. To avoid the crowds, slip into one of the heated stone huts for a soothing massage. Then snag a spot in one of the steaming-hot mineral baths, where you can gaze up at the stars. Even with the crowds, it's worth it.

8 *Do Laundry* 7 p.m.

Laundry (127 11th Street; 970-870-0681; thelaundryrestaurant.com; $$), a gastro-pub with a vintage feel, serves small plates in an old brick laundromat retrofitted with teardrop-shaped light fixtures and Art Deco-style wine racks. Its atmosphere is noisy but festive. Platters of cheeses, cured meats, and fennel-heavy veggies are rich and filling. You may find dishes like savory fried chicken-polenta or hickory-smoked brisket. The bar offers inventive cocktails, like a fiery margarita infused with hot-pepper tequila.

9 *Night on the Riverfront* 9 p.m.

Night life in Steamboat used to consist mainly of sports bars with Western themes and bland menus. But over the past few years, the riverfront street Yampa Avenue has turned into a popular strip of night spots with eclectic bar menus. At **Carl's Tavern** (700 Yampa Avenue; 970-761-2060; carlstavern.com), it's pot roast by day, party atmosphere by night—a roomy and festive space with live bluegrass most weekends and seemingly as many beers on tap as there are oversize TVs. Another favorite is **Sweetwater Grill** (811 Yampa Avenue; 970-879-9500; thesweetwatergrill.com), which has a large fire-pit-equipped back deck overlooking Howelsen Hill and a cozy lounge in front.

SUNDAY

10 *Glade Runner* 9 a.m.

What Steamboat's ski slopes (2305 Mount Werner Circle; 970-879-6111; steamboat.com) lack in open-bowl skiing they make up for in zippy lift lines, carved aspen glades, and silky white Champagne powder. After taking the gondola up to the midstation, head left over to the Storm Peak Express to be whisked up to the summit. Warm up on Buddy's Run, a meandering trail with lots of dips. For fewer crowds, try Frying Pan off the backside. But Steamboat's main attraction is its glades, which are more manageable for intermediate skiers than those on most mountains. Try Shadows or Closet for something less steep. A nice chaser back down to the gondola is Vagabond.

11 *Ski and Skinny Pants* 3 p.m.

Après-ski starts early at Steamboat. Look for the unmarked trailer just north of the gondola called **T Bar** (2045 Ski Time Square Drive; 970-879-6652), surrounded by plastic chairs and picnic tables, around which are seated the usual types: hipsters, ski bums, and shaggy dogs. Its dive bar interior belies its tempting menu of borscht and grilled panini. The bar's ethos, quirky yet simple, is emblematic of Steamboat's rebirth as a resort town in touch with its playful side.

OPPOSITE Carl's Tavern, a home of bluegrass and beer.

ABOVE Shop for Stetsons and rodeo shirts at F. M. Light.

THE BASICS

Take a taxi or shuttle from the Yampa Valley Regional Airport, 22 miles west of Steamboat, or Denver International Airport, 170 miles to the southeast. In town, you won't need a car.

Trailhead Lodge
1175 Bangtail Way
970-879-9000
wvrsteamboat.com
$$$
Roomy suites with kitchenettes and fireplaces; on the mountain.

Home Ranch
54880 County Road 129
970-879-1780
homeranch.com
$$$$
Twenty minutes from Steamboat, cozy cabins surrounded by forests and fields.

Hotel Bristol
917 Lincoln Avenue
970-879-3083
steamboathotelbristol.com
$$
Rustic downtown hotel.

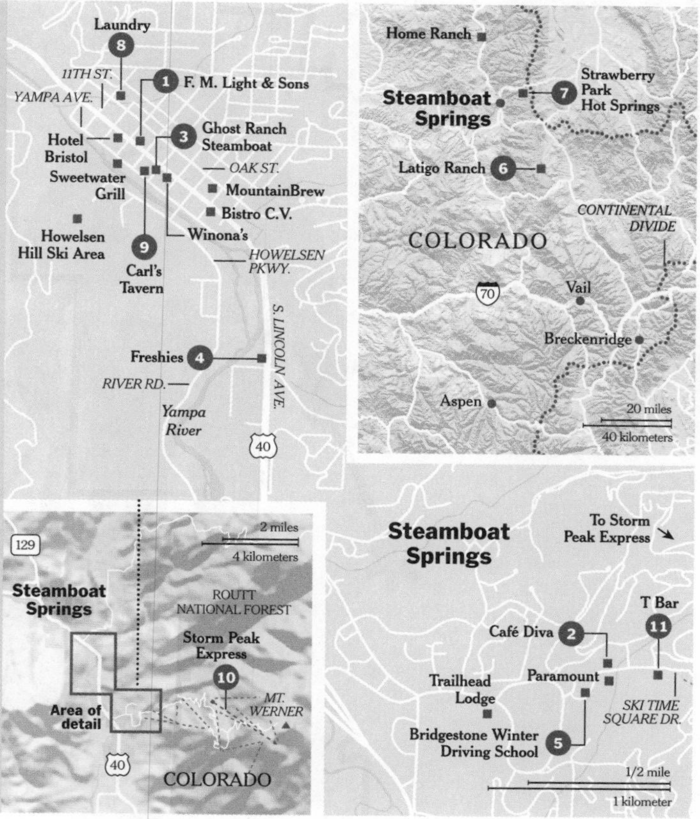

Telluride

Telluride almost begs comparisons with Aspen. A Colorado mining town affixed to a world-class ski resort; rugged locals brushing elbows with the occasional celebrity; white-tablecloth restaurants serving foie gras next to taco dives. "It's like Aspen was back in the '70s, but less pretentious," said Bo Bedford, a self-described Aspen refugee and a manager at the New Sheridan Hotel. "It hasn't gone Hollywood yet." There is, of course, a certain star-studded film festival. And Telluride does count Jerry Seinfeld and Tom Cruise among its regulars. Yet the town stays true to its hardscrabble roots. Dogs roam off-leash, folks rummage for freebies at a so-called Free Box, and residents zip up in flannel instead of fur coats. — BY LIONEL BEEHNER

FRIDAY

1 *Das Boot* 4 p.m.

Ski shops are often staffed by workers straight out of *Bill and Ted's Excellent Adventure*. Not **Boot Doctors** (650 Mountain Village Boulevard; 970-728-8954; bootdoctors.com), where Bob Gleason and his team of "surgeons" run a kind of operating room for your ill-fitting equipment. But don't expect a sterile ward—it looks more like a torture chamber, with pinchers and clawlike tools to stretch, squeeze, and custom-shape any size boots (prices range from about $25 for a boot stretch to $175 for a custom-molded sole).

2 *Broadway Meets Opry* 6 p.m.

Film and theater buffs will take comfort in Telluride's abundance of preserved art-house theaters. Take the intricately stenciled balcony and the maple floors of the **Sheridan Opera House** (110 North Oak Street; 970-728-6363; sheridanoperahouse.com), which dates from 1913. Part '30s vaudeville, part Grand Ole Opry, the stage has been graced with everything from Broadway musicals to bluegrass bands. It is also the hub of the Telluride Film Festival, which brings crowds to town each September.

3 *High Steaks* 8:30 p.m.

If the **New Sheridan** feels like the kind of joint with a secret poker game going on in a smoky backroom, well, that's because it is. But the real draw of this Victorian hotel is its newly refurbished **Chop House Restaurant** (233 West Colorado Avenue; 970-728-9100; newsheridan.com; $$$), which serves large platters of prime steaks. Like the hotel, which was reopened in 2008 after extensive renovations, the musty dining room has been spiffed up with plush booths and crystal chandeliers. After dinner, sneak away next door (there's a secret passage in the back) to the New Sheridan bar, which looks much as it did in 1895—with its crackling fire and carved mahogany bar—but has added a billiard room in back and, yup, a poker table.

SATURDAY

4 *Biscuits and Gravy* 7:30 a.m.

With its red-checkered tablecloths and folksy service, **Maggie's Bakery** (300 West Colorado Avenue; 970-728-3334; $) holds its own against any ski-town greasy spoon. Start the day with a healthy-size biscuit and gravy.

5 *Gold Rush* 9 a.m.

Telluride feels as though it belongs in the Alps—with its 2,000-plus acres of backcountry-like terrain and above-the-tree-line chutes, European-style chalets, and snowy peaks framed by boxy

OPPOSITE Snow-carpeted trails roll past wide meadows and frozen waterfalls in the pocket of southwest Colorado around Telluride.

BELOW Alpino Vino has the feel of an Italian chalet.

canyons and craggy rock formations. Throw in thin crowds and short lift lines, and what's not to like? To warm up, take the Prospect Bowl Express over to Madison or Magnolia — gentle runs that weave through trees below the gaze of Bald Mountain. Or hop on the Gold Hill Express lift to find the mountain's newer expert terrain: Revelation Bowl. Hang a left off the top of the Revelation Lift to the Gold Hill Chutes (Nos. 2 to 5), said to be some of the steepest terrain in North America.

6 *Wine and Cheese* Noon

Telluride does not believe in summit cafeterias, at least not the traditional kind with long tables for diners and deep fryers in the kitchen. Its hilltop restaurants come the size of tree forts. Case in point is **Alpino Vino** (970-708-1120; $$), a spot just off the Gold Hill Express Lift that resembles a chalet airlifted from the Italian Alps. Diners in ski helmets huddle around cherry-wood tables and a roaring fireplace, sipping Tuscan reds, while neatly groomed waiters bring plates of cured meats and fine cheeses. Arrive by noon, as this place fills up fast. For more casual grub, swing by **Giuseppe's** (970-728-7503; $) at the top of Lift 9, which stacks two shelves of Tabasco sauce and a refrigerator full of Fat Tire beer to go with home-style dishes like chicken and chorizo gumbo. After lunch, glide down See Forever, a long, winding trail that snakes all the way back to the village. Detour to Lift 9 if you want to burn off a few more calories.

7 *Full Pint* 5:30 p.m.

A free gondola links the historic town of Telluride with the faux-European base area known as Mountain Village. Just before sunset, hop off at the gondola's midstation, situated atop a ridge. For a civilized drink without cover bands, you'll find **Allred's** (970-728-7474; allredsrestaurant.com), a rustic-chic lodge with craft beers on tap. Grab a window seat for sunset views of the San Juan Mountains.

8 *No Vegans* 8 p.m.

Carnivores should feel at home in Telluride. At some spots, steak knives look like machetes and the beef is said to come from Ralph Lauren's nearby ranch. For tasty Colorado lamb chops, try the **Palmyra Restaurant** (136 Country Club Drive; 970-728-6800; thepeaksresort.com; $$$). Opened in 2009 at the Peaks Resort & Spa in Mountain Village, the glass-walled restaurant has dazzling fire features and romantic valley views. Or, for hearty grub you might find at a firehouse, head into town and loosen your belt at **Oak** (250 W. San Juan Avenue; 970-728-3985; $), a no-frills joint with old wooden tables and a counter where you can order Texas-style barbecued spareribs and breaded-to-order fried chicken.

SUNDAY

9 *Stomping Grounds* 10 a.m.

The snow-carpeted trails that roll past wide meadows and frozen waterfalls in this pocket of southwest Colorado are ideal for snowshoeing. Stock up on snacks and water before riding to the top of Lift 10, where you'll find a warming teepee run by **Eco Adventures** (565 Mountain Village Boulevard; 970-728-7300). Eco offers guided snowshoe tours with ecological lessons thrown in.

10 *Outlaw Tour* 2 p.m.

Did you know that Butch Cassidy robbed his first bank on **Main Street** in 1889? Or that the town's red-light district once had 29 bordellos? These and other historical tidbits give Telluride an added sense of place that's missing from newer, corporate-run resorts. For an entertaining tour, contact **Ashley Boling** (970-728-6639; ashleyboling@gmail.com), a D.J., actor, and self-appointed guide who offers 90-minute tours that are encyclopedic and long on stories. You may see him walking around town in his cowboy hat and red bandanna, guiding little knots of tourists and stopping every few minutes to say hello to friends — unless it's a powder day, in which case Telluride turns into a ghost town.

OPPOSITE Downtown in Telluride, an old mining town attached to a world-class ski resort. Butch Cassidy robbed his first bank on Main Street in 1889.

THE BASICS

Limited service to Telluride Regional Airport; more planes to Montrose Regional, 90 minutes away. Gondolas and your feet will get you around town.

New Sheridan Hotel
231 West Colorado Avenue
970-728-4351
newsheridan.com
$$$
Victorian hotel renovated and reopened in 2008.

Hotel Madeline Telluride
568 Mountain Village Boulevard
970-369-0880
hotelmadelinetelluride.com
$$$
Rustic-style elegance.

Lumière
118 Lost Creek Lane in Mountain Village
970-369-0400
lumierehotels.com
$$$$
Modern boutique hotel; some rooms with breathtaking views.

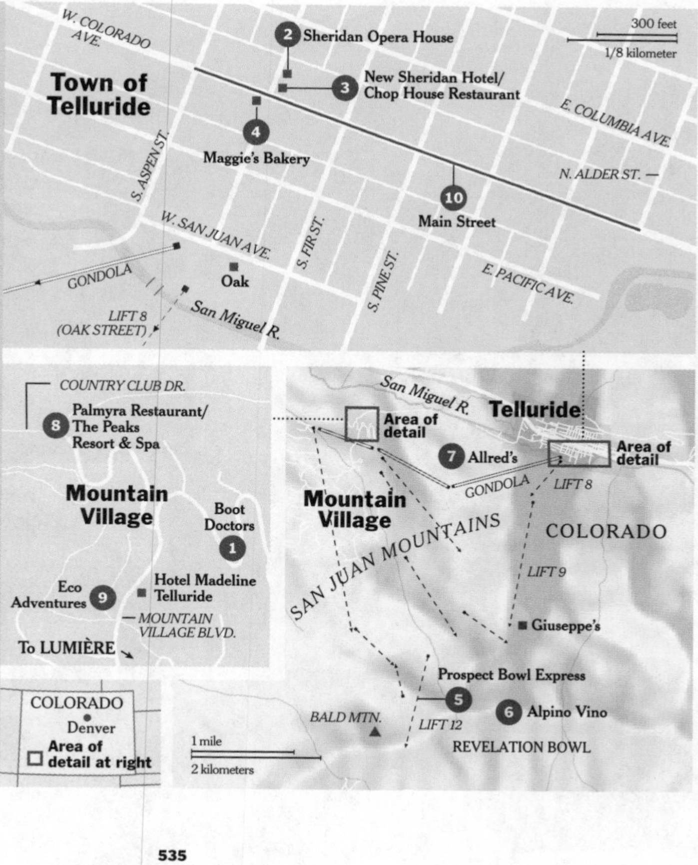

Town of Telluride
W. COLORADO AVE.
2 Sheridan Opera House
3 New Sheridan Hotel/ Chop House Restaurant
4 Maggie's Bakery
10 Main Street
E. COLUMBIA AVE.
N. ALDER ST.
S. ASPEN ST.
W. SAN JUAN AVE.
S. FIR ST.
S. PINE ST.
E. PACIFIC AVE.
Oak
GONDOLA
LIFT 8 (OAK STREET)
San Miguel R.
300 feet
1/8 kilometer

COUNTRY CLUB DR.
8 Palmyra Restaurant/ The Peaks Resort & Spa
Mountain Village
Boot Doctors
1
9 Eco Adventures
Hotel Madeline Telluride
MOUNTAIN VILLAGE BLVD.
To LUMIÈRE

San Miguel R.
Telluride
Area of detail
Area of detail
7 Allred's
GONDOLA
LIFT 8
Mountain Village
SAN JUAN MOUNTAINS
COLORADO
LIFT 9
Giuseppe's
Prospect Bowl Express
5
6 Alpino Vino
BALD MTN.
LIFT 12
REVELATION BOWL
1 mile
2 kilometers

COLORADO
Denver
Area of detail at right

Santa Fe

The Plaza, the heart of old Santa Fe, New Mexico, hasn't changed much since the Spanish settled here 400 years ago, and it's possible to focus a trip entirely on the historic town center, where Native American handicrafts are for sale on every corner. But surrounding it is an increasingly cosmopolitan city. The rest of Santa Fe now offers contemporary art spaces, hot Asian restaurants, and a park designed by a pair of trailblazing architects. Santa Fe is worth loving not just for what it was, but for what it is.

— BY FRED A. BERNSTEIN

FRIDAY

1 *Public Space* 5 p.m.

For a beautifully curated introduction to Santa Fe, visit the **New Mexico History Museum** (113 Lincoln Avenue; 505-476-5200; nmhistorymuseum.org), which includes a gripping display about Los Alamos, where the Manhattan Project was conducted in secret during World War II. A large courtyard with ancient walls and shady trees separates the museum from the Palace of the Governors (palaceofthegovernors.org), the Spanish seat of government in the early 1600s and now a small museum of Colonial and Native American history. The two-museum complex is free on Fridays from 5 to 8 p.m.

2 *White Walls and Wine* 7 p.m.

You'd have to be crazy to pay for a glass of white wine on Fridays. Canyon Road, which angles up from the center of town, has more than 100 galleries, and there are openings every Friday night. According to canyonroadarts.com, the largest category is contemporary representational (think brightly colored paintings of the desert). Check out **Eight Modern** (231 Delgado Street; 505-995-0231; eightmodern.net), where you'll find the geometric scrap-metal constructions of the Santa Fe artist Ted Larsen. The backyard sculpture garden is a great place to marvel at New Mexico's amazingly clear sky and savor its piñon-infused air before heading to dinner.

3 *Ahi Moment* 9 p.m.

Martín Rios is a hometown boy made good. Born in Mexico and raised in Santa Fe, he apprenticed at the Eldorado Hotel and the Inn of the Anasazi — two local stalwarts — and made a brief appearance on *Iron Chef* before opening his own place, **Restaurant Martín** (526 Galisteo Street; 505-820-0919; restaurantmartinsantafe.com; $$), in 2009. The main draw is the food — dishes like ahi tuna tartare and duck breast with smoked bacon polenta and Marcona almonds offer hints of the Southwest, with a dash of global aspiration. But the homey décor makes you want to stick around even after finishing the bittersweet chocolate truffle cake.

SATURDAY

4 *Spice Market* 10 a.m.

The **Santa Fe Farmers' Market** (1607 Paseo de Peralta; 505-983-4098; santafefarmersmarket.com) dates back a half-century and now has a permanent building in the revitalized Railyard district. Everything sold here, including dried chilies, yogurt, and grass-fed meats, is produced in northern New Mexico. The market is part of a bustling district that includes the new Railyard Park by the architect Frederic Schwartz and the landscape architect Ken Smith, both Manhattanites whose taste is anything but quaint. As you wander around, be on the lookout for the **Rail Runner** (nmrailrunner.com), a gleaming passenger train that pulls in from Albuquerque in late morning.

OPPOSITE The Sangre de Cristo Mountains form a backdrop for residences designed by Ricardo Legorreta.

BELOW Don Gaspar Avenue in downtown Santa Fe.

5 *Sustainable Salads* Noon

Santa Fe residents care—as you learned roaming the Farmers' Market—where their food comes from. No wonder **Vinaigrette** (709 Don Cubero Alley; 505-820-9205; vinaigretteonline.com; $$) is an enduring favorite. The brightly colored cafe has a menu based on organic greens grown in the nearby town of Nambé. Choose a base—Caesar, Cobb, and Greek are possibilities—then add diver scallops or hibiscus-cured duck confit. Add a glass of wine for a satisfying meal.

6 *O'Keeffe Country* 1 p.m.

Georgia O'Keeffe's famous landscapes of the New Mexico desert assure that she will always be identified with Santa Fe, and the **Georgia O'Keeffe Museum** (217 Johnson Street; 505-946-1000; okeeffemuseum.org), right off the plaza, holds over 1,000 of her works. The **New Mexico Museum of Art** (107 West Palace Avenue; 505-476-5072; mfasantafe.org), which emphasizes art produced in or related to New Mexico, is also worth a visit. Besides providing a cool afternoon of art appreciation, the museums have stores that offer an alternative to Santa Fe's generally costly shopping, and tourist kitsch.

7 *Riding the Spur* 4 p.m.

Thanks to Santa Fe's sometimes depressing sprawl, it's getting harder and harder to find wide-open spaces. But drive (or bike) to the corner of Galisteo Street and West Rodeo Road, where there's a small parking lot. Then begin pedaling due south, in the direction of Lamy (about 12 miles away). What starts as an asphalt path morphs into a dirt bike trail that swerves around a 19th-century rail spur. There are some pretty steep hills, but they're short, and the momentum from a downhill is usually enough to handle the next uphill. (If only life were like that!) The scenery is always gorgeous, especially in late afternoon, when the sun is low in the sky.

ABOVE The Rail Runner train connects Santa Fe to Albuquerque.

BELOW The distinctive Southwestern look of Santa Fe.

Mellow Velo (132 East Marcy Street; 505-995-8356; mellowvelo.com) rents mountain bikes.

8 *Tapas With Strangers* 8 p.m.

La Boca (72 West Marcy Street; 505-982-3433; labocasf.com; $$) is one of downtown Santa Fe's most popular new restaurants — thanks to its contemporary tapas, plus larger dishes like cannelloni filled with crab, scallop, and Manchego. You'll find yourself sharing tips on what to order — and even forkfuls of delicious eats — with strangers.

SUNDAY

9 *Free-Range Peacocks* 10 a.m.

For a big breakfast and an early start, drive south on Cerrillos Road about 10 miles past the Interstate, until you arrive at the **San Marcos Café** (3877 State Road 14; 505-471-9298; $$). Dozens of peacocks, turkeys, and hens roam the property (which also houses a feed store), providing an Old MacDonald-like backdrop for crowd-pleasers like eggs San Marcos, a cheese omelet in a bath of guacamole, beans, and salsa. While you're at the Railyard, check out **SITE Santa Fe** (1606 Paseo De Peralta; 505-989-1199; sitesantafe.org), a huge, multi-leveled contemporary art space with provocative installations that change regularly.

10 *Kitsch to Contemporary* Noon

If you ever thought that item you found at a roadside stand was one of a kind, **Jackalope** (2820 Cerrillos Road; 505-471-8539; jackalope.com), a

ABOVE Pancho Villa's death mask at the history museum.

BELOW The Santa Fe Farmers' Market.

sprawling indoor-outdoor flea market, will disabuse you of that notion. There are hundreds of everything — look for items like punched-copper switch plates and tote bags that depict Michelle Obama smiling on a swing.

11 *Bring Your Own Adobe* 1 p.m.

It's difficult to spend time in Santa Fe without thinking about buying a home (or second home) here. So check out **Zocalo** (Avenida Rincon; 505-986-0667; zocalosantafe.com), a striking development by the Mexican architect Ricardo Legorreta, who also designed the Visual Arts Center of the Santa Fe University of Art and Design (santafeuniversity.edu). He is known for crisp geometry and super-bright colors — a welcome sight in this city of browns and terra cottas. To appreciate Zocalo, you don't really have to be in the mood to buy. Consider this real estate voyeurism, combined with a crash course in contemporary architecture.

ABOVE Revel in kitsch at the Jackalope, a sprawling indoor-outdoor flea market.

OPPOSITE Outside the San Marcos Café.

THE BASICS

Santa Fe has a tiny airport with limited service. Most visitors fly into Albuquerque and drive about an hour to Santa Fe.

Hotel St. Francis
210 Don Gaspar Avenue
505-983-5700
hotelstfrancis.com
$$
Billed as the oldest hotel in Santa Fe. Fully renovated in 2009.

The El Rey Inn
1862 Cerrillos Road
505-982-1931
elreyinnsantafe.com
$$
Retro-chic 1930s-style motel with nicely furnished rooms.

Hilton Santa Fe Golf Resort & Spa
20 Buffalo Thunder Trail
505-455-5555
buffalothunderresort.com
$$
Part of a new casino complex 15 minutes north of town.

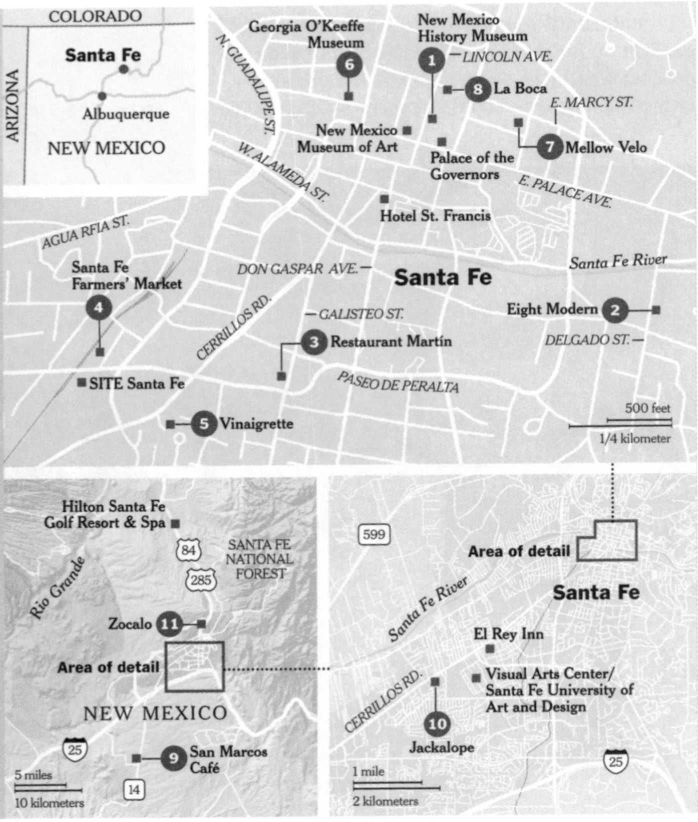

COLORADO
ARIZONA
Santa Fe
Albuquerque
NEW MEXICO
Georgia O'Keeffe Museum 6
New Mexico History Museum 1
LINCOLN AVE.
8 La Boca
E. MARCY ST.
N. GUADALUPE ST.
New Mexico Museum of Art
Palace of the Governors
7 Mellow Velo
W. ALAMEDA ST.
E. PALACE AVE.
Hotel St. Francis
AGUA FRIA ST.
Santa Fe Farmers' Market 4
DON GASPAR AVE.
Santa Fe
Santa Fe River
Eight Modern 2
GALISTEO ST.
CERRILLOS RD.
3 Restaurant Martín
DELGADO ST.
SITE Santa Fe
PASEO DE PERALTA
5 Vinaigrette
500 feet
1/4 kilometer
Hilton Santa Fe Golf Resort & Spa
84
285
SANTA FE NATIONAL FOREST
Rio Grande
Zocalo 11
Area of detail
NEW MEXICO
25
9 San Marcos Café
14
5 miles
10 kilometers
599
Area of detail
Santa Fe River
Santa Fe
El Rey Inn
CERRILLOS RD.
Visual Arts Center/ Santa Fe University of Art and Design
10 Jackalope
25
1 mile
2 kilometers

Albuquerque

New Mexico's biggest city has come back into its own. Thanks to tax breaks and great scenery, the TV and film industry is well established: scenes for Joss Whedon's mega-budget film The Avengers *were shot here, and TV watchers recognize Albuquerque as the backdrop for* Breaking Bad. *For visitors, the sprawl can seem daunting, but it is tempered by new bike paths. On the main drag, Central Avenue, neon signs from Route 66's heyday glow over revitalized, pedestrian-friendly neighborhoods. And along the banks of the Rio Grande, farmland provides a quiet oasis, not to mention heirloom beans, corn, and more to feed the city's vibrant organic movement.*

— BY ZORA O'NEILL

FRIDAY

1 *Mother Road* 3 p.m.

At night, Albuquerque's revived downtown can be a bleary seven-block bar crawl. By day, though, you can appreciate the ornate buildings financed by the railroad boom, like the exuberant Pueblo Deco **KiMo Theatre** (423 Central Avenue Northwest; 505-768-3522; cabq.gov/kimo), which opened as a movie palace in 1927 and is now the city's public arts center. Enter through the business office to admire cow skull wall sconces and pueblo drum chandeliers. Nearby, drop in at classic shops like **Maisel's** (510 Central Avenue Southwest; 505-242-6526; skipmaisels.com), an emporium of American Indian crafts that's just the place to pick up a turquoise-and-silver bolo tie. Look for the '30s murals above the display windows, by artists from surrounding pueblos. **The Man's Hat Shop** (511 Central Avenue Northwest; 505-247-9605; manshatshop.com) is stacked to the ceiling with ten-gallons, fedoras, and more. A short drive south, stop off to see what's showing at the **National Hispanic Cultural Center** (1701 Fourth Street Southwest; 505-246-2261; nhccnm.org).

2 *Healing Potions* 6 p.m.

Go early to get a seat along the edge of the roof deck at the **Parq Central** hotel, a renovated 1926 hospital for railroad employees, tuberculosis patients, and the mentally ill. The menu at its **Apothecary Lounge** (806 Central Avenue Southeast; 505-242-0040; hotelparqcentral.com) notes the place is "not a licensed pharmacy." Instead, it prescribes potions like a dreamy margarita made with prickly-pear juice and elderflower liqueur. As the sun sets, watch the east-side Sandia ("Watermelon") Mountains turn a luscious shade of pink.

3 *Home Grown* 8 p.m.

For a taste of old-school Albuquerque, head to **Golden Crown Panaderia** (1103 Mountain Road Northwest; 505-243-2424; goldencrown.biz; $), for empanadas, Mexican-style bolillos, and pizza with a crust of blue corn or green chili (or chile, as it's usually spelled in New Mexico). Salads are tossed with greens snipped from a tangled indoor garden. For dessert, get a classic anise-laced biscochito cookie and a double-shot espresso milkshake.

4 *Beer and Atmosphere* 10 p.m.

The drinking wing of **Marble Brewery** is called Marble Pub (111 Marble Street Northwest; 505-243-2739; marblebrewery.com), and it is a consummate New Mexican bar: benches, banjo players or salsa drummers, and lots of dogs. Rehydrate, after dancing, with a goblet of barrel-aged ale. Over in the Nob Hill district, east of the University of New Mexico, the longer-established brewpub **Kellys** (3222 Central Avenue Southeast; 505-262-2739; kellysbrewpub.com) is set in a 1939 Ford service station. Find a seat outside, weather permitting, by the vintage gas pumps and watch the fashion parade: flip-flops, graying ponytails, lavish tattoos.

SATURDAY

5 *Lucky Strike* 9 a.m.

In many cities, farm-to-table produce and a chef-owner with Chez Panisse credentials would add up to hipster overload. But in Albuquerque, **Sophia's Place** (6313 Fourth Street Northwest; 505-345-3935) feels like a comfortable family restaurant with an especially interesting take on familiar Mexican dishes (duck enchiladas with tomatillo-serrano salsa, taco salad with sirloin, salmon B.L.T.). For

OPPOSITE Hot-air balloon traffic is heaviest during the annual Albuquerque International Balloon Fiesta, but ballooning is popular all year round.

breakfast, there are gems like lacy blueberry pancakes with pine-nut butter.

6 *Rolling on the River* 10:30 a.m.

Sixteen paved miles of biking bliss, the Paseo del Bosque trail in the city's lowlands hugs the Rio Grande. Pick up your wheels at **Stevie's Happy Bikes** (4685 Corrales Road; 505-897-7900; corralesbikeshop.com). Perhaps a retro three-speed tandem? Stevie can suggest a route, zigzagging along the tree-lined irrigation channels of Corrales, a village within the city, to reach the trail. One destination is **Los Poblanos Farm Shop** (4803 Rio Grande Boulevard Northwest; 505-938-2192; lospoblanos.com), the store at the Los Poblanos inn and organic farm. Lavender lotions and soaps are a specialty.

7 *Clang, Clang, Clang* 3 p.m.

Even if a faux-trolley tour bus doesn't normally appeal to you, hop aboard the adobe-look **ABQ Trolley** (303 Romero Street Northwest; 505-240-8000; abqtrolley.com). The two owner-operators (one talks and the other drives and rings the bell) return happy waves from locals and blast Chuck Berry as they cruise Route 66. The tour features locations for *Breaking Bad* and tales of a young Bill Gates, who co-founded Microsoft here with Paul Allen before he moved back to Seattle. Special outings share Albuquerque lore in the form of talks on public art, ghost stories around Halloween, and tours to see holiday luminarias, the paper-bag lanterns that cast a glow on winter nights.

8 *Red Meat* 6 p.m.

Carne adovada—pork stewed in earthy New Mexican red chili—is the lifeblood of **Mary & Tito's** (2711 Fourth Street Northwest; 505-344-6266; $). Its recipe hasn't changed in decades, nor has its décor—the combination won it a James Beard America's Classic award. Try the carne adovada as a turnover, wrapped in flaky dough and fried.

SUNDAY

9 *Up in the Air* 5:45 a.m.

Since 1972, when the first Balloon Fiesta convened, Albuquerque has been hot-air-balloon heaven, with friendly winds and ample sunshine. Take a dawn flight with **Rainbow Ryders** (505-823-1111; rainbowryders.com). The bird's-eye view takes in the Sandias and dormant volcanoes, but most remarkable is the sensation of drifting just a few feet above the muddy waters of the Rio Grande. Fortify yourself afterward at the **Grove** (600 Central Avenue Southeast, Suite A; 505-248-9800; thegrovecafemarket.com; $). With pancakes or a chocolate-date scone.

10 *Church Music* 10 a.m.

Free espresso fuels the congregation at **Sunday Chatter** (at the Kosmos, 1715 Fifth Street Northwest; 505-234-4611; chatterchamber.org), a Sunday-morning chamber music and poetry series. Founded in 2008 by the cellist Felix Wurman, just

ABOVE Pick up a 10-gallon hat from the Man's Hat Shop.

OPPOSITE ABOVE KiMo theater, designed in Pueblo Deco style.

BELOW Fresh baked at Golden Crown Panaderia.

two years before his death, it was originally called the Church of Beethoven. Wurman's vision of a weekly ritual without the strictures of religion has become one of the city's best-loved musical events. Arrive early to score the best seats, a row of thrift shop easy chairs on one wall of the warehouse turned art space.

11 *Sweet and Hot* 1 p.m.

The decades-old **Frontier Restaurant** (2400 Central Avenue Southeast; 505-266-0550; frontierrestaurant.com; $) occupies the better part of a city block. The Frontier's walls are adorned with portraits of John Wayne, and its booths are occupied by every social stratum of the city. Standard order at the counter: breakfast burrito with bacon, fresh-squeezed orange juice, and a killer sweet roll dripping with molten cinnamon goo. You can even take a frozen pint of New Mexico green chili home on the plane.

THE BASICS

The Albuquerque International Sunport is about a 10-minute drive from downtown.

Los Poblanos Inn
4803 Rio Grande Boulevard Northwest
505-344-9297
lospoblanos.com
$$
Agriturismo, New Mexican style, set on an organic farm. Rooms balance brick and adobe with Alexander Girard textiles.

Andaluz
125 Second Street Northwest
505-242-9090
hotelandaluz.com
$$
Built in 1939 by the New Mexico native Conrad Hilton and recently renovated. Rooms have faux-Moorish doorways and Frette linens.

Böttger Mansion of Old Town
110 San Felipe Northwest
505-243-3639
bottger.com
$$
Victorian inn with period decorations.

To Stevie's Happy Bikes
9 Rainbow Ryders
Los Poblanos Farm Shop
5 Sophia's Place
Los Poblanos Inn
COLORADO
Santa Fe
ARIZONA
Albuquerque
NEW MEXICO
MEXICO
TEXAS
Rio Grande
COORS BLVD. NW
MONTANO RD. NW
RIO GRANDE BLVD. NW
FOURTH ST. NW
SECOND ST. NW
448
85
25
Albuquerque
6 Paseo del Bosque trail
8 Mary & Tito's
CORONADO FWY.
40
Golden Crown Panaderia
10 Sunday Chatter
3
ABQ Trolley
7
MOUNTAIN RD. NW
Böttger Mansion of Old Town
4 Marble Brewery
Frontier Restaurant
Andaluz
Area of detail
11
The Grove
CENTRAL AVE.
Kellys
2 Parq Central/ Apothecary Lounge
Man's Hat Shop
FIFTH ST. NW
Maisel's
SIXTH ST. SW
CENTRAL AVE.
1 KiMo Theater
National Hispanic Cultural Center
GOLD AVE. SW
1 mile
2 kilometers

Paso
MONTE D
SHOP
SIDEWALK SALES PERMIT
MEMBER 2008
Dinero por Oro y Plata!
Dinero
Oro Y
OPE
ABIERTO
POR MES

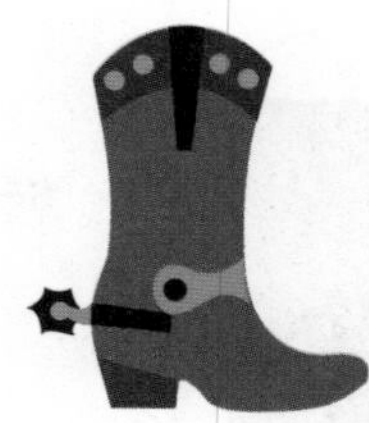

El Paso

Situated at the intersection of Texas, Mexico, and New Mexico, El Paso is a city with a distinct flavor. It juxtaposes authentic Mexican culture with a growing hipster scene. Once the storied heart of the Old West (and playground of Billy the Kid), El Paso has recently gained much of the big-city feel of its larger neighbor across the border, Ciudad Juárez. It has come into its own with new theaters, restaurants, and nightclubs, many of them transplants from Juárez, which found itself at the center of the Mexican drug war.
— BY IZA WOJCIECHOWSKA

FRIDAY

1 *Wine Country* 4 p.m.

Though El Paso's summers, with days that often reach into the 100s, may seem unforgiving for grape-growing, it turns out that zinfandels take quite nicely to the sun. Stop by **Zin Valle Vineyards** (7315 Canutillo La Union Road; 915-877-4544; zinvalle.com) or the neighboring **La Viña Winery** (4201 South Highway 28; 575-882-7632; lavinawinery.com) for generous tastings. Both sit along the historic Don Juan de Oñate Trail, a section of El Camino Real that marks the route that Oñate, the explorer and conquistador, forged in 1598 to settle north of the Rio Grande. A drive down this road reveals majestic pecan groves and vast fields of cotton, chili peppers, and corn.

2 *Eat Local* 7 p.m.

With Juárez right across the highway, it's a no-brainer that El Paso has always been a prime spot for Mexican food. And though enchiladas and tortas still prevail, the past few years have begun to see a locavore, foodie culture spread through the city. And why not? With plenty of undeveloped land still surrounding El Paso, there's room to cultivate nearly everything. **Tom's Folk Cafe** (204 Boston Avenue; 915-500-5573; tomsfolkcafe.com; $) epitomizes the trend with its local meat, veggies, and breads; wine-bottle candlesticks; and nouveau Southern food. After an order of hush puppies stuffed with pulled pork, try an oversized burger with Brie, bacon, and blueberry jam or pan-seared snapper with crawfish ragout.

3 *Indie Scene* 9 p.m.

New music venues are part of El Paso's night-life scene, and with the Coachella music festival to the west and Austin City Limits festival to the east, El Paso could be on its way to becoming a hot spot on indie bands' tours. The **Lowbrow Palace** (111 Robinson Avenue; thelowbrowpalace.com) caters to the college crowd and regularly features local bands as well as touring acts. **Tricky Falls** (209 South El Paso Street; 915-351-9938; trickyfalls.com) is a music space in a gorgeous historic building. Above it is **Bowie Feathers** (209 South El Paso Street; 915-351-9909), which also hosts musicians. It's a bar and hipster haven with black leather booths and funky wall art.

SATURDAY

4 *Farmers' Morning* 9 a.m.

Drive into the desert for brunch at **Ardovino's Desert Crossing** (1 Ardovino Drive; 575-589-0653; ardovinos.com; $$), and hang out on the patio

OPPOSITE A pawn shop on El Paso Street downtown.

RIGHT A cross and Christ figure at the peak of Mount Cristo Rey, in New Mexico, overlook El Paso. In the city, trains rumble by at the foot of the mountain.

beneath the big blue sky. Mix and match menu items like prickly pear mimosas, caramelized grapefruit, and Jackpot Waffles, topped with chicken, bacon, and sautéed apples. Leave room for red-wine-infused ice cream with chocolate cake, and watch the train rumble by at the foot of Mount Cristo Rey. If you're here between May and October, check out the adjacent farmers' market, which features local produce and artisan crafts like ocotillo-flower soap, raspberry chipotle jam, and such edible desert delicacies as cactus fruit or yucca.

5 *Desert Trails* 11 a.m.

El Paso's beauty stems from the inescapable mountains that surround the city. Head to the **Franklin Mountains State Park** (1331 McKelligon Canyon Road; 915-566-6441; tpwd.state.tx.us/state-parks/franklin-mountains) to hike trails replete with cactuses, agaves, and lizards. Explore McKelligon Canyon if you enter the park on the east side of the city, or begin a trail from the Transmountain Road entrance on the west.

6 *Arts and Culture* 1 p.m.

A serious push over the last few years to revitalize the downtown is finally bearing fruit. Renovated historical buildings are getting their due, and fresh establishments are breathing new life into classic El Paso haunts. Visit the free **El Paso Museum of Art** (1 Arts Festival Plaza; 915-532-1707; elpasoartmuseum.org) for its collection of Southwestern and local artwork. Next door is the **Plaza Theater** (125 Pioneer Plaza; 915-534-0600; theplazatheatre.org), which was the pride of El Paso when it opened in 1930. The Plaza survived a decline in the '50s and a near-demolition in the '80s and has made a triumphant return as a beautiful, colorful setting for Broadway shows and concerts by the El Paso Symphony Orchestra. For more lowbrow local flavor, wander down El Paso Street, which is lined with pawn shops and Mexican stores full of cheap clothes, cowboy boots, and oddities.

7 *Cocktail Hour* 5 p.m.

Historic El Paso lurks in the city's old, classy bars. Have a mojito beneath the rotunda of vintage Tiffany glass at the Camino Real Hotel's **Dome Bar** (101 South El Paso Street; 915-534-3000; caminorealelpaso.com/dining), or settle in with a top-shelf drink or cigar at the luxurious **Café Central** (109 North Oregon Street; 915-545-2233; cafecentral.com), which opened in 1918.

8 *Sharing Tapas* 8 p.m.

Across the street from an old locomotive on display in the downtown entertainment district is a cobbled block of dimly lighted restaurants. **Tabla** (115 Durango Street; 915-533-8935; tabla-ep.com; $$) is a pleasing package with its modern décor, a rotation of custom-infused liquors, and an extensive menu of tapas. Its mantra is "share," and after sharing pork confit with goat cheese polenta, grilled asparagus with Serrano ham and salsa verde, and huge pieces of bruschetta loaded with smoked salmon, you'll also be sharing exclamations of delight.

9 *Dance, Dance, Dance* 11 p.m.

Since Mexico's drug war pushed night life over the border from Juárez, the clubbing scene has shifted to downtown El Paso. **Lotus** (201 North Stanton Street; 915-503-2335; lotusep.com) is a sleek and ultramodern club with three floors, D.J.'s, and a huge Buddha sculpture presiding over the dance floor. The nearby **Garden** (511 Western Street; 915-544-4400; thegardenep.com) has a daytime dining patio that is transformed into an outdoor club on weekends. Merrymakers also gravitate to drinks spots like **Hope and Anchor** (4012 North Mesa Street; 915-533-8010; hopeandanchorelpaso.com), which draws crowds with drink specials, and the **Hoppy Monk** (4141 North Mesa Street; 915-307-3263; thehoppymonk.com), which has craft brews on tap.

SUNDAY

10 *Border-Town Brunch* 10:30 a.m.

Pile green chilies, chorizo, avocado, and chipotle onto eggs and serve with a side of black beans, and you have a true Southwestern breakfast. **Ripe Eatery** (910 East Redd Road; 915-584-7473; ripeeatery.com;

$$), a surprisingly chic spot in a nondescript strip mall, stands out for its Southwest Scramble and Brisket Ranchero Eggs Benedict. It can also supply a cold Chelada (beer, Bloody Mary mix, and lime). Stop by **Valentine's Bakery** (6415 North Mesa Street; 915-585-8720) for Mexican pastries.

11 *2 Countries, 3 States* 1 p.m.

Take a ride along Scenic Drive, which winds through the mountains with views of the city and deposits you near the **Wyler Aerial Tramway** (1700 McKinley Avenue; 915-566-6622; tpwd.state.tx.us/state-parks/wyler-aerial-tramway). A public tram is a rare item in Texas, and this one gives you a four-minute ride to a high peak where there are views of the convergence of two countries and three states (Texas; New Mexico; and Chihuahua State, Mexico).

OPPOSITE Tiffany glass above the Dome Bar in the richly decorated, century-old Camino Real Hotel. Jazz musicians play in the bar most nights.

ABOVE An assortment of Mexican pastries at Valentine's Bakery on El Paso's west side.

THE BASICS

Drive to El Paso on Interstate 10 or fly into El Paso International Airport and rent a car.

Camino Real Hotel
101 South El Paso Street
915-534-3000
caminorealelpaso.com
$
Opened in 1912 as the ultimate in luxury; original, vintage lobby is bedecked with chandeliers and ornate golden molding.

DoubleTree Hotel
600 North El Paso Street
915-532-8733
doubletreeelpasohotel.com
$
A recent addition to El Paso's downtown skyline. Its rooms and public terrace provide good city views.

El Paso Marriott
1600 Airway Boulevard
915-779-3300
marriott.com
$$
Near the airport, with pool and fitness center.

1 To Zin Valle Vineyards and La Viña Winery/ Don Juan de Oñate Trail
E. REDD RD.
10 Ripe Eatery
Franklin Mountains State Park 5
N.M.
OKLA.
TEXAS
El Paso
Dallas
Austin
MEXICO
El Paso
N. MESA ST.
MCNUTT RD.
85
Valentine's Bakery
McKelligon Canyon
NEW MEXICO
180
10
Wyler Aerial Tramway 11
ALABAMA ST.
Sunland Park
Ardovino's Desert Crossing/ Farmers' Market 4
ARDOVINO DR.
Area of detail
54
Scenic Drive
2 miles
4 kilometers
MEXICO
To El Paso Marriott
Area of detail
Ciudad Juárez
Rio Grande
Hoppy Monk
1/4 mile
1/2 kilometer
Hope and Anchor
N. MESA ST.
Tom's Folk Cafe 2
Lowbrow Palace 3
BOSTON AVE.
ROBINSON AVE.
N. OREGON ST.
DoubleTree Hotel
N. STANTON ST.
CAMPBELL ST.
N. EL PASO ST.
PIONEER PLAZA
9 Lotus
Plaza Theater
10
El Paso Museum of Art 6
Café Central
7 Camino Real Hotel/ Dome Bar
Garden
DURANGO ST.
WESTERN ST.
Tabla 8
Tricky Falls/ Bowie Feathers
1/4 mile
1/2 kilometer

San Antonio

San Antonio, the United States' seventh-largest city, features a threesome of popular attractions: the River Walk (a meandering canal lined with restaurants and bars), Market Square (said to be the largest Mexican-style market outside of Mexico), and the Alamo (no explanation necessary). Beyond those obvious tourist stops, this old city also offers Latino art, 19th-century-style shopping, salsa-dancing, and plenty of that famous Texas hospitality.

—BY DAN SALTZSTEIN

FRIDAY

1 *Shopping as It Was* 3 p.m.

La Villita historic district (South Alamo Street at East Nueva Street; lavillita.com), just off the River Walk, still feels like the little village it once was but is now crammed with artisanal shops, many of which are housed in lovely mid-19th-century buildings. The **Casa Clasal Copper Gallery** (Building No. 11; 210-271-3856; lavillita.com/copper) sells everything copper; a gorgeous set of hammered ewers started at about $40. **Alice Knight** (No. 17; 210-930-5527; aliceknight.com) sells Knight's playful and sometimes goofy paintings, as well as her delicate handmade-paper masks. On one shopping day the artist's husband, Jack, was running the store. Is he an artist as well? "She lets me paint the edges," he said.

2 *Italy Comes to Texas* 5:30 p.m.

Five-thirty? What is this, the early-bird special? No, it's **Il Sogno Osteria** (Pearl Brewery Complex, 200 East Grayson Street; 210-212-4843; $$), and since it doesn't take reservations, the crowds line up early. The restaurant is Andrew Weissman's wildly successful Italian follow-up to his popular, now closed La Rêve. The industrial-chic space fills up with families and couples, some barside, gazing at the wood-burning oven in the open kitchen. Antipasti might include an addictive white bean purée, and the lasagna with wild mushrooms can be a satisfying pasta option. The Nutella tart, a holdover from La Rêve, is achingly decadent.

3 *More Salsa* 9 p.m.

South Alamo Street, a short but colorful jumble of galleries, shops, and restaurants, is the main strip of the Southtown neighborhood, a diverse and welcoming pocket that's cherished by many locals. Let the beat and the warm bodies pull you into **Rosario's Café y Cantina** (910 South Alamo Street; 210-223-1806; rosariossa.com), a festive Mexican restaurant that pulsates with live salsa music and energetic dancing on Friday nights, especially on each month's First Friday, when the neighborhood sponsors a street fair of art and music. In a town famous for its margaritas, Rosario's are among the tastiest.

SATURDAY

4 *Brewery Without Beer* 9:30 a.m.

Starting your Saturday at a brewery? Not to worry. Though it produced beer for over a century, **Pearl Brewery** (200 East Grayson Street; 210-212-7260; pearlbrewery.com) closed in 2001 and after an elaborate renovation reopened as a mixed-use complex. In addition to a few restaurants (Il Sogno included) and a branch of the Culinary Institute of America, there are a growing number of shops, including **Melissa Guerra** (303 Pearl Parkway; 210-293-3983; melissaguerra.com), a kitchenware store owned by the cookbook author, and the **Twig Book**

OPPOSITE Early morning at the Alamo, before the day's onslaught of eager tourist crowds.

RIGHT Museo Alameda, a Smithsonian affiliate, displays Latino and Chicano art.

Shop (306 Pearl Parkway; 210-826-6411; thetwig.indiebound.com), an airy spot that offers a nice variety of best sellers and Texas-themed publications. There is also a Saturday-morning farmers' market (pearlfarmersmarket.com) with local vendors selling cheeses, salsa, herbs, nuts, baked goods, and all kinds of produce. Stroll and savor the aromas.

5 *Burgers With Conscience* Noon

Don't oversample at the market, because one of the more unusual dining places in town is a few minutes away in the Five Points neighborhood. **The Cove** (606 West Cypress Street; 210-227-2683; thecove.us; $) is a restaurant, car wash, coin laundry, and music spot. Its sloppy and satisfying Texas Burger (with refried beans, chips, grilled onion, avocado, and salsa) won mention in *Texas Monthly*. The Cove is also notable for its dedication to S.O.L.—sustainable, organic, local—ingredients, and it practices what it preaches with dishes like grilled tilapia tacos or a salad of roasted organic beets, goat cheese, and walnuts.

6 *Spirit of the Smithsonian* 2 p.m.

San Antonio has a broad visual art scene that ranges from contemporary to folk, with a special concentration on Latino work. There's a First Friday art walk; nonprofit centers like **Artpace** (artpace.org); and the **McNay Art Museum** (mcnayart.org), which has an impressive collection especially strong in modern and contemporary art. At the **San Antonio Museum of Art** (200 West Jones Avenue; 210-978-8100; samuseum.org), the Nelson Rockefeller Wing for Latin American Art has both folk art from across the Americas and splashy contemporary paintings.

7 *Her Name Is Rio* 5 p.m.

After the Alamo, the most popular attraction in town is probably the **River Walk**, a four-mile stretch of paths that snakes through downtown along the canals (thesanantonioriverwalk.com). Sure, it's touristy, but if you avoid the often overpriced restaurants and bars that line it, a stroll can be lovely, particularly as the sun sets and hanging lights illuminate picturesque bridges.

8 *Eating Up North* 7 p.m.

To satisfy a Tex-Mex craving, head out of town to the Far North area, where you'll see the full extent of San Antonio's sprawl. Amid miles of highway loops, malls, and planned communities, find family-friendly **Aldaco's Stone Oak** (20079 Stone Oak Parkway; 210-494-0561; aldacos-stoneoak.com; $$), which serves big portions in a large, noisy space. A patio looks toward Texas Hill Country. After your shrimp enchiladas, follow the green glow at Plaza Ciel, a nearby strip mall, to the **Green Lantern** (20626 Stone Oak Parkway; 210-497-3722), San Antonio's contribution to the speakeasy trend. There's no sign, but the low-lighted room and old-school drinks attract young professionals. Order something from the classics list, like a well-made Sazerac.

SUNDAY

9 *The Tourist's Mission* 10 a.m.

If you're a first-timer in San Antonio, or you just love the story of the Texans who fought to the death and want to hear it again, Sunday morning can be a good time to hit the **Alamo** (Alamo Plaza; thealamo.org). You won't lack for company—2.5

million people a year visit this holiest of Texas civic shrines — and the parking may cost you. But the old walls are still there, and admission is free.

10 *Brisket Brunch* Noon

Texas's most beloved barbecue is served about an hour north in Hill Country, but the **Smokehouse** (3306 Roland Avenue; 210-333-9548; thesmokehousebbqsa.com; $) represents San Antonio proudly. You'll smell the proof from the parking lot: this is the real deal. Friendly staff members work the 40-foot-long mesquite-wood pits. Order a sandwich or a platter by the pound, including the succulent, charred-on-the-outside brisket.

11 *For the Birds* 2 p.m.

Walk off those calories at **Brackenridge Park** (3910 North St. Mary's Street), a 340-plus-acre green space on the west side of town. The park's sunken Japanese Tea Garden offers a bit of serenity, while the bustling **San Antonio Zoo** (sazoo-aq.org) is particularly child-friendly, with an aviary where visitors can feed, and play with, brightly colored lorikeets. A different sort of Texas hospitality, but an entertaining one for sure.

OPPOSITE Creative decorating on the River Walk, the beloved pathway that snakes for four miles through downtown.

ABOVE Alice Knight, an artist who makes playful handmade-paper masks, at her gallery in La Villita.

THE BASICS

Major airlines serve San Antonio's busy airport. In the city, get around by car.

Valencia Riverwalk
150 East Houston Street
866-842-0100
hotelvalencia-riverwalk.com
$$$
A friendly staff, comfortable beds, and valet parking offset the dark, moody décor.

Riverwalk Vista Bed & Breakfast
262 Losoya Street
210-223-3200
riverwalkvista.com
$$
Individually designed rooms in the historic Dullnig building.

JW Marriott San Antonio Hill Country Resort & Spa
23808 Resort Parkway
210-403-3434
jwsanantonio.com
$$$
Upscale accommodations.

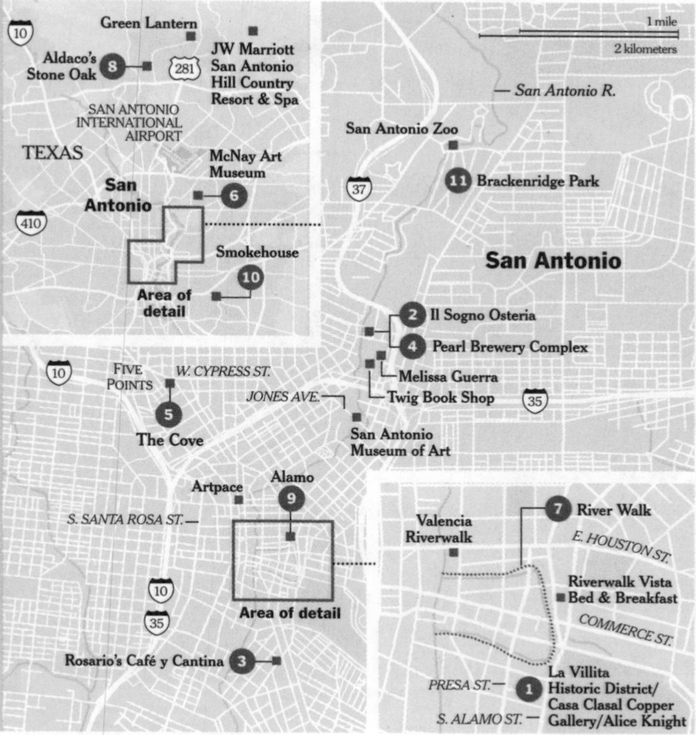

U. S. POST-OFFICE
1850 LUCKENBACH, TX. 1971
OPEN 9 AM

Texas Hill Country

To get a feeling for the Texas Hill Country, where cool mingles with tradition, and industriousness and idleness are equally esteemed values (depending on the time of day), head out among the limestone knolls full of live oak groves and cypress-lined creeks, and to the gritty pin-dot towns built largely of native stone. Here you'll find a delicious tension between rural and refined. Inns and restaurants are bringing a clever touch to Lone Star hospitality and mythology, and with the vineyards and boutique farms (lavender, olives), some people make comparisons to Napa Valley or even Provence. But those assessments ignore something fundamental: the Hill Country—being Texas at its finest—is like nowhere else in the world.
—BY JEANNIE RALSTON

FRIDAY

1 *Water Music* 3 p.m.

For a dramatic Hill Country landscape, many visitors go to Enchanted Rock, an enormous meatloaf-shaped piece of granite outside of the central town of Fredericksburg. **Pedernales Falls State Park** (2585 Park Road 6026, Johnson City; 830-868-7304; tpwd.state.tx.us/state-parks/pedernales-falls), just east of Johnson City, is less known but equally spectacular. Cutting through a shallow canyon here, the Pedernales River tumbles down a series of limestone shelves, with the water collecting in turquoise pools among giant boulders. The soundtrack—the rumble of cascading water—is just as exhilarating as the view.

2 *The Meat Master* 7 p.m.

At **Cooper's Old Time Pit Bar-B-Que** (604 West Young Street, Llano; 325-247-5713; coopersbbqllano.com; $$), one of the premier barbecue joints in Texas, let your fingers do the ordering. Stop at one of the pickup-bed-size grills on the front patio and point at your meat of choice: mesquite-smoked brisket, cabrito, prime rib, pork ribs, sausage—or all of the above. Inside, dig in at picnic tables surrounded by mounted deer heads—another reminder you're in serious carnivore country.

3 *Raise a Glass* 10 p.m.

The best Hill Country night life is in Fredericksburg, and the choicest spot is **Lincoln Street Wine Market** (111 South Lincoln Street, Fredericksburg; 830-997-8463; lincolnst.com), which maintains a Texas-big selection of 300-plus types of wine. The atmosphere is pleasantly unpretentious, every wine is available by the glass, and on weekends there's live music on the patio.

SATURDAY

4 *Guten Morgen* 9 a.m.

On top of the strong Mexican influence that's usual in Texas, the Hill Country has a German overlay, thanks to immigrants who arrived starting in the 1830s. Get a taste of this heritage at the **Old German Bakery and Restaurant** (225 West Main Street, Fredericksburg; 830-997-9084; oldgermanbakeryandrestaurant.com; $). For breakfast, try crepelike German pancakes, potato pancakes, or apple strudel.

5 *Presidential Treatment* 10 a.m.

History buffs will love the superbly packaged **National Museum of the Pacific War**

OPPOSITE Tarry in Luckenbach for good Texas music.

BELOW Cooper's Old Time Pit Bar-B-Que in Llano.

(pacificwarmuseum.org) in downtown Fredericksburg, but to immerse yourself in the specific history and beauty of this part of Texas, head to the **LBJ Ranch** at Lyndon B. Johnson National Historical Park (199 State Park Road 52, Stonewall; 830-868-7128; nps.gov/lyjo), off Highway 290 in Stonewall. The 36th president spent about 25 percent of his term at what was called the Texas White House, and it's easy to see why. Your driving permit (available at the state park adjacent to the national park) comes with a CD that describes what you're seeing as you meander around the 674 acres: Johnson's reconstructed birthplace, the one-room school where he learned to read, and his grave in the family cemetery. After Lady Bird Johnson's death in 2007, the National Park Service opened part of the family home, where you'll still find traces of Johnson's power among the late-'60s furnishings, like the presidential seal on the big man's chair.

6 *Blanco Boffo* Noon

The geographic hub of Blanco — a town still geared more to working ranchers than to tourists — is the imposing 127-year-old stone courthouse, which appeared in the Coen brothers' remake of *True Grit.* But the social hub is the **Redbud Cafe** (410 Fourth Street, Blanco; 830-833-0202; redbud-cafe.com; $), on the main square, where you can order everything from fat burgers to portobello sandwiches to Middle Eastern salads. Try one of the eight beers on tap from the Blanco-based Real Ale Brewing Company. On the wall is a chart left over from the building's many years as a hardware store that recorded monthly rainfall levels from 1900 to 1999. Adjoining the restaurant is **Brieger Pottery**, which sells hefty but graceful stoneware crafted by the Redbud's owners, Jan and Jon Brieger.

7 *Strike Nine* 1 p.m.

The **Blanco Bowling Club Cafe** (310 Fourth Street; 830-833-4416; blancobowlingclub.com) is one of the few places in the Hill Country where German nine-pin bowling is still played. By advance appointment with the bartender, you can try your skill on lanes that are throwbacks to pre-automated times (the pinsetter is usually a local teenager). Follow your game with another treat: the cafe's pies with meringue piled high like airy volcanoes.

8 *Wine Time* 4 p.m.

These days wineries are almost as common in the Hill Country as those ranch windmills that look like tall tin daisies. You can't go to them all — and still expect to operate a car — so head to the two best. The wood-and-stone tasting room at **Becker Vineyards** (464 Becker Farms Road, Stonewall; 830-644-2681; beckervineyards.com) is surrounded by 46 acres of grapes and lavender. **Grape Creek Vineyards** (10587 East U.S. Highway 290, Fredericksburg; 830-644-2710; grapecreek.com) echoes Tuscany with stucco and stone buildings capped by red-tile roofs.

9 *Top of the Hill* 7 p.m.

Rose Hill Manor (2614 Upper Albert Road, Stonewall; 830-644-2247; rose-hill.com; $$$$), a Georgian-style mansion that is more Deep South than Deep in the Heart of Texas, sits on a rise with expansive views over hayfields in the Pedernales River Valley. It also occupies another lofty position: it's the top spot around for an extravagant meal. The four-course menu changes weekly, but always features stand-out dishes like an arugula, oyster mushroom, and candied pecan salad; a creamy potato soup with braised pork bellies; pan-roasted sea bass with soba noodles; and low-country mud pie.

10 *Willie Sang Here* 10 p.m.

Luckenbach, Texas (412 Luckenbach Town Loop, Fredericksburg; luckenbachtexas.com), isn't just the title of the Waylon Jennings and Willie Nelson anti-stress, anti-materialism anthem. It's a real place off Farm to Market Road 1376 — a few old buildings including a general store and a dance hall in a clearing among the trees. If you stay a while — which you should since you'll hear a lot of good Texas music — you'll be glad that the only glitz comes from the party lights strung around

the dance hall. After a night here two-stepping across the worn wood floor, you'll feel you've hit on something genuine that can only be found in Texas, and you will be right.

SUNDAY

11 *No Postman Here* 10 a.m.

At first glance you might mistake the **Welfare Cafe** (223 Waring Welfare Road, Welfare; 830-537-3700; welfaretexas.com/welfare-cafe; $$$) for a derelict building. But inside this old former post office and general store is one of the region's best restaurants. Search the brunch menu for the Welfare Benedict (with gulf shrimp and spicy hollandaise) or an omelet. Fortified, drive on to **Comfort,** another town with a reassuring abstract noun for a name. Its historic district is packed with buildings from the 1800s, many of them designed by the architect Alfred Giles. Wander through the shops, and finish with a prickly pear cactus drink (nonalcoholic) at **Comfort Pizza** (802 High Street; 830-995-5959), a renovated stone filling station that bears a word across its awning that should sum up how you'll feel at this point: "Comfortable."

OPPOSITE The beauty of the Hill Country lures Texans out of their cities, especially Dallas and San Antonio, for trips amid green hills and quiet creeks.

ABOVE Quintessential Texas: trying out a seat atop a longhorn. Luckenbach is a real place, not just the title of a Waylon Jennings and Willie Nelson song.

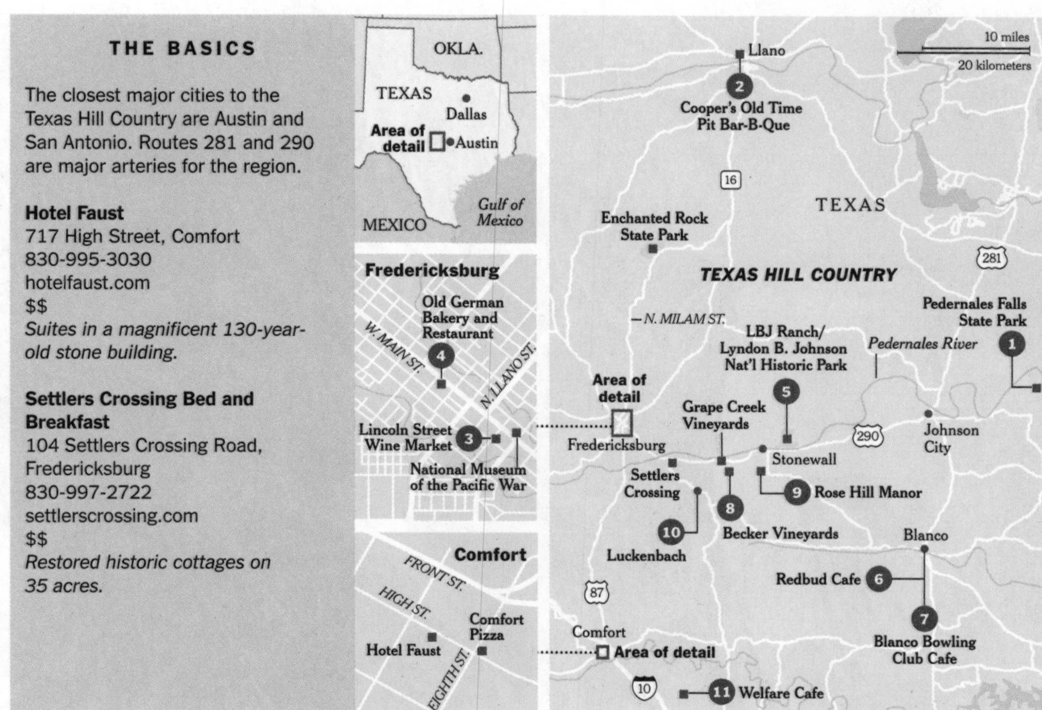

THE BASICS

The closest major cities to the Texas Hill Country are Austin and San Antonio. Routes 281 and 290 are major arteries for the region.

Hotel Faust
717 High Street, Comfort
830-995-3030
hotelfaust.com
$$
Suites in a magnificent 130-year-old stone building.

Settlers Crossing Bed and Breakfast
104 Settlers Crossing Road, Fredericksburg
830-997-2722
settlerscrossing.com
$$
Restored historic cottages on 35 acres.

Austin

The unofficial motto of Austin, Texas, "Keep Austin Weird," blares from bumper stickers on BMWs and jalopies alike, on T-shirts worn by joggers along Lady Bird Lake, and in the windows of locally owned, chain-defying shops and restaurants. A college town known for its liberal leanings and rich music scene, Austin asserts its independent spirit in a largely conservative state. It clings to its tolerance of eccentricity in the face of rapid development including high-tech flagships and fleets of new high-rise condos downtown. And while its openhearted citizens, with their colorful bungalows and tattoos, continue to do their part, it has little to fear from encroachment of the staid and ordinary. As one local put it: "As long as Austinites keep decorating their bodies and cars, we're going to be fine." — BY JAIME GROSS

FRIDAY

1 *Dress the Part* 3 p.m.

If you forgot to pack your Western wear, make a beeline for **Heritage Boot** (1200 South Congress Avenue; 512-326-8577; heritageboot.com), where Jerome Ryan and his team of "boot elves" fashion fanciful boots out of exotic leathers like bull shark and caiman, using vintage 1930s to '60s patterns. With colorful stitching, hand-tooling, and puffy, butterfly-shaped inlays, they are instant collectors' items—and priced accordingly, from a few hundred dollars to around $2,000.

2 *Saucy Platters* 5 p.m.

Barbecue is a local sport, and there are a lot of competing choices. For a classic pit experience —meaning you can smell the smoke and sauce as soon as you pull into the state-fair-size parking lot—drive 25 miles southwest to the **Salt Lick** (18300 Farm to Market Road 1826, Driftwood; 512-858-4959; saltlickbbq.com; $$), settle in at a communal picnic table, and order the all-you-can-eat platter, piled high with brisket, ribs, and sausage. If you prefer to stay in downtown Austin, check out **Lambert's Downtown Barbecue** (401 West Second Street; 512-494-1500; lambertsaustin.com; $$). Carved out of a brick-walled general store that dates from 1873, it has raised the bar (and provoked outrage among purists) with its newfangled "fancy barbecue"—think brown-sugar-and-coffee-rubbed brisket and maple-and-coriander-encrusted pork ribs.

3 *Fine Home for Fine Arts* 8 p.m.

Just off the south shore of Lady Bird Lake (named for Lady Bird Johnson, the former first lady) is the **Long Center for the Performing Arts** (701 West Riverside Drive; 512-474-5664; thelongcenter.org), which has one of the largest, most acoustically tuned stages in Texas. It's home to the Austin Symphony, Austin Lyric Opera, and Ballet Austin. There's also a smaller theater spotlighting local musicians, improv troupes, and theater companies. Even if you don't attend a performance, it is worth stopping by for a glimpse of the glittering skyline views from the building's front terrace.

SATURDAY

4 *Hot and Cold* 9 a.m.

Ease into the morning on the shaded porch at **Jo's Hot Coffee and Good Food** (1300 South Congress; 512-444-3800; joscoffee.com; $). Try a migas taco (eggs, cheese, peppers, and onions) accompanied by an Iced Turbo, proof that not all of the coffee is hot.

5 *Bicycle Friendly* 10 a.m.

Explore the city at a leisurely pace by renting a bicycle from **Mellow Johnny's Bike Shop** (400

OPPOSITE Cycling the Veloway in bluebonnet season.

BELOW Get your custom cowboy boots, crafted in traditional patterns, at Heritage Boot.

Nueces Street; 512-473-0222; mellowjohnnys.com). In addition to selling and renting bikes, the shop stocks accessories like wicker baskets, messenger bags, and colorful racing jerseys. If you ask, staff members will chart an interesting route along Austin's miles of urban bike trails. A favorite is the **Veloway** (veloway.com), where cyclists roll past blooming bluebonnets in the spring.

6 *Munch and Browse* 2 p.m.

Some of Austin's best lunch food is dished out of Airstreams and food trucks by both amateur and professional chefs. You can look for a list on austinfoodcarts.com, or just be on the lookout as you explore South Congress, an appealing neighborhood for shopping or just window shopping. Find rare and collectible vinyl, from 99 cents to $1,000, at **Friends of Sound** (1704 South Congress Avenue; 512-447-1000; friendsofsound.com), down an alley off the main drag. Quirky souvenirs, like a duck decoy or an antique beaver top hat, abound at **Uncommon Objects** (1512 South Congress Avenue; 512-442-4000; uncommonobjects.com), a sprawling emporium with a flea market aesthetic and a giant pink jackalope out front.

7 *Bats!* 7:30 p.m.

From early spring through late fall, the **Congress Avenue Bridge** hosts a Halloween-worthy spectacle: at dusk, more than a million Mexican free-tailed bats pour out from under the bridge and head east to scavenge for insects (austincityguide.com/content/congress-bridge-bats-austin.asp). The best spot for viewing the exodus is from the park at the southeastern end of the bridge, so you can see their flitting forms backlit by the glowing sky. To hear an estimate of the bats' flight time on a particular evening, dial 512-327-9721, an informational line maintained by Bat Conservation International (batcon.org).

8 *Seasoned With Humor* 8:30 p.m.

Before becoming a winner on Bravo's *Top Chef* and vaulting to international fame, Paul Qui was already a culinary sensation in Austin as an executive chef at two contemporary Japanese sister restaurants, Uchi and Uchiko. In 2013, when he opened his own restaurant, **Qui** (1600 East 6th Street; 512-436-9626; quiaustin.com; $$), Austinites' devotion to his playful and creative cuisine followed him. The menu changes daily, but expect it to be entertaining reading, with dishes like Rabbit 7 Ways, Filipino Ceviche, and Fish in a Bag (albacore fillet, peanut curry, bouquet garni). Dessert might be Avocado Qui Lime Pie or a Cheddar cheese ice cream sandwich.

9 *Performance Anxiety* 10 p.m.

The sheer quantity and variety of music in Austin on any given night can be daunting. Step One is to consult Internet listings (ask at your hotel for advice on the best local music Web site currently in operation), but two spots that reliably deliver a good time are the **Broken Spoke**, an old-time honky-tonk dance hall (3201 South Lamar Boulevard; 512-442-6189; brokenspokeaustintx.com), and the retro red-walled **Continental Club** (1315 South Congress Avenue; 512-441-2444; continentalclub.com), which dates from 1957 and has roots, blues, rockabilly, and country music.

ABOVE Austin is a music town with statuary to match. The blues guitarist Stevie Ray Vaughan stands at Lady Bird Lake.

RIGHT Saturday night at the Broken Spoke.

SUNDAY

10 *Take a Dip* 10 a.m.

Wake up with a bracing swim in the natural, spring-fed **Barton Springs Pool** (2101 Barton Springs Road; 512-476-9044; austintexas.gov/department/barton-springs-pool), a three-acre dammed pool that has a water temperature of about 70 degrees year-round. There's sunbathing (sometimes topless) on the grassy slopes, a springy diving board, and century-old pecan trees lining the banks. Afterward, park yourself on the patio at **Perla's Seafood & Oyster Bar** (1400 South Congress Avenue; 512-291-7300; perlasaustin.com; $$) for a decadent lobster omelet and an oyster shooter spiked with rum and honeydew.

11 *Wildflower Country* 1 p.m.

Texas is proud of the masses of wildflowers, and you can find out why at the **Lady Bird Johnson Wildflower Preserve** (4801 La Crosse Avenue, Austin; 512-232-0100; wildflower.org), a University of Texas research center that is also a public botanical garden and spa. If you're curious about Lady Bird and her husband, check out the **Lyndon Baines Johnson Library and Museum** (2313 Red River Street; 512-721-0200; lbjlibrary.org). The permanent exhibition includes a multimedia-enhanced parallel journey through President Johnson's life, including a display on his sudden elevation to the presidency after the assassination of John F. Kennedy and an animatronic version of Johnson telling jokes.

THE BASICS

Bicycles are handy in the city, but to venture very far you will need a car.

Kimber Modern Boutique Hotel
110 The Circle
512-912-1046
kimbermodern.com
$$$
Stylish and eye-catching; winner of a design award from Texas Society of Architects.

The Driskill
604 Brazos Street
512-474-5911
driskillhotel.com
$$$
The grande dame of Austin hotels; opulent lobby and attractively furnished rooms.

Austin Motel
1220 South Congress
512-441-1157
austinmotel.com
$$
Keeps the hip hotel scene on South Congress Avenue real, with kitschy rooms and friendly service.

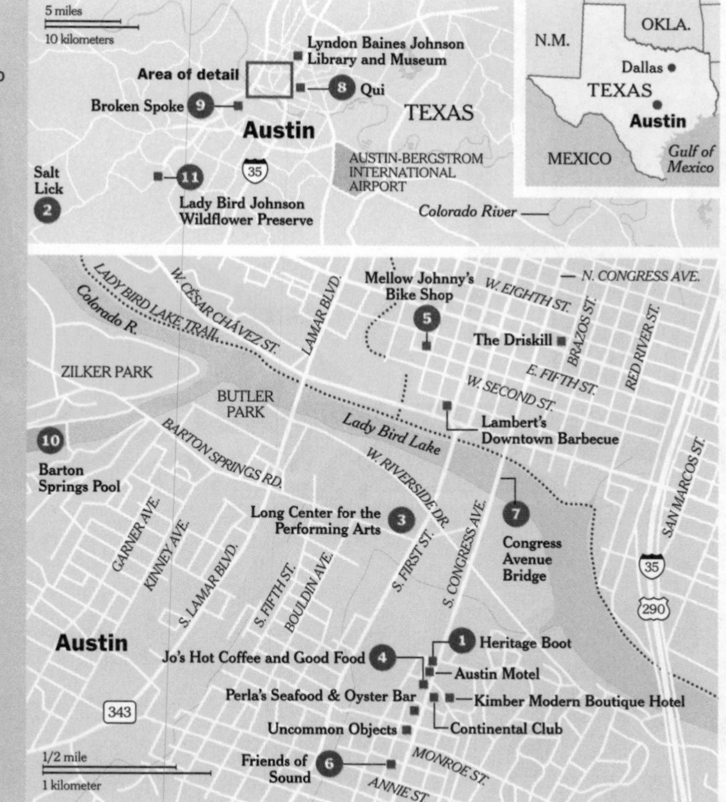

Houston

A snarl of superhighways and skyscrapers, Houston is easily dismissed as a corporate campus — home to Fortune 500 giants like Halliburton and Waste Management and formerly to a company known as Enron. Its generic towers sprawl to the horizon. The Johnson Space Center, where the world's eyes were fixed as NASA directed the moon landing from its control center, is 25 miles south of downtown. But this Texas megalopolis has also been inching back to its urban core. Cool art galleries have sprung up in once blighted neighborhoods. Midcentury modern buildings have been saved and restored. And former factories have been turned into buzzing restaurants and bars.
— BY DENNY LEE

FRIDAY

1 *Park It Downtown* 5:30 p.m.

Houston may be a sea of office towers, but this subtropical city is also surprisingly green. Hundreds of parks carpet the city, and one of the newest, a 12-acre park called **Discovery Green** (discoverygreen.com), is quickly becoming the heart of the city's still sleepy downtown. Opened in 2008, the park serves as a true public space; elderly couples stroll around the artificial lake as toddlers roll down grassy knolls. For sunset cocktails, follow the area's young professionals to the **Grove** (1611 Lamar Street; 713-337-7321; thegrovehouston.com), a modern restaurant inside the park, which offers treehouse-like views of the skyline.

2 *Gulf of Tex-Mex* 8 p.m.

The city's young chefs are working overtime to step out of the shadow of Texas barbecue. Among the most celebrated is Bryan Caswell, the chef and owner of **Reef** (2600 Travis Street; 713-526-8282; reefhouston.com; $$), a seafood restaurant with a Southern twist. Housed in a former car dealership with soaring windows and ceilings, the restaurant creates a dramatic space for winning dishes like roasted grouper with corn pudding and grilled peach. The dining room hums with an eclectic crowd — men in white suits eating ceviche, couples on dates, well- dressed families celebrating birthdays.

3 *Slice of Austin* 10 p.m.

Sports bars and mega-clubs fuel much of the city's night life, but a clutch of down-to-earth bars can be found along the tree-lined streets of Montrose. **Poison Girl** (1641 Westheimer Road; 713-527-9929) has pinball machines, a long shelf of whiskeys, and a dirt-packed backyard jammed with 20-somethings in vintage Wranglers and Keds. Down the street is **Anvil Bar and Refuge** (1424 Westheimer Road; 713-523-1622; anvilhouston.com), which styles itself as a classic cocktail bar, though it can feel like a meat market on weekends. A handful of gay bars are also nearby, including the oldie but still rowdy **611 Hyde Park Pub** (611 Hyde Park Boulevard; 713-526-7070).

SATURDAY

4 *Drilling for Art* 11 a.m.

With all those petrodollars sloshing around, it's no surprise that contemporary art has an eager benefactor in Houston. The grande dame is still the **Menil Collection** (1515 Sul Ross Street; 713-525-9400; menil.org), opened in 1987 to house the collection of Dominique de Menil, an heiress to an oil-equipment fortune. Blue-chip galleries include the **Devin**

OPPOSITE The Chapel of St. Basil, designed by Philip Johnson, is part of Houston's remarkable collection of midcentury modern architecture.

RIGHT A downtown view from the Grove restaurant at Discovery Green, one in Houston's profusion of parks.

Borden Hiram Butler Gallery (4520 Blossom Street; 713-863-7097; dbhbg.com) and the **Sicardi Gallery** (1506 West Alabama Street; 713-529-1313; sicardi.com). Scrappy artists, meanwhile, have carved out studios in downtown warehouses. Some of their work can be seen at the **Station Museum** (1502 Alabama Street; 713-529-6900; stationmuseum.com), which displays younger artists inside a big metal shed.

5 *Global Grills* 1:30 p.m.

While the city's sizable Vietnamese community is now scattered, traces of Little Saigon still remain in Midtown, a mixed-use neighborhood dotted with banh mi joints. A retro-favorite is **Cali Sandwich** (3030 Travis Street; 713-520-0710; $), a ho-hum cafeteria with 1970s-style vertical blinds and prices to match: the freshly made sandwiches include barbecue pork. If you're hankering for genuine Texas BBQ, drive north to **Pizzitola's Bar-B-Cue** (1703 Shepherd Drive; 713-227-2283; pizzitolas.com; $). It may not be as packed as the several outposts of Goode's Houston barbecue empire, but Pizzitola's is the real deal, judging by the wood pits that have been charring ribs out back for 70-plus years.

6 *Pottery to Boots* 3 p.m.

Malls rule in Houston—the biggest, the Galleria, offers 2.4 million square feet of brand names. Off-brand shopping requires a bit more driving. For one-of-a-kind home furnishings, head to **Found** (3433 West Alabama Street; 713-522-9191; foundforthehome.com), which takes old industrial objects like hay feeders and turns them into architectural objets. **Sloan/Hall** (2620 Westheimer Road; 713-942-0202; sloanhall.com) carries an odd array of art books, bath products, and pottery—some by Texas artisans. **Tejas Custom Boots** (208 Westheimer Road; 713-524-9860; tejascustomboots.com) is the place to go for real Texas footwear.

7 *Southwestern Redux* 7:30 p.m.

Robert Del Grande is considered culinary royalty here, credited with pioneering Southwestern cuisine in the 1980s. His **RDG + Bar Annie** (1800 Post Oak Boulevard; 713-840-1111; rdgbarannie.com; $$-$$$) is a multiplex of a restaurant with bars, lounges, and dining rooms that attracts a glamorous crowd. The menu is bold and brash, with dishes like lobster meatballs with a rémoulade sauce and grilled rib-eye steak with a smoked Cheddar sauce. **Underbelly** (1100 Westheimer Road; 713-528-9800; underbellyhouston.com; $$$-$$$$), a much-praised newer spot, describes its raison d'être as "telling the story of Houston food." Small plates accomplish this mission by reflecting the city's diversity: Korean braised goat with dumplings; Vietnamese-style pork meatballs; cornmeal-crusted chicken livers with raw vegetables in spicy Thousand Island dressing.

ABOVE Brick-and-stone tradition at Rice University.

LEFT Sloan/Hall, a clever independent store on Westheimer Road.

8 *Wine and Ice* 10 p.m.

A party corridor has formed along Washington Avenue. Some of the drinking establishments are dive bars with the feel of the Texas "ice house" —informal places traditionally known for specializing in cold beer. A more upscale spot is **Max's Wine Dive** (4720 Washington Avenue; 713-880-8737; maxswinedive.com), which has a long, inexpensive wine list.

SUNDAY

9 *Bottomless Mimosas* 10 a.m.

A cafe tucked inside a nursery (it's called Thompson + Hanson) may sound precious, but so what? **Tiny Boxwood's** (3614 West Alabama Street; 713-622-4224; tinyboxwoods.com; $$) does a fantastic Sunday brunch. Situated close to the posh River Oaks neighborhood, the sun-washed dining room and vine-covered patio draw a handsome and self-assured crowd that mingles easily around a communal table. Chalkboard specials include leafy salads and a delicious breakfast pizza made with pancetta, goat cheese, and an egg, baked sunny side up in a wood oven. Pick up a cactus on the way out.

10 *Modernist Drive-By* Noon

Despite Houston's lack of zoning (or maybe because of it), the city has a remarkable collection of midcentury modern homes and office towers —some well maintained, others verging on collapse.

ABOVE For one-of-a-kind home furnishings, head to Found, which turns old industrial objects into home décor items.

BELOW The Brochstein Pavilion at Rice University.

Landmarks include the gridlike campus for the University of St. Thomas, designed by Philip Johnson. But many more are unknown, like the eerily abandoned **Central Square** building in downtown (2100 Travis Street) or the brawny **Willowick** tower, now condos, in River Oaks (2200 Willowick Road). Piece together your own architectural tour with **Houston Mod** (houstonmod.org), a preservation group that maintains a resourceful Web site with Google maps and photos.

ABOVE Cooling off at the Discovery Green park.

OPPOSITE Rice University balances its academic rigor with a richly decorated main campus.

11 *Glass Houses* 2 p.m.

The skyline goes up, up, up every year. But notable architecture also takes place near the ground. The campus at **Rice University**—a neo-Byzantine maze of rose-hued brick and cloisters—got a new glass heart in 2008 when the **Brochstein Pavilion** (dining.rice.edu/brochsteinpavilion/) opened near the central quad. A Kubrick-esque box with floor-to-ceiling windows, it houses a cafe and media lounge, and has a fine-mesh trellis that extends like a mathematical plane in space. The structure is only one story, but it feels much taller—proof that not everything in Houston has to be big.

THE BASICS

Fly in and rent a car.

Hotel Zaza Houston
5701 Main Street
713-526-1991
hotelzazahouston.com
$$
Playful design and polished service in the lively Museum District.

Aloft Houston by the Galleria
5415 Westheimer Road
713-622-7010
alofthouston.com
$$
New with a pool and gym, in the Uptown district.

Hotel Icon
220 Main Street
713-224-4266
hotelicon.com
$$
A mix of boutique and classic hotel style.

2002
NANCY LEE BASS
COWGIRL HALL
NATIONAL
AND HALL OF FAME

Fort Worth

How much art can you look at in one weekend? Of all American cities that might pose this dilemma, Fort Worth, Texas, traditionally a cow town overshadowed by neighboring Dallas, might be the least expected. But with oil-wealthy patrons eager to build its cultural endowment with sought-after artworks and interesting contemporary architecture to hold them, Fort Worth has become a place to go for art immersion. If you fear museum fatigue, take heart. The city's public art galleries don't overwhelm; they're on a uniformly intimate scale. And there's enough cowboy spirit left in town to give you a break from high culture whenever you want to take one. — BY RICHARD B. WOODWARD

FRIDAY

1 *Sundance* 5 p.m.

Fort Worth is dominated by a few families, none mightier than the billionaire Bass clan, famous for giving generously to George W. Bush's campaigns and for revitalizing the north end of the city. See some of their handiwork in **Sundance Square** (sundancesquare.com). Starting with two square blocks they bought in 1978, it has expanded to more than 35 square blocks dominated by a pair of Brutalist skyscrapers designed by Paul Rudolph in the '70s and now holding the headquarters of the Bass businesses. David Schwarz, the family's favorite architect, has contributed buildings in the Texas Deco style (blending Art Deco with state symbols like the star), including Bass Performance Hall, a home to opera, symphony, touring Broadway shows, and the quadrennial piano competition begun by and named after a local hero, Van Cliburn.

2 *Romance of the West* 6 p.m.

At the **Sid Richardson Museum** in Sundance Square (309 Main Street; 817-332-6554; sidrichardsonmuseum.org), take your time looking at the 38 oil paintings by Frederic Remington and Charles Russell. The museum displays only a tiny sample of the romantic taste of Sid Richardson, a millionaire oilman and Bass relative who collected work on Indian and cowboy themes. If you'd like a different take on Western tradition, take a 10-minute drive to the **National Cowgirl Museum and Hall of Fame** (1720 Gendy Street; 817-336-4475; cowgirl.net), which celebrates Western women, from ranchers to celebrity pop stars.

3 *Saloon Chef* 7 p.m.

Chef Tim Love's **Lonesome Dove Western Bistro** (2406 North Main Street; 817-740-8810; lonesomedovebistro.com; $$$), near Fort Worth's traditional economic heart, the Stockyards, is a very modern pairing of *Iron Chef* cooking and cowboy chic. The décor is reminiscent of an Old West saloon, with a long bar and a tin ceiling, and the staff may be wearing cowboy hats. It's hard to say what the cattle drivers who used to come through Fort Worth would make of the cuisine, including dishes like a chili-rubbed pork chop with Yukon Gold-Swiss Chard Gratin and crispy onions, or beef tenderloin stuffed with garlic and accompanied by plaid hash and a Syrah demi-glace.

SATURDAY

4 *Breakfast for All* 9 a.m.

Don't be dismayed if there's a long line at the **Paris Coffee Shop** (704 West Magnolia Avenue; 817-335-2041; pariscoffeeshop.net; $). It seats more than 100, so tables turn over quickly. A Fort Worth institution since the Depression era, it seems to cater to everyone in town. Who could resist a place that offers green tea as well as cheese grits and has ads on the menu for everything from music lessons to bail bondsmen?

OPPOSITE *High Desert Princess*, by Mehl Lawson, outside the National Cowgirl Museum and Hall of Fame.

RIGHT Breakfast at the Paris Coffee Shop.

5 *Art of America* 10 a.m.

This is your day for serious art appreciation in the **Cultural District**, about five miles west of Sundance. Start at the **Amon Carter Museum of American Art** (3501 Camp Bowie Boulevard; 817-738-1933; cartermuseum.org). Carter, who made his fortune in newspapers and radio, was a Fort Worth booster who hated Dallas so much he reportedly carried his lunch when forced to visit, to keep from spending money there. His bequest financed what is now one of the leading collections of American art in the country, especially strong in Western paintings, 19th-century photographs, and Remington sculptures. The museum's original 1961 building by Philip Johnson was expanded in the late '90s.

6 *Art and Water* Noon

The **Modern Art Museum of Fort Worth** (3200 Darnell Street; 817-738-9215; themodern.org) has been an island of tranquility since it opened a new building in 2002. The architect, Tadao Ando, oriented the building around a shallow pool so that several of the wings extend outward and seem to float on the water. Have brunch at its **Café Modern** (817-840-2157; themodern.org/cafe; $$), which attempts to serve dishes worthy of the setting—consider the Moroccan chicken salad or mushroom goat cheese crepes. Then explore the galleries, arrayed with a select group of postwar and contemporary works—usual suspects like Jackson Pollock and Dan Flavin, as well as rarities in American museums, like the German Minimalist sculptor Ulrich Rückriem. Whether in the sunlit bays beside the water, where you may find a lead floor piece by Carl Andre, or in a cul-de-sac where a wooden ladder-like sculpture by Martin Puryear reaches between floors, the building is still very much the star.

7 *Art and Light* 3 p.m.

The **Kimbell Art Museum** (3333 Camp Bowie Boulevard; 817-332-8451; kimbellart.org) provides an unrivaled museum experience combining first-rate architecture and first-rate art. From the street, the 1972 building, designed by Louis I. Kahn, offers a plain travertine exterior that will not prepare you for the

soaring harmonies inside. To step into the lobby is to enter a Romanesque church of a museum. Long slits and diffusing louvers in the barrel-vaulted ceiling allow the light to both cut spaces dramatically and softly spill over them. The collections, from all periods and places, are noteworthy for both aesthetic quality and historical depth. A pre-Angkor Cambodian statue is less a representative object than a stunningly beautiful one. European paintings — with masterpieces by Bellini, Mantegna, Caravaggio, Velázquez, de la Tour, Goya, Cézanne — are mostly presented without glass.

8 *Steak and Wine* 7 p.m.

You're not finished yet with cowboy-inspired cooking. **Reata** (310 Houston Street; 817-336-1009; reata.net; $$$) is Texas big, spread over several floors of an old building in the heart of Sundance Square. The fourth-floor bar has a panoramic skyline view. Reata's entrees run to steaks and chops, its wine list is extensive, and its desserts are tempting and calorie-laden.

9 *Hang With the Herd* 9 p.m.

Billy Bob's Texas (2520 Rodeo Plaza; 817-624-7117; billybobstexas.com), housed in a former cattle barn and touted as the world's largest honky-tonk, should be visited at least once, and perhaps only once. Walk around and select your entertainment option: play pool or the 25-cent slot machines, watch live bull riding in a ring or sports on TV, eat barbecue or popcorn, shop for cowboy hats, try your luck at outmoded carnival games, drink at any of 32 bars, or dance and listen to country music on the two musical stages. A few hours at Billy Bob's may not measure up to an afternoon viewing Fort Worth's art collections. But as you merge with the herd (capacity is more

OPPOSITE ABOVE AND ABOVE The Modern Art Museum and the Kimbell Art Museum are islands of tranquility that invite contemplation of both the architecture and the artworks.

OPPOSITE BELOW AND BELOW Pool playing and bull riding at Billy Bob's, an outsize honky-tonk in a former cattle barn. It can entertain 6,000 Texans at a time.

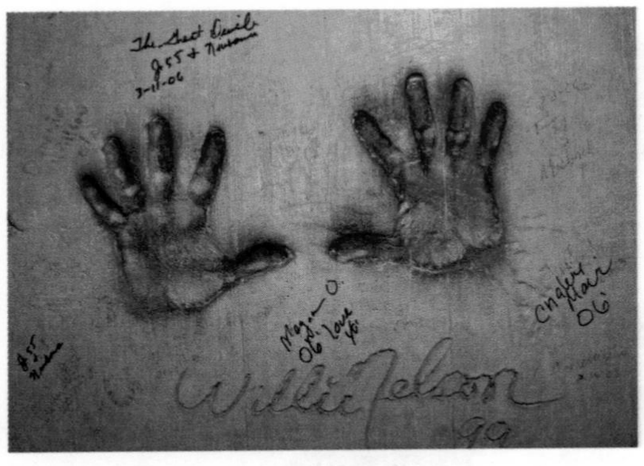

than 6,000), sipping bourbon and watching the gliding two-steppers on the dance floor, it feels like a much more authentic and less imported experience —much more like Texas.

SUNDAY

10 *Texans Also Garden* 11 a.m.

Spend some peaceful hours at the **Fort Worth Botanic Garden** (3220 Botanic Garden Boulevard; 817-392-5510; fwbg.org), home to more than 2,500 species of native and exotic plants that flourish in its 23 specialty gardens. A favorite, the Japanese Garden, is a treat for the senses with koi-filled pools, stonework, and waterfalls. If it's springtime, expect flowering trees and migrating birds—perhaps, if you're lucky, a tree full of cedar waxwings on their way north.

ABOVE Country musicians' handprints on the walls at Billy Bob's are Fort Worth's answer to movie stars' footprints in concrete in Hollywood. These were made by Willie Nelson.

OPPOSITE Texas exuberance on the dance floor.

THE BASICS

Fly into Dallas/Fort Worth International Airport or drive from Dallas. Get around by car.

Renaissance Worthington
200 Main Street
817-870-1000
marriott.com
$$$
In Sundance Square, with 474 rooms and 30 suites at a variety of prices.

The Ashton
610 Main Street
817-332-0100
theashtonhotel.com
$$
Attractive boutique hotel with 39 rooms.

Omni Fort Worth
1300 Houston Street
817-535-6664
omnihotels.com
$$$
Skyline views and a rooftop garden.

Dallas

Dallas may not be a world-class city, but it's pulling out all the stops to get there. Rich with oil money, it has pumped millions of dollars into civic projects, including the AT&T Performing Arts Center, a recent addition to the 68-acre Arts District. Meanwhile, glamorous subterranean bars and edgy Asian restaurants are giving the city a cosmopolitan aura. But when it comes to entertainment, its No. 1 attraction is still the Cowboys, now in their new, $1.2 billion football stadium featuring one of the largest retractable roofs and one of the largest high-definition televisions in the world. — BY LUISITA LOPEZ TORREGROSA

FRIDAY

1 *Architecture Park* 3 p.m.

See what Dallas is happily showing off these days. Go on a walking tour of the **Dallas Arts District** (thedallasartsdistrict.org), a 19-block area straddling downtown office skyscrapers and uptown luxury hotels. A prime attraction of the district is the **AT&T Performing Arts Center** (2403 Flora Street; 214-954-9925; attpac.org), a four-venue complex for music, opera, theater, and dance in a parklike setting. A drum-shaped opera house was designed by Norman Foster and a cube-shaped theater is by Rem Koolhaas. To take it all in, find a bench at the **Nasher Sculpture Center** (2001 Flora Street; 214-242-5100; nashersculpturecenter.org), a museum designed by Renzo Piano with a lush garden that features works from a collection including Rodin, Henry Moore, and George Segal.

2 *Trend-Setter Cocktails* 7:30 p.m.

Size up the city's trend setters and assorted poseurs in their alligator boots and butter-soft tailored jackets at the **Rattlesnake Bar**, a plush lounge with mahogany-paneled walls and chocolate-brown leather sofas at the **Ritz-Carlton, Dallas** (2121 McKinney Avenue; 214-922-4848; ritzcarlton.com/dallas). Order the Dean's Margarita with organic agave nectar, nibble on spring rolls with achiote pulled pork, and watch heads turn whenever a posse of lanky blondes in skinny jeans and designer heels sidles up to the bar.

3 *Southwest Supreme* 8 p.m.

Not so long ago, Dallas was a culinary wasteland, save for its famous barbecue. But in recent years, celebrity chefs like Nobu Matsuhisa, Tom Colicchio, and Charlie Palmer have planted their flags here, joining a fresh crop of hometown talent. At the top is **Fearing's** (2121 McKinney Avenue; 214-922-4848; fearingsrestaurant.com; $$$$), a casual but chic restaurant in the Ritz-Carlton that serves imaginative Southwest-rooted cuisine. Opened in 2007, Fearing's gained national acclaim at the time: Zagat named it No. 1 in domestic hotel dining, and Frank Bruni, the restaurant critic for *The New York Times*, called it one of the country's top 10 new restaurants outside New York. Expect dishes like lobster coconut bisque and wood-grilled Australian lamb chops on pecorino polenta.

4 *Party High* 10:30 p.m.

There are still men's clubs, honky-tonks, and jukebox joints in Dallas, but the city's night life has gotten decidedly sleeker and flashier, with

OPPOSITE Vertigo can be a concern for swimmers at the Joule Hotel. Cantilevered out from the building, the rooftop pool juts out 10 stories above the sidewalk.

RIGHT Size up the city's trend setters and assorted poseurs in their alligator boots at the Rattlesnake Bar, a plush watering hole at the Ritz-Carlton.

velvet-roped discos and bottle-service lounges. If you want a stellar view of the stars and the city's bright lights, go to the rooftop bar of the **Joule** hotel (1530 Main Street; 214-748-1300; thejouledallas.com). It features bedlike sofas and cocoonlike chairs arrayed along a slender, cantilevered swimming pool that juts out 10 stories above the sidewalk. Or, for an even better view, go to **FiveSixty**, Wolfgang Puck's Asian-style restaurant in the glowing ball atop the 560-foot-high **Reunion Tower** (300 Reunion Boulevard; 214-741-5560; wolfgangpuck.com). The rotating bar, which serves a dozen kinds of sake, offers magnificent views of a skyline edged in colorful lights and the suburban sprawl beyond.

ABOVE A contemplative viewer takes in a sculpture at the Dallas Museum of Art. The city's rich cultural life reveals itself in museums and performing arts.

BELOW Forty Five Ten, the epitome of chic Dallas boutiques. The prices are shocking, but it's worth a visit.

SATURDAY

5 *Morning Glory* 10 a.m.

Need a breath of fresh air after a late night out? Head to the **Katy Trail** (entrance at Knox Street at Abbott Avenue; 214-303-1180; katytraildallas.org), a 3.5-mile greenway that winds through the city's wooded parks and urban neighborhoods. Built along old railroad tracks, the trail is a favorite of young and old, bikers and runners, stroller-pushing parents and dog walkers.

6 *Slower Food* Noon

Chicken-fried everything may be a staple in Texas, but in Dallas organic salads and other light fare are just as popular. A trendy spot is **Rise No. 1** (5360 West Lovers Lane; 214-366-9900; risesouffle.com; $$), a charming bistro with a grass-green facade that serves up wonderful soufflés — a slow-paced antidote to Dallas's manic drive-and-shop lifestyle. Try the truffle-infused mushroom soufflé with a glass of dry white.

7 *Retail Overload* 2 p.m.

Shopping is a sport here, and there are more stores than just Neiman Marcus. For slow-paced window shopping, stroll around **Inwood Village** (West Lovers Lane and Inwood Road; inwoodvillage.com), a landmark 1949 shopping center with an eclectic range of signature stores. Retail highlights include **Rich Hippie** (5350 West Lovers Lane, No. 127; 214-358-1968; richhippie.com) for retro and avant-garde clothing like a finely tooled pink leather jacket. But perhaps the chicest boutique is **Forty Five Ten** (4510 McKinney Avenue; 214-559-4510; fortyfiveten.com). The prices are shocking but it's worth a visit. One shopper's finds included a vintage trolley case by Globe-Trotter and an iron vase by the Texan artist Jan Barboglio.

8 *Mex-Mex* 8 p.m.

One of the most popular Dallas spots for original Mexican fare is **La Duni Latin Cafe** (4620 McKinney Avenue; 214-520-7300; laduni.com; $$), which offers terrific dishes like tacos de picanha (beef loin strips on tortillas). For Tex-Mex in a party atmosphere, with mariachi bands, hefty margaritas, and house-made tortillas, travel to East Dallas for **Mexico Lindo** (7515 East Grand Avenue; 214-319-9776; mexicolindodallas.com; $$).

9 *Night Moves* 10 p.m.

There are plenty of ways to close out the evening in Dallas. You could mingle with a well-dressed crowd and enjoy a classic cocktail and some jazz or sultry vocalizing at the urbane **Library Bar** in the Landmark Restaurant of the Warwick Melrose Hotel (3015 Oak Lawn Avenue; 214-521-5151; landmarkrestodallas.com). For indie bands, try **Dada Dallas** (2720 Elm Street; dadadallas.com), in

BELOW Dallas Cowboys Stadium, the focus of most of the city's energy on home-game Sundays.

the Deep Ellum neighborhhood. Or stay up late at **J.R.'s Bar & Grill** (3923 Cedar Springs Road; 214-528-1004; partyattheblock.com), a cavernous gay club with a scuffed dance floor, where nothing gets going before midnight.

ABOVE The Morton H. Meyerson Symphony Center in the 19-block Arts District.

OPPOSITE Fearing's, a chic, casual restaurant with imaginative Southwest-rooted cuisine. Celebrity chefs have planted their flags in Dallas, joining a fresh crop of hometown talent.

SUNDAY

10 *Sports Madness* 11:30 a.m.

If it's Sunday in Dallas, do as the locals do and hit a sports bar. There are dozens in town, if not hundreds, but a favorite is the **McKinney Avenue Tavern** (2822 McKinney Avenue; 214-969-1984; thematonline.com), affectionately nicknamed the Mat. There is a carved-wood bar with two dozen or so rickety tables fronting the 30-odd television screens that show nothing but sports, day and night. When the Cowboys play, the joint is bedlam. Rule No. 1: Go early, stay late.

THE BASICS

Fly into busy Dallas-Fort Worth Regional Airport.

Rent a car for exploring.

Ritz-Carlton, Dallas
2121 McKinney Avenue
214-922-0200
ritzcarlton.com/dallas
$$$$
Reliable luxury, a fine restaurant, and a spa.

The Joule
1530 Main Street
214-748-1300
thejouledallas.com
$$$$
Trendy spot with a jazzy basement nightclub, a Charlie Palmer restaurant, and a rooftop bar with a pool.

The Belmont
901 Fort Worth Avenue
214-393-2300
belmontdallas.com
$$
A moderate-priced alternative restored to bring back 1940s charm while providing modern amenities.

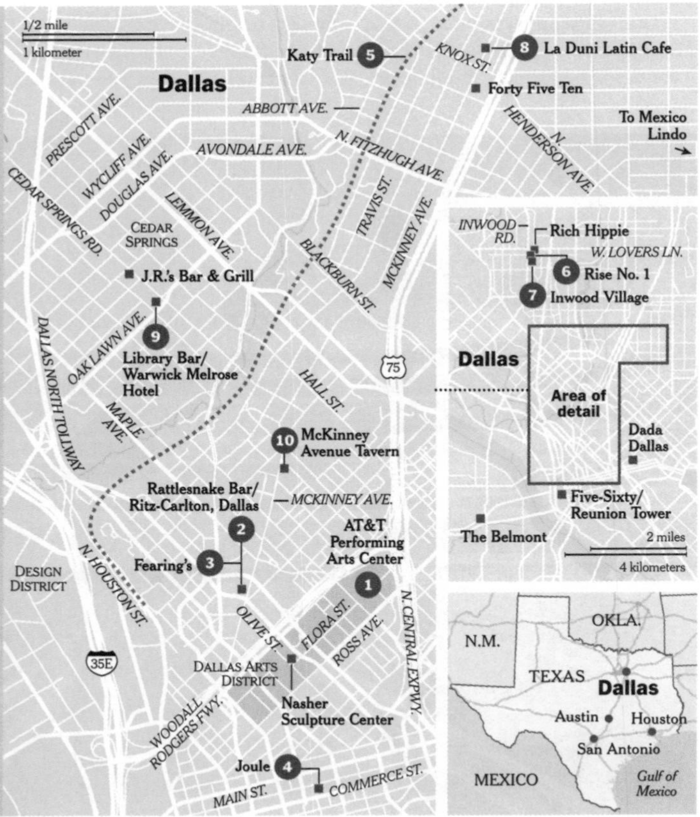

Victoria
694
the San Juan Islands
684
678
Northwes
Seattl
Homer
702
698
Juneau
the Oregon Coast
664
Kauai
730
HONOLULU
706
710
Kailua
NO
636
Berkeley
Silicon Valley
626
Molokai
714
Maui
720
598
Downtown
588
Malibu
594
Santa Monica
724
Hilo

688 VANCOUVER
WEST
COAST
SEATTLE
672
668 PORTLAND
e Mendocino Coast
Napa Valley
648
Marin
County
640
654
Sacramento
Lake
tahoe
660
630
SAN FRANCISCO
622
armel
BIG SUR
616
Palm Springs
612
Santa
602
Barbara
HOLLYWOOD
582 LOS ANGELES
608 San Diego

Fewest

Los Angeles

Angelenos like to tell visitors, "It's a great place to live but I wouldn't want to visit here." Granted, it's tough to decide what to see and do in a city that encompasses 470 square miles. Fortunately, there is always an under-the-radar restaurant, a funky theater, or a splashy store to discover. And you never have to leave the iconic landmarks behind. — BY LOUISE TUTELIAN

FRIDAY

1 *Stop and Shop* 4 p.m.

The hilly Los Feliz area, just northeast of Hollywood, is an old neighborhood reborn with a hip veneer. A walk along North Vermont Avenue turns up an intriguing trove of vintage clothes, handmade jewelry, antique textiles, books, and much more. **New High (M)Art** (1720 North Vermont Avenue; 323-638-0271; newhighmart.com), an industrial-style space filled with world music and the faint perfume of incense, stocks an eclectic mix. For sale one afternoon were a vintage French army camo jacket and a necklace made from hand-painted leather flags. **Skylight Books** (1818 North Vermont Avenue; 323-660-1175; skylightbooks.com) caters to the many artists, writers, musicians, and actors in the neighborhood — and anyone else who loves a carefully curated arts bookstore. Browse the stacks and you'll see a monograph on Richard Meier next to a tome on *Mad* magazine posters. And don't step on Franny, the resident cat.

2 *Friendly Fare* 6 p.m.

Little Dom's (2128 Hillhurst Avenue; 323-661-0055; littledoms.com; $$-$$$) is the best of homey and hip, a bar/bistro with an inventive menu. The fare is mostly Italian-American, but since the executive chef, Brandon Boudet, hails from New Orleans, there's a dash of the South as well. Pappardelle with house-made sausage? No problem. But Boudet also serves up a succulent fried oyster sandwich with hot sauce mayo, y'all.

3 *Bright Lights, Big City* 8 p.m.

Get the big picture at the **Griffith Park Observatory** (2800 East Observatory Avenue; 213-473-0800; griffithobservatory.org), with its view of the entire Los Angeles basin. Visitors line up for a peek into a massive Zeiss telescope with a 12-inch reflector that reveals celestial sights like the rings of Saturn. The Samuel Oschin Planetarium shows employ laser digital projection and state-of-the-art sound. A show about the brilliant aurora borealis — accompanied by Wagner's *Ride of the Valkyries* — is a cosmic experience.

4 *Alive and Swingin'* 10 p.m.

Featured in the movie *Swingers*, with Vince Vaughn and Jon Favreau, the **Dresden** (1760 North Vermont Avenue; 323-665-4294; thedresden.com/lounge.html) is a welcome throwback to an earlier era, with its upscale 1960s rec room décor and stellar bartenders. You're here to see Marty and Elayne, jazz musicians who also perform pop, standards, and the occasional show tune, with a changing array of guest artists, on Friday and Saturday nights in the lounge. The crowd is a cocktail shaker of twenty-somethings on dates, middle-aged couples with friends, and college kids. Somehow, it all goes down very smoothly.

SATURDAY

5 *From Canyon to Canyon* 10 a.m.

Joni Mitchell doesn't live here anymore, but Laurel Canyon retains its '70s image as a

OPPOSITE The endless sprawl of Los Angeles. In a city of 470 square miles, there's always something to do.

BELOW At the Griffith Park Observatory, stargazers line up for a peek at celestial sights like the rings of Saturn.

self-contained artistic enclave (albeit a more expensive one now). Its social hub is the **Canyon Country Store** (2108 Laurel Canyon Boulevard; 323-654-8091), a grocery/deli/liquor store marked by a flower power-style sign that pays homage to its hippie roots. Sip organic oak-roasted espresso at the Canyon Coffee Cart, buy a picnic lunch, and head for the high road — Mulholland Drive. The serpentine road follows the ridgeline of the Santa Monica Mountains, and every curve delivers a spectacular vista of the San Fernando Valley and beyond. Drop down into **Franklin Canyon Park** (2600 Franklin Canyon Drive; 310-858-7272; lamountains.com), 605 acres of chaparral, grasslands, and oak woodlands with miles of hiking grounds. Heavenly Pond is a particularly appealing picnic spot.

ABOVE Skylight Books in Los Feliz, just northeast of Hollywood, caters to writers, artists, musicians, and actors.

BELOW The crowd at the Dresden, where Marty and Elayne perform on weekends, is a cocktail shaker of 20-somethings on dates, clumps of middle-aged friends, and college kids.

6 *The Hills of Beverly* 1 p.m.

The stores range from Gap to Gucci, but you don't need deep pockets to enjoy Beverly Hills. **Prada** (343 North Rodeo Drive; 310-278-8661; prada.com), designed by Rem Koolhaas, delivers a jolt of architectural electricity. The 50-foot entrance is wide open to the street, with no door (and no name, either). A staircase peopled with mannequins ascends mysteriously. On the top level, faux security scanners double as video monitors and luggage-carousel-style shelves hold merchandise. At the **Paley Center for Media** (465 North Beverly Drive; 310-786-1091; paleycenter.org/visit-visitla), enter your own private TVland. At the center's library, anyone can screen segments of classic TV and radio shows, from *The Three Stooges* to *Seinfeld* as well as documentaries and specials. When it's time to cool your heels, head for the **Beverly Canon Gardens** (241 North Canon Drive), a public park masquerading as a private Italian-style garden. Adjacent to the

Montage Hotel, the Gardens have plenty of benches, tables, and chairs, and a large Baroque fountain adding a splashing soundtrack.

7 *Full Exposure* 4 p.m.

The incongruous setting of corporate high-rises is home to the under-appreciated **Annenberg Space for Photography** (2000 Avenue of the Stars; 213-403-3000; annenbergspaceforphotography.org), an oasis of images. One enthralling group show was by nature photographers shooting under Arctic oceans, on a volcano, and deep within Florida swamps. Another featured photographs by Herb Ritts, Mary Ellen Mark, Chuck Close, and other documentarians of beauty and style. The space itself is open and airy, with an iris-like design on the ceiling to represent the aperture of a lens.

8 *Unleashed* 6 p.m.

Don't knock it till you've tried it. Only a restaurant unequivocally named **Animal** (435 North Fairfax Avenue; 323-782-9225; animalrestaurant.com; $$-$$$) can sell diners on dishes like pig ear with chili, lime, and a fried egg, or rabbit legs with mustard and bacon. Or something else if inspiration strikes: the menu doesn't get printed until a half-hour before opening. The place is nondescript with no name on the storefront (it's four doors up from Canter's Deli), but once you've tried the fat pork-belly sliders with crunchy slaw on a buttery brioche bun, you'll beat a path there again.

9 *The Silent Treatment* 8 p.m.

Dedicated to finding, screening, and conserving unusual films (can you say, *"Killer Klowns from Outer Space"*?), the 120-seat **Silent Movie Theater** (611 North Fairfax Avenue; 323-655-2510; cinefamily.org) is like a quirky film class held in a club. Where else can you claim a well-worn couch and pour a cocktail from a punch bowl while waiting for show time? Insider tip: Regulars bring their own bottles of wine.

SUNDAY

10 *Breakfast by the Beach* 10 a.m.

Berries and Brussels sprouts abound at the **Santa Monica Farmers' Market** (2640 Main Street; Santa Monica; 310-458-8712; smgov.net/portals/farmersmarket), but there are also 10 stands where local restaurateurs sell dishes prepared on the spot. Among the best are Arcadie's sweet or savory crepes, Carbon Grill's hefty burritos, and

ABOVE Basking poolside at the eco-chic Palomar boutique hotel on Wilshire Boulevard, near the University of California at Los Angeles.

the Victorian's custom omelets. A live band might be playing any genre from jazz to zydeco. Finish with a scone from the Rockenwagner bakery stand and munch it on the beach, only a block away.

11 *Secret Waterways* 1 p.m.

One of the loveliest walks in west Los Angeles is one visitors hardly ever take: a stroll among the **Venice canals.** The developer Abbot Kinney dug miles of canals in 1905 to create his vision of a Venice in America. The decades took their toll, but the remaining canals were drained and refurbished in 1993. The surrounding neighborhood is now on the National Register of Historic Places. Charming footpaths crisscross the canals as ducks splash underneath. On the banks, mansions stand next to small bungalows. Residents pull kayaks and canoes up to their homes. It's quiet, serene, and hidden. Hollywood? Where's that?

ABOVE Spindly palms and an evening sky in Los Feliz.

OPPOSITE Within its expanse of 470 square miles, Los Angeles has room for places that can feel remote, like this trail in the Santa Monica Mountains.

THE BASICS

Fly into Los Angeles, Burbank, or Long Beach. You can't get by without a car — preferably one with a GPS.

The Farmer's Daughter Hotel
115 South Fairfax Avenue
323-937-3930
farmersdaughterhotel.com
$$
Cool country-hipster hotel in shopping nirvana.

The Avalon Hotel
9400 West Olympic Boulevard
310-277-5221
viceroyhotelgroup.com/avalon
$$-$$$
Luxe spa style a walk away from Beverly Hills sites.

The Palomar
10740 Wilshire Boulevard
310-475-8711
hotelpalomar-lawestwood.com
$$-$$$
Eco-chic boutique hotel.

LOS ANGELES
LOS ANGELES
JEWELRY PLAZA
ONE WAY
FOR LEASE
(310) 467-3863
DIAMONDS
LOS ANGELES

Downtown Los Angeles

The sprawl, the scale, all that freeway time—for many, Los Angeles is an acquired taste. But not downtown. New York-like in its density and mishmash, the long-blighted center has become an accessible, pedestrian-friendly destination in recent years; Angelenos walk around en masse, using their actual legs. The immense L.A. Live entertainment complex is largely responsible for this comeback, but the studiously vintage bars and imaginative restaurants that seem to open every other day are also part of the revival. Skid Row and the drifts of homeless camps haven't vanished altogether, and the grittiness still varies by block. But this part of town is alive again, in ways that make sense even to an outsider.

— BY CHRIS COLIN

FRIDAY

1 *Do the Crawl* 4 p.m.

The Downtown Art Walk—a party-in-the-streets bonanza that draws thousands of revelers the second Thursday of every month—is one way to experience the area's robust art scene. But you can do your own art walk anytime, and you should. Lured by low rents, a number of impressive galleries have found a home here, many of them on Chung King Road, a pedestrian alley strung with lanterns in Chinatown. For starters, look in at **Jancar Gallery** (No. 961; 213-625-2522; jancargallery.com), **Charlie James Gallery** (969 Chung King Road; 213-687-0844; cjamesgallery.com), and **Coagula Curatorial** (974 Chung King Road; 424-226-2485; coagulacuratorial.com). The shows are intimate and occasionally provocative, featuring a broad array of contemporary artists: William Powhida, Orly Cogan, and others.

2 *The City at Its Brightest* 7:30 p.m.

Whether you're catching a Lakers game, touring the Grammy Museum, or attending a concert at the Nokia Theater, there is always something splashy to do at the 27-acre, $2.5 billion sports and entertainment behemoth that is **L.A. Live** (800 West Olympic Boulevard; 213-763-5483; lalive.com). Just strolling the Tokyo-ish Nokia Plaza—20,000 square feet of LED signage—is diverting. An array of restaurants and bars is clustered at the periphery, but many visitors prefer just to stroll around this giant pedestrian zone, trying to take it all in.

3 *A Late, Great Bite* 10 p.m.

The Gorbals (501 South Spring Street; 213-488-3408; dynamic-ink.com/gorb; $$) is one of the more fantastic — and odd — downtown dining options. The chef and owner, a previous *Top Chef* winner, is part Scottish and part Israeli, and his hybrid concoctions are terrific. On one visit, banh mi poutine merged Quebec and Vietnam in ways criminally neglected until now. Bacon-wrapped matzo balls, anyone? The restaurant is tucked into the lobby of the old Alexandria Hotel, a well-worn but charming landmark where Bogart, Chaplin, and Garbo once roamed the halls.

SATURDAY

4 *On the Nickel* 9 a.m.

The maple bacon doughnut is a stand-out on the breakfast menu at the new but ageless **Nickel Diner** (524 South Main Street; 213-623-8301; nickeldiner.com; $). The rest is mostly well-executed diner food. What's remarkable is the location—until recently, this block was one of Skid Row's most notorious. It's a testament to downtown's revival that the intersection of Main

OPPOSITE Broadway in downtown Los Angeles, a pedestrian-friendly destination rebounding from 20th-century decline.

RIGHT Fabric in the Fashion District, a 100-block mix of wholesale-only shops and designer retail discounts.

and Fifth (hence "Nickel") is now home to a place where people line up for tables.

5 *Nice Threads* 10:30 a.m.

The 100-block **Fashion District** mixes high and low seamlessly. Though many shops sell wholesale only, you can still find a wide selection of deeply discounted designer clothes, fabric, and accessories. The jumbled shops and warehouses at Ninth and Los Angeles Streets are a start (feel free to bargain). Don't miss the rowdier **Santee Alley** (thesanteealley.com), a chaotic open-air bazaar where cheap meets weird in a thoroughly Los Angeles way. Energetic vendors hawk the impressive (perfect knock-off handbags) and the odd (toy frogs emblazoned with gang insignias). Find a higher-end experience around the corner at **Acne Studios** (855 South Broadway; 213-243-0960; acnestudios.com), a branch of a Swedish fashion brand. Dripping with 21st-century cool, it draws shoppers to the Art Deco spaces of the Eastern Columbia Building. For an expedition tailored to your particular agenda, contact **Urban Shopping Adventures** (213-683-9715) for a guided shopping trip.

ABOVE Find the outdoor stairway on Frank Gehry's Walt Disney Concert Hall and climb its curves to a rooftop garden.

OPPOSITE ABOVE Drinks at Seven Grand, one of the retro bars inspired by downtown's colorful history.

OPPOSITE BELOW The Nickel Diner, a busy spot in a revived area that not so long ago was part of Skid Row.

6 *Accessible Architecture* 1 p.m.

The arrival of the conductor Gustavo Dudamel at the Los Angeles Philharmonic has brought new crowds to the symphony, but the **Walt Disney Concert Hall** (111 South Grand Avenue; 323-850-2000; laphil.com) — Frank Gehry's deconstructivist celebration of all that is big, curvy, and shiny — deserves a visit even without a ticket. Bring a picnic and wind your way along the semi-hidden outer staircase up to an excellent city vista and rooftop garden oasis. Free guided tours and self-guided audio tours are available most days. Check first (musiccenter.org) for schedules.

7 *Lazy Bones* 7 p.m.

Since 2010, **Lazy Ox Canteen** (241 South San Pedro Street; 213-626-5299; lazyoxcanteen.com; $$-$$$) in Little Tokyo has been the kind of tucked-away gastropub people love to insist is the city's best. Casual and buzzing, the bistro has a long menu featuring adventurous delicacies, from trotters to crispy pigs' ears to lamb neck hash. It's hard to pin the cuisine to a specific origin, but a penchant for bold, meat-centric comfort food is evident. Get several small plates.

8 *Pick a Show, Any Show* 8:30 p.m.

If you're downtown for a performance, chances are it's a sprawling affair at L.A. Live. But a handful of smaller settings offer funkier alternatives. The **Redcat Theater** (631 West Second Street; 213-237-2800; redcat.org) plays host to all manner of experimental performances — one Saturday in winter featured theater, dance, puppetry, and live music from a Slovene-Latvian art collaboration. **Club Mayan** (1038 South Hill Street; 213-746-4287; clubmayan.com), an ornate old dance club most nights, occasionally hosts mad events like Lucha VaVoom, which combines burlesque and Mexican wrestling. And the **Smell** (247 South Main Street; thesmell.org), a likably grimy, volunteer-run space, hosts very small bands circled by swaying teenagers.

9 *Drink as if It's Illegal* 10:30 p.m.

Was Los Angeles a hoot during Prohibition? No need to guess, thanks to a slew of meticulously old-timey new bars that exploit the wonderful history of old Los Angeles. From upscale speakeasy (the **Varnish**; 118 East Sixth Street; 213-622-9999; thevarnishbar.com) to converted-power-plant chic (the **Edison**; 108 West Second Street; 213-613-0000; edisondowntown.com) to an old bank vault (the **Crocker Club**; 453 South Spring Street; 213-239-9099; crockerclub.com), these spiffy places do set decoration as only Los Angeles can. And fussily delicious artisanal cocktails are as plentiful as you'd imagine. The well-scrubbed will also enjoy the swanky **Seven Grand** (515 West Seventh Street, second floor; 213-614-0737; sevengrandbars.com), while the well-scuffed may feel more at home at **La Cita Bar** (336 South Hill Street; 213-687-7111; lacitabar.com).

SUNDAY

10 *Handsome Wake-Up* 10 a.m.

The brand is familiar to coffee aficionados at many coffee shops around the country, but **Handsome Coffee Roasters** (handsomecoffee.com) has its own shop here (582 Mateo Street; 213-621-4194). You can watch the roaster at work behind a glass wall while you eat a pastry and sip expertly made espresso in the subway-tiled coffee bar.

11 *Big Art* 11 a.m.

It's de rigueur these days for every city to have a public gallery specializing in contemporary art. But Los Angeles was in the vanguard with its **Museum of Contemporary Art**, which opened in 1979. Since then, it has developed a renowned collection, including works by Rothko, Oldenburg, Lichtenstein, and Rauschenberg, as well as a reputation for exciting special exhibitions. The museum is spread over three locations; downtown is the main one (250 South Grand Avenue; 213-626-6222; moca.org).

ABOVE If an art piece is much older than the first baby boomer, you're not likely to find it in the Museum of Contemporary Art, which is rich in works by Rothko, Oldenburg, Lichtenstein, and Rauschenberg.

OPPOSITE Downtown skyscrapers aglow in the Los Angeles night. About half a million people go to work every day in downtown's clusters of office towers and civic buildings. In the off hours, it's now also a place to play.

THE BASICS

Flights to Los Angeles are easy to book from anywhere. Walking works better than it used to, but you may still want a car.

Ritz-Carlton
900 West Olympic Boulevard
213-743-8800
lalive.com/stay/ritzcarlton
$$$$
Half of a gleaming new two-hotel complex rising above L.A. Live.

JW Marriott
900 West Olympic Boulevard
213-765-8600
lalive.com/stay/jwmarriott
$$
The other half of the same hotel complex.

Figueroa Hotel
939 South Figueroa Street
213-627-8971
figueroahotel.com
$$
Moroccan-themed.

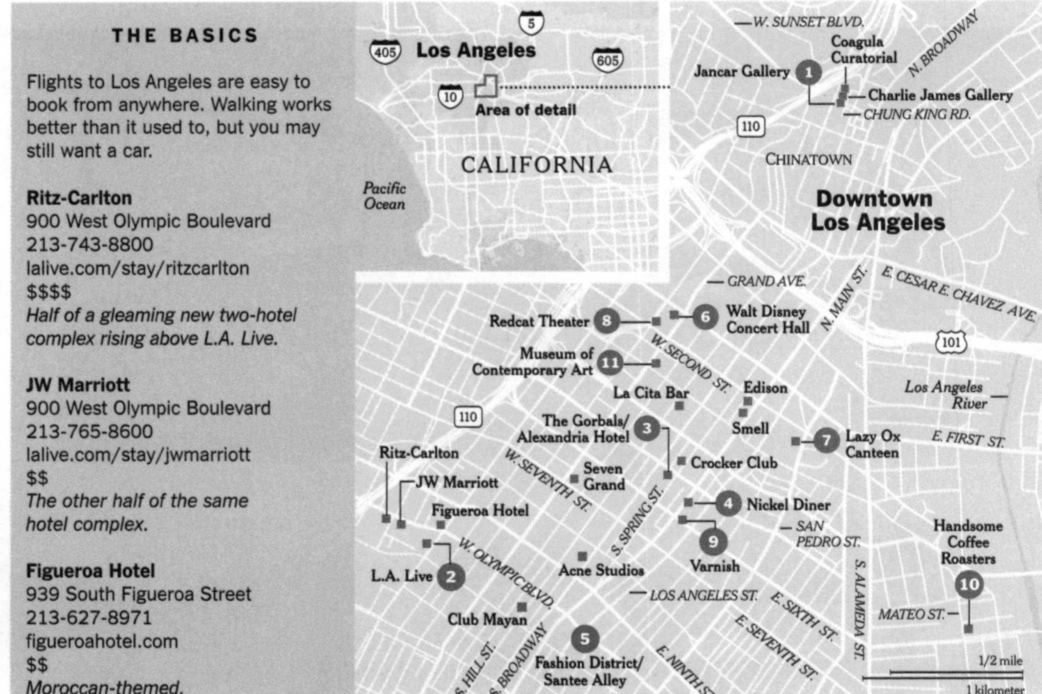

ONE WILSHIRE

Santa Monica

When Los Angelenos think of the perfect beach town, they think of Santa Monica. With its classic amusement pier, glittering bay, and surfers bobbing on swells, it certainly looks the part. But take a short walk inland, and there's a town asserting its unique identity: eight square miles and about 100,000 people surrounded by districts of the City of Los Angeles, but stubbornly remaining a separate city. A well-preserved Mission-style bungalow sits around the corner from a steel performance space by Frank Gehry. Shops sell goods ranging from vintage Parisian wedding gowns to a whimsical map made entirely of license plates. Enjoy the games and famed carousel of the Santa Monica Pier, and then step back from the beach to sample the city's variety the way Santa Monicans do.

— BY FRED A. BERNSTEIN AND LOUISE TUTELIAN

FRIDAY

1 *Landscape and Seascape* 4 p.m.

James Corner, an architect of the High Line park in Manhattan, has transformed a former parking lot into **Tongva Park** (tongvapark.squarespace.com), a stunning 6.2-acre space with observation decks, sculptural art, fountains, play areas, and winding walkways. For a sense of the setting that made Santa Monica, take a stroll in **Palisades Park** (Ocean Avenue at Santa Monica Boulevard; smgov.net/parks) and wander off on one of the sinuous paths overlooking the beach and Santa Monica Pier.

2 *Oyster Shack* 6 p.m.

The **Blue Plate Oysterette** (1355 Ocean Avenue; 310-576-3474; blueplatesantamonica.com; $$), one of the dozen or so Santa Monica restaurants that face the ocean, may be the most ocean-y, with its raw bar and daily specials like pan-seared rainbow trout. The casual blue-and-white restaurant, with a tin-pressed ceiling and blackboard menus, draws a chic, flip-flop-wearing crowd.

3 *The View That Moves* 8 p.m.

At sunset, the most thrilling view in town is at the beach, from the top of the solar-powered, 130-foot-high Pacific Wheel, the Ferris wheel at the **Santa Monica Pier**. Yes, it's touristy, and yes, it might be crowded, but it is, after all, the city's iconic symbol. As you glide upward, watching the entire city of Santa Monica, and far beyond, slide into view, the whole scene will be bathed in the sunset-colored glow. If you prefer a view that's not mobile, head south into Venice to the rooftop lounge of the **Hotel Erwin** (1697 Pacific Avenue; 310-452-1111; hotelerwin.com), where the banquettes seem to hang over the beach. Gaze at a Santa Monica panorama while sipping a cocktail. You can reserve a table through the hotel's Web site.

SATURDAY

4 *Duck for Breakfast* 8 a.m.

The lines spill out the door, so arrive early at **Huckleberry Bakery and Café** (1014 Wilshire Boulevard; 310-451-2311; huckleberrycafe.com; $$). Breakfast favorites include green eggs and ham, made with pesto and prosciutto, and duck hash with sunny-side-up eggs. The cheerful room, with wooden tables and colorful accents, feels like a large country bakery.

5 *Into the Mountains* 9 a.m.

The Backbone Trail, a 69-mile system, roughly follows the crest of the Santa Monica Mountains north

OPPOSITE Palisades Park, overlooking the Pacific Ocean.

BELOW The Isaac Milbank House, designed by the firm that did Grauman's Chinese Theater, is one of the Craftsman-style houses on Adelaide Drive designated as city landmarks.

from **Will Rogers State Historic Park** just north of Santa Monica (1501 Will Rogers State Park Road, off West Sunset Boulevard, Pacific Palisades; 310-454-8212; nps.gov/samo/planyourvisit/backbonetrail.htm). Hikers can take an easy, sage-scented, two-mile loop from the parking lot at Will Rogers up to Inspiration Point, a sensational overlook of Santa Monica Bay from the Palos Verdes Peninsula to Point Dume in Malibu. Do it on a clear day, and you'll see Catalina Island and the white dots of sails. Behind are the slopes of the Santa Monica Mountains, and in the distance, the high-rises of downtown Los Angeles. Up here, the muted chattering of birds and the hum of insects are the only sounds.

6 *Builders and Shoppers* Noon

Back in northern Santa Monica, natural sights give way to architectural ones. Two houses designated as city landmarks are the Craftsman-style **Isaac Milbank House** (236 Adelaide Drive)—designed by the same firm that did Grauman's Chinese Theater in Hollywood—and the stucco **Worrel House** (710 Adelaide Drive), which was built in the mid-1920s and has been described as a "Pueblo-Revival Maya fantasy." Some of the city's best shopping is nearby on Montana Avenue. It's all one-of-a-kind at **Marcia Bloom Designs** (1527 Montana Avenue; 310-393-0985; marciabloomdesigns.com), a gallery/boutique with whimsical gypsy-like skirts, casual Southwestern styles, and statement tops, scarves, gloves, bags, and caps—all of it crafted by the artist-owner herself. **Rooms & Gardens** (No. 1311-A; 310-451-5154; roomsandgardens.com) sells furniture, antiques, and accessories like pillows fashioned from antique Indian saris.

7 *Art Lovers, Art Buyers* 3 p.m.

For an art-filled afternoon, start at **Bergamot Station** (2525 Michigan Avenue; 310-453-7535; bergamotstation.com), built on the site of a former trolley-line stop. The highlight of this complex of art galleries is the **Santa Monica Museum of Art** (310-586-6488; smmoa.org). Off the 3rd Street Promenade, find the unconventional **Adamm's Stained Glass Studio & Art Gallery** (1426 4th Street; 310-451-9390; adammsgallery.com), an interesting spot that even locals often overlook. The work of more than 175 glass artists is for sale, from gem-like paperweights to frilly perfume bottles and sculptural chandeliers.

8 *Bistro Evenings* 8 p.m.

There are lots of stylish hotels in Santa Monica, and some of them offer very good food. A case in point is **Fig** (101 Wilshire Boulevard; 310-319-3111; figsantamonica.com; $$$), a contemporary American bistro at the Fairmont Miramar Hotel. The menu features seasonal ingredients and dishes like a halibut "chop" or snap peas with mint. There is seating indoors, in an elegant room with starburst mirrors, as well as on the terrace with views of the ocean through the lush gardens. The huge Moreton Bay fig tree, from which the restaurant gets its name, will make you feel like climbing.

9 *Disco Nights* 11 p.m.

Santa Monica may be known for sunshine, but there's plenty to do after dark. For a taste of the local night life, head to **Zanzibar** (1301 Fifth Street; 310-451-2221; zanzibarlive.com), a cavernous club that manages to be both cozy and contemporary. It is also the rare venue that seems able to please young and old—you could imagine Joni Mitchell on the dance floor with her grandkids. The D.J.'s play a mix of hip-hop, R&B, and top 40. Even the décor has crossover appeal; hanging from the ceiling are perforated copper lanterns (for a vaguely African feeling) and disco balls.

SUNDAY

10 *No Wet Suit Needed* 10 a.m.

Even in warm weather, the waters of Southern California can be frigid. For a more comfortable swim, duck into the **Annenberg Community Beach House** (415 Pacific Coast Highway; 310-458-4904; annenbergbeachhouse.com), a sleek public facility that opened in 2010. The pool is spectacular, and you can buy a day pass for a reasonable price. If

you've got to get in your laps after October, your best bet is the public **Santa Monica Swim Center** (2225 16th Street; 310-458-8700; smgov.net/aquatics), where the adult and children's pools are kept at 79 and 85 degrees, respectively.

11 *Sunday Retail* Noon

Amid the sneaker stores and used book shops of artsy Main Street, in the Ocean Park neighborhood, look for the Frank Gehry-designed steel boxes of **Edgemar** (2415-2449 Main Street; edgemarcenter.org), which house retail tenants and a performance space around an open courtyard. Gehry's retail footprint in Santa Monica has shrunk since his **Santa Monica Place**, designed in 1980, was replaced by a new version (395 Santa Monica Place; santamonicaplace.com), a glassy open-air retail complex that often has live music, HDTV displays, or seasonal events. If shopping makes you hungry, head for the top level and the **Curious Palate** market, which has a cafe with an artisanal, farm-to-table menu.

OPPOSITE Ocean-view dining at Santa Monica Place, a glassy new open-air version of a California shopping mall.

ABOVE At sunset, the best view in town is at the beach, from the top of the solar-powered, 130-foot-high Pacific Wheel, the Ferris wheel at the Santa Monica Pier.

THE BASICS

Santa Monica is about a 20-minute drive from Los Angeles International Airport. There's a terrific bus system (bigbluebus.com), but most visitors find it more convenient to drive.

The Ambrose
1255 20th Street
310-315-1555
ambrosehotel.com
$$$
Feels like a Mission-style hideaway with stained-glass windows.

Hotel Shangri-La
1301 Ocean Avenue
310-394-2791
shangrila-hotel.com
$$$$
A storied, bright-white apparition on bluffs high above the Pacific.

Shore Hotel
1515 Ocean Avenue
310-458-1515
shorehotel.com
$$$$
Across Ocean Avenue from the pier.

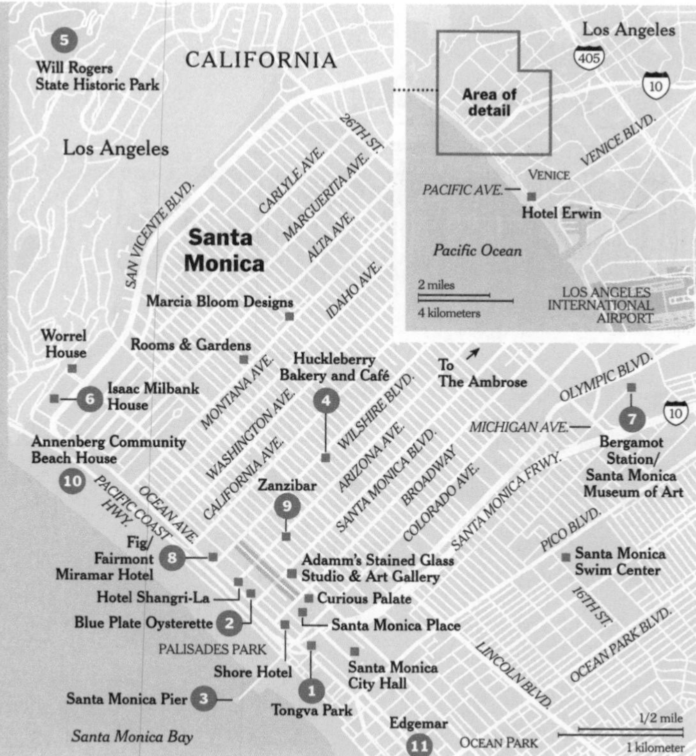

Malibu

Locals call it "the Bu"—a laid-back, celebrity-filled strip of a city that sparkles in the collective consciousness as a sun-drenched state of mind. With the busy Pacific Coast Highway running through and no discernible center of town, some of the best of Malibu, which has around 13,000 residents, can disappear in a drive-by. The staggering natural beauty of the sea and mountains is obvious, but pull off the road and stay awhile, and you'll find more: a world-class art museum, local wines, top-notch restaurants, and chic shops.
— BY LOUISE TUTELIAN

FRIDAY

1 *The Wind, the Waves...* 5 p.m.

What's so appealing about Malibu's little slice of coast? Visit **Point Dume State Preserve** (Birdview Avenue and Cliffside Drive; 310-457-8143; parks.ca.gov), and you'll see. A modest walk to the top of this coastal bluff rewards you with a sweeping view of the entire Santa Monica Bay, the inland Santa Monica Mountains, and, on a clear day, Catalina Island. A boardwalk just below the summit leads to a platform for watching swooping pelicans and crashing waves. To feel the sand between your toes, drive down Birdview Avenue to Westward Beach Road and park at the very end of the lot on your left. You'll be looking at Westward Beach, a gem that most visitors miss. Strike a yoga pose. Sigh at will.

2 *Chasing the Sunset* 7 p.m.

Little known fact: Most of Malibu faces south, not west. That means sitting down at just any seaside restaurant at dusk won't guarantee seeing a sunset over the water. But the aptly named **Sunset Restaurant** (6800 Westward Beach Road; 310-589-1007; thesunsetrestaurant.com) is a sure bet, with just the right orientation. Claim a white leather banquette, order a carafe of wine and select a tasting plate of cheeses, and settle in for the light show.

3 *Shore Dinner* 9 p.m.

If you're going to spot a celebrity, chances are it will be at **Nobu Malibu** (3835 Cross Creek Road, in the Malibu Country Mart; 310-317-9140; nobumatsuhisa.com; $$$), one of the famed chef Nobu Matsuhisa's many restaurants. The sushi is sublime, and the entrees measure up. Reservations are essential. The front room is convivial but noisy; the subtly lighted back room is quieter.

SATURDAY

4 *Walk the Pier* 9 a.m.

The 780-foot-long **Malibu Pier** (23000 Pacific Coast Highway; 888-310-7437; malibupiersportfishing.com) is the most recognizable (and, arguably, only) landmark in town. Take a morning stroll out to the end, chat with the fishermen, and watch surfers paddle out. You'll be walking on a piece of Malibu history. The pier was originally built in 1905 as a loading dock for construction material, and it was a lookout during World War II. It crops up in numerous movies and TV shows.

5 *Bronze for the Ages* 10 a.m.

The **Getty Villa** (17985 Pacific Coast Highway; 310-440-7300; getty.edu) is just over the city's southern border in Pacific Palisades, but no matter: it shouldn't be missed. The museum, built by J. Paul Getty in the 1970s to resemble a first-century Roman country house, contains Greek, Roman, and Etruscan vessels, gems, and statuary, some dating back to 6500 B.C. On the second floor is a rare life-size Greek bronze, *Statue of a Victorious Youth*, a prize of the

OPPOSITE Beach and pier at Malibu, the little slice of Pacific coast that celebrities like to call their own.

BELOW Kai Sanson, a surfing instructor, initiates students into the ways of the waves.

museum. In the outside peristyle gardens, watch the sun glint off bronze statues at the 220-foot-long reflecting pool. Admission is free, but parking is limited, so car reservations are required.

6 *Magic Carpet Tile* 1 p.m.

Even many longtime Angelenos don't know about the **Adamson House** (23200 Pacific Coast Highway; 310-456-8432; adamsonhouse.org), a 1930 Spanish Colonial Revival residence that's a showplace of exquisite ceramic tile from Malibu Potteries, which closed in 1932. Overlooking Surfrider Beach with a view of Malibu Pier, the house belonged to a member of the Rindge family, the last owners of the Malibu Spanish land grant. Take a tour and watch for the Persian "carpet" constructed entirely from intricately patterned pieces of tile. Other highlights: a stunning star-shaped fountain and a bathroom tiled top to bottom in an ocean pattern, with ceramic galleons poised in perpetuity on pointy whitecaps in a sea of blue.

7 *Vino With a View* 4 p.m.

The drive to **Malibu Family Wines** (31740 Mulholland Highway; 818-865-0605; malibufamilywines.com) along the serpentine roads of the Santa Monica Mountains is almost as much fun as tipping a glass once you get there. Set on a serene green lawn, the tasting room is really a covered outdoor stone and wood counter. Sidle up and choose a flight of four styles. Or buy a bottle and lounge at one of the tables. (Tip: Regulars request the horseshoes or bocce ball set at the counter.) And don't miss the collection of vintage pickup trucks spread around the property.

8 *Can You Say Olé?* 7 p.m.

Located in the chic **Malibu Lumber Yard** shopping arcade (the piles of two-by-fours are long gone) you'll find **Café Habana Malibu** (3939 Cross Creek Road; 310-317-0300; cafehabana.com/malibu), the West Coast hermana of famed Café Habana in the West Village and Habana Outpost in Brooklyn. The sleek, solar-powered bar and café serves flavorful Mexican/Cuban fare from 11 a.m. to — most nights — an unheard-of 1 a.m. in early-to-bed L.A. (There's Wednesday karaoke and a nightclub vibe after dark.) Locals tout the fish tacos and charred cheese-covered corn on the cob, and its killer margaritas and mojitos. Yes, the guacamole is the price of a diner entree, but the star-sightings are free.

SUNDAY

9 *Ride the Surf* 10 a.m.

Surf shops offering lessons and board rentals line the Pacific Coast Highway (P.C.H. in local lingo), but Kai Sanson of **Zuma Surf and Swim Training** (949-742-1086; zumasurfandswim.com) takes his fun seriously. Sanson, a Malibu native, will size you up with a glance and gear the instruction to your skills. There's a price for the lessons, but his tales of growing up in Malibu are free. Locals also give high marks to **Malibu Makos Surf Club** (310-317-1229; malibumakos.com).

10 *Brunch in Style (or Not)* Noon

Put on your oversize sunglasses if you're going to **Geoffrey's Malibu** (27400 Pacific Coast Highway; 310-457-1519; geoffreysmalibu.com; $$$). Geoffrey's (pronounced Joffreys) is the hot meeting spot for the

ABOVE The curve of the Pacific beach in Malibu. The houses lining the waterside are worth millions.

BELOW Tasting the reds at Malibu Family Wines.

well-heeled with a hankering for a shiitake mushroom omelet or lobster Cobb salad. Its Richard Neutra-designed building overlooks the Pacific, and every table has an ocean view. Or if you just want to kick back with *The Malibu Times*, head to **Coogie's Beach Café** (23750 Pacific Coast Highway in the Malibu Colony Plaza; 310-317-1444; coogiescafe.com; $$) and carbo-load with Coogie's French Toast: bagels dipped in egg whites with cinnamon sugar and served with peanut butter and bananas.

11 *Shop Like a Star* 2 p.m.

Whether it's diamonds or designer jeans you're after, the open-air **Malibu Country Mart** (3835 Cross Creek Road; malibucountrymart.com) is the place to cruise for them. Its more than 50 retail stores and restaurants include Ralph Lauren, Juicy Couture, and Malibu Rock Star jewelry. In an adjacent space is the luxe **Malibu Lumber Yard** shopping complex (themalibulumberyard.com), with stores like Alice + Olivia and Tory Burch.

ABOVE The Getty Villa museum, built by J. Paul Getty to resemble a first-century Roman country house.

THE BASICS

Malibu is 25 miles or a 45-minute drive (with minimal traffic) from Los Angeles International Airport. A car is essential.

Malibu Beach Inn
22878 Pacific Coast Highway
310-456-6444
malibubeachinn.com
$$$
A blend of chic and Zen tranquillity with waves breaking below.

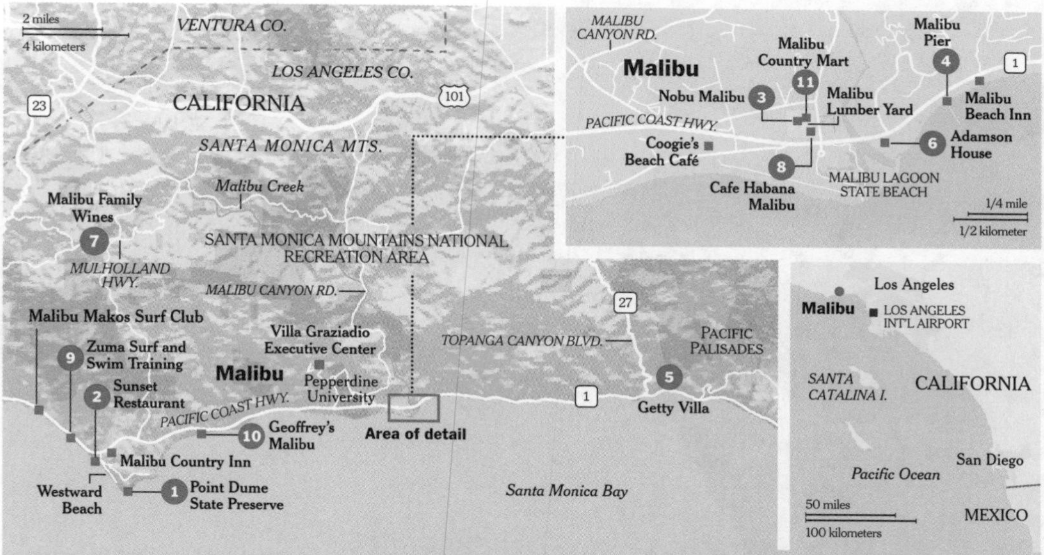

Casa Malibu Inn on the Beach
22752 Pacific Coast Highway
310-456-2219
$$
A hideout for celebrities from Lana Turner to Jamie Lee Curtis.

Villa Graziadio Executive Center
Drescher Graduate Campus of Pepperdine University
24255 Pacific Coast Highway
310-506-1100
villagraziadio.com
$$$
Views of the ocean and mountains.

Santa Barbara

Santa Barbara may be tiny—its 90,000 residents could be seated in the Los Angeles Coliseum—but it packs Oprah-like cachet. Indeed, the queen of daytime TV and other A-listers have made this former outpost of Spain's American dominions their second home. Posh hotels, seven-figure mansions, and trendy boutiques have opened along the so-called American Riviera, catering to members of the Hollywood set who drive up every weekend to frolic among the languorous palms and suntanned celebrities. But don't let the crush of Ferraris and Prada fool you. With its perpetually blue skies and taco stands, Santa Barbara remains a laid-back town where the star attraction is still the beach.

— BY FINN-OLAF JONES

FRIDAY

1 *Lingering Glow* 5 p.m.

Santa Barbara's main beaches face southeast, but you can still catch the Pacific sunset by driving along Cliff Drive until it takes you to secluded **Hendry's Beach**. Hemmed by vertiginous cliffs that turn deep orange as the sun sets, the beach is popular with locals, surfers, and dolphins. Order a rum punch at the **Boathouse at Hendry's Beach** (2981 Cliff Drive; 805-898-2628; boathousesb.com), where you can still feel the warmth of the sun (or is it the fire pit?) long after it has set.

2 *Making Friends* 8 p.m.

Fresh California cuisine is the rule in this region of outstanding vineyards, luscious orchards, and right-off-the-boat seafood. Some of the freshest is at **Brophy Brothers Restaurant and Clam Bar** (119 Harbor Way; 805-966-4418; brophybros.com; $$$), which overlooks the harbor. Sit at the long communal table and strike up a conversation with your new friends. The night I was there, I was offered a job by a local developer. While I didn't take the job, I did sample the clam chowder ("The best in town," I was told about five times), followed by a terrific grilled swordfish with artichoke sauce. Hmmm, what was that starting salary again?

OPPOSITE Sunset at Hendry's Beach. The main beaches in town face southeast, but at Hendry's the shore angles west, and the cliffs glow orange as the sun goes down.

RIGHT La Super Rica, pronounced by Julia Child to be the best of several good places in Santa Barbara to get a fresh and authentic homemade taco.

SATURDAY

3 *Bike to Brunch* 10 a.m.

Rent a bike at **Wheel Fun Rentals** (23 East Cabrillo Boulevard; 805-966-2282; wheelfunrentals.com) and roll along the ocean to the **East Beach Grill** (1118 East Cabrillo Boulevard; 805-965-8805; $), a greasy but bright breakfast institution popular with surfers, cyclists, and skaters, who swear by its banana wheat germ pancakes with eggs and bacon.

4 *Sacred Mission* 11:30 a.m.

It's hard not to feel awed when driving up the hill to **Mission Santa Barbara** (2201 Laguna Street; 805-682-4713; sbmission.org), a 1786 landmark with ocher-colored columns that is known as the Queen of the 21 original Spanish missions built along the California coastline. Escape the crowds by wandering outside the flower-scented Sacred Garden. If there's a docent around, ask if you can see the glazed terra-cotta sculpture of St. Barbara watching over Mary and Jesus. A masterpiece from 1522, it was discovered three years ago in a storage room

that was being cleaned out. It is now installed in an alcove in the garden's private portico.

5 *Taco Heaven* 1 p.m.

Locals argue endlessly about the city's best taco joint. Julia Child threw her weight behind **La Super Rica** (622 North Milpas Street; 805-963-4940; $), ensuring perpetual lines for its homemade tortillas filled with everything from pork and cheese to spicy ground beans. **Lilly's** (310 Chapala Street; 805-966-9180; lillystacos.com; $), a tiny spot in the center of town run by the ever-welcoming Sepulveda family, serves tacos filled with anything from pork to beef eye. And **Palapa** (4123 State Street; 805-683-3074; palaparestaurant.com; $) adds fresh seafood to the equation in its cheery patio just north of downtown, where the grilled sole tacos are fresh and light. Try all three places and join the debate.

6 *Paper Chase* 3 p.m.

Walt Disney's original will. A letter by Galileo. Lincoln's second Emancipation Proclamation (the 13th Amendment). The **Karpeles Manuscript Library and Museum** (21 West Anapamu Street; 805-962-5322; rain.org/~karpeles; free) was started by David Karpeles, a local real estate tycoon, and has one of the world's largest private manuscript collections. If this whets your appetite for collecting, wander seven blocks to **Randall House Rare Books** (835 Laguna Street; 805-963-1909; randallhouserarebooks.com), where the ancient tomes and rare documents have included a signed calling card from Robert E. Lee ($4,500) and the first official map of the State of California ($27,500).

ABOVE AND OPPOSITE Three views of Mission Santa Barbara, known as the Queen of the 21 original Spanish missions built along the California coast. Escape the crowds by wandering outside in the flower-scented Sacred Garden.

LEFT A guest room at San Ysidro Ranch, the longtime celebrity hangout where John F. Kennedy took his bride, Jacqueline, on their honeymoon.

7 *Shop Like the Stars* 5 p.m.

The main shopping drag, State Street, is filled with the usual chain stores like Abercrombie & Fitch. The consumerist cognoscenti head for the hills, to the Platinum Card district of **Montecito**, where you'll find local designers and one-off items along the eucalyptus-lined Coast Village Road. Highlights include **Dressed** (No. 1253; 805-565-1253; dressedonline.com), a small boutique that counts Teri Hatcher and Britney Spears among the fans of its resortwear look, which might include items like an earthy necklace made of bamboo coral by a local jeweler, Corrina Gordon. Next door, **Angel** (No. 1221; 805-565-1599; wendyfoster.com) sells casual sportswear with a youthful vibe and hot accessories like tie-dyed hair ties.

8 *Celebrity Dining* 8 p.m.

J.F.K. and Jackie honeymooned there, Hollywood luminaries like Groucho Marx were regulars, and in 2007 the **San Ysidro Ranch** reopened after a $150 million renovation by a new owner, the Beanie Babies creator Ty Warner. Warner added an enormous terrace, a 4,000-bottle wine cellar, and a lot of buzz by redoing the **Stonehouse** restaurant (900 San Ysidro Lane; 805-565-1700; sanysidroranch.com; $$$$). Expect to see the T-shirt-with-blazer set sitting around an open fire while dining on dishes like warm mushroom salad, juniper-dusted venison loin, and

fresh pastries. Take a post-dinner stroll around the terraced gardens where many of the ingredients were grown.

9 *Glamorous State* 11 p.m.

State Street heats up after 11 o'clock as college students and moneyed folk from the glittering hills descend to its bars and nightclubs. **Wildcat Lounge** (15 West Ortega Street; 805-962-7970; wildcatlounge.com), a retro bar with red-vinyl banquettes, is the place to mingle with the university crowd and local bohos grooving to house music. Cater-corner is **Tonic** (634 State Street; 805-897-1800; tonicsb.com), an airy dance club that draws students in chinos and recent graduates in designer T-shirts to

its cabanas. The international set heads to **Eos Lounge** (500 Anacapa Street; 805-564-2410; eoslounge.com) to dance to world music in a tree-shaded patio that looks like Mykonos on the Pacific.

SUNDAY

10 *Paging Moby-Dick* 10 a.m.

From December to February, some 30,000 gray whales migrating down the Pacific Coast from Alaska to Baja California through a five-mile gap among the Channel Islands, a cluster of rocky isles 20 or so miles off the coast. Catch a glimpse of the commute — and see breaching whales rise from the sea around you — from the decks of the ***Condor Express***, a high-speed catamaran that makes daily whale-watching trips (301 West Cabrillo Boulevard; 805-882-0088; condorexpress.com). Porpoises, sea lions, and the occasional killer whale join in on the fun.

ABOVE Towering palms along Cabrillo Boulevard near Stearns Wharf. Cabrillo follows the beach in the center of town.

OPPOSITE Mission Santa Barbara dates to 1786.

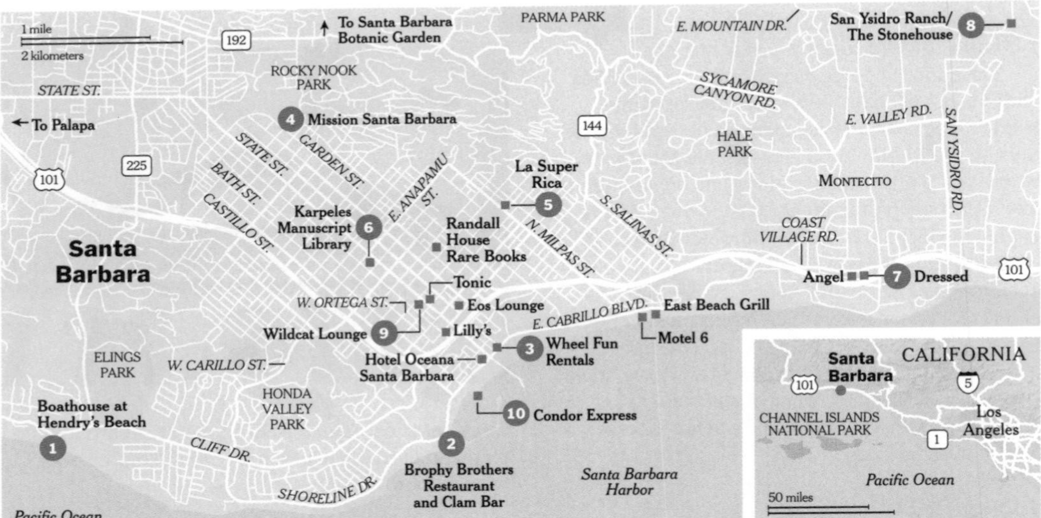

1 mile
2 kilometers
192
To Santa Barbara Botanic Garden
PARMA PARK
E. MOUNTAIN DR.
San Ysidro Ranch/ The Stonehouse 8
ROCKY NOOK PARK
STATE ST.
SYCAMORE CANYON RD.
To Palapa
4 Mission Santa Barbara
144
E. VALLEY RD.
SAN YSIDRO RD.
HALE PARK
225
101
STATE ST.
GARDEN ST.
E. ANAPAMU ST.
La Super Rica 5
MONTECITO
BATH ST.
CASTILLO ST.
Karpeles Manuscript Library 6
Randall House Rare Books
N. MILPAS ST.
S. SALINAS ST.
COAST VILLAGE RD.
Santa Barbara
Tonic
Angel 7 Dressed
101
W. ORTEGA ST.
Eos Lounge
E. CABRILLO BLVD.
East Beach Grill
Wildcat Lounge 9
Lilly's
Motel 6
3 Wheel Fun Rentals
ELINGS PARK
W. CARILLO ST.
Hotel Oceana Santa Barbara
HONDA VALLEY PARK
Boathouse at Hendry's Beach 1
10 Condor Express
CLIFF DR.
2 Brophy Brothers Restaurant and Clam Bar
SHORELINE DR.
Santa Barbara Harbor
Pacific Ocean
Santa Barbara
CALIFORNIA
101
5
CHANNEL ISLANDS NATIONAL PARK
Los Angeles
1
Pacific Ocean
50 miles
100 kilometers

THE BASICS

Fly into Santa Barbara Airport, or for more choice of flights, into Los Angeles International Airport, a two-hour drive away on scenic Highway 101. Rent a car.

Hotel Oceana Santa Barbara
202 West Cabrillo Boulevard
805-965-4577
hoteloceanasantabarbara.com
$$$
Modern rooms clustered around gardens and facing the beach.

San Ysidro Ranch
900 San Ysidro Lane
805-565-1700
www.sanysidroranch.com
$$$$
Still attracts celebrities from J. Lo to Gwyneth Paltrow.

Motel 6 Santa Barbara-Beach #1
443 Corona Del Mar
805-564-1392
motel6.com
$-$$
The first Motel 6.

San Diego

Like its urban rival Los Angeles, San Diego is not so much a city as a loose collection of overlapping (and sometimes colliding) communities bound by arterial, life-giving freeways. It's a military town in Coronado; a surf town in funky, eclectic Ocean Beach; and a border town in the historic Mexican-American neighborhood of Barrio Logan. If San Diego has a cohesive identity at all, it's a shared embrace of an easy, breezy Southern California casualness. With its lack of pretension, the city is often seen by outsiders as a kind of Pleasantville — a bland, happy place with an exceptional amount of sunshine. Depending on how deep you look, that may be all you see. But there are, after all, worse things than Spanish tiles, palm trees, tropical blooms, year-round flip-flops, fresh fish tacos, and bonfires on the beach. — BY FREDA MOON

FRIDAY

1 *View Across the Bay* 4:30 p.m.

Sitting above the water on a stilted deck on Harbor Island, **C Level** (880 Harbor Island Drive; 619-298-6802; cohnrestaurants.com/islandprime) looks across San Diego Bay to the Naval ships at Coronado, downtown's towering skyline, and the tall ships at the Maritime Museum. Have a cool drink and enjoy snacks like rice-paper-wrapped prawns and steamed mussels with chorizo. Afterward, take a giddy ride on the Giant Dipper wooden roller coaster at Belmont Park (belmontpark.com), a vintage amusement park on the beach in Mission Bay.

2 *Pork Shop* 7 p.m.

Carnitas' Snack Shack (2632 University Avenue; 619-294-7675; carnitassnackshack.com; $), a popular spot with local crowds, is a glorified taco stand serving pork-centric comfort food — including carnitas tacos with guacamole and salsa fresca, braised Duroc pork belly with a frisée, apple and radish salad, a steak sandwich on jalapeño and Cheddar cheese bread — from a takeout window in North Park. The shack is a squat structure with outdoor tables and heat lamps around back and a giant sculpture of a metal pig adorning its roof.

3 *Just About Normal* 8:30 p.m.

For dessert, head for Adams Avenue and try the house-made Mexican chocolate or banana walnut ice cream at the mom-and-pop **Mariposa Ice Cream** (3450 Adams Avenue; 619-284-5197; mariposaicecream.com) or the exotic Mexican-style popsicles, called paletas, in flavors like lavender lemonade, salted caramel, and mango-chile at **Viva Pops** (3330 Adams Avenue; 619-795-1080; ilovevivapops.com). Both shops close at 9 p.m. on weekends. You're in the buzzing Normal Heights neighborhood, so do some more exploring. Stop in at **Lestat's Coffee House** (3343 Adams Avenue; 619-282-0437; lestats.com), and check the events calendar for the attached concert space, which hosts local music acts, comedy shows, and open mic nights.

4 *Old School, New Age* 10:30 p.m.

In South Park, rockabillies and old-timers take turns playing shuffleboard at **Hamilton's Tavern** (1521 30th Street; 619-238-5460; hamiltonstavern.com), which has a daunting 28 taps, two cask beer engines, and some 200 bottled beers, and claims to be the city's oldest alehouse. Or, instead, have an only-in-California experience at **Kava Lounge** (2812 Kettner Boulevard; 619-543-0933; kavalounge.com), a New Age bar, dance club, and arts space that promotes "future planetary night life" in the form of vegan cocktails, experimental dance music, and class

OPPOSITE AND RIGHT Eye catchers in a Navy Town: *Unconditional Surrender*, by Seward Johnson, and the decommissioned aircraft carrier *Midway*, now a museum, occupying space along the San Diego Embarcadero.

offerings that include "Ballet for Belly Dancers" in a nondescript building identifiable only by the Eye of Providence painted above its entrance.

SATURDAY

5 *To the Shore* 9 a.m.

Cruise up the coast to the **Cottage** in La Jolla (7702 Fay Avenue; 858-454-8409; cottagelajolla.com; $$), a would-be surf bungalow with an umbrella-canopied patio, which makes use of the Western bounty with dishes like lemon ricotta pancakes; polenta with tomato relish, kale pesto, goat cheese sauce, and chives; and soy chorizo hash with scrambled eggs, black beans, and queso fresco. After breakfast, continue north to the 2,000-acre **Torrey Pines State Natural Reserve** (12600 North Torrey Pines Road; 858-755-2063; torreypine.org), home to the torrey pine, one of the rarest species of pine in the world; sandstone cliffs shaped by the sea; and a lagoon that hosts migrating seabirds.

6 *Mission Viejo* Noon

Founded in 1769 as the first of California's 21 missions, the **Mission Basilica San Diego de Alcala** (10818 San Diego Mission Road; 619-281-8449; missionsandiego.com) has a bloody and politically complicated past. Today it is an exceptionally peaceful place—an active parish on a hillside carpeted with ice plants, with a Spanish-style garden at its center and a gift shop that sells Mexican folk art like milagros (religious charms) and Talavera pottery. For lunch, head north to the **Island Style Cafe** (5950 Santo Road; 858-541-7002; islandstylecafe.com; $), a home-style Hawaiian cafe with fabric orchids on the tables and tropical landscape prints on the walls. Try the Korean-style fried chicken thighs, served with classic sides like macaroni salad, and a glass of POG (passion-orange-guava juice).

7 *Easy Does It* 4 p.m.

Back downtown, stroll along the **Embarcadero**, a two-mile stretch of downtown waterfront where a gentle sea breeze will lull you into a zombie-like state in no time. You'll pass *Unconditional Surrender*, a giant sculptural rendering of Alfred Eisenstaedt's famous VJ Day photo of a sailor kissing a nurse. The decommissioned aircraft carrier *Midway* sits nearby and can be admired from Tuna Harbor Park, a shady nook next to the touristy but tasty **Fish Market** restaurant (750 North Harbor Drive; 619-232-3474; thefishmarket.com; $$).

8 *Sea and Sky* 7 p.m.

In the perennial debate over where to find San Diego's best fish tacos, the line at **Blue Water Seafood Market & Grill** (3667 India Street; 619-497-0914; bluewaterseafoodsandiego.com; $) is one indication. The menu reads like a choose-your-own aquatic adventure, listing a dozen kinds of seafood including Scottish salmon, Hawaiian albacore, and Alaskan halibut; six kinds of marinade (among them: chipotle, blackened, and "bronzed"); and four preparations: salad, sandwich, plate, or tacos. After you've eaten, have a nightcap next door at **Aero Club** (3365 India; 619-297-7211; aeroclubbar.com), a charmingly divey whiskey bar with some 600 bottles climbing the wall and toy airplanes hanging from the ceiling. Or eat a bit earlier and head up to Mission Hills to **Cinema Under the Stars** (4040 Goldfinch Street;

ABOVE The Pacific from Sunset Cliffs.

RIGHT You could ride, but walking is also a nice way to make your way down the central thoroughfare of Balboa Park.

619-295-4221; topspresents.com), an open-air theater with zero-gravity lounge chairs, for an 8 p.m. movie.

SUNDAY

9 *Very Old California* 9 a.m.

Take a slow Sunday drive down the coast, past the sandstone Sunset Cliffs to the **Cabrillo National Monument** (1800 Cabrillo Memorial Drive; 619-557-5450; nps.gov/cabr). Walk the two-mile Bayside Trail along a rocky point of sage scrub and maguey plants, near where in 1542 Juan Rodriguez Cabrillo led the first European expedition to the coast of what is now California.

10 *Park and Ride* Noon

With 15 museums, one of the country's most-respected zoos, and 1,200 acres of hills, gardens, forests, and ravines, **Balboa Park** (1549 El Prado; 619-239-0512; balboapark.org) cannot be fully explored in a weekend, much less an afternoon. But, for an overview, **San Diego Fly Rides** (1237 Prospect Street; 619-888-3878; sandiegoflyrides.com) uses high-end electric bikes, which can travel up to 20 m.p.h., to cover nine miles of ground on its two-hour Spanish Twist tour.

ABOVE Strolling the Embarcadero, a breezy two-mile stretch of waterfront. As the sculpture seems to suggest, fish is often on the menu at the restaurants nearby.

THE BASICS

Numerous airlines fly to San Diego. Or drive two hours from Los Angeles.

Hotel Indigo
San Diego-Gaslamp Quarter
509 Ninth Avenue
619-727-4000
hotelindigo.com
$$
A 3,800-square-foot green roof, free wireless, and a terrace bar.

Andaz San Diego
600 F Street
619-849-1234
sandiego.andaz.hyatt.com
$$$
Modern rooms, a four-story nightclub, and a flashy Philippe Starck-Katsuya Uechi restaurant.

Hotel del Coronado
1500 Orange Avenue
619-435-6611
hoteldel.com
$$$$
Beachside grande dame.

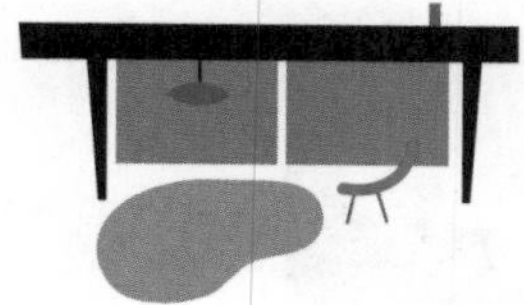

Palm Springs

Palm Springs was once the miles-from-Hollywood getaway that Malibu is now: a place for '60s movers and shakers to eat, drink, and sunbathe poolside while they awaited calls from studio execs. Today, after some hard-earned changes, this California desert town nestled in the Coachella Valley is becoming a destination for laid-back cool once again. The revival of modernism that inspired makeovers of its midcentury hotels, restaurants, and shops brought a revival of style, and the desert sun has never lost its appeal. Now Palm Springs attracts visitors who are just as happy climbing canyons as sipping cocktails on a lounge chair amid the design and architectural treasures of the past.

— BY ERICA CERULO

FRIDAY

1 *Cruising on Two Wheels* 3 p.m.

Because of its modest size, Palm Springs can easily become familiar over a couple of days, or even a few hours. Start your trip with a self-guided bike tour. **Big Wheel Tours** (760-779-1837; bwbtours.com) rents bicycles and can arrange bike and hiking tours. Free maps are available at the **Palm Springs Visitors Center** (777 North Palm Canyon Drive; 760-778-8418; palm-springs.org). To scope out the dramatic terrain and local hot spots, pedal the Downtown Loop, which can be done in less than an hour, or the 10-mile Citywide Loop that takes you past the Moorten Botanical Gardens.

2 *Austria and Beyond* 7 p.m.

At **Johannes** (196 South Indian Canyon Drive; 760-778-0017; johannesrestaurants.com; $$$), the chef Johannes Bacher bills the food as modern Austrian, combining classic Central European specialties like spaetzle and sauerkraut with decidedly borrowed ingredients and flavors, ranging from polenta to wasabi. But one of the best dishes is also the most traditional: a heaping plate of Wiener schnitzel with parsley potatoes, cucumber salad, and cranberry compote.

3 *Partying Poolside* 9:30 p.m.

Back when Frank Sinatra held raucous shindigs at his Twin Palms home, Palm Springs was known for its party scene. These days, the best drinking establishments are in hotels. The white stucco exterior of the **Colony Palms Hotel** (572 North Indian Canyon Drive; 760-969-1800; colonypalmshotel.com) conceals a welcoming hideaway with stone walkways, towering palms, and, when needed, patio heaters. At the buzzing restaurant **Purple Palm**, ask to be seated by the pool and order a plate of Humboldt Fog chèvre, organic honey, and local dates with your drink to top off the night.

SATURDAY

4 *Modernist America* 9:30 a.m.

Along with the moneyed 20th-century tourists came eye-catching buildings: hotels, commercial spaces, and vacation homes. Next to a hopping Starbucks on the main drag sits one of the city's oldest architectural touchstones: a concrete bell tower salvaged from the long-gone Oasis Hotel, which was designed by Lloyd Wright (son of Frank) in 1924. This spot is also where Robert Imber, the often seersucker-clad architectural guru and one-man show behind **PS Modern Tours** (760-318-6118; psmoderntours@aol.com), starts his three-hour excursions, which provide a survey of the city's key structures with a focus on the midcentury sweet

OPPOSITE Indian Canyons, a natural oasis on the Agua Caliente Indian Reservation just outside Palm Springs.

RIGHT The Kaufmann House, designed by Richard Neutra.

spot. Design enthusiasts can catch glimpses of the iconic Albert Frey-designed Tramway Gas Station, Richard Neutra's 1946 Kaufmann Desert House, and the mass-produced but stunning Alexander homes that your guide identifies by pointing out the four key components—"garage, breezeway, windows, wall"—in their various arrangements. Reserve well in advance.

5 *Chic Cheek* 1 p.m.

The wait for brunch at **Cheeky's** (622 North Palm Canyon Drive; 760-327-7595; cheekysps.com; $$) should be a tip-off: the bright, streamlined space, which feels airlifted from L.A.—in a good way—is popular. The standard eggs and waffles are spiced up with ingredients like beet relish, homemade herbed ricotta, and sour cherry compote.

6 *Used Goods* 3 p.m.

Stroll **Palm Canyon Drive**, a strip that's terrific for high-end vintage shopping, if a little dangerous for those who quickly reach for their credit cards. Among the many stores that focus on better-with-age décor, just a few have mastered the art of curating. At **a La MOD** (844 North Palm Canyon Drive; 760-327-0707; alamod768.com), nearly 70 percent of the merchandise, which is heavy on Lucite and lighting, is sourced locally, according to the shop's owners. Across the street, **Modern Way** (745 North Palm Canyon Drive; 760-320-5455; psmodernway.com) stocks an eclectic collection of larger pieces like Arthur Elrod couches, Verner Panton cone chairs, and Hans Olsen dining sets. For something you can actually take home, shop **Bon Vivant** (766 North Palm Canyon Drive, No. 3; 760-534-3197; gmcb.com), where the charming proprietors make you feel like a genuine collector for purchasing an $18 engraved brass vase or a $5 tie clip.

7 *Stay Silly* 5 p.m.

At the **Palm Springs Yacht Club**, at the **Parker Palm Springs** hotel (4200 East Palm Canyon Drive; 760-770-5000; theparkerpalmsprings.com), standard spa offerings like deep-tissue rubdowns and wrinkle-fighting facials come with a playful attitude of retro irony. The pampering is real. Expect to pay high-end prices (some treatment packages are well over $300) but go away feeling refreshed and maybe—is it possible?—a little younger.

8 *Friend of the House* 8 p.m.

Most of the favored area restaurants have an old-school vibe: tuxedoed waiters, a headwaiter who has worked there since opening day, and steak-and-lobster specialties. Though **Copley's** (621 North Palm Canyon Drive; 760-327-9555; copleyspalmsprings.com; $$$) might not have the culinary history of nearby Melvyn's Restaurant and Lounge, which opened as an inn in 1935, it has a different sort of storied past—it is housed in what was once Cary Grant's estate. It also has food that incorporates 21st-century flavors (one spring menu included dishes like a duck and artichoke salad with goat cheese, edamame, and litchi).

9 *Toasting Friends* 11 p.m.

The cocktail craze and the microbrew trend have both made their way to the desert, and the cavernous **Amigo Room** at the Ace Hotel (701 East Palm Canyon Drive; 760-325-9900; acehotel.com/palmsprings) is leading the way. In addition to pouring dozens of microbrews, the guys at the bar will measure, shake, and pour classic concoctions like the margarita and more offbeat options like the Figa (fig-infused vodka with Earl Grey and honey tangerine) that reek of late-night innovation. The cool but mellow vibe—supplemented by décor featuring burgundy leather booths and glass tables with inlaid pesos—will keep you ordering.

SUNDAY

10 *Get Close with Cactus* 9 a.m.

Those looking for an early-morning calorie burn might prefer the uphill battles of Gastin or Araby Trail, but a hike through **Tahquitz Canyon** (500 West Mesquite Avenue; 760-416-7044; tahquitzcanyon.com), part of the natural oasis area called Indian Canyons, offers a leisurely alternative. A small entrance fee gets you access to a 1.8-mile loop and the sights and smells that come with it: desert plants, lizards aplenty, and a stunning, 60-foot waterfall. Take a two-hour ranger-led tour or explore the trail at your own pace. You'll see arid desert and cool, palm-lined gorges.

11 *Pink Robots* Noon

For a one-of-a-kind experience that's both entertaining and eye-opening, drive out to the **Kenny Irwin Art and Light Show** (1077 East Granvia Valmonte; 760-774-8344; kennyirwinartist.com), a two-acre backyard sculpture park with massive, lighthearted, and very clever works that have to be seen to be believed. Metal and plastic junk from old vacuum cleaners to shopping carts is transformed with welding and bright paint into giant robots, roller coasters, space vehicles, and even an intimidating version of Santa's sleigh. Visits are by appointment only, so be sure to call in advance.

OPPOSITE Residential architecture of the mid-20th century distinguishes Palm Springs. This example is the Kaufmann House exterior.

ABOVE Hiking at Tahquitz Canyon.

THE BASICS

Several major airlines serve the Palm Springs airport. On the ground, you will need a car.

The Parker Palm Springs
4200 East Palm Canyon Drive
760-770-5000
theparkerpalmsprings.com
$$$$
Old Hollywood glamour in the new Palm Springs.

Riviera Resort & Spa
1600 North Indian Canyon Drive
760-327-8311
psriviera.com
$$$
Vegas-style glitz, 406 Old Hollywood-style rooms.

Saguaro Palm Springs
1800 East Palm Canyon Drive
760-323-1711
thesaguaro.com
$$
A chic and inexpensive option in a former Holiday Inn.

Big Sur

Running southward from Carmel, 150 miles south of San Francisco, to San Simeon, Big Sur's mass of tight mountains pushes brazenly against the Pacific swell. Kelp forests sway at the feet of the rugged sea cliffs. Deep valleys shelter some of California's southernmost redwoods. Writers, artists, dreamers, and hippies have all been drawn here; Henry Miller described it as "a region where one is always conscious of weather, of space, of grandeur and of eloquent silence." Although the rich and famous are now building homes here, the geography prevents sprawl and most of the development is invisible, preserving the feeling of solitude. Big Sur still rewards serendipity, but this is no place to rely upon it: the few lodgings fill quickly. Make your reservations well in advance, allow plenty of time for the drive, and then let the ocean and the mountains take over.

— BY GREGORY DICUM

FRIDAY

1 *View from the Road* 2 p.m.

The only way into and through the Big Sur coast is along winding, breathtaking **California Highway 1**. Its construction here in the 1930s was controversial (sheer cliffs and constant rockfalls attest to the project's audacity), but today it is a testament to the ambition of New Deal public works projects. Though Big Sur is as much an idea as a place, you will know you have arrived when, driving south from Monterey, you cross **Bixby Bridge**. A marvel of concrete spanning a deep coastal gorge, it has appeared in a thousand car commercials, and it's worth a stop if you're into infrastructure: turn out at either end of the span. Other viewpoints abound on the road, so keep your camera at the ready and expect to stop frequently.

2 *Waterside* 5 p.m.

Though the Pacific is everywhere in Big Sur, the enfolding coast guards access like a jealous lover. Beaches nestle in coves backed by fearsome cliffs, and in only a few places is it easy—or even possible—to set foot on them. **Pfeiffer Beach** is one. Take a sharp right turn a quarter-mile south of the Big Sur Ranger Station onto the unmarked Sycamore Canyon Road, and follow it down to a bay sheltered from the ocean's full force by chunky offshore rocks. The fine tan sand here is streaked with purple minerals. Wander in the warm sun and test a toe in the cold water. On one sunny late afternoon, handfuls of college students basked in sweatshirts and sunglasses like style-conscious sea lions. An arch in the rocks serves as a proscenium for the lowering sun and the backlit orange seawater splashes of gentle swells.

3 *Sunset Sustenance* 7 p.m.

Big Sur has remarkably few dining options for a place so visited. Fortunately, some of them are sublime. **Cielo**, the restaurant at the **Ventana Inn** (48123 Highway One; 831-667-4242; ventanainn.com; $$$) takes archly appropriate ingredients—wild Dungeness crab, seasonal local organic vegetables, Sonoma duck, bison from a Wyoming ranch—and turns them into finely wrought California cuisine. Get a table by the big windows, or outside, and enjoy a view of the sun dropping into the rippling waves. Unless it's foggy, of course.

OPPOSITE McWay Falls pours 80 feet onto a perfect, though inaccessible, beach around a blue Pacific cove.

BELOW A yurt at Treebones Resort, a mid-priced lodging option. Land-use restrictions both keep Big Sur beautiful and limit places to stay.

SATURDAY

4 *Grandpa's Eggs Benedict* 9 a.m.

One of Big Sur's heartiest breakfasts is at **Deetjen's** (48865 Highway 1; 831-667-2378; deetjens.com; $$), this coast's original roadhouse. The inn dates to the 1930s, when Grandpa Deetjen built a redwood barn here that grew into a cluster of cabins. The restaurant, open to all, has an unpretentious but efficient and friendly feel that seems the epitome of Big Sur at its best. Eggs Benedict are a specialty, but there's a varied menu that also includes smoked salmon and huevos rancheros. If you're lucky, you can eat by the fire, but resist the urge to sit there all day: it's time to work off that breakfast.

5 *The Redwoods Are Waiting* 10 a.m.

State parks are strung up and down the coast. Many offer short hikes to astounding coastal vistas, while others permit access to the rugged mountain wilderness of the interior. At **Pfeiffer Big Sur State Park** (26 miles south of Carmel on Highway 1), trails lead through dense, damp groves of redwoods and oaks to coastal overlooks, a waterfall, and up to open ridges and mountaintops. The three-mile Oak Grove Trail gives hikers a taste of the diversity of Big Sur landscapes and, with luck, the wildlife: Big Sur is one of the places where majestic California condors have been reintroduced following their near-extinction.

6 *Go for the View* 1 p.m.

Nepenthe (48510 Highway 1; 831-667-2345; nepenthebigsur.com; $$–$$$) has long been a favorite tourist aerie. It is worth a visit on a sunny day for the magnificent views and cheery crowd,

ABOVE A cabin in a redwood grove at Deetjen's, an inn that dates to the 1930s.

RIGHT At Pfeiffer Big Sur State Park, trails lead through dense redwood groves to open ridges and mountaintops.

OPPOSITE Pfeiffer Beach, one of the few accessible Big Sur beaches. Most are below fearsome cliffs.

although the food is undistinguished. Think of it as the price of admission.

7 *Waterfall to the Sea* 2 p.m.

Julia Pfeiffer Burns State Park (on Highway 1; 831-667-2315; parks.ca.gov), not to be confused with Pfeiffer Big Sur State Park, is an all but requisite stop. From the parking area it's an easy stroll to view McWay Falls. The 80-foot-high cataract pours onto a perfect, though inaccessible, beach around a blue Pacific cove. It's the image most likely to come to mind later as you reminisce about Big Sur.

8 *Enlightenment* 3 p.m.

"There being nothing to improve on in the surroundings," Miller wrote of Big Sur in 1957, "the tendency is to set about improving oneself." He could have been describing the **Esalen Institute** (55000 Highway 1), a sort of New Age Harvard founded in 1962, whose campus tumbles down toward a precipitous cliff above the ocean. Seekers and celebrities come for "energy" and Atlantis, registering for workshops in yoga, meditation, and various kinds of self-realization. Participants stay overnight. To get a taste of the place in a shorter time—and work away any lingering stress that has managed to survive Big Sur so far—book a massage (831-667-3002; esalen.org/page/massage-healing-arts; time slots limited and reservations essential). It will give you a rare opportunity to enter the Esalen grounds without committing to a longer stay. You're allowed to arrive an hour early and stay an hour afterward to experience the hot springs.

9 *The Soak* 5:30 p.m.

By now you've emerged refreshed from your bodywork and are soaking (nudity optional but de rigueur) in the **Esalen Hot Springs Baths** (esalen.org/page/esalen-hot-springs). Esalen is known for these legendary tubs. Hugging a seaside cliff, the complex of baths momentarily captures natural hot springs before they pour into the Pacific. Indoors, there are concrete walls, warm and grippy sandstone floors, and floor-to-ceiling windows looking out to sea. Outdoor soaking pools and a living roof lend the baths a sense of belonging in the landscape. From the hot water bathers can look down on sea otters lounging in the kelp. If your brief soak isn't enough, sign up to return between 1 a.m. and 3 a.m., when the baths are open to the public. The hours are inconvenient (the nighttime drive over corkscrew Highway 1 will instantly undo the baths' restorative effects), but breakers below shake the cliff and thousands of stars shine out of a black sky, giving the place the feel of a celestial point of embarkation.

10 *Above It All* 8 p.m.

On the ridgeline hundreds of feet above Pfeiffer Beach, the **Post Ranch Inn** perches in unobtrusive luxe, its cottages spread tactfully over rolling acres of grass and woods. But like the rest of Big Sur, the inn has a charm that has as much to do with its attitude as with the landscape—not every thousand-dollar-a-night resort has an in-house shaman. Even if your wallet places you in a different category from the establishment's target clientele, you will find a welcoming spirit at the inn's restaurant, the **Sierra Mar** (831-667-2800; postranchinn.com; $$$$). Seek a table on the outdoor deck and order the four-course prix fixe dinner.

OPPOSITE A hot spring pool at the Esalen Institute, where you can seek enlightenment or just a relaxing massage.

SUNDAY

11 *Literary Nexus* 11 a.m.

The **Henry Miller Memorial Library** (Highway 1; 831-667-2574; www.henrymiller.org) maintains a reference collection of Miller's work, a bookshop, and a big wooden deck where visitors can enjoy coffee and Wi-Fi. Special events include readings, concerts, art shows, performances, and seminars. It's hardly monumental—little more than a house in the woods before a grassy yard strewn with sculptures and bric-a-brac that might be sculptural. Like much of the rest of Big Sur, the library is a casual place where lounging and artistic pursuit go hand in hand.

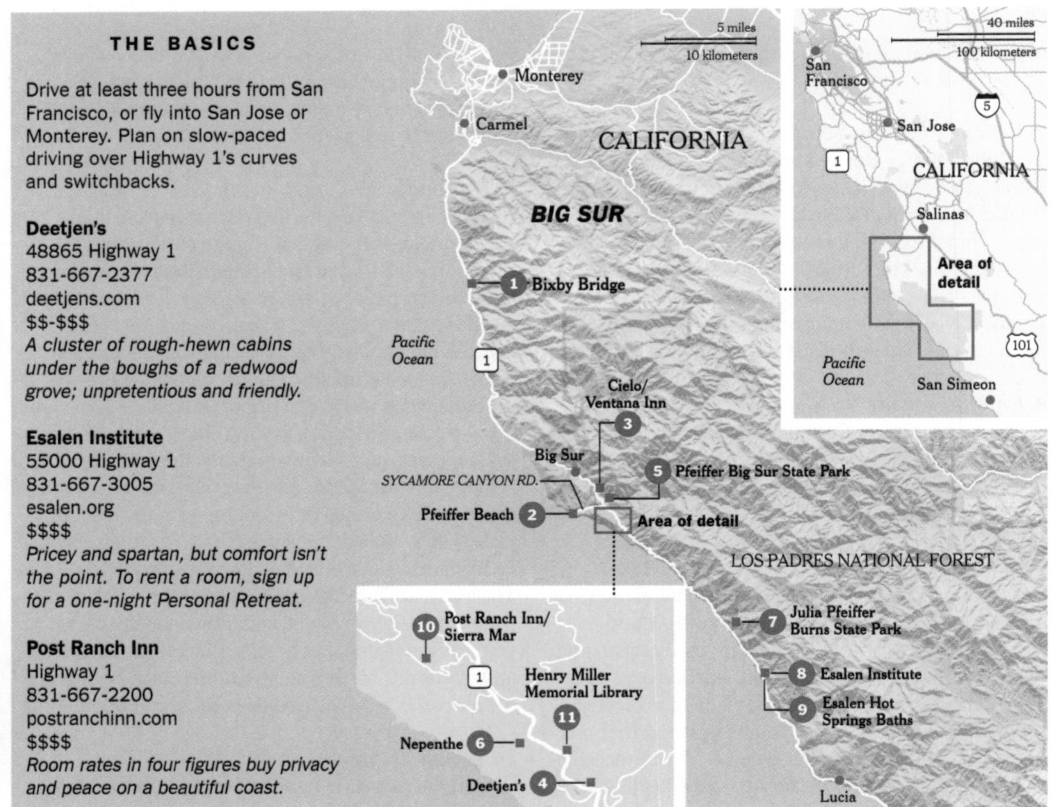

THE BASICS

Drive at least three hours from San Francisco, or fly into San Jose or Monterey. Plan on slow-paced driving over Highway 1's curves and switchbacks.

Deetjen's
48865 Highway 1
831-667-2377
deetjens.com
$$-$$$
A cluster of rough-hewn cabins under the boughs of a redwood grove; unpretentious and friendly.

Esalen Institute
55000 Highway 1
831-667-3005
esalen.org
$$$$
Pricey and spartan, but comfort isn't the point. To rent a room, sign up for a one-night Personal Retreat.

Post Ranch Inn
Highway 1
831-667-2200
postranchinn.com
$$$$
Room rates in four figures buy privacy and peace on a beautiful coast.

Carmel

With its architectural mishmash of storybook English cottages and Swiss Alpine chalets, the small California town of Carmel-by-the-Sea resembles a Disneyland version of Europe. You half expect a bereted Parisian to saunter out of one of the ridiculously cute Euro-themed bistros. But walk a few blocks to Carmel's steep, sandy beach and the view is pure California: a rugged Pacific coastline spangled with rocky outcroppings, ghostly cypress trees, and the electric green slopes of the famed Pebble Beach golf course. The one-square-mile village has no street lights, parking meters, or numbered addresses, but you wouldn't call it low-key. Once a bohemian outpost for people like Jack London, Carmel today is prime real estate, and the surrounding valley is abuzz with top-notch restaurants, boutique wineries, and upscale shops. — BY JAIME GROSS

FRIDAY

1 *Cocktails with Clint* 6 p.m.

Carmel has had its share of boldfaced residents, but few more enduring or beloved than Clint Eastwood, who was the town's mayor from 1986 to 1988 and still lives in the area. You might catch a glimpse of him at his restaurant at **Mission Ranch** (26270 Dolores Street; 831-624-6436; missionranchcarmel.com), his 22-acre property just outside of town, where he's been known to eat with his family and greet old-timers at the piano bar. Order a glass of wine and snag a seat on the heated restaurant patio overlooking a striking tableau: sheep meadows, rolling hills, and the shimmering ocean in the distance.

2 *California French* 8 p.m.

For an intimate dinner with plenty of foodie appeal, try Aubergine, the restaurant at the Relais & Châteaux hotel **L'Auberge Carmel** (Seventh Avenue and Monte Verde Street; 831-624-8578; laubergecarmel.com; $$$$). The French-influenced menu reflects the availability of fresh local produce with dishes like roasted lamb with cranberry bean cassoulet.

OPPOSITE The Point Lobos State Reserve.

RIGHT A landscape painter at Bernardus Winery in vineyard country near Carmel-by-the-Sea.

SATURDAY

3 *Biking for a View* 8 a.m.

Beat the gawking motorists and entry fee for cars by waking early and biking the **17-Mile Drive**, the jaw-dropping corniche that hugs the rocky coastline between Carmel and Pacific Grove. **Adventures by the Sea** (299 Cannery Row, Monterey; 831-372-1807; adventuresbythesea.com) rents bikes and is an easy five miles from the drive's most scenic stretches, which are lined with sandy beaches, golf courses, and a 250-year-old cypress tree sprouting from a seaside boulder.

4 *Mission Museum* 11 a.m.

The **San Carlos Borroméo del Rio Carmelo Mission** (3080 Rio Road; 831-624-1271; carmelmission.org) was founded at its present site in 1771 by Father Junipero Serra and was once the headquarters for the entire California mission system. Known more simply as the Carmel Mission, the site includes a poppy-filled garden, an abalone-strewn cemetery, and a stone Basilica with original 18th-century artworks. At the Mission's **Convento Museum**, you can peer into Father Serra's spartan living quarters—with a table, a chair, and a highly uncomfortable-looking wooden bed—and check out his book collection, identified as "California's first library."

5 *Lunch In-Town* 1 p.m.

Pick up lunch at Carmel's best food shops. **Bruno's Market and Deli** (Sixth Avenue and Junipero Avenue; 831-624-3821; brunosmarket.com) has gourmet tri-tip and barbecued chicken sandwiches. The **Cheese Shop** (Carmel Plaza, Ocean Avenue and Junipero Avenue, lower level; 800-828-9463; thecheeseshopinc.com) stocks picnic fixings, wine, and about 300 cheeses. They'll let you taste as many as you like, or they can assemble a customized cheese plate that you can nibble at the cafe tables out front.

6 *Poodles and Scones* 2 p.m.

In a town known for being dog-friendly, the **Cypress Inn** (Seventh Avenue and Lincoln Street; 831-624-3871; cypress-inn.com) takes the cake with poop bags at the door, bone-shaped biscuits at the front desk, and a *Best-in-Show*-worthy tea service. In addition to serving scones and crustless cucumber sandwiches, the tea service draws a head-spinning parade of Shih Tzus, toy poodles, and other impeccably groomed pups taking tea with their equally well-coiffed owners. Reservations are recommended.

7 *Stuff for Home* 4 p.m.

The 42 hidden courtyards and alleys of Carmel shelter a plethora of stylish galleries and fashionable boutiques. Spend a lazy afternoon wandering and browsing. One shop not to miss is the **Carmel Drug Store** (Ocean Avenue and San Carlos Street; 831-624-3819; carmeldrugstore.com), which has been selling handmade Swiss combs, grandma colognes, and Coca-Cola in glass bottles since 1910. Another high spot is the working studio and gallery of **Steven Whyte**, a local sculptor (Dolores Street between Fifth and Sixth Avenues; 831-620-1917; stevenwhytesculptor.com) who makes hyper-realistic cast-bronze portraits.

8 *Casual Flavors* 8 p.m.

For dinner, make a beeline for one of Carmel's über-charming French or Italian restaurants. **La Bicyclette** (Dolores Street at Seventh Avenue; 831-622-9899; labicycletterestaurant.com; $$$) resembles a rustic village bistro. The compact menu spans Europe with dishes like beef with Gorgonzola-red wine sauce or German sausage with homemade sauerkraut. Also worth a try is **Cantinetta Luca** (Dolores Street between Ocean and Seventh Avenues; 831-625-6500; cantinettaluca.com; $$$), an Italian restaurant popular for its wood-fired pizzas, homemade pastas, all-Italian wine list, and a dozen types of salumi aged on site in a glass-walled curing room.

SUNDAY

9 *Sea Life* 11 a.m.

Legend has it that Robert Louis Stevenson hit on the inspiration for the 1883 novel *Treasure Island* while strolling the beach near Point Lobos. Retrace his steps at **Point Lobos State Reserve** (Route 1, three miles south of Carmel; 831-624-4909;

ABOVE The Cheese Shop stocks picnic fixings, wine, and about 300 different cheeses.

RIGHT A heron at Point Lobos State Reserve.

pt-lobos.parks.state.ca.us), a majestic landscape with 14 meandering trails. Don't forget binoculars: you can spot sea otters, seals, and sea lions year-round, and migrating gray whales December through May. Scuba divers take note: 60 percent of the reserve's 554 acres lies underwater, in one of the richest marine habitats in California. Scuba diving, snorkeling, and kayaking reservations can be booked through the park's Web site.

10 *Sip the Valley* 1 p.m.

Thanks to its coastal climate and sandy, loamy soil, Carmel Valley is gaining renown for its wines. Most of the tasting rooms are clustered in Carmel Valley Village, a small town with a handful of restaurants and wineries 12 miles east of Carmel-by-the-Sea. **Bernardus** (5 West Carmel Valley Road; 831-298-8021; bernardus.com/winery), the granddaddy of area wineries, is known for the breadth and quality of its wines. A relative newcomer, **Boekenoogen Wines** (24 West Carmel Valley Road; 831-659-4215; boekenoogenwines.com), is a small family-owned winery with a few varietals. Teetotalers can opt for topical wine treatments at **Bernardus Lodge** (415 West Carmel Valley Road; 831-658-3560; bernardus.com), where a spa offers chardonnay facials and grape seed body scrubs.

ABOVE Cycling on the winding 17-Mile Drive, which hugs the rocky coastline between Carmel and Pacific Grove.

THE BASICS

Carmel-by-the-Sea is a scenic two-hour drive south of San Francisco.

L'Auberge Carmel
Seventh Avenue and Monte Verde Street
831-624-8578
laubergecarmel.com
$$$$
Winding staircases lead to 20 rooms, many with Japanese soaking tubs.

Cypress Inn
Seventh Avenue and Lincoln Street
831-624-3871
cypress-inn.com
$$$
Co-owned by Doris Day, whose songs are piped through the hotel.

Carmel Valley Ranch
1 Old Ranch Road
831-625-9500
carmelvalleyranch.com
$$$$
Fireplaces, terraces, golf course.

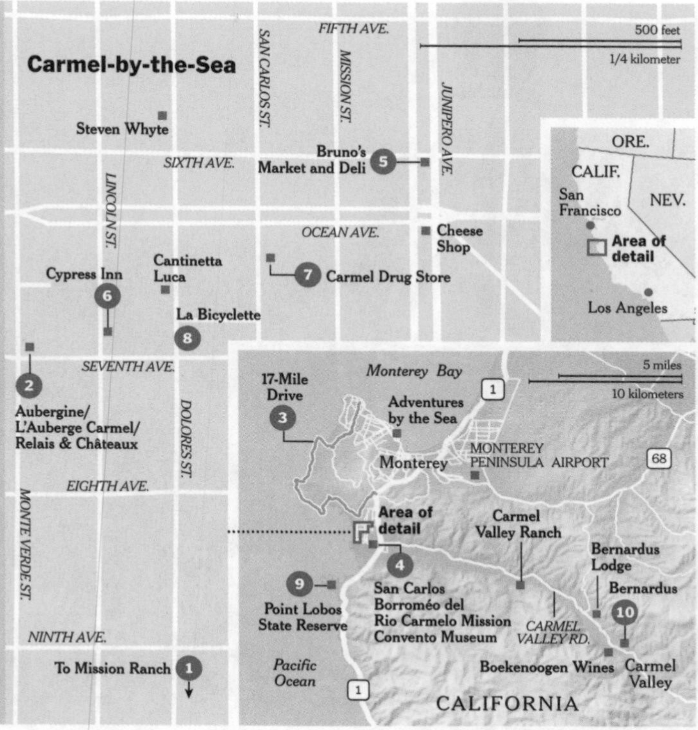

Silicon Valley

Like the high-tech companies that give this hyper-prosperous region its name, Silicon Valley thrives on reinvention. Situated just south of San Francisco Bay, the valley was once home to orchards and vineyards. These days, of course, it bears fruit of a different sort, as the home of tech giants like Apple, Google, and Intel. Buoyed by the resilience of tech companies, the valley's dozen or so cities, which include Mountain View and Palo Alto, continue to evolve from corporate strip malls to urban hubs. The valley now buzzes with cultural spaces, lively restaurants, and the energy of a hyper-educated workforce that has no problem keeping up.
— BY ASHLEE VANCE

FRIDAY

1 *Small Town Downtown* 3 p.m.

San Jose may still call itself the capital of Silicon Valley, but picturesque **Los Gatos** is emerging as its trendier downtown, with historic cottages and upscale boutiques. The chains have begun an invasion, but dozens of independent shops remain, selling fashion, children's clothing, baby duds, shoes, accessories, home décor, and collectors' items. Start your prospecting on North Santa Cruz Avenue at West Main Street and follow your whims as you head north. The people cruising the streets in Los Gatos give off a vibe that matches the bright, charming town, which is full of surprises off the main drag.

2 *Pitch Your Venture* 6 p.m.

Sand Hill Road is one of the valley's main arteries, cutting through Palo Alto, Menlo Park, and Stanford University. As the weekend gets under way, follow the stream of Prius hybrids, Mercedes coupes, and the occasional Tesla electric car to **Madera** (2825 Sand Hill Road, Menlo Park; 650-561-1540; maderasandhill.com), at the Rosewood Sand Hill hotel. The indoor-outdoor bar is a hot spot for venture capitalists to unwind and gossip as they survey their domain on a terrace that looks out on the surrounding mountains. Down a cocktail or three, and find your pluck to pitch that brilliant Web idea you had.

3 *American Fare* 8 p.m.

St. Michael's Alley (140 Homer Avenue, Palo Alto; 650-326-2530; stmikes.com; $$), a few blocks off crowded University Avenue in Palo Alto, has three elegant dining areas, including a bar anchored by an artful hunk of walnut. The business casual attire matches the informal cuisine, which leans toward Californian and American fare. One night's pan-roasted salmon filet, for instance, came with lentils, leeks, rainbow carrots, and mustard herb butter.

4 *Choose Your Libation* 10 p.m.

Shame on Stanford students for allowing such tame bars along their home turf, University Avenue. For a more energized crowd, head to nearby California Avenue. A favorite among Silicon Valley's young titans is **Antonio's Nut House** (321 California Avenue, Palo Alto; 650-321-2550; antoniosnuthouse.com), a low-key neighborhood place where patrons can chuck their peanut shells on the floor, scribble on the walls, and take a photo with a peanut-dispensing gorilla. Down the road is **La Bodeguita del Medio** (463 California Avenue, Palo Alto; 650-326-7762; labodeguita.com), a small Cuban restaurant with a bar that serves sangria and rum, and a room for smoking hand-rolled cigars.

SATURDAY

5 *Engineers Under the Palms* 9 a.m.

The name Silicon Valley may have been coined in the early 1970s, but the tech timeline goes even further

OPPOSITE A view over the valley toward San Francisco Bay.

BELOW The first Apple, at the Computer History Museum.

back here. For a sense of the computer lore of Palo Alto, drive to 367 Addison Avenue and take a look at the humble wood garage where Bill Hewlett and Dave Packard started their company in 1939. The contrast to today's high-tech complexes is glaring. Next swing by 844 Charleston Road, an office building where Fairchild Semiconductor invented a commercial version of the integrated circuit in 1959. Then get to the intellectual center of it all, **Stanford University** (visitor center at Campus Drive and Galvez Street; 650-723-2560; stanford.edu) in time to park and do a little walking around before the 11 a.m. tour of the palm- and oak-shaded campus. The place is so peaceful and gorgeous that you'll find yourself pondering the role of a tranquil environment in the production of high-tech engineers.

6 *Google Brunch* 1 p.m.

Some chefs parlay a reality show into a restaurant. Charlie Ayers used his stint as the top chef of the cafeteria at the Googleplex, Google's headquarters-cum-playground, to open **Calafia Café** (855 El Camino Real, Palo Alto; 650-322-9200; calafiapaloalto.com). It is split down the middle between a sit-down restaurant and to-go counter. The fare is a lunch-style version of Californian comfort food: tacos, salmon, lamb hash, turkey meatloaf, and, of course, a vegetarian menu. The **Googleplex** itself (1600 Amphitheatre Parkway, Mountain View) isn't open to the public, but you can get a glimpse from the public park next to the entrance that peeks inside the laid-back campus.

7 *Computers 101* 3 p.m.

Much of the history of Silicon Valley—and, by extension, the electronic revolution in our daily lives—is now lovingly captured at the **Computer History Museum** (1401 North Shoreline Boulevard, Mountain View; 650-810-1010; computerhistory.org). It's well worth the trip to see some of the early tech devices that are now highly valued antiques, and you'll get a sense of how we got from room-filling mainframes to nanochips.

8 *Vietnamese Plates* 8 p.m.

Thanks to Google and its army of millionaires, Castro Street, the main drag in Mountain View, has undergone a culinary and nightlife revival. Among the bubblier spots is **Xanh** (110 Castro Street, Mountain View; 650-964-1888; xanhrestaurant.com; $$), a sprawling Vietnamese fusion restaurant with a handsome patio and dining rooms bathed in green and blue lights. The playful names on the menu—Duck Duck Good, Truth Serum cocktails—fail to capture the elegance of the dishes, plated in delicate fashion with exotic sauces. On weekends, the bar/lounge turns into a quasi-nightclub, with D.J.'s and more cocktails.

9 *Geek Talk* 10 p.m.

Back in 2010, an Apple software engineer lost an iPhone 4 prototype at **Gourmet Haus Staudt** (2615 Broadway; 650-364-9232; gourmethausstaudt.com), a German beer garden in Redwood City. Images of the prototype were splattered on Gizmodo, foiling the company's well-known obsession with secrecy. The beer garden has since shaken off its notoriety and remains a low-key place for engineers to gab about the newest products of their wizardry.

SUNDAY

10 *Local Harvest* 9 a.m.

Farmers' markets dot the valley on Sundays. One of the most bountiful is the **Mountain View Farmers' Market**, in the parking lot of the town's Caltrain Station (600 West Evelyn; 800-806-3276; cafarmersmkts.com), where flowers, fruits, and

vegetables are sold along with locally raised meats and artisanal cheeses. You can pick up prepared foods to munch on as well, including homemade pork dumplings and fresh samosas.

11 *Up to the Hills* 11 a.m.

It's called a valley for a reason. The Santa Cruz Mountains rise along the valley's western edge and provide a treasure hunt for people willing to explore. Wineries, including the **Thomas Fogarty Winery** (19501 Skyline Boulevard, Woodside; 650-851-6777; fogartywinery.com), sit atop the mountains, offering unrivaled views of the valley. Hikes abound. The **Windy Hill Open Space Preserve** (openspace.org), a 15-minute drive from Stanford in Portola Valley, has a range of trails that cut through 1,312 acres of grassland ridges and redwood forests. By the end of the hike, you'll be able to spot Stanford, the NASA Ames Research Center, and the mega-mansions like a valley pro.

OPPOSITE ABOVE The garage where Hewlett-Packard began.

OPPOSITE BELOW The Computer History Museum surveys the history of computing from the abacus to the iPad.

ABOVE Gourmet Haus Staudt found a place in valley lore when an iPhone prototype was carelessly left behind there.

THE BASICS

Fly into San Jose or San Francisco. Rent a car.

Rosewood Sand Hill
2825 Sand Hill Road
Menlo Park
650-561-1500
rosewoodsandhill.com
$$$$
On a 16-acre estate with stunning rose gardens overlooking the hills.

Avatar Hotel
4200 Great America Parkway
Santa Clara
408-235-8900
avatarhotel.com
$$
Newly remodeled, with Wi-Fi and iPod docks.

Hotel Keen
425 High Street
Palo Alto
650-327-2775
hotelkeen.com
$$
Inexpensive and as inventive as some of its Silicon Valley neighbors.

San Francisco
580
101
San Francisco Bay
CALIFORNIA
280
Gourmet Haus Staudt 9
Redwood City
Menlo Park
Area of detail
880
680
1
Madera/ Rosewood Sand Hill 2
Avatar Hotel
Windy Hill Open Space Preserve
Pacific Ocean
SKYLINE BLVD.
11 Thomas Fogarty Winery
Sunnyvale
Santa Clara
SILICON VALLEY
San Jose
Los Gatos
1 Los Gatos
17
10 miles
20 kilometers
Hotel Keen
UNIVERSITY AVE.
St. Michael's Alley 3
367 Addison Ave.
SAND HILL RD.
6 Calafia Café
Antonio's Nut House 4
EL CAMINO REAL
Stanford University 5
Palo Alto
La Bodeguitadel Medio
1/2 mile
1 kilometer
S. CALIFORNIA AVE.
Googleplex
AMPHITHEATRE PKWY.
Computer History Museum 7
101
Mountain View Farmers' Market/Caltrain Station 10
CENTRAL EXPWY.
Mountain View
Xanh 8

FILA

San Francisco

San Francisco typically wows visitors with its heights. The hills sear themselves into memory after a few up-and-down-and-up-again cable car rides or punishing walks. Then there are the hilltop sights: the sweeping vistas and the picturesque Victorians. But surrounding all of that is coastline, miles of peninsula shore along the Pacific Ocean and the expansive natural harbor of San Francisco Bay. Once a working industrial area with pockets of outright blight, much of the city's waterfront has been polished into another of its pleasures. To sample what it offers, start exploring in the east, south of the Bay Bridge, and loop your way west to the Golden Gate and then south to Ocean Beach. In one weekend romp, you'll join San Franciscans in many of the places they love best—and see what remains of their city's maritime heart.

— BY JESSE MCKINLEY

FRIDAY

1 *A Ride along the Water* 4 p.m.

China Basin, south of the Bay Bridge, is home to an entirely new neighborhood since big changes began around 2000. The University of California, San Francisco has developed its **Mission Bay Campus**, adding handsome new buildings and public art including two soaring steel towers by Richard Serra, a San Francisco native. And the opening of **AT&T Park**, the baseball field that's home to the San Francisco Giants, brought new energy and new monuments including tributes to greats like Willie Mays and Willie McCovey (the basin is often called McCovey Cove). Rent a bike at the **Bike Hut**, a nonprofit outlet at Pier 40 (415-543-4335; thebikehut.org), and pedal the wide promenade along the water.

2 *Embarcadero Imbibing* 5:30 p.m.

Once the home to a raised freeway—demolished after the 1989 Loma Prieta earthquake—and before that a busy wharf area receiving cargo from around the world, the **Embarcadero** is now one of San Francisco's most inviting Friday night spots, filled with workweek-wearied downtown workers ready to relax. Two inviting spots for a drink and appetizers are **Waterbar** (399 Embarcadero; 415-284-9922; waterbarsf.com) and **Epic Roasthouse** (369 Embarcadero; 415-369-9955; epicroasthouse.com). Views of the Bay Bridge are unbeatable at either, but oysters at Waterbar can really set the mood.

3 *Boat to a Bistro* 8 p.m.

Forbes Island (off Pier 39; 415-951-4900; forbesisland.com; $$$) is not an island, but it is an experience. Created from a 700-ton houseboat, it's a floating restaurant complete with an underwater dining room (with portholes), a 40-foot lighthouse, and an outdoor bar within barking distance from local sea lions. Its nautically minded creator and owner, Forbes Thor Kiddoo, pilots the pontoon boat that brings patrons from a nearby pier. The fish chowder is briny and yummy, as is an assortment of turf (including flat steak in a cognac cream sauce) and surf (organic salmon). Kiddoo, a houseboat designer who combines Gilligan's mirth with the Skipper's physique, is a charming host. Don't miss the 360-degree view from the top of the lighthouse; it may be the best—and the most unusual—vantage point in the city.

OPPOSITE On the Embarcadero near the San Francisco Oakland Bay Bridge. Outdoor workouts, often including jogging near the water, are a theme of San Francisco life.

RIGHT The Bay Bridge view from Waterbar.

SATURDAY

4 *Flip, Flop, Fly* 9 a.m.

Yearning for a Saturday-morning workout? Go for a run at **Crissy Field**, once a waterfront airfield and now San Francisco's weekend outdoor gym, with masses of joggers, walkers, and cyclists cruising its paths. It's part of the **Presidio**, formerly a military complex guarding San Francisco Bay and the strategic strait at its entrance — the Golden Gate. Now it's all part of the Golden Gate National Recreation Area. Activities run from the quirky (crabbing classes at the Civil War-era Fort Point, under the Golden Gate Bridge) to the caffeinated (outdoor coffee at the **Beach Hut**, 1199 East Beach; 415-561-7761). But the bounciest option is the **House of Air** (926 Mason Street; 415-345-9675; houseofairsf.com), a trampoline center in one of the repurposed buildings on the main Presidio post. Flanked by a kids' swimming school and an indoor climbing center, the House of Air also features a dodgeball court, a training center, and an old-fashioned bouncy castle for tots.

5 *Chow Time* Noon

Dining at the Presidio has come a long way since the days of reveille at dawn. Several restaurants now dot the northeastern corner, where much of the Presidio's development has occurred since it was transferred to the National Park Service in the mid-1990s. One spot that retains the old military feel is the **Presidio Social Club** (563 Ruger Street; 415-885-1888; presidiosocialclub.com; $$$). As unpretentious as an Army grunt, the club offers old-time drinks (the rye-heavy Sazerac, which dates to 1840) and a pleasantly affordable brunch. A dessert of beignets with hot cocoa can fuel you up for your next offensive.

6 *Union Street Stroll* 2 p.m.

Detour off base to Union Street, long a shoppers' favorite for its locally owned boutiques and home furnishings stores. The owner of **Chloe Rose** (No. 1824; 415-932-6089; chloeroseboutique.com) has a keen eye for silk dresses, chiffon blouses, and gold jewelry. Nearby are **Sprout San Francisco** (No. 1828; 415-359-9205; sproutsanfrancisco.com), which carries clothing, toys, and other items for children, and more women's wear at **Ambiance** (No. 1864; 415-923-9797; ambiancesf.com) and the nearby **Marmalade** (No. 1843; 415-673-9544; marmaladesf.com). Keep strolling for more stores, selling a variety of antiques, jewelry, clothing, and crafts.

7 *Nature and Art* 4 p.m.

Take a walk through the hills and woods on the Pacific coast side of the Presidio, where miles of hiking trails lead to scenic overlooks (presidio.gov). You may also find an artwork or two. The Presidio doesn't need much help being beautiful, but that hasn't stopped artists who have placed installations and sculpture on the grounds. One is Andy Goldsworthy, an environmental British sculptor whose ephemeral pieces in the park include *Spire* — a soaring wooden spike — and *Wood Line*, a serpentine forest-floor sculpture made of eucalyptus.

8 *Dinner at the Edge* 8 p.m.

The **Cliff House** (1090 Point Lobos; 415-386-3330; cliffhouse.com) has been serving visitors at the end of the continent since the Civil War. Still perched on the same rocks, facing shark-fin-shaped Seal Rock and the crashing waves below, the Cliff House underwent a major renovation in 2004. The result was a vastly improved dining experience on two levels, each with commanding views of the Pacific. The **Bistro** ($$), upstairs, serves entrees and cocktails under the watchful eyes of celebrity headshots (Judy Garland, for one, on an autographed glamour shot, sending her "best wishes"). Downstairs is the higher-end **Sutro's** ($$$), where the specialty is seafood dishes like a two-crab sandwich or grilled scallops. Try a Ramos Fizz, a gin cocktail — and purported hangover cure — made with egg whites, half-and-half, and orange juice.

9 *Burning, Man* 10:30 p.m.

Few things say California more than beach bonfires, a proud tradition up and down the coast. In San Francisco, free spirits keep it going at **Ocean Beach**, the wide sand expanse south of Baker Beach (the spot where Burning Man, the now Nevada-based arts fest, was born). While the wind can be biting, the mood at the impromptu fires is usually

OPPOSITE At Crissy Field, a part of the Presidio, masses of joggers, walkers, and cyclists cruise the paths.

BELOW *Spire*, a sculpture by Andy Goldsworthy, at the Presidio. Miles of trails lead to ocean views.

warm as groups congregate with guitars, pipes, and good vibes. Take a blanket and a pullover and watch the stars, surf, and sparks collide.

SUNDAY

10 *Other Side of the Park* 11 a.m.

The western edge of **Golden Gate Park**, facing Ocean Beach, has a Rodney Dangerfield feel, less known and appreciated than the park's cityside flanks. But its offerings are impressive, including a cheap and public nine-hole, par-3 golf course, a lovely bison enclave, and serene fly-fishing ponds. A good place to convene for any park adventure is the **Park Chalet** (1000 Great Highway; 415-386-8439; parkchalet.com; $$$). In this somewhat hidden spot just off Ocean Beach, kids run free in the wilds of the park and parents enjoy a brunch buffet that advertises "bottomless champagne."

ABOVE On the trail that leads from Fort Point, under the Golden Gate Bridge, along the bay to Crissy Field.

OPPOSITE A 21st-century addition, *Cupid's Span*, by Claes Oldenburg and Coosje van Bruggen, frames a view of the Ferry Building clock tower, a more traditional San Francisco landmark.

THE BASICS

Take the BART train from San Francisco International Airport to downtown. Get around the city using taxis and public transportation.

Hotel Vitale
8 Mission Street
415-278-3700
hotelvitale.com
$$$$
Style and luxury on the Embarcadero, across from the landmark Ferry Building.

Harbor Court Hotel
165 Steuart Street
415-882-1300
harborcourthotel.com
$$
Boutique hotel with bay views.

Union Street Inn
2229 Union Street
415-346-0424
unionstreetinn.com
$$$
Quiet and charming bed-and-breakfast.

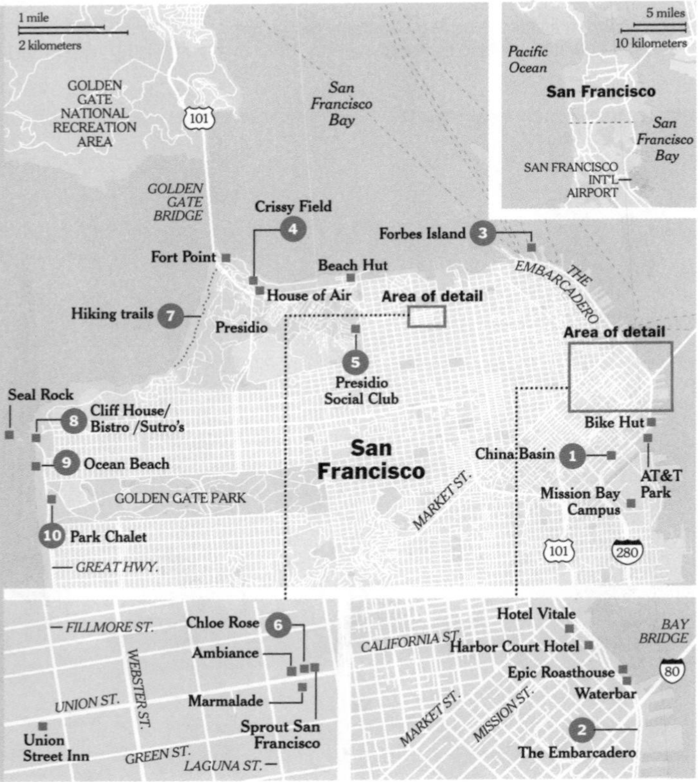

1 mile
2 kilometers
GOLDEN GATE NATIONAL RECREATION AREA
101
San Francisco Bay
GOLDEN GATE BRIDGE
Crissy Field 4
Forbes Island 3
Fort Point
Beach Hut
THE EMBARCADERO
House of Air
Area of detail
Hiking trails 7
Presidio
5 Presidio Social Club
Area of detail
Seal Rock
8 Cliff House/ Bistro /Sutro's
Bike Hut
San Francisco
China Basin 1
9 Ocean Beach
MARKET ST.
AT&T Park
GOLDEN GATE PARK
Mission Bay Campus
10 Park Chalet
GREAT HWY.
101
280
5 miles
10 kilometers
Pacific Ocean
San Francisco
San Francisco Bay
SAN FRANCISCO INT'L AIRPORT
FILLMORE ST.
Chloe Rose 6
Ambiance
WEBSTER ST.
UNION ST.
Marmalade
Union Street Inn
Sprout San Francisco
GREEN ST.
LAGUNA ST.
Hotel Vitale
BAY BRIDGE
CALIFORNIA ST.
Harbor Court Hotel
Epic Roasthouse
80
Waterbar
MARKET ST.
MISSION ST.
2 The Embarcadero

Berkeley

Berkeley, California, sticks in the collective memory as a hotbed of '60s radicalism and '70s experimentation. But anyone who thinks that's the whole picture is in for a surprise. From the main gate of the flagship campus of the University of California to revamped sophisticated boutiques, this city overlooking San Francisco Bay offers variety few towns can match. On College Avenue, the main drag, costumed hipsters mix with high-tech geeks in training, and freelance philosophers rub elbows with label-conscious materialists. Not that the spirit of 1969 has completely gone away. Walk down Telegraph Avenue, and along one block you may encounter activists for Free Tibet, patchouli-scented advocates of homeopathic medicine, and crusty purple-haired free-love followers still eager to convert you to their cause.

— BY JOSHUA KURLANTZICK

FRIDAY

1 *Bookmark This* 5 p.m.

Old and new Berkeley, activists and achievers, all head to **Moe's Books** (2476 Telegraph Avenue; 510-849-2087; moesbooks.com). Founded in 1959 and piled high with used books, Moe's is a place to wander for hours, flipping through choices from out-of-print tomes on 1950s African history to kabbalah manuals. The store also hosts frequent readings.

2 *College-Town Fusion* 8 p.m.

Berkeley's food scene has blossomed well beyond student hangouts. Consider **Iyasare** (1830 Fourth Street; 510-845-8100; iyasare-berkeley.com; $$), where the classy Japanese fusion fare is decidedly un-college-town but the unpretentious crowd makes you feel as if you were eating in someone's home. On the menu, along with sushi and specialties reflecting the cuisine of rural northern Japan, are creative entrees like sea urchin fettucine with smoked miyagi oyster, ikura, black truffle, and shaved bonito.

3 *Cinema Paradise* 10 p.m.

The **Pacific Film Archive** (2621 Durant Avenue; 510-642-0808; bampfa.berkeley.edu) at the Berkeley Art Museum offers one of the most refreshingly unpredictable moviegoing experiences in the Bay Area. At the archive's theater across the street from the museum, you might find a French New Wave festival followed by a collection of shorts from West Africa. The archive is particularly strong on Japanese cinema — and grungy-looking grad students.

SATURDAY

4 *Hill Country* 8 a.m.

This is California, so you'll have to get up early to have prime walking paths to yourself. Wander through the main U.C. Berkeley campus, quiet at this time, and into the lush Berkeley Hills overlooking the university. You'll pass sprawling mansions that resemble Mexican estates, families walking tiny manicured poodles, and students running off hangovers along the steep hills. It's easy to get lost, so take a map; Berkeley Path Wanderers Association (berkeleypaths.org) offers one of the best. If you want a longer walk, try nearby **Tilden Park**, a 2,000-acre preserve that includes several peaks and numerous trails open for mountain biking. Or head to the **University of California Botanical Garden** (200 Centennial Drive; 510-643-2755; botanicalgarden.berkeley.edu), home to more than 12,000 species of plants.

5 *Veggie Bounty* Noon

It's tough choosing from the many farmers' markets in the San Francisco Bay Area, but for the

OPPOSITE At Moe's Books, the stock spills off the tables and all of Berkeley streams in the door.

BELOW Berkeley Bowl, a fruit-and-vegetable heaven.

real deal, head to the **Berkeley Farmers' Market** (Center Street at Martin Luther King Way; ecologycenter.org). The Berkeley market is run by actual farmers and has a workingman's vibe. Afterward, stop by the **Berkeley Bowl Marketplace** (2020 Oregon Street; 510-843-6929; berkeleybowl.com) for a comparison. A veritable fruit-and-vegetable heaven, the Bowl offers a staggering array of peaches, apples, and rows of heirloom tomatoes—pudgy, lumpy, flavorful. Grab a roasted chicken and fresh beet salad at the deli counter, and snack on it while arguing with the various activists who congregate outside the Bowl's doors.

6 *Snake Pit* 3:30 p.m.

For a shopping experience not easily duplicated, drop in at the **East Bay Vivarium** (1827-C Fifth Street; 510-841-1400; eastbayvivarium.com), perhaps the city's strangest attraction. But don't come with a fear of snakes: the massive gallery and store, which specializes in reptiles, amphibians, and arachnids, is like a living nightmare. Strolling through, you'll pass gargantuan boas and more scorpion species than you'd ever imagined.

7 *Rock Out* 5 p.m.

The best views of campus aren't from the 10-story Evans Hall, but from **Indian Rock Park**. Wedged in a residential neighborhood along the city's northeast, the park has large rock outcroppings that offer 360-degree views across Berkeley and Oakland, and over the Bay to San Francisco. For more spectacular sunset views, bring some rope and carabiners: the main outcropping, Indian Rock, is a practice site for rock climbers.

8 *Homage to Alice Waters* 6:30 p.m.

Scoring a reservation at **Chez Panisse** (1517 Shattuck Avenue; 510-548-5525; chezpanisse.com; $$$$), the renowned restaurant created by the groundbreaking chef Alice Waters in 1971, can be a labor-intensive project. A creative, casual alternative is **Gather** (2200 Oxford Street; 510-809-0400; gatherrestaurant.com; $$), very much built on the

OPPOSITE ABOVE Sather Gate, leading into the central campus of the University of California.

OPPOSITE BELOW Entrance to the Pacific Film Archive Theater.

Waters tradition but heading down its own contemporary organic/local ingredients/eco-chic path. The stated aim is to please both vegetarians and omnivores, and even the pizzas, nicely blistered and chewy, shed light on the concept. How about morel pizza topped with fontinella, stinging nettles, and braised leeks?

9 *Berkeley Roots* 8 p.m.

Berkeley may be the perfect town for roots music. The genre of the '60s is not forgotten, although there's no objection to some updating. Shows at **Freight and Salvage Coffeehouse** (2020 Addison Street; 510-644-2020; freightandsalvage.org) feature nationally known musicians performing folk, blue-grass, and modern takes on traditional music like jazz folk and Celtic jazz. Be warned. There's no alcohol. It really is a coffeehouse.

SUNDAY

10 *Fourth and Long* 11 a.m.

Fourth Street is not far from Telegraph, but it's miles away in style. This trendy shopping district has become a chic, open-air mall with funky home décor, local art, and designer fashions. One of the most interesting of the shops and galleries is the **Stained Glass Garden** (1800 Fourth Street; 510-841-2200; stainedglassgarden.com), which carries elegantly curved glassware, dangly jewelry that resembles Calder mobiles, and kaleidoscope-like lampshades.

THE BASICS

Drive across the Oakland Bay Bridge from San Francisco and then into Berkeley. Or fly into Oakland. Public transportation is limited.

Claremont Resort and Spa
41 Tunnel Road
510-843-3000
claremontresort.com
$$$
Built in 1915 in the manner of an English estate. Full-service spa.

Hotel Shattuck Plaza
2086 Allston Way
510-845-7300
hotelshattuckplaza.com
$$
Boutique hotel in a historic building.

Berkeley City Club
2315 Durant Avenue
510-848-7800
berkeleycityclub.com
$$
Built in 1927.

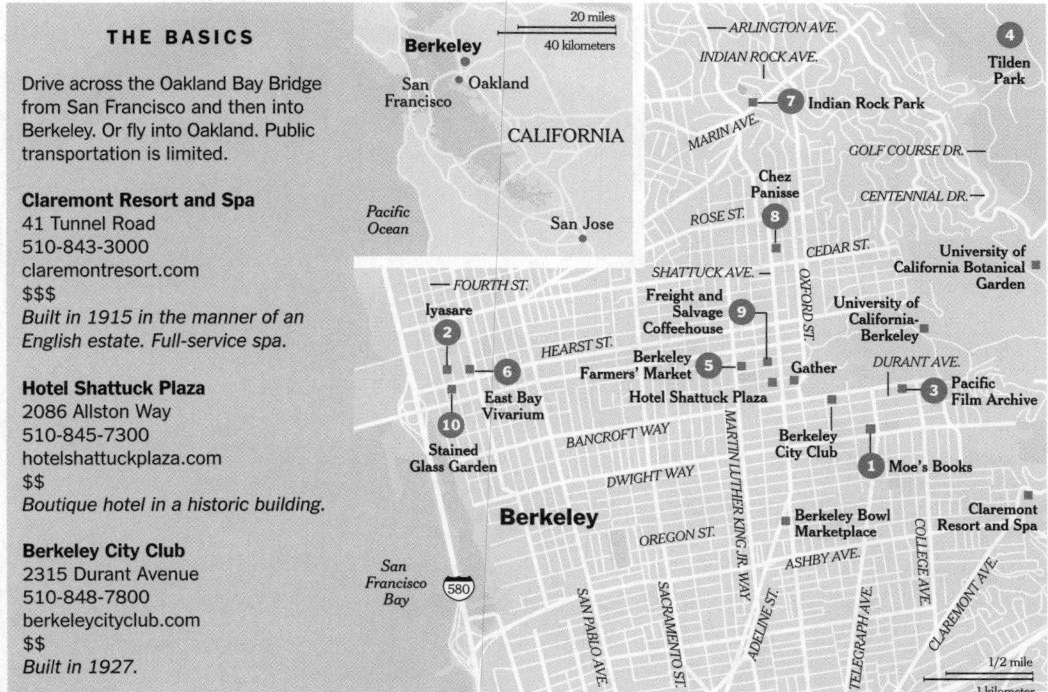

Marin County

Crossing the Golden Gate Bridge from San Francisco, you arrive in Marin even before landing on solid ground. The end of the bridge hangs over the county line (which is at the water's edge on the north shore of the Golden Gate strait), and this introduction is fitting since Marin itself feels suspended—ethereal, privileged, a place apart from the rest of the Bay Area. Fearing the perils of suburban sprawl, Marin invested early and often in conservation. Outside of a handful of small cities (San Rafael and Novato the largest among them), the county is a surprisingly rural landscape of cattle ranches, rolling hills, redwood groves, houseboat communities, and roadhouses. It is among the wealthiest counties in the country, and its affluence is apparent in places like Mill Valley. But Marin also has small towns, like Bolinas and Fairfax, that retain an endearing Northern California eccentricity.

—BY FREDA MOON

FRIDAY

1 *Past and Present* 3 p.m.

The **Marin History Museum** (1125 B Street, San Rafael; 415-454-8538; marinhistory.org), occupying a Victorian house on a hillside in old San Rafael, has an intriguing collection of local mementos and exhibitions about county icons and institutions like the Golden Gate Bridge and the notorious San Quentin Prison. Around the corner, the **Falkirk Cultural Center** (1408 Mission Avenue, San Rafael; 415-485-3328; falkirkculturalcenter.org) is a magnificent Queen Anne mansion with floor-to-ceiling stained-glass windows and a creaky staircase that leads to a gallery featuring local artists.

2 *Dead and Alive* 5 p.m.

Phil Lesh of the Grateful Dead modeled **Terrapin Crossroads** (100 Yacht Club Drive, San Rafael; 415-524-2773; terrapincrossroads.net), in San Rafael's Canal district, after Levon Helm's Midnight Rambles in Woodstock, N.Y. This music space, restaurant, and bar on the waterfront often hosts jam sessions featuring Lesh and his friends. At happy hour, you'll find an exceptional list of Northern California draft beers, half-off pizza from a flaming wood-fired oven, and appetizers like the Hangtown Fry, a taco-size crepe with wilted spinach, crispy fried oysters, and bacon.

3 *For the Soul* 7 p.m.

Occupying an imposing lime green building in downtown San Rafael, **Sol Food** (901 Lincoln Avenue, San Rafael; 415-451-4765; solfoodrestaurant.com; $) is a bright, plant-filled space with communal tables and Puerto Rican classics like shrimp sautéed in a garlic, onion, and tomato sauce, with mofongo (mashed green plantains), salad, and fresh avocado. Sol Food serves no alcohol; order the mango ice tea or Mexican Coke. Save room for dessert at **Fairfax Scoop** (63 Broadway Boulevard, Fairfax; 415-453-3130), an elevator-size ice cream shop where there's almost always a line.

4 *Fairfax for All* 9 p.m.

For an after-dinner drink, head over to **123 Bolinas** (123 Bolinas Street, Fairfax; 415-488-5123; 123bolinas.com), a wine bar across from Bolinas Park that serves small plates, local beer, and regional wines. The bar top is carved from a 100-year-old fallen oak, the furniture is built of reclaimed barn siding, and there's a U.F.O.-shaped fireplace. For something more casual, head to the cycle-centric beer and sausage spot **Gestalt Haus Fairfax** (28 Bolinas Road, Fairfax; 415-721-7895),

OPPOSITE The Marin Headlands from the shore below the Golden Gate Bridge in San Francisco.

RIGHT Pedaling on the Lagunitas Lake loop trail. Marin claims to be the birthplace of mountain biking.

which has board games, a CD jukebox, cyclocross posters on the walls, and 20 or so tap beers. Then sample one of the several lively spots in downtown Fairfax, a 7,500-person town that claims to have had live music every night for more than 30 years.

SATURDAY

5 *Head for the Hills* 9:30 a.m.

Start the day with beignets and chicory coffee at the homey, New Orleans-inspired **Hummingbird** (57 Broadway Boulevard; Fairfax), and then go mountain biking; Marin proclaims itself as the sport's birthplace. Stop by **Sunshine Bicycle Center** (737 Center Boulevard, Fairfax; 415-459-3334; sunshinebicycle.com) to rent a high-performance bike, grab a map, and get directions to the Lagunitas Lake loop (known locally as the Gentleman's Loop), a relatively nontechnical trail that travels past lakes and through chaparral, oak groves, and meadows.

6 *Coastal Picnic* 2 p.m.

Stop into the **Cowgirl Creamery** (80 Fourth Street, Point Reyes Station; 415-663-9335; cowgirlcreamery.com), which sells exceptional cheeses, like triple-cream Red Hawk and Mt. Tam, along with baguettes, charcuterie, and wine, in a restored barn in downtown Point Reyes Station. Then head to **Hog Island Oyster Company** (20215 Highway 1, Marshall; 415-663-9218; hogislandoysters.com), where the shuck-your-own oyster picnic gets you a picnic table and grill, rubber shucking gloves and knife, oyster condiments (lemon, hot sauce, and freshly grated horseradish), and views of Tomales Bay. There are two three-hour time slots each day, and reservations are required, often weeks in advance. For bivalves without the elbow grease (or the planning), go to the **Marshall Store** (19225 Shoreline Highway, Marshall; 415-663-1339; themarshallstore.com; $$), a waterfront seafood shack in a half-buried boat that serves barbecued oysters in chorizo butter, smoked oysters on crostini, and grilled fish tacos.

7 *Down to Drakes* 4 p.m.

Take the **Estero Trail** (nps.gov/pore), one of Point Reyes's lesser-known hikes, through grasslands and a Christmas tree farm and egret rookery. Then descend to a wooden bridge across a narrow inlet of Drakes Estero, an estuary that's a breeding ground for seals. From the bridge, you may spot leopard sharks gliding back and forth at the water's surface. If time allows, continue to Sunset Beach, for a total round-trip hike of eight miles.

8 *Get Fresh* 8 p.m.

Saltwater (12781 Sir Francis Drake Boulevard, Inverness; 415-66-1244; saltwateroysterdepot.com; $$), in the small town of Inverness, is an unusual restaurant. A partnership with Pickleweed Point Community Shellfish Farm, which trains "underserved youth" to work in the oyster industry, the 34-seat bistro was crowd-source-financed. Local wines are on tap, and local fishermen are invited to sell their catch directly at the kitchen door. The menu changes with the harvest and includes artfully executed dishes like local king salmon with garbanzo beans, eggplant relish, and arugula pesto, and crispy lamb tongue with lentils and fingerling potatoes.

SUNDAY

9 *To Market, to Market* 8 a.m.

The Sunday **Marin Farmers Market** (10 Avenue of the Flags, San Rafael; agriculturalinstitute.org) in San Rafael has 160 vendors selling everything from radishes to prepared foods at the **Marin Civic Center**,

Frank Lloyd Wright's last major commission. Pick up breakfast: perhaps a savory pie or enchilada, or waffles from a food truck.

10 *Over the Hill* 10 a.m.

Take your picnic breakfast and join the slow Sunday parade of drivers winding their way **over Mount Tamalpais**. The views, which sweep back toward the bay and then west to Stinson Beach, are worth the crawl. On the coast, stop in at the **Bolinas Museum** (48 Wharf Road, Bolinas; 415-868-0330; bolinasmuseum.org), which opens at noon and has a regional history museum, three contemporary art galleries, and a permanent collection of works by West Marin artists. Another option, for those averse to the drive, is the short but breathtaking 1.7-mile walk through the **Tennessee Valley** to the cliff-flanked Tennessee Beach. And if you have never been to **Muir Woods**, the cathedral-like grove of giant redwoods that is one of California's most revered remnants of its original landscape, this is your chance.

11 *Waterfront Living* 1 p.m.

Tucked away on a dead-end street beside a marina, **Fish** (350 Harbor Drive, Sausalito; 415-331-3474; 331fish.com; $$$) serves a decadent Dungeness crab roll. After you've finished yours, walk the waterfront for a glimpse of Sausalito's well-appointed houseboats.

OPPOSITE ABOVE Hog Island Oyster Company.

OPPOSITE BELOW 123 Bolinas, a wine bar that serves small plates and beer as well as local wines.

THE BASICS

From San Francisco, drive across the Golden Gate Bridge to Marin County.

Mill Valley Inn
165 Throckmorton Avenue
Mill Valley
415-389-6608
marinhotels.com/mill-valley-inn
$$
Surrounded by redwood trees at the foot of Mount Tamalpais.

Gerstle Park Inn
34 Grove Street, San Rafael
415-721-7611
$$
B&B in large English-manor-style house; eight opulent rooms.

Cavallo Point
601 Murray Circle, Fort Baker, Sausalito
415-339-4700
cavallopoint.com
$$$$
In a renovated century-old Army fort above San Francisco Bay.

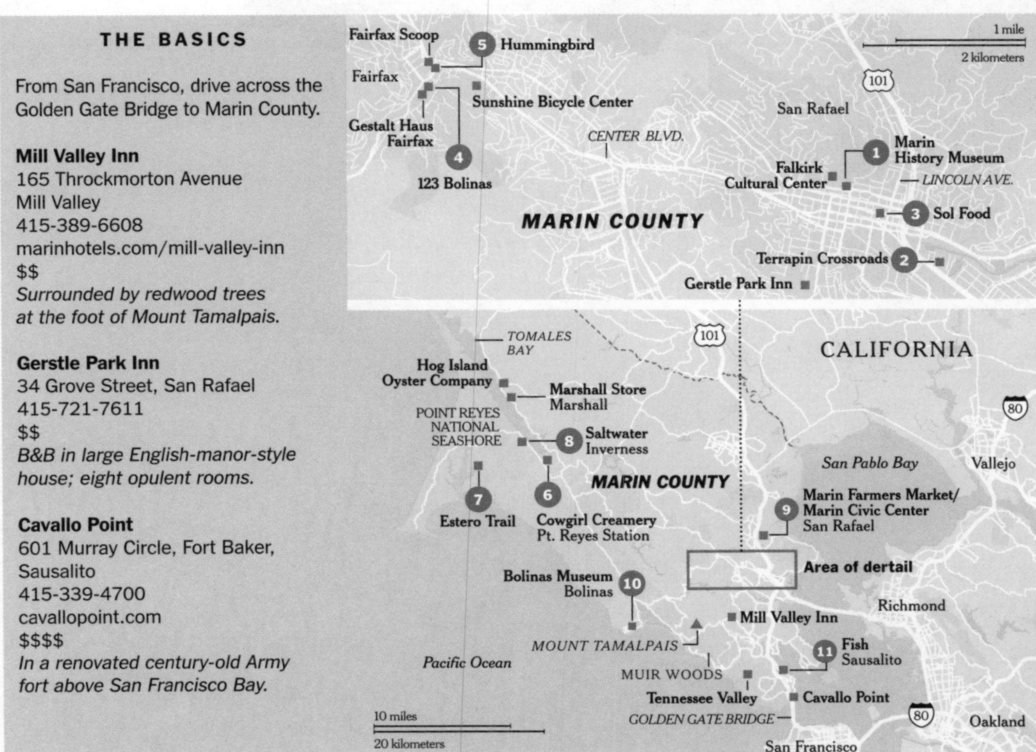

The Mendocino Coast

*Since the '60s and '70s, when a flood of artists, hippies, and back-to-the-landers brought the cosmopolitan counterculture to this corner of Northern California, the Mendocino coast has made appearances on many a television show (*Murder, She Wrote*, most notably, where the small village of Mendocino was the stand-in for a fictional New England town) and movies (*Overboard*, for one). Once a collection of working-class logging, fishing, and ranching communities, the Coast — as it's called by residents — has become a stand-in for California's left-coast eccentricities. It is also widely known for its intoxicants — its celebrated wine, beer, and marijuana. But what really makes this stretch of oceanfront real estate so stirring is its profound windswept natural beauty, which seems to have inspired the local residents to a fierce independence.*

— BY FREDA MOON

FRIDAY

1 *Firehouse Firewater* 5 p.m.

For local lore and a drink, pull up a stool at **Beacon Light by the Sea** (7401 South Highway 1; 707-877-3311), high on a hill near Elk, population 200. Part dive bar, part museum of oddities, "Bobby's place" is run by the Greenwood Ridge fire chief, Bob Beacon, in a back room of his remote fire station. You'll be greeted by a Great Dane and a grand piano. Break away at sunset for a walk on Navarro Beach, where sand castles and driftwood sculptures litter the pebble-strewn shoreline and bonfires burn on clear nights.

2 *Enchanté* 8 p.m.

For dinner, continue up the coast to **Ledford House** in Albion (3000 North Highway 1; 707-937-0282; ledfordhouse.com; $$), a French country bistro in the new California style (local farms, local wines, international influences), with a deck and tall Pacific-facing windows. A husband-wife, maître d'-executive chef team turns out formidable renditions of classics like cassoulet and steak au poivre. The dining room is homey, and there's live jazz every night.

SATURDAY

3 *Spiritual Sustenance* 8 a.m.

Rise early to explore Mendocino village and the wild coast at its edge. Wander the streets of the village, a cluster of low white frame Victorian buildings and old wooden water towers, many of which have been repurposed to house shops, art studios, and even lodging. Take note of the **Mendocino Art Center** (45200 Little Lake Street, Mendocino; 707-937-5818; mendocinoartcenter.org), in case you want to come back later to check out its galleries and watch artists at work. Venture out on the narrow footpaths of **Mendocino Headlands State Park**, which wraps around the village at the water's edge, and walk along the rocky, wind-lashed headlands to the picturesque Blowhole. Nearby, there's an imposing Tiki sculpture; do as the locals do and place an offering in the mouth of the carved kahuna. Or watch the swells come ashore from the driftwood "Love Bench" above Portuguese Beach.

4 *Bialy in the Morning* 9 a.m.

For a light breakfast, linger over espresso and a house-made bialy at **GoodLife Cafe and Bakery** (10485

OPPOSITE Paths at Mendocino Headlands lead out to the edges of rocky promontories.

RIGHT Water craft at rest outside Liquid Fusion Kayaking, where novices can take lessons in sea kayaks.

Lansing Street; 707-937-0836; goodlifecafemendo.com). For a more substantial meal, drive to **Eggheads** (326 North Main Street; 707-964-5005; $$) in Fort Bragg — a cramped Wizard of Oz-themed diner with menu items like Dorothy's Revenge, a supremely rich Dungeness crab eggs Benedict.

5 *Seaworthy* 10 a.m.

All who have witnessed the frothing Pacific know that its name — from the Spanish for peaceful — is a misnomer. Here, the sea is as violent as it is beautiful. **Liquid Fusion Kayaking** (32399 Basin Street, Fort Bragg; 707-962-1623; liquidfusionkayak.com) in Noyo Harbor teaches novices to ride the white water with a three-hour surf kayaking session. For a more leisurely paddle, rent a Polynesian-style outrigger at **Catch a Canoe & Bicycles Too** (44850 Comptche-Ukiah Road; 707-937-0273; catchacanoe.com) and glide up Big River.

6 *Take Out* 1 p.m.

At **Jenny's Giant Burger** (940 North Main Street, Fort Bragg; 707-964-2235; $), a classic roadside stand with vinyl stools, pick up a cheeseburger and a chocolate malt to go. Drive north to **MacKerricher State Park** (24100 MacKerricher Road, Fort Bragg; 707-937-5804; parks.ca.gov) to eat beside cattail-lined, fish-stocked Lake Cleone. Then walk south along the former log-haul road to where the pavement disintegrates into the sand dunes at **Inglenook Fen Ten Mile Dunes Preserve.** Another approach is to rent a bike in town and ride the length of the trail, crossing the nearly century-old Pudding Creek Trestle, an elegant lattice bridge that is now a pedestrian and bike path.

7 *Coastal Counterculture* 3 p.m.

Back in Fort Bragg, climb the stairs to the **Triangle Tattoo & Museum** (356B North Main Street, Fort Bragg; 707-964-8814; triangletattoo.com), where Madame Chinchilla and Mr. G have compiled exhibitions dedicated to Maori tattoos, circus skin art, and vintage ink machines. For contemporary installation art pieces and paper made from discarded textiles or local invasive species like pampas grass, visit the **Lost Coast Culture Machine** (190 East Elm Street, Fort Bragg; 707-961-1600; lostcoastculturemachine.org), a collective founded by a transplanted Brooklynite. There's more shopping in Fort Bragg's compact downtown, including the **Bookstore and Vinyl Cafe** (353 North Franklin Street; 707-964-6559), which has a lovingly curated selection of used books.

8 *Beer Country* 5 p.m.

The **Taproom** at the **North Coast Brewing Company** (444 North Main Street, Fort Bragg; 707-964-3400; northcoastbrewing.com) has wooden booths and a 12-beer sampler that includes the brewery's flagship Red Seal Ale. For a wider selection of regional beers, plus excellent New York-style pizza, head to **Piaci Pub and Pizzeria** (120 West Redwood Avenue, Fort Bragg; 707-961-1133; piacipizza.com). Or travel south to the **Wine Bar[n]** at Glendeven Inn (8205 North Highway 1, Mendocino; 707-937-0083; glendeven.com), which pours a wide variety of local wines by the glass each afternoon.

9 *In Good Company* 7 p.m.

Until 2002, Fort Bragg was a company town with a coastline consumed by a sprawling lumber mill. The second story of the former company store, a redwood building with a cathedral-like interior, is now home to **Mendo Bistro** (301 North Main Street; 707-964-4974; mendobistro.com; $$), a New American restaurant that serves dishes like barbecued lamb shoulder with cornmeal fried tomatoes, pickled onions, and mint, or pappardelle with pesto, cherry tomatoes, corn, and black olives.

10 *All That Jazz* 8:30 p.m.

For live music and an after-dinner latte, go to **Headlands Coffeehouse** (120 Laurel Street; 707-964-1987; headlandscoffeehouse.com), a local institution with a monthly art show and a loyal

ABOVE Llamas amble at Glendeven Inn, south of Mendocino. If you're not staying at the inn, drive out in the evening to sample vintages in its wine bar.

following that has helped to revitalize Fort Bragg's once-decaying downtown. Just across the alley, **V'Canto** (124 East Laurel Street; 707-964-6844) is an Italian restaurant-lounge with a welcoming bar and a well-considered wine list.

SUNDAY

11 *The Long Road Home* 10 a.m.

Take Highway 1 out of Mendocino County, stopping at **Queenie's Roadhouse Cafe** (6061 South Highway 1, Elk; 707-877-3285; queeniesroadhousecafe.com; $$) for breakfast food like organic allspice-laced corned beef hash or waffles with fresh fruit and yogurt dressing. Continue south to Point Arena, stopping at the 115-foot **Point Arena Lighthouse** (pointarenalighthouse.com). Rebuilt in 1907 after an earlier lighthouse was damaged in the same great 1906 earthquake that also devastated San Francisco, the current structure is said to have been the first steel-reinforced concrete lighthouse in the country. Three miles south of town, take the overgrown path to **Schooner Gulch State Beach** for one final walk along the water's edge.

ABOVE The view from Ledford House, a French country bistro in Albion, is out over the Pacific Ocean. The fare is farm-to-table, with local foods and wines.

THE BASICS

To reach the Mendocino coast from San Francisco, drive north on U.S. Highway 101 and turn onto Highway 128 at Cloverdale to get to the coastal road, Highway 1.

Mendocino Hotel & Garden Suites
45080 Main Street
707-937-0511
mendocinohotel.com
$$-$$$$
Victorian rooms and cottages with up-to-date amenities; overlooks the ocean and headlands.

Westport Hotel and Abalone Pub
38921 North Highway 1, Westport
877-964-3688
westporthotel.us
$$
Rejects television sets, in-room phones, and radios in favor of the sound of the growling Pacific.

Napa Valley

If you don't know where to look, the Napa Valley of California can seem uninspiring: big, Disney-ish wineries, lines four deep at the tasting rooms, and one too many tour buses. But nudge just a little off the tourist track, and you're instantly back in the rolling, bucolic paradise that first beckoned wine growers decades ago—quirky little vineyards, tiny towns, and a genuinely slower pace, despite the massive industry all around. In the bright days of summer and the misty moodiness of winter, this 30-mile-long region hums with life—and invites an air of reflection perfectly suited to those big California reds. — BY CHRIS COLIN

FRIDAY

1 *Vintage Cycling* 2 p.m.

Rent a bicycle at the **Calistoga Bike Shop** (1318 Lincoln Avenue, Calistoga; 707-942-9687; calistogabikeshop.com) and do some exploring. Some of the prettiest local roads are found around Calistoga, a funky and unstuffy town on the northwest tip of the valley—a bit of whiskey before the pinot. For your first taste of Napa Valley wine, pedal two miles to the Michael Graves-designed **Clos Pegase Winery** (1060 Dunaweal Lane, Calistoga; 707-942-4981; clospegase.com) and feel the terroir under your tires.

2 *Sling Some Mud* 5 p.m.

Calistoga's name has been mud, or at least synonymous with it, ever since the Gold Rush pioneer Sam Brannan dipped into the Wappo tribe's ancient mud baths. Some claim the volcanic ash and geothermally heated water rejuvenate the pores; others find relief from aches and pains. At a minimum, it's fun and weird to float in hot goop with cucumbers on your eyes. With a manicured lawn and white cottages, the **Indian Springs Resort and Spa** (1712 Lincoln Avenue; 707-942-4913; indianspringscalistoga.com) resembles a colonial hill town under the British Raj and claims the title of the oldest continually operating spa in California.

3 *The Food Is Local, Too* 8 p.m.

Stay in Calistoga for dinner at **JoLe Farm to Table** (1457 Lincoln Avenue; 707-942-5938; jolerestaurant.com; $$), which aims to live up to its name with seasonal cuisine made from organic locally farmed ingredients. Selections change frequently, but you might find scallops with leeks, mushrooms, and pancetta or chicken fried quail with Cobb salad. The wine list, naturally, also leans local.

SATURDAY

4 *Sizing Up the Grapes* 10 a.m.

Time to hit the vineyards. With hundreds to choose from in this valley, there's no perfect lineup. But some stand out for personality, memorable wines, or both. Make your first stop at **Casa Nuestra** (3451 Silverado Trail North, St. Helena; 707-963-5783; casanuestra.com; appointments required). This is a small family winery, and with your sips of chenin blanc or tinto you can expect a taste of old California informality—just ask the goats out front that clamor for snacks, emboldened by having a blend named after them (Two Goats Red).

5 *Chefs in the Cellars* 11 a.m.

From Casa Nuestra it's a short drive to the **Culinary Institute of America at Greystone** (2555 Main Street, St. Helena; 707-967-1100; ciachef.edu/california), the California campus of the chef-training school in Hyde Park, New York. It's not a winery, but it occupies a picturesque century-old stone building that was

OPPOSITE Oak barrels in a cave at Quintessa. Stop in to see how its Bordeaux-style wines are made.

BELOW Grapes on the vine at a Napa vineyard.

originally the Christian Brothers' Greystone Cellars, and its shop and the campus are worth a look around.

6 *Main Street Retail* Noon

You could have lunch at the Culinary Institute's restaurant, but you'll want to stop anyway in the precious town of St. Helena, a shopaholic's delight, so you may as well eat there. Have an avocado and papaya salad or a burger with house-made pickles at **Cindy's Backstreet Kitchen** (1327 Railroad Avenue; 707-963-1200; cindysbackstreetkitchen.com; $$). Then shop Main Street. **Footcandy** (No. 1239; 877-517-4606; footcandyshoes.com) carries Jimmy Choos and Manolo Blahniks with heels as high as stemware. **Woodhouse Chocolate** (No. 1367; 707-963-8413; woodhousechocolate.com) sells handmade artisanal chocolates in an elegant space that looks more like a jewelry shop. And the local interior designer Erin Martin has bronze sculptures, porcelain lamps, and other housewares at her shop, **Martin Showroom** (No. 1350; 707-967-8787; martinshowroom.com).

7 *Back to the Grapes* 2 p.m.

Large wineries often suffer in the character department, but not **Quintessa** (1601 Silverado Trail; Rutherford; 707-967-1601; quintessa.com). From the graceful crescent facade to the fascinating tours of its production facilities, this 280-acre estate makes a great stop—and it produces wonderful Bordeaux-style wines. For drop-dead gorgeous scenery, swing by **Frog's Leap** (8815 Conn Creek Road, Rutherford;

ABOVE The misty moodiness of the Napa Valley.

LEFT Cycling the quiet roads near Calistoga, the unstuffy town on the valley's northwest tip.

OPPOSITE Mustard, a winter crop growing amid the rows of leafless vines.

707-963-4704; frogsleap.com) and its five acres of lush gardens, orchards, beehives, chickens, photovoltaic cells, and everything else that puts this among Napa's more forward-thinking operations. And for unforgettable architecture, visit **Quixote Winery** (6126 Silverado Trail, Napa; 707-944-2659; quixotewinery.com). Its turreted, multicolored, cartoonlike building was designed by Friedensreich Hundertwasser, Vienna's late 20th-century answer to Antoni Gaudí. Appointments are required at each of these vineyards, and all have tasting fees.

8 *Riverfront Dining* 8 p.m.

For memorable fare and setting, go to **Angèle** in the city of Napa (540 Main Street; 707-252-8115; angelerestaurant.com; $$$), a converted boathouse on the Napa River where locals and tourists come to get away from the tourists. French brasserie classics like braised rabbit and cassoulet are served under a beamed ceiling and warm lighting. Regulars can be spotted ordering the off-menu burger with blue cheese. Needless to say, the wine list is varied and extensive.

9 *Make It Swing* 9:30 p.m.

The city of Napa rolls up its sidewalks after dark, but **Uva** (1040 Clinton Street; 707-255-6646; uvatrattoria.com) makes an exception for free live jazz every Saturday until midnight. Photos of old jazz greats crowd the walls, and you can tap along from the swanky dining room or the crowded bar.

SUNDAY

10 *The Overview* 6 a.m.

By this time, you've noticed that the Napa Valley is beautiful country, with corduroy-pattern vineyards carpeting its rolling golden hills and the Napa River easing its way from north to south. There's no better way to see it than from a slow-floating hot-air

balloon. Several companies will take you up and away for $200 or more per person; one standby is **Napa Valley Balloons** (4086 Byway East, Napa; 707-944-0228; napavalleyballoons.com). After a ride lasting about an hour, you will be served a Champagne brunch. The balloons leave early in the morning to catch favorable air currents.

11 *Art of Winemaking* 11 a.m.

For a nontipsy perspective on wine, drive up the winding, woodsy road to the ivy-covered **Hess Collection** (4411 Redwood Road, Napa; 707-255-1144; hesscollection.com), the winery and contemporary art museum built by the Swiss multimillionaire Donald Hess. Tours of the bright gallery, which are self-guided and free, take you past works by Frank Stella, Robert Motherwell, and Francis Bacon. At one point, a window provides a view of the fermentation tanks — the suggestion that wine equals art is not lost. Judge for yourself: the tasting room, just off the lobby, specializes in mountain cabernets.

ABOVE Dining at the Calistoga Inn Restaurant & Brewery, an outpost of beer in the wine country.

OPPOSITE Ballooning over the Napa Valley, an exhilarating adventure for a Sunday morning.

THE BASICS

The Napa Valley is about 50 miles north of San Francisco, just over an hour's drive. Make someone in your group the designated driver.

Indian Springs Resort and Spa
1712 Lincoln Avenue, Calistoga
707-942-4913
indianspringscalistoga.com
$$$
Retro glamour in an authentic, century-old spa. Olympic-size mineral springs pool.

River Terrace Inn
1600 Soscol Avenue, Napa
707-320-9000
riverterraceinn.com
$$$
Well-appointed rooms; close to riverside walks.

Auberge du Soleil
180 Rutherford Hill Road, Rutherford
707-963-1211
aubergedusoleil.com
$$$$
Spa, pool, tennis court, and terraces with valley views.

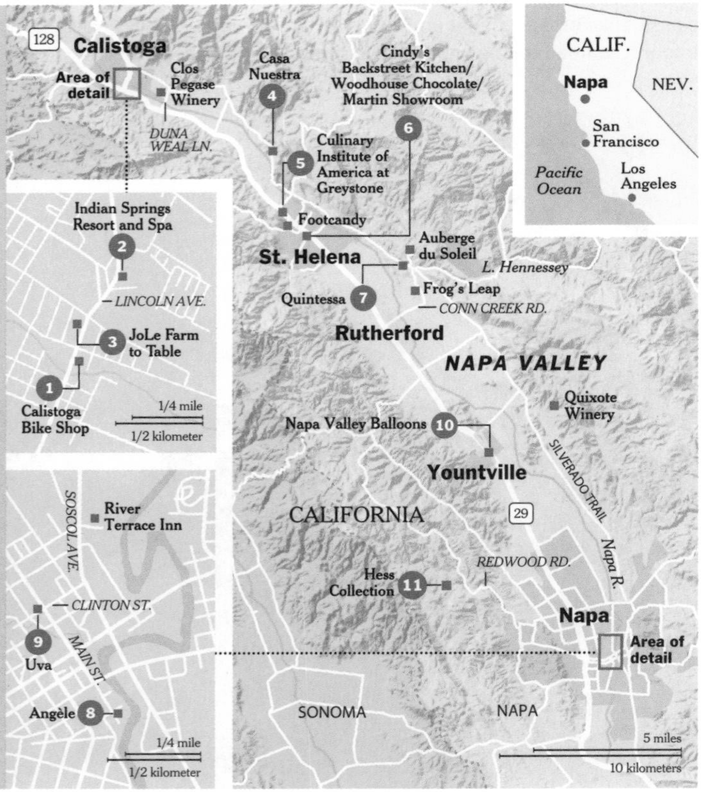

ESTERN PACIFIC
913
4466

Sacramento

California's governors and legislators may argue aggressively at its center, but the rest of Sacramento, California's capital city, has a gentle, small-town charm. Situated at the confluence of the Sacramento and American Rivers, it grew into a city as the gateway to the California Gold Rush and prospered as the home of railroad barons. What visitors will notice today is a strong theater tradition, delightful restaurants, a vibrant art scene, and a wealth of greenery — residents proudly claim that Sacramento has more trees per capita than any city in the world besides Paris. — BY BETH GREENFIELD

FRIDAY

1 *What Could Go Wrong?* 4 p.m.

Who says California's capital is prone to disarray? A stroll through the **California State Capitol** (10th and L Streets; 916-324-0333; capitolmuseum.ca.gov) — a neo-Classical confection of Corinthian and other classic columns, parget plasterwork, and mosaic floors — conveys the feeling that everything is in grand order. Painstakingly restored in the 1970s, the interior is graced with numerous artworks, including presidential portraits, WPA murals, and a stunning marble statue of Columbus and Queen Isabella by Larkin Goldsmith Mead. Outside is a lush park. A 250-pound bronze statue of a grizzly bear was brought by Arnold Schwarzenegger to guard the door to the governor's office. Wander at a leisurely pace while government employees rush by.

2 *Farm to Table* 6:30 p.m.

To dine in modern elegance, head a few blocks to the **Ella Dining Room and Bar** (1131 K Street; 916-443-3772; elladiningroomandbar.com; $$), which is draped with dramatic scrims of white linen. The restaurant emphasizes local produce, a sensible choice given that Sacramento sits amid some of the world's richest farmland. The menu includes dishes like pappardelle with poached egg and prosciutto in preserved lemon butter sauce or Sonoma duck breast with lentils and roasted pears. You could also have a soothing elderflower gimlet and a chocolate-rich dessert.

3 *Act Three* 8 p.m.

Sacramento has a healthy theater scene, judging by the well-chosen plays at the intimate **B Street Theatre** (2711 B Street; 916-443-5300; bstreettheatre.org). Past productions have included *The Maintenance Man*, a comedy about divorce by Richard Harris, a prolific British playwright, and *Entertaining Mr. Sloane*, a tale of seduction and sibling rivalry by Joe Orton. Draw out the drama with a nightcap at **Harlow's** (2708 J Street; 916-441-4693; harlows.com), where you'll find live rock or jazz downstairs and purple backlighting and plush and inviting seats in the Momo Lounge upstairs.

SATURDAY

4 *Mimosa Brunch* 10 a.m.

The **Tower Cafe** (1518 Broadway; 916-441-0222; towercafe.com; $$) sits across the street from the original (and, sadly, defunct) Tower Records. Get there early, and you'll have a better chance of

OPPOSITE The exhibits dwarf the visitors at the California State Railroad Museum. Visitors can climb aboard the restored locomotives and railroad cars.

RIGHT Bond with the American River with a morning of riding along its shores on the Jedediah Smith Memorial Bike Trail, a 32-mile loop.

snagging an outdoor table under the shady mimosa tree. But you could also do a lot worse than sitting indoors—where you'll be surrounded by an eclectic collection of objets d'art including African beaded belts, Mexican Day of the Dead sculptures, and 1930s travel posters. Dive into toothsome specialties like the Mexican scramble, blueberry cornmeal pancakes, or chorizo burrito.

5 *Buffet of Art* 11:30 a.m.

The **Crocker Art Museum** (216 O Street; 916-808-7000; crockerartmuseum.org) is the perfect museum for a weekend getaway: compact yet diverse, including works from prehistoric to modern times. Oswald Achenbach's painting *Festival and Fireworks by Moonlight*, circa 1855, has a fiery luminescence so true that you expect to feel heat rising off the canvas. In the contemporary gallery, the Mexican artist Rufino Tamayo's *Laughing Woman*, from 1950, is dark and whimsical. The original building, an 1872 Victorian Italianate mansion, is absolutely grand, and a 2010 addition that tripled the museum's size works in tasteful counterpoint.

6 *Boats and Trains* 1:30 p.m.

Old Sacramento (oldsacramento.com), a historic district with costumed cowboys and Old West facades, is a hokey, tourist-mobbed scene. But two spots stand out: the **Pilothouse Restaurant** (1000 Front Street; 916-441-4440; deltaking.com; $$) and the **California**

ABOVE The Crocker Art Museum opened in 1885 as a gift from Margaret E. Crocker. Her family also included Charles Crocker, one of California's railroad barons.

State Railroad Museum (Second and I Streets; 916-445-6645; csrmf.org). The restaurant is on the *Delta King*, a 1920s riverboat-turned-floating-hotel, and offers dishes like a Shrimp Louie salad or fish and chips. The museum contains restored locomotives and railroad cars that you can climb aboard, including a 1937 stainless-steel dining car with white linen, fancy china, and a vintage menu offering a "lamb chop, extra thick" for 80 cents.

7 *Shop Midtown* 4 p.m.

Midtown, the area bordered roughly by 17th and 29th Streets and H and P Streets, is Sacramento's hippest district. Stop into boutiques like **Dragatomi** (2317 J Street; 916-706-0535; dragatomi.com) for designer collectibles like Kidrobot. Midtown is also home to art galleries, so if you're not in town for a Second Saturdays Art Walk, pop into a few, including **b. sakata garo** (923 20th Street; 916-447-4276; bsakatagaro.com) or the **Center for Contemporary Art Sacramento** (1519 19th Street; 916-498-9811; ccasac.org).

8 *Capital Cuisine* 6:30 p.m.

For a taste of Sacramento's new culinary scene, make reservations at **Grange** (926 J Street; 916-492-4450; grangesacramento.com; $$$), an airy restaurant in the Citizen Hotel. Michael Tuohy uses local ingredients to make seasonal dishes like risotto with morels and fava beans, grilled sturgeon with polenta and shiitake mushrooms, or slow-smoked pork shoulder with turnips.

9 *Closer to Wine* 8:30 p.m.

If the art gods are on your side, you'll be in town for a **Second Saturday Art Walk**, when galleries stay open until 10 p.m. with live music, food vendors, and, of course, vino. Though most of the action is in Midtown, around K Street, galleries in other neighborhoods get involved, too; it's best to check in with the art walk's map, on its Web site (2ndsaturdaysacramento.com). Any other Saturday, remind yourself how close you are to California wine country with a trip to **Revolution Wines** (2831 S Street; 916-444-7711; revolution-wines.com), a tiny industrial-chic winery with free tastings, or **Downtown & Vine** (1200 K Street; 916-228-4518; downtownandvine.com), which has California wines by the glass.

10 *Sutter's Fort, and Folly* 10 p.m.

Stop in at the city's original center to see how Sacramento got its start. In the early 1840s, an eccentric adventurer named Johann Augustus Sutter built

OPPOSITE BELOW Old Sacramento, a historic district with touristy shops behind Old West facades.

ABOVE The rotunda in the California State Capitol, both working center of government and restored landmark.

an adobe stronghold, still standing and now open as **Sutter's Fort State Historic Park** (2701 L Street; suttersfort.org). He called it New Helvetia and attracted a few followers. All went well until 1848, when he decided to build a sawmill 50 miles to the east, and the builders found gold. In the ensuing gold rush, Sutter's fields were trampled and his horses stolen. He missed out on the gold, too.

ABOVE An indoor-outdoor view of passersby and reflected diners at the Grange restaurant in the Citizen Hotel.

OPPOSITE The city skyline and the placid Sacramento River in an evening glow.

SUNDAY

11 *Bike the River* 10 a.m.

Bond with the American River by riding along the **Jedediah Smith Memorial Bike Trail**, a 32-mile loop that snakes along the water and through a series of parks featuring sand dunes, oak groves, picnic areas, and fishing nooks. **Practical Cycle** (114 J Street; 916-706-0077; practicalcycle.com), in Old Sacramento, has rentals.

THE BASICS

Fly into Sacramento International Airport or drive about 80 miles from San Francisco. Drive or ride a bicycle on the smooth, flat streets.

The Citizen Hotel
926 J Street
916-447-2700
citizenhotel.com
$$
Designer boutique hotel in California's Joie de Vivre collection, site of popular Grange restaurant and Scandal bar.

Inn & Spa at Parkside
2116 6th Street
916-658-1818
innatparkside.com
$$$
Eleven elegant rooms and a spa in a 1936 mansion.

Delta King
1000 Front Street
916-444-5464
deltaking.com
$$
Hotel aboard a riverboat in Old Sacramento.

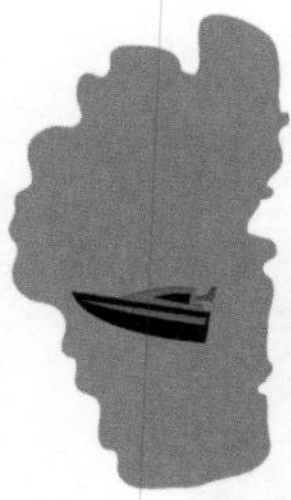

Lake Tahoe

Politics and religion aside, 200,000 people can't be wrong. According to the California Tahoe Conservancy, that's the estimated crowd at Lake Tahoe on a busy summer weekend. That's enough people to make you rethink your vacation plans, but Tahoe never feels too frantic. Maybe it's the enormous mountain lake standing center, proudly straddling California and Nevada, that lets you know right away who's in charge, but the weekenders who flood the 72 miles of shoreline instinctively bow to nature's pace. And there's that other little fact, too — far less provable, but widely asserted: There's nothing quite like a weekend spent circling Tahoe. The endless activities of summer are standard enough, but they're set to a Sierra backdrop of soaring evergreens and crystalline water worthy of a thousand poets. Throw in the late-night siren call of the Nevada casinos, and it's a tough act to follow.

— BY CINDY PRICE

FRIDAY

1 *Deeper Shades of Blue* 3 p.m.

Wordsmiths have beat themselves silly trying to capture the true color of Lake Tahoe, so take your pick — cobalt, azure, electric, sapphire. Suffice it to say that it's pretty darn blue. And cold. Even in late summer, the water averages 65 to 70 degrees, given the many mountain streams that slither into it. Judge for yourself on a guided kayak trip out of Sand Harbor, Nevada, with the **Tahoe Adventure Company** (530-913-9212; tahoeadventurecompany.com), which offers individual tours that are part geology lesson and part history lesson. Paddle out past the children cannonballing off the rocks, and learn about the lake's underlying fault lines — and the tsunami that may have burst forth there sometime in the last 10,000 years.

2 *Drama on the Sand* 7 p.m.

Shake yourself dry, slip on your flip-flops, and head up the beach to the **Lake Tahoe Shakespeare Festival** (Sand Harbor State Park, Nevada; 775-832-1616; laketahoeshakespeare.com). Patrons pile up on the inclined sand banks, carrying towels, wine, and fat dinner spreads. You can bring your own, or check out the food court and beer garden. The plays are staged at dusk, the lake deftly employed as a silent witness to the unfolding action. If you miss the play, you don't have to miss the beautiful park.

OPPOSITE Set high in the Sierra Nevada, Lake Tahoe is the largest alpine lake in North America.

RIGHT The lake straddles California and Nevada. At the Cal Neva Resort, the border divides a fireplace chimney.

SATURDAY

3 *Frank's Joint* 11 a.m.

Swing by the **Cal Neva Resort, Spa, and Casino** (2 Stateline Road, Crystal Bay, Nevada; 775-832-4000; calnevaresort.com). Frank Sinatra owned this hotel for three short years (from 1960 to 1963), but he left a wealth of scandal in his wake. The resort, called the Cal-Neva Lodge when Sinatra owned it, rests on the state line, and the property is marked down the center. After falling on hard times, it closed for remodeling in 2013. The owners promised that their renovation is also one part restoration, so if it has reopened by the time you arrive, you should still be able to poke your head into the old Celebrity Showroom, where Frank and his buddies performed. Marilyn Monroe often sat up front, and members of the hotel staff say she overdosed on sleeping pills here two weeks before her death, amid a swirl of rumors of sex and foul play. Secret passages running below the hotel lead to the closets of Cabin 3 (Marilyn's) and Cabin 5 (Frank's). The Chicago mobster Sam Giancana is said to have used the tunnels to conduct business.

4 *High Noon* 12 p.m.

It's noon on the lake, and you're 6,225 feet above sea level. A cheeseburger washed down with an ice-cold Anchor Steam is not only agreeable; it's mandatory. You're now in California, coming down the west side of the lake. Find your way through Tahoe City and take a right just past Fanny Bridge (called "rump row" for the line of backsides that forms as people lean over the railing to stare at the Truckee River and its fish). **Bridgetender Tavern and Grill** (65 West Lake Boulevard, Tahoe City; 530-583-3342; $) is home to one of the juiciest cheeseburgers on the lake as well as a generous outdoor patio that winds along the Truckee.

5 *Just Drift Away* 2 p.m.

Follow the hoots of laughter across Fanny Bridge and arrive at the **Truckee River Raft Company** (185 River Road, Tahoe City; 530-584-0123; truckeeriverraft.com) for a lazy afternoon on the river. You can paddle, but the ride is best enjoyed as one long floating party. Families drift alongside groups of friends with tubes lashed together as they bask and pass each other beer. A little more than halfway, you might find a shallow, standing-room-only party complete with makeshift stickball games (the paddles double as bats).

6 *Cocktail of the Brave* 7 p.m.

South Lake Tahoe isn't known as a gastronomic hotbed, but the sushi bar at the **Naked Fish** (3940 Lake Tahoe Boulevard, South Lake Tahoe; 530-541-3474; thenakedfish.com; $$) offers ace rolls and a frisky pre-casino crowd. Kick your night off with an appetizer of barbecued albacore and the surprisingly tasty house drink, the Money Shot, which involves a bolt of hot sake, a drizzle of ponzu sauce, fish eggs, a Japanese mountain potato, and a few other nerve-racking ingredients.

7 *Poker Faces, Old and New* 10 p.m.

Itching for the dull tumble of dice on felt, or the shudder and snap of a fresh deck of cards being shuffled? You'll have no trouble finding it. South Tahoe's casinos are snuggled against each other along the border of Stateline, Nevada. Refurbishing has made them sexier. Witness the vampy **MontBleu Resort Casino & Spa** (55 Highway 50; 775-588-3515; montbleuresort.com), a.k.a. the old Caesar's sporting a slap of paint and a fresh attitude, or the swank bar at **Harveys Resort Casino** (18 Lake Tahoe Boulevard; 775-588-2411; harveystahoe.com). Still, old-timers and hipsters might enjoy the old-school ambience and low-limit tables at the **Lakeside Inn and Casino** (168 Highway 50; 775-588-7777; lakesideinn.com).

SUNDAY

8 *Now That's Venti* 10 a.m.

Ride the touristy but must-do **Heavenly Gondola** (Heavenly Mountain Resort; 4080 Lake Tahoe Boulevard, South Lake Tahoe; 775-586-7000; skiheavenly.com), a ski lift that doubles as a sightseeing excursion in summer. Hop on board when it opens and cruise 2.4 miles up the mountain to the observation deck. Grab a very decent mocha at the cafe and soak in the stunning views of the Carson Valley and the Desolation Wilderness—not to mention that big blue thing in the center.

BELOW Warming up at the Bridgetender Tavern and Grill.

9 *Pesto Bread, Just Like Mom's* Noon

There's an art to gathering beach provisions, and Tahoe regulars know there's good one-stop shopping at the **PDQ Market** (6890 West Lake Boulevard, Tahoma, California; 530-525-7411; $), where customers can secure not only the usual Coke and sun block, but also one of the tastiest sandwiches in town. Press through the store, and you'll find a little homegrown operation pushing out delicious sandwiches on fresh-baked breads like jalapeño or pesto. The half-size sandwich, loaded high with shaved meats like pastrami or turkey, is a steal.

10 *Decisions, Decisions* 2 p.m.

Trying to pick the right Tahoe beach is a bit like plucking a date off the Internet. Zephyr Cove is young and likes to party. Meeks Bay is into poetry and likes long walks on the beach. The good news is that each is better looking than the next. For those given to fits of polarity, try **D. L. Bliss State Park** (Highway 89, South Lake Tahoe; 530-525-7277; parks.ca.gov), a camping ground with sheltered coves for swimming and lazing, as well as a few bracing hikes for the restless. The pristine beaches make it hard to resist the former, though. Imagine you've found the turquoise waters of Vieques in the middle of the Black Forest of Germany. Until you dip your hand in, of course.

OPPOSITE ABOVE Learning about the lake on a kayaking tour with Tahoe Adventure Company.

ABOVE A ski lift does summer duty ferrying sightseers.

THE BASICS

Fly to Reno and drive 60 miles or to Sacramento and drive 100 miles.

Mourelatos Lakeshore Resort
6834 North Lake Boulevard
Tahoe Vista, California
530-546-9500
mlrtahoe.com
$$$
Cute hotel on the lake, with a private beach.

Avalon Lodge
4075 Manzanita Avenue
South Lake Tahoe, California
530-544-2285
avalonlodge.com
$$$
Walking distance to casinos.

Marriott's Timber Lodge
4100 Lake Tahoe Boulevard
South Lake Tahoe, California
530-542-6600
marriott.com
$$$
Pool, private beach, fitness center.

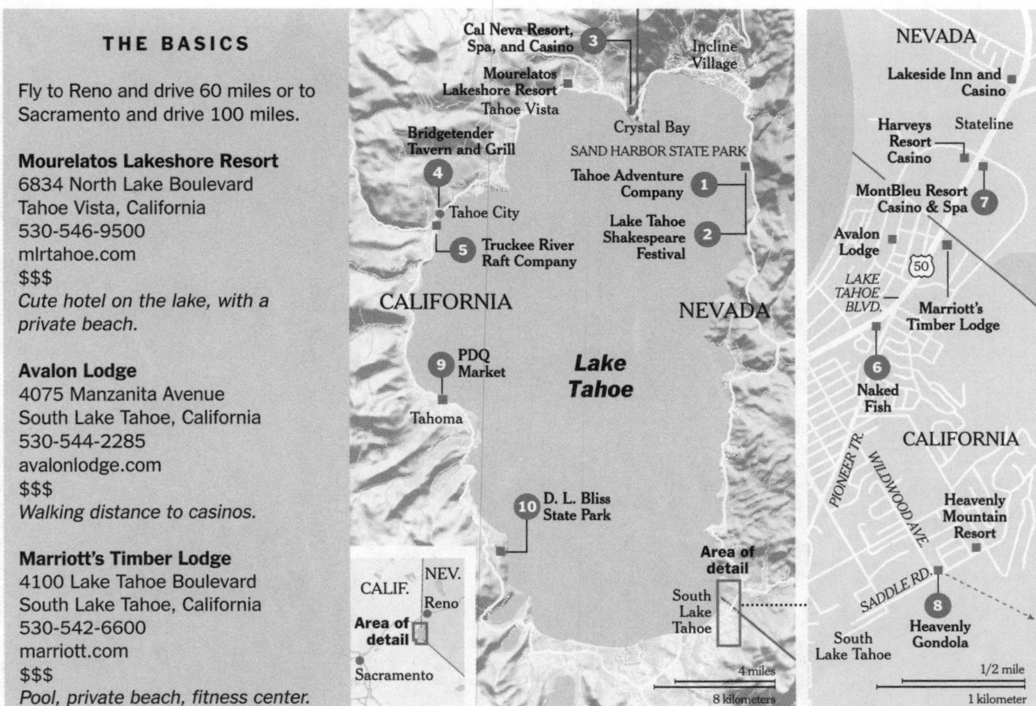

The Oregon Coast

You could drive down the southern third of the Oregon coast in a couple of hours, and you'd think, How beautiful! Highway 101, the Oregon Coast Highway, hugs the shoreline enough to give you views of the sand and windblown trees, rocks and crashing waves that give this stretch its fame. But to instill memories that will make these gorgeous seascapes your own, plan a leisurely weekend of detours and side trips with plenty of time to stop at the beaches and lighthouses, gulp the salt air, and kick back in the harbor towns.

— BY DAVID LASKIN

FRIDAY

1 *Park Land* 1 p.m.

In North Bend, leave Highway 101 to pick up Route 540 and head south as it leaves city streets behind to become the **Cape Arago Highway**. You'll descend quickly into Charleston, a tiny place with a working harbor, a fish-and-chips shack, and tidal shallows raked by whitecaps on windy days. The road—despite its "highway" designation, it's only a few miles long—leads from there to a series of three adjoining oceanside state parks (oregonstateparks.org). Stop at the first, **Sunset Bay**, for beachcombing and your first photo ops, but don't be tempted to stay too long. You'll need time at the next one, **Shore Acres**, to sniff the luxe ivory Elina roses in the well-kept garden of a former private estate perched atop a forbidding cliff.

2 *Cape Arago* 3 p.m.

The last stop on the road, before it loops around to point you back toward Charleston, is **Cape Arago State Park**, where you'll find the rocky headland, topped by a lighthouse, that all of this has been leading to. Hike on one of the cove trails down to the beach and look for seals and tidepools. When you've seen enough, drive back to Charleston and pick up Seven Devils Road, which will lead you to West Beaver Hill Road to complete the loop back to Highway 101.

OPPOSITE Highway 101 winds close to the water's edge along rocky coast south of Cape Sebastian State Park.

RIGHT Surf fishing in Port Orford, a town where every street seems to end in a view of the sea.

3 *Old Town Wine List* 4 p.m.

Find a little West Coast slice of Nantucket in **Bandon**, a town of 3,100 people with terrific beaches to the west and the silvery estuary of the Coquille River to the north and east. Check out the shops and galleries in the compact Old Town before heading to dinner at the **Alloro Wine Bar** (375 Second Street Southeast; 541-347-1850; allorowinebar.com; $$-$$$). It serves superb dishes like feather-light lasagna, sautéed local snapper, and fresh fava beans. Relax over a Walla Walla cabernet or another of the Northwest vintages on the wine list.

SATURDAY

4 *Sea Stacks* 10 a.m.

Take the lightly trafficked **Beach Loop Road** south of town. It parallels the coast for four and a half miles, and although there are a few too many cottages and motels, you forget all about them when you stop to wander on the beach amid fantastically carved sea stacks and watch colorful kites slashing against the sky. After the loop rejoins Highway 101, follow it as it leaves the coast for an inland stretch past ranches and cranberry bogs. When you come to Route 250, the Cape Blanco Road, turn right and drive through rolling sheep pastures reminiscent of Cornwall. It's not far to the sea.

5 *Blown Away* 11 a.m.

State parks are strung along this coast, and you can't hit them all. But **Cape Blanco** is a must-stop—the farthest west point on the Oregon coast, the state's oldest lighthouse, one of the windiest spots in the United States. Be prepared for that wind as you walk toward the stark circa-1870 lighthouse. The view at the headland is worth it, so stand and stare as long as you can withstand the blast.

6 *On the Edge* 1 p.m.

Imagine the shabby picturesque waterfront of an outer Maine island fused onto the topographic drama of Big Sur: that's **Port Orford**. Mountains covered with Douglas firs plunge toward the ocean, and you feel how truly you are at the continent's edge. The town itself has a salty, dreamy, small-town vibe; every street ends in blue sea framed by huge dark green humps of land. Look around and then find lunch. **Griff's on the Dock** (490 Dock Road; 541-332-8985; $$) and the **Crazy Norwegian's** (259 Sixth Street; 541-332-8601; $$) are good bets for fish and chips.

7 *End of the Rogue* 3 p.m.

The Rogue River, known for the whitewater along its 200-mile journey from the Cascades, looks wide, tame, and placid as it meets the sea in **Gold Beach.** The bridge that carries Highway 101 over it is a beauty, multiple-arched, elegant, and vaguely Deco. The city isn't particularly inviting—utilitarian motels hunkering along the strand, a drab dune obstructing views of the ocean. But don't miss the well-stocked **Gold Beach Books** (29707 Ellensburg Avenue; 541-247-2495; oregoncoastbooks.com), which in addition to covering every literary genre has an art gallery and coffee house. **Jerry's Rogue River Museum** (29880 Harbor Way; 541-247-4571; roguejets.com) is worth a look around and has an unusual feature—you can book a jetboat trip on the Rogue there. There's also good hiking just outside town at **Cape Sebastian State Park**, with miles of trails and views down the coast to California.

8 *Gold Beach Dining* 7 p.m.

If you can get a reservation, head out of town for dinner at the **Tu Tu' Tun Lodge** (96550 North Bank Rogue River Road; 541-247-6664; tututun.com; $$$), a fishing resort a few miles upstream on the Rogue. If you're staying in town, try **Spinner's Seafood Steak and Chophouse** (29430 Ellensburg Avenue; 541-247-5160; spinnersrestaurant.com; $$$), which features hefty portions of entrees like grilled duck breast, Alaska halibut, and ribeye steak.

SUNDAY

9 *More and More Scenic* 9 a.m.

Have a filling breakfast at the **Indian Creek Café** (94682 Jerry's Flat Road; 541-247-0680) and get back on the road. From here on it just keeps getting better. About 14 miles south of Gold Beach you will enter **Samuel H. Boardman Scenic Corridor**, a nine-mile roadside corridor along Highway 101 with turnouts overlooking natural stone arches rising from the waves, trailheads accessing the Oregon Coast Trail, and paths winding down to hidden beaches and tide pools. The scenic summa may be **Whaleshead Beach**, a cove with the mystical beauty of a Japanese scroll—spray blowing off the crest of a wave,

ABOVE The harbor in Crescent City, a town just south of the Oregon state line in California.

RIGHT Driftwood piled up by the surf at a beach along Beach Loop Drive in Bandon, Oregon.

massive sea rocks dazzled in the westering sun, and maybe a kid or two making tracks in the sand.

10 *Tsunami Zone* 11 a.m.

Glance around in **Brookings**, by far the toastiest town on the Oregon coast. Its curious microclimate — winter temperatures in the 80s are not unheard of — is a point of pride, as is its park devoted to preserving native wild azaleas. Then push on south into California to **Crescent City**, a place distinguished by its unfortunate history. In 1964 it was struck by a tsunami that destroyed 300 buildings and killed 11 residents. The vulnerability remains in this region of the Pacific coast. In 2011, the harbors in both Brookings and Crescent City were severely damaged by the tsunami that swept away cities in coastal Japan. You're tantalizingly close to California's majestic redwoods here, so turn a few miles inland and make a final stop at **Jedediah Smith Redwoods State Park**, where you can wander among 200-foot-tall trees. Their majesty matches that of the rocky windswept coast you've just left behind.

ABOVE The Patterson Bridge in Gold Beach.

THE BASICS

Small carriers serve airports in North Bend and Crescent City. Driving to Coos Bay from Eugene, Oregon, takes about two and a half hours. Cyclists will find the back roads are good for bike travel.

Bandon Dunes Golf Resort
57744 Round Lake Drive
888-345-6008
bandondunesgolf.com
$$$
Luxurious inn with oceanside golf course.

Bandon Beach Motel
1090 Portland Avenue SW, Bandon
541-347-9451
bandonbeachmotel.com
$-$$
Gorgeous ocean views.

Tu Tu' Tun Lodge
96550 North Bank Rogue River Road, Gold Beach
541-247-6664
tututun.com
$$$
A few miles inland on the Rogue River.

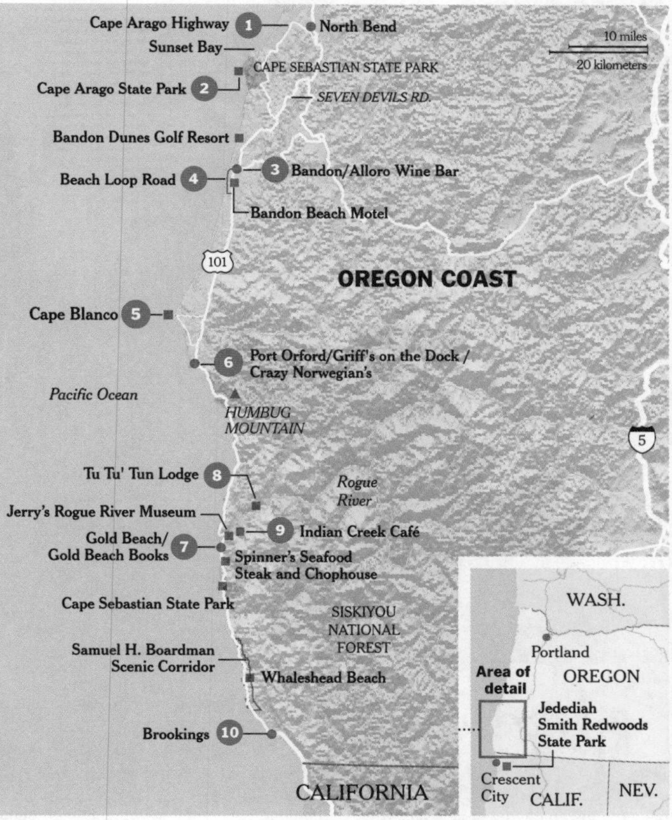

Cape Arago Highway 1
North Bend
Sunset Bay
10 miles
20 kilometers
Cape Arago State Park 2
CAPE SEBASTIAN STATE PARK
SEVEN DEVILS RD.
Bandon Dunes Golf Resort
3 Bandon/Alloro Wine Bar
Beach Loop Road 4
Bandon Beach Motel
101
OREGON COAST
Cape Blanco 5
6 Port Orford/Griff's on the Dock / Crazy Norwegian's
Pacific Ocean
HUMBUG MOUNTAIN
5
Tu Tu' Tun Lodge 8
Rogue River
Jerry's Rogue River Museum
9 Indian Creek Café
Gold Beach/ Gold Beach Books 7
Spinner's Seafood Steak and Chophouse
Cape Sebastian State Park
SISKIYOU NATIONAL FOREST
Samuel H. Boardman Scenic Corridor
Whaleshead Beach
Brookings 10
CALIFORNIA
WASH.
Portland
Area of detail
OREGON
Jedediah Smith Redwoods State Park
Crescent City
CALIF.
NEV.

Portland

"Nice" is an adjective that Portland, Oregon, can't seem to shake. But below the fleece-clad and Teva-wearing exterior lurks a cool and refreshingly unneurotic city that marches to its own cosmopolitan beat. Truth is, Portland doesn't want to be Seattle, its highly caffeinated neighbor to the north. With less traffic, better public transportation, and Mount Hood in its backyard, this self-styled City of Roses doesn't stand in anybody's shadow. Its vibrant downtown overflows with urban pleasures like chic restaurants, funky nightclubs, and sprightly neighborhoods crackling with youthful energy, but nobody's boasting. That's another nice thing about Portland.

— BY DAVID LASKIN

FRIDAY

1 *Fresh Orientation* 6 p.m.

The pastel roses peak in the late spring at the **International Rose Test Garden** (850 SW Rose Garden Way; 503-227-7033; rosegardenstore.org), but the blooms last for months and the view from this hillside terraced garden is fantastic year-round. Even if clouds keep you from seeing Mount Hood, you still get a bird's-eye view of colorful wood-frame houses surrounding a tidy grove of skyscrapers. Breathe in the pine-scented air and stretch your legs on the hillside paths of this precipitous chunk of green, five minutes from downtown by car, or 15 minutes on the efficient MAX Light Rail.

2 *Bistro Bird* 7:30 p.m.

Little Bird (219 SW Sixth Avenue; 503-688-5952; littlebirdbistro.com; $$) is the second Portland restaurant from a favorite Portland chef, Gabriel Rucker, less formal and more affordable than his flagship **Le Pigeon** (738 East Burnside Street; 503-546-8796; lepigeon.com; $$). Little Bird's bright dining room has a pressed-tin ceiling and lace window curtains, and the dishes brought to its tables are "more accessible for the everyday diner," in Rucker's words. The cuisine in both restaurants is French; at Little Bird, that may mean cassoulet, hanger steak with frites, crispy veal sweetbreads, and a sweet corn and fennel crepe with soft-boiled egg, tomatoes, and hollandaise.

3 *Downtown Jazz* 9:30 p.m.

Portland's nightlife scene offers plenty of choices, from torchy lounges to high-decibel indie hang-outs. A much-loved institution is **Jimmy Mak's** (221 NW 10th Avenue; 503-295-6542; jimmymaks.com), an intimate jazz club with a national profile. You'll see high-quality local musicians or jazz stars like Joey DeFrancesco or Louis Hayes. Reserve if you want a table.

SATURDAY

4 *Market to Teahouse* 10 a.m.

Even if you can't stand handcrafted soaps, dangly earrings, gauzy scarves, chunky ceramics, fancy pet bowls, messy street food, and the people who make them, the **Portland Saturday Market** is worth visiting (portlandsaturdaymarket.com). Tucked under the Burnside Bridge, the market is a perfect starting point for a leisurely walk amid the cast-iron buildings of Old Town and into Chinatown. Drop in at stores like **Floating World Comics** (20 NW 5th Avenue; 503-241-0227; floatingworldcomics.com), a shop that approaches comic books as an art form, or **Table of Contents** (33 Northwest 4th Avenue; 503-206-5630; tableofcontents.us), which sells hip clothing and jewelry for men and women. Wend your way to the serene **Lan Su Chinese Garden** (239 NW Everett Street; 503-228-8131; lansugarden.org), where you can refuel with a cup of tea in the ornate teahouse beside Zither Lake.

OPPOSITE A view from the International Rose Test Garden.

RIGHT Portland's skyline from the outskirts.

5 *Walk to Lunch* Noon

Downtown Portland has about five neighborhoods, each with its own mood and flavor, but it isn't very big. In 20 minutes, you can walk from Chinatown in the northwest to the cultural district in the southwest. Which brings you to lunch. At **Southpark Seafood Grill & Wine Bar** (901 SW Salmon Street; 503-326-1300; southparkseafood.com; $$), you can plunk down at the bar for a quick meal and ask for sightseeing suggestions from the young downtown crowd. Seafood holds center stage; check the menu for bouillabaisse or fried calamari with spicy aioli.

6 *Market to Teahouse* 1 p.m.

South Park takes you to the **Portland Art Museum** (1219 SW Park Avenue; 503-226-2811; portlandartmuseum.org), which has an impressive collection of photographs. They run the gamut from 19th-century daguerreotypes to contemporary landscapes. Another strong point in the permanent collection is Japanese scrolls from the Edo period. If you'd like to buy art objects as well as look at them, proceed to the nearby **Russian Art Gallery** (518 SW Yamhill Street; 503-224-5070; russiangalleryportland.com), which carries religious icons for several hundred to several thousand dollars, along with nesting dolls and Gzhel pottery, all imported from Russia.

7 *Roll Out of Town* 3 p.m.

Stash your stuff, don your Spandex and rent a bicycle at **Waterfront Bicycles** (10 SW Ash Street No. 100; 503-227-1719; waterfrontbikes.com) for a ride along the Willamette River. If you're feeling mellow, ride the three-mile loop that goes north on the Waterfront Bike Trail in **Tom McCall Waterfront Park**, across the river via the Steel Bridge to the **Vera Katz East Bank Esplanade**, and back across on the Hawthorne Bridge. For a tougher workout, stay on the East Bank Esplanade and continue south on the **Springwater Corridor** for an 18-mile ride through the city's semirural outskirts. The trail terminates at the town of Boring (its slogan: "An Exciting Place to Live"). A newer trail, in different territory, is the **Banks-Vernonia State Trail** (oregonstateparks.org), which begins in the town of Banks and proceeds 20 miles on former railroad beds, crossing two 80-foot-high trestles along the way. (For that one, you can pick up a bike at Banks Bicycle Repair & Rental at 14175 Northwest Sellers Road; banksbicycles.com.)

8 *Portland Fusion* 8 p.m.

Serious foodies head to **Park Kitchen** (422 NW Eighth Avenue; 503-223-7275; parkkitchen.com; $$$). In a former garage, the restaurant has a warren of dark and cozy rooms that faces an open kitchen. The chef and owner, Scott Dolich, combines elements of French, Italian, and Northwestern cooking in an imaginative fusion all his own. The menu changes with the season, but the tastes are always superb.

9 *Hang Out, Rock On* 10:30 p.m.

Check out the latest indie bands at **Doug Fir Lounge**, connected to the trendy Jupiter Hotel (830 East Burnside Street; 503-231-9663; dougfirlounge.com). It is Portland's primo spot to hang out, drink good local beer, rub shoulders with the young and pierced, and catch emerging groups from all over the country. The room is surprisingly modern and woodsy for a dance club, with gold-toned lighting, a fire pit, and walls clad in Douglas fir logs.

SUNDAY

10 *Petit Déjeuner* 10 a.m.

For a taste of Paris, pop over to **St. Honoré Boulangerie** (2335 NW Thurman Street; 503-445-4342; sainthonorebakery.com; $-$$), a French-style bakery where Dominique Geulin bakes almond croissants, apricot tarts, and Normandy apple toast, a mix of French toast, brioche, and custard. The cafe is airy, with huge windows and lots of wicker. Equally important, the coffee is among the city's finest.

11 *City of Books* 11 a.m.

It says a lot about Portland that **Powell's City of Books** (1005 West Burnside Street; 503-228-4651; powells.com) is one of the city's prime attractions — a bookshop so big that it provides maps to help shoppers find their way around. The dusty, well-lighted store is larger than many libraries, with 68,000 square feet of new and used books. Plan to stay a while.

OPPOSITE ABOVE The Portland Saturday Market in full swing. Portland's vibrant downtown overflows with youthful energy.

ABOVE Comb the shelves at Powell's City of Books.

THE BASICS

Bicycling is encouraged. Excellent public transportation includes light rail to the airport.

The Nines
525 Southwest Morrison Street
877-229-9995
thenines.com
$$$
Cool design, including an art collection, in a downtown building.

Paramount Hotel
808 SW Taylor Street
503-223-9900
portlandparamount.com
$$
Sophisticated style downtown.

Kennedy School
5736 NE 33rd Avenue
503-249-3983
mcmenamins.com/kennedyschool
$$
Stay in an old elementary school, with a chalkboard in your room.

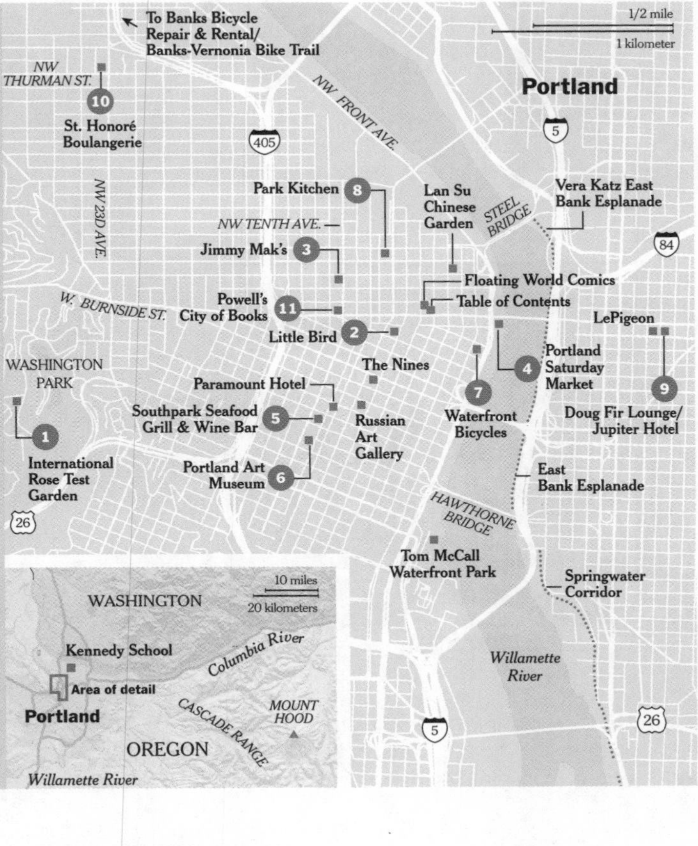

To Banks Bicycle Repair & Rental/ Banks-Vernonia Bike Trail
1/2 mile
1 kilometer
NW THURMAN ST.
10 St. Honoré Boulangerie
405
NW FRONT AVE.
Portland
5
NW 23D AVE.
8 Park Kitchen
NW TENTH AVE.
3 Jimmy Mak's
Lan Su Chinese Garden
STEEL BRIDGE
Vera Katz East Bank Esplanade
84
Floating World Comics
Table of Contents
W. BURNSIDE ST.
11 Powell's City of Books
2 Little Bird
LePigeon
WASHINGTON PARK
The Nines
4 Portland Saturday Market
Paramount Hotel
7 Waterfront Bicycles
9 Doug Fir Lounge/ Jupiter Hotel
5 Southpark Seafood Grill & Wine Bar
Russian Art Gallery
1 International Rose Test Garden
6 Portland Art Museum
East Bank Esplanade
26
HAWTHORNE BRIDGE
Tom McCall Waterfront Park
Springwater Corridor
WASHINGTON
10 miles
20 kilometers
Kennedy School
Columbia River
Area of detail
Portland
CASCADE RANGE
MOUNT HOOD
OREGON
Willamette River
Willamette River
5
26

PACIFIC PLACE STATION

Seattle

Seemingly overnight, whole swaths of downtown Seattle, Washington, and close-in neighborhoods —notably South Lake Union and the Pike-Pine Corridor—have transformed themselves into vibrant enclaves of restaurants, bars, and galleries. With so many converted and repurposed buildings, Seattle's cityscape is starting to look as layered as the wardrobes of its inhabitants. The tarry pitch of this old timber port city has never disappeared; it was just plastered over with grunge flannel, tech money, yuppie coffee, Pacific Rim flavors, and more recently the backyard chickens and chard of urban pioneers. Don't let one of Seattle's famous rainshowers keep you from entering the mix. This is one of the rare American cities where you can be outdoors year-round without either shivering or sweating. — BY DAVID LASKIN

FRIDAY

1 *Park Tower View* 3 p.m.

Volunteer Park (1247 15th Avenue East; 206-684-4075; seattle.gov/parks), a 10-minute cab or bus ride from downtown at the north end of Capitol Hill, has gardens designed a century ago by the Olmsted Brothers, a conservatory bursting with plants from regions around the world, and a squat brick water tower that you can ascend for terrific views of the city below and the mountains and sea beyond. Rain or shine, it's the ideal place for orientation. If hunger strikes, stroll a couple of blocks east through one of Seattle's oldest and prettiest neighborhoods for a slice of lemon Bundt cake and a Stumptown coffee at the cozy, humming **Volunteer Park Cafe** (1501 17th Avenue East; 206-328-3155; alwaysfreshgoodness.com; $$).

2 *Coolest Corridor* 5 p.m.

The Pike-Pine Corridor is Seattle's happiest urban makeover: from a warren of shabby flats and greasy spoons to an arty but not oppressively gentrified hamlet just across the freeway from downtown. When the locally revered **Elliott Bay Book Company** (1521 10th Avenue; 206-624-6600; elliottbaybook.com) abandoned Pioneer Square downtown to relocate here, the literati gasped—but now it looks like a perfect neighborhood fit, what with the inviting communal tables at **Oddfellows** (1525 10th Avenue; 206-325-0807; oddfellowscafe.com; $$) two doors down, and a full spectrum of restaurants, vintage clothing shops, and home décor stores in the surrounding blocks. **NuBe Green** (921 East Pine Street; 206-402-4515; nubegreen.com), which advertises its green credentials, sells all American-made clothing, housewares, and gifts.

OPPOSITE A streetcar rolls along Westlake Avenue in South Lake Union, a thriving urban village within the city of Seattle. The streetcar line connects the neighborhood to downtown.

3 *Fresh and Local* 8 p.m.

One of the most talked-about restaurants in town, **Sitka & Spruce** (1531 Melrose Avenue East; 206-324-0662; sitkaandspruce.com; $$), looks like a classy college dining room with a long refectory table surrounded by a few smaller tables, concrete floors, exposed brick, and duct work. But there's nothing sophomoric about the food. The chef and owner, Matt Dillon, who moved the restaurant to the Pike-Pine Corridor in 2010, follows his flawless intuition in transforming humble local ingredients (smelt, nettles, celery root, black trumpet mushrooms, turnips, pumpkin) into complexly layered, many-textured but never fussy creations like beer-fried smelt with aioli, spiced pumpkin crepe with herbed labneh, and salmon with stinging nettles. Heed your server's advice that entrees are meant to be shared—you will have just enough room for dessert (try warm dates, pistachios, and rose-water ice cream), and you will be pleasantly surprised by the bill.

SATURDAY

4 *Art and Water* 9 a.m.

There used to be two complaints about downtown Seattle: it offered no inspiring parks and no waterfront access worthy of the scenery. The **Olympic Sculpture Park** (2901 Western Avenue; 206-654-3100; seattleartmuseum.org), by the Seattle Art Museum, took care of both problems in one stroke. Masterpieces in steel, granite, fiberglass, and bronze by nationally renowned artists have wedded beautifully with maturing native trees, shrubs, ferns, and wildflowers. Wander the zigzagging

paths and ramps past the massive weathered steel hulls of Richard Serra's *Wake* and Alexander Calder's soaring painted steel *Eagle* until you reach the harborside promenade. From there continue north to a pocket beach and into the adjoining grassy fields of waterfront **Myrtle Edwards Park.** It's all free.

5 *Urban Village* 10:30 a.m.

The development of South Lake Union into a thriving urban village, brainchild of the Microsoft tycoon Paul Allen, is finally alive and kicking. This former industrial no man's land now houses the city's best galleries, an ever increasing collection of dining spots, some nifty shops, and the spanking new Amazon campus. Use the South Lake Union Streetcar to hop from **Gordon Woodside/John Braseth Gallery** (2101 Ninth Avenue; 206-622-7243; woodsidebrasethgallery.com), which specializes in Northwest landscapes, to **Honeychurch Antiques** (964 Denny Way; 206-622-1225; honeychurch.com), with museum-quality Asian art and artifacts, and on to the **Center for Wooden Boats** (1010 Valley Street; 206-382-2628; cwb.org), where you can admire the old varnished beauties or rent a rowboat or sailboat for a spin around Seattle's in-city lake.

6 *Lunch beside the Chief* 1 p.m.

Tilikum Place, with its imposing fountain statue of the city's namesake, Chief Sealth, is Seattle's closest thing to a piazza, and the **Tilikum Place Café** (407 Cedar Street; 206-282-4830; tilikumplacecafe.com; $$) supplied the one missing element—a classy informal restaurant—when it opened. Understated elegance is the byword here, whether in the delicate purée of butternut squash soup with bits of tart apple, the beet salad with arugula and blue cheese, or the light and piquant mushroom and leek tart.

ABOVE AND LEFT A dock and a tool shop at the Center for Wooden Boats, where you can admire classic boats or rent a rowboat or sailboat for a spin around Lake Union, Seattle's in-city lake. The center also offers boatbuilding workshops and other woodworking classes.

7 *Walk on Water* 4 p.m.

You don't have to leave the city limits to immerse yourself in the region's stunning natural beauty. Drive or take a bus 15 minutes from downtown to the parking lot of the **Museum of History and Industry** (2700 24th Avenue East; 206-324-1126; mohai.org) and pick up the milelong **Arboretum Waterfront Trail**. A network of well-maintained paths and boardwalks takes you through thickets of alder, willow, and elderberry into marshy islands alive with the trills of red-winged blackbirds and marsh wrens, and over shallows where kayakers prowl amid the rushes and the concrete pillars of the freeway overhead. If the sun is out, you'll want to prolong the outing with a stroll through the flowering fruit trees in the adjoining **Washington Park Arboretum** (depts.washington.edu/uwbg).

8 *La Dolce Vita* 8 p.m.

Maybe it's the stylish Italian vibe or the pretty people basking in the soft glow of dripping candles, or maybe it's the sumptuous, creatively classic food — whatever the secret ingredient, **Barolo Ristorante** (1940 Westlake Avenue; 206-770-9000; baroloseattle.com; $$$) always feels like a party. The pastas would do a Roman mother proud — gnocchi sauced with braised pheasant, leg of lamb ragù spooned over rigatoni. The rack of lamb with Amarone-infused cherries is sinfully rich, and the seared branzino (sea bass) exhales the essence of the Mediterranean. Don't leave without at least a nibble of cannoli or tiramisù.

9 *The Beat Goes On* Midnight

At **See Sound Lounge** (115 Blanchard Street; 206-374-3733; seesoundlounge.com) young and not

TOP The beach at Myrtle Edwards Park next to the Olympic Sculpture Park in downtown Seattle.

ABOVE Sitka & Spruce looks like a classy college dining room, but there's nothing sophomoric about the food. Humble local ingredients like nettles and smelt are transformed here into sophisticated dishes.

so young Seattle join forces to party to house music spun by a revolving cast of D.J.'s. There's a small dance floor — but the compensation is lots of booths and sofas to crash on. The scene outside can get rowdy in the wee hours, but inside the beat and liquor flow smoothly.

SUNDAY

10 *Bayou Brunch* 10:30 a.m.

Lake Pontchartrain meets Puget Sound at **Toulouse Petit** (601 Queen Anne Avenue North; 206-432-9069; toulousepetit.com; $$), a funky bistro-style spot near the Seattle Center in Lower Queen Anne. Grab a booth and settle in with a basket of hot, crispy beignets; then indulge in something truly decadent, like pork cheeks confit hash topped with a couple of fried eggs or eggs Benedict with crab and fines herbes. You can cleanse your system afterward with a brisk walk up the hill to **Kerry Park** (211 West Highland Drive) for a magnificent farewell view.

ABOVE See Sound Lounge, where Saturday night house music, spun by varying D.J.'s, goes into Sunday morning. The crowd is a mix of young and not so young.

OPPOSITE A stroll near Alexander Calder's steel sculpture, *Eagle*, at the Olympic Sculpture Park downtown. The park is affiliated with the Seattle Art Museum.

THE BASICS

The best and cheapest way to get from the airport to downtown is the new Link Light Rail. Around town, drive or walk and take the bus.

Hyatt at Olive 8
1635 Eighth Avenue
206-695-1234
hyatt.com
$$
New in 2009, with pool, fitness center, and city views.

Pan Pacific Hotel Seattle
2125 Terry Avenue
206-264-8111
panpacific.com
$$$
Light and airy; a 15-minute walk to downtown.

Fairmont Olympic
411 University Street
206-621-1700
fairmont.com/seattle
$$$
The grande dame of Seattle hotels.

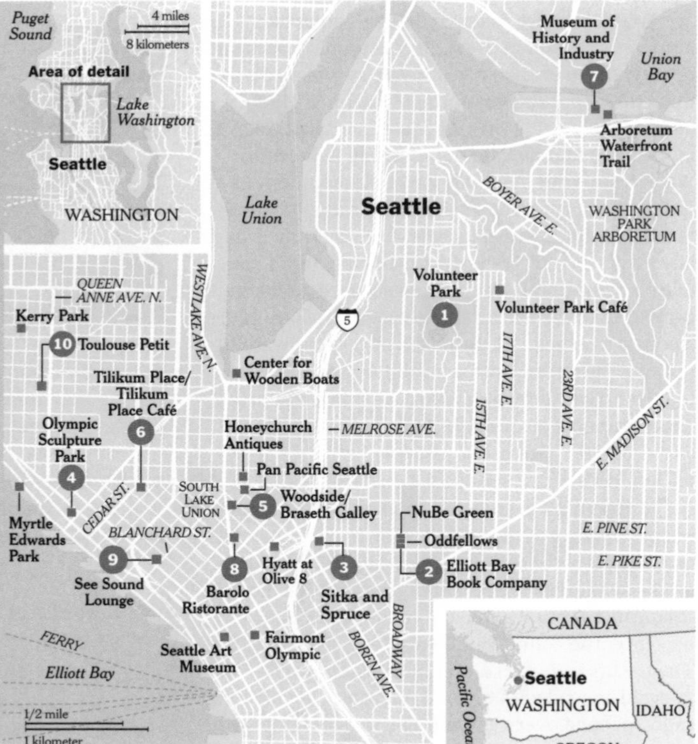

Puget Sound
4 miles
8 kilometers
Area of detail
Lake Washington
Seattle
WASHINGTON
Lake Union
Seattle
Museum of History and Industry
7
Union Bay
Arboretum Waterfront Trail
BOYER AVE. E.
WASHINGTON PARK ARBORETUM
QUEEN ANNE AVE. N.
Kerry Park
10 Toulouse Petit
WESTLAKE AVE. N.
5
Volunteer Park
1
Volunteer Park Café
Center for Wooden Boats
Tilikum Place/ Tilikum Place Café
6
Olympic Sculpture Park
4
Honeychurch Antiques
MELROSE AVE.
17TH AVE. E.
15TH AVE. E.
23RD AVE. E.
E. MADISON ST.
Pan Pacific Seattle
SOUTH LAKE UNION
5 Woodside/ Braseth Gallery
NuBe Green
Oddfellows
CEDAR ST.
Myrtle Edwards Park
BLANCHARD ST.
9 See Sound Lounge
8 Barolo Ristorante
Hyatt at Olive 8
3 Sitka and Spruce
2 Elliott Bay Book Company
E. PINE ST.
E. PIKE ST.
FERRY
Elliott Bay
Seattle Art Museum
Fairmont Olympic
BOREN AVE.
BROADWAY
1/2 mile
1 kilometer
CANADA
Pacific Ocean
Seattle
WASHINGTON
IDAHO
OREGON

Northwest Seattle

Long ago the expanding city of Seattle swallowed up two of its neighbors, and neither of them has ever forgotten. Fremont and Ballard, once cities in their own right, are now Seattle neighborhoods of a particularly independent-minded kind. They're close together, though not contiguous, and still have unique character that resists complete assimilation—arty and free-spirited in Fremont; Nordic and proudly maritime in Ballard. Each is undergoing a kind of 21st-century renaissance, with shops and restaurants moving in, and a new, often young crowd arriving to live or just to play. But in either one, you can still lose yourself so thoroughly that you will barely even remember you're in the same town as the Space Needle. — BY DAN WHITE

FRIDAY

1 *Welcome to Fremont* 3 p.m.

As they cross the orange-and-blue Fremont Bridge on their way from downtown Seattle, drivers are met by a neon Rapunzel, a sign proclaiming Fremont the Center of the Universe, and instructions to set their watches back five minutes. From there on, it's a cross between a family-friendly bohemian enclave and a larger-than-life-size hipster sculpture garden. Don't be surprised if the cast-aluminum commuters standing near the bridge, waiting for a train that has not run for years, are wearing flamboyant clothes and headgear. Ever since ***Waiting for the Interurban*** was installed in 1979, whimsical Fremonters have clad them in continually changing costumes. (During the Abu Ghraib scandal someone put hoods over their heads, but it's not usually that political.) A block to the southeast, beneath the busy Aurora Bridge, the two-ton **Fremont Troll** crouches beneath a support wall, staring with his one eye and squashing a Volkswagen Bug in his left hand. Children sometimes crawl up his forearms and wedge their hands into his nostrils while parents take pictures.

2 *Scrap Art* 3:30 p.m.

You'll see a variety of outdoor art around Fremont —clown statues, dinosaur topiaries, a street sign pointing to Atlantis—but don't miss two more high spots. The seven-ton bronze **statue of Lenin** (Evanston Avenue North and North 36th Street), rescued from an Eastern European scrapyard after the Soviet collapse, loses some of its symbolic power when adorned with lights at Christmas or dressed in drag during Gay Pride Week. Another must-see is the **Fremont Rocket** (601 North 35th Street), a reborn piece of cold war junk pointing 53 feet into the sky. Some Fremontians, still pining for their lost independence, claim that it is aimed at Seattle's City Hall.

3 *Retail Trail* 4 p.m.

Do some exploring on foot. Beneath the rocket, check out **Burnt Sugar** (601 North 35th Street; 206-545-0699; burntsugarfrankie.com), selling handbags, books, and more. Walk west on 35th Street to **Theo Chocolate** (3400 Phinney Avenue North; 206-632-5100; theochocolate.com), a chocolate factory that offers tours and has a retail shop. A bit farther south, find the entrance to the **Burke-Gilman Trail** near where Phinney Avenue intersects with North Canal Street and walk southeast along the Lake Washington Ship Canal amid the joggers and cyclists. Just before you reach the Fremont Bridge, head back north on Fremont Avenue to find shops like **Jive Time Records** (3506 Fremont Avenue North; 206-632-5483; jivetimerecords.com), **Ophelia's Books** (3504 Fremont Avenue North; 206-632-3759; opheliasbooks.com), and **Show Pony** (702 North

OPPOSITE Autumn shopping at the Farmers Market in Ballard, a Seattle neighborhood with an independent streak.

BELOW Cocoa beans at Theo Chocolate in Fremont, another part of town with its own quirky identity.

35th Street; 206-706-4188; showponyseattle.com), a clothing boutique.

4 *Korea Modern* 7:30 p.m.

Revel (403 North 36th Street; 206-547-2040; revelseattle.com; $$) serves contemporary Korean cooking in an artfully designed space. The menu changes, but one example of Revel's fare was a clever take on bibimbap, the traditional rice dish, with asparagus, pistachios, and olives. Desserts are a specialty, too. Stick around after dinner for cocktails at **Quoin**, the attached bar.

SATURDAY

5 *Eggs of the Universe* 9 a.m.

Start the day at **Silence-Heart-Nest** (3508 Fremont Place North; 206-633-5169; silenceheartnest.com; $), a vegetarian cafe. It's a total-immersion experience in itself, with sari-clad wait staff asking diners to ponder business cards printed with inspirational verses while serving sesame waffles and Center of the Universe scrambled eggs. After breakfast, it's time to leave Fremont. Drive northwest on Leary Way, which becomes Northwest 36th Street, and into Ballard, where neighborhood assertion goes in a different direction.

6 *Nordic Pride* 10:30 a.m.

Follow the mazelike layout of the surprisingly beguiling **Nordic Heritage Museum** (3014 Northwest 67th Street; 206-789-5707; nordicmuseum.org) as it snakes through three floors of a former schoolhouse, guiding you past a centuries-old fishing boat and a life-sized replica of an Icelandic sod house. Seafaring Scandinavians were the heart of old Ballard, and although ethnicities are mixed up now, the neighborhood still celebrates Norwegian Constitution Day every May 17 with a parade and much flag-waving. It was water that persuaded reluctant Ballardites to accept annexation in 1907 by a narrow margin — they needed access to Seattle's freshwater supply. Not everyone is reconciled to it even now. On the 100th anniversary, some people wore black armbands.

7 *Cohos on the Move* Noon

The nearly century-old **Hiram M. Chittenden Locks** (3015 Northwest 54th Street; 206-783-7059) help keep the salt water of Puget Sound from despoiling freshwater Lake Washington. They also lift boats from sea level to the lake's 26-foot elevation. Watch yachts and fishing boats steadily rise as the locks fill like a

ABOVE The bar at King's Hardware on Ballard Avenue.

OPPOSITE BELOW The Fremont Troll peers out from under the Aurora Bridge. His left hand is squashing a Volkswagen Bug.

giant bathtub—a sight that can seem surreal. But the irresistible flourish is the glass-lined tunnel that, if you're here in salmon spawning season, lets you spy on cohos and chinooks as they make their way up the fish ladder, a series of ascending weirs. You can press your face a few millimeters away from the fat fish, which clunk into each other, form traffic jams, and sometimes turn their vacant expressions on the humans.

8 *The Sound of Lunch* 1:30 p.m.

Ballard's southern boundary is the Washington Lake Ship Canal, its western boundary is Puget Sound, and **Ray's Cafe**, at Ray's Boathouse Restaurant (6049 Seaview Avenue Northwest; 206-789-3770; rays.com) sits right about where they meet. Grab a table on the outdoor deck and order fish for lunch.

9 *Dunes in the City* 3 p.m.

The maritime spirit feels alive at **Golden Gardens Park** (8498 Seaview Place Northwest; 206-684-4075; seattle.gov/parks/parkspaces/Golden.htm), arguably the loveliest picnic spot in all of Seattle, with sand dunes, a lagoon, secluded benches, occasional sightings of bald eagles, and heart-stopping views of the distant Olympic Mountains at sunset. Walk the paths, find a spot for relaxing, and chill.

10 *Dinner With Alice* 8 p.m.

Oysters from the cold Pacific waters off the coast of Washington are the specialty at the **Walrus and the Carpenter** (4743 Ballard Avenue Northwest; 206-395-9227; thewalrusbar.com; $$$), and the menu lists them by name—baywater sweet, blue pool, sea cow, judd cove. There's more seafood too, as well as meat dishes like steak tartare and duck prosciutto, and desserts like maple bread pudding or roasted dates. This is a festive place, with a convivial crowd enjoying the food, wine, and beer. Lovers of Lewis Carroll's Alice will recognize the source of the fanciful name: a poem in *Through the Looking*

Glass in which oysters are lured from their beds to suffer the same fate they are meeting here. You can finish out the night with Ballard's friendly mix of students, fishermen, professionals, and laborers over drinks at **King's Hardware** (5225 Ballard Avenue Northwest; 206-782-0027; kingsballard.com) or **Hattie's Hat** (5231 Ballard Avenue Northwest; 206-784-0175; hatties-hat.com).

ABOVE Music at Ballard Sunday Farmers Market, which is open year-round.

OPPOSITE Golden Gardens Park in Ballard is one of the loveliest places for an afternoon escape in all of Seattle. The park has sand dunes and views of the Olympic Mountains.

SUNDAY

11 *Sunday Shoppers* 11 a.m.

Ballard's eastern edge feels more contemporary, with dining, shopping, and a lively social scene. Year-round, the **Ballard Sunday Farmers Market** (Ballard Avenue between Vernon Place and 22nd Avenue; ballardfarmersmarket.wordpress.com) brings out vendors and shoppers in a scene that some Ballardites insist surpasses Seattle's well-known Pike Place Market. Spend some time people watching and checking out the quintessentially Pacific Northwestern products on offer: giant radishes, tiny potatoes called spud nuts, jugs of homemade cider, milk from purebred Boer goats, and spiced blackberry wine.

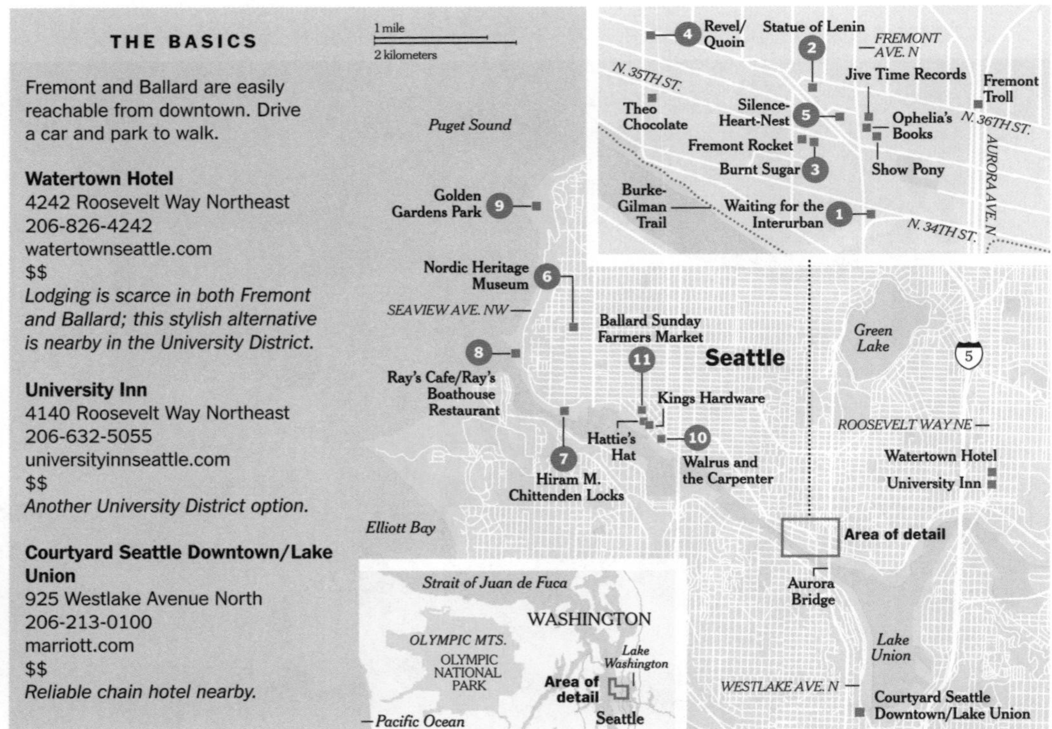

THE BASICS

Fremont and Ballard are easily reachable from downtown. Drive a car and park to walk.

Watertown Hotel
4242 Roosevelt Way Northeast
206-826-4242
watertownseattle.com
$$
Lodging is scarce in both Fremont and Ballard; this stylish alternative is nearby in the University District.

University Inn
4140 Roosevelt Way Northeast
206-632-5055
universityinnseattle.com
$$
Another University District option.

Courtyard Seattle Downtown/Lake Union
925 Westlake Avenue North
206-213-0100
marriott.com
$$
Reliable chain hotel nearby.

The San Juan Islands

You could spend years getting to know the more than 170 San Juan Islands of Washington, but in a single weekend, it's easy to become acquainted with three of the biggest. Lopez, Orcas, and San Juan are jewels of the Pacific Northwest, great for sailing, kayaking, hiking, biking, diving, or just relaxing. Visit, and you'll find out how a quarrel over the killing of a farm animal in the 19th century nearly led to war, spot wildlife in a way you've probably never done before, and find yourself drifting onto island time. — BY BOB MACKIN

FRIDAY

1 *You and the Island* 2 p.m.

Make the pleasant passage by car ferry (206-464-6400; wsdot.wa.gov/ferries) from Anacortes on the mainland to quiet Lopez Island. The eternal lure of the San Juans is their landscapes of forests, hills, and fjords. Thanks to an active land preservation effort, there is plenty of terrain open to the public to explore, and Lopez has its share of beautiful spots. Take a walk at **Lopez Hill** (lopezhill.org/lopezhill.htm), where a web of public trails winds past mossy conifers and madrona trees with peeling cinnamon-red bark, or at the spectacular **Watmough Bay Preserve** (lopezisland.com/parks.htm), where a path leads to a strip of beach on a wooded inlet.

2 *A Table by the Bay* 7 p.m.

Drive to Lopez Village for dinner. The view is fantastic at the **Bay Café** (9 Old Post Road; 360-468-3700; bay-cafe.com; $$), and so is the food. Look out on the bay and the islands beyond as you dig into fresh local fish or locally raised beef or lamb. Make a reservation in advance, and ask for a window table. Residents of other islands make the trip to Lopez just to dine.

SATURDAY

3 *Sea to Summit* 9 a.m.

Start today's explorations on Orcas Island, at **Moran State Park** (3572 Olga Road, Olga; 360-376-2326; parks.wa.gov). In the park is Mount Constitution, which at 2,409 feet is the highest point in the San Juans. The 15-minute drive to the top is full of hairpin turns on a narrow road. But if the weather cooperates, you'll be rewarded with breathtaking views as far as Vancouver, British Columbia; the Cascade and Olympic ranges; and the islands and ships in Puget Sound. The park was granted to Washington in 1921 by Robert Moran, a shipbuilding magnate and former mayor of Seattle. He also had a mansion on Orcas, which you can visit at the **Rosario Resort & Spa** (1400 Rosario Road, Eastsound; 360-376-2222; rosarioresort.com). Moran built the house when doctors told him to retire early, but he wound up living to 86—thanks, it is said, to the serene beauty of Orcas Island.

4 *Some Pig* 11 a.m.

Take the boat to San Juan Island, home of the strange tale of the Pig War. In 1859, an American settler killed a pig belonging to the Hudson's Bay Company, the powerful British corporation that once controlled much of North America. Within two months, more than 400 American troops, dispatched to protect the settler from arrest, faced off against some 2,000 British soldiers, sailors, and marines. But no shots were fired. Small detachments from both nations remained until 1872, when Kaiser Wilhelm I, acting as arbitrator, awarded the islands to the United States, not British Canada. Today, the British and American camps make up the **San Juan Island National Historical Park** (360-378-2902; nps.gov/sajh). During summer, it comes alive as local history buffs don period costumes for historical recreations.

5 *Whale Watch, Minus Boat* 2 p.m.

Pack a picnic, keep binoculars handy, be patient. That's the three-pronged strategy for enjoying your time at **Lime Kiln Point State Park** (1567 Westside Road, Friday Harbor; 360-378-2044; parks.wa.gov). The 36-acre park has Douglas fir, arbutus, and even cactuses along its forest trails. But from late spring to early fall, it may be the world's best place to see orca whales from land. Park your car in the lot and hike the lighthouse trail to the rocky outcrop in the shadow of the Lime Kiln Point lighthouse. Set up your picnic on the rocks and watch for the shiny black and white orcas. If you're lucky, they'll come close enough so that they can also see you. If you miss

OPPOSITE Sunset and serenity in the San Juans.

a pod on parade, you're still likely to see seals and eagles. The lighthouse, built in 1919, is now a whale behavior research center. In summer, park staff members are often available to provide information on the whales and also offer evening tours of the lighthouse; day tours can be arranged.

6 *Purple Pleasure* 4 p.m.

Lavender farming has made its way to the San Juans, so ask if there's lavender oil available when you choose hot stone massage, Swedish massage, reiki, or all three at **Lavendera Day Spa** (285 Spring Street, Friday Harbor; 360-378-3637; lavenderadayspa.com), ideal after a spell of hiking and sitting on rocks. When you've achieved blissful relaxation, make a visit to the **Pelindaba Lavender Farm** (33 Hawthorne Lane, off Wold Road; 360-378-4248; pelindabalavender.com), where you're welcome to tour the rippling purple fields in flowering season.

7 *San Juan Island Locavore* 6 p.m.

This is Washington, and salmon should be on the menu. Expect it at **Coho Restaurant** (120 Nichols Street, Friday Harbor; 360-378-6330; cohorestaurant.com; $$$), along with shellfish from the Straits of Juan de Fuca, meat from a Lopez Island farm, and local produce from several island growers. The desserts are house-made, and the wine list is filled with vintages from Washington, Oregon, and California.

8 *Sculptured Trail* 8 p.m.

A visit to the **Westcott Bay Nature Preserve and Sculpture Park** (Roche Harbor Road, Roche Harbor; thesanjuans.com/san-juan-island-activities/san-juan-workshops) is a great way to spend the late, late afternoon. Scattered along the trails are more than 100 sculptures (by artists from the Pacific Northwest and beyond) looking magical in their open-air setting as the light fades.

SUNDAY

9 *Whale Talk* 10 a.m.

A modest two-story building, the former Odd Fellows Hall in Friday Harbor is the home of the **Whale Museum** (62 First Street North; 360-378-4710; whale-museum.org), a remarkable collection of whale photographs, skeletons, and even some brains. Take a few minutes to listen to the library of whale vocalizations in a phone booth.

ABOVE A ferry system, carrying both passengers and their cars, runs a busy schedule and keeps the islands connected with one another and tied to the mainland.

OPPOSITE Boats docked near Eastsound on Orcas Island.

10 *A Drink of Lavender* Noon

The proprietors of the lavender farm you visited yesterday have cleverly opened the **Pelindaba Lavender shop** in downtown Friday Harbor near the ferry terminal (First Street; 360-378-4248; pelindabalavender.com). The lavender-infused lemonade is the perfect drink to quaff on a summer day's cruise among the San Juans as you make your way back toward the mainland.

11 *Foodie Quest* 4 p.m.

If you have a full free day and a yen for dining at talked-about restaurants, once back on the mainland drive north from Anacortes to Bellingham, where you can catch the ferry to **Lummi Island**. (Although it's only a couple of miles by water from Lopez, there's no direct ferry connection to Lummi from there or any of the other San Juans.) Be sure you have a reservation made weeks in advance for dinner at the celebrated **Willows Inn** (2579 West Shore Drive, Lummi Island; 360-758-2620; willows-inn.com; $$$$). Dinner is prix fixe, much of the food comes from the island, and the presiding cook is Blaine Wetzel, a former chef at the wildly acclaimed Copenhagen restaurant Noma.

THE BASICS

Take the Washington State Ferries from Anacortes, about 80 miles north of Seattle.

Hop from island to island by car ferry, and drive.

Inn on Orcas Island
114 Channel Road, Deer Harbor
360-376-5227
theinnonorcasisland.com
$$$
Eight artfully decorated rooms, cottages, and suites, all facing a bay. Breakfast is included.

Tucker House Inn
275 C Street, Friday Harbor
360-378-2783
tuckerhouse.com
$$$
Rooms, cottages, and suites in century-old buildings.

Rosario Resort and Spa
1400 Rosario Road, Eastsound
rosarioresort.com
$$
Tastefully furnished rooms with sweeping water views.

4 miles
10 kilometers
SAN JUAN ISLANDS
WALDRON ISLAND
Eastsound
Moran State Park
3
Willows Inn
11
Lummi Island
ORCAS ISLAND
Rosario Resort & Spa
8
Westcott Bay Nature Preserve and Sculpture Park
Inn on Orcas Island
Deer Harbor
San Juan Island National Historical Park
BRITISH CAMP
SHAW ISLAND
BLAKELY ISLAND
CYPRESS ISLAND
GUEMES ISLAND
Lime Kiln Point State Park
5
SAN JUAN ISLAND
Area of detail
2
Bay Café
DECATUR ISLAND
Anacortes
Pelindaba Lavender Farm
Griffin Bay
LOPEZ ISLAND
1
Lopez Hill
Rosario Strait
4
San Juan Island National Historical Park
AMERICAN CAMP
Watmough Bay Preserve
Friday Harbor
9
Whale Museum
FIRST ST.
FRONT ST.
SECOND ST.
SPRING ST.
Friday Harbor
10
Pelindaba Lavender shop
Coho Restaurant
7
Tucker House Inn
NICHOLS ST.
C ST.
6
Lavendera Day Spa
VANCOUVER ISLAND
CANADA
Strait of Juan de Fuca
Area of Detail
WASHINGTON
Puget Sound
Seattle
Pacific Ocean
50 miles
100 kilometers

Vancouver

Set against a jaw-dropping confluence of mountains and sea, Vancouver is a Pacific gateway in more ways than one. Traditionally a busy harbor, it is now an active cruise port—an opening to the Inside Passage, with its glacier-carved fjords and wooded islands—as well as Canada's largest cargo port. For outdoor lovers, it is an entry point to wild and beautiful landscapes of temperate rain forest and rocky coast. Sophisticated and cosmopolitan, it also holds a multiethnic population that has arrived from all over the world, and especially from China, bringing a happy mix of cultures and some of the best ethnic restaurants in North America. —BY HANNAH SELIGSON

FRIDAY

1 *Two Views* 4:30 p.m.

Vancouver is a drop-dead-gorgeous city that should be admired from as many vantage points as possible. Start with a glass elevator ride 553 feet up to the **Vancouver Lookout** (555 West Hastings Street; vancouverlookout.com). The circular viewing platform offers 360-degree panoramic views of the downtown skyline, Mount Seymour, Grouse Mountain, Lions Gate Bridge, and seaplanes taking off and landing. Back at ground level, walk to the nearby **Waterfront Station** (601 West Cordova Street; 604-953-3333; translink.ca) and board the SeaBus commuter ferry to North Vancouver. The 15-minute ride has to be one of the most stunning commutes in the world. The boat docks next to the **Lonsdale Quay Market** (123 Carrie Cates; lonsdalequay.com), where vendors sell comestibles from candy and wine to curry and souvlaki. At the **Cheshire Cheese** pub (Lonsdale Quay Market; 604-987-3322; cheshirecheeserestaurant.ca), order a pitcher of sangria, sit on the outdoor deck, and take in the view of downtown, the industrial port, and Burrard Inlet.

2 *Japanese Plates* 8 p.m.

Guu (838 Thurlow Street; 604-685-8817; guu-izakaya.com; $$) is a Vancouver iteration of the Japanese izakaya, a type of after-work pub where alcohol (usually beer) accompanies small plates and conviviality is the rule. At this izakaya, food arrives fast and at a quarter of the price in a trendy restaurant; try dishes like tuna tataki, kimchi fried rice, kabocha croquette, and yaki udon. Sit at the bar and watch meticulous chefs flip, slice, and arrange food on plates with the precision of a martial arts performance. And enjoy the spirited Japanese welcome and goodbye from the servers and chefs as each guest arrives and departs.

3 *Glamour Bar* 10:30 p.m.

Glam it up at the **Yew Seafood and Bar** in the Four Seasons Hotel (791 West Georgia Street; 604-692-4939; yewrestaurant.com), a dramatic space with 26-foot ceilings and a plush lounge area. The ambience is relaxed with a dash of ritzy, but this place is really about the cocktails: for example, the Moscow Mule (vodka, lime, and ginger beer), served in an elegant bronze cup, or the 20th Century (gin, crème de cacao, and lemon).

SATURDAY

4 *Pastries and Greenery* 10 a.m.

Start the morning at **Thierry** (1059 Alberni Street; 604-608-6870; thierrychocolates.com), a traditional French bakery where you can grab an almond croissant and a cappuccino for breakfast and buy macaroons in flavors like chocolate pistachio, coffee, and maple pecan to eat later. Then take the Canada Line (Vancouver's rapid transit system)

OPPOSITE Outdoor lunch on Granville Island, with a metropolitan view across False Creek.

BELOW The Teahouse in Stanley Park, a choice for brunch.

southbound to the 55-acre **VanDusen Botanical Garden** (5251 Oak Street; vancouver.ca/vandusen), home of hundreds of thousands of plants from around the world. Regardless of the blossoms du jour, it's all sublime. Don't miss the hedge maze—see if you can get to the monkey puzzle tree in the middle.

5 *Down-Home Dim Sum* 1 p.m.

For one of the most genuine Asian cultural and culinary experiences in North America, travel to Richmond, a suburb 20 minutes south of Vancouver, for dim sum at **Fisherman's Terrace** (4151 Hazelbridge Way; 604-303-9739; $$) in the sprawling Aberdeen Center. Among the 76 options on the dim sum menu are deep-fried chicken knee with spicy salt, mini sticky rice in bamboo leaves, steamed duck tongue, triple mushrooms in rice noodle wrap, and chilled coconut cake with diced taro. After your meal, browse in the shopping center, which caters to the large Asian-Canadian population in Richmond with shops like a pan-Asian supermarket, a Korean barbecue spot, and an entire store dedicated to Hello Kitty merchandise.

6 *First Nations* 3 p.m.

Before Vancouver became a mecca for immigrants, there were the First Nations—Canadian aboriginals, whose culture and art is very much a presence in the city. To get a sense of the craft work and art that are still being produced, head to **Inuit Gallery** (206 Cambie Street; 604-688-7323; inuit.com) in Gastown, the once-seedy downtown historic district that is now a center of shopping, restaurants, and nightlife. Check out the paintings and prints of Kenojuak Ashevak, an Inuit artist from Canada's Arctic regions; her work, which is known for its

ABOVE The seawall path in Stanley Park.

LEFT Drinks at the Keefer Bar, a dark, sultry place in Chinatown that has Chinese anatomical charts on the walls.

OPPOSITE Vancouver's setting on the calm Burrard Inlet, a long coastal fjord, made it a prosperous port.

geometric shapes and nature imagery, has been used on Canadian stamps. For more forgiving prices, walk across the street to **Hill's Native Art** (165 Water Street; 866-685-5422; hillsnativeart.com), which has a nice selection of jewelry, woodcarvings, sculpture, and prints.

7 *Boutique Collection* 4:30 p.m.

Gastown may be more famous, but **Yaletown**, a former industrial area that is now dotted with shops and high-priced lofts, has its own collection of interesting boutiques. **Chintz & Company** (950 Homer Street; 604-689-2022; chintz.com/t-vancouver.aspx) is a great place to buy jewelry, pillows, and luscious TokyoMilk hand cream. **Revolucion** (1062 Mainland Street; 604-662-4427; revolucionstyle.com) is a men's store with an entire wall of high-end shaving products and grooming kits, as well as the occasional quirky item like a wine caddy in the shape of a woman's foot. A few doors down is **Global Atomic Designs** (1144 Mainland Street; 604-806-6223; globalatomic.com), which sells an array of international designer clothes.

8 *Dressed in Layers* 8 p.m.

When in Vancouver, eat lots of seafood, the unrivaled local specialty. One of the most talked-about places to do this is **Blue Water Cafe** (1095 Hamilton Street; 604-688-8078; bluewatercafe.net; $$$$). If it's available, sample the BC tasting for two, which resembles a four-tiered seafood wedding cake of Dungeness crab salad, scallop ceviche, albacore tuna tartare, and smoked sockeye salmon terrine.

9 *Chinese Medicine* 10:30 p.m.

Near the Chinatown night market, join a hip young crowd at the **Keefer Bar** (135 Keefer Street; 604-688-1961; thekeeferbar.com), a dark, sultry lounge that has Chinese anatomical charts framed

on the walls. The cocktails, which the menu calls "prescriptions" (homage to an apothecary theme), are worth waiting at the crowded bar to order, particularly the intriguingly spicy Chinatown Sour and the Dragon Fly.

SUNDAY

10 *Teahouse With a View* 9:30 a.m.

Spend the morning in **Stanley Park**, a sprawling and busy urban oasis of greenery and water. Begin at the **Teahouse in Stanley Park** (7501 Stanley Park Drive; 604-669-3281; vancouverdine.com/teahouse; $$), a brunch spot well loved for both its location and its Canadian Northwest twists on classic breakfast items. Ask for a table by a window overlooking English Bay and West Vancouver, and don't miss the smoked salmon Benedict.

11 *Bike the Loop* 11 a.m.

Miles of paths and trails lead through the park's stately evergreens and along its Lost Lagoon. The resident wildlife, living within a golf swing of downtown skyscrapers, includes geese, ducks, swans, turtles, and raccoons. If it's sunny, you could soak up some rays at Second Beach at the southwest corner of the park. But to cover the most territory, pick up a bicycle at **Spokes Bicycle Rental** (1798 West Georgia Street; 604-688-5141; spokesbicyclerentals.com) and ride the six-mile loop around the sea wall. Be careful as you contend with inline skaters, but mostly just soak up the fresh sea air and marvel at all the natural wonders of Vancouver.

OPPOSITE Cyclists share the seawall path in Stanley Park with runners and families out for a stroll.

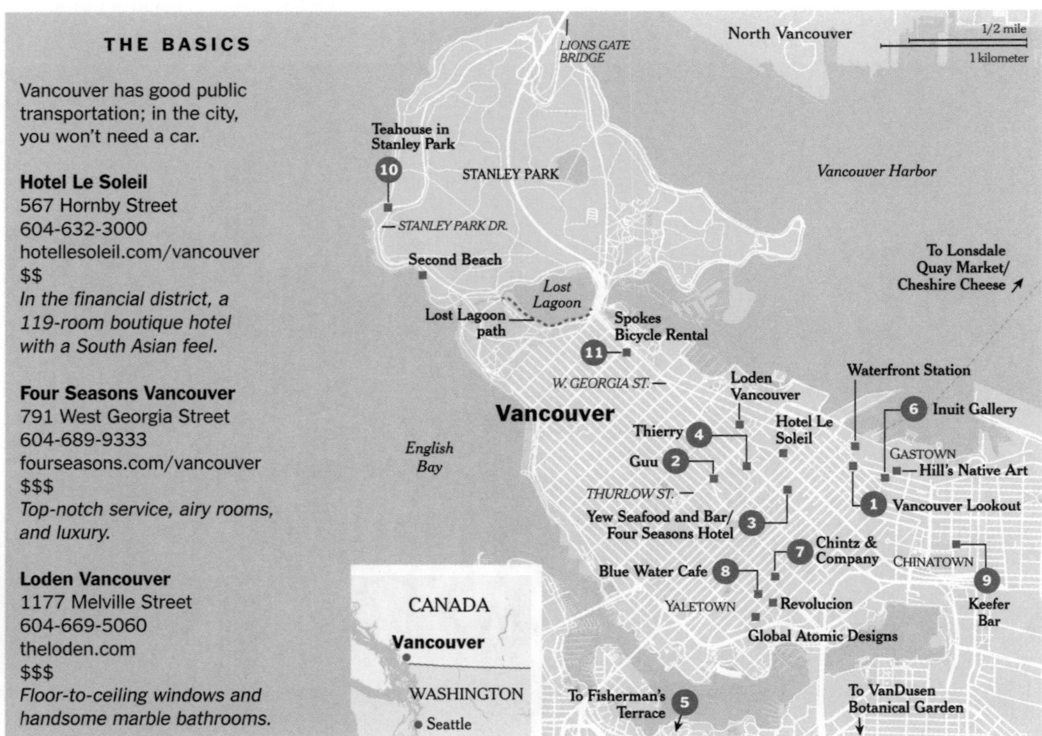

THE BASICS

Vancouver has good public transportation; in the city, you won't need a car.

Hotel Le Soleil
567 Hornby Street
604-632-3000
hotellesoleil.com/vancouver
$$
In the financial district, a 119-room boutique hotel with a South Asian feel.

Four Seasons Vancouver
791 West Georgia Street
604-689-9333
fourseasons.com/vancouver
$$$
Top-notch service, airy rooms, and luxury.

Loden Vancouver
1177 Melville Street
604-669-5060
theloden.com
$$$
Floor-to-ceiling windows and handsome marble bathrooms.

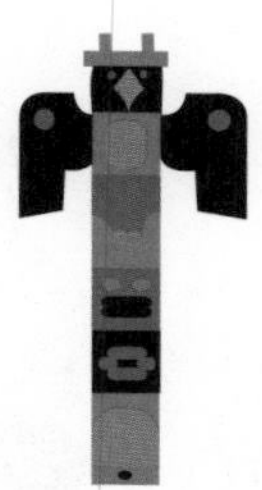

Victoria

Victoria, at the southern tip of Vancouver Island, invites exploration with a lively and compact downtown, abundant parkland, miles of trails and oceanfront, and what has been called the mildest climate in Canada. At the picturesque, boat-lined Inner Harbor, British Columbia's provincial Parliament buildings and the landmark Fairmont Empress hotel overlook the water, stately by day and spectacularly lighted at night. Taking a spin around the Tudor-style neighborhoods (a tribute to the city's English heritage) of suburban Oak Bay, cyclists can stop for picnic lunch near a towering totem pole, a symbol of the area's indigenous people, in Beacon Hill Park. Despite its proximity to Vancouver and to Seattle, Washington, Victoria remains surprisingly uncrowded — a gem of a city with its own unique elegance on vivid display.
— BY BONNIE TSUI

FRIDAY

1 *Overhead Whale Watch* 5 p.m.

Look down for whales as you arrive in **Victoria Harbor** by seaplane from Vancouver, across the Strait of Georgia. There are other ways to get to town, but the view from above is unbeatable both for spotting the pods that make whale-watching boat tours popular in Victoria from April through October and for the panorama of the city as you touch down in the harbor.

2 *Home Cooking* 7 p.m.

The **Clay Pigeon** (1002 Blanshard Street; 250-590-6657; claypigeonrestaurant.com; $$) is a great spot to sample the region's seasonal bounty: seared wild salmon, cornmeal-crusted crispy oysters, tuna Nicoise with cold smoked albacore. The upscale diner-style restaurant also has prosecco and beer on tap and local wines by the glass — try the Mission Hill reserve cabernet sauvignon from the Okanagan Valley. Chase it all down with house-made marshmallows, Nutella cookies, and hot chocolate.

3 *Pick a Neighborhood* 9 p.m.

Get the lay of the land in an after-dinner stroll, starting in Old Town, near the waterfront. In summer, music festivals, art performances, and family-friendly events enliven the courtyard at Market Square, a cluster of home design shops, bakeries, and restaurants in a block of restored buildings. On Johnson Street, 19th-century storefronts mix with places like **Smoking Lily** (569A Johnson Street; 250-382-5459; smokinglily.com), a tiny space that sells hand-screened printed clothing. In the up-and-coming Fernwood neighborhood, a short walk from downtown, **Stage** (1307 Gladstone Avenue; 250-388-4222; stagewinebar.com) is an upscale wine bar that has won over patrons from near and far. It's easy to see why. Its outstanding small plates are made with local, organic ingredients. A favorite: roast acorn squash with capers, raisins, and brown butter.

SATURDAY

4 *A Century in Bloom* 10 a.m.

About 14 miles north of downtown on what once was the site of a limestone quarry that fed the Butchart family's cement manufacturing fortune, **Butchart Gardens** (800 Benvenuto Avenue, Brentwood Bay; 250-652-5256; butchartgardens.com), begun in 1904, now covers 55 acres with 900 varieties of blooms and is open year-round. Among the attractions: a serene Japanese garden, a magnificent rose garden, a hand-carved carousel, and two 30-foot totem poles that were made on-site by Charles Elliott and Doug LaFortune, artists who are members of the Coast Salish Nation.

OPPOSITE Victoria is Britain in the land of totem poles.

BELOW The Vancouver Island coast from Beach Drive.

5 *Sip Like Royalty* 1 p.m.

Built in 1908, the **Fairmont Empress** hotel (721 Government Street; 250-384-8111; fairmont.com/empress-victoria) has long been known for highbrow luxury and elaborate afternoon tea ($$$$), complete with towers of warm buttery scones and its own tea blend. Dance scenes for the 1994 film *Little Women* were filmed in its traditionally decorated rooms, and the pink confection of a tearoom is the very definition of Old World regal, with chandeliers, porcelain lamps, and live piano music. Reserve in advance or risk missing the scrumptious cream puffs (there are three to five seatings daily from noon, depending on the season).

6 *Thunderbirds* 2 p.m.

The **Royal BC Museum** (675 Belleville Street; 250-356-7226; royalbcmuseum.bc.ca) explores every era of British Columbia history, from the reign of woolly mammoths to 20th-century millinery. But with limited time, concentrate on the First Peoples Gallery, with its Native Canadian wood carvings, masks, and even a traditional dwelling. Walk outside to Thunderbird Park, where totem poles of British Columbia's native tribes tower over a manicured lawn. Several of the sculpted figures include the Thunderbird, which plays a role in native mythology.

7 *External Use, Too* 4 p.m.

For another take on tea, schedule a pre-dinner rejuvenating treatment at **Silk Road Tea** in Chinatown (1624 Government Street; 250-704-2688; silkroadteastore.com). This tranquil shop has an in-house organic spa downstairs—try the sea-salt spa scrub with green tea—and sells loose teas, a colorful array of serving sets, and other tea paraphernalia.

8 *French Connection* 7 p.m.

At the beloved **Brasserie L'École** (1715 Government Street; 250-475-6260; lecole.ca; $$), in what was once a Chinatown schoolhouse, dark, rich hardwood floors and deep maroon walls set an intimate stage for French country dishes like mussels with French fries, endive salad topped with bacon and a mustard wine dressing, and Sooke trout with warm farro and kale salad. The menu changes seasonally, but a staple is the charcuterie and cheese course.

9 *After-Dinner Drinks* 9 p.m.

There's no shortage of excellent waterfront bars and pubs, and you can sample a palette of wildly diverse flavors. **Canoe Brewpub** (450 Swift Street; 250-361-1940; canoebrewpub.com), in a brick-and-timber establishment with a patio, has its own brews. Hungry night owls can find tasty seafood and white bark wheat ale to go with it at **Ferris' Oyster Bar and Grill** (536 Yates Street; 250-360-1824; ferrisoysterbar.com), where the lines are often out the door. A few blocks from the water, you'll find all manner of creative cocktails at **Veneto Tapa Lounge** (653 Pandora Avenue; 250-383-7310; venetodining.com). You might try the Hell's Bells, a spicy concoction of muddled bell pepper with Blanco tequila and honey, with a touch of habanero shrub.

SUNDAY

10 *Pedal Power* 9:30 a.m.

Rent a bicycle from **Cycle BC Rentals** (685 Humboldt Street; 250-380-2453; cyclebc.ca) and tour the countryside on the **Galloping Goose Regional Trail**, which stretches 34 miles from downtown Victoria to Leechtown, a former mining village that is now a ghost town. Built on abandoned railway track and trestles, the trail passes from urban back roads to hidden waterways, rain forests, farmland, and rocky slopes where bald eagles roost.

11 *Sushi With Panorama* Noon

At the tip of a promontory in Oak Bay, the **Marina Restaurant** (1327 Beach Drive; 250-598-8555; marinarestaurant.com; $$) serves morning food along with a stellar view of Mount Baker on the mainland in the state of Washington. Along with more traditional brunch fare, there's a sushi bar.

OPPOSITE The Fairmont Empress, a symbol of Victoria, serves afternoon tea in a pink confection of a tearoom.

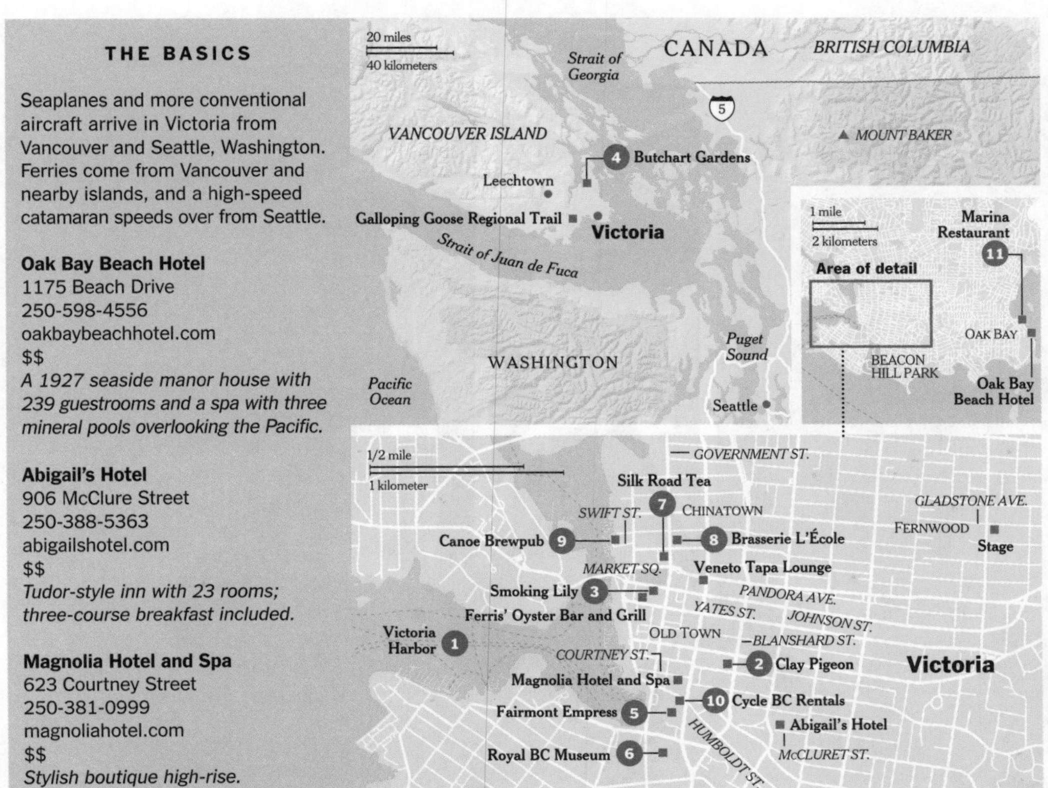

THE BASICS

Seaplanes and more conventional aircraft arrive in Victoria from Vancouver and Seattle, Washington. Ferries come from Vancouver and nearby islands, and a high-speed catamaran speeds over from Seattle.

Oak Bay Beach Hotel
1175 Beach Drive
250-598-4556
oakbaybeachhotel.com
$$
A 1927 seaside manor house with 239 guestrooms and a spa with three mineral pools overlooking the Pacific.

Abigail's Hotel
906 McClure Street
250-388-5363
abigailshotel.com
$$
Tudor-style inn with 23 rooms; three-course breakfast included.

Magnolia Hotel and Spa
623 Courtney Street
250-381-0999
magnoliahotel.com
$$
Stylish boutique high-rise.

FR

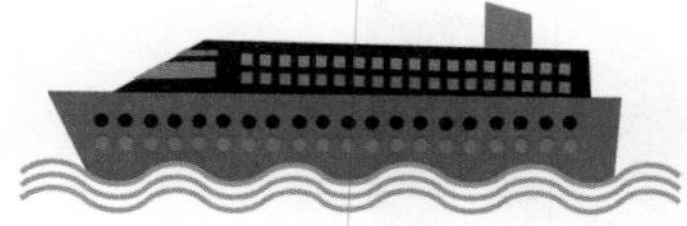

Juneau

Residents of Juneau, Alaska, brag that their town is the most beautiful state capital city in America, and they have a strong argument. Juneau is inside the Tongass National Forest, part of the world's largest temperate rain forest. Old-growth groves and glaciers lie within the municipal limits, snow-capped mountains loom overhead, and whales and other marine wildlife are a short boat ride away. The town itself is a working state capital with a utilitarian feel, but gold rush-era buildings, art galleries, quality regional theater, and fresh seafood make pleasant complements to Juneau's stunning surroundings. — BY CORNELIA DEAN

FRIDAY

1 *Back to the Ice Age* 3 p.m.

Nature beckons. But some preparations are required. On your way into town, stop at **Western Auto-Marine** (5165 Glacier Highway; 907-780-4909; westernautojuneau.com) for a pair of brown rubber, calf-high Xtra Tuf Boots, a must-have item in any Alaskan's wardrobe. Thus prepared, start your Juneau explorations at the entrance to **Switzer Creek and Richard Marriott Trails** (midway on Sunset Street). On the hillside, evergreens in even ranks give way to a hodge-podge of trees of different species, sizes, and shapes. This change marks the boundary between second-growth timber, on land logged decades ago, and an old-growth forest, untouched since the end of the last ice age. Hike up the trail — it's not too strenuous — and discover for yourself why environmentalists are so keen to save these ancient woods, home to an amazingly rich variety of plant and animal life. (Keep to the wooden planks at the base of the trail, and be glad you have your boots. The bog, or muskeg, is plenty wet.)

2 *Fish Don't Get Fresher* 6:30 p.m.

Locals say Juneau is not much of a restaurant town because so many people dine on fish they catch themselves. But when they want fish prepared for them, they head to the **Hangar on the Wharf Pub & Grill** (2 Marine Way; 907-586-5018; hangaronthewharf.com; $$-$$$). The building's exterior of plain blue clapboard isn't designed to impress, but the harborside location offers dazzling views of the Gastineau Channel and the mountains of Douglas Island west of downtown. There's halibut on the menu, of course, and salmon (guaranteed wild-caught) and king crab.

OPPOSITE A navigational buoy near Juneau makes a convenient perch for Steller sea lions and a bald eagle.

RIGHT Cruise ships turn their sterns toward town at the end of daylong stops in Juneau's harbor.

3 *Indoor Drama* 8 p.m.

Take in a play at the **Perseverance Theatre**, a nonprofit repertory company across the Gastineau Channel on Douglas Island (914 Third Street, Douglas; 907-364-2421; perseverancetheatre.org). A pillar of Juneau's cultural life since 1979, Perseverance stages high-quality classic and contemporary plays, and the prices are low.

SATURDAY

4 *Seeing Sea Life* 9 a.m.

What better way to start your Saturday than with some close-up views of Juneau's wildlife? A number of companies offer whale-watching trips from Auke Bay, a short car (or bus) ride north of downtown. Find one offering a trip up the Lynn Canal to **Berners Bay**, and you are sure to see Steller sea lions basking on a rocky haul-out, harbor seals bobbing in the water, and harrier hawks, geese, and ducks. Also watch for eagles nesting along the shores. Most companies guarantee you will see whales; chances of spotting humpbacks are best in late spring when the herring-like fish called eulakon ("hooligan" in a local Native language) are running.

5 *Up North, Down South* Noon

Back in town, enjoy a taste of old Juneau at the **Triangle Club** (251 Front Street; 907-586-3140; triangleclubbar.com; $). Order a hot dog and some Alaskan Amber — one of the local beers brewed and bottled right in town. If the Triangle looks a bit louche for your tastes, try **El Sombrero** around the corner (157 South Franklin Street; 907-586-6770; $$), a Juneau institution. This modest place has been dishing out generous helpings of Mexican standards since the oil boom began in the 1970s.

6 *They Came First* 1:30 p.m.

For some historical perspective, visit the **Alaska State Museum** (395 Whittier Street; 907-465-2901; museums.state.ak.us), which houses a collection covering the Athabascans, Aleuts, and other Alaska Natives, the state's history as a Russian colony, and the gold rush that helped create Juneau. The museum's store stocks Native crafts including baskets, prints, and dolls. Keep walking farther from the port and you'll come upon what is probably Juneau's least-known gem: the lichen-covered tombstones in **Evergreen Cemetery** (601 Seater Street; 907-364-2828). Joseph Juneau and Richard Harris, the prospectors who founded the city, are buried here, and the cemetery was also the site of the funeral pyre of Chief Cowee, the Auk who led them to Juneau's gold.

7 *Arts and Crafts* 3 p.m.

When cruise ships are in town, the locals say they stay out of "waddling distance" of the piers. And with good reason: most of the shops that line the streets of downtown are filled with mass-produced "Native" items for the tourist trade. But not all. The **Juneau Artists Gallery** (175 South Franklin Street; 907-586-9891; juneauartistsgallery.net), a co-operative shop, sells jewelry, prints, pottery, drawings, and other work. Be sure to chat with the gallery staff — each is an artist and a member of the co-op. For apparel a little more exotic than the ubiquitous Alaska-themed sweatshirt, try **Shoefly & Hudsons** (109 Seward Street; 907-586-1055; shoeflyalaska.com), which offers unusual designs in footwear, handbags, and accessories. (People in Juneau say it was one of Sarah Palin's favorite shops when she was the governor.) But the city's most unusual retail outlet is **William Spear Design** (174 South Franklin Street; 907-586-2209; wmspear.com), a purveyor of tiny enamel pins, zipper pulls, and other items — many with edgy political messages.

8 *On the Page* 4:30 p.m.

If your shopping interests are geared more toward the written word, you are in luck: Juneau is friendly to independent bookstores. One in downtown is the **Observatory** (299 North Franklin Street; 907-586-9676; observatorybooks.com), perched up the hill from the harbor. From a tiny blue house not much younger than the town itself, the shop's proprietor, Dee Longenbaugh, offers an extensive stock of books on Alaska, particularly the southeast region. She prides herself on her collection of maps and charts as well as works on regional plants, animals, and geology.

9 *Alaskan Mediterranean* 7 p.m.

With its high ceiling and wood floors, **Zephyr** (200 Seward Street; 907-780-2221; zephyrrestaurant.com; $$$) is Juneau's most elegant restaurant. It

ABOVE AND BELOW Spectacular scenery courtesy of Juneau's in-town glacier, the Mendenhall Glacier. Downstream, Nugget Falls cascades from the glacial melt, while upstream the glacier itself holds onto its frozen grandeur.

serves fish, of course, but Mediterranean style: for example, the halibut provençale, with tomatoes and olives. There are also options like mushroom risotto. The desserts are rich, so save some appetite. After dinner, you can get back into the gold rush mood with a game of pool and an Alaskan pale ale in the bar of the **Alaskan Hotel** (167 South Franklin Street; 907-586-1000; thealaskanhotel.com).

SUNDAY

10 *Coffee and a View* 9 a.m.

Grab a coffee and a pastry at the downtown location of the **Heritage Coffee Company** chain (174 South Franklin Street; 907-586-1087; heritagecoffee.com) before donning your boots and heading out to Juneau's in-town glacier, the **Mendenhall Glacier**, off Glacier Spur Road. Dress warmly—cool air flows constantly off the 12-mile stream of ice, and it is typically five or 10 degrees cooler here than in town. In part because of global warming, the glacier is retreating perhaps as much as 100 feet a year. Even from the visitor center (8510 Mendenhall Loop Road; 907-789-0097), you can see the kinds of rock and soil it deposited as it moved inland. But if you are feeling energetic, try the Moraine Trail for a first-hand look at what glaciers leave behind.

ABOVE Tourists cruise South Franklin Street.

THE BASICS

There are no roads to Juneau, which traditionally was reached by sea. Major airlines serve its airport. Rent a car at the airport.

Westmark Baranoff
127 North Franklin Street
907-586-2660
westmarkhotels.com
$$
Part of an Alaska and Yukon chain, caters to business types and tourists.

The Juneau Hotel
1200 West 9th Street
907-586-5666
juneauhotels.net
$$
A comfortable all-suites option.

Pearson's Pond Luxury Inn and Adventure Spa
4541 Sawa Circle
907-789-3772
pearsonspond.com
$$$$
Out of town and loaded with amenities.

Homer

As you round the final bend on the Sterling Highway in Alaska and reach the town of Homer, the view of Kachemak Bay stops you dead. Across the water, jagged mountains cut by fjords lead right to the rocky coastline, and forests lead to alpine tundra, then glaciers that glint in the sunlight. On the Homer side of the bay, fields full of purple lupine, white yarrow, and goldenrod lead to beaches. Snow-capped volcanoes across a nearby inlet come into view. Homer is called the End of the Road, the Halibut Fishing Capital of the World, or the Cosmic Hamlet by the Sea, depending on whom you happen to ask. Located on the Kenai Peninsula, a 220-mile drive south of Anchorage, Homer is a small town of homesteaders and artists, fishermen and ex-hippies, with a sprinkling of outlaws and seers. These categories frequently overlap, creating a funky, dynamic community that is a bit eccentric even by Alaskan standards. — BY MARIA FINN

FRIDAY

1 *Across the Water* 4:30 p.m.

The road on the Homer Spit, a four-mile-long sliver of land jutting into the bay, leads to the boat harbor and **Kachemak Bay Ferry** (907-399-2683; halibut-cove-alaska.com/ferry.htm). Catch the ferry, the *Danny J*, for a ride across Kachemak Bay to **Halibut Cove**, a small community that has no roads, only wooden boardwalks. The *Danny J* has a wildlife tour to Halibut Cove at noon and a 5 p.m. service that takes people there for the evening. Before dinner, stroll the boardwalks and drop in at the **Halibut Cove Experience Fine Art Gallery** (907-296-2215; halibutcoveexperience.com), which shows the works of Halibut Cove artists. Some of this area's local artists also fish commercially, a way of life reflected in the salmon mosaics and drawings and the occasional halibut or herring painting.

2 *Taste of the Bay* 6:30 p.m.

The **Saltry** restaurant (907-399-2683; halibut-cove-alaska.com/saltry.htm; $$$) in Halibut Cove serves seafood caught locally and vegetables grown in a patch out back. There is seating indoors or outside on a covered deck that overlooks the moored boats. The Saltry has a brief list of wines to go with its main event, the seafood. Try a huge appetizer platter of tart pickled salmon or mildly spiced halibut ceviche, and an entree of grilled halibut or another Pacific cod brandade.

OPPOSITE Homer has been called the End of the Road and the Cosmic Hamlet by the Sea.

3 *Beer on the Spit* 9 p.m.

To while away a few hours in an atmosphere of conviviality (if not urbanity), drop in at the **Salty Dawg Saloon** (4380 Homer Spit Road; 907-235-6718; saltydawgsaloon.com), a dive bar and Alaska institution. It's the place where tourists and locals drink, sing, and get silly together.

SATURDAY

4 *Tempting Aromas* 8 a.m.

Anyone cutting back on carbs should avoid **Two Sisters Bakery** (233 East Bunnell Avenue; 907-235-2280; twosistersbakery.net) in Homer's Old Town near Bishop's Beach. But the salty ocean air carrying wafts of pecan sticky buns, savory Danishes, and fresh-brewed coffee makes this place hard to resist.

5 *Natural Alaska* 10 a.m.

Get into the forest on an early guided hike at the **Wynn Nature Center** (East Skyline Road; 907-235-6667; akcoastalstudies.org/wynn-nature-center.html), which is part of the nonprofit Center for Alaskan Coastal Studies, established in 1982. The bears and moose may be elusive, but the wildflowers and trees stay in place, ready for your guide's interpretation. (The coastal studies center also offers full-day nature tours from its Peterson Bay Field Station, leaving from Homer Harbor and including a forest hike, talks about indigenous people and fantastical rock formations, and a glimpse of the sea life exposed at low tide.)

6 *Lunch and a Book* Noon

You'll be back in town in time for lunch at the cozy **Mermaid Cafe** (3487 Main Street; 907-235-7649; mermaidcafe.net; $$), where tapas choices may include salmon sliders and falafel. After

your meal, browse next door at the **Old Inlet Bookshop** (oldinletbookshop.com), located at the same address.

7 *Paddling the Bay* 2 p.m.

From the Homer harbor, take a water taxi ride across the bay to **Yukon Island**, where you can launch a kayak into the smooth waters of Kachemak Bay. There, translucent jellyfish pulse below the sea's surface and bald eagles perch on rocky balustrades. On clear days the volcanoes Iliamna and Augustine can be seen. Take a half-day tour with **True North Kayak Adventures** (5 Cannery Row Boardwalk, Homer Spit Road; 907-235-0708; truenorthkayak.com). Alison O'Hara, the owner and a longtime guide in Kachemak Bay, teaches how to approach the sea otters resting in kelp beds and identifies the seabirds. You may see porpoises, whales, and seals. (There are also full-day and three-quarter-day options.)

ABOVE The beach at Kachemak Bay.

BELOW A fresh catch of halibut is prepared for market on a dock along the Homer Spit.

OPPOSITE Catch the ferry to Halibut Cove.

8 *The Homestead* 8 p.m.

Locals describe the **Homestead Restaurant** (at the 8.2-mile marker on East End Road; 907-235-8723; homesteadrestaurant.net; $$$) as the best in the state. Menus change weekly, but expect a variety of local seafood: perfect oysters, clams, Alaska scallops, Alaskan king crab. Another specialty, predictably, is halibut, Homer's favorite fish. Dishes are nicely presented, and the wine list is extensive.

SUNDAY

9 *Cosmic Cuisine* 7:30 a.m.

Brother Asaiah Bates, a follower of South Asian mysticism, arrived in Homer in 1955 from California. He and others with him vowed not to wear shoes or cut their hair until world peace had been achieved and world hunger eradicated. They were called Barefooters. Although the group broke up, Brother Asaiah stayed on, becoming a local sage. He dubbed Homer "the Cosmic Hamlet by the Sea," and although he died in 2000, a small cafe, the **Cosmic Kitchen** (510 Pioneer Avenue; 907-235-6355; $), shows that his legacy lives on in many forms, even in the breakfast burrito. A homemade salsa

bar offers condiments for the breakfasts of burritos with chorizo or huge plates of huevos rancheros accompanied by fresh hash browns.

10 *Head of the Bay* 8:30 a.m.

Just about the only way to get to the head of Kachemak Bay is on horseback. **Trails End Horse Adventures** (53435 East End Road; 907-235-6393) takes visitors down a steep switchback that leads to the beach, and then past the Russian Orthodox village of Kachemak Selo. The tour continues on to the Fox River Flats. Turning toward the Homer Hills, the horses follow a narrow path flanked by elderberry bushes that open into a breathtaking site that was a Barefooters homestead in the 1950s and is now abandoned. Bald eagle chicks peer down from cottonwood trees and clusters of wildflowers dot the open fields. It feels like timeless Alaska.

THE BASICS

By road, Homer is 220 scenic miles southwest of Anchorage. Small planes from regional airlines land at the Homer Airport. If you fly in, rent a car.

Land's End Resort
4786 Homer Spit Road
907-235-0400
lands-end-resort.com
$$-$$$
At the tip of the Homer Spit, with 80 rooms, a restaurant, and a spa.

Hoedel's House & Cabin
4526 East Hill Road
907-235-8859
homerbandb.com
$$
Cozy, well-equipped lodgings with bay views in a cottage and a cabin.

Alaskan Suites
3255 Sterling Highway
907-235-1972
alaskansuites.com
$$$
Breathtaking views from modern cabins with wide-screen TVs and small kitchens.

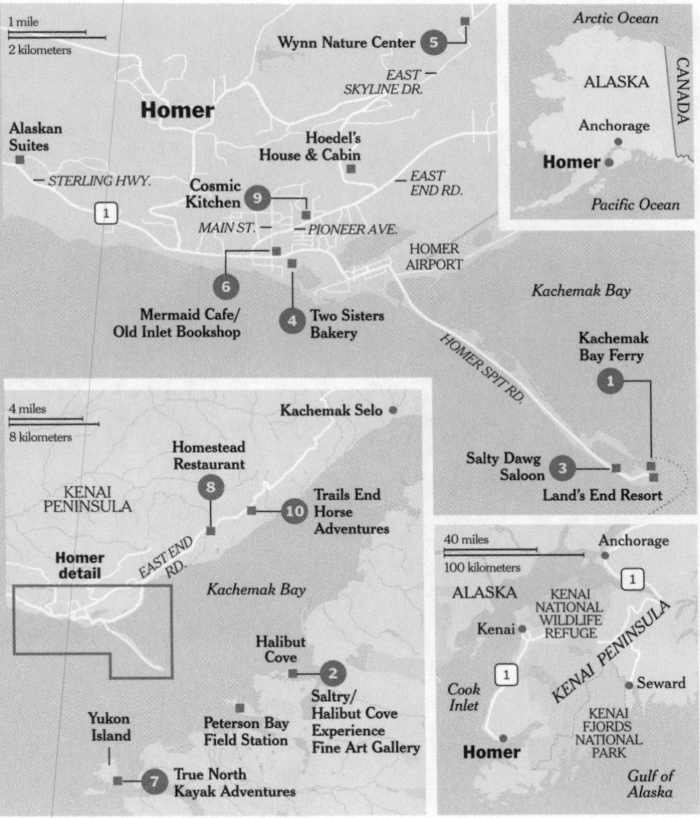

1 mile
2 kilometers
Homer
5 Wynn Nature Center
EAST SKYLINE DR.
Alaskan Suites
Hoedel's House & Cabin
STERLING HWY.
9 Cosmic Kitchen
EAST END RD.
1
MAIN ST.
PIONEER AVE.
HOMER AIRPORT
6 Mermaid Cafe/ Old Inlet Bookshop
4 Two Sisters Bakery
Kachemak Bay
HOMER SPIT RD.
1 Kachemak Bay Ferry
3 Salty Dawg Saloon
Land's End Resort

Arctic Ocean
ALASKA
CANADA
Anchorage
Homer
Pacific Ocean

4 miles
8 kilometers
Kachemak Selo
8 Homestead Restaurant
KENAI PENINSULA
10 Trails End Horse Adventures
Homer detail
EAST END RD.
Kachemak Bay
Halibut Cove
2 Saltry/ Halibut Cove Experience Fine Art Gallery
Peterson Bay Field Station
Yukon Island
7 True North Kayak Adventures

40 miles
100 kilometers
Anchorage
1
ALASKA
KENAI NATIONAL WILDLIFE REFUGE
Kenai
KENAI PENINSULA
1
Seward
Cook Inlet
KENAI FJORDS NATIONAL PARK
Homer
Gulf of Alaska

Honolulu

It's a cosmic irony that the longest, most grueling nonstop in the United States ends in the sweetest arrival of all. Jet-lagged, rumpled mainland travelers land in Honolulu having flown 2,500 miles from California—5,000 miles if from the East Coast. But they will have flown past Diamond Head and over the surfers and paddlers of Waikiki Beach, and their first inhalations of Hawaiian air are likely to be scented with tuberose and plumeria. Add to these timeless enchantments the ethnic restaurants and fine art galleries and hula dancers at sunset, and you have a city in full bloom. So what if you miss the mangoes of summer? There are whales and surf meets in the winter, gardenias in the spring, and cultural festivals and farmers' markets year-round. — BY JOCELYN FUJII

FRIDAY

1 *A Spa without Walls* 3 p.m.

Embrace Honolulu with vigor at **Kapiolani Park**, at the foot of Diamond Head, the volcanic tuff cone and landmark the Hawaiians named Leahi. Work up a sweat with the joggers and rugby players while white terns soar above the ironwoods. Top that off with a sunset swim across the street, at the beach fronting the New Otani Kaimana Beach Hotel.

2 *Hawaiian Sound* 6 p.m.

Sandy feet are not an anomaly at **Duke's Restaurant and Barefoot Bar** (2335 Kalakaua Avenue; 808-922-2268; dukeswaikiki.com), where the stars of Hawaiian music play nightly at sunset. Maunalua, a trio offering contemporary Hawaiian music, usually plays on Fridays, and the guitarist-vocalist Henry Kapono, the self-proclaimed "wild Hawaiian," is the Hawaiian-rock attraction on Sundays. The open-air spot has a vintage surfer feel and wall-to-wall tributes to the Olympic swimming legend Duke Kahanamoku.

3 *Seafood Hong Kong Style* 7:30 p.m.

Follow the scent of jasmine, plumeria, and tuberose to the lei stands that line Maunakea Street, where vendors sell fragrant garlands amid Chinese herb shops, Asian grocery stores, and artists' galleries. At the busy **Little Village Noodle House** (1113 Smith Street; 808-545-3008; littlevillagehawaii.com; $), the sizzling scallops have a kick and the tofu pot stickers have a following. Vegetarian choices abound, and even traditional Chinese offerings like broccoli beef and noodles, kung pao chicken, and walnut shrimp are tastier—and healthier—than the norm.

4 *From Tattoos to Dragons* 9:30 p.m.

The **Dragon Upstairs** (1038 Nuuanu Avenue; 808-526-1411; thedragonupstairs.com), an intimate jazz club, is a Chinatown hotspot in a former tattoo parlor lined with red walls, dragon masks, and glass-shard sculptures by Roy Venters, the Andy Warhol of Honolulu. Affixed to the wall is a large glittery dragon, a former stage prop for opera. While the mood is friendly and upbeat, it's the music that soars: some of the best jazz in town can be heard here, and because many in the audience are musicians, you can count on hearty improv and guest artists.

SATURDAY

5 *Diamond Head for Foodies* 9 a.m.

Yes, it's possible to have breakfast on the slopes of Diamond Head—at Honolulu's busiest Saturday market. A bonanza for early-bird foodies, the **Farmers' Market at Kapiolani Community College**

OPPOSITE A paddleboarder near Diamond Head.

BELOW Waikiki, the gorgeous beach that made Honolulu a world-famous vacation spot, is flanked by high-rise hotels as it curves toward Diamond Head.

(4303 Diamond Head Road; 808-848-2074; hfbf.org) is an essential stop for many a local food lover. Take your own bag and go early to find parking. The rainbow of products is edible Hawaii in full color, whether it's persimmons, homemade ginger and guava drinks, mangoes, goat cheese, local honey, or scones and banana bread.

6 *All About the Art* 11 a.m.

To glimpse the private passions of the late reclusive billionaire Doris Duke, take a peek at **Shangri La** (shangrilahawaii.org), her oceanfront estate on the other side of Diamond Head. Two-hour tours of the Islamic museum there (reservations required) begin and end at the **Honolulu Museum of Art** (900 South Beretania Street; 808-532-8701). A 15-minute shuttle ride takes you to the site, where a Mughal garden quiets the mind and 13th-century Persian tiles line the walls of the central courtyard. The 8th- to 20th-century artifacts are integrated into the architecture, so you can stand at a 13th-century prayer niche, called a mihrab, and then sit in the gleaming Turkish Room, where Duke, a tobacco heiress, entertained guests after dinner.

7 *The Plate and the Art* 1:30 p.m.

The **Honolulu Museum of Art Café** (900 South Beretania Street; 808-532-8734; honolulumuseum.org/394-pavilion_cafe; $$) scores high points for its Mediterranean menu and its alfresco location next to a waterfall and Jun Kaneko sculptures. The menu, while not fancy, is ideal: white bean salad with arugula and wilted radicchio, hearty sandwiches (feta, tapenade, tomato; chopped salmon steak), a pasta of the day, and desserts like chocolate pot de crème and fresh fruit crisp. At the museum shop a few steps away are books, cards, textiles, and handmade jewelry.

8 *Sunset Serenade* 5:30 p.m.

Halekulani's House Without a Key (2199 Kalia Road; 808-923-2311; halekulani.com) is a magnet at sunset. A century-old kiawe tree is gracefully backlighted by the late afternoon sun, the mai tais are heroic, and the views of the ocean and Diamond Head make you forget about the neighboring high-rises. When the hula dancer Kanoe Miller takes the stage, small talk ceases. It could be a postcard from the 1940s, the heyday of Waikiki.

9 *Wong's Way* 8 p.m.

In the face of many rivals, and despite its lack of an ocean view and adequate waiting space, **Alan Wong's** (1857 South King Street; 808-949-1939; alanwongs.com; $$$$) is the local temple of fine dining. The koa-paneled room with open kitchen has a subdued ambience that puts the spotlight squarely on the food. To fresh local ingredients and familiar, even nostalgic, ethnic traditions, Wong adds sophisticated touches: ahi sashimi appears as a high-rise tartare; "California roll" is really Kona lobster; tomato soup is a yin-yang swirl of yellow and red; and fresh seafood can be crusted, poached, sautéed, and served in diverse preparations. Ginger, lemongrass, black beans, wasabi, and chili pepper are among Wong's signature flavors, but be ready for anything, as the menu changes by the day. Wong, one of the twelve founders of the Hawaii regional cuisine organization, is a devoted supporter of local farmers and food producers.

SUNDAY

10 *The Turning Point* 10 a.m.

The **Makapuu Point Trail**, at the easternmost part of Oahu, is the tour de force on a drive full

of special moments. Pack sunscreen and a hat as you head south along Kalanianaole Highway past Hanauma Bay and Sandy Beach. Koko Head Crater on the left has created striated cliffs that nearly run into the lava shoreline, and you're driving between them both. Once past Sandy Beach, park at the Ka Iwi State Park lot and follow the trail to Makapuu Point along a two-mile 500-foot ascent. The 1909 Makapuu Lighthouse completes the package with views of the eastern coast and small offshore islands.

11 *The Buzz About Burgers* 12:30 p.m.

Continue the drive along the windward coast, where sea turtles feed among fishermen and snorkelers. About 20 minutes from Makapuu, you'll reach **Kailua Beach**, lined with ironwoods and dotted with paddlers and windsurfers. The local watering hole, **Buzz's Original Steakhouse** (413 Kawailoa Road; 808-261-4661; buzzsoriginalsteakhouse.com; $$), is across the street, with a charming veranda and a tree growing through the center of the dining room. While Buzz's is basically a burger joint, there are some standouts, like kiawe-grilled fresh fish burgers. Bloody marys and beer flow freely from the koa and bamboo bar.

OPPOSITE ABOVE Hike up the slopes of Diamond Head for 360-degree views.

OPPOSITE BELOW The lights of downtown Honolulu, a metropolitan enclave in an island paradise.

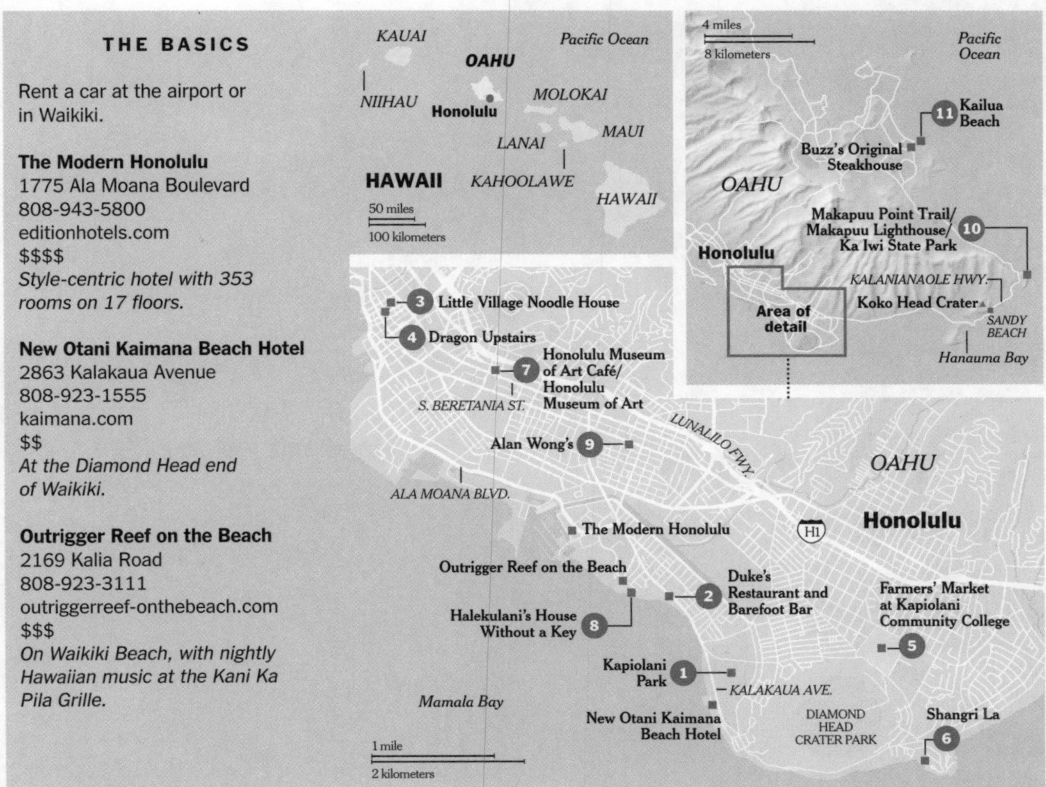

THE BASICS

Rent a car at the airport or in Waikiki.

The Modern Honolulu
1775 Ala Moana Boulevard
808-943-5800
editionhotels.com
$$$$
Style-centric hotel with 353 rooms on 17 floors.

New Otani Kaimana Beach Hotel
2863 Kalakaua Avenue
808-923-1555
kaimana.com
$$
At the Diamond Head end of Waikiki.

Outrigger Reef on the Beach
2169 Kalia Road
808-923-3111
outriggerreef-onthebeach.com
$$$
On Waikiki Beach, with nightly Hawaiian music at the Kani Ka Pila Grille.

Kailua

The guidebooks say Kailua is basically a beach. But there's a town wrapped around the beach, and, around that, a whole other side of the 600-square-mile island of Oahu — the windward side, a world away from Waikiki. Kailua is barely half an hour from Honolulu, but separated from it by a soaring ribbon of razorback mountains, the Koolau Range. The green lava wall is pierced near its summit by two sets of highway tunnels, like airlocks in time and space. You will probably come from the Honolulu side, which is dry and sunny, its postcard loveliness folded among high-rises, offices, airport, and freeways. Emerge on the Kailua side — greener, quieter, lower, and slower, with marshes and palms and perfect Kailua Bay.
— BY LAWRENCE DOWNES

FRIDAY

1 *View to Windward* 3 p.m.

On your way in, leave the freeway at the Pali Highway (Route 61) exit and drive north, climbing steadily with the green, fluted mountain walls closing in — silvered with mist and plunging waterfalls when it rains. When highway builders, in the 1950s, reached the knife-edged Koolau summit, or pali, they punched tunnels through it and all but did away with the meandering mountain-goat path down the other side, with its treacherous winds and rock slides. After you go through the second tunnel, the windward side is before you: lush terrain of old fishponds, streams, marshes, soft volcanic cinder cones, and the blue, isle-dotted Kailua Bay. Stop at the **Nuuanu Pali State Wayside** (hawaiistateparks.org/parks/oahu/nuuanu.cfm), a lookout well-marked by signs. You're looking down here from a thousand-foot precipice, a view that dazzled Mark Twain. And this is where, in 1795, King Kamehameha's army, invaders from the Big Island, pushed the army of Chief Kalanikupule to the pali's brink. The only way out was to plummet, which hundreds did. A plaque recounts the battle.

2 *Beach First* 4 p.m.

Once you're in Kailua, waste no time getting to **Kailua Beach Park** (Kailua Road and South Kalaheo Avenue). As you walk toward the bay, you'll see a field of impossible blue, sky down to water, and a broad crescent beach. The sand is cottony and cool by the naupaka shrubs at the top of the beach, sloping down to firm wet velvet under the foam. Overhead, great frigatebirds, 'iwa in Hawaiian, hover in the whipping trade winds. Don't look for surfers here: the waves are gentle, good for swimming and body-surfing. This is also a good place to get out on the water on a paddle board or in a sea kayak. **Kailua Sailboards and Kayaks** (130 Kailua Road; 808-262-2555; kailuasailboards.com) provides rentals and lessons.

3 *Ice and Spice* 6 p.m.

A five-minute walk from the park is **Island Snow** (130 Kailua Road; 808-263-6339; islandsnow.com), where President Obama and his daughters come for shave ice when they're on vacation in Kailua. His favorite flavors are supposedly lime, guava-orange, and cherry. You might like the coconut, with sweetened azuki beans. It won't spoil your dinner, which you might want to have at **Saeng's Thai Cuisine** (315 Hahani Street; 808-263-9727; restauranteur.com/saengs; $), an attractive place with cloths on the tables, pad Thai and spring rolls on the menu, and Thai iced tea (herbal teas with cream and sugar). There's also a full bar.

OPPOSITE The Lanikai Pillbox Trail, a mildly strenuous hike leading up to a panoramic view and the remains of concrete coastal lookouts built in World War II.

BELOW A team of paddlers in a racing canoe in Kailua Bay. Outrigger canoe racing is a part of the Hawaiian Islands' living Polynesian heritage.

SATURDAY

4 *Sunrise Islands* 5:30 a.m.

Get up before dawn for Pacific sunrise watching. If you have jet lag operating in your favor, it will be easy. When the spectacle is over, enjoy a swim on the quiet, nearly deserted beach. Even at 6 a.m. the water is bathtub warm. Lie on your back and contemplate **Flat Island** off to the right, close-in, temptingly swimmable, and the Mokulua islets, **Moku Nui** and **Moku Iki**, a kayak trip away. Girding the bay to the left is a humpbacked volcanic crater, the Mokapu Peninsula, looking like the snake that swallowed an elephant in *The Little Prince*. It's a United States Marine base that has served as Obama's vacation gym.

5 *Early Risers* 7 a.m.

Kailua is a morning town, and by now runners are on the beach and ambling couples are walking dogs and clutching cups of coffee. Hit **Kalapawai Market** (306 South Kalaheo Avenue; 808-262-4359; kalapawaimarket.com), near the park entrance, for Kona coffee, bagels, and the morning paper. Or take the short walk to **Cinnamon's** (315 Uluniu Street; 808-261-8724; cinnamons808.com; $$) for an omelet, steak and eggs, or French toast. **Agnes' Portuguese Bake Shop** (46 Hoolai Street; 808-262-5367; agnesbakeshop.com) has the best malasadas (Portuguese doughnuts).

6 *An Older Oahu* 10 a.m.

Kailua was a thriving population center before European contact, a playground for chiefs, rich in farming and fish. For a plunge into antiquity, visit **Ulupo Heiau** (hawaiistateparks.org/parks/oahu/ulupo.cfm), a massive temple built of lava stone perhaps 400 years ago. Once it was neatly terraced with wooden altars and statues and sacrifices. The surviving platform, 150 feet by 140 feet with walls up to 30 feet high, is a staggering work of ancient hand-to-hand rock laying. Get there from the parking lot of the YMCA (1200 Kailua Road). For another hint of the original Hawaii, drive to **Ho'omaluhia Botanical Garden** (45-680 Luluku Road, Kaneohe; 808-233-7323;), which is replanted in native species.

7 *Island Retail* Noon

There's not a lot of shopping in Kailua, but it's worth poking around amid the shops and lunch spots downtown. **BookEnds** (600 Kailua Road; 808-261-1996), in the Kailua Shopping Center, has an excellent section on Hawaiian history and guidebooks for bird- and fish-spotting. **Global Village** (539 Kailua Road; 808-262-8183; globalvillagehawaii.com) is one of the shops with clothing and jewelry that fit the island vibe, and homegrown places sell art and antiques.

8 *Some Like Waves* 2 p.m.

Investigate another beach. **Kalama Beach Park** (248 North Kalaheo Avenue) is far quieter and more secluded than Kailua Beach, and if you like bigger waves, you'll be happier here. Or head out to the beach at **Waimanalo**, a short drive into a more Hawaiian state of mind. Oahu's windward side has local fishermen, dancers, musicians, artists — native Hawaiian families rooted for generations, with names like Mahoe, Aluli, and Pahinui. In Waimanalo, some houses fly the Hawaiian sovereignty flag, salving wounds unhealed since the overthrow of the native kingdom by the United States in 1893.

9 *Square Meal* 7 p.m.

After an active day, you should have enough appetite for **Buzz's Original Steak House** (413 Kawailoa Road; 808-261-4661; buzzsoriginalsteakhouse.com; $$) and its all-American fare: steak, ribs, lobster tail. It's across the street from Kailua Beach Park.

SUNDAY

10 *Above the Bay* 9 a.m.

Get an overview on the **Lanikai Pillbox Trail**, a short, mildly strenuous hike to a ridgeline along a smooth-sloped cinder cone just above Lanikai Beach (kailuachamber.com/beaches). Trailhead signs are near the entrance to **Mid Pacific Country Club** (266 Kaelepulu Drive). The red-dirt trail starts out crumbly and steep. It's a dry, hot hike, with cactus flowers and pili grass and butterflies. All the water is below you: Kaelepulu Stream, leading to the bay; Kawainui Marsh, the island's largest; the cobalt blue beyond the reef. At the summit are the hulks of two concrete pillboxes built in World War II as coastal lookouts. They're a good place to rest, drink, soak it all in.

11 *Beach Farewell* Noon

Revive back in town with brunch at **Crepes No Ka Oi** (131 Hekili Street; 808-263-4088; crepesnokaoi.com; $$). You can choose sweet, savory, or both; breakfast crepes include eggs, cheese, and meat. Afterward, stop at the beach for a last gathering of those sensations of surf and warmth, of sun squinting and salt smell, to take home to the mainland with you.

OPPOSITE Kalapawai Market, a place to stop for coffee, bagels, and the morning paper on the way to a day of sun and ocean at Kailua Beach Park.

ABOVE Playing in the warm waves of Kailua Bay. Each in its own way, both ocean and sky here are an impossible blue.

THE BASICS

Drive to Kailua from Honolulu on Routes H-1 and 61. Kailua has no hotels, but it has bed-and-breakfasts and vacation-home rentals. Look for legal, licensed accommodations.

Pat's Kailua Beach Properties
808-262-4128
patskailua.com
$-$$$$
Clean lodgings close to Kailua Beach Park and Lanikai.

Sheffield House Bed & Breakfast
131 Kuulei Road
808-262-0721
hawaiisheffieldhouse.com
$$
Close to Kailua Beach, shopping, and restaurants.

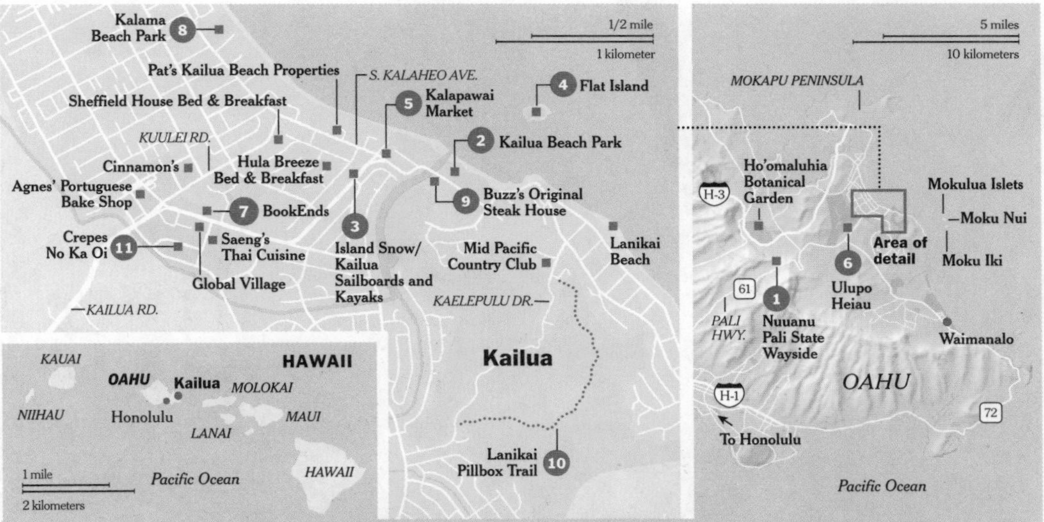

Hula Breeze Bed & Breakfast
172 Kuumele Place
808-469-7623
vrbo.com/235628
$$
Guesthouse a few blocks from the beach.

Molokai

You've got to really want to go to Molokai, a steppingstone Hawaiian island between Oahu and Maui. Its stunning beaches and rugged jungle interior invite exploration, and the tragic tale of its leper colony, where native Hawaiians used to be summarily exiled, inspire an unavoidable curiosity. But hotel rooms are few, tourist amenities scarce, and developers actively discouraged. Yet for those who remember an older Hawaii — magical, sensuous, isolated — or for those who want to find some sense of how things were on Maui, the Big Island, and Kauai before they were drawn into the hustle and flow of Oahu, Molokai is more than worth the trouble. Its lifestyle is more traditionally Polynesian, its people reserved, but when their veneer is cracked, warm and full of an ancient joie de vivre. — BY CHARLES E. ROESSLER

FRIDAY

1 *The Moccasin* 1 p.m.

Pick up your rental car in the lava-rock terminal of tiny **Hoolehua Airport**, in the center of Molokai, and drive west on Highway 460 to **Maunaloa**, an old cattle ranching settlement. You won't encounter much traffic on this 10 miles of road, or anywhere on Molokai, which has 7,400 residents. The island is shaped roughly like a moccasin, 10 miles wide and 38 miles long from east to west. While eastern Molokai has a wet climate and junglelike foliage, the west end is arid with scrub vegetation. But it is rich in Hawaii's mythical history. Puu Nana, east of Maunaloa, is revered as the birthplace of the hula, which its practitioners consider to be a sacred dance, and every May dancers arrive to celebrate it. Molokai is also famous for its kahuna, powerful priests who could either provide life-giving herbal remedies or pray a healthy person to death.

2 *Clear Waters* 3 p.m.

Go for a swim at tiny **Dixie Maru Beach** at the lower end of a string of idyllic beaches that line the west coast. Ignore the temptation to swim at **Papohaku**, two gorgeous miles of 100-yard-wide sandy beach; it harbors danger from sharp hidden coral reefs and swift, treacherous rip currents. Dixie Maru, not much more than a protected cove, is enticing in its own way: clear, deep-blue water with a calming undulation. If you take a careful walk over the lava rocks framing the left side of the bay, you may get lucky and spot a honu (a sea turtle) bobbing and weaving along the shoreline. This area was once dominated by a resort called Molokai Ranch, but it closed in 2008 after Molokai residents rejected a plan for its expansion.

3 *Try the Opakapaka* 6 p.m.

A bare-bones place reminiscent of a '50s diner, with old Coca-Cola decals on the wall, the **Kualapuu Cookhouse** (102 Farrington Avenue, Highway 470; 808-567-9655; $$-$$$) is a Molokai institution, serving fresh fish, beef, pork, and chicken dishes. Mahi-mahi and opakapaka (pink snapper) are local catches, subject to availability. The restaurant does not sell alcohol, but you can bring your own wine. Eat outdoors — you might share a picnic table with other customers who can tell you about life on the island. There may be live music — perhaps a ukelele and a one-string, gut-bucket bass — but be warned: the restaurant closes early.

SATURDAY

4 *Island Market* 10 a.m.

Saturday morning offers an opportunity to mix with the locals at the **Molokai Farmers Market** (Ala

OPPOSITE AND RIGHT Kaluapapa National Historic Park, the former leper colony that forms the core of Molokai's story of beauty and tragedy. A limited number of visitors are allowed; they arrive by mule ride or on foot.

Malama Street) in what passes for a downtown in tiny Kaunakakai, the island's largest town. On a short street lined with stands, browse in a convivial, relaxed atmosphere for papaya and poi, T-shirts, animal carvings, and shell jewelry. Molokai never surrendered to tourist-first faux aloha spirit: the people here are genuine. They call Molokai the Friendly Island, but it can turn into the surly island to the outsider who ignores local protocol. The outdoor market is an opportunity to take in the local color and meet the locals on neutral ground.

5 *Fishponds and Spears* Noon

Have lunch at **Molokai Pizza** (15 Kaunakakai Place, just off Highway 460, Kaunakakai; 808-553-3288), which boasts the best pan pizza on the island, along with deli sandwiches on its own bread. Then set out to explore the south shore, driving east from Kaunakakai on Route 450, the East Kamehameha V Highway. In the first 20 miles you'll see 19th-century churches and some of the 60 ancient fishponds that dominate the southern coast. The Hawaiians who built them seven or eight centuries ago used lava rocks to surround and trap fish attracted to underground streams. At Mile Marker 20, stop at **Murphey's Beach**, a popular snorkeling spot. Watch locals spearfishing for dinner while children frolic on the sand, shouting and laughing.

6 *Old Ways* 2 p.m.

The last seven miles of the trip to the east end rival Maui's famous Road to Hana in adventure and beauty. The pulse quickens as you drive inches away from the ocean on the one-lane road. Inland views are a window onto a traditional Hawaii. Foliage is dense, and families have their horses and goats tied close to the road. On many of their one-acre plots, gardens and fruit trees vie for space with chickens, dogs, rusted car skeletons, and modest homes. Fishing nets and hunting accouterments, including dog kennels, attest to the survival of old ways of finding food; wild pigs, goats, and deer are the hunters' prey.

7 *The Far East* 3 p.m.

The road ends at **Halawa Park** in the spectacular Halawa Valley, surrounded by mountains and ocean. The isolated beaches in the bay are good for a dip in summer and great for big-wave surfing in winter. In the verdant valley, an ancient complex of terraces and taro patches, built by the Polynesians who first settled this island, helped sustain life on Molokai

ABOVE The verdant, isolated Halawa Valley.

OPPOSITE ABOVE An ancient Molokai fishpond.

OPPOSITE BELOW A fisherman casts his net on a school of fish in Honouli Wai Bay.

from about 650 A.D. to the mid-20th century, when other job opportunities lured residents away. What remained of the taro was destroyed by a tsunami in 1946 and floods in the 1960s. You can learn about attempts to restore it — and can hike to lovely Moalua Falls — if you have some extra time and arrange a private tour (book at Hotel Molokai in Kaunakakai; about $80). On your drive back, go a half-mile or so past Kaunakakai to **Kaiowea Park** to see the **Kapuaiwa Coconut Grove**, a cluster of tall coconut palms that remain from 1,000 of their kind planted here in the 1860s by King Kamehameha V.

8 *Night Life* 7 p.m.

Find Molokai's weekend social scene at the casual **Hula Shores** restaurant in the Hotel Molokai (1300 Kamehameha V Highway, Kaunakakai; 808-660-3408; hotelmolokai.com; $$). Try a local dish like kalua pork and cabbage or hibachi chicken and listen to live music, likely to feature ukeleles. The adjoining tiki bar, only yards away from the tranquil Pacific, conveys a feeling of timelessness as you sway in a hammock, one of three catching the slight breeze. If you're still out and about at 10, join the line at **Kanemitsu Bakery** (79 Ala Malama Avenue; 808-553-5855) waiting for hot French bread. It's what's happening Saturday night in Kaunakakai.

SUNDAY

9 *The Colony* 10 a.m.

Drive up Highway 470 to the north shore. Much of it is impenetrable, with soaring cliffs pitched

straight down 2,000 feet. In the center is **Kalaupapa National Historic Park** (nps.gov/kala), a small peninsula where native Hawaiian victims of leprosy were dropped off by ship and isolated. It was also the home of Father Damien, now St. Damien of Molokai, the 19th-century priest and Hawaiian folk hero who worked with the lepers until he contracted their disease and died. The unique community that developed there has a small-town New England feel, with tidy churches and modest homes belying past horrors. It is open to small numbers of visitors by permit; they can hike a cliff trail down or go with **Molokai Mule Ride** (808-567-6088; muleride.com) Monday through Saturday. Get a good view from the **Kalaupapa Overlook**, 1,700 feet above the peninsula in **Palaau State Park**. If you know the story, the sight of the village below sets the mind racing with searing images of lepers being tossed overboard offshore and ordered to sink or swim to the peninsula—never to leave again.

ABOVE Ignore the temptation to swim at Papohaku, two gorgeous miles of 100-yard-wide sandy beach. It harbors danger from sharp hidden coral reefs and rip currents.

OPPOSITE The grave of Father Damien, now St. Damien of Molokai, at Kalaupapa National Historic Park. He devoted his life to the people exiled to a leper colony there.

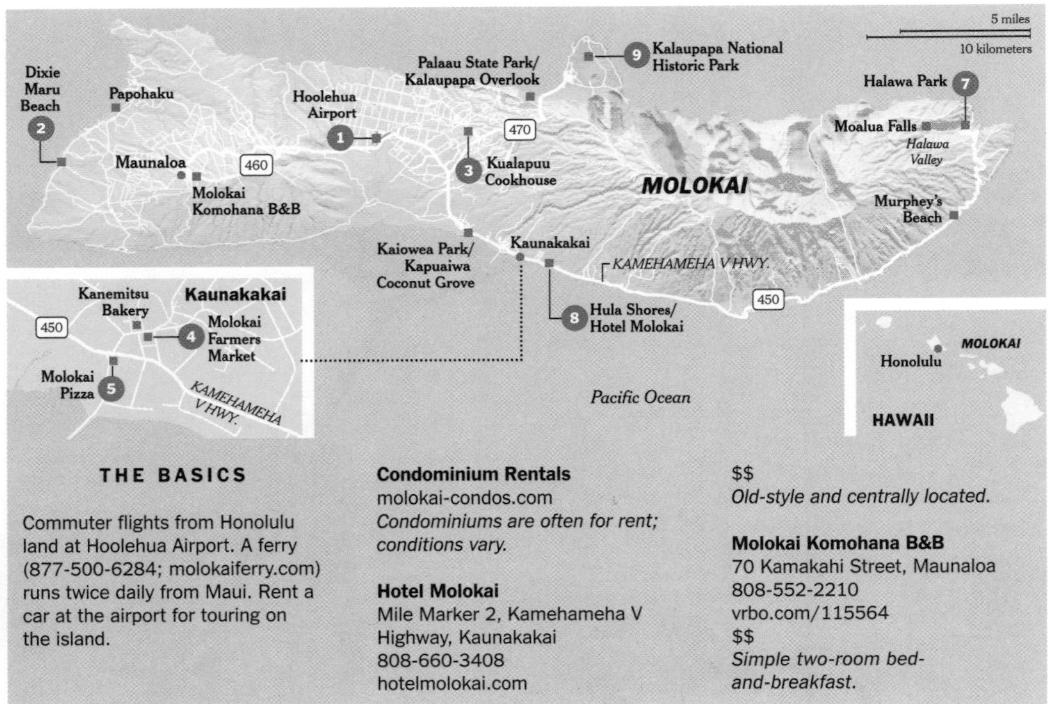

THE BASICS

Commuter flights from Honolulu land at Hoolehua Airport. A ferry (877-500-6284; molokaiferry.com) runs twice daily from Maui. Rent a car at the airport for touring on the island.

Condominium Rentals
molokai-condos.com
Condominiums are often for rent; conditions vary.

Hotel Molokai
Mile Marker 2, Kamehameha V Highway, Kaunakakai
808-660-3408
hotelmolokai.com
$$
Old-style and centrally located.

Molokai Komohana B&B
70 Kamakahi Street, Maunaloa
808-552-2210
vrbo.com/115564
$$
Simple two-room bed-and-breakfast.

Maui

"I went to Maui to stay a week and remained five," Mark Twain wrote in 1866. Whether lazing on a warm sugary beach, gazing awestruck at a Haleakala sunrise, or snorkeling to the song of humpback whales, visitors to Maui today would likely feel the same. And while it is known for its sparkling coastline and fertile green interior, Hawaii's second-largest island appeals equally to the urbane. Resorts hugging the south and west shores claim some of the state's finest restaurants, shops, and spas. A thriving arts community keeps culture and creativity in high gear. In upcountry Maui, on the slopes of the 10,000-foot Haleakala, you can sample just-picked fruit or walk among fields of lavender. Mark Twain had it right: it's not an easy island to leave. — BY JOCELYN FUJII

FRIDAY

1 *Beauty and the Beach* 2:30 p.m.

Tucked between the condo-studded town of Kihei and the upscale resort of Wailea, the white-sand beach of **Keawakapu** is south Maui's hidden jewel. Lined with lavish Balinese- and plantation-style homes, this half-mile playground has gentle waves, talcum-soft sands, and free public parking along South Kihei Road. If it's winter when you take a dip there, listen for the groans and squeaks of the humpback whale, a haunting, mystifying song.

2 *Drive-by Birding* 4 p.m.

For a glimpse of Maui's remarkable biodiversity, take a stroll on the boardwalk at the **Kealia Pond National Wildlife Refuge** (Milepost 6, Mokulele Highway 311; 808-875-1582; fws.gov/kealiapond), a 700-acre natural wetland and seabird sanctuary. Among the birds that shelter here are endangered Hawaiian stilts, black-crowned night herons, and Hawaiian coots, as well as migrating birds like ruddy turnstones.

3 *Fresh and Italian* 6 p.m.

The owners of a popular former Maui pizzeria took their business upscale with **Matteo's Osteria** (161 Wailea Ike Place, Wailea; 808-891-8466; matteosmaui.com; $$), a wine bar and cafe offering dozens of wines by the glass and a variety of Italian dishes from Spaghetti Bolognese (with beef from Maui cattle) to local ahi with Calabrese tapenade. The locals who loved the pizza can still find it at lunch.

4 *Fine Arts* 7 p.m.

The stellar collection of contemporary art (including Jun Kaneko, Toshiko Takaezu, and a bevy of island superstars) at **Four Seasons Resort Maui** at Wailea (3900 Wailea Alanui Drive; 808-874-8000; fourseasons.com/maui) is reason enough to go there. Add designer cocktails, live Hawaiian music, hula, and jazz in the open-air Lobby Lounge, and it becomes a seduction. Take the self-guided audio tour through half of the 68-piece art collection, then settle in for martinis and musical magic at the bar by the grand piano. Live nightly entertainment covers a gamut of musical tastes. (If you want a romantic view, time your visit to catch the setting sun.)

SATURDAY

5 *Upcountry Adventures* 9 a.m.

Jump start your morning at **Grandma's Coffee House** in the village of Keokea (9232 Highway 37, or Kula Highway; 808-878-2140; grandmascoffee.com), on the slopes of Haleakala volcano. On a wooden deck with million-dollar views, you can sip Grandma's

OPPOSITE A windy beach on Maui, an island known for its sparkling coastline and fertile green interior.

BELOW Kula Country Farm Stand sells just-picked fruit, like pineapple and guavas, along with homemade mango bread.

Original Organic, an espresso roasted blend from the family's fifth-generation coffee farm. Then move on to the **Kula Country Farm Stand** (Highway 37, or Kula Highway, across from Rice Park; 808-878-8381), a green-and-white produce stand selling just-picked fruit. Here's a chance to pick up fresh mangos (in season), rare pineapple guavas, and homemade mango bread before heading to lavender fields a few twists and turns away. With its view, acres of lavender, and fragrant jellies, scones, potions, and creams, **Ali'i Kula Lavender Farm** (1100 Waipoli Road; 808-878-3004; aklmaui.com) is a multisensory delight.

6 *Hot Art* Noon

Art is hot in **Makawao**, the cowboy town turned art colony that is about 1,600 feet above sea level on the slopes of Haleakala. Here you will find old wooden storefronts, mom-and-pop restaurants, chic boutiques, and hippie herb shops. At **Hot Island Glass** (3620 Baldwin Avenue; 808-572-4527; hotislandglass.com), the furnace burns hot and glass-blowing is performance art as molten glass evolves into jellyfish, bowls, and oceanic shapes. Next door, Maui artists display their work in the airy plantation-style space of **Viewpoints Gallery** (3620 Baldwin Avenue; 808-572-5979; viewpointsgallerymaui.com).

7 *Put the Top Down* 3 p.m.

The hourlong drive from Maui's hilly upcountry to Lahaina, a popular resort town on the island's west coast, provides nonstop entertainment. With the shimmering Pacific on your left and the chiseled valleys of the West Maui Mountains to the right, you will be hard-pressed to keep your eyes on the road. Once you reach **Black Rock**, a lava outcropping north of Lahaina in the resort named Kaanapali, you'll find equally compelling underwater sights. Grab a snorkel and explore this Atlantis-like world of iridescent fish, spotted eagle rays, and giant green sea turtles.

8 *Farm to Fork* 7:30 p.m.

Peter Merriman of **Merriman's Kapalua** (One Bay Club Place; 808-669-6400; merrimanshawaii.com; $$$) is a pioneer in Hawaii regional cuisine, a culinary movement blending international flavors with local ingredients. The oceanfront restaurant features jaw-dropping views of Molokai island, and the menu highlights local ingredients, whether chèvre from upcountry goats, Maui lehua taro cakes, or line-caught fish from nearby waters. Look for kalua pig ravioli or wok-charred ahi so fresh that it tastes as if it were cooked on the beach. With the opening of his newer Monkeypod Kitchen in Wailea, featuring handcrafted beers and food (house-made hamburger buns, made-from-scratch pies and juices), Merriman has both coastlines covered.

9 *Tiki Torches* 9:30 p.m.

The old Hawaii—tikis and plumeria trees around buildings without marble and bronze—is elusive in today's Hawaii, but you'll find it at **Kaanapali Beach Hotel**'s oceanfront **Tiki Courtyard**, where the **Tiki Bar** (2525 Kaanapali Parkway; 808-667-0111; kbhmaui.com) offers authentic Hawaiian entertainment nightly. Hula by Maui children, lilting Hawaiian music by local entertainers, and the outdoor setting under the stars are a winning combination, especially when warmed by genuine aloha.

RIGHT Jumping off the cliffs of Black Rock, a lava outcropping just north of Lahaina.

SUNDAY

10 *Make It to Mala* 9 a.m.

Brunch at **Mala Ocean Tavern** (1307 Front Street, Lahaina; 808-667-9394; malaoceantavern.com; $$) is like being on the ocean without leaving land. At this casual restaurant, you're practically sitting on the water, enjoying huevos rancheros with black beans or lamb sausage Benedict while dolphins frolic in the ocean and turtles nibble at the shore. Ask for a table outdoors.

11 *Fly Like an Eagle* 11 a.m.

For an adrenaline finish, head to the heights of West Maui, where **Kapalua Ziplines** (2000 Village Road; 808-756-9147; kapaluaziplines.com) offers an unusually long zip-line course. Beginners need not fear, as the two-and-a-half-hour zip (about $170) requires virtually no athleticism. The four-hour trip (about $190) is not for the weak-kneed. The zip line takes you over bamboo forests, gulches, and ridges, with the luscious coastline in the distance.

OPPOSITE ABOVE Find a touch of the old Hawaii — tikis and plumeria trees under the stars — at Kaanapali Beach Hotel's tiki bar. The lilting Hawaiian music is genuine.

ABOVE At Black Rock, grab a snorkel. Below the surface are iridescent fish, spotted eagle rays, and giant turtles.

THE BASICS

Kahului Airport on Maui is served by most major domestic airlines. Major agencies have airport car rentals.

The Four Seasons Resort Maui at Wailea
3900 Wailea Alanui
808-874-8000
fourseasons.com/maui
$$$$
Elegant rooms and suites, seaside massages, and three restaurants.

Hyatt Regency Maui Resort & Spa
200 Nohea Kai Drive, Lahaina
808-661-1234
maui.hyatt.com
$$$$
Irrepressibly flamboyant sprawling resort.

Mana Kai Maui
2960 South Kihei Road
808-879-1561
crhmaui.com
$$
With ocean views, full kitchens, and car-condo deals, a great value.

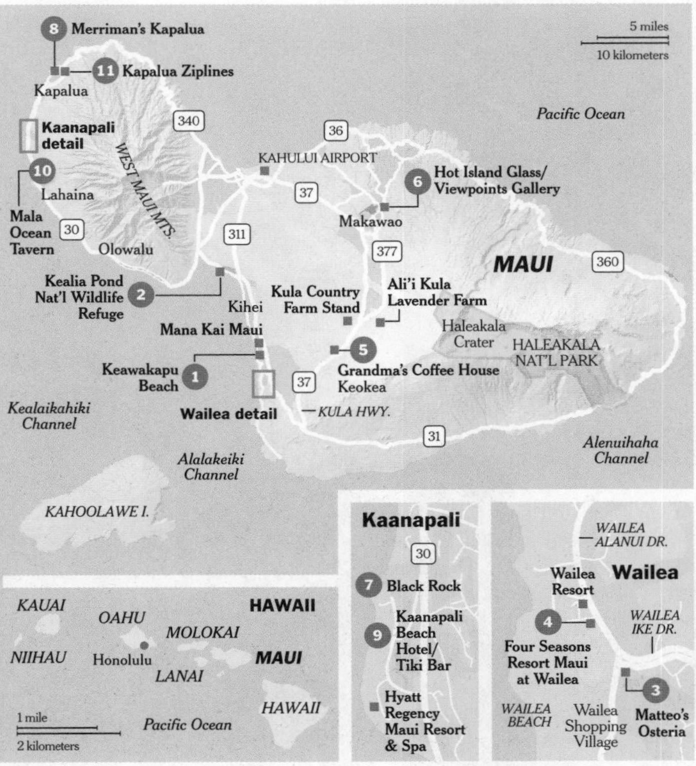

Hilo

Of all the tropical postcard places in the Hawaiian Islands, Hilo, on the Big Island of Hawaii, may have the least to offer the traditional tourist. And that's exactly the reason to go. The center of power of Kamehameha the Great, the king who unified the islands in the early 19th century, Hilo combines history and raw natural power to offer a rich alternative to the resort scene. Orchids and anthuriums, fostered by the wet climate, grow amid some of the most magnificent geographic features on earth, and the city exudes a genuine, small-town warmth and prototypical Aloha spirit. No one works the tourist hustle, and the visitors don't come to vegetate. There's too much to see and do in a natural wonderland where some of the world's tallest mountains, as measured from sea bottom, dominate magnificent landscapes of beach and garden, rain forest and desert, with flowing lava adding more territory every day. — BY CHARLES E. ROESSLER

FRIDAY

1 *Down by the Banyans* 5 p.m.

Cruise down **Banyan Drive**, through a cathedral of monstrous banyan trees labeled with the names of celebrities who planted them, including Babe Ruth and Amelia Earhart. Park near Queen Liliuokalani Gardens, a 30-acre formal Japanese garden with a teahouse and pond, and cross the footbridge to Coconut Island for a good late afternoon photo op looking back at the city and bay, with Mauna Kea volcano in the background. Back on the bayfront, keep walking, passing young boys fishing with bamboo poles while elders work two or three large rods each. It's O.K. to watch, but don't talk. These locals don't work for a tourist bureau; they come down here for peace and solitude — and maybe dinner. Out on the bay, you may see teams of paddlers in 45-foot outriggers. The King Kamehameha statue in **Wailoa River State Park** is similar to the famous one in Honolulu, minus the mob.

2 *Fish Worth Flying For* 8 p.m.

Islanders sometimes fly in from Honolulu for the aholehole, or Hawaiian flagtail, a reef fish raised in ponds for the tables at the **Seaside Restaurant and Aqua Farm** (1790 Kalanianaole Avenue; 808-935-8825; seasiderestaurant.com; $$-$$$). Ask to be seated on the patio and watch the egrets roosting in a small tree for the night. You can't go wrong with the catch of the day, which might be ahi, mahi-mahi, or opakapaka (blue snapper).

SATURDAY

3 *The Blissful Mist* 8 a.m.

Get up early and take a five-minute ride up Waianuenue Avenue to **Rainbow Falls**, where early morning affords the best chance to catch an ethereal rainbow rising from the mist. Refreshed with negative ions, head back to town and park near the **Hilo Farmers Market** at the corner of Mamo Street and Kamehameha Avenue (hilofarmersmarket.com). You won't be early; vendors begin to arrive at 3 a.m. to set up stalls selling exotic produce like atemoya and jackfruit. Sample a suman, a Filipino sticky-rice sweet wrapped in a banana leaf and cooked in coconut milk.

4 *Another Side of Paradise* 9:30 a.m.

Stroll Kamehameha Avenue, checking out **Sig Zane Designs** (122 Kamehameha Avenue; 808-935-7077;

OPPOSITE Hawaii Volcanoes National Park near Hilo on the island of Hawaii — the Big Island.

BELOW The statue of King Kamehameha I, the unifier of the Hawaiian islands, in Hilo. The city was the king's power base.

sigzane.com), with floral-themed contemporary Hawaiian fashions, and **Burgado's Fine Woods** (808-969-9663), with exquisite koa furniture, and the **Dreams of Paradise Gallery** (808-935-5670; dreamsofparadisegallery.com), both in the S. Hata Building (308 Kamehameha Avenue). Take a few steps to the **Pacific Tsunami Museum** (130 Kamehameha Avenue; 808-935-0926; tsunami.org), particularly poignant after the disastrous tsunami in Japan in 2011 and the earlier Indian Ocean tragedy in 2004. The museum explains the physics of these "harbor waves" and documents tsunami devastation in Hilo in 1946 and 1960. A 25-minute video recounts the terror of the survivors, some of whom are docents at the museum.

5 *Munching the Mochi* Noon

Pick up an inexpensive two-course lunch to go, starting with a deliciously authentic bento at the **Puka Puka Kitchen** (270 Kamehameha Avenue; 808-933-2121). For dessert, walk to the **Two Ladies Kitchen** (274 Kilauea Avenue; 808-961-4766) and get the best mochi in the islands. You can see this glutinous rice sweet being made in the tiny shop as five workers scurry around with the hot mixture sticking to big ladles. All the flavors are ono (Hawaiian for delicious), but savor the strawberry, if it's available. Pack the food in the car and make the 45-minute drive southwest to **Hawaii Volcanoes National Park** (Highway 11; 808-985-6000; nps.gov/havo), where you can dine alfresco in the picnic area.

6 *Look Out for the Lava* 1 p.m.

Get information on current conditions from the visitor center at the park entrance. Though lava is likely to be flowing somewhere in the park, the 45-minute drive on Chain of Craters Road can end in frustration if Madame Pele, the temperamental Fire Goddess, isn't sending it that way. Another choice is

ABOVE Clouds of steam and gases surge into the night sky as lava from the Kilauea volcano pours into the ocean.

LEFT Shopping at Sig Zane Designs on Kamehameha Avenue for Zane's floral-themed Hawaiian clothing and textiles.

11-mile **Crater Rim Drive**, which circles the Kilauea Caldera. Stop at the park's **Thomas A. Jaggar Museum** for a refresher course in volcanology. You'll pass through desert flora, moonscapes, and rain forest and find incredible crater views. Take in the **Thurston Lava Tube**, formed as a lava flow left behind a hardened outer crust.

7 *Free-Range and Local* 7 p.m.

Find your way to the **Hilo Bay Cafe** (123 Lihiwai Street; 808-935-4939; hilobaycafe.com; $$), a local favorite and locavore haven that grew out of a strip-mall health food store and is now located near a country club. Start with cocktails and dine on the likes of pan-seared scallops with crème fraîche, black truffle tomato relish, capellini in brown butter, and tobiko. Or perhaps the coconut-crusted tofu with sauteed vegetables, rice, and sweet chili sauce. The menu suggests wine pairings — or, in the case of the local free-range beef burger, a beer pairing: Guinness.

ABOVE A steaming volcanic cone near Hilo.

BELOW Hiking in the lava fields at the end of Chain of Craters Road in Volcanoes National Park.

SUNDAY

8 *Back to the Garden* 9 a.m.

Drive north on Route 19 and turn onto the Scenic Route at Onomea Bay. Drive slowly past distortions of normal plants — huge Alexandra palms, king-size gingers, and hearty African tulip trees — to the **Hawaii Tropical Botanical Garden** (27-717 Old

Mamalahoa Highway; 808-964-5233; htbg.com). You're ahead of the crowd, so relish the peace in a tropical wonderland resplendent with bromeliads, heliconias, brilliant gingers, and delicate, buttery orchids. The garden holds more than 2,000 exotic species from all over the tropics.

9 *Water Rush* 11 a.m.

Akaka Falls State Park (end of Akaka Falls Road; 808-974-6200; hawaiistateparks.org) provides a final opportunity to inhale nature's gifts on the Big Island. It's a short drive off Route 19 through the tiny former plantation town of Honomu. Take the 20-minute circular hike through bamboo groves, fern banks, and jungle flowers to view two beautiful waterfalls. The more impressive is Akaka, which tumbles 420 feet into a turbulent gorge eaten away by centuries of aquatic pounding. It's a no-frills tourist spot breathtaking in its raw simplicity—a perfect last taste of Hilo.

ABOVE Inside the Thurston Lava Tube, formed as a lava flow left behind a hardened outer crust.

OPPOSITE Hike through bamboo groves, fern banks, and jungle flowers to Akaka Falls, which tumbles 420 feet.

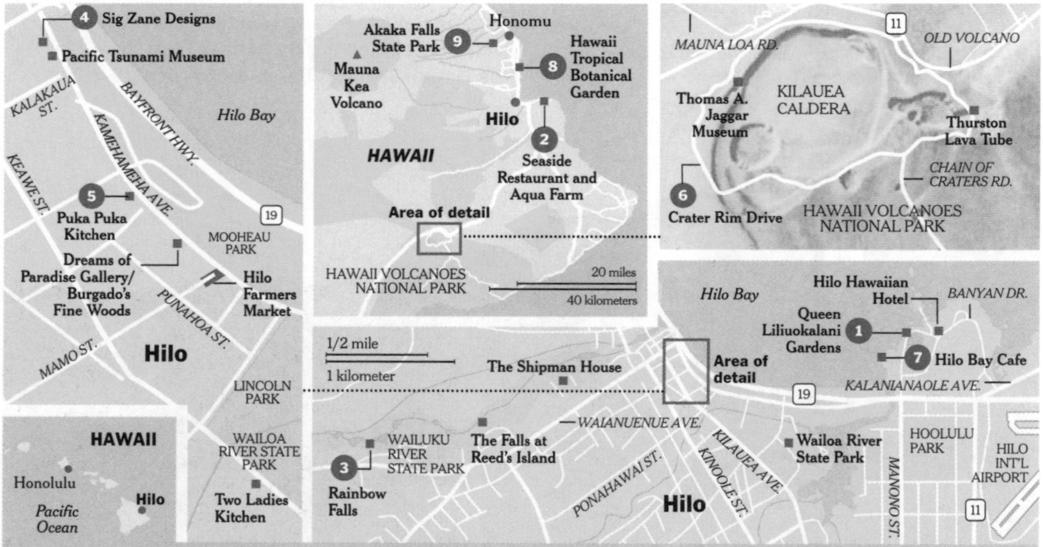

THE BASICS

Hilo is a 50-minute flight from Honolulu and six to seven hours from Los Angeles. When you arrive, rent a car.

The Shipman House
131 Kaiulani Street
808-934-8002
hilo-hawaii.com
$$$
A classic Victorian house refurbished as a bed-and-breakfast.

Hilo Hawaiian Hotel
71 Banyan Drive
808-935-9361
castleresorts.com
$$
Views of Hilo Bay from some of the 286 rooms.

The Falls at Reed's Island
286 Kaiulani Street
808-635-3649
reedsisland.com
$$$$
Inn hidden away next to a waterfall a mile from downtown Hilo.

Kauai

Kauai is a hot spot, and its beautiful North Shore, where majestic mountains meet the surging sea, is hottest. Two or three decades ago, when Maui was the place, Kauaians grinned and thought, "Good, we've got ours and we're going to keep it that way." Now, residents make their livings catering to tourists and pampering the movie stars and magnates who are collecting North Shore trophy homes. But with 60,000 people, this is still the least populated of the four major Hawaiian islands, and its spacious white beaches ring a lush, untrammeled interior. Kauai roads may not be marked, and numbers are rarely posted, so it helps to memorize the two most important directional words — mauka, meaning toward the mountains, and makai, for toward the ocean. When you ask directions, be ready for an answer like this: "Go a mile to the big mango tree, take a left, and head makai."

— BY CHARLES E. ROESSLER

FRIDAY

1 *Big Stretch* 5 p.m.

Your drive from the airport, north and then west on the Kuhio Highway following the curves of the coast, will take you through small towns and lush tropical countryside, with the bonus of a few coastal views, all the way to Hanalei, the last town on the North Shore. (Don't be surprised if you also see a rooster or two — wild chickens, descendants of escapees from domesticated flocks, are abundant on Kauai.) But for the best reward, stay with the highway past Hanalei, all the way until it ends at Kauai's northwest tip. On the last stretch, the road narrows, shrinking to one-lane bridges over inlets and streams, against a misty backdrop of volcanic hills and cliffs. It ends at **Haena State Park** (hawaiistateparks.org), where reef-protected Ke'e Beach offers a serene spot to take in the remains of the day. If there's time and conditions are mellow, it's a short swim out to the reef for some quality snorkeling.

2 *Feast at Sunset* 6:30 p.m.

When you enter the **St. Regis Princeville** (5520 Ka Haku Road; 808-826-9644; princeville.com) make your way straight to the **Makana Terrace** (stregisprinceville.com/dining/makana-terrace; $$$) to take in the sweeping Hanalei Bay view. Settle in, order the signature cocktail, blending passion fruit and Champagne, and look out across the water. The mountains on the other side stood in for Bali Hai in the movie *South Pacific*. (Be sure to arrive before sunset.) You may also see some surfers if the waves are right — the North Shore is popular for surfing and all of its relatives — windsurfing, body-boarding, stand-up paddling. Stay for a buffet dinner ($$$), or move indoors in the hotel to the **Kauai Grill** ($$$), where the frequently changing menu includes entrees like soy-glazed short ribs with papaya-jalapeno puree. After dinner, walk down to the beach, spectacular under a full moon.

SATURDAY

3 *Morning by the Sea* 7:30 a.m.

Take a stroll on the Princeville walking path, paralleling the road leading into the planned community of **Princeville**, and look out over the Robert Trent Jones Jr. golf course. At this time of day there is a good chance of seeing double rainbows in the direction of the misty mountains.

OPPOSITE AND BELOW Hanalei Bay and the pier at Hanalei on a cloudy day in December. Magnates and movie stars have arrived, but Kauai is still the least populated of the four main Hawaiian islands.

ABOVE Houses along the golf course in the North Shore planned community of Princeville.

BELOW Kauai is popular for surfing and all of its relatives — windsurfing, body-boarding, stand-up paddling.

OPPOSITE The cliffs of the Na Pali Coast, inaccessible by road. One way to see them is on a scenic helicopter ride.

4 *Botanicals* 9:30 a.m.

Limahuli Gardens in Haena (5-8291 Kuhio Highway; 808-826-1053; ntbg.org/gardens/limahuli.php), one of five National Tropical Botanical Gardens in the country, is in a valley where, 1,800 years ago, the first Hawaiians, with taro as their staple, developed a complex, hierarchical social system. On your self-guided tour, amid native plants like the ohia lehua tree and imports from Polynesia like breadfruit and banana trees, you can see the lava-rock terraces where taro was grown, fed by a series of fresh-water canals. You will also find exquisite vistas; the Polynesians chose a lovely spot. Guided tours are at 10 a.m.; reservations are required.

5 *Nene Spotting* 11 a.m.

Jutting out from the North Shore, the **Kilauea Lighthouse** (end of Kilauea Lighthouse Road; 808-828-0168; fws.gov/kilaueapoint) provided a life-saving beacon for the first trans-Pacific flight from the West Coast in 1927. Now it is part of the

Kilauea Point National Wildlife Refuge and offers both an unobstructed view of striking shoreline and a chance to spot dolphins, sea turtles, and whales. Birders who visit here check off species like the red-footed booby, the great frigatebird, and the nene, or Hawaiian goose.

6 *Saddle Up* Noon

Grab an ono (delicious) ahi wrap or other takeout lunch at **Kilauea Fish Market** (4270 Kilauea Lighthouse Road, Kilauea; 808-828-6244; $) to eat a few miles mauka as you listen to instructions for your two-hour horseback ride at the **Silver Falls Ranch** (2888 Kamookoa Road; 808-828-6718; silverfallsranch.com). Imagine what life must have been like for the cowboys who raised cattle for islanders in years past. As you meander through fern and eucalyptus toward Mount Namahana, the stately peak of an extinct volcano, listen for the small streams that trickle along, hidden by the ferns. This is the Kauai that most visitors miss and most locals love (about $100 to $125; call ahead for directions and reservations).

7 *Kauaians' Favorite Beach* 4 p.m.

Another local favorite is **Kalihiwai Beach**, at the end of Kalihiwai Road, where a wide river empties into the ocean, and joggers, boogie boarders, and dog owners share a piece of the shore. There are no amenities but you can take a dip or body surf in the shore break. And this late in the afternoon, you shouldn't need sun block if you want to stretch out and catch a few Z's or watch the seabirds work the ocean.

8 *Laid-Back Fine Dining* 7 p.m.

Postcards (5-5075 Kuhio Highway; 808-826-1191; postcardscafe.com; $$-$$$) offers mostly organic food in the picturesque town of Hanalei. Start with the taro fritters with pineapple ginger chutney, and try grilled fish with peppered pineapple sage or shrimp enchiladas. The modest portions leave room for a piece of banana and macadamia nut pie.

SUNDAY

9 *A Flyover* 9 a.m.

Get on board with **Sunshine Helicopters** (808-245-8881; sunshinehelicopters.com/kauai/tours/kauai.html) at the tiny Princeville Airport on Highway 56 and soar into the heart of Kauai. The trip takes just 50 minutes, but you'll revisit it in dreams. You fly along the dark walls of Waialeale Crater, home to the Hawaiian gods and shoulder to the wettest spot on Earth (more than 450 inches of rain a year), Mount Waialeale (pronounced way-AH-lay-AH-lay). Among the waterfalls plunging around and below you as you sweep along the mountain faces is one that appeared in *Jurassic Park*. You soar over Waimea Canyon; knife into valleys once inhabited by the ancient

Hawaiians, now home to wild pigs and goats; and glide along the dramatic Na Pali Coast. Expect to pay in the neighborhood of $300 per person.

10 *Ship the Orchids Home* Noon

As you head back to the Lihue Airport, stop in the town of Kapaa for high-end aloha shirts and skirts at **Hula Girl the Vintage Collection** (4-1340 Kuhio Highway; 808-822-1950); glass art at **Kela's** (4-1354 Kuhio Highway; 808-822-4527; glass-art.com); or works by Hawaii-based artists at **Aloha Images** (4504 Kukui Street; 808-821-1382). At **Mermaids Cafe** (4-1384 Kuhio Highway; 808-821-2026; mermaidskauai.com; $$), order a focaccia sandwich or a tofu coconut curry plate. Make one last stop at **Orchid Alley** (4-1383 Kuhio Highway; 808-822-0486; orchidalleykauai.com) and have some tropical flowers shipped home to meet you on the mainland.

ABOVE Sunset at Ke'e Beach in Haena State Park, the last stop on the road west on the North Shore.

OPPOSITE The road to Ke'e narrows in the last stretch, shrinking to one-lane bridges over inlets and streams, against a misty backdrop of volcanic hills and cliffs.

THE BASICS

Lihue, the Kauai airport, is a 25-minute flight from Honolulu. The North Shore is a 40-minute drive north from the airport along Route 56. Rent a car to get around.

Princeville at Hanalei
5-3900 Kuhio Highway
808-826-9644
stregisprinceville.com
$$$$
Overlooks Hanalei Bay and has hosted many a celebrity.

Sealodge Condominiums
3700 Kamehameha Road
800-585-6101
hestara.com
$$
In Princeville, condo units with sea views.

Hanalei Bay Resort
5380 Honoiki Road
808-826-6522
tradingplaces.com/rentals
$$
156 rooms and condo units.

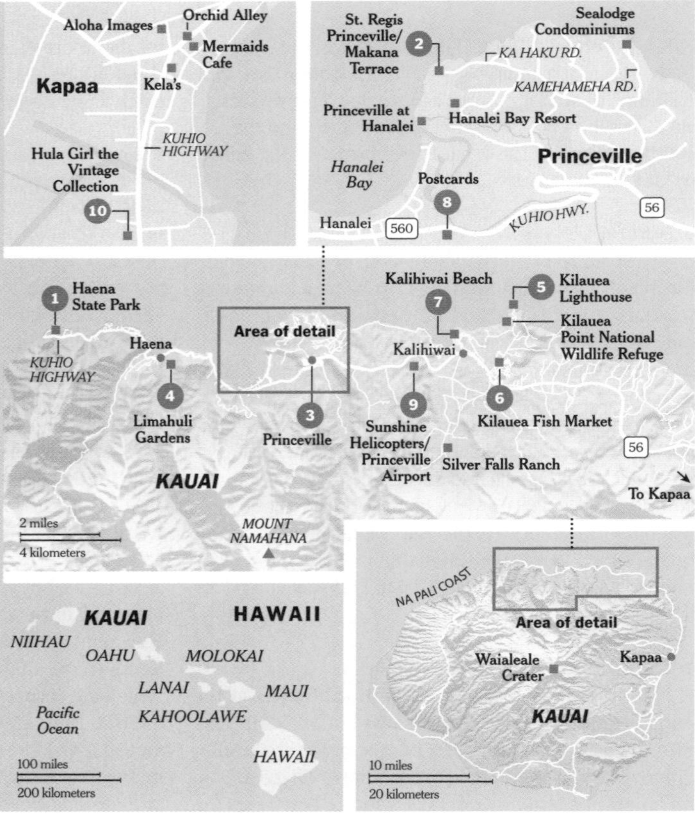

Aloha Images
Orchid Alley
Mermaids Cafe
Kapaa
Kela's
KUHIO HIGHWAY
Hula Girl the Vintage Collection
10

St. Regis Princeville/ Makana Terrace
2
Sealodge Condominiums
KA HAKU RD.
KAMEHAMEHA RD.
Princeville at Hanalei
Hanalei Bay Resort
Princeville
Hanalei Bay
Postcards
8
KUHIO HWY.
Hanalei
560
56

1 Haena State Park
KUHIO HIGHWAY
Haena
4 Limahuli Gardens
Area of detail
3 Princeville
Kalihiwai Beach
7
Kalihiwai
9 Sunshine Helicopters/ Princeville Airport
Silver Falls Ranch
5 Kilauea Lighthouse
Kilauea Point National Wildlife Refuge
6 Kilauea Fish Market
56
To Kapaa
KAUAI
MOUNT NAMAHANA
2 miles
4 kilometers

KAUAI
HAWAII
NIIHAU
OAHU
MOLOKAI
LANAI
MAUI
KAHOOLAWE
Pacific Ocean
HAWAII
100 miles
200 kilometers

NA PALI COAST
Area of detail
Waialeale Crater
Kapaa
KAUAI
10 miles
20 kilometers

Indexes

BY DESTINATION

BY STATE OR PROVINCE

ACTIVE OUTDOORS

AFTER DARK

ATMOSPHERE

CITY SIGHTS

CULTURE

ONE OF A KIND

HISTORY

NATURE'S GRANDEUR

SPECIAL INTERESTS

SPECIALTY MUSEUMS

SHOPPING

TOURS

WRITERS

PHOTOGRAPHERS

ADDITIONAL PHOTO CREDITS

Cory Aronec Photography 359; Tom Brewster Photography 613, 614; Dan Dry 288; Stan Grossfeld/The Boston Globe 120; Dan Harper 358; Getty Images (Tim Bewer/Lonely Planet Images 348; Walter Bibikow/AWL Images RM 434; Chris Cheadle/All Canada Photos 694; David Cheresna/Flickr RF 370; Richard Cummins/Lonely Planet Images 436 (below); Mark Daffey/Lonely Planet Images 84; Mitch Diamond/Photodisc 476; Franz Marc Frei/LOOK 337; Geoffrey George/Flickr RF 582; Universal Images Group 302; Christian Heeb/AWL Images RM 18; Dennis K. Johnson/Lonely Planet Images 554; Jumper 364; Caleb Kenna/Aurora Open 146; Don Klumpp/age fotostock RM 212; Zubin Li 512; Amanda Lynn/First Light 376; A. Messerschmidt 542; Ethan Miller 8; Michael N. Paras/age fotostock RM 38; Dave Reede/All Canada Photos 356; Paul J. Richards/AFP 199; George Rose 334 (above); Stephen Saks/Lonely Planet Images 282; Joel Sartore/National Geographic Creative 436 (above); Randy Wells/The Image Bank 684; Jeremy Woodhouse 327); ©The Hoberman Collection 244; ©2008 Adam Kuehl Photography 221; Andy Newman/Florida Keys News Bureau 258; Courtesy of the Omaha Convention and Visitors Bureau 435; Jennifer Patrick 583, 584; Visit Savannah (VisitSavannah.com) 220

Acknowledgments

We would like to thank everyone at *The New York Times* and at TASCHEN who contributed to the creation of this book and to its revision for this second edition.

For the book project itself, special recognition must go to Nina Wiener, Anne Sauvadet and Eric Schwartau at TASCHEN, the dedicated editors behind the scenes; to Natasha Perkel, the *Times* artist whose clear and elegantly crafted maps make the itineraries comprehensible; to Phyllis Collazo of the *Times* staff, whose photo editing gave the book its arresting images; and to Olimpia Zagnoli, whose illustrations and illustrated maps enliven every article and each regional introduction.

Guiding the transformation of newspaper material to book form at Taschen were Marco Zivny, the book's designer; Josh Baker with Marco Zivny, art directors; David Knowles, layout designer; Frauke Kaiser, production manager; Sean Monahan, who created the region maps; and Mari Rustan, Jonathan Newhall, and Robert Noble for editorial assistance.

Steve Bailey copy-edited the manuscript. Fact-checking for the book was in the hands of Patrick Jude Wilson. Heidi Giovine helped keep production on track at critical moments.

But the indebtedness goes much further back, and deeper into the *New York Times* staff and the list of the newspaper's many contributors. This book grew out of the work of all of the editors, writers, photographers, and others whose contributions and support for the weekly *36 Hours* column built a rich archive over many years.

For this legacy, credit must go first to Stuart Emmrich, who created the column in 2002 and then refined the concept over eight years, first as the *Times* Escapes editor and then as Travel editor. Without his vision, there would be no *36 Hours*. His successors in the role of Travel editor, Danielle Mattoon and then Monica Drake, have brought steady leadership to the column and support to the *36 Hours* books.

Suzanne MacNeille, the direct editor of *36 Hours* at *The Times*, and her predecessors, Denny Lee and Jeff Klein, have guided *36 Hours* superbly through the world by assigning and working with writers, choosing and assigning destinations, and assuring that the weekly column would entertain and inform readers while upholding *Times* journalistic standards. The former Escapes editors Amy Virshup and Mervyn Rothstein saw the column through many of its early years, assuring its consistent quality.

The talented *Times* photo editors who have overseen images and directed the work of photographers for *36 Hours* include Jessica De Witt, Lonnie Schlein, Gina Privitere, Darcy Eveleigh, Laura O'Neill, Chris Jones, and the late John Forbes.

Among the many editors on the *Times* Travel and Escapes copy desks who have kept *36 Hours* at its best over the years, three who stand out are Florence Stickney, Steve Bailey, and Carl Sommers. Editors of the column on nytimes.com have been Alice Dubois, David Allan, Miki Meek, Allison Busacca, Danielle Belopotosky, Samantha Storey, and Josh Robinson. Fact-checkers for the weekly column have included Emily Brennan, Rachel Lee Harris, Rusha Haljuci, Nick Kaye, Anna Bahney, and George Gustines.

Finally, we must offer a special acknowledgment to Benedikt Taschen, whose longtime readership and interest in the *36 Hours* column led to the partnership of our two companies to produce this book.

— BARBARA IRELAND AND ALEX WARD

Editor Barbara Ireland
Project management Alex Ward
Photo editor Phyllis Collazo
Maps Natasha Perkel
Spot illustrations Olimpia Zagnoli
Editorial coordination Nina Wiener and Eric Schwartau
Art direction Marco Zivny and Josh Baker
Layout and design Marco Zivny
Production Horst Neuzner and Frauke Kaiser

Hohenzollernring 53, D–50672 Köln, www.taschen.com
ISBN 978-3-8365-5489-3 Printed in Latvia

VANCOUVER
CANADA
WEST COAST
Seattle
MIDW
& GREA
WELCOME TO Fabulous
SAN FRANCISCO
LAS VEGAS
Denver
SOUTHWEST
& ROCKY MOUNTAINS
LOS ANGELES
ALASKA
HAWAII
MEXICO